Introduction to German Law

**General Editors of the Series: Prof. Tuğrul Ansay
& Prof. Don Wallace, Jr.**

List of the Introduction books published are as follows:

Introduction to German Law
Third Edition

Edited by

Joachim Zekoll
Gerhard Wagner

Published by:
Kluwer Law International B.V.
PO Box 316
2400 AH Alphen aan den Rijn
The Netherlands
E-mail: international-sales@wolterskluwer.com
Website: lrus.wolterskluwer.com

Sold and distributed in North, Central and South America by:
Wolters Kluwer Legal & Regulatory U.S.
7201 McKinney Circle
Frederick, MD 21704
United States of America
Email: customer.service@wolterskluwer.com

Sold and distributed in all other countries by:
Air Business Subscriptions
Rockwood House
Haywards Heath
West Sussex
RH16 3DH
United Kingdom
Email: international-customerservice@wolterskluwer.com

Printed on acid-free paper.

ISBN 978-90-411-9098-7

e-Book: ISBN 978-90-411-9114-4
web-PDF: ISBN 978-90-411-9115-1

Printed in the United Kingdom.

Editors

Gerhard Wagner holds the chair of Private Law, Commercial Law, and Law and Economics at Humboldt Universität zu Berlin, Germany, since 2013. From 1999 to 2013, he was the director of the Institute of Civil Procedure and Conflict Management at the University of Bonn, Germany. During the academic year 2010–2011, he was Visiting Professor of Law at the University of Chicago Law School, Illinois, USA. From 2009 through 2014, he also served as Professor of Fundamentals of Private Law at Erasmus University, Rotterdam, The Netherlands

Joachim Zekoll holds the chair of Private Law, Civil Procedure, and Comparative Law at Goethe University in Frankfurt am Main, Germany, since 2001. From 1992 until 2001, he was on the faculty of the Tulane University School of Law (New Orleans, USA), serving as the John Minor Wisdom Professor of Law from 1999 until 2001. From 2003 to 2007, concurrently with his appointment in Frankfurt, he was the A.D. Freeman Professor of Law at Tulane University.

Contributors

Prof. Dr. Georg Borges is Professor of Civil Law, Legal Informatics, and Commercial Law, Saarland University, Faculty of Law, Saarbrücken, Germany.

Prof. Dr. Gerhard Dannecker is Professor of Criminal Law and Criminal Procedure, University of Heidelberg Faculty of Law, Heidelberg, Germany.

Dr. Wolfgang Hau is Professor of Private Law, German, International, and Comparative Civil Procedure, Ludwig-Maximilians-University Munich, Germany, and part-time judge at the Higher Regional Court of Munich.

Prof. Dr. Tatjana Hörnle is Professor of Criminal Law, Criminal Procedure, Jurisprudence and Comparative Law, Humboldt University of Berlin, Faculty of Law, Germany.

Prof. Dr. Marcel Kau, LL.M. (Georgetown), is Associate Professor of Public Law, Public International Law, European Law, and Constitutional History, University of Konstanz Faculty of Law, Konstanz, Germany.

Dr. Harald Koch was Professor (Emeritus) of Civil Law, Civil Procedure,Private International and Comparative Law at Rostock University and Humboldt University Berlin, Germany, and retired Judge on the Rostock Court of Appeals (Oberlandesgericht).

Prof. Dr. Jürgen Kohler is Professor of Private Law and Civil Procedure, University of Greifswald Faculty of Law, Greifswald, Germany.

Prof. Dr. Johannes Köndgen is Professor (Emeritus) of Comparative Law and Commercial Law, University of Bonn Faculty of Law, Bonn, Germany.

Prof. Dr. Dieter Martiny is Professor (Emeritus) of Civil Law, Private International Law, and Comparative Law, European University Viadrina Faculty of Law, Frankfurt (Oder), Germany.

Prof. Dr. Julian Roberts is a Rechtsanwalt in Munich and a barrister in 10 Old Square, Lincoln's Inn, London, UK.

Prof. Dr. Johannes Saurer, LL.M. (Yale) is Professor for Public Law, Environmental Law, Law of Infrastructure, and Comparative Law, University of Tübingen.

Prof. Dr. Rolf Sethe, LL.M. (London) is Professor of Civil Law, Commercial and Business Law, Faculty of Law, University of Zurich, Switzerland.

Dr. Kurt Siehr is Professor Emeritus of Private Law, Comparative Law, and Private International Law, University of Zurich Faculty of Law, Zurich, Switzerland. He now lives in Hamburg and is working at the Max Planck Institute of Comparative and International Private Law there.

Prof. Dr. Dennis Solomon, LL.M. (Berkeley) is Director of the Institute for International and Foreign Law and Professor of Civil Law, Private International and Comparative Law at the University of Passau Faculty of Law, Passau, Germany.

Rita Vavra, LL.M. (Columbia), is a research assistant and PhD candidate at the Department of Criminal Law, Criminal Procedure, Jurisprudence and Comparative Law, Humboldt University of Berlin, Germany.

Prof. Dr. Manfred Weiss is Professor of Labor Law and Civil Law, Johann Wolfgang Goethe University, Faculty of Law, Frankfurt am Main, Germany.

Prof. Dr. Wolfgang Wurmnest, LL.M. (Berkeley) is Professor of Private Law, Commercial Law, Private International and Comparative Law, University of Augsburg Faculty of Law, Augsburg, Germany.

Prof. Dr. Reinhard Zimmermann is Director at the Max Planck Institute for Foreign and Private International Law, Hamburg, Germany, and Professor of Civil Law, Roman Law, and Comparative Law, University of Regensburg Faculty of Law, Regensburg, Germany.

Summary of Contents

Summary of Contents

Preface

The goal of this book is to provide an introduction of the most important areas of German law for foreign readers – be they practitioners, scholars, or students. Each chapter was written by one or several experts and presents an overview of the basic concepts and rules shaping German law in the respective field. After an initial characterization of the German legal system and culture, it covers fourteen specific topics of private and public law as well as procedural law. Each contribution provides a bibliography referring the reader to the most important literature for more detailed research.

This book is the third edition of *Introduction to German Law*. First published in 1996 by Werner Ebke and Matthew Finkin, its successor (published by Joachim Zekoll and Mathias Reimann) appeared under the same title in 2005. In the thirteen years that have passed since the second edition was completed, German law has again undergone substantial change. This is due mainly to three related factors. First, European Union law has continued to shape and change German private and public law in significant ways. Second, the German legislature has remained very active over the past thirteen years. Responsive not only to directives from Brussels and to judgments rendered by the European Court of Justice, but also to the forces of globalization and to demands for law reform on the purely domestic level, German lawmakers have left virtually no area addressed in this volume untouched. Third, the Constitutional Court as well as the Federal Supreme Court have handed down numerous decisions that added important changes to the legal landscape in Germany.

We are indebted to our secretaries and collaborators, Gisela Amend-Khaskhoussi (Frankfurt), and Dr. Bettina Rentsch (Berlin) for valuable assistance in the process of editing this volume.

Joachim Zekoll, Frankfurt am Main
Gerhard Wagner, Berlin
July 2018

CHAPTER 1

Characteristic Aspects of German Legal Culture

Reinhard Zimmermann[*]

TABLE OF CONTENTS

---

[*] The manuscript was submitted in the autumn of 2017 and reflects law and literature as of that date.

1

§1.01   THE CONSTITUTIONAL MONSTROSITY

If there is a specifically German legal culture, it is of relatively recent origin. Germany only became a modern nation-state in 1871, after Bismarck, by means of the Franco-Prussian war, had welded together the North German Federation (that had itself only been established five years earlier) and the South German States. Austria, of course, did not become part of the new German Empire, since it had effectively been dismissed from 'German' constitutional history in 1866. In that year, Prussia had crushingly defeated the Austrian army at Königgrätz and had thus brought to an end the constitutional regime established in 1815 at the Congress of Vienna. That regime had been based on the *Deutscher Bund*, a federation of forty-one formally independent 'German' states, among them one Empire (Austria), five kingdoms (Prussia, Bavaria, Saxony, Hannover, and Württemberg), one electorate (Hesse), seven Grand-Duchies (including Luxemburg), a whole range of duchies and principalities, and also the four Free Cities (Hamburg, Bremen, Lübeck, and Frankfurt); the latter were much loved among Romantic intellectuals.

This may appear to be a complex mélange today, but it replaced an infinitely more bewildering system of government that had, after a long period of decline, finally collapsed in 1806 under the Napoleonic onslaught.[1] It had been known as the Holy Roman Empire of German Nation and traced its lineage to Charlemagne's coronation as 'Roman' Emperor by the Bishop of Rome, Pope Leo III, on Christmas Day of the year 800. The Carolingian Empire had soon disintegrated, but the idea of a supreme ruler of the occidental world, who was regarded as a successor to the Roman Emperors, lived on. In 962 Otto I, German king (not king of Germany), was crowned Roman Emperor, and effectively established what was to become a fundamental feature of German constitutional history: the combination of German kingship and 'Roman' Empire. The universalist claim inherent in the concept of being 'Emperor' contributed to the fact that the (elected) German rulers were never in a position to establish a national kingdom along the French or English model.

The Holy Roman Empire, especially during the one and a half centuries following the Peace of Westphalia, has been said to have been neither holy, nor Roman, nor even

---

1. For the constitutional history of Germany, *see* Otto Kimminich, *Deutsche Verfassungsgeschichte* (2nd ed. 1987); Dietmar Willoweit, *Deutsche Verfassungsgeschichte* (7th ed. 2013).

an Empire. The famous Natural lawyer Samuel Pufendorf referred to it as a constitutional monstrosity.[2] It consisted of between 300 and 320 sovereign states as well as some 1,400 territories that were directly subordinate to the Empire. Even after the secession of Switzerland and of the (Northern) Netherlands, the Empire comprised territories such as the 'Spanish' Netherlands, Lorraine and Burgundy, Bohemia, Moravia, and parts of Northern Italy; and the Habsburgs, who had been elected to the Emperorship ever since 1438, also ruled the Kingdom of Hungary. Many 'foreign' potentates had a say in Imperial affairs, among them the British king, in his capacity as king of Hanover, and the king of Sweden, who had gained large parts of Pomerania, the duchy of Bremen and some other areas as a result of the Thirty Years' War. As time wore on, the old *Reich* was growing weaker and weaker before the territorial lords; and though it had provided an institutional framework for peaceful coexistence and dispute resolution,[3] it was increasingly perceived to be a tattered collection of outdated and highly inefficient institutions, bogged down by elaborate procedures and laborious protocol. It represented hardly more than an unduly ornate façade.

§1.02 FROM CIVIL LAW TO CIVIL CODE

This was reflected in the way in which the law developed. If the German king was Roman Emperor, it was not at all unnatural that the Imperial law should be Roman law. This ideological connection obviously helped the process of what is usually referred to as the 'reception' of Roman law.[4] But if Roman law was indeed 'received' in all imperial territories, that did not, of course, transform it into a German legal system. Since the days of the so-called Renaissance of the 12th century,[5] when the Glossators had started intellectually to penetrate the entire body of Roman law that had escaped the turmoil of the *Völkerwanderung*, its influence had spread northwards and westwards, and Roman legal learning soon formed a major component of what has come to be known as the Roman-Canon *ius commune*. Law, in the Middle Ages, was not conceived of as a system of rules enacted for, and exclusively applicable within, a specific territory, and thus the *ius commune* provided the cornerstone for the emergence of an essentially unified, European legal tradition.[6]

---

2. *De statu imperii Germanici*, 1667 (German translation by Horst Denzer, *Die Verfassung des deutschen Reiches*, 1976).
3. Barbara Stollberg-Rilinger, *Das Heilige Römische Reich deutscher Nation: Vom Ende des Mittelalters bis 1806* (5th ed. 2015); Hans-Peter Haferkamp, 'Holy Roman Empire', in: Jürgen Basedow, Klaus J. Hopt & Reinhard Zimmermann (eds), *The Max Planck Encyclopedia of European Private Law* (2012), pp. 835 et seq.
4. The authoritative discussion on the reception of Roman law and generally on the history of private law in Germany is Franz Wieacker, *Privatrechtsgeschichte der Neuzeit* (2nd ed. 1967) (English translation by Tony Weir, *A History of Private Law in Europe*, 1995). For the significance of Roman law in Germany and in European history in general, *see* Paul Koschaker, *Europa und das römische Recht* (4th ed. 1966); Reinhard Zimmermann, 'Roman Law in the Modern World', in: David Johnston (ed.), *The Cambridge Companion to Roman Law* (2015), pp. 452 et seq.
5. The significance of which has been stressed by Harold J. Berman, *Law and Revolution. The Formation of the Western Legal Tradition* (1983).
6. This point has been elaborated by Helmut Coing in various publications; cf., in particular, his *Europäisches Privatrecht*, vol. I (1985); and *see* Manlio Bellomo, *The Common Legal Past of*

It was only with the rise of rationalism and nationalism that the intellectual world of the European *ius commune* started to disintegrate.[7] The enlightened rulers of the two most influential states within the 'Roman' Empire set the wheels in motion to enchant their subjects with a codification, both rational and comprehensive, that would enable them to know their rights and duties within society. The Prussian *Allgemeines Landrecht* of 1794 and the Austrian *Allgemeines Bürgerliches Gesetzbuch* were radically different in many respects (particularly as far as the style of legal drafting is concerned), but they were both inspired by a desire to leave behind the subtleties of Roman legal disputes and to emphasize the responsibility of the territorial ruler for the administration of justice. In 1804 the codification movement received a further powerful impulse with the enactment of the *Code Napoléon (Code civil)*.[8] In the course of the 19th century, several other German states attempted to codify their private law, but only the kingdom of Saxony managed to enact a civil code. That was in 1865, a mere six years before the foundation of the German Reich.[9]

At that stage, the legal landscape of Germany still looked very patchy. Austria (to be pushed out of the *Deutscher Bund* in 1866) had its *Allgemeines Bürgerliches Gesetzbuch*. The Prussian territories (including, for instance, Westphalia, Bayreuth, and Ansbach) were governed by the *Prussian Allgemeines Landrecht*. In the Rhine-Province, in Alsace, and Lorraine the *Code civil* applied.[10] The Grand Duchy of Baden had adopted the *Badisches Landrecht* which was based on a translation of the *Code civil*. Some places in Bavaria lived according to Austrian law, while in parts of Schleswig-Holstein Danish law prevailed. Most of the remaining German territories (comprising, in 1890, close to 30% of the population of the *Deutsches Reich*) still

---

Europe, 1000–1800 (1995); Reinhard Zimmermann, 'Roman Law and the Harmonisation of European Private Law', in: Arthur Hartkamp et al. (eds), *Towards a European Civil Code* (4th ed. (2011), pp. 27 et seq.); Alfons Bürge, 'Das römische Recht als Grundlage für das Zivilrecht im künftigen Europa', in: Filippo Ranieri (ed.), *Die Europäisierung der Rechtswissenschaft* (2002), pp. 19 et seq.; Nils Jansen, 'Ius Commune', in: *Max Planck Encyclopedia* (n. 3), pp. 1006 et seq.

7. For a general discussion, *see* Helmut Coing, *Europäisches Privatrecht*, vol. II (1989); Klaus Luig, 'Usus Modernus', in: *Max Planck Encyclopedia* (n. 3), pp. 1755 et seq. The disintegration became visible in the emergence of a new type of legal literature; *see* Klaus Luig, 'The Institutes of National Law in the Seventeenth and Eighteenth Century', *Juridical Review* 17 (1972) 193 et seq.

8. On the codes of the age of the 'law of reason' (*Vernunftrecht*), *see* Wieacker/Weir (n. 4), 257 et seq.; Konrad Zweigert & Hein Kötz, *An Introduction to Comparative Law* (translated by Tony Weir, 3rd ed. 1998), pp. 80 et seq., 135 et seq. On the phenomenon of codification in general, *see* Reinhard Zimmermann, 'Codification: The Civilian Experience Reconsidered on the Eve of a Common European Sales Law', in: Wen-Yeu Wang (ed.), *Codification in International Perspective: Selected Papers from the 2nd IACL Thematic Conference* (2014), pp. 11 et seq. The codifications, however, did not succeed in pushing back the influence of Roman law. For the continuity between the *ius commune* and French law, *see* James Gordley, 'Myths of the French Civil Code', *American Journal of Comparative Law* 2 (1994) 459 et seq.; on the 'pandectification' of Dutch, Prussian and Austrian law, *see* Reinhard Zimmermann, *Roman Law, Contemporary Law, European Law: The Civilian Tradition Today* (2001), pp. 3 et seq.

9. For all details concerning the history of codification in 19th-century Germany, *see* Barbara Dölemeyer, in: Helmut Coing (ed.), *Handbuch der Quellen und Literatur der neueren europäischen Privatrechtsgeschichte*, vol. III/2 (1982), pp. 1421 et seq.

10. *See* the contributions in Reiner Schulze (ed.), *Französisches Zivilrecht in Europa während des 19. Jahrhunderts* (1994), and in *idem* (ed.), *Rheinisches Recht und Europäische Rechtsgeschichte* (1996); Elmar Wadle, *Französisches Recht in Deutschland* (2002).

administered justice according to the *ius commune* (*gemeines Recht*).[11] Yet the *ius commune* was only applicable *in subsidio*, and countless more specific territorial or local laws could therefore govern a particular dispute: from 13th-century texts like Eike von Repgow's famous *Sachsenspiegel* or the *Jütsche Low* to Baron von Kreittmayr's *Codex Maximilianeus Bavaricus Civilis* of 1756 (which became the *Bayerisches Landrecht*), from the *Neumünsterische Kirchspielgebräuche* to the *Nassau-Katzenelnbogensche Landesordnung*.[12] Thus, for example, there were all in all more than 100 different regulations concerning succession upon death. This was not, of course, a very convenient state of affairs; nor did it seem worthy of a modern united nation-state that its citizens, to quote a famous quip of Voltaire, had to change their law as often as they changed their post-horses. Thus, it is hardly surprising that the preparation of a German Civil Code immediately became a matter of great practical as well as symbolic significance in the years after 1871.

§1.03 THE QUEST FOR GERMAN LEGAL UNITY

The quest for German national legal (as well as political!) unity was not new, however. One of its first harbingers had been A.F.J. Thibaut, a professor of Roman law at Heidelberg.[13] In the wave of patriotism that swept the German states after they had finally shaken off the Napoleonic yoke, he had published a pamphlet in which he urged the introduction of a general German civil code, modelled on the French *Code civil*, which could pave the way towards political unity. This proposition – which eventually did not gain acceptance – was opposed, particularly prominently, by the man who was to emerge as Germany's most celebrated jurist of the century. Friedrich Carl von Savigny in his famous essay entitled *Vom Beruf unserer Zeit für Gesetzgebung und Rechtswissenschaft* [Of the Vocation of our Time for Legislation and Legal Science][14] did not, of course, argue that Germany should remain, legally, the patch-work quilt that it was. 'As to what we aim at, we are in agreement', he wrote, '[for] we want a national community whose scientific endeavours focus upon one and the same object'. But, he added, the right way towards this goal was not a piece of legislation but rather an 'organically progressive legal science which may be common to the whole nation'.

---

11. For an overview of the laws applicable in Germany at the end of the 19th century, *see* 'Anlage zur Denkschrift zum BGB', in: Benno Mugdan (ed.), *Die gesammten Materialien zum Bürgerlichen Gesetzbuch für das Deutsche Reich*, vol. I (1899), pp. 844–845; and *see* the *Allgemeine Deutsche Rechts- und Gerichtskarte* (1896) (re-edited in 1996 by Diethelm Klippel).
12. For a comprehensive study of the application of the various laws prevailing in Germany in the practice of the courts (covering the early modern period), *see* now Peter Oestmann, *Rechtsvielfalt vor Gericht: Rechtsanwendung und Partikularrecht im Alten Reich* (2002); on the relationship between statutory law and common law in general, *see* Reinhard Zimmermann, 'Statuta sunt stricte interpretanda? Statutes and the Common Law: A Continental Perspective', *Cambridge Law Journal* 56 (1997) 315 et seq.
13. On whom *see* Christian Hattenhauer, Klaus-Peter Schroeder & Christian Baldus (eds), *A.F.J. Thibaut (1772–1840)* (2017).
14. Both Savigny's and Thibaut's programmatic essays (the latter of which was entitled 'Über die Nothwendigkeit eines allgemeinen bürgerlichen Rechts für Deutschland') are easily accessible in Hans Hattenhauer (ed.), *Thibaut und Savigny: Ihre programmatischen Schriften* (2nd ed. 2002).

Savigny himself[15] laid the foundations for this kind of 'legal science' (*Rechtswissenschaft*) when he turned his attention (and that of his followers) to the Roman law of the antiquity and started to rid its contemporary version of all the accretions and distortions brought about by some 800 years of scholarship and legal practice.

The result of Savigny's legal historicism was a new approach to legal scholarship. It was dubbed 'pandectist' because it used the most important body of the Roman legal sources, the Digest (Greek synonym: *Pandectae*), to build an internally consistent and logical system of concepts, rules and principles.[16] The pandectist school secured the leading place for Germany in the world of 19th-century legal scholarship; it was much admired by lawyers all over Europe and exercised significant influence on legal developments in countries like France, Italy, and Austria.[17] Above all, however, it was the fulcrum for the emergence of a national community of scholars,[18] of German legal unification on a scholarly level. The flip side of this coin, incidentally, was the condescending and neglectful attitude that the German professoriate tended to adopt towards the territorial laws – even if they were as important as the Prussian civil code.

But the legislatures and governments of the various states joined in the *Deutscher Bund* were not entirely inactive either. They were attempting to accommodate the needs of an expanding economy that was operating increasingly on a supraregional level. The advent of machinery and urbanization facilitated the production processes

---

15. On Savigny, on his concept of law, and on his influence on 19th-century German legal scholarship, *see* Joachim Rückert, *Idealismus, Jurisprudenz und Politik bei Friedrich Carl von Savigny* (1984); Horst Heinrich Jakobs, *Die Begründung der geschichtlichen Rechtswissenschaft* (1992); Joachim Rückert, 'Savignys Konzeption von Jurisprudenz und Recht, ihre Folgen und ihre Bedeutung bis heute', *Tijdschrift voor rechtsgeschiedenis* 61 (1993) 65 et seq.; Benjamin Lahusen, *Alles Recht geht vom Volksgeist aus: Friedrich Carl von Savigny und die moderne Rechtswissenschaft* (2012); cf. also the contributions in *American Journal of Comparative Law* 37 (1989) 1 et seq.
16. For details, *see* Wolfgang Wilhelm, *Zur juristischen Methodenlehre im 19. Jahrhundert* (1958); Franz Wieacker, *Pandektenwissenschaft und Industrielle Revolution* (1966); Mathias Reimann, 'Nineteenth Century German Legal Science', *Boston College Law Review* 31 (1990) 837 et seq.; Jan Schröder, *Recht als Wissenschaft* (2nd ed. 2012), pp. 193 et seq.; Thomas Rüfner, 'Historical School', in: *Max Planck Encyclopedia* (n. 3), pp. 830 et seq.; Hans-Peter Haferkamp & Tilman Repgen (eds), *Wie pandektistisch war die Pandektistik?* (2017). On the pandectist systematization of private law, *see* Jan Peter Schmidt, 'Pandektensystem', in *Max Planck Encyclopedia* (n. 3), pp. 1238 et seq.
17. Cf., as far as France is concerned, the comprehensive study by Alfons Bürge, *Das französische Privatrecht im 19. Jahrhundert* (1991), pp. 150 et seq.; for Austria: Werner Ogris, *Der Entwicklungsgang der österreichischen Privatrechtswissenschaft im 19. Jahrhundert* (1968); for Italy: the contributions in Reiner Schulze (ed.), *Deutsche Rechtswissenschaft und Staatslehre im Spiegel der italienischen Rechtskultur während der zweiten Hälfte des 19. Jahrhunderts* (1990). For further references to literature concerning other European countries and the United States, *see* Reinhard Zimmermann, 'Savigny's Legacy: Legal History, Comparative Law, and the Emergence of a European Legal Science', *Law Quarterly Review* 112 (1996) 580, n. 18.
18. The rise of the Roman law professoriate in the early 19th century made Germany the quintessential country of professorial law; it thus became, in the words of Jack Dawson, the only region in Europe to build its law on academic treatises. For details *see* James Q. Whitman, *The Legacy of Roman Law in the German Romantic Era* (1990); Stefan Vogenauer, 'An Empire of Light? Learning and Lawmaking in the History of German Law', *Cambridge Law Journal* 64 (2005) 481 et seq. For the position at the end of the 19th century, *see* the memorandum by Emil Friedberg, *Die künftige Gestaltung des deutschen Rechtsstudiums nach den Beschlüssen der Eisenacher Konferenz* (1896), pp. 7–8, translated in Zimmermann, *Civilian Tradition* (n. 8), 7–8.

and the rising *bourgeoisie* favoured open markets promoting the free interplay of economic forces. Legal unification therefore was required, first and foremost, in the trade-related fields of law. A first significant step in this direction was the establishment of a German Customs Union in 1833. In 1848 the law of negotiable instruments was unified by means of the *Allgemeine Deutsche Wechselordnung*[19] and between 1861 and 1866 nearly all the states of the *Deutscher Bund* adopted the draft of a General German Commercial Code (*Allgemeines Deutsches Handelsgesetzbuch*) that had been completed in 1861.[20] A draft law of obligations (*Dresdener Entwurf*) was published in 1865. Although it was never adopted, it significantly influenced the German Civil Code.

After the creation of the *Deutsches Reich* a streamlined procedural and organizational framework for the uniform and efficient administration of justice was established: the four *Reichsjustizgesetze*[21] concerned the unification of the court system (*Gerichtsverfassungsgesetz*), of the law of bankruptcy (*Konkursordnung*), civil procedure (*Zivilprozeßordnung*) and criminal procedure (*Strafprozeßordnung*). They all came into force in October 1879. While they have been amended on various occasions, three of these acts have remained on the statute book until today; the *Konkursordnung* has been replaced by a new insolvency code (*Insolvenzordnung*) in 1999. 1 October 1879 also saw the opening of a Supreme Appeal Court for the entire *Reich* in all civil and criminal matters: the *Reichsgericht*.[22] Its seat was Leipzig, a city with a distinguished legal tradition which had the advantage of being outside of, but still sufficiently close to, the political capital of the *Reich* (Berlin). Its first president was Eduard von Simson, a Prussian lawyer of Jewish descent who had been baptized in his early youth. He had presided over the German National Assembly of 1848 that had met in the Frankfurt *Paulskirche* and had also been president of the Imperial Parliament.[23]

---

19. *See* Ulrich Huber, 'Das Reichsgesetz über die Einführung einer allgemeinen Wechselordnung für Deutschland vom 26. November 1848', *Juristenzeitung* 1978, 785 et seq.

20. Christoph Bergfeld, 'Preußen und das Allgemeine Deutsche Handelsgesetzbuch', *Ius Commune* 14 (1987) 101 et seq.; Andreas M Fleckner, 'Allgemeines Deutsches Handelsgesetzbuch (ADHGB)' in: *Max Planck Encyclopedia* (n. 2), pp. 51 et seq.; and *see* Karsten Schmidt, *Das HGB und die Gegenwartsaufgaben des Handelsrechts* (1983). For the modernization of commercial law in the 19th century in general, *see* Karl Otto Scherner (ed.), *Modernisierung des Handelsrechts im 19. Jahrhundert* (1993); Arnold J.Kanning, *Unifying Commercial Laws of Nation-States* (2003), pp. 46 et seq.

21. On which *see* Peter Landau, 'Die Reichsjustizgesetze von 1879 und die deutsche Rechtseinheit', in: *Vom Reichsjustizamt zum Bundesministerium der Justiz: Zum 100jährigen Gründungstag des Reichsjustizamtes* (1977), pp. 161 et seq.

22. On which *see*, on the occasion of its 100th anniversary, Arno Buschmann, '100 Jahre Gründungstag des Reichsgerichts', *Neue Juristische Wochenschrift* 1979, 1966 et seq.; Elmar Wadle, 'Das Reichsgericht im Widerschein denkwürdiger Tage', *Juristische Schulung* 1979, 841 et seq. On the *Reichsgericht's* predecessor, the Supreme Commercial Court, first of the *Norddeutscher Bund* and later of the *Reich* (it existed from 1870–1879), *see* Herbert Kronke, 'Rechtsvergleichung und Rechtsvereinheitlichung in der Rechsprechung des Reichsoberhandelsgerichts', *Zeitschrift für Europäisches Privatrecht* 5 (1997) 735 et seq.; Andreas M. Fleckner, 'Reichsoberhandelsgericht (with Reichsgericht)', in: *Max Planck Encyclopedia* (n. 3), pp. 1438 et seq.

23. On Eduard von Simson, *see* James E. Dow, *A Prussian Liberal: The Life of Eduard von Simson* (1981); Bernd-Rüdiger Kern & Klaus-Peter Schroeder (eds), *Eduard von Simson (1810–1899)* (2001). On the rise of Jewish lawyers and lawyers of Jewish descent in 19th-century Germany, *see* Peter Landau, 'Juristen jüdischer Herkunft im Kaiserreich und in der Weimarer Republik', in: Helmut Heinrichs, Harald Franzki, Klaus Schmalz & Michael Stolleis (eds), *Deutsche Juristen jüdischer Herkunft* (1993), pp. 133 et seq.; Reinhard Zimmermann, 'Was Heimat hieß, nun heißt

The scene was thus set for what was to be the crowning symbol of German legal unity: a civil code common to the whole nation. Its gestation period was twenty-six years.[24] A First Commission consisting of eleven judges, officials, and professors (among them the most famous pandectist scholar of his time, Bernhard Windscheid)[25] produced a draft that was published in 1888. It aroused a vigorous public debate and encountered sharp criticism as being too abstract, pedantic, and 'doctrinaire'. The leading 'Germanist' of the day, Otto von Gierke, mourned the absence of even 'a drop of socialist oil'.[26] A second commission (this time containing some non-lawyers, among them three members of the landed gentry) was appointed in 1890. The second draft did not, however, substantially differ from the first one. The Imperial Parliament debated the code in 1896 and made a few amendments here and there: the words 'and hares' were deleted in the section relating to damage caused by game, the right of pursuit of the owner of a swarm of bees was modified. The Social Democrats eventually voted against the code because it did not specifically deal with labour relations. Nevertheless, the Civil Code (*Bürgerliches Gesetzbuch*, BGB) was adopted with a comfortable majority and signed into law by Emperor Wilhelm II. It came into force on what many people believed to be the beginning of a new era: 1 January 1900. On that day, the *Deutsche Juristenzeitung* carried the heading: '*Ein Volk. Ein Reich. Ein Recht*' (One People. One Empire. One Law), and Ernst von Wildenbruch celebrated the great event with an impassioned poem.[27] It marked the apogee of the age of legal nationalism.

---

es Hölle': The emigration of lawyers from Hitler's Germany: political background, legal framework and cultural context, in: Jack Beatson & Reinhard Zimmermann, *Jurists Uprooted: German-Speaking Emigré lawyers in Twentieth Century Britain* (2004), pp. 9 et seq.

24. For details, *see* Werner Schubert, in: Horst Heinrich Jakobs & Werner Schubert (eds), *Die Beratung des Bürgerlichen Gesetzbuchs in systematischer Zusammenstellung der unveröffentlichten Quellen: Materialien zur Entstehungsgeschichte des BGB* (1978), pp. 27 et seq.; Barbara Dölemeyer, 'Das Bürgerliche Gesetzbuch für das Deutsche Reich', in: Coing (n. 9), 1572 et seq.; Michael John, *Politics and Law in Late Nineteenth Century Germany: The Origins of the Civil Code* (1989); Hans-Peter Haferkamp, 'Bürgerliches Gesetzbuch (BGB)', in: *Max Planck Encyclopedia* (n. 3), pp. 120 et seq.; and *see* the charming account by Frederic W. Maitland, 'The Making of the German Civil Code', in: Herbert A.L. Fisher (ed.), *The Collected Papers of Frederic William Maitland*, vol. III (1911), pp. 474 et seq. Cf. also the table in Mathias Schmoeckel, Joachim Rückert & Reinhard Zimmermann (eds), *Historisch-kritischer Kommentar zum BGB*, vol. I (2003), pp. XXVII–XXVIII.

25. Windscheid wrote the leading pandectist textbook of his time. This three-volume treatise has remained a monument: Bernhard Windscheid, *Lehrbuch des Pandektenrechts* (9th ed. 1906, edited by Theodor Kipp). For an important re-evaluation of Windscheid as a jurist, *see* Ulrich Falk, *Ein Gelehrter wie Windscheid* (1989); cf. also Joachim Rückert, 'Methode und Zivilrecht bei Bernhard Windscheid (1817–1892)', in: Joachim Rückert & Ralf Seinecke (eds), *Methodik des Zivilrechts von Savigny bis Teubner* (2nd ed. 2012), pp. 97 et seq.; Friedrich Klein, *Bernhard Windscheid 26.6.1817–26.10.1892: Leben und Werk* (2014).

26. Otto von Gierke, *Die soziale Aufgabe des Privatrechts* (1889), p. 11; for comment, *see* Tilman Repgen, *Die soziale Aufgabe des Privatrechts: Eine Grundfrage in Wissenschaft und Kodifikation am Ende des 19. Jahrhunderts* (2001). On the emergence of two separate branches of Savigny's Historical School, i.e., the 'Romanists' and the 'Germanists', *see* Zimmermann, *Civilian Traditon* (n. 8), 18 et seq. For the history of criticism of the BGB, *see* Dieter Schwab, 'Das BGB und seine Kritiker', *Zeitschrift für Neuere Rechtsgeschichte* 22 (2000) 325 et seq.

27. *Deutsche Juristen-Zeitung* 1900, XXI.

§1.04 ONE NATION: ONE LAW

It is a remarkable feature of our modern academic life that whilst it would be manifestly absurd to refer to German chemistry or French mathematics, it has for the past hundred years been taken for granted that there are, in principle, as many legal systems (and consequently: legal scholarships) in Europe as there are national states. This is, at least partly, another aspect of the intellectual heritage of the 'historical school' of jurisprudence: that the law of a country has come to be regarded as a characteristic expression of its national spirit. The national code, which was taken to constitute an autonomous interpretational space, was attributed sole, supreme, and unquestioned authority, and all the energies of those legal academics interested in the application and development of private law were channelled into the task of expounding the code and of discussing the court decisions based on its provisions. This is what has happened in Germany after 1900. Mountains of literature have been compiled on every detail of the civil code,[28] but in the process the basic historical unity of European legal scholarship has largely been forgotten. The history of the *ius commune* was held to have ended with the enactment of the national codifications, and exploration of the Roman sources was thus regarded as an end in itself.[29] Legal history emerged as a proper discipline in its own right and has since achieved an unparalleled level of sophistication. But it has become a highly specialized type of scholarship, increasingly unwilling and unable to maintain an intellectual contact with the legal profession. The historical approach to law that was still so characteristic of 19th-century legal science has largely been abandoned in Germany (as elsewhere);[30] at the same time, the national particularization of legal scholarship has shaped the minds and attitudes of several new generations of lawyers. This state of affairs is still reflected in our modern law curricula and examination regulations, in the appointment requirements for law teachers, and the prerequisites for entry into the legal profession.[31] German law professors, by and large, train German lawyers, who in turn use German legal literature when drafting their opinions or handing down their judgments.

---

28. Even by 1899, i.e., before the Civil Code had entered into force, the librarian of the *Reichsgericht*, Georg Maas, published a bibliography that listed approximately 4,000 titles over 324 pages.
29. On the neo-humanistic turn of legal history, *see* Koschaker (n. 4), 290 et seq.; Zimmermann, *Civilian Tradition* (n. 8), 22 et seq. The disjunction between legal history and modern doctrine strongly resonates in modern methodological debates; *see*, for example, Reinhard Zimmermann, 'Roman and Comparative Law: The European Perspective', *Journal of Legal History* 16 (1995) 21 et seq.; Mathias Reimann, 'Rechtsvergleichung und Rechtsgeschichte im Dialog', *Zeitschrift für Europäisches Privatrecht* 7 (1999) 496 et seq.; Johannes Liebrecht, 'Rechtsgeschichte', in: *Max Planck Encyclopedia* (n. 2), pp. 1245 et seq. and *see* the contributions to Pio Caroni & Gerhard Dilcher (eds), *Norm und Tradition: Welche Geschichtlichkeit für die Rechtsgeschichte?* (1998).
30. Zimmermann, *Civilian Tradition* (n. 8), 40 et seq.; Eugen Bucher, 'Rechtsüberlieferung und heutiges Recht', *Zeitschrift für Europäisches Privatrecht* 8 (2000) 394 et seq.; for the Netherlands, *see* Willem Zwalve, 'Teaching Roman Law in the Netherlands', *Zeitschrift für Europäisches Privatrecht* 5 (1997) 393 et seq.
31. For criticism, Hein Kötz, 'Europäische Juristenausbildung', *Zeitschrift für Europäisches Privatrecht* 1 (1993) 268 et seq.; Axel Flessner, 'Deutsche Juristenausbildung', *Juristenzeitung* 1996, 689 et seq.; *idem*, 'Juristische Methode und europäisches Privatrecht', *Juristenzeitung* 2002, 14 et seq.

What has been said here about private law applies, *mutatis mutandis*, to the other legal subjects to be treated in this book. They are part of a national jurisprudence that finds its basis in a statutory enactment of, at least, its leading principles. Civil procedure and criminal procedure, as has been pointed out already, are governed by two codifications, both dating back to 1879. The Criminal Code (*Strafgesetzbuch*) came into effect in 1871 (a revised version was enacted in 1975), the Commercial Code (*Handelsgesetzbuch*), like the BGB, on 1 January 1900. The Introductory Act to the BGB (EGBGB) attempted to codify the private international law (conflict of laws).[32] The law of business associations and companies is regulated partly by the Commercial Code and partly by special statutes. The tradition of German constitutions laid down in a constitutional charter goes back to the National Assembly of 1848 (*Paulskirche*). The German Empire and the Weimar Republic had written constitutions, their modern successor is the *Grundgesetz* (Basic Law) of 1949. The rules of administrative law are found in a whole variety of scattered enactments; the matter has largely been left to the individual States rather than the federal legislature. Thus, it is only in the field of labour law that we find a somewhat special situation. All attempts at drafting a comprehensive labour code appear to have been abandoned. There are a multitude of special statutes (apart, of course, from the rules relating to the contract of services in the BGB), but much of what constitutes modern labour law has been developed by the courts. Thus, the Federal Labour Court is usually referred to as the real architect of modern labour law.

§1.05   THE STYLE AND SYSTEM OF THE GERMAN CIVIL CODE

Since, however, all of these topics will be dealt with in separate chapters, we will continue to focus our attention on the general private law. In a way, of course, this bias towards private law (as well as the strict separation between private law and public law on a conceptual level) is in itself a characteristic feature of the civilian tradition.[33] And while it may be criticized, it still provides a fair idea of what may be dubbed German legal culture. This is particularly true of the German Civil Code.[34] Somewhat dry and uninspiring in its tone and rather aloof from the social and political issues of the day,

---

32. A comprehensive reform has entered into effect in 1986; it has subsequently repeatedly been amended and supplemented – today *see* Art 3-48 EGBGB. Of increasing significance are the efforts to harmonize private international law within the European Union; *see* the Rome I, II, and III Regulations as well as the European Regulation concerning the law of succession, easily accessible in Oliver Radley-Gardner, Hugh Beale & Reinhard Zimmermann (eds), *Fundamental Texts on European Private Law* (2nd ed 2016), pp. 59 et seq.

33. Thus, for instance, it is only very recently that the history of public law in Germany has been written; *see* the four-volume treatise by Michael Stolleis, *Geschichte des öffentlichen Rechts in Deutschland*, vol. I (1600–1800) (2nd ed. 2012); vol. II (1800–1914) (1992); vol. III (1914–1945) (1999); vol. IV (1945-1990) (2012); cf. also, for a brief account, Michael Stolleis, *Öffentliches Recht in Deutschland: Eine Einführung in seine Geschichte 16.–21. Jahrhundert* (2014).

34. For an assessment, *see* Max Kaser, 'Der römische Anteil am deutschen bürgerlichen Recht', *Juristische Schulung* 1967, 337 et seq.; Franz Wieacker, *Industriegesellschaft und Privatrechtsordnung* (1974); Zweigert, Kötz & Weir (n. 8), 143 et seq.; Rolf Stürner, 'Der hundertste Geburtstag des BGB: Nationale Kodifikationen im Greisenalter?', *Juristenzeitung* 1996, 741 et seq.; Michael Martinek & Patrick L. Sellier (eds), *100 Jahre BGB – 100 Jahre Staudinger* (1999); Okko Behrends

it is of very considerable technical solidity. Its high level of doctrinal refinement, its intellectual maturity, and its remarkable sense of legislative self-restraint have made it an enduring monument to 19th-century legal scholarship. The BGB is not addressed to the layman. Its prose is neither beautiful nor easily comprehensible. Not everywhere, of course, are its sentences as convoluted as in § 164 II ('In the case where the will to act in another person's name is not apparent, the absence of the agent's will to act in his own name is not taken into account'), not everywhere does one find a string of cross-references as complex as in § 2013 I. But the BGB is marked by a degree of conceptual abstraction that has caused, and continues to cause, both admiration and disapproval. Technical terms tend to be used in one and the same sense, the way in which a sentence is constructed indicates where the burden of proof lies, and many provisions of the code can only be understood properly when they are read in conjunction with other provisions in far-away corners of the code. The internal logic of this kind of arrangement is usually impeccable, but it does not promote the code's comprehensibility.

The BGB consists of five books: general part (§§ 1–240), obligations (§§ 241–853), property (§§ 854–1296), family law (§§ 1297–1921) and succession (§§ 1922–2385). This way of subdividing the general private law can ultimately be traced back to the famous threefold classification introduced by Gaius in his Institutes: *personae, res, actiones*, with *res* being conceived of as the law of the patrimony in a broad sense and thus comprising the law of property in a narrower sense, succession, and obligations. In the course of the subsequent centuries, this system underwent considerable change and refinement.[35] One of its central features remains the differentiation between the law of obligations and of property which represents the translation into substantive law of the dichotomy between the Roman *actiones in rem* and *in personam*. Of Roman origin, too, is the concept of a law of obligations, embracing particularly contract and delict, but also what the Romans termed quasi-contract and quasi-delict.[36] Family law and the law of succession (both contextual rather than conceptual categories) owe their recognition as separate systematic entities to the Natural lawyers.

The most original and characteristic contribution of 19th-century scholarship to the disposition of private law as reflected by the BGB is Book I, the general part.[37] It has left its mark not only on the code but on German legal scholarship as a whole (and on most legal systems influenced by German law). To abstract and bring forth a body of general rules has great systematic advantages as well as severe inherent dangers. It has a rationalizing effect and contributes to the clarity of legal analysis. On the other hand,

---

& Wolfgang Sellert (eds), *Der Kodifikationsgedanke und das Modell des Bürgerlichen Gesetzbuches (BGB)* (2000); Uwe Diederichsen & Wolfgang Sellert (eds), *Das BGB im Wandel der Epochen* (2002).

35. For details, *see* Reinhard Zimmermann, *The Law of Obligations: Roman Foundations of the Civilian Tradition* (paperback edition 1996), pp. 24 et seq.

36. *See* Zimmermann (previous note), pp. 10 et seq.

37. On which *see* Mathias Schmoeckel, 'Der Allgemeine Teil in der Ordnung des BGB', in: Mathias Schmoeckel, Joachim Rückert & Reinhard Zimmermann (eds), *Historisch-kritischer Kommentar zum BGB*, vol. I (2003), pp. 123 et seq.; Jan Peter Schmidt, 'General Part', in *Max Planck Encyclopedia* (n. 3), pp. 774 et seq.

it tends to render the law inaccessible. Thus, many of the general rules about the law of obligations are not, in fact, to be found in Book II, but in the general part (Book I): how contracts are to be concluded, the effect of *error* or *metus* on the validity of contracts, capacity to contract, interpretation, etc. And if, for instance, a dispute concerning the sale of a movable object between an 'entrepreneur' (*Unternehmer*, as defined today in § 14 BGB) and a consumer (*Verbraucher*, § 13 BGB) has arisen, the special rules concerning consumer sales may be relevant (§§ 474 ff.), as may be the more general (but still fairly special) rules provided for the contract of sale (§§ 433 ff.), the general part of the law of obligations (§§ 241 ff.), the general part of the BGB (more particularly §§ 104 ff.), and, as far as the transfer of ownership is concerned, the law of property (Book III, particularly §§ 929 ff., dealing with the transfer of ownership in movable things). The hierarchy of rules applicable to a specific case, incidentally, is determined by the rule of *lex specialis derogat legi generali*.

The general part is a child of legal formalism; legal philosophies based on social ethics are bound to reject this abstract, technical, and unconcrete way of structuring law and legal analysis. As far as in particular the BGB is concerned, additional criticism can be levelled against the content of its general part; for it does not contain rules about the basic principles of legal behaviour, about the exercise of rights in society, the sources of law, or the powers of a judge; instead, a variety of topics are included, which foreign lawyers would hardly expect there, such as the law of associations, foundations, extinctive prescription (limitation of actions), or the giving of security.

§1.06   WINDS OF CHANGE

The BGB has now been in force for close to one hundred and twenty years and it is not surprising, in view of the vast changes in the general conditions of life over that period, that it has been amended in many respects. Thus, in particular, the field of family law has been fundamentally reshaped. Around seventy significant amendments have left hardly a single aspect of it unchanged.[38] Family law is probably more intimately linked to norms and practices of a specific period and society than any other of the core-areas of private law, and the Christian(-Protestant) and patriarchal views still prevailing in the second half of the 19th century have given way to more permissive sentiments. Recognition of the equality of sexes has led to a legal model of marriage based on partnership rather than domination, as well as to a significant change in the marital property regime; the discrimination against illegitimate children has been abandoned; the age of majority was reduced from 21 to 18 years in order to accommodate the desire of young grown-ups fully to participate in public and commercial life; the role-model of the married woman performing the function of a house-keeper was removed from the statute book (if not from the reality of married life); fault was replaced by irretrievable

---

38. For an overview, *see* Dieter Schwab, *Wertewandel und Familienrecht* (1993) (reprinted in *idem, Geschichtliches Recht und moderne Zeiten* (1995), pp. 257 et seq.); Rainer Frank, '100 Jahre BGB – Familienrecht zwischen Rechtspolitik, Verfassung und Dogmatik', *Archiv für die civilistische Praxis* 200 (2000) 401 et seq.; Elisabeth Koch, in: *Münchener Kommentar zum Bürgerlichen Gesetzbuch* (7 th ed., vol. VIII, 2017), *Einleitung*, nos 64 et seq.

breakdown of the marriage as the central consideration for granting a divorce; the maintenance claims of the needy spouse after divorce were also largely detached from considerations of fault in the breakdown of the marriage; fifteen extraordinarily complex provisions concerning pension rights adjustment after divorce were introduced (and have ever since managed to test the powers of comprehension of the average lawyer to the utmost);[39] adoption was recognized as a means of taking care of children without a (suitable) home rather than of perpetuating the name and property of the adoptive parents' family; the concept of parental power was replaced by parental care, and the 'welfare of the child' was emphasized as the core concern within parent-child-relationships; the legal position of transsexual persons had to be improved; persons incapable of dealing with their own affairs are no longer simply placed under guardianship but are being 'looked after' (*betreut*); the law concerning the determination of the family name underwent two major reforms before it could be regarded as reflecting the fundamental equality of man and woman (and as having irremediably lost its function of disclosing the underlying family relationships);[40] and homosexual partnerships came to be recognized in the form of a legal institution effectively resembling marriage without, however, being called marriage (*Gesetz über die Eingetragene Lebenspartnerschaft* of 2001 – literally: Act on Registered Life Partnerships). A statement by the German Chancellor, Mrs Merkel, in the course of a panel discussion prompted a cascade of events which resulted in the opening up of the legal institution of marriage for homosexual couples in the summer of 2017. The respective act (*Gesetz zur Einführung des Rechts auf Eheschließung für Personen gleichen Geschlechts*) was passed by the German Parliament in June and entered into force on 1 October 2017.

These are but a number of the more important examples. Some of the changes have become necessary as a result of the enactment of the Basic Law of 1949, while in other cases the Basic Law had to be invoked to protect established institutions against excessive reformist zeal. Nowhere have the premises of constitutional law had a greater impact on private law than in the area of family law. The catalyst for reform has usually been the Constitutional Supreme Court,[41] which has declared numerous provisions of the BGB to be invalid: as insufficiently taking account of the fact that the care and upbringing of children is a natural right of, and a duty primarily incumbent upon, the parents (Article 6 II GG); as disregarding the 'equal rights' provision of Article 3 II GG; as infringing the personality rights of children; and for many other reasons. Of great significance in setting the parameters for law reform has also been the provision of Article 6 I GG according to which 'marriage and family shall enjoy the

---

39. In the course of a fundamental structural reform in 2009, the respective provisions have been removed from the BGB. The *Gesetz über den Versorgungsausgleich* (Act concerning pension rights adjustment) now contains 54 provisions.
40. Cf. Uwe Diederichsen, 'Die Neuordnung des Familiennamensrechts', *Neue Juristische Wochenschrift* 1994, 1089 et seq.; and *see* the amusing comments by Dieter Schwab, 'Statt einer Glosse: Der Name ist Schall und Rauch', *Zeitschrift für das gesamte Familienrecht* 1992, 1015 et seq.
41. *See* Dieter Henrich, 'Familienrechtsreform durch die Verfassungsgerichte', *Zeitschrift für Rechtsvergleichung* 1990, 241 et seq.; Joachim Gernhuber & Dagmar Coester-Waltjen, *Lehrbuch des Familienrechts* (6th ed. 2010), pp. 31 et seq.

special protection of the state'. Where parliament has tried to shirk its duty of reforming the law, the courts have not hesitated to step into the breach. Thus, most famously, they tackled the task of bringing family law into conformity with the equal rights provision of Article 3 II GG after the Federal Parliament, neglectful of Article 117 I GG, had failed to do so by the end of March 1953.[42] This judicial regime was subsequently replaced by the Equal Rights Act of 1957.

Until recently it would have been true to claim that the other books of the BGB have, by and large, weathered the storms of legal development. They have, for just over one hundred years, provided the doctrinal foundations of the modern German law of obligations, property, and succession. The BGB's remarkable resilience throughout the 20th century, with all its upheavals and changes in political regime, has often been noted either critically or as confirmation of the inherent strengths of that code. For a very long time, there have been relatively few changes in the actual wording of Books I–III and V. The formal requirements for drawing up a will have been relaxed, the position of the surviving spouse in the law of instestate succession has been improved, and the provisions on lease and employment contracts have been considerably modified and supplemented (but the development of the law on residential leases has largely, and that of labour law has just about completely, taken place outside the framework of the BGB).[43] Animals have been elevated to a special status; they are no longer 'things' but the rules relating to 'things' apply *mutatis mutandis*.[44] In 1979, the legislature managed to disfigure the law of special contracts by a regulation of contracts relating to package holidays (§§ 651a–651l BGB) that has created more problems than it has solved. Other major amendments relate to the law of land tenure (§§ 585 ff. BGB) and contracts concerning bank transfer, bank payments and current accounts (§§ 676a ff. BGB; today *see* §§ 675c–676c (28 provisions!)). Outside the BGB, a 'secondary system of private law'[45] has grown up based on special statutes, by means of which the social model underlying the BGB has been adapted to modern conditions. Apart from competition law, labour law, and 'social lease law', the law of consumer protection deserves to be mentioned in this context. Among its core components are the statutes on standard contract terms,[46] doorstep sales and similar transactions, and consumer credit, but also other statutes such as the ones dealing with liability for defective products, time-share agreements, and distance sales.[47] It is often overlooked that this

---

42. *See* Jan Kropholler, *Gleichberechtigung durch Richterrecht* (1975).
43. The *Mietrechtsreformgesetz* (Act Reforming Lease Law) of 2001 has led to a partial reintegration of the law relating to residential leases into the BGB; *see* now §§ 535–580a BGB, with §§ 549–577a being devoted to special rules on residential leases.
44. 90a BGB (on which *see* Jürgen Ellenberger, in: Palandt, *Bürgerliches Gesetzbuch* (76th ed. 2017), § 90 no. 1: 'a sentimental pronouncement without any effective legal content').
45. Stürner, *Juristenzeitung* 1996, 742.
46. The pertinent political and academic discussions preceding the enactment of the *Gesetz zur Regelung der Allgemeinen Geschäftsbedingungen* (Standard Terms of Business Act) of 1976 had been dominated by the notion of consumer protection. None the less, the Act was not confined to contracts concluded between consumers; it was also, at least in principle, made to apply to businessmen. For background *see*, e.g., Hein Kötz, 'Der Schutzzweck der AGB-Kontrolle – Eine rechsökonomische Skizze', *Juristische Schulung* 2003, 209 et seq.
47. For details of the development, *see* Reinhard Zimmermann, *The New German Law of Obligations* (2005), pp. 171 et seq.

tradition of excluding from the general private law codification subjects, which were considered to be of a special nature because they fly in the face of basic principles underpinning the system of private law, goes back to the Historical School, and that therefore neither the statute on instalment sales of 1894 nor the one imposing strict liability for personal injuries sustained in the operation of a railway (the Imperial Law of Liability, *Reichshaftpflichtgesetz*) were included in the code. The latter statute provided a deviation from the principle of letting losses lie where they have fallen, unless they are attributable to somebody else's fault;[48] the former one could hardly be reconciled with the basic precepts of classical contract doctrine.[49] It has, in fact, remained controversial until today whether, or to what extent, such matters have attained the kind of structural and conceptual stability required for a codification or are at all suitable for incorporation into the general civil law. The tendencies towards a 'materialization' of the German law of contract,[50] however, are evident, not only in the special statutes outside the BGB, but also in the application of the provision invalidating transactions *contra bonos mores* to instalment credit contracts, or to suretyship contracts entered into by impecunious wives or children of the main debtor, and in the development and use of institutions of judge-made law such as *culpa in contrahendo*.

§1.07 TURNING THE CIVIL CODE INTO A BUILDING SITE

Today, however, the picture has changed dramatically. This is due, largely, to the most momentous reform that has affected the BGB since its inception. It has been brought about by the statute modernizing the German law of obligations (*Gesetz zur Modernisierung des Schuldrechts*), which entered into effect on 1 January 2002.[51] The history of the idea to effect a comprehensive reform of the German law of obligations reaches back to the late 1970s when the Minister of Justice requested a number of academic opinions which were published in 1981 and 1983.[52] The project was then limited to three notorious problem areas: extinctive prescription, breach of contract, and liability for defects in contracts of sale and contracts for work. A special Commission, appointed

---

48. This had acquired, in the course of the 19th century, the status of an unquestionable, axiomatic truth: Zimmermann (n. 35), 1034–1035. On the historical background of the Imperial Law of Liability and on the pattern of ad hoc legislation as the appropriate means of accommodating the need for a stricter-than-normal type of liability in exceptional instances, *see* Zimmermann (n. 35), 1130 et seq.
49. On which *see* James Gordley, *Philosophical Origins of Modern Contract Doctrine* (1991), pp. 161 et seq.
50. On which *see* Claus-Wilhelm Canaris, 'Wandlungen des Schuldvertragsrechts – Tendenzen zu seiner "Materialisierung"', *Archiv für die civilistische Praxis* 200 (2000) 273 et seq.
51. For an easily accessible collection of the various drafts and the motivations of the draftsmen, *see* Claus-Wilhelm Canaris (ed.), *Schuldrechtsreform 2002* (2002); for comment *see*, e.g., Peter Huber & Florian Faust, *Schuldrechtsmodernisierung* (2002); Ingo Koller, Herbert Roth & Reinhard Zimmermann, *Schuldrechtsmodernisierungsgesetz 2002*, (2002). For an account in English, *see* Zimmermann (n. 47), pp. 30 et seq.
52. Bundesminister der Justiz (ed.), *Gutachten und Vorschläge zur Überarbeitung des Schuldrechts*, vol. I (1981); vol. II (1981); vol. III (1983).

in 1984 by the Federal Minister of Justice, presented its final report in 1992.[53] After that, however, the élan to enact the reform proposals appeared to peter out (as had previously happened with much less ambitious projects), and the report of the reform commission was not very broadly discussed.

It therefore caused considerable surprise when in September 2000 a 630-page 'discussion draft' of a statute modernizing the law of obligations was published by the Federal Department of Justice. This draft was triggered by the enactment of *Directive 1999/44/EC of the European Parliament and Council on certain aspects of the sale of consumer goods and associated guarantees* and the need for that directive's implementation by 1 January 2002. In some respects, the 'discussion draft' considerably deviated from the proposals submitted by the reform commission; in other respects, it went beyond the reform agenda covered by the latter; and, for the rest, it had not been brought up to date and had thus missed more than ten years of legal development. Immediately, therefore, severe criticism was levelled against the 'discussion draft'.[54] Two working groups were then established by the Minister of Justice. They revised the draft, in some areas very substantially.[55] A government draft was published in early May 2001. Though it was pushed through Parliament by way of an accelerated procedure, it was again repeatedly changed. Thus, for example, the Council of State Governments submitted proposals for 150 amendments, of which the Government accepted about 100. The statute was finally approved by the Federal Parliament in October and by the Council of State Governments in early November 2001 and it was promulgated on 26 November 2001. A little more than five weeks later it entered into force. The period left to German courts and legal practice to adjust to the new civil code can hardly be regarded as generous. After the BGB in its original version had been promulgated, a period of more than three years was regarded as adequate before the new code took effect.[56]

The following core areas of the law of obligations and of the general part of the BGB have been affected: extinctive prescription, breach of contract, contracts of sale, contracts for work,[57] credit transactions, and restitution after termination for breach of contract. The Standard Contract Terms Act and a number of special statutes aiming at the protection of the consumer have been integrated into the BGB. Some legal doctrines which had been developed over the past hundred years and had come to be generally recognized have also now found their home in the text of the BGB. All of these reforms were well-intentioned. They attempted to iron out a number of grave and widely

---

53. Bundesminister der Justiz (ed.), *Abschlußbericht der Kommission zur Überarbeitung des Schuldrechts* (1992).
54. *See* the contributions published in Wolfgang Ernst & Reinhard Zimmermann (eds), *Zivilrechtswissenschaft und Schuldrechtsreform* (2001).
55. *See* the contributions published in *Juristenzeitung* 2001, 433 et seq.
56. Generally on the process of preparing legislation in Germany, *see* Reinhard Zimmermann, 'Text und Kontext – Einführung in das Symposium über die Entstehung von Gesetzen in rechtsvergleichender Perspektive', *RabelsZ* 78 (2014) 315 et seq.
57. For all details, *see* Zimmermann (n. 47), pp. 39 et seq., 79 et seq., 122 et seq; Reinhard Zimmermann, 'Restitution after Termination for Breach of Contract: German Law after the Reform of 2002', in: Andrew Burrows & Lord Rodger of Earlsferry (eds), *Mapping the Law: Essays in Memory of Peter Birks* (2006), pp. 323 et seq.

perceived deficiencies of the code, they were supposed to render the law clearer and 'more in keeping with the times'[58] and they were designed to bring the German law of obligations in line with international developments and thus to render a contribution to the Europeanization of private law.[59]

These aims, however, have only partly been achieved. This is true, particularly, of the law of prescription (which is practically by far the most important issue on the reform agenda) and of the law of breach of contract (which is the most interesting area, doctrinally). The diversity, and eccentricity, of the individual prescription periods in the old code had brought about serious distortions in core areas of the law of obligations and had created a host of intricate but substantially unnecessary difficulties.[60] The new regime (based, essentially, on a short general prescription period which does not run as long as the creditor does not know, and cannot reasonably know, of the identity of his debtor and of the facts giving rise to his claim) constitutes a considerable improvement but it has not been implemented consistently. The extraordinarily tight time schedule has also made it impossible to devote sufficient attention to a number of important points of detail.[61] The fragmented and excessively complicated way of dealing with the problem of breach of contract, revolving unhappily around a pandectist concept of 'impossibility' and other specific types of breach, was also widely regarded as an unfortunate feature of the BGB.[62] However, the new rules are not distinguished by the simplicity of their structure either. Nonetheless, the courts have, by and large, managed to cope with the legal problems arising in their practical application.[63] As far as the inclusion of a number of (but not all!) special private law statutes into the BGB is concerned,[64] even the most cursory glance at the new BGB indicates that use of the term 'integration' would be a remarkable euphemism. What used to be the Standard Contract Terms Act now occupies the place of §§ 305–310 BGB. Thus, the rules of the previous act, covering a variety of issues such as formation of contract, interpretation and fairness control, have all been shoved into one place. No attention has been paid to the fact that the BGB is based on a systematic structure. The contrast with the careful and meticulous way in which the BGB in its original version was prepared is evident.

All of this has to be seen against the background of further amendments of the BGB effected either shortly before or in the course of 2002. Thus, for example, a reform of the law relating to damages has been implemented.[65]

---

58. Hans A. Engelhard (the then Minister of Justice), 'Zu den Aufgaben einer Kommission für die Überarbeitung des Schuldrechts', *Neue Juristische Wochenschrift* 1984, 1201 et seq.
59. *See* Herta Däubler-Gmelin (the then Minister of Justice), 'Die Entscheidung für die so genannte Große Lösung bei der Schuldrechtsreform', *Neue Juristische Wochenschrift* 2001, 2281 et seq.
60. *See* Reinhard Zimmermann, 'Extinctive Prescription in German Law', in: Erik Jayme (ed.), *German National Reports in Civil Law Matters for the XIVth Congress of Comparative Law in Athens* (1994), pp. 164 et seq.
61. For a comparative analysis *see* Zimmermann (n. 47), pp. 122 et seq.
62. *See*, e.g., Zweigert, Kötz & Weir (n. 8), 488 et seq.; but *see* Ulrich Huber, *Leistungsstörungen*, vols. I and II (1999).
63. *See* Markus Arzt, Beate Gsell & Stephan Lorenz, *Zehn Jahre Schuldrechtsmodernisierung* (2014).
64. On the policy considerations for and against such move, *see* Wulf-Henning Roth, 'Europäischer Verbraucherschutz und BGB', *Juristenzeitung* 2001, 475 et seq.
65. For details, *see* Gerhard Wagner, *Das neue Schadensersatzrecht* (2002).

Further reforms have followed, many of them based on the necessity of implementing directives enacted by the European Union. If the experience is anything to go by, the future for the integrity and resilience of the BGB does not look bright.[66] Thus, Ulrich Huber has emphasized the 'indifference, superficiality and arrogance' of the legislature in dealing with traditional core areas of the law.[67] There have also repeatedly been objections to the surprise character of far-reaching amendments implemented hastily and without adequate public discussion.[68] It is obvious today that the BGB, once acclaimed for its durability and technical perfection, has been turned into a permanent building site.[69] But then, perhaps, it may be better for a modern code of private law to resemble a building site than a museum.

§1.08   THE PROVINCE OF LEGISLATION DETERMINED

It would be utterly wrong, even in a codified legal system, to measure the advances of private law in the 20th century[70] merely by looking at amendments to the code and at the enactment of specific statutes. Unlike the fathers of the Prussian code the draftsmen of the BGB were no longer obsessed with the idea that they had to provide an exhaustive regulation – from first principles down to the finest details – for every imaginable set of facts.[71] They did not aim at comprehensiveness. Nor did they contemplate the abolition of legal scholarship. They were keenly aware of the distinction between the 'political' and the 'technical' element of private law which had once been introduced by Savigny in order to mark off the province of legislation from

---

66. *See* Hans Hermann Seiler, 'Bewahrung von Kodifikationen in der Gegenwart am Beispiel des BGB', in: Okko Behrends & Wolfgang Sellert (eds), Der Kodifikationsgedanke und das Modell des Bürgerlichen Gesetzbuches (BGB) (2000), pp. 105 et seq.
67. Ulrich Huber, 'Das Gesetz zur Beschleunigung fälliger Zahlungen und die europäische Richtlinie zur Bekämpfung von Zahlungsverzug im Geschäftsverkehr', *Juristenzeitung* 2000, 966–967.
68. *See*, for example, Wolfgang Ernst, 'Deutsche Gesetzgebung in Europa – am Beispiel des Verzugsrechts', *Zeitschrift für Europäisches Privatrecht* 8 (2000) 767 et seq.
69. Wulf-Henning Roth, *Juristenzeitung* 2001, 488.
70. *See* generally Karl Kroeschell, *Rechtsgeschichte Deutschlands im 20. Jahrhundert* (1992). A history of private law during the time of the Weimar Republic has been written by Knut Wolfgang Nörr, *Zwischen den Mühlsteinen: Eine Privatrechtsgeschichte der Weimarer Republik* (1988); on German legal history in the post-war period, *see* Rainer Schröder, 'Rechtsgeschichte der Nachkriegszeit', *Juristische Schulung* 1993, 617 et seq.; Joachim Rückert, 'Abbau und Aufbau der Rechtswissenschaft nach 1945', *Neue Juristische Wochenschrift* 1995, 1251 et seq.; Dieter Simon (ed.), *Rechtswissenschaft in der Bonner Republik* (1994); Dieter Medicus, 'Entscheidungen des BGH als Marksteine für die Entwicklung des allgemeinen Zivilrechts', *Neue Juristische Wochenschrift* 2000, 2921 et seq. For a comprehensive assessment, *see* the contributions to Mathias Schmoeckel, Joachim Rückert & Reinhard Zimmermann (eds), Historisch-kritischer Kommentar zum BGB, vol. I (2003), vols. II 1 and II 2 (2007) and vols. III 1 and III 2 (2013).
71. On the principled nature of the BGB, *see* Joachim Rückert, 'Das BGB und seine Prinzipien: Aufgabe, Lösung, Erfolg', in: Mathias Schmoeckel, Joachim Rückert & Reinhard Zimmermann (eds), *Historisch-kritischer Kommentar zum BGB*, vol. I (2003), pp. 34 et seq.

that of 'legal science'.[72] Time and again, we therefore find statements in the *travaux préparatoires* that a particular problem should be left to legal scholarship rather than be resolved by the code itself.

Moreover, the fathers of the BGB refrained from defining and regulating purely doctrinal questions – central as they might be. Thus, we find neither definition nor explanation of basic concepts such as legal capacity, contract, declaration of intention, damage, causation, or unlawfulness; freedom of contract is not even mentioned. Matters of legal construction (is performance merely a factual act or is it a contract?) are avoided, as far as possible. Many basic propositions have not been included in the code as being self-evident. Thus, for instance, the BGB merely sets out the three different types of error that it regards as operative but does not mention that a mere error in motive cannot give rise to a right of rescission (as Savigny had pointed out, error in motive does not affect the will of the contracting party but relates to the preliminary process of the formation of such a will).[73] The BGB, in this as in many other cases, merely marks certain fixed points but does not attempt to prescribe the details of a comprehensive doctrine. Moreover, as has repeatedly been observed, the BGB is characterized by a considerable degree of abstraction, both as far as style and content are concerned.[74] It refrains from a case by case regulation of the individual problems encountered in real life but rather provides abstract conceptual tools which can usefully be employed for a variety of new and unforeseen situations. In fact, the BGB has turned out to be conspicuously weak and outdated where it, exceptionally, departs from this approach: where it deals with individual concerns such as the law of the flight of the bees (§§ 961 ff.) or where it used to take us into the 19th-century world of cab drivers and messengers, of domestic servants, day labourers and journeymen (§ 196, old version, in force until 1 January 2002). The language, too, in which the BGB is drafted, usually maintains a level of abstraction that leaves much room for interpretation and scholarly refinement. In addition, of course, the draftsmen of the code have made use of the device of inserting a number of provisions merely containing general standards of behaviour, most famously § 138 I BGB (*boni mores*)[75] and § 242 BGB (good faith).[76]

All of this contributes to a considerable built-in flexibility which immediately sets the scene not for confrontation but for an alliance between legislation and legal

---

72. For details, *see* Horst Heinrich Jakobs, *Wissenschaft und Gesetzgebung im bürgerlichen Recht nach der Rechtsquellenlehre des 19. Jahrhunderts* (1983); Hans Hermann Seiler, 'Rechtsgeschichte und Rechtsdogmatik', in: Karsten Schmidt (ed.), *Rechtsdogmatik und Rechtspolitik* (1990), pp. 117 et seq.
73. On Savigny's doctrine concerning error, *see* Martin Josef Schermeier, *Die Bestimmung des wesentlichen Irrtums von den Glossatoren bis zum BGB* (2000), pp. 483 et seq.
74. Cf., e.g., Folke Schmidt, 'The German Abstract Approach to Law', *Scandinavian Studies in Law* 9 (1965) 133 et seq.
75. On the application of which *see* Hans-Peter Haferkamp, in: Mathias Schmoeckel, Joachim Rückert & Reinhard Zimmermann (eds), *Historisch-kritischer Kommentar zum BGB*, vol. I (2003), § 138, nos 1 et seq.
76. On which *see* Simon Whittaker & Reinhard Zimmermann, 'Good faith in European contract law: surveying the legal landscape', in: Reinhard Zimmermann & Simon Whittaker (eds), *Good Faith in European Contract Law* (2000), pp. 18 et seq.

scholarship.[77] Even more importantly, however, the code itself suggests the point of reference for the most congenial kind of legal scholarship: the Roman-Canon *ius commune* in its 19th-century pandectist version. For those who drafted the BGB did not, on a doctrinal level, intend their code to constitute a fresh start, a break with the past. On the contrary: they largely aimed at setting out, containing and consolidating 'the legal achievements of centuries',[78] as they had been processed and refined by pandectist legal learning. Horst Heinrich Jakobs has, therefore, pointedly referred to the BGB as a codification 'which does not contain the source of law in itself but has its source in the legal scholarship from which it was created'.[79] The BGB was designed to provide a framework for an 'organically progressive legal science'[80] which was itself an organic product of the tradition of pandectist learning. This, incidentally, supports the claim of those who argue that the BGB is much less specifically 'German' than is often assumed; that it merely constitutes both a local variation and a transitional stage within an ongoing tradition; that legal history and modern law are not two different worlds; and that the elucidation of the history of legal doctrines and institutions remains an important prerequisite for laying the foundations of a contemporary European scholarship in private law.[81]

§1.09   CASE LAW IN A CODIFIED SYSTEM

The Imperial Court (*Reichsgericht*), too, did not regard the BGB as the great watershed in German legal history. It cautiously developed the law and started to adapt it to new circumstances. Usually there were either overt or covert lines of continuity linking the new law to the old: either because the judges simply perpetuated their earlier case law, or because they extended a line of development which had its origin in the 19th

---

77. Cf. the contributions by Jan Schröder and Okko Behrends in: Okko Behrends & Wolfram Henkel (eds), *Gesetzgebung und Dogmatik* (1989); Vogenauer, Cambridge Law Journal 64 (2005) 481 et seq.; Reinhard Zimmermann, 'Wider die verderbliche Einseitigkeit': Einführung in das Symposium 'Dialog zwischen Rechtswissenschaft und Rechtsprechung', RabelsZ 77 (2013) 300 et seq.
78. *See* Bernhard Windscheid, 'Die geschichtliche Schule in der Rechtswissenschaft', in: *idem*, *Gesammelte Reden und Abhandlungen* (edited by Paul Oertmann, 1904), pp. 75–76: 'We want to have the code and also the legal achievements of centuries: we will take care of that as genuinely historical jurists. As historical jurists we know that the code will be no more than a moment in the development, more tangible, certainly, than the ripple in a stream but, none the less, merely a ripple in the stream.'
79. Jakobs, *Wissenschaft und Gesetzgebung* (n. 79), 160. This does not mean that the draftsmen of the BGB did not in many instances abandon outdated doctrines and institutions; sometimes they also resolutely opted for a new regulatory pattern (even, or perhaps particularly, in the law of succession, an area usually regarded as stable and resistant to change; for the German parentelic system, taken over from Austria, *see* Reinhard Zimmermann, 'Intestate Succession in Germany', in: Kenneth G.C. Reid, Marius J. de Waal, and Reinhard Zimmermann (eds), *Intestate Succession* (2015), pp. 180 et seq.; a very similar story can be told about the compulsory portion).
80. *Supra*, text following n. 15.
81. For a more detailed discussion, and for further references, *see* Reinhard Zimmermann, 'Heard melodies are sweet, but those unheard are sweeter … ', *Archiv für die civilistische Praxis* 193 (1993) 121 et seq.; *idem*, 'Savigny's Legacy: Legal History, Comparative Law and the Emergence of a European Legal Science', *Law Quarterly Review* 112 (1995) 576 et seq.; *idem*, 'Europa und das römische Recht', *Archiv für die civilistische Praxis* 202 (2002) 243 et seq.

century.[82] Among the tools used by the courts were the undisguised appeal to general legal intuition or common sense, the reading of tacit conditions into a contract (a device which has been popular at all times and in many countries), and the construction of fictitious contracts.[83] The practice of the *Reichsgericht*, even in the early years of the 20th century, was not characterized by positivistic narrowness in the application of the code. At the same time, it was one of the great achievements of the Court to avoid a break in continuity.

Today, of course, the BGB has become enveloped in thick layers of case law which anybody who wishes to apply the law has to be thoroughly familiar with.[84] Drafting mistakes, internal inconsistencies and gaps have been discovered in the code. The proper interpretation of the words and phrases used by the draftsmen of the code had to be settled. The details of many abstract provisions had to be worked out, atypical situations to be accommodated. Some provisions had to be extended, others to be restricted in their scope of application. Entirely new and unforeseen legal problems had to be solved: What are the legal consequences of artificial insemination?[85] Can the birth of a child conceivably be regarded as a damaging event?[86] May the transfer fee for a professional soccer player be reclaimed if the German soccer association withdraws his licence to play?[87] Can a shop owner sue a person caught in the act of shoplifting for the reward promised and paid to those who caught the thief?[88] Changed societal *mores* and evaluations had to be accommodated. The modern cult of the motor vehicle or the increasing 'commercialization' of leisure time, particularly holidays, has been reflected in the development of the law of damages.[89] Unjustified enrichment, delictual liability, the law of damages: areas such as these, where the code provides hardly more than general principles, have become pockets of a typical case-law jurisprudence.[90]

But the courts have done much more. They have introduced entirely new legal institutions of which we find only a few scattered points of departure in the code. The

---

82. For details, *see* the contributions to Ulrich Falk & Heinz Mohnhaupt (eds), *Das Bürgerliche Gesetzbuch und seine Richter* (2000); Zimmermann, *Civilian Tradition* (n. 8), 53 et seq.
83. *See* the references in Reinhard Zimmermann, 'Das Bürgerliche Gesetzbuch und die Entwicklung des Bürgerlichen Rechts', in: Mathias Schmoeckel, Joachim Rückert & Reinhard Zimmermann (eds), *Historisch-kritischer Kommentar zum BGB*, vol. I (2003), vor § 1, no. 17. At no. 16 a number of examples are given substantiating the proposition that, contrary to a widely held opinion, judges in 19th-century courts had also managed 'to procure for themselves the flexibility which is so indispensable for the judge' (Bernhard Windscheid & Theodor Kipp, *Lehrbuch des Pandektenrechts*, vol. I (9th ed. 1906), § 28 note 4); cf. also Regina Ogorek, *Richterkönig oder Subsumtionsautomat? Zur Justiztheorie im 19. Jahrhundert* (1986).
84. John P. Dawson, *The Oracles of the Law* (1968), pp. 432 et seq. refers to 'Germany's Case-Law Revolution'.
85. BGHZ 87, 169 and subsequent cases.
86. BGHZ 76, 249; more recently, *see* BGHZ 124, 128; BGH, *Neue Juristische Wochenschrift* 2002, 2636 et seq.
87. BGH, *Neue Juristische Wochenschrift* 1976, 565; *see* Zimmermann & Whittaker (n. 76), 578 et seq.
88. BGHZ 75, 230.
89. Cf., e.g., BGHZ 56, 214; 63, 98; Dieter Medicus & Jens Petersen, *Bürgerliches Recht* (25th ed. 2015), nos 822 et seq.
90. The commentary by Gerhard Wagner on § 823 in *Münchner Kommentar zum Bürgerlichen Gesetzbuch*, 7th ed., vol. 6 (2017), extends over more than 1,000 marginal numbers (and is not even the longest commentary).

German equivalent of frustration of contract (*Wegfall der Geschäftsgrundlage*) was recognized, initially, in response to the problems posed by the consequences of the First World War on the performance of long-term contracts. It has become an established feature of the German legal landscape, even though the draftsmen of the code had rejected its predecessors of the pre-code *ius commune* period, the *clausula rebus sic stantibus* and Bernhard Windscheid's 'presupposition' doctrine.[91] *Culpa in contrahendo* and the contract with protective effects vis-à-vis third parties have installed themselves in the grey area between contract and delict, and positive malperformance has been introduced as a specific type of breach of contract, supplementing the system of remedies provided by the code.[92] Often these new institutions have been designed to circumvent provisions of the code which have turned out to be inappropriate or inconvenient. One of the reasons why the German courts have felt compelled to extend the province of the law of contract beyond its natural borderline into the adjoining law of delict lies in the odd, but practically important, distinction relating to liability for the fault of third parties: § 278 BGB provides for a strict liability in contract, whereas the defendant in a delictual action can exonerate himself by showing that no *culpa in eligendo, custodiendo* or *inspiciendo* was attributable to him.[93] The 'right to an established and operating business' (*Recht am eingerichteten und ausgeübten Gewerbebetrieb*) has been smuggled into the list of rights and interests protected according to § 823 I BGB in order to sidestep the decision that pure economic loss is not, in principle, recoverable in delict.[94] A complex body of law concerning transfer of ownership *in securitatem debiti* has been developed because the principle entrenched in § 1205 BGB, that a pledge must be delivered to the creditor, has turned out to be impractical.[95] A delictual action has been made available where an object that has been bought is destroyed as the result of a defect in an individual and identifiable part of it. The true reason for this development is the desire to help disappointed purchasers whose warranty claims under the contract of sale have prescribed as a result of the extraordinarily harsh prescription rule of § 477 BGB (old version).[96]

---

91. RGZ 103, 328; Klaus Luig, 'Die Kontinuität allgemeiner Rechtsgrundsätze: Das Beispiel der clausula rebus sic stantibus', in: Reinhard Zimmermann, Rolf Knütel & Jens Peter Meincke (eds), *Rechtsgeschichte und Privatrechtsdogmatik* (2000), pp. 171 et seq.; Zimmermann (n. 35), 579 et seq.; *idem, Civilian Tradition* (n. 8), 80 et seq. Since 1 January 2002 the doctrine has found a statutory home in § 313 BGB.

92. Zimmermann, *Civilian Tradition* (n. 8), 88 et seq., 92 et seq., 95 et seq. *Culpa in contrahendo* has today found a statutory basis in § 311 II, III BGB, while the doctrine of positive malperformance has been absorbed by the general notion of 'breach of duty' (*Pflichtverletzung*): § 280 BGB. The doctrinal device of a contract with protection effects has not found a home in the code; it is based either on what is usually referred to as *ergänzende Vertragsauslegung* (supplementary interpretation) or regarded as an instance of judicial development of the law legitimated by § 242 BGB (good faith).

93. Zimmermann (n. 35), 1120 et seq. (1125–1126); *idem, Civilian Tradition* (n. 8), 72 et seq.

94. Zimmermann (n. 35), 1036 et seq.; *idem, Civilian Tradition* (n. 8), 63 et seq.

95. Klaus Luig, 'Richter secundum, praeter oder contra BGB? Das Beispiel der Sicherungsübereignung', in: Falk & Mohnhaupt (n. 82), 383 et seq.; Zimmermann (n. 37), 116.

96. *See* Zimmermann (n. 60), 170. For a comparative study, *see* Hartwin Bungert, 'Compensating Harm to the Product Itself', *Tulane Law Review* 66 (1992) 1179, 1217 et seq. Even after the abolition of the six-month period of § 477 BGB in the course of the reform of the law of extinctive prescription the courts have not changed direction; *see* Hein Kötz & Gerhard

The famous 'general provisions' of the BGB have, of course, provided the most convenient space for judicial law making. In the process, however, they have been taken far beyond the scope of application originally allotted to them. The standard of 'good faith' (*Treu und Glauben*), for instance, appears only in a seemingly rather marginal provision (§ 242), where it relates specifically to the manner in which an obligation has to be performed. Soon, however, the courts seized upon the rule and converted it into a provision governing, and transforming, the German law of contract. By 1961 the details of its application had reached such a degree of complexity that a standard commentary on the BGB devoted a whole volume of about 1,400 pages, largely in small print, to the compilation, classification, and analysis of the rules and institutions derived from it.[97] The '*boni mores*' clause of § 138 I has been used to combat unfair standard contract terms[98] and it continues to be a valuable tool in the hands of courts that are willing to protect the economically weaker party within a contract from exploitation. It has thus heralded a shift of emphasis from freedom of contract to social responsibility. By falling back on § 138 I in order to sidestep the restrictive requirements of the usury provision of § 138 II, the courts have, at the same time, begun to re-emphasize the idea of equality of exchange.[99] In a startling decision of 1993 the Federal Constitutional Court has enjoined the civil courts to police the content of contracts which are unusually burdensome for one of the two parties and which result from structurally unequal bargaining power.[100] That decision has prompted the Federal Supreme Court to invalidate a surety's obligation in terms of § 138 I in situations where the conclusion of the contract of suretyship cannot be said to be the result of an act of free self-determination. This can be the case, particularly, where close relatives have stood surety for the main debtor's obligations and where the amount of the main debt far exceeds the economic possibilities of the surety.[101]

Wagner, *Deliktsrecht*, 13th ed. (2016), nos 151 et seq. This may be due to the fact that damages claims based on latent defects continue to be under a different (i.e., stricter) prescription regime than delictual claims.

97. Wilhelm Weber, in: Staudinger, *Kommentar zum BGB* (11th ed. 1961), § 242. Very influential in the process of domesticating the unruly horse and in paving the way towards a more orderly and rational analysis has been Franz Wieacker, *Zur rechtstheoretischen Präzisierung des § 242 BGB* (1956). Cf. also John Dawson, 'The General Clauses, Viewed from a Distance', *Rabels Zeitschrift* 41 (1977) 441 et seq.; Whittaker & Zimmermann (n. 76), 22 et seq.

98. Cf., e.g., Ludwig Raiser, *Das Recht der Allgemeinen Geschäftsbedingungen* (1935), pp. 302 et seq. After the Second World War, the courts started to base the policing of unfair standard contract terms on § 242 BGB; *see*, for the development prior to the enactment of the Standard Contract Terms Act in 1976 (*see* above, n. 47) Sibylle Hofer, in: Mathias Schmoeckel, Joachim Rückert & Reinhard Zimmermann (eds), *Historisch-kritischer Kommentar zum BGB*, vol. II 2 (2007), §§ 305–310, nos 7 et seq.

99. Christian Armbrüster, in: *Münchener Kommentar zum BGB*, vol. I (7th ed. 2015), § 138, nos 112 et seq.; Zimmermann (n. 35), 269 et seq.

100. BVerfGE 89, 214.

101. For discussion, *see* Mathias Habersack & Reinhard Zimmermann, 'Legal Change in a Codified System: Recent Developments in German Suretyship Law', *Edinburgh Law Review* 3 (1999) 272 et seq.

§1.10   JUDICIAL LAW-MAKING: PROBLEMS, PREMISES, PERSPECTIVES

[A]   The Constitutionalization of Private Law

General provisions such as §§ 138, 242 BGB constitute the most important as well as the most convenient ports of entry for the values of the community. Under the Nazi-dictatorship this was a curse as much as it is a blessing under the Basic Law. The concept of an indirect horizontal effect (*mittelbare Drittwirkung*) of the fundamental rights contained in the first part of the Basic Law[102] has led to an infusion of constitutional values into private law. At the same time, however, it has increasingly placed the Federal Constitutional Court into the position of a Supreme adjudicator in private law matters: a development which has been severely criticized by a number of private law professors.[103] One of the most dramatic examples of the impact of constitutional values on the shape of modern private law has occurred in the area of the law of delict. Influenced by the totalitarianism of the Nazi-regime the draftsmen of the Basic Law entrenched the respect for human dignity and the right to personal freedom, very prominently, in its first two articles. Soon the argument began to gain ground that these constitutional provisions were of fundamental importance not only in the field of public law; and since their spirit was to pervade every branch of the legal system, they should also be given effect on the level of the private law. More particularly, delictual protection of the personality was deemed to be desirable, and even necessary. It was introduced in 1954 by the Federal Supreme Court via the phrase 'or other right of another' (*oder ein sonstiges Recht eines anderen*) contained in § 823 I BGB[104] and has, since then, been reaffirmed on numerous occasions. Yet, a further, and even more spectacular, step was taken. In spite of the fact that 253 BGB (old version) in conjunction with §§ 823 I, 847 BGB (old version) explicitly confined the aggrieved claimant to a claim for the pecuniary loss that he had suffered, the Federal Supreme Court has been so bold as to award financial compensation for non-pecuniary harm in all cases where the intrusion into the plaintiff's personality right has been grave and objectively serious.[105] The elimination of damages for immaterial loss from the

---

102. It was developed by Günter Dürig, 'Grundrechte und Zivilrechtsprechung', in: *Festschrift für Hans Nawiasky* (1956), pp. 158 et seq. and has been adopted by the Federal Constitutional Court in the *Lüth*-decision: BVerfGE 7, 198; on which *see* David P. Currie, *The Constitution of the Federal Republic of Germany* (1994), pp. 181 et seq. For a summary of the debate about the horizontal effect in English, *see* Basil S. Markesinis, 'Privacy, Freedom of Expression, and the Horizontal Effect of the Human Rights Bill: Lessons from Germany', *Law Quarterly Review* 115 (1999) 47 et seq.; for a discussion in comparative and European perspective, *see* Chantal Mak, *Fundamental Rights on European Contract Law* (2008), pp. 25 et seq., 45 et seq.
103. *See*, e.g., Uwe Diederichsen, 'Das Bundesverfassungsgericht als oberstes Zivilgericht – ein Lehrstück der juristischen Methodenlehre', *Archiv für die civilistische Praxis* 198 (1998) 171 et seq.
104. BGHZ 13, 334. Ironically, this seminal decision concerned a letter written on behalf of a former Nazi minister of economic affairs who felt insulted by a newspaper article dealing with his activities in pre-war and post-war Germany. On the phrase 'or other right of another' in § 823 I BGB, *see* Zimmermann, *Civilian Tradition* (n. 8), 57 et seq.
105. BGHZ 26, 349 (the case of the 'gentleman horse-rider'); BGHZ 35, 363 (the case of the ginseng roots).

protection of personality would, in the opinion of the Court, have meant that injury to the dignity and honour of a human being would remain without a satisfactory sanction by the civil law and such a state of affairs could no longer be considered to be in conformity with the fundamental value system established by the Basic Law.[106]

[B]   The Re-Emergence of Ideas

In a broader, historical perspective, these developments can hardly be regarded as surprising. The very rigorous attitude adopted by the draftsmen of the BGB towards infringements of a person's honour and good reputation was based on relatively short-lived notions of contemporary upper class society.[107] It has not stood the test of time, and the courts have managed to bring German law back into the mainstream of European legal tradition, as represented, in this case, by the history of the *actio iniuriarum*.[108] The courts have also, for example, at least partly, endorsed the idea of equality of exchange, even though the draftsmen of the code had rejected the time-honoured device of *laesio enormis*.[109] The *clausula rebus sic stantibus* has re-entered German law through the window, although it had been thrown out by the door.[110] A modern version of the Roman *fiducia* has slipped into German law, in spite of the fact that the fathers of the BGB had attempted to ensure that a right of pledge could not be granted without transfer of the object to the creditor.[111] Even as accomplished a codification as the BGB is not detached from the ebb and flow of legal development; and the re-appearance of supposedly outmoded ideas is not a rare phenomenon.[112]

[C]   Theory and Practice of Interpretation

The methodological background to the German 'case-law revolution' is provided by Philipp Heck's *Interessenjurisprudenz* (an interpretation guided by the interests underlying the law),[113] which was based on Rudolf von Jhering's sociological and anti-formalistic approach to the law[114] and which was transformed into a *Wertungs-jurisprudenz* (an interpretation focusing on the values underlying the law) after

---

106. For details, *see* Zweigert, Kötz & Weir (n. 8), 688 et seq.; Basil S. Markesinis & Hannes Unberath, *The German Law of Torts: A Comparative Treatise* (2002), pp. 415 et seq.
107. *See* Zimmermann (n. 35), 1090 et seq.
108. Zimmermann (n. 35), 1085 et seq.
109. Zimmermann (n. 35), 259 et seq.
110. *Supra*, text to n. 91.
111. *Supra*, text to n. 95.
112. Cf. Theo Mayer-Maly, 'Die Wiederkehr von Rechtsfiguren', *Juristenzeitung* 1971, 1 et seq.; Peter Stein, 'Judge and Jurist in the Civil Law: A Historical Interpretation', in: *idem, The Character and Influence of the Roman Civil Law* (1988), pp. 142 et seq.; Reinhard Zimmermann, 'Civil Code and Civil Law', *Columbia Journal of European Law* 1 (1994/95) 91 et seq.
113. On Heck, *see* Heinrich Schoppmeyer, *Juristische Methode als Lebensaufgabe: Leben, Werk und Wirkungsgeschichte Philipp Hecks* (2001), pp. 89 et seq.
114. On Rudolf von Jhering, the great methodological innovator in 19th-century German jurisprudence, *see* Nils Jansen & Mathias Reimann, 'Begriff und Zweck in der Jurisprudenz', *Zeitschrift für Europäisches Privatrecht* 26 (2018) 89 et seq.

1945.[115] Textbooks on legal methodology[116] tell us how the courts may proceed: that they have to take account of the literal meaning of the words and of the grammatical structure of a sentence, of the legislative history and of the systematic context of a legal rule. Above all, however, they are guided by the design or purpose that lies behind a rule: the 'teleological' method of interpretation. We read about 'wide' and 'narrow' interpretation, interpretation in conformity with the constitution, comparative interpretation and 'harmonizing' interpretation under the auspices of European law.[117] With the proliferation of European directives affecting private law, the significance of interpreting statutory provisions of national law implementing those directives in conformity with them increases.[118] Under the surface, many of the maxims, or *regulae iuris*, concerning interpretation of the *ius commune* still live on.[119] Little, however, can be said as to when or why a court is using the one or the other approach,[120] or how certain preconceived ideas and value judgments can, or cannot, be prevented from influencing the judgment.[121] But German courts go far beyond what may legitimately be dubbed 'interpretation'. They regard it as their duty to fill both patent and latent 'gaps' in the law, often by resorting either to the device of analogical reasoning or that of 'teleological reduction'. They even resort to judicial law-making *praeter legem* and thus transcend both the intentions of the draftsmen of the statute in question and its objective 'rationale'.[122] This obviously leads on to the wider question whether German courts are allowed to disregard the law. Article 97 I GG makes clear that the subjection of the judge to the law is inextricably linked with, and has to be regarded as a necessary

---

115. Jens Petersen, *Von der Interessenjurisprudenz zur Wertungsjurisprudenz* (2001).
116. The leading one is Karl Larenz & Claus-Wilhelm Canaris, *Methodenlehre der Rechtswissenschaft* (3rd ed. 1995); cf. also Ernst A. Kramer, *Juristische Methodenlehre* (5th ed. 2016); Bernd Rüthers, Christian Fischer & Axel Birk, *Rechtstheorie* (9th ed. 2016); Franz Reimer, Juristische Methodenlehre *(2016)*. A monumental account on legal methods in comparative perspective is Wolfgang Fikentscher, Methoden des Rechts in vergleichender Darstellung, 5 vols. (1975–1977); an equally monumental work on statutory interpretation in historical and comparative perspective is Stefan Vogenauer, *Die Auslegung von Gesetzen in England und auf dem Kontinent: Eine vergleichende Untersuchung der Rechtsprechung und ihrer historischen Grundlagen*, 2 vols. (2001). In English, *see* the discussion by Dawson (n. 84), 479 et seq. At its bi-annual meeting in Würzburg in 2013, the association of private law professors of German language (*Zivilrechtslehrervereinigung*) comprehensively explored the legal methodology of private law; the papers are published in Gerhard Wagner & Reinhard Zimmermann (eds), 'Methoden des Privatrechts', *Archiv für die civilistische Praxis* 214 (2014) 1 et seq.
117. For the latter, *see* Walter Odersky, 'Harmonisierende Auslegung und europäische Rechtskultur', *Zeitschrift für Europäisches Privatrecht* 2 (1994) 1 et seq.
118. *See* Claus-Wilhelm Canaris, 'Die richtlinienkonforme Auslegung und Rechtsfortbildung im System der juristischen Methodenlehre', in: *Festschrift für Franz Bydlinski* (2002), pp. 47 et seq.; Wulf-Henning Roth, Christian Jopen, 'Die richtlinienkonforme Auslegung', in: Karl Riesenhuber (ed.), *Europäische Methodenlehre* (3rd ed., 2015), pp. 263 et seq.
119. Hans Hattenhauer, 'Zur Rechtsgeschichte und Dogmatik der Gesetzesauslegung', in: Reinhard Zimmermann, Rolf Knütel & Jens Peter Meincke (eds), *Rechtsgeschichte und Privatrechtsdogmatik* (2000), pp. 129 et seq.; Vogenauer (n.116), 430 et seq.
120. For a comprehensive discussion as to how the German courts normally proceed, *see* Vogenauer (n. 116), 248 et seq.
121. Josef Esser, *Vorverständnis und Methodenwahl in der Rechtsfindung: Rationalitätsgarantien der richterlichen Entscheidungsfindung* (1970).
122. For details, *see* Larenz & Canaris (n. 116), 187 et seq. A specificity of German legal methodology is the distinction between interpretation and judicial development of the law, on which the treatise by Larenz & Canaris and most other works are based.

prerequisite for, the hallowed judicial independence. Article 20 III GG, on the other hand, provides that the judiciary is to be bound by law and justice (*Gesetz und Recht*) and thus evokes the memory of those twelve years in German legal history when law and justice emphatically did not coincide. Whatever the constitutional lawyers may have to say about the matter,[123] both the existence and the legitimacy of judge-made law are very widely acknowledged today and even judicial law-making *contra legem* is tolerated in exceptional situations.[124]

Judge-made law, of course, is case law and so we widely find today a typical case-law approach prevailing:[125] the recognition of 'leading cases' as starting points for new developments and principles, distinguishing and arguing from case to case. 'Herrenreiter', 'Schwimmerschalter', 'Jungbullen', 'Flugreise', 'Hühnerpest', 'Funkenflug', 'Kartoffelpülpe', 'Seereise' and many others have become household names for German lawyers[126] – since cases are never cited by the names of the litigants but, somewhat dully, by the place and page of publication, leading cases have come to be remembered by a characteristic feature of the underlying factual situation. A doctrine of *stare decisis* does not, in general, exist in German law[127] but, of course, decisions of the Federal Supreme Court have an authority for the lower courts which in actual practice is more than merely 'persuasive'. The Federal Supreme Court, too, is not bound by its own previous decisions but, for obvious reasons, tends to overrule them as rarely as possible.[128] Occasionally, the Court hints at a future change of opinion in order to reduce possible surprise and embarrassment for potential litigants.

[D]   The Style of German Court Decisions

But there are further mechanisms for safeguarding certainty of law. One of them, of course, is the hierarchical structure of the court system which, as long as the litigants are prepared to take their case that far, allows the Federal Supreme Court to have the last word in most matters of any significance (unless, of course, it can be argued that

---

123. Cf. Jörn Ipsen, *Richterrecht und Verfassung* (1975); Horst Dreier, Art. 20 (*Demokratie*), nos 140 et seq., Art 20 (*Rechtsstaat*) nos 101 et seq. and 175 et seq., in *idem* (ed.), *Grundgesetz: Kommentar*, vol. II (3rd ed. 2015).

124. The award of a financial compensation for non-pecuniary harm resulting from an infringement of the 'general right of personality' (*see* above, n. 104) is one of the most blatant examples of judicial law-making *contra legem*. The Federal Constitutional Court has, however, condoned what effectively amounted to a judicial derogation of § 253 BGB (old version); *see* BVerfGE 34, 269 (*Soraya*). But see subsequently BVerfGE 65, 182 reversing BAG, *Neue Juristische Wochenschrift* 1979, 774 (concerning how claims based on social redundancy plans have to be treated if the employer falls insolvent).

125. Of fundamental importance for the German discussion has been Josef Esser, *Grundsatz und Norm in der richterlichen Fortbildung des Privatrechts* (2nd ed. 1964).

126. For a characteristic expression of this phenomenon, *see* Haimo Schack & Hans-Peter Ackmann, *Höchstrichterliche Rechtsprechung zum Bürgerlichen Recht* (5th ed. 2004); and see the appendix listing 'especially important decisions' in Medicus & Petersen (n. 89), nos 499 et seq.

127. On the methodological and theoretical implications of interpretative change in a codified system, *see* Reinhard Zimmermann & Nils Jansen, 'Quieta movere: Interpretative Change in a Codified System', in: *The Law of Obligations: Essays in Celebration of John Fleming* (1998), pp. 285 et seq.

128. A number of examples are discussed by Zimmermann & Jansen (previous note), 287 et seq.

a decision of the Federal Supreme Court disregards one of the fundamental rights enshrined in the Basic Law, in which case the matter may be brought before the Federal Constitutional Court). Another one is the necessity for all courts to provide reasons for their decisions and thus to expose their arguments to (academic) criticism.[129] A German judgment is supposed to appear as an act of an impartial as well as impersonal public authority furnishing the official and objective interpretation rather than personalized opinions of the individual deciding justices. Thus it is drafted in a uniform and dispassionate style without personal flavour.[130] The judges never write in the first person, and concurring or dissenting opinions are not permitted, except in decisions of the Federal Constitutional Court. The decision emanates from the court (or, in actual fact, from one of its divisions, i.e., for the Federal Supreme Court, from one of its 'senates' for matters of private law (*Zivilsenate*)) rather than from individual judges (whose names are not even mentioned in the case reports). The typical German judgment, like its French counterpart, attempts to deduce the result of a case from the pertinent legal rules. But, like its English counterpart, it is discursive in character. All legal problems raised by the facts of the case are comprehensively discussed, the pertinent case law and academic literature are thoroughly considered. A German decision, at the Regional Appellate or Federal Supreme Court level, addresses itself as much to the legal community (including the community of legal scholars) as to the parties of the individual case.

[E]   Bench and Chair

That leads on to a further characteristic feature of German legal culture: the close cooperation between courts and legal writers in developing the law.[131] Learned monographs and commentaries, legal textbooks, and articles in law reviews: all forms of scholarly writing are carefully noted and taken into consideration by the courts, and one need be neither dead nor particularly prominent in order to be quoted by the Federal Supreme Court. It is merely the applicability and the persuasiveness of the argument that counts. German legal scholarship, in turn, is typically 'doctrinal' in nature:[132] it expands, develops, refines, or criticizes a specific doctrine of German law

---

129. *See* also Dawson (n. 84), 433 et seq.
130. For a comparative analysis of judicial styles, *see* Hein Kötz, *über den Stil höchstrichterlicher Entscheidungen* (1973); *idem*, 'Scholarship and the Courts: A Comparative Survey', in: *Comparative and Private International Law: Essays in Honour of John Henry Merryman* (1990), pp. 183 et seq.; Jutta Lashöfer, *Zum Stilwandel in richterlichen Entscheidungen* (1992). And *see* the comments by Basil S. Markesinis, 'Conceptualism, Pragmatism and Courage: A Common Lawyer Looks at Some Judgments of the German Federal Court', *American Journal of Comparative Law* 34 (1986) 349 et seq.
131. *See* above, n. 77. For an interesting study relating to company law, *see* Wulf Goette, 'Dialog zwischen Rechtswissenschaft und Rechtsprechung in Deutschland am Beispiel des Gesellschaftsrechts', *RabelsZ* 77 (2013) 309 et seq.
132. *See*, e.g., Nils Jansen, 'Rechtsdogmatik im Zivilrecht', in: *Enzyklopädie der Rechtsphilosophie* (online, 2011); Christian Bumke, Rechtsdogmatik (2017). For a more general assessment of what is characteristic for legal scholarship in Germany, see the contributions to Christoph Engel and Wolfgang Schön (eds), *Das Proprium der Rechtswissenschaft* (2007).

(like 'Fremdbesitzerexzeß im Eigentümer-Besitzer-Verhältnis' or 'Saldotheorie')[133] and, in the process, discusses all the relevant decisions of the courts. It provides – usually – sophisticated foundations for both the existing and the future case law. The complexity and high level of technical refinement of (much of) German legal writing renders access by outsiders notoriously difficult. Elegance in style and presentation is not generally considered to be worth striving for, and witticisms are usually frowned upon. Unconventional forms of legal scholarship have tended for a long time, to be marginalized.[134] Economic analysis has now, however, established itself as an alternative (or perhaps rather: supplementary) perspective for private law regulation and dispute resolution.[135]

§1.11 THE PERVERSION OF THE LAW

[A] The Unjust Positive Law and the Precepts of Justice

The fixation of German lawyers on doctrinal exegesis with the 'positive law' as its central, and largely unquestioned, starting point[136] has been blamed for the subdued and uncritical, if not outright supportive, attitude which German lawyers have displayed during the darkest period in German history, the years of the so-called 'Third Reich'. The 1950s saw a revival of Natural law thinking that even influenced decisions of the Federal Supreme Court.[137] It was a pointed reaction against a legal formalism which had not concerned itself with substantive value-judgements and which had thus lost the ability to draw fundamental distinctions between good and evil or between law

---

133. Occasionally a new doctrine or new approach is 'discovered'. On legal discoveries, *see* Hans Dölle, 'Juristische Entdeckungen', in: *Verhandlungen des 42. Deutschen Juristentages* (1958), pp. 131 et seq.; on legal discoverers, *see* Thomas Hoeren (ed.), *Zivilrechtliche Entdecker* (2001).

134. One of the most interesting 'unconventional' approaches in modern German legal history was the *Freirechtsbewegung* (Free Law Movement); for a recent re-assessment, *see* Marietta Auer, 'Der Kampf um die Wissenschaftlichkeit der Rechtswissenschaft', *Zeitschrift für Europäisches Privatrecht* 23 (2015) 773 et seq.

135. For an assessment of various different 'perspectives' (both traditional and unconventional) on private law, see the contributions to Gerhard Wagner and Reinhard Zimmermann (eds), 'Perspektiven des Privatrechts', *Archiv für die civilistische Praxis* 216 (2016) 1 et seq. (based on the biannual meeting of the *Zivilrechtslehrervereinigung* in Cologne in 2015). For the economic analysis of law cf. also Horst Eidenmüller, *Effizienz als Rechtsprinzip* (4th ed. 2015); for the historical perspective Nils Jansen, 'Tief ist der Brunnen der Vergangenheit': Funktion, Methode und Ausgangspunkt historischer Fragestellungen in der Privatrechtsdogmatik', *Zeitschrift für Neuere Rechtsgeschichte* 27 (2005) 202 et seq.; for comparative law, *see* Thomas Coendet, *Rechtsvergleichende Argumentation* (2012). Legal sociology is a largely neglected field of study in Germany; and the impact of legal philosophy (or legal theory) on private law is also comparatively underdeveloped; but *see* now Marietta Auer, *Der privatrechtliche Diskurs der Moderne* (2014).

136. The classical account on the rise of 'positivism' (first 'scholarly positivism' and then 'textual positivism') in 19th-century German law is Wieacker & Weir (n. 4), pp. 341 et seq., 363 et seq.

137. *See* the critical discussion by Franz Wieacker, 'Rechtsprechung und Sittengesetz', *Juristenzeitung* 1961, 337 et seq.; Arthur Kaufmann, 'Die Naturrechtsrenaissance der ersten Nachkriegsjahre – und was daraus geworden ist', in: *Die Bedeutung der Wörter: Festschrift für Sten Gagnér* (1991), pp. 105 et seq.; Lena Foljanty, *Recht oder Gesetz: Juristische Identität und Autorität in der Naturrechtsdebatte der Nachkriegszeit* (2013).

and justice; and it was encouraged also by the public renunciation, in 1946, of unlimited positivism on the part of one of its most influential exponents during the time of the Weimar Republic. Gustav Radbruch had been professor of criminal law and legal philosophy in Kiel and Heidelberg before he was dismissed by the Nazi Government in May 1933, and in the early 1920s he had also been member of the *Reichstag* for the Social Democratic Party and Minister of Justice.[138] In his philosophical writings he had always insisted on the 'formal' character of justice and had emphasized certainty of law as the key aspect of legal validity. Having experienced the atrocities committed in the name of a particularly venomous combination of racism, nationalism, and totalitarianism, he coined what has come to be known as the Radbruch formula: where the discrepancy between the positive law and justice reaches a level so unbearable that legal certainty, as a value safeguarded by the positive law, can no longer be regarded as significant, the positive law has to make way to justice because it is 'false law', or non-law.[139]

But positivism was hardly the real culprit, certainly not the only one. Nor were the lawyers merely detached and uncritical observers. The national-socialist regime did not force itself onto an unwilling nation. It was cautiously welcomed or even greeted enthusiastically by a majority of the population, and among that majority there were the mainstream lawyers. The new rulers immediately embarked on a programme of purging the legal professions of what they regarded as racially or politically unsuitable elements – the German law faculties, for instance, lost more than a quarter of their members.[140] Many of them left Germany and had to try to reorient themselves in a strange new environment.[141] These purges elicited hardly any adverse comment. The process of 'aryanization' of the German law professoriate offered considerable chances of advancement for the younger generation of scholars. Some of them eagerly embraced the golden opportunity of contributing to the new era of national grandeur, no one more so than the highly opportunistic Carl Schmitt, one of the rising stars of constitutional law during the Weimar Republic. He celebrated the Nuremberg laws as

---

138. An edition of Radbruch's collected works has appeared in 20 volumes (1987 et seq.). On the life and work of Radbruch, *see* Arthur Kaufmann, *Gustav Radbruch: Rechtsdenker, Philosoph, Sozialdemokrat* (1987); cf. also Gustav Radbruch, *Der innere Weg: Aufriß meines Lebens* (1951).
139. Gustav Radbruch, 'Gesetzliches Unrecht und übergesetzliches Recht', *Süddeutsche Juristenzeitung* 1946, 105 et seq.; *idem, Vorschule der Rechtsphilosophie* (2nd ed. 1959), p. 33.
140. For details concerning the 'purge' of the German law faculties and on the 'nazification' of legal life in Germany, *see* Reinhard Zimmermann, '"Was Heimat hieß, nun heißt es Hölle": The emigration of lawyers from Hitler's Germany: political background, legal framework and cultural context', in: Jack Beatson & Reinhard Zimmermann (eds), *Jurists Uprooted: German-Speaking Emigré Lawyers in Twentieth Century Britain* (2004), pp. 46 et seq.
141. For an assessment of the influence of the German émigré scholars on American law cf. Ernst C. Stiefel & Frank Mecklenburg, *Deutsche Juristen im amerikanischen Exil (1933–1950)* (1991); Marcus Lutter, Ernst C. Stiefel & Michael H. Hoeflich (eds), *Der Einfluß deutscher Emigranten auf die Rechtsentwicklung in den USA und in Deutschland* (1993); for England, see the contributions to the volume edited by Beatson & Zimmermann (previous note). Cf. also Leonie Breunung & Manfred Walther, *Die Emigration deutschsprachiger Rechtswissenschaftler ab 1933: Ein bio-bibliographishes Handbuch*, vol. 1 (2012).

'the constitution of freedom'[142] and reminded German lawyers that by fighting the Jew, they were doing the work of the Lord.[143]

[B] German Lawyers and the 'Third Reich'

The history of the perversion of the legal system[144] after 1933 is as sad as it is complex. Attempts to come to grips with the past only started in the late 1960s. Onedimensional or monocausal explanations have remained highly unsatisfactory. Among practising lawyers as well as law professors there were certainly those who tried to do their best, according to traditional standards of morality, within a largely hostile environment. They refused to be influenced by the new ideology, even if they occasionally had to pay lip service. Often they were unable to pursue the career that would normally have been their first choice. Others were simply unconcerned about the broader issues and continued to do their job as if nothing had happened. They contributed to an image of normality within a highly anomalous situation.[145] Then, of course, there were the fellow travellers who saw attractive career opportunities. But there was also a sizeable group of lawyers and professors who actively supported the new system, both politically and in their capacity as judges or law teachers. Not that they had all been appointed by the Nazi rulers. It is well known that many members of the legal professions (particularly of the judiciary and the civil service) had been at best sceptical of, and at worst outright hostile towards, the Weimar democracy. That was reflected, for instance, in the cavalier treatment of right wing political extremists by the criminal

---

142. Carl Schmitt, 'Die Verfassung der Freiheit', *Deutsche Juristen-Zeitung* 1935, 1133.
143. Carl Schmitt, 'Die deutsche Rechtswissenschaft im Kampf gegen den jüdischen Geist', *Deutsche Juristen-Zeitung* 1936, 1193 et seq. On Carl Schmitt, *see* Bernd Rüthers, *Entartetes Recht: Rechtslehren und Kronjuristen im Dritten Reich* (1988), pp. 99 et seq.; *idem, Carl Schmitt im Dritten Reich: Wissenschaft als Zeitgeist-Verstärkung* (2nd ed. 1990); Anna-Maria Gräfin von Lösch, *Der nackte Geist* (1999), pp. 429 et seq.; Reinhard Mehring, *Carl Schmitt – Aufstieg und Fall: Ein Biographie* (2009).
144. To quote the title of the influential book by Fritz von Hippel, *Die Perversion von Rechtsordnungen* (1955). For more recent studies *see* Bernhard Diestelkamp & Michael Stolleis (eds), *Justizalltag im Dritten Reich* (1988); Bernd Rüthers, 'Recht als Waffe des Unrechts – Juristische Instrumente im Dienst des NS-Rassenwahns', *Neue Juristische Wochenschrift* 1988, 2825 et seq.; Ralf Dreier & Wolfgang Sellert (eds), *Recht und Justiz im 'Dritten Reich'* (1989); Lothar Gruchmann, *Justiz im Dritten Reich 1933–1940* (3rd ed. 2001); Franz Jürgen Säcker (ed.), *Recht und Rechtslehre im Nationalsozialismus* (1992); Michael Stolleis, *Recht im Unrecht* (1994) (American edition published in 1998 under the title *The Law under the Swastika*); cf. also the study by Rainer Schröder, '… aber im Zivilrecht sind die Richter standhaft geblieben!' *Die Urteile des OLG Celle aus dem Dritten Reich* (1988) and the overview by Michael Stolleis, 'Nationalsozialistisches Recht', in: *Handwörterbuch zur deutschen Rechtsgeschichte*, vol. III (2nd ed. 2016), cols. 1806 et seq. For the perversion of a supposedly 'value-neutral' and technical subject such as tax-law, *see* Reimer Voß, *Steuern im Dritten Reich: Vom Recht zum Unrecht unter der Herrschaft des Nationalsozialismus* (1995). On the dichotomy between law and justice see, in this context, Bernd Rüthers, *Das Ungerechte an der Gerechtigkeit* (3rd ed. 2009).
145. *See* the analysis by Ernst Fraenkel, *Der Doppelstaat* (reprint 1984, the English original 'The Dual State' appeared in 1941).

courts.[146] These lawyers were now willing to lend a helping hand in building the new society. They drafted the notorious 'Nuremberg laws' and wrote learned commentaries on them, they hailed the *Führer* as the supreme legislator and guardian of the law[147] and they set about drafting a 'people's code' (*Volksgesetzbuch*)[148] better suited to a national spirit emanating from a 'people's community based on blood and soil' (*Gemeinschaft von Blut und Boden*) than the BGB. Significantly, point 19 of the National Socialist Party Programme had demanded, as early as 1920, the replacement of the received Roman law, which was seen as serving a 'materialistic philosophy of life',[149] by a legal system based on the German people's community values.[150] This was partly implemented by drafting enactments based on vaguely defined notions of the 'public welfare' (*Gemeinwohl*).[151]

The Nuremberg laws, and the subtle casuistry to which they gave rise, provide examples of the type of legislation that could be expected from the Nazi-rulers.[152] In a way, however, these and many other acts of legislation suffused with Nazi-ideology still preserved a semblance of the rule of law: they were publicly enacted, commented upon, interpreted by the courts and could even be used, sometimes, as a safeguard against ideological zealots. There were other areas, however, where the rule of law had been replaced by the arbitrary use of power and by unchecked violence. And then, of course, there were many fields where the old law still prevailed. The Civil Code provides the best example. Here, during the 1920s, the courts had started to use the 'general provisions' of the BGB for far-ranging judicial interventionism, most famously, perhaps, in their attempts to deal with the consequences of the First World War on the performance of long-term contracts.[153] Perspicacious critics had started to realize that

---

146. Cf. Hugo Sinzheimer, Ernst Fraenkel, *Die Justiz in der Weimarer Republik: Eine Chronik* (1968); Ingo Müller, *Furchtbare Juristen: Die unbewältigte Vergangenheit unserer Justiz*, (1987), pp. 19 et seq.; and *see* the documents in: *Im Namen des Volkes. Justiz und Nationalsozialismus: Katalog zur Ausstellung des Bundesministers der Justiz* (1989), pp. 7 et seq., 28 et seq.

147. For a notorious statement, *see* Carl Schmitt, 'Der Führer schützt das Recht', *Deutsche Juristen-Zeitung* 1934, cols. 945 et seq., after the Nazis had, in the early summer of 1934, killed about one hundred persons who were regarded as hostile to their rule (so-called Röhm-*Putsch*).

148. On which *see* Hans Hattenhauer, 'Das Volksgesetzbuch', in: *Festschrift für Rudolf Gmür* (1983), pp. 255 et seq.; Gerd Brüggemeier, '"Oberstes Gesetz ist das Wohl des deutschen Volkes: Das Projekt des "Volksgesetzbuches"', *Juristenzeitung* 1990, 24 et seq.; and *see* Werner Schubert (ed.), *Volksgesetzbuch* (1988).

149. In the 1930s, Roman Law was regarded by those in the Nazi-party, who cared for these matters, as corrupted by Jews and as a bastion of everything that was now odious: individualism, formalism, liberalism, sophistry, and the cult of the letter.

150. *See* Peter Landau, 'Römisches Recht und deutsches Gemeinrecht: Zur rechtspolitischen Zielsetzung im nationalsozialistischen Parteiprogramm', in: Michael Stolleis & Dieter Simon (eds), *Rechtsgeschichte im Nationalsozialismus: Beiträge zur Geschichte einer Disziplin* (1989), pp. 11 et seq.

151. For the implementation of point 24 of the National Socialist Party Programme ('Gemeinnutz geht vor Eigennutz' – public welfare has priority over self-interest), *see* Michael Stolleis, *Gemeinwohlformeln im nationalsozialistischen Recht* (1974).

152. For startling intellectual links to the American race legislation, *see* now James Q. Whitman, *Hitler's American Model: The United States and the Making of Nazi Race Law* (2017).

153. RGZ 107, 78; Bernd Rüthers, *Die unbegrenzte Auslegung: Zum Wandel der Privatrechtsordnung im Nationalsozialismus* (12th ed. 2012), pp. 40 et seq.; Rudolf Meyer-Pritzl, in: Mathias Schmoeckel, Joachim Rückert & Reinhard Zimmermann (eds), *Historisch-kritischer Kommentar*, vol. II/2 (2007), §§ 313–314, nos 18 et seq.

this kind of recourse to the general provisions could conceivably entail grave 'dangers for state and law'.[154] These misgivings were fully confirmed by what happened after 1933. General standards such as those contained in § 138 BGB (*boni mores*) and § 242 BGB (good faith) were among the most convenient points of departure for imbuing the legal system with the spirit of the new, 'national' (*völkisch*) legal ideology.[155] A study of the history of private law within those years reveals the frightening flexibility of the methodological tools available to lawyers inspired by ideological premises and preconceptions. The 'unlimited interpretation' was an important key to the insidious perversion of the legal system by those charged with its preservation.

[C]   Reluctance to Glance in the Mirror

The quest for *Lebensraum* and racism were the central, and interrelated, fountainheads of Hitler's ideology.[156] The first, ultimately, meant war, the second was to culminate in the gas chambers of Auschwitz. When the war was over and the Jews had been 'exterminated', Germany was ruined, both physically and morally. Yet, the pace of the *physical* reconstruction astounded the world. Germany became the country of the proverbial economic miracle (*Wirtschaftswunder*). None the less, for many of those who had emigrated, Germany was not a country to which they wanted to return.[157] Those who had remained often took great umbrage if émigrés expected the Germans to confess their guilt and moral failure. These sentiments erupted with particular vehemence when Germany's most famous writer, Thomas Mann, publicly declined to follow a fellow writer's exhortation to return to Germany and, like a good doctor, help cure the wounds inflicted on the German nation.[158] Mann rejected the simplistic separation between the Nazi-rulers and a large majority of Germans who had, in a way, become Hitler's first victims, and he considered any genuine communication between those who had experienced the pandemonium from outside and who had taken part in it to be fraught with difficulties. The attempt to pick up the thread as if those twelve

---

154. Justus Wilhelm Hedemann, *Die Flucht in die Generalklauseln: Eine Gefahr für Recht und Staat* (1933). A few years later, and under the influence of national-socialist legal thinking, Hedemann radically changed his views; he now referred to the general provisions as 'shining ever more brightly' on the firmament of German private law; cf. Heinz Mohnhaupt, 'Justus Wilhelm Hedemann als Rechtshistoriker und Zivilrechtler vor und während der Epoche des Nationalsozialismus', in: Michael Stolleis & Dieter Simon, *Rechtsgeschichte im Nationalsozialismus: Beiträge zur Geschichte einer Disziplin* (1989), pp. 107 et seq.
155. The seminal publication on the subject is Bernd Rüthers, *Die unbegrenzte Auslegung: Zum Wandel der Privatrechtsordnung im Nationalsozialismus* (1st ed. 1968, 7th ed. 2012). For § 138 BGB, *see* now Jens Wanner, *Die Sittenwidrigkeit der Rechtsgeschäfte im totalitären Staat: Eine rechtshistorische Untersuchung zur Auslegung und Anwendung des § 138 Absatz 1 BGB im Nationalsozialismus und in der DDR* (1996), pp. 88 et seq.; *Historisch-kritischer Kommentar*/Haferkamp (n. 83), § 138, nos 23 et seq.
156. Ludolf Herbst, *Das nationalsozialistische Deutschland 1933–1945* (1996).
157. Only between four and five percent of those who had been persecuted for racial reasons (and that was the large majority of all émigrés) returned to one of the three successor states of the 'Greater' German *Reich* after the *Anschluß*. For details, and for a discussion of the obstacles impeding remigration, *see* Zimmermann (n. 140), 61 ff.
158. *See* Klaus Schröter (ed.), *Thomas Mann im Urteil seiner Zeit: Dokumente 1891 bis 1955* (1969), pp. 334 et seq.

years had never happened was, to him, 'the sign of a certain naiveté and insensitiv-ity'[159]

Yet, by and large, Thomas Mann's analysis was correct. For in many respects the Federal Republic of Germany, its politicians, its cultural élites and West- German society in general, did indeed attempt to live 'as if those twelve years had never happened'. Thus, for instance, the legal system was not completely remoulded but only the openly national-socialist acts of legislation were repealed. As a result, many of the old textbooks could appear in new editions, with only minor and, one might be inclined to say, cosmetic adjustments.[160] The ideological veneer with which their authors had attempted to demonstrate their political correctness had been removed. 'Denazifica-tion' also did not leave too many traces on the composition of the legal establishment. Some of the most prominent and vociferous supporters of the Nazi-regime were removed from their posts, but by the early 1950s all the others, as long as they had not reached retirement age, 'were back at their old desks'.[161] Some of the academics who had jumped on the Nazi bandwagon turned away from politically sensitive subjects. Others who had been fellow-travellers apologetically maintained that they had been caught up in the great excitement; that they had merely been commenting on the positive law; or that they had subtly sprinkled their reservations between the lines of their books and articles.[162] All of them had one thing in common: the reluctance to glance in the mirror.[163] Even those who recognized and seriously regretted the aberrations of their early years were not normally inclined to talk about them. And most of those who did not have to hide anything, also for a variety of different reasons, took the pragmatic approach of letting sleeping dogs lie:[164] They tended to turn their energies to more constructive tasks than to investigate the details of an unfortunate past from which German law had now happily emerged. Thus, it took a long time before 'those twelve years' in the history of German law became the subject of scholarly attention and before it was increasingly accepted that they could not simply be repressed or eliminated from the collective memory.[165] There persists a fairly

---

159. Thomas Mann, 'Brief nach Deutschland [Warum ich nicht nach Deutschland zurückgehe]', in: *idem*, Essays VI (1945–1950), edited and with commentary by Herbert Lehnert (2009), p. 76.
160. *See* Joachim Rückert, 'Abbau und Aufbau der Rechtswissenschaft nach 1945', *Neue Juristische Wochenschrift* 1995, 1251 et seq.
161. Michael Stolleis, *Reluctance to Glance in the Mirror: The Changing Face of German Jurispru-dence after 1933 and post-1945* (The Maurice and Muriel Fulton Lecture Series of the Law School, University of Chicago) (2001), p. 8. The path towards a far-reaching re-integration of the old élites was paved, first, by the way in which the denazification procedures were, in practice, gradually converted into rehabilitation procedures (*see*, e.g., Gertrude Lübbe-Wolff, in: Horst Dreier (ed.), *Grundgesetz: Kommentar*, vol. III (2000), Art. 139, no. 7) and then, for those who had been employed in the civil service before 1945, by an Act passed by the Federal Parliament in 1951 specifying the provision of Art. 131 GG: *see* Lübbe-Wolff, Art. 131, no. 5; Rückert, *Neue Juristische Wochenschrift* 1995, 1256.
162. Stolleis (previous note), 10–11.
163. To quote the title of Michael Stolleis' booklet.
164. Stolleis (n. 161), 11.
165. For an overview of the efforts undertaken by German legal historiography to come to terms with the period of the 'Third Reich', *see* Rainer Schröder, 'Die Bewältigung des Dritten Reiches durch die Rechtsgeschichte', in: Heinz Mohnhaupt (ed.), *Rechtsgeschichte in den beiden deutschen Staaten* (1988–1990) (1991), pp. 604 et seq.

wide-spread uneasiness that in spite of denazification and in spite of the trials against the 'war criminals', the legal system had ultimately proved unable to cope with the actions of those implicated in the atrocities of the 'Third *Reich*'; and that although everything possible has been done to prevent a recurrence of those events, we are still, essentially, at a loss as to how to explain them.

[D]   Another Aberration

This uneasiness, incidentally, has not been alleviated by the fact that the German legal system had to wrestle, for a second time within fifty years, with the legal and ideological consequences of yet another regime inspired by a totalitarian ideology and based on a fundamental disregard for human rights and the rule of law.[166] According to which law do the actions of the marksmen along the 'antifascist wall' protecting the German Democratic Republic have to be judged?[167] Can those who shot a fugitive defend themselves by claiming that they were ordered to do so? But did these orders not violate the Natural Law?[168] And is it just to punish the individual officer who fired the shot while the politicians in charge of the entire system remain largely unscathed? The release of Erich Honecker[169] was watched with mixed feelings by many observers from both the East and West of Germany. Germany's reunification has given rise to more problems than originally envisaged. From a legal point of view, incidentally, we are not dealing with a 'reunification' but with an accession of what used to be the German Democratic Republic to the Federal Republic of Germany. As a result, West German law has, in principle, become applicable to the five new *Länder* and to East Berlin. Thus, for instance, the BGB has been reintroduced.[170] It had been superseded, in part, by a family code in 1965 and, for the remainder, by a socialist civil code in

---

166. Klaus Lüderssen, *Der Staat geht unter – das Unrecht bleibt?* (1992); Walter Odersky, *Die Rolle des Strafrechts bei der Bewältigung politischen Unrechts* (1992); Josef Isensee (ed.), *Vergangenheitsbewältigung durch Recht* (1992).

167. BGHSt 39, 1; BGHSt 39, 168; BVerfGE 95, 96.

168. Cf. the discussion by Joachim Hruschka, 'Die Todesschüsse an der Berliner Mauer vor Gericht', *Juristenzeitung* 1992, 665 et seq.; Klaus Adomeit, 'Die Mauerschützenprozesse – rechtsphilosophisch', *Neue Juristische Wochenschrift* 1993, 2914 et seq.; Hartmut Horstkotte, 'The Role of Criminal Law in Dealing with East Germany's Past: The Mauerschützen Cases', in: Werner F. Ebke & Detlev F. Vagts (eds), *Democracy, Market Economy, and the Law: Legal, Economic and Political Problems of Transition to Democracy* (1995), pp. 213 et seq.; Robert Alexy, *Der Beschluß des Bundesverfassungsgerichts zu den Tötungen an der innerdeutschen Grenze vom 24. Oktober 1996* (1997). More generally on 'pre-positive' law as object and task of legal science, *see* Joachim Hruschka, 'Vorpositives Recht als Gegenstand und Aufgabe der Rechtswissenschaft', *Juristenzeitung* 1992, 429 et seq.

169. On the basis of *Verfassungsgerichtshof des Landes Berlin* (Berlin Constitutional Court), *Neue Juristische Wochenschrift* 1993, 515 et seq.; on which *see*, for example, the discussion by Eckart Klein & Andreas Haratsch, 'Landesverfassung und Bundesrecht – BerlVerfGH, NJW 1993, 515', *Juristische Schulung* 1994, 559 et seq.; cf. also BVerfG, *Neue Juristische Wochenschrift* 1993, 1577.

170. For a discussion of the problems on the level of private and commercial law arising from the transition from a socialist to a free market economy, *see* Norbert Horn, *Das Zivil- und Wirtschaftsrecht im neuen Bundesgebiet* (2nd ed. 1993); cf. also *idem*, Die Rolle des Zivilrechts im Prozess der Wiedervereinigung Deutschlands, *Archiv für die civilistische Praxis* 194 (1994) 190 et seq.

1975.[171] Again, however, the courts in the German Democratic Republic had paved the way for these reforms by interpreting many of the BGB's provisions in the light of Marxist ideology.[172]

§1.12   LEGAL EDUCATION IN GERMANY

[A]   Hereditas Borussica

A legal culture is shaped considerably by the way in which lawyers are trained. Thus, the emergence of the 'learned' lawyer is one of the characteristic features of the Western legal tradition as a whole.[173] To this day, lawyers continue to be educated at a university, in Germany as much as in France or Italy. Nineteenth-century German universities were the leading contemporary exponents of legal learning in the traditional sense, and German pandectism has been enormously influential in moulding the modern legal mind: both within and outside of Germany. Yet, at the same time, legal education in Germany[174] displays a variety of features which have tended to set it apart from other European countries. They have contributed to the sophistication of German law but have also led to a remarkable rigidity and (international) isolation. The training of lawyers has, for more than a century, been the subject of continued discussions among German legal practitioners and academics. Sporadically, these discussions have culminated in calls for far-reaching reforms. This happened, for instance, in the early 1970s and again in 1990.[175] Throughout the 1990s, various individuals and interest

---

171. Jörn Eckert & Hans Hattenhauer (eds), *Das Zivilgesetzbuch der DDR* (1995).
172. For a brief legal history of the 'German Democratic Republic', *see* Kroeschell (n.77), 152 et seq.; for the development of private law, *see* Rainer Schröder (ed.), *Zur Zivilrechtskultur der DDR*, vol. I (1999); vol. II (2000); vol. III (2001). A history of how justice was administered in East Germany, based on the files of the city Wismar between 1945 and 1989, has been written by Inga Markovits, *Gerechtigkeit in Lüritz* (2006).
173. Stefan Vogenauer, 'Legal Scholarship', in: *Max Planck Encyclopedia* (n. 3), pp. 1077 et seq. On the historical development of the legal training, *see* Thomas Rüfner, 'Historischer Überblick: Studium, Prüfungen, Berufszugang der Juristen in der geschichtlichen Entwicklung', in: Christian Baldus, Thomas Finkenauer & Thomas Rüfner (eds), *Bologna und das Rechtsstudium* (2011), pp. 3 et seq.
174. For discussions in English, *see* Jutta Brunnée, 'The Reform of Legal Education in Germany: The Never-Ending Story and European Integration', *Journal of Legal Education* 42 (1992) 399 et seq.; Juergen R. Ostertag, 'Legal Education in Germany and the United States – A Structural Comparison', *Vanderbilt Journal of Transnational Law* 26 (1993) 301 et seq.; Ingo von Münch, *Legal Education and the Legal Profession in Germany* (2002); Stephan Korist, 'Legal Education in Germany Today', *Wisconsin Law Journal* 24 (2006) 86 et seq.
175. Cf., in particular, the comprehensive survey and the reform proposals, eventually largely rejected, by Winfried Hassemer, Friedrich Kübler, 'Welche Maßnahmen empfehlen sich – auch im Hinblick auf den Wettbewerb zwischen Studenten aus den EG-Staaten – zur Verkürzung und Straffung der Juristenausbildung?', in: *Verhandlungen des 58. Deutschen Juristentages*, vol. I (1990), pp. E 1 et seq. For a more conservative view, *see* Horst-Diether Hensen & Wolfgang Kramer, under the same title and at the same place, pp. F 1 et seq. Both papers were presented for consideration at the *Deutscher Juristentag*, a biannual meeting of all German legal professions (on the history of which *see* Hermann Conrad, 'Der deutsche Juristentag 1860–1960', in: *Hundert Jahre deutsches Rechtsleben: Festschrift Deutscher Juristentag*, vol. I (1960), pp. 1 et seq.).

groups have expressed their dissatisfaction with the *status quo*.[176] In 1998 a group of more than twenty academics and practitioners under the chairmanship of Ernst-Wolfgang Böckenförde tabled a model curriculum which was distinguished by its strong emphasis on foundational subjects.[177] This initiative was as unsuccessful as an attempt by the conference of German ministers of justice to merge the two phases of the present legal training system.[178] On 1 July 2003, however, a reform bill finally entered into effect which, while essentially perpetuating the traditional system, introduced some significant modifications.[179] It has not, however, stopped the reform discussions;[180] indeed, a reform of the reform appears to be imminent.[181]

The basic pattern of German legal education, which has been preserved with extraordinary tenacity, still reflects its origins in 18th-century Prussia.[182] It owes its existence to the need to train a homogeneous, highly qualified, and loyal body of

---

176. *See*, for example, Hein Kötz, 'Zehn Thesen zum Elend der deutschen Juristenausbildung', *Zeitschrift für Europäisches Privatrecht* 4 (1996) 565 et seq.; Axel Flessner, 'Deutsche Juristenausbildung', *Juristenzeitung* 1996, 689 et seq.; Ernst- Wolfgang Böckenförde, 'Juristenausbildung – auf dem Weg ins Abseits', *Juristenzeitung* 1997, 317 et seq.; Hans-Uwe Erichsen, 'Thesen zum Elend und zur Reform des Jurastudiums', *Jura* 1998, 449 et seq.; Filippo Ranieri, 'Reform der Juristenausbildung ohne Ende?', *Juristenzeitung* 1998, 831 et seq.
177. The so-called *Ladenburg*-model: *see Neue Juristische Wochenschrift* 1998, 2797 et seq. (based on the *Ladenburg*-manifesto; *see Neue Juristische Wochenschrift* 1997, 2935 et seq.).
178. Ulrich Goll, 'Praxisintegrierte Juristenausbildung als Chance', *Zeitschrift für Rechtspolitik* 2000, 38 et seq.
179. *See infra* under [F].
180. *See*, e.g., Matthias Kilian, *Juristenausbildung* (2015), pp. 51 et seq. The most significant reform proposals are contained in the recommendations of the *Deutscher Wissenschaftsrat* (German Council for Science and Humanities) under the title *Perspektiven der Rechtswissenschaft. Situation, Analyse, Empfehlungen* (Perspectives of Legal Scholarship in Germany. Current situation, Analyses, Recommendations) (2012), pp. 53 et seq. For comment, *see* the contributions to *Juristenzeitung* 2013, 693 et seq. Most recently, *see* Friedhelm Hufen, 'Der wissenschaftliche Anspruch des Jurastudiums', *Juristische Schulung* 2017, 1 et seq. – The English version of the recommendations of the *Deutscher Wissenschaftsrat* contains a useful glossary on the terminology concerning accademics in Germany (pp. 7 et seq.).
181. *See* Joachim Lege, 'Zum Stand der Koordinierung der Juristenausbildung', *Juristenzeitung* 2017, 88 et seq. – Mainstream German legal education has not been affected by what is often referred to as the 'Bologna process'. None the less, a number of institutions (particularly *Fachhochschulen* – universities of applied sciences) have started to offer Bachelor- and Master-degrees in law; they do not, however, provide access to the classical legal professions. *See* Kilian (n. 180), 54 et seq.; *Deutscher Wissenschaftsrat, Perspektiven der Rechtswissenschaft* (n. 180, English version), pp. 56 et seq.; and *see* Heiner Schöbel (Head of the Bavarian Examination Office for Law) 'Einführung des Bologna-Modells in der deutschen Juristenausbildung?', in Baldus, Finkenauer & Rüfner (n. 173), pp. 253 et seq. (expressing the widely prevailing scepticism towards an introduction of the Bologna-model for law in Germany).
182. On the history of legal education in Germany *see* Gerhard Dilcher, 'Die preußischen Juristen und die Staatsprüfungen: Zur Entwicklung der juristischen Professionalisierung im 18. Jahrhundert', in: *Festschrift für Hans Thieme* (1986), pp. 295 et seq.; Hans Hattenhauer, 'Juristenausbildung – Geschichte und Probleme', *Juristische Schulung* 1989, 513 et seq.; Ina Ebert, *Die Normierung der juristischen Staatsexamina und des juristischen Vorbereitungsdienstes in Preußen (1849–1934)* (1995); Filippo Ranieri, 'Juristen für Europa: Wahre und falsche Probleme in der derzeitigen Reformdiskussion zur deutschen Juristenausbildung', *Juristenzeitung* 1997, 801 et seq.; Peter Krause, 'Geschichte der Justiz und Verwaltungsausbildung in Preußen und Deutschland', in: Christian Baldus, Thomas Finkenauer & Thomas Rüfner (eds), *Juristenausbildung in Europa zwischen Tradition und Reform* (2008), pp. 95 et seq.; for an overview, *see* also Kilian (n. 180), pp. 21 et seq.

executive and judicial officers to administer a far-flung and fairly heterogeneous territory. Thus, a 'preparatory service', run by the State, was introduced to equip university graduates with the necessary practical skills to perform their various functions; this preparatory service was also made a mandatory requirement for admission as a private legal practitioner or notary; the academic legal training at the universities was subjected to detailed regulation; and the State assumed responsibility not only for the examination at the end of the preparatory service but also for the one concluding the academic legal training. What used to be a genuine university degree was thus, essentially, converted into an entrance examination for the preparatory service which, in turn, became the needle's eye through which candidates for all legal professions had to pass. The glory and the misery of German legal training have remained intimately linked to these constituent features.

[B]   The State Examination: A Key Feature of German Legal Training

German law students continue to conclude their university studies, usually lasting between ten and eleven semesters, not by obtaining a university degree but by passing a 'first legal examination' (*Erste Juristische Prüfung*) which used to be, and still very largely is, a State examination. It is run in all of the 16 German states (*Länder*) by a specific office within the administration of justice of the respective state (*Landesjustiz-prüfungsamt*) which also appoints the examiners. For more than 100 years professors have participated in the process of examining. As a result, the papers are normally graded by one practitioner (usually an appeal court judge, or a senior member of the state administration) and by one professor, and each panel for oral examinations is usually composed of professors as well as practitioners. In most states, students are required to write six (formerly eight) five-hour papers, which can cover the entire disciplinary spectrum within the three fields of private law, public law, and criminal law, as far as it is part of the obligatory curriculum. In each of these papers the student is usually presented with a set of hypothetical facts and has to provide a reasoned legal opinion as evidence of the fact that he or she does not just *know* the law (including, in particular, the relevant legal doctrines) but that he is able to *apply* it. The characteristic emphasis on application rather than regurgitation of what has been learnt is underlined by the fact that the text of all relevant codes and statutes are always available to students in the course of their examination. After all papers have been graded, each student whose aggregate mark reaches a certain minimum level has to submit to an oral examination. An oral examination session, which lasts several hours, is attended by up to five students who are examined, in turn, by several examiners in private law, public law, and criminal law. Once again, the focus is on legal reasoning. At the end of a long and gruelling morning, often lasting well into the afternoon, each student receives individual marks for the different parts of his oral examination; these marks, together with those obtained in the written tests, provide the basis for calculating the aggregate mark. The eccentric German grading scale for legal examinations ranges from 0 to 18 points, with 0 to 3 points indicating failure, while the designations for passing an examination are 'sufficient' (*ausreichend*: 4–6 points), 'satisfactory' (*befriedigend*: 7–9 points), 'fully satisfactory' (*voll befriedigend*: 10–12 points), 'good' (*gut*: 13–15 points), and 'very good' (*sehr gut*: 16–18 points).[183]

Legal education in Germany is traditionally regulated by the various German states; the Federation only provides a general framework.[184] As a result, the details differ from state to state, both as far as the procedure and the substantive content of the state examination is concerned. Thus, for example, while the German Judiciary Act determines that students have to be familiar with 'the core areas of private law, criminal law, public law, and procedural law, including the relationships with European law, legal methodology, and the philosophical, historical, and social foundations', the legal training and examination regulations of the various states specify what exactly counts as core area (labour law, company law, the different branches of administrative law, which of the many specific crimes in the criminal code?). By regulating the admission requirements for the traditional legal professions, the State is thus determining the agenda of the academic legal training. For in whatever way the law faculties might like to see their own mission, their primary function is to prepare their students for the first examination. Unfortunately, however, they are neither particularly well-placed nor ideally equipped to attain this aim.

[C] Students, Professors, and the Private Cram Schools

To start with, there are no university entrance examinations. Anybody who has graduated from Secondary School comprising the 'secondary level II' (*Gymnasium*), i.e., who has attended twelve or thirteen years of school and successfully passed the *Abitur*, may apply for admission to a faculty of law. All applicants have a right to be admitted, though not necessarily at the university of their first or second choice. The ceiling figures fixed by state regulation for the individual law faculties are high;[185] they far exceed the maximum capacity for which the faculties have originally been designed. First- or second-year courses with 300 or 400 students are the rule rather than the exception. All faculties operate according to their own model curricula; these do not, however, differ from each other in significant respects.

In principle, students are free to choose which courses they want to take at what time. They do not have to attend lectures at all, as long as they formally register for a

---

183. This is determined in a regulation with the unwieldy title *Verordnung über eine Noten- und Punkteskala für die erste und zweite juristische Prüfung*, known under the even more unwieldy abbreviation JurPrNotSkV. As far as the aggregate mark for the state examination is concerned, the designations at the upper and of the scale are different ('fully satisfactory': 9–11.5 points; 'good': 11.5–13.99 points; 'very good': 14–18 points). In calculating the aggregate mark, the marks for the oral part of the examination usually count one-third, those of the written tests two-thirds.

184. *See* §§ 5 et seq. of the *Deutsches Richtergesetz* (German Judiciary Act); cf. also § 4 *Bundesrechtsanwaltsordnung* (Federal Lawyers' Act), § 5 *Bundesnotarordnung* (Federal Act concerning Notaries Public), both of them referring to the Deutsches Richtergesetz. It is highly significant for the German legal training tradition that the key requirements for a legal qualification are laid down in the *Judiciary* Act.

185. *See* the statistics provided by von Münch (n. 174), 79–80.

certain number of courses and obtain a certain number of certificates by means of writing tests or home exams. In theory, they are largely free to determine for themselves how best to organize their studies. Since, however, they lack the experience required for independent academic study, many of them actually start to drift. German professors, in turn, do not find it congenial to teach huge classes with ill-equipped and badly motivated students and do not always put in an inspired performance during their mandatory eight to ten hours of teaching per week.[186] Also, traditionally they prioritize research rather than teaching, since it is very largely on the basis of their research record (as well as on their ability to attract external funding for their research) that they manage to secure attractive offers from other universities (allowing them either to accept those offers, or to re-negotiate the conditions for staying where they are). A distinguished detachment from the hustle and bustle of university life is not an uncommon attitude among German professors, in law as much as elsewhere.[187]

As a result of these, and a variety of other, contributing factors, the large majority of students have traditionally been driven into the arms of private cram school teachers which have for some generations been an unfortunate but well-established part of German legal education.[188] These cram schools (*Repetitorien*) charge substantial fees (which universities do not do) and enforce a rigorous work discipline (which law faculties do not do either). They are not interested in sophisticated academic discourses but teach the nitty-gritty of the case-method: how to tackle hypothetical sets of facts such as those presented in the State examination. For a German law student does not only have to have a very broad and detailed knowledge of substantive law (statutes, case law, legal doctrine) and to be able to apply that knowledge in one single,

---

186. The teaching year in the State University consists of about thirty weeks divided into two semesters.
187. German Professors are normally civil servants of the state within which their university is situated. While relatively well paid (in comparison with professors in other European countries, though not in comparison with lawyers practising in international law firms, or public notaries), they may, within limits, engage in private practice. They are much sought after to provide expert opinions, they are involved in high-profile litigation or arbitration, or they serve as (part-time) judges in a Regional Appeal Court (Oberlandesgericht). Hardly any professor will, however, contemplate giving up his chair for full-time legal practice or for appointment as a regular judge. Elevation to the Bench of the Federal Constitutional Court (Bundesverfassungsgericht) presents an exception. About half the sixteen judges of that Court are usually law professors who, for the period of their court tenure, cease to be full-time teachers. – Professors are paid according to a special salary scale. The one in force since 2005 (introduced by an act with the attractive title *Professorenbesoldungsreformgesetz* was, in part, struck down by the Federal Constitutional Court in a decision of 14 February 2012 as evidently disregarding the established principle of 'adequate alimentation' concerning civil servants. The reform legislation thus required has the even more attractive title of *Professorenbesoldungsneuregelungsgesetz*.
188. *See* Wolfgang Martin, *Juristische Repetitorien und staatliches Ausbildungsmonopol in der Bundesrepublik Deutschland* (1993); Kilian (n. 180), pp. 151 et seq. (who relates, on the basis of a survey conducted among lawyers admitted to legal practice between 2004 and 2010, that 86% of them have attended a *Repetitorium* – in spite of the fact that many law faculties have themselves mounted ambitious repetition courses preparing their students for the first legal examination; cf. also Thorsten Deppner, Matthias Lehnert & Friederike Wapler, *Examen ohne Repetitor* (2011).

comprehensive examination at the end of his studies; equally important is the mastery of a highly formalized 'method' of preparing a legal opinion and 'solving the case',[189] that is enforced with unrelenting rigour. This method is designed to ensure that the student considers the case under all relevant legal aspects, that he explores every conceivable argument either supporting or defeating the plaintiff's claim and that, in the process, he avoids discussing any issue that is not strictly relevant. Of central importance is the notion of an *Anspruch* ('claim')[190] by means of which the leading 19th-century scholar Bernhard Windscheid managed to remould the Roman *actio* into a term of substantive, rather than procedural law.[191] It invariably provides the point of departure for any case analysis in German law and has, more generally, become one of the fundamental conceptual pillars of modern private law doctrine.[192] This way of thinking is designed to cure students of any temptation to approach the case with a naïve and unselfconscious sense of what is right and wrong. It nurtures a mental discipline that is widely regarded as a specific attribute of lawyers. It both requires and encourages a style of writing that is precise, detached and 'neutral'; or, as may also be said, entirely colourless and devoid of any literary grace and personal flavour. And it possesses a sublime, if faintly pedantic, inherent logic.

It is not probably surprising, under those circumstances, that in the first legal examination there is regularly a startlingly high failure rate. While, until the middle of the 1970s, it used to be below 20%, it has over the years risen to close to 30%, occasionally even slightly above that margin.[193] More than two-thirds of those who pass merely achieve a result of 'sufficient' or 'satisfactory'. All in all, the average mark, counting all those who sit for the first examination, is not quite 6 points.[194]

[D]   The 'Preparatory Service' and Legal Practice

Those who have passed the first examination usually start with their 'preparatory service' or practical legal training (*Referendardienst*). It takes two years and is intended to introduce them to the various legal professions and to school them in the art of

---

189. For a comprehensive instruction concerning private law cases *see* Uwe Diederichsen & Gerhard Wagner, *Die BGB-Klausur* (9th ed. 1998); Dirk Olzen & Rolf Wank, *Zivilrechtliche Klausuren-lehre und Fallrepetitorium* (8nd ed. 2015).

190. Defined in § 194 I BGB as 'the right to demand an act or an omission from another' ([D]*as Recht, von einem anderen ein Tun oder Unterlassen zu verlangen*).

191. *See* Bernhard Windscheid, *Die Actio des römischen Civilrechts vom Standpunkte des heutigen Rechts* (1856); Bernhard Windscheid & Theodor Kipp, *Lehrbuch des Pandektenrechts* (9th ed. 1906), §§ 43, 106.

192. For a general discussion, *see* Dieter Medicus, 'Anspruch und Einrede als Rückgrat einer zivilistischen Lehrmethode', *Archiv für die civilistische Praxis* 174 (1974) 313 et seq.; Bernhard Großfeld, 'Examensvorbereitung und Jurisprudenz', *Juristenzeitung* 1992, 22 et seq.; Jan Schapp, 'Das Zivilrecht als Anspruchssystem', *Juristische Schulung* 1992, 537 et seq. In his tremendously successful book *Bürgerliches Recht: Eine nach Anspruchsgrundlagen geordnete Darstellung zur Examensvorbereitung* (now continued by Jens Petersen: 25th ed. 2015), Dieter Medicus has provided an analysis of the BGB which is strictly based on the various *Ansprüche* recognized in German private law.

193. Kilian (n. 180), pp. 136 et seq., with speculations about the cause of this increase.

194. Kilian (n. 180), pp. 133.

drawing up pleadings, drafting administrative acts, writing judgments, etc. The *Referendardienst* is run entirely by the State, which contributes towards the maintenance of the trainees (*Rechtsreferendare*). The latter have to complete a number of obligatory stages (with a civil division of a court, a criminal division of a court or public prosecutor, an office within the public administration, and with a lawyer in private practice), plus one or two optional stages. In addition, *Rechtsreferendare* are required to attend practical legal training courses run by judges or civil servants.

The preparatory service ends with the second State examination (*Zweite Staatsprüfung*) which follows a pattern similar to the first. Up to eleven (Bavaria) five-hour tests have to be written over a period of less than three weeks and, after these tests have been marked, an oral examination takes place which lasts several hours. This time, only judges, senior civil servants, and senior practising lawyers serve as examiners. Again, candidates receive a final overall mark (on the same scale as for the first examination) which determines their professional prospects. Even at that stage, between 10% and 20% of all candidates fail (they may repeat the examination once). Only around 20% receive a distinction of 'fully satisfactory' or better, i.e., a mark of 9 points or above; only around 2% attain a distinction of 'good' or 'very good'.[195] In hardly any other field is the final grade as significant for an aspiring youngster's career prospects as in the law; some career options are effectively closed for those who have not at least achieved 9 points.

Those who pass may call themselves *Assessor*. They are fully qualified lawyers and may now try to secure an appointment as a judge (the judiciary in Germany constitutes a career office within the civil service), as a notary public, as a public prosecutor, or as an adviser in the legal department of a firm. Alternatively they may join a law firm or open their own office as a private practitioner. They have survived two intense and remorseless examinations and have received a rigorous training 'to think like a lawyer'. In reality, however, they have been taught to think like a judge; for in the course of their legal training, particularly at the university, the focus has generally been on the impartial assessment of a legal conflict. Yet, paradoxically, only a minority of *Assessoren* embark on a judicial career. But even as private practitioners representing party interests they have to be committed ultimately to serving justice in a higher and more disinterested sense. This, at least, is the ideology behind what must appear to an outsider to be a somewhat skewed approach to legal training.

But quite a few lawyers do not even enter one of the traditional legal professions. Law is still regarded as one of the best general educations available and lawyers are therefore widely taken to be well qualified for senior management positions, for appointments within the civil service, and for other careers. At the same time, however, it is obvious that the market cannot absorb around 8,000 newly qualified lawyers every year.[196] And even those who can be absorbed have bought their career

---

195. *See* Kilian (n. 180), pp. 209 et seq.
196. Even though the number of judges in Germany is high compared to that, for example, in the United Kingdom, only a very small percentage of those who have passed both State examinations are appointed as members of the judiciary. By the end of 2014, there were 20,301 judges in active service in Germany. A career path that enjoys great exclusivity and prestige (as well as a very good income) is that of notary public. Admission is severely restricted and available

opportunities at a cost: they are normally well beyond twenty-five years of age and, if they have obtained a postgraduate degree at a foreign university[197] and/or a doctorate, beyond the age of thirty.

[E]   A Career in Itself: The Path to the Chair

A doctorate is a much appreciated extra qualification for those who want to enter legal practice, for German clients tend to be impressed by academic titles.[198] A doctorate may, however, also be the starting point for what remains one of the most prestigious legal careers: that of a law professor. But the path to the first 'call' to a chair is extraordinarily arduous. The potential member of the academic community must have received high grades in the legal examinations. His (much more often than her) thesis – written, normally, within a period of between two and three years – must have received the distinction of *magna cum laude*, or *summa cum laude*; normally it will have been published as a book. This is followed by some years of apprenticeship with an established professor. For that purpose, the latter usually makes available one of the posts of 'academic assistant' (*wissenschaftlicher Assistent*) attached to his university chair or Max Planck Institute[199] (unless the postdoc has been successful with an application for a scholarship, granted e.g., by the *Deutsche Forschungsgemeinschaft* (German Research Foundation)). The assistant, on the one hand, has to do a limited number of tutorials and to support the incumbent of the chair in his research projects. On the other hand, he has to work on a second thesis called *Habilitation* which has to constitute an even more fundamental and original contribution to knowledge. Completion of that work can easily take five years. The *Habilitation* has to be accepted by the faculty, to which the professor, under whose *aegis* the work is written, belongs. The faculty bestows on its new member the *venia legendi*, i.e., the permission to teach a legal subject in his own responsibility.

After some tense months (hopefully not years) during which he may have acted as a substitute for a professor in another faculty and during which he may have given

---

only to the very best. Thus, for example, in the city state of Hamburg, in 2016 only seventy-four notaries were practising, compared to 10,231 *Rechtsanwälte* (private practitioners). In the same year, a total of more than 165,000 *Rechtsanwälte* were practising in Germany (i.e., close to 200 per 100,000 inhabitants). Many of those who have passed their examination with a below average mark and who are unable to secure employment in an established law firm, in a business enterprise, insurance company, etc. are struggling hard to make a living. For comprehensive statistical material, broken down by states, *see* Kilian (n. 180), pp. 347 et seq.; cf. also the figures in von Münch (n. 174), pp. 56 et seq.

197. For details, *see* Kilian (n. 180), pp. 248 et seq.

198. On all questions concerning and surrounding doctoral degrees in Germany, *see* Ingo von Münch & Peter Mankowski, *Promotion* (2013); cf. also Kilian (n. 180), pp. 231 et seq. The number of successfully completed proceedings for the degree of doctor of laws (Dr iur.) has constantly increased from 511 in 1985 to 1,906 in 2005. Since then, the number has decreased; in 2013 the figure was 1,438.

199. Max Planck Institutes are a unique feature of the German academic landscape. They are independent bodies under the umbrella of the Max Planck Society, a private organization mainly financed by the State. The mission of these Institutes is foundational research. Throughout Germany, there are eight Max Planck Institutes entirely or partly devoted to law.

a variety of presentation lectures, the 'private lecturer' (*Privatdozent*) receives his first 'call' to a professorship or chair. (As his reputation spreads, he will apply to, and may expect to receive offers from, other universities.) A healthy convention requires faculties to choose applicants from outside rather than to appoint in-house candidates. By the time an academic starts teaching as an associate or full professor, he is usually between 35 and 40 years old. He is exceptionally well qualified (as a researcher; much less so as a teacher), has written two major monographs as well as a variety of articles, case notes, and book reviews; but he has never been in a position of independent responsibility, academic or otherwise.

[F]   Changes

The peculiarities of the German legal training system, particularly its rigid regulation by the State and the system of State examinations, have largely, so far, prevented the forty-five law faculties in Germany from competing with each other by developing their own characteristic profiles. Students, by and large, receive the same type of legal training everywhere. They tend to choose a university because it is in an attractive city or close to the mountains, because it has a long tradition (or, conversely, because it is one of the new universities with, possibly, more modern buildings and better equipment), because it is very big (and can thus offer a broad variety of optional courses and 'focus areas') or because it is fairly small (which makes it easier to establish contacts between staff and students), because it is the place where their parents have studied, where the traditional student fraternities continue to exist or, very often, simply because it is close to home.[200] Law faculty rankings have started to be published in the second half of the 1990s; however, they are widely regarded as not very sophisticated and as methodically suspect. Teaching evaluations have also only established themselves comparatively recently.

The reform legislation of 2003 has, however, made a number of changes to the traditional system.[201] It has attempted to provide a better preparation for private legal practice as a *Rechtsanwalt* and (cautiously) to emphasize the international and interdisciplinary dimensions of the law. In particular, it has brought about a significant change in the rules for the first examination. For 30% of the aggregate mark, mentioned above, now result from grades determined by the individual law faculties in their own academic responsibility and concerning 'focus areas' (*Schwerpunktbereiche*) offered as part of the *curriculum* and to be chosen by every student. (Before the reform, the examination in an optional subject had been part of the normal first state examination.) The grades obtained for the university part of the first examination are significantly better than those in the State examination relating to the obligatory subjects (5.0% as

---

200. For a characteristic comment, *see* Victor Ehrenberg, in: Hans Planitz (ed.), *Die Rechtswissenschaft der Gegenwart in Selbstdarstellungen*, vol. I (1924), p. 60: 'When would German law students ever have been guided, in the choice of their university, by the quality of a faculty?'
201. For an assessment, *see* Ute Mager, 'Die Ausbildungsreform von 2002: Ziele, Inhalte, Erfahrungen und Folgerungen für weitere Reformen', in: Baldus, Finkenauer & Rüfner (n. 173), pp. 239 et seq.

opposed to 0.1% 'very good'; 19.4% as opposed to 2.9% 'good'; 32.3% as opposed to 13.5% 'fully satisfactory' for the year 2015).[202]

This is the reason why the university component of the first examination, which is shown separately on the first examination certificate, is often taken less seriously by prospective employers, scholarship agencies, etc. The impending reform of the 2003 reform[203] thus intends to reduce its weight from 30% to 20%; in addition, it sets out to standardize the way in which the law faculties organize the 'focus areas' and assess their students' performances. And it sets out to do what has, again and again, been demanded: to reduce the range of obligatory subjects required for the two legal examinations.

But there have been other important developments affecting legal education and the legal professions. In October 2000 the first private institution offering legal education in Germany was opened. The Bucerius Law School in Hamburg is financed largely by a wealthy private foundation (*Zeit-Stiftung*) but also, partly, by tuition fees paid by its students and funds raised from law firms and other sponsors. It offers an interesting alternative to what used to be a monopoly on legal education by the traditional State universities[204] and has quickly acquired an excellent reputation. Also, recently, the Federal legislature has attempted to downgrade the significance of the *Habilitation* for an academic career.[205] German law faculties, none the less, effectively continue to insist on a second major monograph as a prerequisite for appointment to a chair; for the time being, they even continue with their traditional *Habilitation*-procedure. In addition, another career-track has been opened up for academics by introducing so-called junior professorships.[206] The profession of private practitioners in law (*Rechtsanwalt*) has also changed significantly over the past twenty-five years. New forms of co-operation between *Rechtsanwälte* (such as the establishment of a company with limited liability)[207] and between *Rechtsanwälte* and members of related professions (such as tax consultants or accountants: partnership association)[208] have been established. Legal practitioners may now advertise their services (though the – dispassionately drafted – advertisement may only contain factual information and must relate to the professional activities of the practitioner or his firm),[209] and they may apply for the title of *Fachanwalt* (i.e., legal practitioner in a specialized field of expertise).[210] Legal practitioners from Member-States of the European Union may

---

202. Bundesamt für Justiz, 'Ausbildungsstatistik', available online. The aggregated grades for the first examination in total are, for 2015: 0.13% 'very good'; 2.94% 'good'; 13.52% 'fully satisfactory', 27.6% 'satisfactory'; 25.2% 'sufficient'; 30.6% 'failed'. There were a total of 12.744 participants.
203. *See supra*, n. 181.
204. *See* von Münch (n. 174), 31 et seq., 82 et seq.; Sascha Leske, 'Bucerius Law School in Hamburg – Ein neuer Weg in der Juristenausbildung', *Juristische Schulung* 2001, 414 et seq.; Christoph Luschin, 'A German Ivy: The Bucerius Law School', Southwestern Journal of International law 19 (2012), 1 et seq., 20 et seq.
205. § 44 *Hochschulrahmengesetz*.
206. §§ 45, 47 *Hochschulrahmengesetz*.
207. §§ 59c et seq. *Bundesrechtsanwaltsordnung*.
208. *Gesetz über Partnerschaftsgesellschaften Angehöriger Freier Berufe* (1994).
209. §§ 6 et seq. *Berufsordnung für Rechtsanwälte*.
210. *Fachanwaltsordnung* (1999).

under certain circumstances practise in Germany without having passed the First and Second State examinations.[211] Most importantly, perhaps, a wave of mergers, first between German firms but then also increasingly between German and international law firms, has swept over the legal profession.[212] Thus, for example, the firm of Freshfields Bruckhaus Deringer now consists of over 25 offices (five of them in Germany) with more than 2,500 practitioners (over 500 of them in Germany). Twenty-five years ago, such dimensions were unheard of in Germany. Other German law firms have become part of large transnational alliances.[213]

§1.13   BROADENING THE HORIZON

The growing international orientation of legal practice at the top level reflects a development which has characteristically started to shape private and commercial law over the past thirty or forty years. For private law in Europe has acquired an increasingly European character.[214] The Council and the Parliament of the European communities have enacted a string of directives deeply affecting core areas of German law.[215] Increasingly, therefore, rules of German law have to be interpreted from the point of view of the relevant community legislation underpinning it.[216] The case law of the European Court of Justice, too, acquires an ever greater significance for the development of German private law. For some time, the prospect of a European contract code has seriously been pursued;[217] and even if that project has now collapsed, it has left behind a number of 'textual layers', i.e., successive attempts to establish academic restatements of European contract law.[218]

The internationalization of private law is also vigorously promoted by the uniform private law based on international conventions covering significant areas of commercial law. The United Nations Convention on Contracts for the International Sale of Goods, in particular, has been adopted by about eighty-five states (amongst

---

211. This is as a result of the Directive of the European Union on the Right of Establishment of Legal Practitioners (1998); on which see Martin Henssler, 'Der lange Weg zur EU-Niederlassungsrichtlinie für die Anwaltschaft', Zeitschrift für Europäisches Privatrecht 7 (1999) 689 et seq.; von Münch (n. 174), 65 et seq. (who also lists the admission requirements in Germany for practitioners from other EU states).

212. See von Münch (n. 174), 71 et seq.

213. For the alliance operating under the name CMS, see von Münch (n. 174), 73.

214. See, e.g., Nils Jansen, 'European Private Law', in: Max Planck Encyclopedia (n. 3), 637 et seq.

215. For private law, see the directives collected in Oliver Radley-Gardner, Hugh Beale & Reinhard Zimmermann, Fundamental Texts on European Private Law (2nd ed. 2016).

216. Supra n. 118.

217. See, for example, Jürgen Basedow, 'Das BGB im künftigen europäischen Privatrecht: Der hybride Kodex', Archiv für die civilistische Praxis 200 (2000) 445 et seq.; Martin Schmidt-Kessel, 'European Civil Code', in: Max Planck Encyclopedia (n. 3), 153 et seq.; Horst Eidenmüller et al., 'The Proposal for a Regulation on a Common European Sales Law: Deficits of the Most Recent Textual Layer of European Contract Law', Edinburgh Law Review 16 (2012) 301 et seq.

218. Nils Jansen, The Making of Legal Authority: Non-legislative Codifications in Historical and Comparative Perspective (2012); Reinhard Zimmermann, '"Wissenschaftliches Recht" am Beispiel (vor allem) des europäischen Vertragsrechts', in: Christian Bumke & Anne Röthel (eds), Privates Recht (2012), pp. 21 et seq.

them twenty-one member-states of the European Union); in Germany it entered into force on 1 January 1991 and has started to generate a significant amount of case law.[219] In the first (legal) examination familiarity with the basic principles of European Union law is required.[220] A significant number of students spend a period of one or two semesters at a law faculty in another member-state of the European Union under the auspices of the successful Erasmus/Erasmus+ programmes.[221] Also, it has become very popular, particularly among young lawyers with top grades and aiming for employment in one of the big law firms, to acquire an additional, post-graduate qualification in other countries, particularly in Great Britain or the United States.[222] Conversely, the number of foreign students at German law faculties is increasing. More and more faculties have sought to obtain a 'Euro'-profile by offering a broad range of language courses, by establishing international summer schools or integrated programmes on an undergraduate and post-graduate level,[223] by flagging out chairs for European private law, or European legal history, or by creating research centres in European private law. Legal periodicals have been established pursuing the objective of promoting the development of a European private law[224] and textbooks have been written analysing particular areas of private law under a genuinely European perspective and dealing with the rules of German, French, or English law as local variations of a common theme.[225] Interest has been rekindled in the 'old' European ius commune, and legal historians are busy rediscovering the common historical foundations of modern private law and restoring the intellectual contact with comparative and modern private lawyers.[226] Yet, all these developments have not fundamentally changed the specifically German approach towards legal education, legal thinking, and legal writing. A comprehensive internationalization is still one of the challenges faced by legal scholarship in Germany today.[227]

---

219. *See* the regular reports by Ulrich Magnus beginning in *Zeitschrift für Europäisches Privatrecht* 3 (1995) 202 et seq.; most recently, *see Zeitschrift für Europäisches Privatrecht* 25 (2017) 140 et seq.
220. Heino Schöbel, 'Privatrecht und Europarecht in der Ersten Juristischen Staatsprüfung', Zeitschrift für Europäisches Privatrecht 3 (1995) 139 et seq.
221. Generally on study periods abroad, as far as law students are concerned, Kilian (n. 180), 115 et seq.
222. For details, *see* Kilian (n. 180), pp. 248 et seq.
223. *See*, for example, Stefan Grundmann, Jacqueline Dutheil de la Rochère & John Phillips, 'The European Law School (Network)', *European Review of Private Law* 2009, 249 et seq.
224. Zeitschrift für Europäisches Privatrecht, since 1993; cf. also Europäische Zeitschrift für Wirtschaftsrecht, since 1989.
225. *See*, in particular, Hein Kötz, Europäisches Vertragsrecht (2nd ed. 2015) (English translation by Gill Mertens & Tony Weir, European Contract Law, 2nd ed. 2017); cf. also Christian von Bar, Gemeineuropäisches Deliktsrecht, vol. I (1996); vol. II (1999) (English translation: The Common European Law of Torts, vol. I (1999); vol. II (2001)); Peter Schlechtriem, *Restitution und Bereicherungsausgleich in Europa*, vol. I (2000); vol. II (2001); Filippo Ranieri, *Europäisches Obligationenrecht* (3rd ed. 2009).
226. *See*, e.g., Reinhard Zimmermann, 'Europa und das römische Recht', Archiv für die civilistische Praxis 202 (2002) 243 et seq.
227. For an instructive analysis of the strengths and weaknesses of legal scholarship in Germany, *see* the study by the *Deutscher Wissenschaftsrat*, referred to *supra*, n. 180.

APPENDIX

It may not be inappropriate to append to this essay some remarks of a more practical nature. They are designed to help foreign lawyers orient themselves in the complex world of German legal materials.

The only formal source of law, of course, is legislation (including subordinate legislation). All statutes are published in the official law gazette of either the Federation (*Bundesgesetzblatt*) or the State by which they have been issued. Since, however, it is much too cumbersome always to refer to the law gazettes, private publishing houses sell compilations of the most important statutes. Two of the compilations are owned by virtually every German lawyer who has ventured beyond the first or second year of study: *Schönfelder, Deutsche Gesetze* (containing around 100 statutes in the fields of private law, commercial law, criminal law, and procedural law, including, for example, the BGB (*Bürgerliches Gesetzbuch* – German Civil Code), HGB (*Handelsgesetzbuch* – Commercial Code), and StGB (*Strafgesetzbuch* – Criminal Code))[228] and *Sartorius, Verfassungs- und Verwaltungsgesetze der Bundesrepublik Deutschland* (with the most important federal statutes in the fields of administrative and constitutional law)).[229] *Schönfelder* and *Sartorius* are hefty loose-leaf tomes in a characteristic red cover. They are updated several times a year; and the regular sale of the supplements earns their publishing house a fortune. Since administrative law is largely a matter for the individual States, each of them has its own equivalent of the *Sartorius*; the one for Bavaria, for instance, is called *Ziegler/ Tremel, Gesetze des Freistaates (!) Bayern* (loose-leaf). Within their area of specialization, lawyers normally also make use of more convenient, pocket-size editions of certain of the central statutes.[230]

German statutes are normally subdivided into sections, referred to as *Paragraph* (§); the German Constitution (*Grundgesetz*, or 'Basic Law'), however, is composed of the more dignified 'articles'. Each section (or article) may be broken down into sub-sections (*Absatz*; indicated, for short, by a Roman numeral), each sub-section into sentences (*Satz*; indicated by an Arabic numeral). Thus, for instance § 305 I 1 BGB refers to section 305, first sub-section, first sentence of the German Civil Code.

Most of the important cases of the various Federal courts are published in a quasi-official series edited, normally, by members of the respective court; thus, there are *Entscheidungen des Bundesverfassungsgerichts* (abbreviated *BVerfGE*, followed by the volume number and page reference),[231] *Entscheidungen des Bundesgerichtshofes in Zivilsachen*[232] (*BGHZ*), *Entscheidungen des Bundesgerichtshofes in Strafsachen*

---

228. Schönfelder, *Deutsche Gesetze: Sammlung des Zivil-, Straf- und Verfahrensrechts* (loose-leaf ed.), C.H. Beck, Munich. In January 2002, Schönfelder was effectively split into two volumes (though the second one is merely entitled 'supplementary volume') with a number of statutes of particular relevance for practice as *Rechtsanwalt*. The main volume consists of around 4,000 pages. The 167th supplement has appeared in January 2017.
229. Also published by C.H. Beck, Munich. There are two further volumes for International Treaties and European Union Law (Sartorius II) and for further administrative statutes (Sartorius III). Also for the original Sartorius (I) there is now a supplementary volume.
230. *See, e.g., BGB – Bürgerliches Gesetzbuch (Beck-Texte im dtv)* (79th ed. 2017).
231. Mohr Siebeck, Tübingen, most recently vol. 141 (2017).
232. Karl Heymanns Verlag, Köln-Berlin; currently (spring 2017) in its 210th volume.

(*BGHSt*), *Entscheidungen des Bundesarbeitsgerichts (BAGE)*, etc. Most of the decisions published in these series are also reported, though often in a shortened version, in one or several law journals. These journals sometimes also publish cases not included in the 'official' series and important cases from the lower courts. Today, the more recent decisions (in the case of the Federal Constitutional Court from 1998, in the case of the Federal Supreme Court from 2000) are available online.

Legal writing usually takes one of five forms: commentaries, textbooks, monographs, legal articles, and case annotations. Commentaries (*Kommentare*) are one of the most useful and convenient research tools.[233] They relate to a specific code or statute and follow the order of §§ or Articles of that code or statute. Each section is first cited verbatim and then elucidated in detail. The relevant case law and legal literature is referred to and the reader is thus presented with a more or less comprehensive picture of the *interpretatio moderna* of that § or Article as well as with the relevant sources for further research. The commentator is not normally supposed to advance extravagant opinions of his own.

As far as the BGB is concerned, we find commentaries of all shapes and sizes: many more than one could ever wish for.[234] The standard commentary in one volume is *Palandt*. It has become a household name and is certainly one of the more remarkable institutions of German legal culture in the field of private law. Since the date of its first appearance in 1939[235] the team of commentators has undergone repeated changes; at the moment it is composed of ten authors, one of them a professor of Bucerius Law School, two notaries public, five (active or retired) presiding judges in Regional Appeal Courts, and one judge in the Federal Supreme Court. Every year a new edition is produced[236] and since almost every judge and every private practitioner in the field of private law will want to have his own copy, we are dealing here with another big money-spinner for Germany's leading legal publisher. One copy of the massive grey tome (3,247 pages in small print) sells for €115.00. The *Palandt* is a stunning achievement. It is always up to date, it is as concise as it is comprehensive and it is well-balanced in its views. On the other hand, however, it is almost incomprehensible to outsiders since it uses a very refined and technical telegraphese and is riddled with unfamiliar abbreviations.[237] The small print type does not enhance its readability either. *Palandt* focuses on court decisions (as constituting the law in action); references to legal literature are sparse. It is the quintessential practitioner's commentary which

---

233. For the cultural history of the commentary, *see* David Kästle-Lamparter, *Die Welt der Kommentare* (2016).
234. For criticism, *see* Reinhard Zimmermann, 'Juristische Bücher des Jahres', *Neue Juristische Wochenschrift* 2011, 3557.
235. On the history of *Palandt, see* Dieter Medicus, 'Palandt – 50. Auflage', *Neue Juristische Wochenschrift* 1991, 887 et seq.; cf. also the *Festschrift zur 75. Auflage des Kurz-Kommentars Palandt, Bürgerliches Gesetzbuch* (2016). Otto Palandt (1877–1952) was a prominent lawyer who, after 1933, turned to national socialism; he thus became head of department in the Imperial Ministry of Justice and President of the Imperial Legal Examination Board.
236. Currently the 76th ed. 2017, is in use.
237. For a typical example, *see* Überbl v § 194, n. 17: 'Die VerjEinrede ist unbeachtl, wenn sie gg das Verbot unzuläss RAusübg verstößt'; for criticism, *see* Jürgen Basedow, 'Euro-Zitrone für den Palandt?' *Zeitschrift für Europäisches Privatrecht* 1 (1993) 656 et seq.

has, however, managed to become equally indispensable for the German academic. With only some slight exaggeration it may be said: 'Quidquid non agnoscit Palandt, non agnoscit curia'.

In its own way also a masterpiece of conciseness is *Jauernig* (now in its 16th edition, 2015), a short commentary written by a team of five authors (all of them professors). It provides a reliable overview of the current state of case law and legal doctrine and is written in full sentences and without too many abbreviations. Thus, it is probably today the most convenient, and affordable, key to modern German private law for neophytes.

The *Münchener Kommentar zum Bürgerlichen Gesetzbuch* has managed to establish itself, within a surprisingly short time, as probably the leading multi-volume commentary.[238] The seventh edition started to appear in 2015 and will consist of twelve volumes with a total of about 28,000 pages; each of these volumes is written by between ten and twenty professors and senior practitioners.

A commentary on an even larger scale than *Münchener Kommentar*, and a phenomenon in its own right, is *Staudinger*. It was initiated by Julius von Staudinger (1836–1902), a senior practitioner, in 1898, i.e., two years before the BGB entered into force. After it had taken twenty-six years to complete the 12th edition, the publishers (Sellier – de Gruyter) have given up the idea of publishing new editions; instead, the volumes are individually revised. Thus, for example, the volume on testamentary executors (§§ 2197–2228 BGB) has appeared simply as 'Neubearbeitung 2016' (revised edition 2016). Today, the *Staudinger* consists of 105 volumes, with a total of more than 70,000 pages. A phalanx of around 180 commentators is involved in this gigantic project. Staudinger, of course, provides a most thorough compilation of material and extensive analysis. Many of its volumes contain masterly expositions which leave no question unanswered. The commentary to § 823 BGB (by Johannes Hager),[239] for example, comprises over 1,300 marginal notes, spread over 1,100 pages.[240]

Commentaries make it fairly easy to discover the law on a particular topic; provided, of course, one knows where to look. This, in turn, depends on some degree of familiarity with the BGB. Essentially, of course, a commentary follows the sequence of its sections. When it comes to legal doctrines *praeter legem*, however, certain conventions have evolved as to where they are discussed. Thus, for example, the contract with protective effect vis-à-vis third parties is normally discussed within the context of § 328 BGB (contract in favour of a third party), forfeiture (*Verwirkung*) in the context of § 242 BGB (good faith), and transfer of ownership *in securitatem debiti* in the context of § 930 BGB (transfer of ownership by constructive delivery).

---

238. It is edited by Franz Jürgen Säcker, Roland Rixecker, Hartmut Oetker & Bettina Limperg, i.e., two professors, the President of the Regional Supreme Court of the Saarland, and the President of the Federal Supreme Court; and it is published by C.H. Beck, Munich.
239. § 823 A–D (revised ed. 2017), § 823 E-II, 824, 825 (revised ed. 2009).
240. Spin-offs of the Staudinger are a useful synoptic overview of the various amendments that the provisions of the BGB have undergone between 1896 and 1998 (*BGB-Synopse 1896–1998* (1998)), and a collection of treatises on the cornerstones of private law: Michael Martinek (ed.), *Eckpfeiler des Zivilrechts* (revised ed. 2014/2015).

Only *Jauernig*, incidentally, confines itself mainly to the Civil Code. The other commentaries also deal with a variety of statutes closely related to the core of private law. *Palandt*, among others, includes the Introductory Law to the German Civil Code (EGBGB), the Products Liability Act, the Sectional Titles Act, and the Act on Registered Life Partnerships. Even broader in scope is the *beck-online-Großkommentar zum Zivilrecht*. It is intended to rival the *Staudinger*, even if it does not appear in print. In fact, its only purpose appears to be to have available a king-size commentary[241] for the database of C.H. Beck, after the Staudinger was licensed exclusively to the rival database *juris* as from 2015.

Different in character from all the other commentaries is the Historical Commentary on the BGB of which the first volume has appeared in 2003.[242] It aims at making available to the modern reader the tradition and the historical experiences on which the BGB as well as present day German legal doctrine rest. It thus provides the basis for a critical re-evaluation of that doctrine, and also specifies the position of German private law within the broader European context.

For every area of German private law there are a wide variety of textbooks. For the general part of the BGB, for example, one has the choice between approximately twenty textbooks of all sizes and levels. German textbooks range from fairly unpretentious student readers to standard reference works such as those of the 'green series' produced by C.H. Beck: Wolf & Neuner on the general part of the BGB,[243] Larenz on the law of obligations,[244] Baur & Stürner on the law of property,[245] Gernhuber & Coester-Waltjen on family law,[246] Lange & Kuchinke on succession,[247] von Bar on private international law,[248] Rosenberg, Schwab & Gottwald on civil procedure,[249] etc. The problem with these literary flagships is that some of them are out of date. One book that has managed to mould the minds of generations of law students since it first appeared in 1968 is *Dieter Medicus, Bürgerliches Recht*; it is now in its 25th edition (by Jens Petersen) 2015, and continues to be the best and clearest comprehensive analysis of the major problem areas of German private law on an advanced level.[250] The appellation

---

241. The *beck-online-Großkommentar zum Zivilrecht*, which is still in the process of being set up, will have a total of 25 editors and more than 400 authors – the hypertrophy of legal commenting. Apart from that, incidentally, C.H. Beck also has a more moderately sized online commentary under the title *Beck'scher Online Kommentar*.
242. Mathias Schmoeckel, Joachim Rückert & Reinhard Zimmermann (eds), *Historisch-kritischer Kommentar zum BGB*, vol. I (2003), vols. II/1 and II/2 (2007), vols. III/1 and III/2 (2013). Three further volumes are projected.
243. Manfred Wolf & Jörg Neuner, Allgemeiner Teil des Bürgerlichen Rechts (11th ed. 2016).
244. Karl Larenz, *Lehrbuch des Schuldrechts*, vol. I (14th ed. 1987); Karl Larenz, *Lehrbuch des Schuldrechts*, vol. II/1 (13th ed. 1986); Karl Larenz & Claus-Wilhelm Canaris, *Lehrbuch des Schuldrechts*, vol. II/2 (13th ed. 1994).
245. Jürgen F. Baur & Rolf Stürner, Sachenrecht (18th ed. 2009).
246. Joachim Gernhuber & Dagmar Coester-Waltjen, *Lehrbuch des Familienrechts* (6th ed. 2010).
247. Heinrich Lange & Kurt Kuchinke, *Erbrecht* (5th ed. 2001).
248. Christian von Bar, *Internationales Privatrecht*, vol. I (1987); vol. II (1991); the second edition of vol. I (2003) is by von Bar und Peter Mankowski.
249. Leo Rosenberg, Karl-Heinz Schwab & Peter Gottwald, *Zivilprozeßrecht* (17th ed. 2010).
250. Dieter Medicus has also written textbooks on the general part of the BGB (*Allgemeiner Teil des BGB* (11th ed. (by Jens Petersen) 2016)) and on the general and special parts of the law of

'*Kurz-Lehrbuch*' can, sometimes, be misleading: Ebenroth on succession (1992) comprises 1,116 pages, and books such as Gerhard Kegel on private international law (9th ed. (by Klaus Schurig) 2004) or Thomas Oppermann on European community law (7th ed. (by Claus-Dieter Classen & Martin Nettesheim) 2016) have attained authoritative status.

Monographs on every conceivable aspect of German law are often based on a thesis (for either a doctorate or a *Habilitation*); typically they appear as part of a series (*Schriftenreihe*) run by Mohr Siebeck, Duncker & Humblot, and other publishing houses.

Law journals provide the major outlet for legal articles. Unlike most American law reviews, they are not run by students. Each German law journal has a board of editors which consists, depending on the nature of the journal, of law professors and/or senior practitioners. The editorial work is either done in its entirety by the editors themselves (and their academic assistants); or it is divided between the editors, who determine the general academic and editorial policy, and a professional editorial office provided by the publishing house producing the journal. The number of law journals is very large already; none the less, it is growing larger every year. The titles range from *Der bayerische Bürgermeister* to the *Archiv für Rechts- und Sozialphilosophie*. Typically, German law journals specialize in a specific area of the law, such as family law, administrative law, criminal law, or even nature conservation law, zoning law, the law relating to civil servants, cars, or limited liability companies. Some journals, such as *Deutsche Richterzeitung* or *Deutsche Notarzeitschrift* concern themselves with issues affecting a specific legal profession. There are also three law journals aimed primarily at a student audience (among them, as the oldest one, *Juristische Schulung*, founded in 1960 and published by C.H. Beck, Munich).

General law journals are surprisingly rare. The *Neue Juristische Wochenschrift (NJW)*[251] is supposed to fall into that category and to provide a general overview of recent developments in all the major fields of law; as its name indicates, it appears every week and devotes a large part of every issue to case reports. But though over the years it has grown considerably in size (the volume for 2016 runs to 3,808 pages) and though it probably remains the law journal that is most widely subscribed to, particularly among practitioners, it has left the detailed coverage of more and more subjects to specialized 'daughter' journals, such as *Neue Zeitschrift für Strafrecht, Neue Zeitschrift für Verwaltungsrecht* or *Neue Zeitschrift für Arbeitsrecht*. The disintegration of the *NJW* thus reflects, and promotes, the increasing particularization of German legal scholarship. The other major general law journal, the *Juristenzeitung (JZ)*[252] has a somewhat more academic orientation: thus, for example, an inaugural lecture is a piece a young author would want to be published there. The entire field of private law is covered by the venerable *Archiv für die civilistische Praxis (AcP)*[253] which will

---

obligations (*Schuldrecht I, Allgemeiner Teil* (21st ed. (by Stephan Lorenz) 2016); Schuldrecht II, Besonderer Teil (18th ed. (by Stephan Lorenz) 2017)). They, too, are distinguished by their clarity of presentation.

251. Published by C.H. Beck, Munich.
252. Published by Mohr Siebeck, Tübingen.
253. *Ibid.*

complete its 217th volume in 2017; it is one of very few journals prepared to publish comprehensive studies of fifty or sixty pages on, say, the law of property or obligations. The most prestigious German journals in comparative law and legal history are *Rabels Zeitschrift für ausländisches und internationales Privatrecht (RabelsZ)* which is edited by the Max Planck Institute for Comparative and International Private Law in Hamburg[254] and the *Zeitschrift der Savigny-Stiftung für Rechtsgeschichte (SZ or ZSS)*[255] (which is split, for outdated historical reasons, into three separate annual volumes – referred to, quaintly, as *Abteilungen* – for Roman law, the history of German(ic) law and Canon law).

Another characteristic feature of the German legal landscape is its *Festschriften*. They constitute collections of essays presented, traditionally, to distinguished academics on a specific occasion, in Germany normally their 70th birthday. A *Festschrift*, usually a source of joy for its recipient, is often welcomed wearily by the broader legal community. Although it is notoriously difficult to find a publisher, *Festschriften* are presented to more and more scholars, and even to senior practitioners, on more and more occasions, and it seems to be widely though that the sheer size of a *Festschrift* as well as the number of authors who have contributed to it indicate the prestige of its recipient. *Festschriften* are usually so expensive that hardly any individual lawyer or legal scholar can afford to buy them. Few of them have a clear and well-defined thematic focus, and as a result of these and other factors, *Festschriften* are sometimes cynically regarded as distinguished burial grounds for legal ideas.[256]

It has been mentioned above that the *travaux préparatoires* constitute a valuable source of information on the meaning of the provisions of a code. As far as the BGB is concerned, we have a set of motivations emanating from the First Commission (referred to as *Motive*) and another one compiled by the Second Commission (generally known as *Protokolle*). Both of them have been published individually. But there is also the very useful edition by Benno Mugdan, *Die gesammten Materialien zum Bürgerlichen Gesetzbuch für das Deutsche Reich*, 1899, in six volumes which reproduces both *Motive* and *Protokolle* (as well as some other relevant sources, such as the debates in the Imperial Parliament). The genesis of every individual section contained in the BGB has now been traced and made available by Horst Heinrich Jakobs and Werner Schubert in an exemplary fashion.[257] In addition, Werner Schubert has organized a reprint of the preliminary drafts of the reporters appointed for the First Commission and their motivations.[258] They contain a wealth of comparative material and are a rich source for the state of contemporary doctrinal discussions.

---

254. Published by Mohr Siebeck, Tübingen. On the Max Planck Institutes, *see supra*, n. 199.
255. Published by Böhlau-Verlag, Wien-Köln-Weimar.
256. For comment *see*, e.g., Jürgen Basedow, 'Juristisches Lexikon: Festschriftfähigkeit', *Zeitschrift für Europäisches Privatrecht* 19 (2011) 228 et seq.
257. Horst Heinrich Jakobs & Werner Schubert, *Die Beratung des Bürgerlichen Gesetzbuchs in systematischer Zusammenstellung der unveröffentlichten Quellen*, 16 vols. (1978–2002).
258. Werner Schubert (ed.), *Die Vorlagen der Redaktoren für die erste Kommission zur Ausarbeitung des Entwurfs eines Bürgerlichen Gesetzbuches*, 15 unnumbered vols. (1980–1986).

Sadly, there is not much general literature on German law in English. E.J. Cohn's *Manual of German Law* (2 vols. 1968 and 1971)[259] is outdated. The same is true of Dieter Medicus' national report on the Federal Republic of Germany in volume I of the *International Encyclopedia of Comparative Law* (completed in 1972).[260] In 1982 Norbert Horn, Hein Kötz and Hans Leser, three distinguished professors of private and comparative law, produced a more modern work providing an introduction to German private and commercial law.[261] More comprehensive in its coverage is Nigel G. Foster and Satish Sule, *German Legal System and Laws*, 4th ed. 2010.[262] Zweigert and Kötz, *An Introduction to Comparative Law* (3rd ed. 1998, as translated by Tony Weir)[263] remains a classic from which much of the spirit of German law and many characteristic features of its law of obligations can be gleaned. Literature in English covering more specific areas of German law will be referred to in the respective sections of this book. Even at this stage, however, the volumes inspired by Basil Markesinis on the German law of obligations,[264] Peter L. Murray & Rolf Stürner, *German Civil Justice* (2004), and David Currie's lucid exposition of German constitutional law[265] must be mentioned. Markesinis' work provides an excellent opportunity to familiarize oneself with German decisions, since a great number of them have been translated into English. There are English versions of some of the major German codes, such as the Criminal Code and the Civil Code[266] available online. Romain, *Wörterbuch der Rechts- und Wirtschaftssprache*[267] is particularly useful as a dictionary of legal and commercial terms. Dietl & Lorenz, *Wörterbuch Recht, Wirtschaft & Politik*[268] contains succinct commentaries in English and German in addition to the translations of the terms but is considerably more expensive.

Legal texts – even apart from the Palandt – probably contain more abbreviations than texts in any other discipline. The standard work for decoding German legal

---

259. Oceana Publications, London.
260. J.C.B. Mohr, Tübingen.
261. Clarendon Press, Oxford; translation by Tony Weir.
262. Oxford University Press. Cf. also Gerhard Dannemann, *Introduction to German civil and commercial law* (1993); Raymond Youngs, *Sourcebook on German Law* (2nd ed. 2002); Howard D. Fisher, *The German Legal System and Legal Language* (6th ed. 2015); Gerhard Robbers, *An Introduction to German law* (6th ed. 2017) (with useful glossary on pp. 251 et seq.).
263. Clarendon Press, Oxford.
264. Basil S. Markesinis, Hannes Unberath & Angus Johnson, *The German Law of Contract: A Comparative Treatise* (2nd ed. 2006); Basil S. Markesinis, Hannes Unberath, The Law of Torts: A Comparative Treatise (4th ed. 2002); Gerhard Dannemann, The German Law of Unjustified Enrichment and Restitution: A Comparative Introduction *(2009)*.
265. David P. Currie, *The Constitution of the Federal Republic of Germany* (1994); cf. also Donald P. Kommers & Russell A. Miller, *The Constitutional Jurisprudence of the Federal Republic of Germany* (3rd ed. 2012); Justin Collins, *Democracy's Guardians: A History of the German Federal Court*, 1951–2001 (2015).
266. Simon Goren, *The German Civil Code* (revised edition 1994); the work includes a translation of the Introductory Act to the Civil Code and the Act of Liability for Defective Products, but is now in large parts out of date.
267. Vol. I English – German, 5th ed. 2000 by Alfred Romain, Hans Anton Bader & B. Sharon Byrd; vol. II German – English, 4th ed. 2002 by Alfred Romain, B. Sharon Byrd & Carola Thielecke.
268. Vol. I English – German, 7th ed. 2016 by Clara-Erika Dietl, Egon Lorenz & Stefan Hans Kettler; vol. II German – English, 5th ed. 2005 by Clara-Erika Dietl & Egon Lorenz.

abbreviations is Hildebert Kirchner, *Abkürzungsverzeichnis der Rechtssprache.*[269] Comprehensive lists for abbreviations used in private law can also, however, be found in commentaries such as *Palandt* or *Jauernig*.

The market for legal online services is dominated in Germany by two big databases. One of them is *beck-online. DIE DATENBANK*, which was founded in 2001. A great variety of 'modules' are on offer, either covering certain areas of the law or aimed at certain professions (or the universities: *Hochschulmodul*). A module can be purchased for a flat rate. Apart from that there is the database *beck-eBibliothek* which contains digital versions of many standard textbooks. The other major legal database is *juris* (*juristisches Informationssystem für die Bundesrepublik Deutschland* – legal information system for the Federal Republic of Germany). Established originally within the Federal Ministry of Justice, it was moved to an independent limited liability company (juris GmbH) in 1985. Like *beck-online*, *juris* operates on the basis of modules which a user can subscribe to. Particularly the decisions of German and European courts and all statutes of the Federation as well as of the individual states are easily accessible through *juris*. Both databases are very popular in legal practice, among law students, and the younger generation of academics. Since just about all universities subscribe to *beck-online* and *juris*, a significant part of the legal sources and the legal literature can be called up on every computer covered by the licence. It is likely that the success and wide-spread use of these databases – especially among younger lawyers – has been aided by the opportunity for law students to apply for an e-fellows' scholarship: among other benefits, the scholarship provides free access to *beck-online* and *juris* not only at the university campus but also from home.

---

269. 8th ed. by Eike Böttcher 2015.

CHAPTER 2

Constitutional Law

Marcel Kau

TABLE OF CONTENTS

§2.01 THE HISTORY OF THE GERMAN BASIC LAW

[A] The Process of Adoption

After World War II the Allied Powers divided Germany into four occupational zones. Over time, however, the so-called Länder, smaller entities with state functions on a regional level, were created in every zone to support the occupying powers in their attempt to uphold public order and – in the Western parts of Germany – to establish democratic structures and the rule of law. The idea of reestablishing Germany as a whole soon became prominent, but failed because of growing estrangement between the USSR and the Western Allies. Even among the latter some might have held the position that a divided Germany was favorable for the time being. During the London Conference of December 1947, the Western Allies made a last futile attempt to prevent the division of Germany into different States. Following the failure of this conference, the three Western Allies (i.e., the United States, the United Kingdom, and France) suggested that the Prime Ministers of the West German *Länder* create a constituent assembly for the Western part of Germany. The aim was to build a federal government whose political and constitutional independence and sovereignty would gradually increase over the ensuing decades. The Prime Ministers of the Länder agreed to this plan only on a provisional basis, as they still hoped for a unified German State within the prewar borders. This had consequences for the name of the constitutive document, which was entitled "Basic Law" (*Grundgesetz, GG*) rather than "Constitution" (*Verfassung*) in order to emphasize its provisional character – until, as the preamble of the Basic Law then stated, the German people "achieve in free self-determination the unity and freedom of Germany." The provisional character of the document also affected the procedure for its creation, i.e., it was drafted by delegates of the *Länder* and adopted by the *Länder* parliaments rather than by a national constituent assembly.

The constitutional deliberations took place in two steps. From August 10 to 23, 1948, a Constitutional Convention of experts appointed by the Prime Ministers of the *Länder* shaped a first draft at Herrenchiemsee. Subsequently, a Parliamentary Council (*Parlamentarischer Rat*) of sixty-five deputies, elected by the western *Länder* legislatures, was assembled to revise this draft which they did to some extent. The members of the Parliamentary Council agreed upon the final version on May 8, 1949. Subsequently, the Basic Law was adopted by the *Länder* parliaments and came into force on May 24, 1949. By this, the Federal Republic of Germany (FRG) was established only shortly before a separate East German State, the German Democratic Republic (GDR), was founded on October 7, 1949 under the auspices and control of the USSR.

[B]   The Basic Law after Reunification

Since several provisions of the Basic Law required the West German authorities to pursue the ultimate goal of a reunification of Germany (so-called Wiedervereinigungs-gebot), especially the German Constitutional Court upheld the doctrine of uninter-rupted existence of the traditionally established German State, however limited for the time being to a diminished territory. In so doing, the Constitutional Court followed its constitutional obligations and preserved *inter alia* the perspective of future German unity. The hope for reunification was eventually fulfilled and since October 3, 1990, the Basic Law is applicable in Germany as a whole, which now consists of the territory of the FRG and the former GDR. When the Berlin wall came down on November 9, 1989, discussions concerning the future relations between the two States started immedi-ately. Due to the immense legal, social and economic differences between these States, some advocated an interim solution. Others, however, favored rapid reunification either under the Basic Law or under a new constitution. The Basic Law contained provisions for both "unification projects." Article 146 GG stipulated – reflecting to the provisional character of the Basic Law – that the Basic Law itself "shall cease to be in force on the day on which a constitution by a free decision of the German people comes into force." In contrast, Article 23 GG made provision for other parts of Germany to access to the constitutional order of the Basic Law and become part of the FRG. The governments of the two German States finally decided to unite the two German States by accession of the GDR to the territory covered by Article 23 of the Basic Law, which appeared to be the faster and considerably easier constitutional way to realize reunification. Subsequently, the Basic Law was modestly revised to accommodate the new political and constitutional situation.

The process of accession took place in stages. An important prerequisite was achieved by the Treaty between the FRG and the GDR Establishing a Monetary, Economic and Social Union beginning July 1, 1990; it established the common free market and the Deutsche Mark as common currency. On August 23, 1990, the East German *Länder* assembled in the Parliament of the GDR, the People's Chamber (*Volkskammer*), and declared accession to the FRG under the Basic Law. According to the Treaty on the Establishment of German Unity (Unification Treaty), the Basic Law took effect in all acceded territories of Germany on October 3, 1990, in accordance with Article 23 GG. At this moment, the GDR ceased to exist.

The different socioeconomic and legal-political development of the two German States over the previous forty years called for flexibility in assimilating West German legal and social principles to the East German situation. Accordingly, the Unification Treaty contained more than 1000 pages on a broad range of topics dealing with the integration of East Germany under West German law. The general concept was that GDR provisions presently in force should remain in effect for a transition period even if such provisions deviated from the Basic Law. Only if fundamental constitutional principles were violated the contravening provisions were null and void.

Two major constitutional issues were addressed in the Unification Treaty. The first concerned the vast and mostly illegitimate expropriations of private property in the former GDR. The second concerned the right of abortion, which had been less restricted in the GDR than in the FRG. The latter was settled by a new abortion law, which more or less upheld former West German standards. The settlement of the effects of expropriations turned out to be more difficult. Due to political necessities – allegedly the USSR had demanded to adhere to the expropriations carried out under Soviet occupation between 1945 and 1949 – and the financial and social interests at stake, sophisticated solutions were needed. As a general rule, a political decision was made to give restitution of property precedence over compensation. The remaining legal problems, especially the question of compensation for expropriations between 1945 and 1949, had to be settled in due course with the ultimate assistance of the Federal Constitutional Court (FCC).

From a constitutional point of view, unification was completed on October 3, 1990. Germany as a whole was reunited, which also meant that no further territorial claims would be raised. This was confirmed by the 2-plus-4-treaty of September 12, 1990 between the FRG and the GDR on the one side and the United States, the UK, France, and the USSR on the other side. Later this was affirmed in bilateral treaties between the united Germany and Poland and the Soviet Union, respectively. Accordingly, Article 23 GG was repealed, foreclosing any constitutional way to an accession of former German territories.

[C]   Amendments since 1994

In 1994, the Basic Law was amended. The new provisions strengthened the legislative and administrative role of the *Länder*, provided for a transfer of power to the European Union (EU) in cooperation with the *Länder*, and added new constitutional guidelines for legislature. In particular, a legal basis for affirmative action was established in provisions calling for the advancement of equal opportunity for women and for the reduction of existing disadvantages in Article 3 section 2 cl. 2 Basic Law. A new clause prohibiting discrimination on grounds of disabilities was also included (cf. Article 3 section 3 cl. 2 GG). After a protracted discussion, environmental protection was included among the constitutional principles which every legislative and administrative decision has to respect. However, a clause on minorities, previously contained in the Constitution of the GDR for special ethnic groups, was not adopted due to a lack of the necessary majority of two-thirds of the members of parliament.

The next major amendment of the Basic Law was made in 1998. The fundamental right of the inviolability of the home in Article 13 GG was modified to allow the so-called grand eavesdropping operation (*Großer Lauschangriff*). Under certain closely defined circumstances, acoustic surveillance of communication at home is now permitted to state authorities. Ever since it has been discussed whether the amendment is unconstitutional. Much later, the FCC held only some of the incriminated provisions in the criminal procedure law unconstitutional, but the core provisions were deemed constitutional and in particular not to violate human dignity, which is a centerpiece of the Basic Law.

Women became entitled to join every branch of the military in 2000, when Article 12a IV of the Basic Law was changed. Previously, women could only join medical and musical army corps and could not carry arms. Now women can also join combat units and have the right to carry arms, though they still cannot be required to do so. The Federal Government was forced to pass this amendment by a decision of the European Court of Justice (ECJ).

In 2002, the protection of animals finally became a constitutional principle in addition to environmental protection in Article 20a GG. Every legislative, administrative and judicial decision is bound by this principle which has to be recognized beside several other principles. With the amendment, Germany became the first member of the EU to grant animal protection constitutional rank.

Later constitutional amendments were strongly focused on German federalism (Föderalismus-Reform I and II). In 2006, for example, the emphasis was on changing the division of legislative and administrative competences between the federal government (Bund) and the *Länder*. Three years later, in 2009 further amendments affected the financial constitution of the Basic Law (Finanzverfassung) creating new provisions governing the distribution of taxes and revenues between the two levels of government. In 2017, these rules underwent a thorough transformation again. Simultaneously, constitutional legislation was adopted introducing a new procedure before the FCC (Article 21 II GG) with the purpose of excluding parties with hostile attitude toward the constitutional order from public party funding.

§2.02   THE STRUCTURE OF THE BASIC LAW

The Basic Law outlines in considerable detail the political and legal system of the FRG. It consists of fourteen chapters. The first chapter (Articles 1–19) contains the Basic Rights (*Grundrechte*) of individuals. Chapter II (Articles 20–37) determines the fundamental structural principles of the Federation and the *Länder*. Chapters III to VI (Articles 38–69) contain *inter alia* provisions concerning the main organs of the State, which are the Federal Parliament (*Bundestag*), the Federal Council (*Bundesrat*), the Federal President (*Bundespräsident*), the Federal Government (*Bundesregierung*), and the Federal Chancellor (*Bundeskanzler*). Chapter VII (Articles 70–82) deals with federal legislation, Chapter VIII (Articles 83–91) with the implementation of federal laws and with federal administration. Chapter IX (Articles 92–104) regulates the administration of the federal judiciary, Chapter X (Articles 104a–115) deals with finance, Chapter Xa (Articles 115a–115l) with defense. Chapter XI (Articles 116–146) contains transitional and concluding provisions.

§2.03   THE FUNDAMENTAL STRUCTURAL PRINCIPLES OF THE FRG

The basic provision governing the constitutional organization of the FRG is Article 20 I-III GG. It establishes the principles of representative democracy, separation of powers (*Gewaltenteilung*), the rule of law (*Rechtsstaatlichkeit*), federalism, and the welfare or "social" state (*Sozialstaatlichkeit*). Article 20 GG provides in pertinent part:

(1) The FRG shall be a democratic and social federal State.
(2) All public authority emanates from the people. It shall be exercised by the people through elections and referenda and by specific legislative, executive, and judicial bodies.
(3) The legislature shall be bound by the constitutional order, the executive and the judiciary by law and justice.

This provision enjoys special protection. Any amendment abridging the principles laid down in this article is prohibited (Article 79 III GG). Such absolute protection is granted by the Basic Law only to the most fundamental principles of the constitutional order, i.e., the division of the Federation into *Länder*, their participation in the legislative process, and the protection of human dignity. As a result of the 1994 revision of the Basic Law, the protection of the environment (Article 20a GG) has been added to these principles and the constitutional order.

[A]   Democracy

Article 20 II GG defines German democracy as a representative one; this means that State authority is exercised by representative bodies. In fact, only two provisions in the Basic Law grant the people direct legislative power: Article 29 GG requires a referendum in case the boundaries of the *Länder* shall be modified – a provision which has never been applied so far. The second is Article 146 GG: In the unlikely case that a new constitution terminating the Basic Law will be adopted, the German people has to confirm it through a referendum. Democratic representation is basically limited to voting rights, in particular, the right to elect the Federal Parliament (*Bundestag*) every four years. All other state organs derive their authority from the parliament either directly, by vote – like the Federal Government – or at least indirectly, by means of an "uninterrupted chain of legitimation" reaching from the Federal Parliament to the State organ in question.

According to Article 38 GG, the members of the Federal Parliament shall be elected in general, direct, free, equal, and secret elections. On the one hand, direct elections preclude a system of electing delegates predetermined to elect, as practiced in the electoral college of the U.S. election system. Equality of vote, on the other hand, requires all votes to have the same voting power in principle. Half of the members of the Federal Parliament are elected directly in each district on the basis of a majority vote while the other half is elected on the basis of proportional representation, i.e., drafted from party lists. All voters have two votes accordingly. Since the splitting of the two votes by awarding them to different parties can lead to so-called overhang seats (*Überhangmandate*), pursuant to a decision of the FCC, the other parties obtain compensating seats in exchange. Consequently, the Federal Parliament usually consists of far more members than the 598 originally foreseen by the Federal Election Act (*BundeswahlG*). For example, in its 19th session (2017–2021) the *Bundestag* consists of 709 members altogether and in the 18th session (2013–2017) there were 630 members instead of 598.

In general, foreign nationals are not entitled to vote in elections to the Federal Parliament. Yet, since 1997 citizens of Member States of the EU (so-called Union citizens) have a right to vote and to be elected in municipal elections according to Art. 28 I 3 GG and in the elections to the European Parliament (*section 6 EuWG*).

[B]   The Rule of Law

The rule of law (*Rechtsstaatsprinzip*) is a fundamental part of the constitutional system of the FRG. The executive and the judiciary are bound by legislation. The legislature is bound by the Constitution. Although Article 20 GG does not mention the term "rule of law" explicitly, Article 28 GG does so, by stating that the "constitutional order in the *Länder* shall conform to the principles of the republican, democratic and social State governed by the rule of law in accordance with the Basic Law." The principle of the separation of powers among the legislative, executive, and judicial branches of government, as laid down in Article 20 II GG, is deemed to secure the rule of law. An important aspect of the rule of law principle is also laid down in Articles 20 III and 93 I GG subjecting legislation to judicial review by the FCC (*Bundesverfassungsgericht*).

[1]   Legal Certainty and the Ban on Retroactive Legislation

Legal certainty is one of the most important requirements of the rule of law. Administrative decisions, in which an individual is awarded benefits (e.g., a license, social benefit, or subsidy) can be modified or repealed *ex post facto* only under certain, legally defined conditions, even where the administrative authority may have reason to believe that its earlier decision was legally unsound or even unlawful.

Retroactive legislation is only permitted within certain limits. These rules are among the most important law-making constraints directly derived from the rule of law principle.[1] There is an explicit stipulation in the Basic Law (Article 103 II GG) prohibiting punishment for an act committed before it was made a legal offense. In other words, the definition of the crime and the sanction must be laid down by law before the act in question was committed. As to retroactive legislation in general, the Basic Law does not contain any explicit provision. The guidelines given by the FCC[2] are based upon inferences drawn from the general principle of the rule of law contained in the Basic Law. The FCC considers laws retroactively imposing a burden to be generally unconstitutional, with a few narrowly defined exceptions, e.g., where an individual had reason to expect the new regulation at the time the retroactive law came into force. A government announcement is ordinarily not sufficient to legitimate retroactive legislation. However, the situation may be different when a parliamentary decision has

---

1. Volkmar Götz, *Bundesverfassungsgericht und Vertrauensschutz*, in: Bundesverfassungsgericht und Grundgesetz, Festschrift aus Anlass des 25-jährigen Bestehens des Bundesverfassungsgerichts, vol. 2, p. 421 (1976).
2. *See* BVerfGE 13, 261.

already been made in the *Bundestag* and simply requires further procedural steps, such as the consent of the *Bundesrat* and the *Bundespräsident*, before the law takes effect.[3]

[2]   The Rule of Law and the Government

The principle of the rule of law – as addressed to the government – is best expressed by the separation and division of powers, both on a horizontal and a vertical basis. Tripartite government, the provision of checks and balances, is – according to Locke and Montesquieu – the hallmark of modern constitutionalism.[4]

Every branch of government is required to remain within its jurisdiction, i.e., its sphere of institutional competence. This is a basic principle in most, if not all, constitutions of the democratic type. It is the responsibility of the parliament, elected by the people, to decide important questions of state conduct[5] and fundamental public policies as long as it remains within the limits of the Constitution. An act of parliament takes precedence over all other acts of state. The executive branch is bound by the Constitution, statutory law, and equity in the sense of general principles of written and unwritten legal constraints (Article 20 III GG). The tendency of the modern rule of the legal State – the State governed by law – is to impose an ever closer net of legal constraints upon the executive:[6]

- Constitution and law are binding upon every executive action (Article 20 III GG).
- Delegated legislation may be executed only in a restricted manner according to constitutional law (Article 80 GG).
- Executive action against a person can be taken only on the basis of statutory law.
- The relevant statute has to provide a sufficiently clear and detailed basis for any encroachment of areas that are protected by basic rights.
- No State action must be excessive; intrusions into basic rights (or public benefits) have to be proportional to the reason for the intrusion.
- All actions of governmental agencies must be "transparent," open to the public, and every citizen whose rights are affected must be given the reasons for the action.[7]
- The exercise of State authority as a permanent function shall, as a rule, be entrusted to members of the public service whose status, service, and loyalty are governed by public law (Article 33 IV GG).

---

3. Volkmar Götz, Legislative and Executive Power under the Constitutional Requirements Entailed in the Principle of the Rule of Law, in: New Challenges to the German Basic Law (Christian Starck ed. 1991), p. 145.
4. Konrad Hesse, Grundzüge des Verfassungsrechts der Bundesrepublik Deutschland (20th ed. 1999), p. 85.
5. Klaus Stern, Das Staatsrecht der Bundesrepublik Deutschland, vol. 1 (2nd ed. 1984), p. 956.
6. Ulrich Karpen, The Rule of Law, in: The Constitution of the Federal Republic of Germany: Essays on the Basic Rights and Principles of the Basic Law with a Translation of the Basic Law (Ulrich Karpen ed. 1988), p. 176.
7. Philip Kunig, Das Rechtsstaatsprinzip (1986), p. 198.

[C]   Federalism

The FRG consists of sixteen *Länder*: Baden-Württemberg, Bavaria, Berlin, Branden-
burg, Bremen, Hamburg, Hessen, Lower Saxony, Mecklenburg-Western Pomerania,
North-Rhine Westphalia, Rhineland-Palatinate, Saarland, Saxony, Saxony-Anhalt,
Schleswig-Holstein and Thuringia.

[1]   History of Federalism

Federal systems have different roots in history. The origins of the Swiss Federation, to
give an example, lie in the 13th century. Switzerland started as a loose confederacy of
rural and municipal associations bound together in a democratic tradition. Federalism
in Germany, one of the important constitutional ideas of the 19th century, is attributable to the attempt to steer a middle course between two historical extremes:
fragmented diversity and unity. The 17th and 18th centuries were the centuries of
extreme diversity, a diversity which exceeded even regional and ethnic distinctions. In
the period of absolutism, the dying Holy Roman Empire disintegrated into a loose
association of some 300 independent and mutually distant states, principalities, and
free cities. Most of these entities were in fact centralized states, the prince having
supreme domestic power and the state being independent in foreign affairs. This
situation was hardly conducive to the realization of nationhood. The French Revolution created the model of *la grande nation* and *la republique unie et indivisible*, and
Napoleon as the ruler of Europe spread it to the neighboring countries. German
constitutionalism in the 19th century sought both nationhood and diversity of regional
groups and cultures. There was fear both of French centralism as well as of past
German disunity.[8] Federalism was an instrument for achieving both ends. In 1871,
German unification was finally brought about in the form of a strong federal union – via
the earlier and weak North German Confederation – established under Bismarck's
leadership and accompanied by the rise of Prussia.[9]

If the Constitution of the Bismarckian Empire had been characterized by strong
federalist and weaker democratic features, the Weimar Republic (1919–1933) presented the opposite model: a watered-down version of federalism with strong democratic elements. The steam roller of the Hitler regime leveled out the remnants of
federalism and violently destroyed democracy and the idea of State based on the rule
of law. But Nazism was ultimately unable to uproot the seeds of either. They rose with
the essential support of the Western Allies to new life after the devastations caused by
Nazism and war.[10]

The roots of federalism in Germany can be found, to some extent, in the historical
experiences and in efforts to avoid a centralistic State like the *Third Reich*. But

---

8. Ulrich Karpen, *Federalism*, in: The Constitution of the Federal Republic of Germany: Essays on
   the Basic Rights and Principles of the Basic Law with a Translation of the Basic Law (Ulrich
   Karpen ed. 1988), p. 207.
9. Ernst Rudolf Huber, *Deutsche Verfassungsgeschichte seit 1789*, vol. 3 (1963), p. 785.
10. Ulrich Karpen, *supra* note 8, p. 208.

federalism is also intended to help to preserve the regional, historical and cultural ties of the inhabitants of different regions, even if several *Länder* were artificial entities, created by the Allies after World War II. They are not totally homogeneous states and, in many cases, the geographical boundaries between the *Länder* were drawn in an arbitrary manner. The *Länder* differ in size and economic strength. For this reason, Article 29 GG stipulates that "boundaries may be modified to ensure that the *Länder*, by virtue of their size and capacity, can effectively perform their functions." However, the assertiveness of the *Länder* governments and a growing self-confidence has rendered provisions like Article 29 GG widely unused, since the last attempt to merge two *Länder* – Berlin and Brandenburg – failed in 1994.

[2] Federal Features

Federalism in the FRG is characterized by a distribution of power between the Federation and the *Länder*, the latter possessing state quality independent of the Federation. Both the Federation and the *Länder* have their own state organs of legislation, administration and judiciary that perform tasks on their own according to a distribution of powers determined by the Basic Law.

As defined in the Basic Law, the division of power between the three levels of government, the Federation (*Bund*), the constituent states (*Länder*), and local authorities, applies in three fields.

[a] Legislation

In the distribution of legislative powers, the *Bund* plays a dominant role and, with some exceptions for *Länder* autonomy such as school and educational affairs, cultural policy, and most police powers. The legislative interests of the *Länder* on the federal level are considered in the second chamber of the German legislature, namely the Federal Council or *Bundesrat*.

The Constitution provides that the Federal Council shall consist of members of the *Länder* cabinets. The vote of a *Land* must be cast as en bloc, thus enhancing its influence by bringing on its whole weight upon a legislative issue of the federal government. In principle, the Federal Council enjoys only a suspensive veto, which may be overridden in the *Bundestag*. However, in certain cases explicitly foreseen in the constitution, e.g., tax and revenue issues, the Federal Council has an absolute veto and the *Bundestag* is not able to adopt legislation in these fields without its consent;[11] this is when the Federal Council acts as a "genuine" second chamber (Articles 77 and 78 GG).

---

11. Hesse, *supra* note 4, pp. 263 et seq.

[b]   Administration

The main responsibility with respect to administration rests with the *Länder*. While the *Bund* has an administrative structure of its own in a limited number of areas (such as foreign policy and defense), most federal laws are executed by the administrative authorities of the *Länder*. This not only vests the *Länder* with administrative discretionary powers, it also explains why a large amount of the federal laws require the consent of the *Bundesrat*, providing it with an absolute veto in those cases as well. Local administrations in the municipalities depend directly on the *Länder* governments, but they enjoy considerable discretionary powers of their own in matters of purely local interest.

[c]   Finance

Some taxes or shares of taxes are allocated directly to the municipalities, while other taxes go to the *Länder* or to the *Bund*. Some tax is shared between the three levels. For example, income and corporation taxes are shared in a fixed proportion between the three levels of government, and the value added tax (VAT) is divided between the *Bund* and the *Länder* according to a formula which is often subject to highly controversial negotiations that need to take place every year. A fixed proportion of the revenue from the VAT goes to the EU, thus adding a supra-national element to the fiscal picture. The municipalities are notoriously financially weak because they have to provide most public services but have relatively low tax revenues of their own. In order to secure uniform living standards in Germany, there are arrangements for financial equalization between the "rich" and the "poor" *Länder* (by the so-called horizontal compensation scheme, *horizontaler Finanzausgleich*), and between *Bund, Länder* and municipalities (the so-called vertical compensation scheme, *vertikaler Finanzausgleich*).

In general, the German federal system is based on the principle of subsidiarity (*Subsidiaritätsprinzip*), which means that problems should be addressed at the level of government where they emerge. Additionally, it is required that the administrative power is vested in the respective government entity. A higher level will take over only if it competent according to the law and problems cannot be solved locally while the higher level is better suited to succeed in doing this.

[d]   Federal Structure

The Basic Law displays fundamental federalist characteristics throughout.[12]

> (1) Election of Judges of the FCC
>   The Basic Law provides for the establishment of a FCC (*Bundesverfassungs-gericht*) (Articles 92–95 GG). Each chamber of the federal legislature – the *Bundestag* and the *Bundesrat* – elects one half of the court's judges. The

---

12. *See* generally Karpen, *supra* note 8, p. 209.

tribunal decides *inter alia* legal disputes between the Federation and the *Länder* or between different *Länder* making it the highest arbiter in struggles in the realm of federalism.

(2) Amendments to the Constitution

The *Länder* participate in the adoption of the Constitution and amendments to it (Article 79 II GG). To be valid, amendments to the Constitution require a two-third majority in both houses of parliament. Amendments to the Constitution are generally "inadmissible" if they disrespect the federal nature of government, i.e., the division of the *Bund* into *Länder*, the principle of participation of the *Länder* in legislation and the basic principles upon which the State is founded, that is, civil rights and the democratic and federal character of the State as laid down in Articles 1 and 20 GG. However, modest changes and adjustments in the complex scheme of German federalism are not infringing on the so-called "eternity"-guarantee of Article 79 III GG (*Ewigkeitsgarantie*).

(3) Election of the President

The Federal President of the Republic (*Bundespräsident*) is elected by a Federal Convention (*Bundesversammlung*) (Article 54 GG) consisting of all members of the *Bundestag* and an equal number of members elected by the *Länder* legislatures according to their partisan allocation. The President may be impeached before the FCC after the *Bundestag* or the *Bundesrat* have initiated the procedure with the required majorities (Article 61 GG).

(4) Federal Civil Service

Civil servants in leading federal positions are to be employed in an equitable ratio from all the *Länder* and persons employed in other Federal Offices normally have to be chosen from the *Länder* in which they are employed (Article 36 GG). This provision has a particularly federalist character.

(5) Federal Enforcement of *Länder* Obligations

If a *Land* fails to fulfill its constitutional or legal obligations toward the *Bund*, the federal government may take measures to force the *Land* to fulfill its obligations (*Bundeszwang*), but it may do so only with the consent of the *Bundesrat* (Article 37 GG). Prior to such a step, the dispute must, however, be submitted to the FCC. The federal enforcement of a *Land's* obligations is, therefore, subject to the approval of two distinctly federalist institutions – the FCC and the Federal Council.

[3]   *Nonfederal and Antifederal Features*[13]

Some provisions of the Basic Law underline the legal and constitutional coherence of the nation and the states. Thus, for example, Article 28 GG provides that "the constitutional order in the *Länder* must conform to the principles of the republican,

---

13. *See* generally Karpen, *supra* note 8, p. 210.

democratic and social State based on the rule of law principle." The Federal Constitution, therefore, determines the basic features of the constitutions of the *Länder* (principle of homogeneity).[14] In addition, also local government must comply with the principles set forth in the Basic Law. Consequently, the Constitution requires counties and municipalities to "have a representative assembly resulting from general, direct, free, equal and secret elections" (Article 28 GG). By doing so, the principle of democratic rule and the essential requirement of democratic elections are also binding on local governments.

The Constitution, however, also pursues an antifederalist approach in subjecting changes in the geographic boundaries of the *Länder* to the final jurisdiction of the Federation, requiring the approval by the *Bundestag* and a referendum, after the *Länder* concerned have "been heard" (Article 29 GG). Article 30 GG provides that "the exercise of the powers of the state and the performance of the state functions shall be the concern of the *Länder*, insofar as the Basic Law does not otherwise prescribe and permit." In a more detailed manner, Articles 70, 83 and 92 GG apply the same principle of distribution of powers to the legislative, executive and judicial branches of government. According to the "supremacy clause" of Article 31 GG, federal law supersedes state law. This provision, giving the *Bund* legislative precedence over the *Länder*, is conditioned upon the requirement that federal law must be constitutional, especially that the federal government must have legislative authority. Taking into account the fact that the majority of legislative powers is vested in the Federation, the provisions mentioned above have the consequence that the corpus of federal law is much larger and more vital for society and government than the law of the *Länder*.

[D]   Local Autonomy

Federalism has to be understood as a barrier against usurpation of power vis-à-vis the local government and other social institutions enjoying legal autonomy, e.g., corporations of public law, universities, social security carriers, and independent public law broadcasting corporations. Federalism, in other words, is the most important element of a vertical division of powers.[15] By virtue of Article 28 II GG, municipalities are guaranteed the right to regulate all local affairs within the limits of the law, and self-government is considered to be a realization of the principle of subsidiarity and the struggle for more democratic participation.[16]

The local government system consists of municipalities (*Städte* and *Gemeinden*) and counties (*Kreise*). At the moment, there are about 16,000 municipalities and 420 counties in Germany. Local municipalities have different sizes and structures. They can be small rural communities or modern cities ("model of the standard municipality"). Larger municipalities in this group, such as cities, have a distinctive position corresponding to special provisions in the law of municipalities and fulfill all tasks that

---

14. *See* Theodor Maunz & Reinhold Zippelius, *Deutsches Staatsrecht* (30th ed. 1998), p. 120.
15. *See* generally Ulrich Karpen, *Application of the Basic Law*, in: Main Principles of the German Basic Law (Christian Starck ed. 1983), p. 69.
16. Karpen, *supra* note 15, p. 71.

would, in a rural area, otherwise be the obligation of a county. This is especially true for the so-called cities independent of a county (*kreisfreie Städte*). Counties are administrative units, originally in rural areas, but nowadays also contiguous with larger cities. Counties have the task of supporting the municipalities assigned to within their territories and take on projects that require greater administrative capacity.

The local authorities (*Kommunalkörperschaften*) belong to the organization of their respective state.[17] Local authorities are[18] associations for a special purpose, administrative units for singular, special purposes (e.g., water supply, waste disposal) or for unique situations, for example, in a region that has certain planning problems, especially for areas with an agglomeration of facilities.[19]

Article 28 II GG ensures that Germany will have municipalities as an element in the structure of its public administration. A municipality is an administrative unit of a special type that is characterized by the following criteria:[20]

– A fixed sovereign territory. The territory's size is characterized by the fact that its inhabitants can feel an attachment to their municipality and to ensure its efficiency in fulfilling its administrative tasks. In reality, there are huge differences in this regard between small rural areas and larger cities. Yet, even in a city, the residents have a special interest in local politics that differs from that in state or federal politics.

– Personal membership of the residents. The membership of a municipality includes all residents living in its territory and having the right to vote. The guarantee of local autonomy is meant to support the "democratic structures, from the bottom up."[21] In recent years criticism has evolved that the right to vote only extends to German nationals and EU citizens as nationals of Member States of the EU whereas nationals from other countries, for example Turkey or African countries, are not included into the local democratic community.[22] Given the fact that acquiring the German citizenship has been facilitated considerably during the last decades – it only takes seven or eight years after residing lawfully in Germany – every resident has a realistic chance of acquiring the position of a resident of the local community.

– Status as an entity in law. Municipalities are legal entities. Their legal capacity bestows upon them flexibility and security in legal transactions because they have standing in legal proceedings in order to protect their rights in court. However, municipalities are not just legal persons, they are more specifically legal persons under public law that have the particular form of public law

---

17. *See* Walter Rudolf, in: *Allgemeines Verwaltungsrecht* (Hans-Uwe Erichsen & Wolfgang Martens eds. 10th ed. 1995), p. 698.
18. Eberhard Schmidt-Assmann, *The Constitution and the Requirements of Local Autonomy*, in: New Challenges to the German Basic Law (Christian Starck ed. 1991), p. 170.
19. Hans J. Wolff, Otto Bachof, Rolf Stober & Winfried Kluth, *Verwaltungsrecht II* (7th ed. 2010), p. 169.
20. *See* Schmidt-Assmann, *supra* note 18, p. 171.
21. BVerfGE 52, 95, 111.
22. Cf. Hans Meyer, *Grundgesetzliche Demokratie und Wahlrecht für ansässige Nichtdeutsche*, JZ 2016, p. 121.

entities organized with regard to a constituency. As such, they exercise state power and have jurisdiction over their constituencies and other persons or entities in their areas.

The guarantee of a legal position in Article 28 II GG does not prevent the Federation from dissolving individual municipalities or from forming new ones by "territorial restructuring." Such reforms have occurred every now and then in the history of German statehood. Yet, they are permitted only for sufficiently important reasons of public interest and only after the affected municipality has been heard.[23] In any case, even after such a reform, the municipality as an administrative unit representing the local area, must meet the characteristics described.[24]

Autonomy is guaranteed in all matters affecting the local community. Local matters are such that "have their roots" in the local community or have a special relation to it and can be regulated autonomously and independently.[25] Accordingly, matters such as local area planning as well as the construction and maintenance of local roads are tasks of the local community. On the other hand, questions of foreign policy, defense, or national economic policy are clearly not within their sphere. The municipalities have no unlimited general political mandate.[26]

[E]   The Principle of "Social Justice"

[1]   The Origin of "Social Justice"

It is commonplace, even in historical context, that the Basic Law's reference to "social justice" does not allow drawing concrete substantive conclusions as to the content or function of the principle. The origin of the general idea of social justice as a goal to be pursued by the State is to supplement individual rights especially in those cases where individuals cannot preserve their own livelihood, diminishing their opportunity to make full use of their individual liberties. In other words, the State's support of social justice was meant to ensure an opportunity to effectively participate in social life.

The concept of State intervention into the socioeconomic structure on the one hand and individual rights on the other have been twins in sociopolitical development ever since economic liberalism became a basic feature of German society in the 19th century. The "social rights" of the Weimar Constitution have evolved into a system of social security – a free market economy grown into a "free and social market economy" (*freie und soziale Marktwirtschaft*) – including a network of State institutions for public welfare, they are the result and expression of an inherent tension between leaving

---

23. BVerfGE 50, 95, 134; 52, 95, 120.
24. Eberhard Schmidt-Assmann & Hans Christian Röhl, in: *Besonderes Verwaltungsrecht* (Eberhard Schmidt-Assmann, 13 ed. 2011), p. 113.
25. BVerfGE 8, 122, 134; 52, 95, 120.
26. BVerfGE 79, 127, 147.

persons free to exercise their individual intellectual, physical, and economic capabilities and placing limits upon the results of the exercise of these freedoms.[27]

[2] *"Social Justice" as a Norm Describing a Goal to Be Pursued by the State*

The existence of constitutional policy goals (*Staatszielbestimmungen*) reflects not only the experiences of the political past, it also formulates a pattern for the political and legal framework. Certainly, political goals or programs cannot be laid down or even enumerated in a constitution. Their definition may be left to the political and legislative process; in a system of democratic government, the formation of politically relevant opinions originates from society, is channeled by political parties and the electoral processes, and is finally defined and executed by the government. The Basic Law proclaims certain goals as *minima* that have to play a role in decision-making on all levels of public action. However, it is not easy to determine the weight which these goals shall have in making a choice between alternatives. As a rule, one may say that their significance varies according to the intensity by which a conceivable structure of a given normative guideline can be identified.[28] Admittedly, the responsible State organs have considerable discretion in assessing the core areas and key aspects of their legislative or administrative activities. As a minimum, the social state principle requires to provide for the basic or essential needs of the residents. However, there is a high probability that several welfare benefits conferred by law are not required by the Social state principle but exceed the constitutional obligations considerably.

Germany has developed a specific idea of a social state (*Sozialstaat*) over time. The Basic Law primarily constitutes a basis and starting point for multiple and widespread legislative activities. On the one hand, social benefits are financed by taxes, including inheritance tax. The social state is inherently a tax State, provided that it does not abuse the function of social distribution. It is worth noting here that after two World Wars, economic needs could not have been met without the support of the state.[29] Insofar as the principle of social justice is seen as a normative directive to legislation, there is, for all practical purposes, in fact only limited judicial control. The FCC has never declared any social legislation to be incompatible with the principle of social justice as such.[30] The protection of the security of data, prevention of cruelty to animals, the prohibition of discrimination of disabled people or unmarried couples were not considered to be novel social goals, nor was the obligation to advance the welfare of children or the care for the elderly. On the contrary, the FCC has on several occasions held that the principle of the social state connected with the constitution's

---

27. Philip Kunig, *The Principle of Social Justice*, in: The Constitution of the Federal Republic of Germany: Essays on the Basic Rights and Principles of the Basic Law with a Translation of the Basic Law (Ulrich Karpen ed. 1988), p. 191.
28. Kunig, *supra* note 27, pp. 194, 195.
29. Günter Dürig, *An Introduction to the Basic Law of the Federal Republic of Germany*, in: The Constitution of the Federal Republic of Germany: Essays on the Basic Rights and Principles of the Basic Law with a Translation of the Basic Law (Ulrich Karpen ed. 1988), p. 21.
30. Kunig, *supra* note 27, p. 198.

highest value, the protection of human dignity, establishes a right to a "subsistence minimum" which has to be provided by the government.[31] In recent years, the FCC has extended its jurisdiction on the "subsistence minimum" to the welfare assistance provided for asylum seekers in Germany.[32]

§2.04   THE STATE ORGANS

[A]   The Federal Parliament (*Bundestag*)

The *Bundestag*, the lower house of parliament, represents the German people and is the highest political institution of the FRG. It is the principal and sole representative organ in all legislative matters although its powers have been somewhat restricted in favor of the Federal Council (*Bundesrat*) and the Federal Government (*Bundesregierung*) in comparison with the corresponding organ in the Weimar Republic. The members of the Federal Parliament are elected in a general, direct, free, equal, and secret election for a four-year term. They shall be, according to Article 38 GG, "representatives of the whole people; they shall not be bound by any instructions, only by their conscience."

[1]   *The Autonomy of the* Bundestag

The rights of the *Bundestag*, according to the German Constitution, are based on the experiences of the English Parliament in its struggle against the Crown in the 17th century. At the center stands its autonomy, i.e., its right of self-regulation in all affairs and its complete independence from other constitutional organs. This applies in particular to the election of the President of the *Bundestag* and his or her deputies, the determination of its rules of procedure (*Geschäftsordnung*), and the formation of the necessary committees. No other institution may exercise authority within the confines of the *Bundestag* building. In particular, police powers are exercised exclusively by the President of the *Bundestag* (Article 40 II GG).

[2]   *The Competence of the* Bundestag

The competence of the *Bundestag* is not explicitly delineated in a single provision of the Constitution. It can, however, be described as follows: the *Bundestag*, as the highest constitutional organ representing the will of the electorate, has broad competences, limited only by the competence of other constitutional organs. The principal functions of the *Bundestag* include:

- election of certain organs, particularly the heads of the executive;
- control over the executive;

---

31. BVerfGE 125, 175, 213 (Hartz IV).
32. BVerfGE 132, 134, 157 (AsylBLG).

- enacting legislation, determining the budget, and giving approvals;
- representation of the people.

[3]   The Rights of a Member of the Bundestag

The fundamental principle of the "free mandate" (Article 38 I 2 GG) is central to the rights of each Member of the *Bundestag* (MdB). MdBs are subject only to their conscience and are not bound by any instructions or directives. This ideal, however, does not entirely correspond to political realities. The interest of the MdBs in their reelection makes them dependent on the support of their party and parliamentary group. The "free mandate" is protected by the indemnity and immunity of the MdB. Indemnity (Article 46 I GG) exempts the MdB from any criminal, civil and disciplinary liability for remarks made in Parliament. Immunity (Article 46 II-IV GG) protects the MdB against immediate judicial and police measures. Therefore, criminal prosecutions against an MdB require the Council of Elders (*Ältestenrat*) of the *Bundestag* to decide on the lifting of immunity, which is regularly done if the proceedings appear justified. In order to secure the mutual independence of the highest organs of State, certain combinations of concurrent membership in those organs are forbidden on grounds of incompatibility. Most importantly, concurrent membership in both *Bundestag* and *Bundesrat* is not permitted. Likewise, membership in the *Bundestag* is incompatible with the position of Minister or Senator of a *Bundesland* (state). On the other hand, it is common for the Federal Chancellor and the cabinet ministers to be simultaneously members of the *Bundestag*. In exceptional and rare cases, it is even permitted that a Member of the *Bundestag* simultaneously is a Member of the *Landtag* of a state.

[4]   Parliamentary Groups

The organization of the *Bundestag* through parliamentary groups (*Fraktionen*) is a result of the constitutional expression of democracy as exercised through the political parties and the State. A political party may form a parliamentary group if it holds at least 5% of the seats in the *Bundestag*. The legal competence of a parliamentary group is wide, especially including the power to make recommendations and motions. The parliamentary group plays a crucial political role in transforming the political will of the party to the Parliament. However, the parliamentary group is also a part of the Parliament and is therefore, at least indirectly, an organ of the State.

The parliamentary groups are subdivided into working groups. These working groups contain the specialists of the particular parliamentary party, divided according to subject matter areas, e.g., foreign policy defense, economy, employment, budget and finance. The compromises reached in the working groups often determine the position of the parliamentary group in the *Bundestag*. Here, the party in government usually pushes through its program by virtue of its majority, as long as the parliamentary group itself is united. The decisions of the *Bundestag* are therefore considerably dependent on the opinions of the working groups within the parliamentary groups.

[5]   Committees

Committees are support organs (suborgans) of Parliament, constituted to carry out preparatory work for parliamentary proceedings. Certain committees are mandatory, for example, the Committees on Foreign Affairs and Defense (Article 45a GG) and the Petitions Committee (Article 45c GG). Under Article 44 of the Basic Law, a special "investigation committee" (*Untersuchungsausschuss*) is to be appointed by the *Bundestag* if one quarter of its members demand the formation of such a committee. Investigation committees can be a powerful instrument in the hands of the opposition to control and influence the government. All decisions of an investigation committee are made with a simple majority of the vote. The committee representatives of the government are able to exclude the public and limit the scope of the inquiry. However, investigation committees can only determine factual questions. They cannot pronounce any judgments; but factual determinations of these committees bind the courts, which are restricted to the legal interpretation of the factual situation forming the basis of the inquiry.

In recent years, so-called Enquête commissions have achieved particular importance. Under § 56 of the *Bundestags Geschäftsordnung*, such commissions are appointed for the preparation of decisions in significant subject areas, e.g., genetic engineering.

[6]   The Constitution and the Parties

In the FRG, the political parties are among the most influential actors in the democratic state. Their freedom of action represents a vital part of the democratic system. This development makes it necessary to set limits to the parties' exercise of power. An attempt to trust blindly in the free play of political forces would be tantamount to ignoring the lessons of history and underestimate the latent inclination towards monopolization of power. The object of constitutional law and of the statute governing political parties is to preserve the openness and the transparency of political decision-making. Such difficult matters as the internal organization of parties, the administration of their finances, their relationship with the executive branch, and their competitiveness – as well as the treatment to be accorded so anticonstitutional and undemocratic parties – require a set of rules.

The Basic Law furnished the political parties with a proper position and function in the constitution of the state, for the first time in the constitutional history of Germany. After a constitutional amendment in 2017 Article 21 GG provides:

(1) The political parties shall help to form the political will of the people. They may be freely established. Their internal organization shall conform to democratic principles. They shall publicly account for the sources and use of their funds.

(2) Parties which, by reason of their aims or the conduct of their adherents, seek to impair or abolish the free democratic order or to endanger the existence of

the FRG shall be unconstitutional. The FCC shall rule on the question of unconstitutionality.

(3) Parties which, by reason of their aims or the conduct of their adherents, seek to impair or abolish the free democratic order or to endanger the existence of the FRG, are to be excluded from public funding. Upon exclusion, tax privileges of the party and of contributions in favor of the party are dispensed with.

(4) The FCCs decides on the issue of unconstitutionality according to section 2 and on the exclusion from public funding according to section 3.

(5) Details shall be regulated by federal law.

Up to the present, the Court has declared two parties to be unconstitutional: the Neo-Nazi *Sozialistische Reichspartei* (SRP) in 1952 and the Communist Party of Germany (*Kommunistische Partei Deutschlands*) in 1956. In both instances, the Federal Government, led by Chancellor Konrad Adenauer, initiated the proceeding before the FCC. As the Court put it in the first of these cases:

The behavior of the (SRP) party and its members, as well as the personal and organizational relationships between the SRP and the NSDAP, demonstrates that the goal of the SRP is to overthrow the free democratic order. The very same circles which made it possible for Hitler to lead Germany into the abyss are now again trying to assert their political leadership. They cherish his means and recommend the same ways that resulted in Germany's being torn apart. In a very unconcerned manner they declare their approval of Hitler … The SRP is thus unconstitutional in the sense stipulated in Article 21 II GG. … The party, therefore, must be dissolved.[33]

Article 21 III and IV GG were introduced after the 2017 party ban proceeding against the right wing party NPD failed for formal reasons. Although the proceedings to declare it unconstitutional ultimately were not successful, the FCC expressed its readiness to accept a procedure stripping such parties from public funding at least.[34] Therefore, the constitutional amendment opened the gate for the FCC to decide on excluding political parties from public funding as a new constitutional procedure. Subsequently, a first proceeding pursuant to Article 21 III GG was introduced by the Federal Council against the NPD in 2018.

In addition to the Constitution, which sets out the main points of legislation relating to political parties, the *Parteiengesetz* has now become one of the most important frameworks for political expression. Pursuant to the legal definition set out in section 2 of that law, political parties are associations of citizens who set out to influence either permanently or for a long period of time the formation of political opinions at the Federal or *Land* level and to participate in the representation of the people in the *Bundestag* or state parliaments (*Landtage*), provided that they offer a

---

33. BVerfGE 2, 1, 78.
34. BVerfG, 1/17/2017, 2 BvB 1/13, NJW 2017, 611; cf. Jan Philipp Schaefer, *Das Parteiverbot im Lichte der Europäischen Menschenrechtskonvention*, AöR, Vol. 141 (2016), p. 594; Uhle, *Das Parteiverbot gem. Art. 21 II GG*, NVwZ 2017, p. 583; Gusy, *Verfassungswidrig, aber nicht verboten*, NJW 2017, p. 601.

sufficient guarantee of seriousness of their aims, particularly in regard to the scale and strength of their organization, the number of registered members and their image in public opinion.

Political associations are not deemed to be parties if their registered seat is located abroad or if most of their members or executive committee members are aliens. This provision limits the number of associations in the FRG that possess the status of a political party and all the resulting rights and duties.[35]

[B]   The Federal Council (*Bundesrat*)

As noted above, federal legislative power is vested in two organs: the *Bundestag*, chosen by direct elections, and the Federal Council (*Bundesrat*). It is through the latter that the *Länder* participate in the legislative and administrative functions of the Federation. The members of the *Bundesrat* are members of the governments of the *Länder*; they are delegated by the *Länder* and subject to their instructions (Article 51 I GG). Each state has at least three votes. States with more than 2 million inhabitants have four, states with more than six million inhabitants have five, and states with more than seven million inhabitants have six votes (Article 51 II GG).

The *Bundesrat* does not take part in the legislative process on an equal footing with the *Bundestag*. However, it has the right to introduce bills and to give its views on bills initiated by the Federal Government. Acts passed by the *Bundestag* will be referred to the *Bundesrat* which, regularly, may only exercise a suspensive veto; its objections can be overridden by a new vote in the *Bundestag* (Article 77 IV GG). In enumerated cases, however, a bill can only pass if the *Bundesrat* consents. It then has an absolute veto power. Differences between the *Bundestag* and the *Bundesrat* may be reconciled in a special mediation committee (*Vermittlungsausschuss*) composed of an equal number of members of both the *Bundestag* and *Bundesrat*. In accordance with Article 77 GG, the *Bundesrat* can request a meeting within fourteen days after the receipt of the bill from the *Bundestag*.

[C]   The Federal Chancellor (*Bundeskanzler*) and Cabinet

Executive authority in the FRG is vested in the Federal Chancellor (*Bundeskanzler*) and the Federal Ministers who together are referred to in the Basic Law as the *Bundesregierung* or cabinet. The Federal President (*Bundespräsident*) is the head of state, but, as indicated below, he has only very limited powers. Under the Basic Law, the essential political power is vested in the Chancellor. He or she decides on the number of ministers and appoints all cabinet ministers who, in turn, are directly responsible to him or her. In addition the Rules of Procedure of the Federal Cabinet (*Geschäftsordnung der Bundesregierung*) have to be approved by the Federal President.

The Chancellor is constitutionally responsible for setting "national policy guidelines." He could theoretically maintain his position in the face of an opposition holding

---

35. Walter Keim, *The Law on Political Parties* (1982), p. 5.

a majority of votes in the *Bundestag*. This stems from the fact that under the constitutional provisions for the so-called constructive vote of no confidence (*konstruktives Misstrauensvotum*), the Chancellor may not be removed unless the no confidence vote is accompanied by the election of a successor by a majority of the members of the *Bundestag*. So far, this has happened only once – in 1982. The Chancellor's powers under the Constitution, combined with a regular four-year tenure and the legacy of strong leadership provided by West Germany's first Chancellor, Konrad Adenauer, have led many observers to characterize the FRG as a "chancellor democracy." Later experiences have led to the conclusion that the effective use of the Chancellor's constitutional powers strongly depends on his personality and political standing. In any case, it has to be noticed that Germany is a representative democracy with the characteristic feature that the Federal Government with the Chancellor at the helm depends heavily on a reliable majority in the Bundestag. A change of coalition or a surprising scandal, therefore, can spur the wheel of politics and entail the loss of the parliamentary majority which dooms the fate of the Chancellor and his or her cabinet.

One of the most powerful instruments of executive leadership today is the Office of the Federal Chancellor (*Bundeskanzleramt*), which is analogous to the White House Office of the President of the United States and to some extent also to the Offices of the British and Canadian Prime Ministers. Originally a small secretariat serving the Chancellor's personal needs, it has developed into an agency of major political importance as could be seen, for example, in the Refugee Crisis of 2015. It contains departments mirroring to the various federal ministries, as well as others engaging in long-term social and economic planning, in the coordination of policies relating to the EU and in coordinating internal security and overseeing the secret services. Its staff of some 500 civil servants keeps the Chancellor informed on domestic and foreign affairs, coordinates policy making among the Federal Ministers and monitors the implementation of cabinet decisions. The office is headed by a "chief of staff" (*Kanzleramtsminister*), usually a personal confidant of the Chancellor. Finally, the Chancellor is served by a Federal Press Secretary (*Bundespressechef*), who in turn heads the Federal Press and Information Office (*Bundespresse- und Informationsamt*).

The Chancellor is elected by a majority of the *Bundestag* in a secret ballot. Owing to the operation of the German party system, he has frequently also been the chairman or the chairwoman of his or her party outside of parliament. One decisive constitutional feature of the Basic Law, especially responsible for the remarkable stability despite of being a representative democracy, refers to the majority required to elect the Chancellor. According to Article 63 II GG, a majority of the votes of the members of the Bundestag – currently 355 of 709 – is required to become Chancellor of the FRG. The rationale of this provision lies in the idea that acquiring such a convincing majority of the members of the *Bundestag* – and not only of the members present – at the beginning of the parliamentary term, all united behind the head of the Federal Government has good chances to last for the whole or most of the election period.

As Article 65 GG shows, the predominance of the Chancellor can, theoretically, be matched by the cabinet acting as a collegial organ with the Chancellor then reduced to the status of a *primus inter pares* when votes are taken. This was, for example, the case under several "*Große Koalitionen*" ("great coalitions") between 1966 and 1969, and later between 2005 and 2009, and since 2013. In other words, whether a "chancellor democracy" prevails or whether the power of ultimate decision-making lies with the cabinet, depends on whether or not the government consists of a coalition in which the Chancellor (together with his political friends inside and outside the cabinet) has to take the views expressed by the coalition partner into consideration as well as on the personality of the incumbent.[36] In any case, it must be observed that the constitutionally strong position of the Chancellor does not always reflect his or her real power concerning the outcome of the latest polls or the maneuvers of the current coalition partner.

[D]   The Federal President (*Bundespräsident*)

Unlike the U.S. President or the President of France, the *Bundespräsident* is a nongoverning head of state, provided with mostly representative duties and only called to have decisive power in times of emergency and in the process of starting or ending legislative terms. Under the Constitution, the President (*Bundespräsident*) has few immediate responsibilities. However, the President is not quite such an "apolitical" constitutional institution as he is occasionally portrayed. In case of a threat of a minority government, the President alone has the authority to decide, according to his own political and constitutional judgment, between accepting a minority government or dissolving the *Bundestag* (Articles 63 IV and 68 I GG). The President does not have an independent role in shaping policy; rather, he serves a primarily representative and integrative function which, as such, is not comprehensively defined. It is clear, however, that the constitutional position of the President is that of an independent and superior constitutional organ, and that the President likewise is bound to uphold the constitutional order – which can be significant in the exercise of his authority. The President is the head of state, though he does not participate in meetings of the Federal Government. His duties and responsibilities lie above all in the representation of the State, in particular abroad (Article 59 I GG). He is responsible for the execution of legislation, the appointment and dismissal of members of the government, and the declaration of a state of legislative emergency in accordance with Article 81 GG. He is, however, denied participation in political leadership. This indicates an implied duty of reservation on political questions, and neutrality vis-à-vis party politics. Article 82 GG requires countersignature of the President to legislation in which, however, he is bound to perform by the political decision making competence of the government.

The President is the representative of the Federal Republic abroad and is responsible in particular for the conclusion of international treaties, according to Article 59 I GG. However, he is not responsible for shaping foreign policy. In contrast, the legislature and the government have authority in foreign affairs. Consequently, the authority under Article 59 I GG refers neither to the substantive aspect of foreign policy nor to the negotiation of international treaties, but rather to the formal act of conclusion

---

36. Donald P. Kommers, *Chancellor, Cabinet and President*, in: Politics and Government in the Federal Republic of Germany, Basic Documents (Carl-Christoph Schweitzer ed. 1984), p. 50.

of treaties that have been negotiated by the government. Whether a treaty is subject to ratification is determined by Article 59 II GG. In the case of treaties not subject to ratification, the President is directly responsible for their conclusion, according to Article 59 I GG, but not for the treaty negotiations. He can – and regularly does – delegate his authority to conclude treaties to a representative like the Chancellor or the Minister of Foreign Affairs.

[E]   Structure of the Court System

The German court system differs from that of other federations, such as the United States of America, as all the trial and intermediate appellate courts are state – as opposed to federal – courts; only the courts of last resort are on the federal level. All courts may hear cases based on law enacted on the federal level, though there are some areas of administrative law over which the *Länder* have exclusive control (cf. section 137 VwGO). The federal courts assure the uniform application of national law by the lower courts. In addition to the courts of general jurisdiction for civil and criminal cases, the highest of which is the Federal Supreme Court (*Bundesgerichtshof*), there are four court systems with specialized jurisdiction – in administrative, labor, social security, and tax matters.

While all courts have the power and the obligation to review the constitutionality of government action and legislation within their jurisdiction, only the FCC (*Bundesverfassungsgericht*) may declare legislation unconstitutional. Other courts must suspend proceedings if they find a statute unconstitutional and must submit the question of constitutionality to the FCC for decision (Article 100 I GG).

Without the FCC, the Constitution would be of little value. All government institutions are obliged to adhere to the Constitution, but without the FCC there would be no one to determine whether or not that obligation has been breached. The normative power of the Constitution is therefore established as a political reality only through the Constitutional Court. This is particularly true with regard to fundamental rights (*Grundrechte*). The FCC has turned the necessarily broad and vague articles of the Constitution into a living and working element of social and legal reality. It is due to the Constitutional Court that most of the fundamental rights do not simply lie idle, as it was the case under the Weimar Constitution, but guide and control all public activities. The Court has, by the force of its decisions, contributed significantly to the translation of the principles of the Constitution into a free democratic order in both government and society.

The decisions of the FCC apply not only *inter partes*, as in civil judgments, but bind all constitutional organs, courts and authorities at both the federal and state levels. It is a subject of controversy whether the decision alone is binding or whether the grounds for the decision are binding as well. A middle ground position is that not all the grounds of decision are necessarily binding, but only those that form the constitutional core of the decision and are reflected in the operative provisions of a judgment.

The responsibilities of the Constitutional Court are for the most part set out in the Basic Law itself, particularly in its Article 93 GG. Detailed procedural rules are provided in the FCC Act (*Bundesverfassungsgerichtsgesetz*). Section 13 of this Act contains a complete summary of all types of procedures available in the FCC. The Court never takes up a case on its own initiative, but acts solely upon an application. The question of who has standing to lodge an application with the Court depends on the particular kind of dispute.

According to Article 93 I GG, anyone claiming that his fundamental rights have been violated by a public authority may file a complaint of unconstitutionality (*Verfassungsbeschwerde*) with the Court. Public authority in this context includes legislation, administration and judicial decisions. In other words, laws, acts of administration, and court rulings may be attacked through a constitutional complaint after exhausting the necessary remedies of the respective jurisdiction. The main requirement for an application to be admissible is the allegation that a fundamental constitutional right has been violated. The "possibility theory" maintains that this allegation must be substantiated, i.e., that in light of the facts presented a breach of fundamental rights appears at least possible. Whether there has been such a breach is a question of proof and is not decided at the preliminary admissibility stage. The rights of the citizen contained in Article 33 (equal civil status, professional civil service), Article 38 (elections), Article 101 (inadmissibility of ad hoc tribunals), Article 103 (court hearings, inadmissibility of retroactive criminal legislation and double jeopardy) and Article 104 (legal guarantees in the event of detention) may also be the subject of a complaint of unconstitutionality as described above.

§2.05   THE RESPONSIBILITIES OF THE EXECUTIVE

[A]   State Administration

Articles 83–86 GG refer only to the implementing (*gesetzesakzessorische*) administration with respect to the implementation of Federal legislation. Conversely, the administration of state legislation is not addresses in the Basic Law. As can be concluded from Articles 30, 83 GG the Länder are usually responsible for the administration of laws, with the explicit exception of Federal administration according to Article 87 GG. Thus, Article 30 GG contains the general principle of Länder power and competence which is supplemented with respect to legislation by Article 70 GG, with respect to administration by Article 83 GG and for the practice of the judiciary by Article 92 GG. Therefore, the administration is the primary responsibility of the *Länder*.

The *Länder* do this usually as a matter of their own concern (Articles 83 and 84 GG). This means that the administrative authorities of the *Länder* are supervised by the state government (*Landesregierung*). The supervision of state administration by the Federal Government is limited to the question of legality of administrative activities and provides no authority to give directions, apart from an exception under Article 84 V GG. After all, the Federal Government may – with the consent of the Federal Council – promulgate general rules for the executive branch. These rules comprise both organizational provisions which regulate structure and internal order, responsibilities and procedure of authorities, and administrative guidelines regarding the interpretation of legislation to be implemented, as well as the exercise of discretion. According to the prevailing view, administrative guidelines are not legal norms, but have above all a limited relevance relating to the principle of equal application of the law. Nevertheless, it must be clear that administrative guidelines help shaping the application and interpretation of legal provisions in practice.

[B] Implementation of Laws by the *Länder* for the Federation (*Bundesauftragsverwaltung*)

Contrary to the state implementation of federal legislation as a matter of the states' own concern, the Constitution provides for state implementation on behalf of the federal government in particular areas, e.g., in Article 87 II 1 GG (federal defense), Article 87c GG (nuclear energy), Article 87d II GG (air transport), Article 89 II 3 GG (federal waterways) and Article 90 II GG (federal highways). In these areas, the *Land* is bound by the instructions and subject to the supervision of the Federal Government (Article 85 III and IV GG). In general, directions are to be addressed to the highest state authority (Article 85 III GG). Consequently, even here, the organization of administrative authorities remains primarily in the hands of the *Länder*. At any rate, the federal branch of government is bound to handle its supervising powers with utmost restraint, which goes far beyond mere courtesy towards the *Länder*. Rather, the federal government is obliged to indicate early in the process that a problem might arise or a dispute is upcoming before offering advice or even giving orders and directives.

[C] Federal Administration (*Bundeseigene Verwaltung*)

The Federal Government has far more limited administrative powers than the *Länder*. Its areas of responsibility include in particular the foreign service, the treasury with respect to federal taxes and revenues, the military, the aviation administration and the Federal Bank (*Bundesbank*). Apart from these areas, the Federal Government may only form federal agencies under the conditions set forth in Article 87 III GG. One must distinguish between independent legal entities and federal authorities with and without an administrative substructure: agencies as independent legal entities may be established in all areas of federal legislative jurisdiction, by simple legislation. The same is true for Federal agencies without an administrative substructure. There are federal administrative agencies which are responsible for the whole of Germany and which are organizationally independent from any Federal Ministry. Their organizational independence does not, however, mean autonomy from directions of the controlling Federal Ministry. On the other hand, according to Article 87 III GG, the establishment of new federal agencies (with an administrative substructure) is only permissible when new tasks arise in areas within the competence of the Federal Government, and even then only with the consent of the *Bundesrat*. These obstacles are so great that so far scarcely any use has been made of this possibility.

[D]   Joint Tasks of the Federal Government and the Länder, and "Mixed Administration"

Despite the extensive cooperation of the Federal Government and the *Länder* in the area of legislation and administration, the German Constitution adheres to a "separation principle" whereby the Federal Government and the *Länder* remain separate not only as organizations but also with respect to the fulfillment of their tasks. There is in fact a general prohibition of "mixed administration" – an administrative organization in which a Federal authority is subordinate to a state authority, or in which federal and state authorities cooperate by agreement. The reason for this extensive prohibition of a "mixed administration" is to provide for accountability with respect to the democratic process. Voters are supposed to be able to discern which branch of which government is responsible for a specific measure and to hold it accountable in the next election. By establishing "mixed administrations," accountability would be obscured with detrimental effects for democratic principles.

A rare exception are "joint tasks" (*Gemeinschaftsaufgaben*) of the Federal Government and *Länder*, but Article 91a–91e GG limit and shape the scope of such joint tasks.

§2.06   FUNDAMENTAL RIGHTS

[A]   The Classical Function of Fundamental Rights

The classical functions of fundamental rights are subdivided into distinct relationships between an individual and the State. One may distinguish between:

- *status negativus*;
- *status positivus*; and
- *status activus*.[37]

"*Status negativus*" describes a situation in which the individual is given freedom from the State and can, without governmental support, solve his or her problems, regulate social participation, and carry out his or her business. This freedom is guaranteed through the Constitution's fundamental rights to the extent that they protect the individual against State interference and allow the individual freely to pursue his legal interests. "*Status positivus*" describes the situation in which the individual cannot exercise freedom without the help of the State or is otherwise dependent on provisions made by the State. Fundamental rights apply insofar as rights to services, procedure, and participation are guaranteed. "*Status activus*" is the situation in which the individual's freedom operates in or for the State as in the rights and duties of voter and elected official or in the entry into the civil service or into other employment in the public sector.

---

37. Michael Kloepfer, *Verfassungsrecht – Grundrechte*, p. 26.

[B]   The Binding Force of Fundamental Rights and the Limits of those Rights

The threshold question is who is subject to these fundamental rights. Article 1 III GG binds the State in its legislative, executive and judicial functions; it states clearly that the fundamental rights are "directly binding law." This is a deliberate change from the Weimar Constitution in which the fundamental rights were regarded merely as policy objectives.

Fundamental rights, however, do not necessarily have a horizontal effect. They are not directly applicable in contract law but they do shape it: they serve both as a driving force and as guidelines for legislation, administration and the judiciary. They also influence civil law. No civil law provision may contradict the fundamental rights and every law must be interpreted in accordance with their spirit.[38] The general clauses (*Generalklauseln*) of the civil code serve as media for the transmission of the fundamental rights into private relationships; these clauses can thus be described as "ports of entry" for the fundamental rights into the civil law.[39]

The fundamental rights and freedoms are not unrestricted. If that were the case, conflicts would arise not only with the interests of the general public, but also with the interests of other individuals. Therefore the fundamental rights are subject to limitation in certain circumstances. These limitations are governed by the proportionality principle (*Grundsatz der Verhaltnismässigkeit*). The proportionality principle requires that any government interference with fundamental rights be appropriate, necessary and reasonable, i.e., proportional in the narrow sense. Interference is *appropriate* if it promotes the objective in any way: it does not have to be the best means of doing so but it has to be a contribution in pursuing the aforementioned objective. *Necessary* means that there is no way of achieving this objective that would be less intrusive to the rights of the citizen equally appropriate. Therefore, the *necessary*-standard requires government authorities to choose among several means that are equally appropriate the one that is least invasive to the rights of the individual. *Reasonableness* means, eventually, that the interference must be commensurate with the object sought to be achieved, which requires striking the proper balance between means and ends. Within the jurisdiction of the FCC the proportionality principle has grown to be a generally applied constitutional yardstick for government action.

[C]   The Principal Fundamental Rights

[1]   *Freedom of the Person*

According to the Constitutional Court[40] the right to freedom of the person, as guaranteed in Article 2 I GG in connection with Article 1 I GG, functions to secure the

---

38. BVerfGE 7, 198.
39. *See also* Reinhard Zimmermann, *An Introduction to German Legal Culture (with special reference to private law), supra* p. 1, 18 (Ch. X.1.); Michael Kloepfer, *supra* note 37, p. 74.
40. BVerfGE 54, 153.

narrow personal sphere of life and the maintenance of basic needs, which are not conclusively guaranteed by the traditional rights. This need arises also in view of modern developments and new risks for human personality. This category comprises, for example, the protection of human dignity, the right to one's own image and spoken words, the right to one's own genetic code, as well as the right to self-determination in terms of sexuality and sexual orientation.

[2]   Equal Rights Principle

The general equality principle does not mean that all people are always to be treated the same, but rather that it is the duty of public authorities to differentiate only for convincing reasons. The prohibition of Article 3 I GG can be formulated as follows: like is to be treated alike, and unlike is to be treated unlike, i.e., according to differences and characteristics. The equality principle is breached when there is no good reason arising from the nature of things or other evident grounds for the differentiation or unequal treatment, in short when a decision must be described as arbitrary.

Several legal principles are derived from the principle of equality. The general principle of equality to the law as a whole.[41] Its effects in criminal law, tax law, civil law, labor law, social welfare law or procedural law cannot be considered in detail here, but a few secondary principles derived from the equality principle shall be outlined.[42]

[a]   The Binding Effect of Previous Decisions

The principle of equality requires continuity and prevents arbitrariness through a change of practice or in the application of law. If the legislature, executive or judiciary decides and applies the law according to certain principles, these have to be applied equally in deciding or regulating comparable subsequent cases. Only overwhelming reasons for the abandonment of the previous maxim of decision can supply a sufficient basis for a different application of the law – and a basis for future decisions.

[b]   Equal Participation

Article 3 I GG assures equal treatment in the sharing of public benefits. It would apply, for example, where individuals or specific groups are excluded from these benefits, e.g., for the granting of subsidies, the admission to public institutions or to schools and universities.[43]

---

41. BVerfGE 35, 272.
42. Thomas Würtenberger, *Equality*, in: The Constitution of the Federal Republic of Germany: Essays on the Basic Rights and Principles of the Basic Law with a Translation of the Basic Law (Ulrich Karpen ed. 1988), p. 85.
43. BVerfGE 33, 331.

[c]   *Equality of Educational Opportunities under the Rule of Law and the*
        Sozialstaatsprinzip

The traditional equality of opportunity according to the rule of law demands an equal chance for all in education and training, in admission to university education, in examinations and the like, regardless of economic or other differences between individuals. What is required is equal treatment corresponding to capability and skill. The social equality of opportunities (*sozialstaatliche Chancengleichheit*) aims at equality in actual educational opportunities by breaking down economic barriers. Public benefits, such as government loans and grants for students are designed to achieve this objective.[44]

[d]   *Equal Chances for Political Parties*

The principle of equal opportunity for political parties to compete for political influence is derived from Article 3 GG, more specifically from the principle of universality and equality of suffrage,[45] and particularly to an even greater extent from Article 21 I GG. Public authorities are obligated to treat the political parties equally in granting access to public institutions or to public benefits. A graded equality of opportunities (*abgestufte Chancengleichheit*) is nonetheless permitted; it allocates the amount of public services available to the political parties in proportion to their importance.[46]

[e]   *Equal Opportunities in the Competition for Public Opinion*

The legislature has to create conditions to ensure that a variety of opinions can be expressed in both the public and private broadcasting media, corresponding to their importance. A disproportional or one-sided influence of particular programs on public opinion must be avoided.[47]

[f]   *Equitable Taxation*

The principle of tax equity, resulting from Article 3 I GG, requires tax burdens to be apportioned according to financial capability.[48] Those financially better off have to pay higher taxes (in percentage of their income) than the financially weaker taxpayers. In that case equality is proportional. The principle of tax equity is infringed, for instance, if circumstances which diminish the financial capabilities of an individual taxpayer are not taken into account.[49]

---

44. To the most part reaffirmed by BVerfG of December 19, 2017 (numerus clauses II).
45. BVerfGE 24, 340.
46. BVerfGE 14, 132; 24, 340; 47, 225.
47. BVerfGE 73, 118.
48. BVerfGE 6, 70; 26, 310; 50, 391.
49. BVerfGE 67, 298.

[3]   *Freedom of Religion*

This area of protection covers the freedom to form, to hold and to express a belief or philosophy of life, as well as to act according to it. Also included is the freedom not to adhere to any faith and to refuse to recognize any particular belief or philosophy.

[4]   *Freedom of Speech*

The guarantee of freedom of speech protects the expression of a "statement." This freedom includes all value judgments, regardless of the particular topic. Neither is it relevant whether or not the statement is correct as long as it is not a "factual statement." The Constitution protects every opinion, conviction, comment, evaluation, judgment, whatever subject or person may be concerned.[50] In principle the protection applies whether the opinion is geared towards private or public affairs, whether or not it is deemed of importance or value. As the FCC held,[51] to differentiate between valuable and worthless contributions contradicts freedom of speech in a democratic and pluralistic society. It is the subjectivity of the evaluation that is essential to the right of expression. One would misunderstand the connection between freedom of speech and democracy if one were to protect only political discourse.[52] In contrast "factual statements" defined as information on facts are not covered by the freedom of speech provided that there are no elements of value judgments included. In the case that "factual statements" are combined or intertwined with value judgments or opinions – for example, by choosing powerful or evaluating expressions – the impossibility of separating between both parts renders the whole statement an opinion.

[5]   *Freedom of the Press*

The press includes all printed works intended for circulation. The legal definitions in the Press Acts of the *Länder (Landespressegesetze)* correspond to this definition. Thus "press" covers not only periodical publications (newspapers and magazines) but also one-time publications such as books, flyers, leaflets, stickers, and posters. Freedom of the press covers all stages of production, from procurement of information to the circulation of news and opinions. Consequently, it also protects auxiliary activities important to the functioning of the press, though the Constitutional Court usually limits this to internal press activities, i.e., those organizationally integrated with the publishing business. External activities are generally protected by other fundamental rights, particularly Article 12 I GG (freedom of profession).

---

50. Christian Starck and Andreas L. Paulus, in: Hermann von Mangoldt, Friedrich Klein & Christian Starck, *Grundgesetz*, vol. 1 (7th ed. 2018), p. 76.
51. BVerfGE 33, 15.
52. Starck & Paulus, *supra* note 50, p. 578.

[6] Freedom of the Arts

The efforts by the judiciary and by academics to develop a generally applicable definition of art have been fruitless so far; it is increasingly argued that such a definition is impossible. The case law of the FCC is based on the assumption that art can be defined.[53] In recent years, however, the Court has emphasized the "impossibility of generally defining art."[54] The Court uses various concepts of art concurrently:

- a materially artistic idea;
- a formal expression of a concept of art by which the fundamental element of the work is its ability to be categorized according to the particular type, e.g., painting, sculpture, poetry or theater;
- an open-ended concept in which the characteristic feature of an artistic expression is that it is possible to draw further meanings from the representation in a continuous process of interpretation such that the work provides a practically inexhaustible, multi-layered communication of information.[55]

[7] Freedom of Assembly

The act of assembly requires the coming together of at least two persons. In addition, there has to be an internal connection, or an internal, intellectual link between these persons. This latter feature differentiates an assembly from a mere crowd. Such a connection is expressed through the pursuit of a common purpose related to forming or expressing an opinion. This protects the discussion of private as well as public affairs.

[8] Freedom of Association

Article 9 GG speaks of associations (*Vereine*) and companies (*Gesellschaften*). The concept of association is further described in § 2 I of the Association Act as an "association, which a majority of natural or legal persons have joined for a period of time to follow a common purpose and to submit themselves to an organized formation of will." The legal form of the association is not decisive; it includes informal associations formed by citizens as well as highly organized groups. The constitutive elements are:

- membership is voluntary (associations formed under public law are excluded from the protection of Article 9 I GG);

---

53. The Federal Constitutional Court stated in BVerfGE 30, 188: "The fundamental element of artistic activity is the free creative form in which impressions and experiences of the artist are brought to direct view through the medium of a particular use of forms." Cf. Kau, *Polizeiliches Filmverbot im Spannungsverhältnis von Kunst- und Meinungsfreiheit*, AöR, Vol. 140 (2015), p. 31.
54. BVerfGE 67, 225.
55. BVerfGE 67, 225, 226.

- membership serves a common purpose; this purpose can be freely determined and may relate to art, culture, society, politics or socializing;
- membership unites several natural or legal persons with a certain organizational stability; this allows the formation of a common will that can manifest itself in any manner.

[9]   Protection of Private Property

Article 14 GG protects the existence but not the acquisition of property rights; acquisition is protected by the provisions of Article 12 GG (freedom of occupation). Article 14 GG also protects the use as well as the preservation of property. Expropriation is only permitted where it is based on a legislative act of parliament for the good of the general public and only against just compensation.

For purposes of constitutional protection, the concept of property is disputed.[56] It is commonly held that the private law notion of property cannot be applied without modification within the constitutional context. The FCC therefore has argued that it is necessary to develop a special constitutional concept of property.[57] Basically the notion of property as guaranteed by the Constitution must be derived from the Basic Law itself. Therefore the notion of property in the constitutional sense cannot be derived directly from ordinary statutes ranking below the Constitution. An individual or personal interpretation of the right to property has prevailed in the decisions of the FCC. In the words of the Court:

> The historical as well as the actual meaning of the guarantee of property is that of a fundamental right, which is intimately related to individual freedom. In the context of the fundamental rights its function is to give the individual a free range within the area of proprietary interests and to enable the individual to shape his life on the basis of responsibility.[58]

As a consequence, the genesis of the case law of the FCC concerning Article 14 GG is a history of the expansion of constitutional protection of property ownership. The concept of property in Article 14 GG is not restricted to real estate and movables but covers all vested property rights. Even the right to a commercial enterprise has been held by the Constitutional Court to fall under the concept of property. Subjective public rights are also included in the definition. However, such a right must exist in relation to a service, or relate exclusively to a claim which the State grants in furtherance of its obligation to provide for the welfare of its citizens.[59] Consequently, the constitutional guarantee of property comprises:

---

56. Gunnar Folke Schuppert, *The Right to Property*, in: The Constitution of the Federal Republic of Germany: Essays on the Basic Rights and Principles of the Basic Law with a Translation of the Basic Law (Ulrich Karpen ed. 1988), p. 108.
57. BVerfGE 58, 300 (*Nassauskiesung*).
58. BVerfGE 24, 367, 389 (*Hamburger Deichordnung*); BVerfGE 31, 229, 239 (*Urheberrecht*).
59. BVerfGE 53, 289.

- property in movables, immovables, and claims;
- intellectual property (copyrights, patents, trademarks);
- industrial and commercial property;
- the right to social security benefits based on contributions by the beneficiary.[60]

§2.07   AMENDMENTS TO THE BASIC LAW

The Basic Law may be amended only by a law expressly modifying or supplementing its text (Article 79 I cl. 1 GG). This ensures that there is always transparency as to which constitutional rules are in force and applicable. An amendment of the Basic Law must win the approval of two-thirds of the members of the *Bundestag* and two-thirds of the votes of the *Bundesrat*. Amendments fundamentally affecting the division of the Federal Republic into *Länder*, their participation in the legislative process, or the principles laid down in Articles 1 and 20 GG are prohibited.

§2.08   THE EU FROM THE PERSPECTIVE OF THE GERMAN
CONSTITUTIONAL COURT[61]

[A]   Maastricht and the Need for an Act of the *Pouvoir Constituant*

The transfer of sovereignty occasioned by the Treaty of Maastricht (1992) was the predominant topic in the public discussion during the early 1990s. In Germany, a growing number of scholars questioned whether the existing constitutional law permitted an accession to the Treaty. As a result, the Constitution was amended on December 21, 1992, to authorize the further transfer of competences from the Federal Republic to the European Union (then still: European Community). The newly created Article 23 GG enables the Federal Republic "with a view to establishing a united Europe" to participate in the development of the EU, which is committed to democracy, the rule of law, social and federal principles as well as to the principle of subsidiarity. It ensures protection of basic rights in EU law comparable in substance to the protection provided by the Basic Law.

This was the principal constitutional basis on which Germany acceded to the EU.[62]

---

60. Schuppert, *supra* note 56, p. 109.
61. Kay Hailbronner, *The European Union from the Perspective of the German Constitutional Court*, German Yearbook of International Law 37 (1995), p. 93.
62. Matthias Herdegen, *Die Belastbarkeit des Verfassungsgefüges auf dem Weg zur Europäischen Union*, EuGRZ 1992, 589; Fritz Ossenbühl, *Maastricht und das Grundgesetz –eine verfassungsrechtliche Wende?*, DVB1. 1993, 629; Rupert Scholz, *Grundgesetz und europäische Einigung*, NJW 1992, 2593.

Starting from the individual right of a German citizen to participate in elections, the FCC, in its Maastricht-decision, examined whether this right had in fact been rendered meaningless as there were no significant competences left to the *Bundestag*.[63]

An analysis of the Maastricht Treaty led the Constitutional Court to a characterization of the EU as a "confederation of allied States" for the purpose of realizing an ever closer union of the peoples of Europe, organized as States. It explicitly rejected the concept of a European federal State based on the people of one European nation as an integral part of the Maastricht Treaty, though the Court took pains to explain that it was not its task to decide on the possible future development of the Union.

[B]   The Principle of Limited Powers

The Constitutional Court proceeds from the undisputed principle that the Union Treaty and the EC Treaty (presently: TEU and TFEU) follow the principle of limited powers. Therefore, in the Court's view, a Treaty goal is not enough in and of itself to create an extension of duties and powers. This principle can hardly be criticized. It is rather the practice of this principle by the European institutions and in particular the ECJ that raises concern. It is the dynamic extension of the existing treaties by a broad interpretation of today's Article 352 TFEU and the concept of implied powers of the Communities allowing a maximum exploitation of EU powers or the doctrine of *effet utile* that troubles the Constitutional Court. Later in the judgment on the Lisbon Treaty (2009) these objections are surfaced.

[C]   Democracy in the EU and the Role of the German *Bundestag*

The democratic principle – not subject to change or amendment under the Basic Law – requires that the carrying out of State functions and the exercise of public authority is derived from the people and that the officials performing such activities are fundamentally answerable to the people. The German Constitutional Court acknowledged that in the EU a democratic legitimization cannot be organized in the same way as it is within a Member State. In contrast to the prevailing view that democratic legitimization – primarily based on democratically elected governments – must be strengthened through an extension of the European Parliament's rights, the Court emphasized the role of the national parliaments, although it did not exclude an extension of the powers of the European Parliament. If the EU – which is described as a union of the peoples of Europe – carries out its sovereign duties, and thereby exercises sovereign powers, it is in the first place the nationals of the Member States through their national parliaments who have to provide democratic legitimization. At the same time, the democratic principle does not prevent the transfer of sovereign powers to the EU. In the Court's view, however, this process is limited by the essence

---

63. BVerfGE 89, 155; v. Münch, *Staatsrecht I*, Rdnr. 967; Frowein, *Das Maastricht-Urteil und die Grenzen der Verfassungsgerichtsbarkeit*, ZaöRV 54 (1994), 1.

of the democratic principle requiring that functions and powers of substantial importance must remain for the German *Bundestag*. An excessive delegation of functions and powers to the Union would effectively weaken democracy at the national level so that the parliaments of the Member States could no longer legitimate the sovereign power exercised by the Union.

[D] The Lisbon Judgment of the Constitutional Court (2009)

Similar to the judicial handling of the Maastricht Treaty also the Treaty of Lisbon (2007/2009) raised intricate constitutional and European law related issues which ultimately had to be settled by the Constitutional Court.[64] The first holding of the court in its Lisbon judgment addressed the question if the FRG would exceed its authority derived from the Basic Law by transferring further powers upon the EU. In this context, the FCC established mainly two points: First, the domestic legislation accompanying the Lisbon treaty (so-called *Begleitgesetze*) was deemed to be too weak to ensure the democratic rights of the *Bundestag* and the Bundesrat. Therefore, new legislation was required. Under the new rules, both legislative chambers must approve in advance decisions of the federal government to consent to comprehensive and groundbreaking changes of the EU's legal framework and governance. *Inter alia*, this referred to every unanimous vote in the council, the abandoning of unanimity in favor of majority voting and substantial expansions of European authority by using, for example, the so-called bridging clauses of the Treaty on the European Union (TEU).[65] In order to ensure that substantial legislative power continues to be vested in the competent German institutions, the Constitutional Court carved out specific legislative areas which remain foreclosed to European legislation (e.g., citizenship law, police and military powers, budget law, and criminal law). As a result, the crucial issues of the Treaty with all its sweeping changes of the EU were in fact not struck down by the court.[66] Only the easy-to-correct domestic legislation was critically assessed and changes demanded. Whether the various democratic safeguards such as the foreclosed areas of legislation really will seriously constrain or tame the authority of the EU institutions and the behavior of the German government in the Council appears, however, quite doubtful. The multiple activities undertaken to ameliorate the consequences of the several

---

64. Rudolf Streinz, Christoph Ohler & Christoph Hermann, *Der Vertrag von Lissabon*, 118 ff., 2010 (3rd ed.); Thomas Oppermann, *Die Europäische Union von Lissabon*, DVBl. 2008, p. 473; Jörg Philipp Terhechte, *Der Vertrag von Lissabon*, EuR 2008, p. 143; Armin Hatje & Anne Kindt, *Der Vertrag von Lissabon*, NJW 2008, p. 1761; Ekkhard Pache & Franziska Rösch, *Der Vertrag von Lissabon*, NVwZ 2008, p. 473.

65. Frank Schorkopf, *Die Europäische Union im Lot*, EuZW 2009, p. 718; Thomas Oppermann, *Den Musterknaben ins Bremserhäuschen!*, EuZW 2009, p. 473; Christoph Schönberger, *Lisbon in Karlsruhe: Maastricht's Epigones At Sea*, GLJ 2009, p. 1201; Martin Nettesheim, *Ein Individualrecht auf Staatlichkeit?*, NJW 2009, p. 2867; Klaus Gärditz & Christian Hillgruber, *Volkssouveränität und Demokratie ernst genommen*, JZ 2009, p. 872; Claus-Dieter Classen, *Legitime Stärkung des Bundestags oder verfassungsrechtliches Prokrustesbett?*, JZ 2009, p. 881.

66. Donald P. Kommers & Russel A. Miller, *The Constitutional Jurisprudence of the Federal Republic of Germany*, 2012 (3rd ed.) pointing to this as "anticlimactic conclusion."

European crises after 2009 do not attest to a new culture of restraint on the European level.[67]

[E]   The EU under the Supervision of the Constitutional Court?

The subject criticized most heavily is the Constitutional Court's assumption of its prerogative to decide on the limits of the Union's powers and the concept of a "cooperative relationship with the European Court of Justice" in the protection of basic rights (*Grundrechte*). This has even increased after the Lisbon judgment stipulating areas foreclosed to EU legislation. One of the major objections of the petitioners against the Maastricht Treaty as against the Lisbon Treaty had been that the basic concept of an "ever closer union" does not clarify the extent to which Germany has assented to the transfer of sovereign powers. The Court has accepted the constitutional assumption that the extent of powers transferred to the Union must be predictable and certain, as it has pointed out before.[68] While this sounds reasonable in theory, already the subsequent decisions of the FCC on the ESM[69] and the policies of the European Central Bank[70] underscored the impression that the Court will refrain from interfering with the EU's regulating and governing power in the future. Even though the Constitutional Court might theoretically oppose the expansion of EU powers, until now it has always resisted to actually annul measures of the EU.

As far as the protection of basic rights is concerned, the Constitutional Court had in earlier days assumed that an effective protection of such rights is also secured by the ECJ, with respect to the exercise of the sovereign powers by the EU itself (Solange II).[71] Therefore, the guarantee of the essential content of these rights against the EU institutions fell in the competence of the ECJ instead of the domestic FCC. Some years later the Court changed its mind and overruled this broad holding with its judgment on the Maastricht Treaty stating that it deems itself competent to declare void unlawful European measures (so-called "*ausbrechende Rechtsakte*" or *ultra vires*-measures).[72] However, when the situation arose to actually exercise the control as announced the Court refrained from doing so.[73] The reason for this restraint obviously lies in the fact that it is much easier to threaten to exercise control than actually doing so and thereby produce a serious crisis in the EU. In fact, the threshold to ascertain that a basic rights situation has occurred justifying the Constitutional Court to step in is extremely high, some legal commentators have stated that it will be hardly ever reached.[74]

---

67. BVerfGE 123, 267 (Lissabon Treaty).
68. BVerfGE 58, 1, 37; 68, 1, 98.
69. BVerfGE 132, 195 (ESM).
70. BVerfGE 134, 366 (OMT).
71. BVerfGE 73, 339, 386–387 (Solange II).
72. BVerfGE 89, 155 (Maastricht).
73. BVerfGE 102, 147 (Bananenmarktordnung); 126, 286 (Honeywell).
74. Cf. Rudolf Streinz, in: *Grundgesetz-Kommentar*, 2018 (Michael Sachs ed., 19th), Art. 23 MN 43.

After all, the relationship between the FCC and the ECJ is described by the former, somewhat ambiguously, as a "cooperative relationship" in which the latter guarantees protection of basic rights in every individual case for the entire area of the EU. The German Constitutional Court can therefore be seen as having restricted itself to a general guarantee of those constitutional standards that cannot be protected otherwise. Constitutional confrontations between the two courts are, until now, avoided with utmost care.

SELECTED BIBLIOGRAPHY

[A]   Constitutional Law

Hans-Wolfgang Arndt & Thomas Fetzer, *Öffentliches Recht* (16th ed. 2013).
Peter Badura, *Staatsrecht* (5th ed. 2012).
Ernst Benda, Werner Maihofer & Hans-Jochen Vogel, *Handbuch des Verfassungsrechts der Bundesrepublik Deutschland* (2nd ed. 1994).
Albert Bleckmann, *Staatsrecht II – Die Grundrechte* (4th ed. 1997).
Christoph Degenhart, *Staatsrecht I* (32nd ed. 2016).
Konrad Hesse, *Grundzüge des Verfassungsrechts der Bundesrepublik Deutschland* (20th ed. 1999).
Peter M. Huber & Andreas Vosskuhle (eds.), v. Mangoldt/Klein/Starck, *Grundgesetz* (7th ed. 2018).
Josef Isensee & Paul Kirchhof, *Handbuch des Staatsrechts*, vols. I–X (3rd ed. 2003–2015).
Alfred Katz, *Staatsrecht* (18th ed. 2010).
Thorsten Kingreen & Ralf Poscher, *Staatsrecht II* (33rd ed. 2018).
Michael Kloepfer, *Verfassungsrecht I – Grundlagen, Staatsorganisation, Bezüge zum Völker- und Europarecht* (2011).
Michael Kloepfer, *Verfassungsrecht II – Grundrechte* (2010).
Hartmut Maurer, *Staatsrecht* (7th ed. 2017).
Michael Sachs, *Grundgesetz-Kommentar* (19th ed. 2018).
Michael Schweitzer, *Staatsrecht III* (8th ed. 2004).
Klaus Stern, *Das Staatsrecht der Bundesrepublik Deutschland*, vols. I–V (1980–2000).
Ingo von Münch & Ute Mager, *Staatsrecht*, vols. I–II (8th ed. 2016, 6th ed. 2002).

[B]   European Union Law

Hans-Wolfgang Arndt, *Europarecht* (7th ed. 2004).
Albert Bleckmann, *Europarecht* (6th ed. 1997).
Georg Jochum, *Europarecht* (3rd ed. 2016).
Waldemar Hummer, Bruno Simma, Christoph Vedder & Frank Emmert, *Euro- parecht in Fällen* (3rd ed. 1999).
Gert Nicolaysen, *Europarecht I* (2nd ed. 2002).

Thomas Oppermann & Claus Dieter Classen & Martin Nettesheim, *Europarecht* (10th ed. 2010).

Michael Schweitzer & Waldemar Hummer, *Europarecht* (4th ed. 1993).

Rudolf Streinz, *Europarecht* (10th ed. 2016).

Rudolf Streinz, *EUV/EGV-Kommentar* (2nd ed. 2012).

CHAPTER 3
Administrative Law

Johannes Saurer[*]

TABLE OF CONTENTS

---

[*]   I would like to thank Manuel Dueñas, Claudio Seis, Anja Widmann and the editors for their help with this chapter.

97

§3.01   INTRODUCTION

[A]   The Doctrinal Legacy of the 19th Century

Key concepts of German administrative law were first established during the German *Kaiserreich* of 1871 (until 1918), when Germany was still a constitutional monarchy (or monarchical *Rechtsstaat*), and not yet a democracy. Particularly important is the work of Otto Mayer (1846–1924), the author of the most influential comprehensive treatise in the history of German administrative law.[1] Inspired by the *acte administrative* in

---

1. Otto Mayer, *Deutsches Verwaltungsrecht*, Vols. 1 and 2 (1895 and 1896).

French administrative law, Mayer developed the concept of the "administrative act" (*Verwaltungsakt*) as the doctrinal core of administrative law.[2] Mayer intended on the one hand to provide the monarchical executive with a stable legal instrument to determine rights and duties of the individual legal subject. On the other hand, he wanted to provide the individual with legal certainty and reliability of state action. To that extent, Mayer conceived of the administrative act as the basic legal form and common denominator of a colorful variety of empirical administrative actions. Moreover, Mayer emphasized the principle of statutory authorization for administrative action (*Gesetzesvorbehalt*). The concept of Georg Jellinek (1851–1911) on subjective-public rights[3] granted to the individual by the state provided the foundations for a rights based approach to administrative law.[4] While the constitutional basis of administrative law has changed fundamentally under the democratic, internationally integrated constitutional order of the Basic Law (*Grundgesetz*, GG),[5] the above mentioned legal institutions are a doctrinal legacy of the 19th century that is still present in today's administrative law.[6]

[B] Constitutionalization: Administrative Law under the Basic Law

Under the Basic Law of May 23, 1949, fundamental rights and the constitutional principles of a democratic federal state became very important. Administrative Law underwent an enduring process of "constitutionalization." Administrative law was ever more understood as "concretized constitutional law," as Fritz Werner, then-President of the Federal Administrative Court, framed it.[7] Examples of the strong substantive influence of fundamental rights include the expansion of the protection of legitimate expectations from the law of social security to economic regulation (*Vertrauensschutz*),[8] the universalization of the concept of proportionality (*see infra* §3.02[C][4]), the introduction of fundamental rights into so-called specific administrative relations (*besondere Gewaltverhältnisse*) concerning citizens in prisons,[9] the military and schools,[10] and the doctrinal implications of the fundamental right to property for construction law (*see infra* §3.03[B]). Procedural aspects of constitutionalization include the notion of fundamental rights protection through procedural rights

---

2. Mayer, *supra* note 1, Vol. 1, pp. 94 et seq.
3. Georg Jellinek, *System der subjektiven öffentlichen Rechte* (1892).
4. Armin von Bogdandy & Peter M. Huber, *Evolution and Gestalt of the German State*, in: Max Planck Handbooks in European Public Law (von Bogdandy/Huber/Cassese eds. 2017), pp. 196, 217.
5. BGBl. 1949, 1; BGBl. 2017 I, 2347.
6. *See*, also for 19th century doctrines that have been given up, *infra* §3.01[B]; §3.02[C][1] and [D][4].
7. *See* Fritz Werner, *Verwaltungsrecht als konkretisiertes Verfassungsrecht*, DVBl. 1959, pp. 527 et seq.
8. BVerwGE 1, 159.
9. BVerfGE 33, 1.
10. The original doctrine exempted subjective rights entirely from "specific administrative relationships," *see*, again, Mayer, *supra* note 1, Vol. 1, p. 102.

("*Grundrechtsschutz durch Verfahren*")[11] and the expansion of judicial review of administrative action under the influence of the right to effective judicial review guaranteed in Article 19 IV GG.

[C]   Europeanization: Administrative Law and the Legal Order of the European Union

With the Treaty of Rome of 1957, the Single European Act of 1986, the Treaty of Maastricht of 1992 and the Treaty of Lisbon of 2007, European integration became ever closer. Simultaneously, the process of "Europeanization" of German administrative law became ever more intense.[12] The strong influence of EU law follows from the principle of "indirect administration" of EU law. The EU treaties assign only very limited administrative resources to EU bodies such as the Commission and EU agencies. Rather, the Member-States bear the prime responsibility for the implementation of EU law.[13] In general, Member-States are free to determine procedural rules and administrative organization (so-called procedural autonomy).[14] However, they must adhere to the EU principle of equivalence. That principle "requires the same remedies and procedural rules to be available to claims based on [EU] law as are extended to analogous claims of a purely domestic nature" and the EU principle of effectiveness that requires that "national remedies and procedural rules do not render claims based on EU law impossible in practice or excessively difficult to enforce."[15] Examples for Europeanization of German administrative law include the limitation of legitimate expectations under the influence of EU state aid law,[16] the expansion of state liability,[17] the integration of national administrative authorities into the networks of the "European administrative compound"[18] or the expansion of the concept of individual rights.[19]

---

11. BVerfGE 53, 30.
12. For the analysis of constitutionalization and Europeanization as "two phases of German public law after 1949" *see* Rainer Wahl, *Verfassungsstaat, Europäisierung, Internationalisierung* (2003), pp. 411 et seq.
13. According to Art. 197 Sec. 1 TFEU the "effective implementation of Union law by the Member States [is] essential for the proper functioning of the Union."
14. Thomas von Danwitz, *Europäisches Verwaltungsrecht* (2008), pp. 302 et seq.
15. *See* Opinion of AG Jääskinen, delivered on February 7, 2013, Case C-536/11, ECLI:EU:C:2013:67, at 3.
16. ECJ, Judgment of February 2, 1989, Case 94/87, ECR 1989, 175 (Alcan I); ECJ, Judgment of March 20, 1997, Case C-24/95, ECR 1997, I-1591 (Alcan II).
17. ECJ, Judgment of November 19, 1991, Joined Cases C-6/90 and C-9/90, ECR 1991 I-5357 (Francovich); ECJ, Judgment of September 30, 2003, Case C-224/01, ECR 2003 I-10239 (Köbler).
18. Eberhard Schmidt-Aßmann & Bettina Schöndorff-Haubold (eds.), *Der Europäische Verwaltungsverbund*, 2005.
19. ECJ, Judgment of July 25, 2008, Case C-237/07, ECR 2008, I-6221 (Janecek); ECJ, Judgment of May 30, 1991, Case C-361/88, ECR 1991, I-2567; ECJ, Judgment of May 30, 1991, Case C-59/89, ECR 1991, I-2607.

[D]   Administrative Tasks

The scope and nature of administrative tasks is constantly evolving. For most of the 19th century – the era of the monarchical *Rechtsstaat* (*see supra* §3.01[A]) – the dominant administrative task was to further the public good through specific interventions aimed at correcting negative developments in society (interventive administration, *Eingriffsverwaltung*). Beginning in the 19th and continuing over the 20th century to the present, the so-called service administration (*Leistungsverwaltung*) became ever more important. Administrative authorities were increasingly faced with a growing need for the improvement of public infrastructure concerning railroads, streets, airway transportation as well as energy generation and energy supply. The modern social security administration emerged. Since the 1970s the administrative tasks of protection of the environment, sustainable management of natural resources and preservation of living conditions for future generations have been added to the list of administrative tasks (*see infra* §3.03[D]). Since the 1990s, administrative tasks within the "regulatory state" emerged. The state adopted a new role in the fields of network infrastructures and services such as telecommunication, postal services and railroads. Frequently influenced by European law, the state allowed for substantial or formal privatization of the aforementioned sectors. However, the legal design of the new markets included the emergence of new administrative authorities vested with powers to regulate the market processes in the interest of certain goals of the public good (*see infra* §3.03[E]).

The multifaceted, constantly evolving nature of administrative tasks has prevented the adoption of a single, universally accepted definition of "administration." Many scholars prefer a negative definition, in which administration is the state function that is neither legislative, nor judicial, nor governmental.[20]

[E]   General Administrative Law and Special Areas of Administrative Law

The distinction between general and special parts of the law (*Allgemeine und Besondere Teile*) has a long-standing tradition across all areas of German law. Most notably, the German Civil Code (*Bürgerliches Gesetzbuch, BGB*) and the Federal Criminal Code (*Strafgesetzbuch, StGB*) are organized along this distinction, and law school courses are taught accordingly.

In administrative law, this distinction is less explicit. A codified equivalent to BGB and StGB with textual references to general and special parts is missing. However, since the days of Otto Mayer, administrative law scholarship aims to join ranks with the "sister disciplines" of private and criminal law when it comes to examining and

---

20. *See* Hartmut Maurer & Christian Waldhoff, *Allgemeines Verwaltungsrecht* (19th ed. 2017), pp. 1 et seq.

systematizing overarching legal principles.[21] Moreover, the Federal Code of Administrative Court Procedure (*Verwaltungsgerichtsordnung, VwGO*)[22] and the Federal Administrative Procedure Act (*Verwaltungsverfahrensgesetz, VwVfG*)[23] actually function to some extent as codified general parts because they provide rules guiding the application of special administrative law. Accordingly, this distinction of general administrative law and special areas of administrative law also plays an important role in the law schools' curricula.

§3.02   GENERAL ADMINISTRATIVE LAW

[A]   Sources of Administrative Law

Administrative lawmaking occurs at every level of the hierarchy of norms. On top of this hierarchy is the Basic Law (*Grundgesetz*), the federal constitution that enjoys supremacy over every provision of ordinary (administrative) law. In addition to the fundamental rights guarantees and constitutional principles (Articles 1 et seq. and 20 GG) the *Grundgesetz* contains general provisions on the allocation of administrative tasks and powers between the federal and the state level (Articles 83 et seq. GG), prescribes detailed provisions on the federal administration (Articles 86 et seq. GG) and constitutes the framework for executive rulemaking (Articles 80 and 82 GG).

At the intermediate level of the hierarchy of norms are parliamentary statutes on administrative law matters. Some take the form of (partial) codifications. For example, the Federal Code of Administrative Court Procedure (VwGO) establishes abstract rules on personal and substantive requirements to obtain justice in administrative matters. The (federal) Administrative Procedure Act (VwVfG) – just as the equivalent administrative procedure acts in the sixteen German states (*Länder*)[24] – is a procedural codification that sets out the general legal principles governing the two central forms of administrative action (the administrative act and the administrative contract) and provides the framework for administrative procedure.[25] Most federal and state statutes, however, only address issues arising in specific areas of administrative law (*see infra* §3.03). Below the level of statutes, there are legal forms of executive rulemaking (statutory regulations; administrative directives; ordinances), but also individualized administrative acts and administrative contracts (*see infra* §3.02[D]). Last, but not least, the federal constitution acknowledges the strong impact of EU law on German law (*see* Article 23 GG). As a consequence, EU law may prescribe new administrative law or set aside existing administrative law on all levels of the hierarchy of norms.

---

21. Mayer, *supra* note 1, Vol. 1 (3rd ed. 1924), p. 20; for a modern adaption *see* Eberhard Schmidt-Aßmann, *Das allgemeine Verwaltungsrecht als Ordnungsidee* (2nd ed. 2006), p. 2.
22. BGBl. 1960 I, 17; BGBl. 2017 I, 3546.
23. BGBl. 1976 I, 1253; BGBl. 2017 I, 2745.
24. *See*, e.g., Administrative Procedure Act for Baden-Württemberg (*Landes-Verwaltungsverfahrensgesetz, LVwVfG*), GBl. BW 1977, 227; GBl. BW 2015, 324.
25. For the purposes of this chapter, references to the VwVfG regularly cover both the federal VwVfG and the state versions.

Due to the vast body of statutes and executive rules, customary law plays only a minor role in modern German administrative law, for example in the law of state liability, where legislative ambitions failed over a significant period (*see infra* §3.02[F]).

[B]   Organization

In the Federal Republic of Germany, administrative tasks are allocated according to the principle of "executive federalism."[26] According to the default rule in Article 83 GG, the *Länder* are responsible for the implementation of federal legislation as long as the Basic Law itself does not provide or permit otherwise. In addition, each of the *Länder* implements its own state legislation.

[1]   Federal Administration

Administrative entities at the federal level are the exception to the rule (Article 83 GG). However, the Basic Law does allow for federal administration in a variety of sectors. In some cases, federal administration is even explicitly required.

Article 86 GG distinguishes between direct and indirect federal administration (*unmittelbare und mittelbare Bundesverwaltung*).[27] Direct federal administration includes all federal administrative authorities that are under the legal and political control of the federal government and are no genuine legal persons under public law (*juristische Personen des öffentlichen Rechts*). According to Article 87 I GG, direct federal administration governs the Foreign Service (*Auswärtiger Dienst*), the Federal Financial Administration (*Bundesfinanzverwaltung*), the Federal Border Police (*Bundesgrenzschutz*) and "central offices" for purposes of information and communication in the security, anticrime and antiterrorism sector (*Zentralstellen*). Additional areas of direct federal administration include the Federal Administration of the Military (*Bundeswehrverwaltung*, Article 87b GG) and federal administration of infrastructure concerning air traffic (Article 87d GG), railroads (Article 87e GG), waterways (Article 87f GG) and highways (Article 90 GG).

Article 87 III 1 GG vests the federal legislature with the power to create new federal administrative authorities with nationwide jurisdiction *(Selbständige Bundesoberbehörden)* in all areas of federal legislative competences. As an inherent limitation of federal administrative powers, those authorities have no subordinated sectoral authorities. Because the legislative authority spelled out in Article 87 III GG is frequently invoked, federal administration spreads widely beyond the instances explicitly provided for in Articles 87 et seq. GG. Examples include the Federal Office for Motor Vehicles (*Kraftfahrt-Bundesamt*),[28] the Federal Cartel Office (*Bundeskartellamt*),[29] the

---

26. von Bogdandy/Huber, *supra* note 4, p. 219.
27. For the terminology *see* Maurer/Waldhoff, *supra* note 20, pp. 604 et seq., pp. 628 et seq.
28. BGBl. 1951 III, No. 9230-1.
29. BGBl. 1957 I, 1081.

Federal Office for Protection against Radiation (*Bundesamt für Strahlenschutz*)[30] and the Federal Net Agency for the regulation of electricity, gas, telecommunication, postal services and railroads (*Bundesnetzagentur*).[31]

Indirect federal administration includes all federal administrative authorities that are genuine legal persons under public law (*juristische Personen des öffentlichen Rechts*). Articles 86 and 87 GG explicitly mention federal corporations and institutions (*Körperschaften und Anstalten des öffentlichen Rechts*) as examples of indirect administration. While corporations do have a formal membership and are organized along the principle of self-government, institutions lack those features. The most important practical examples of federal corporations are the federal social insurance institutions that organize and guarantee health insurance, pensions (*Rentenversicherung*) and unemployment insurance. The benefits of these federal social insurance institutions apply to most employees of German enterprises and many members of the public service sector in their membership. Examples include the German Federal Film Board (*Filmförderungsanstalt*)[32] in the administration of cultural affairs and the German Federal Institute for Risk Assessment (*Bundesinstitut für Risikobewertung*).[33] The Basic Law implicitly allows for the legislative establishment of additional forms of indirect administration, for example public foundations (*Stiftungen des öffentlichen Rechts*).[34]

Under certain conditions, the Basic Law also allows for the provision of public services through private law entities owned by the state. For example, the single most important railway company, Deutsche Bahn AG, operates as stock company under private law (*Aktiengesellschaft*) and yet remains entirely in federal public ownership.[35]

[2]   State Administration

The bureaucracies of the *Länder* are the most important actors in German administrative law. They carry out state legislation, but also the bulk of federal legislation (*see supra* §3.02[B] before [1]). The distinction of direct and indirect administration does also apply, but does play out differently. Within the *Länder* administration, the municipalities are the most important indirect administrators. State administration is mostly organized in hierarchical three-tier structures of bureaucracy with the respective state ministry at the top level, regional governments at the intermediate level and local administrations at the lowest level.[36] However, some *Länder* have opted for different organizational structures. The three city-states (*Stadtstaaten*) Berlin, Hamburg and Bremen, which are state and municipality at the same time, are organized as

---

30. BGBl. 1989 I, 1830.
31. BGBl. 2005 I, 1970.
32. BGBl. 2016 I, 3413.
33. BGBl. 2013 I, 1324.
34. *See*, e.g., the public foundation "*Stiftung Preußischer Kulturbesitz*" – the administrator of museums, libraries and archives that formerly belonged to Prussia, BGBl. 1957 I, 841.
35. In 2017, the Deutsche Bahn AG and its subsidies had around 195,000 employees, 187,000 of the working full-time, *see* www.deutschebahn.com/de/konzern/konzernprofil/zahlen_fakten/mitarbeiter.html (visited April 3, 2018).
36. *See*, e.g., for North Rhine-Westphalia www.land.nrw/de/land-und-leute/landesverwaltung-nordrhein-westfalens (visited April 3, 2018).

administrative unities rather than in tiered structures. Some of the territorial states have opted for two-tier structures of administrative organization without regional governments, but with an emphasis on sectoral administrative authorities with state-wide competences.[37]

As a rule, the *Länder* carry out federal legislation in their own right regarding organizational details, regulation of administrative procedure and the exercise of discretion. Accordingly, sectoral federal statutes are regularly supplemented by corresponding *Länder* statutes or regulations on organizational and procedural matters. For example, the state government of Baden-Württemberg has issued a regulation that specifies the organizational scheme of administrative authorities for the implementation of the Federal Immission Control Act (BImSchG).[38] Only in the exceptional cases of state administration "on behalf" of the federal government (*Bundesauftragsverwaltung*) can the federal government issue instructions addressed at the state bureaucracies (Article 85 III GG). One example of this type of administration, which requires an explicit authorization in the Basic Law is state administration of certain highways of federal significance (Article 90 III GG).

[3] Local Administration

From the point of view of citizens and enterprises, local administration through municipalities and counties is the most visible form of administration. Indeed, most *Länder* statutes on administrative organization assign the implementation of (federal and state) legislation routinely to local authorities in municipalities and counties. This shows that local administration is formally an element of state legislation. The degree of oversight of higher-ranking administrative authorities over municipalities varies across different areas of the law.

[C] Selected Principles of Administrative Law

[1] Principle of Legality

The principle of legality (*Gesetzmäßigkeit*) ensures that all actions of administrative authorities are grounded in statutory authorization. This principle consists of two key elements both of which are rooted in constitutional law. The first element is the supremacy of statutes over administrative actions (*Vorrang des Gesetzes*). This element is constituted in Article 20 III GG which states that the executive is bound by law and justice. It affirms the understanding of the present normative order as a "hierarchy of norms." Accordingly, administrative authorities have to adhere to the content of statutes. The second element is the requirement that any administrative action be statutorily authorized (*Gesetzesvorbehalt*). This requirement is an emanation of the

---

37. *See*, e.g., for Lower Saxony www.mi.niedersachsen.de/themen/verwaltungsmodernisierung_ organisation_landesverwaltung/aufbau_landesverwaltung/aufbau-der-landesverwaltung-6126 5.html (visited April 3, 2018).
38. GBl. BW 2010, 406.

principle of democracy (Article 20 I and II GG) and the principle of *Rechtsstaat* (Article 28 I GG). According to the Federal Constitutional Court's "doctrine of essential matters" (*Wesentlichkeitstheorie*), the requirement calls for the regulation of "essential" aspects in important areas of the law by way of parliamentary statutes.[39] In addition, the Basic Law requires statutory authorization as an indispensable prerequisite for the interference with fundamental rights (*see*, e.g., Article 2 I and II GG, Article 5 II GG and Article 12 I GG).

[2]   The Treatment of General Legal Terms

Administrative law statutes often contain broad terms to achieve the legislative intent. For example, the Federal Code of Public Economic Law (*Gewerbeordnung, GewO*)[40] requires the administrative authority to intervene against a particular business if the business owner proves to be "not reliable" and certain additional aspects are given (§ 35 I GewO). The Federal Building Code (*Baugesetzbuch, BauGB*)[41] calls for the enactment of a land-use plan as soon as and to the extent that such plan is "necessary" for the order of urban development (§ 1 III BauGB). Further examples of general legal terms that many administrative law statutes employ are "public interest" and "public good."

The use of such general legal terms raises the question of which standard of judicial review should apply in cases in which a particular administrative interpretation is challenged in court. As a rule, the fundamental right of effective judicial review (Article 19 IV GG) vests the courts with the power to review and, if necessary, to discard the administrative authority's interpretation of a general legal term.[42]

A limitation of this judicial review power only applies in exceptional cases such as examination decisions in school or professional education[43] or decisions by administrative boards composed of representatives of social interests.[44]

[3]   Exercise of Discretion

Many administrative law statutes grant discretion to administrative authorities in order to find flexible solutions for the factual situation at issue. For example, the *Länder* statutes on public construction law (*Landesbauordnungen, LBO*) grant discretion to the competent authority to decide upon the fate of a building which was built contrary to the law. If there is no other way to ensure compliance with the law, authorities can (but do not necessarily have to) order the demolition of the building in whole or in part.[45] Prior to reaching a decision, the competent authority will weigh the gravity of

---

39. BVerfGE 40, 237, 249 et seq.; 49, 89, 126; 95, 267, 307 et seq.
40. BGBl. 2017 I, 3562.
41. BGBl. 2017 I, 3634.
42. BVerfGE 84, 34, 49 f.; NVwZ 2011, 1062, 1064.
43. BVerfGE 84, 34, 49 et seq.; 84, 59; BVerwGE 75, 275; 8, 272.
44. BVerwGE 91, 211, 215 et seq.
45. *See* Section 65 Sent. 1 LBO BW, GBl. BW 2010, 357; GBl. BW 2017, 612.

the infringement at issue against the legal interests affected and will then decide on whether to demolish the building or refrain from doing so. The administrative procedure acts at the federal and state level require that the administrative authority exercise its discretion in line with the purpose underlying the grant of discretion and within the given legal limits (§ 40 VwVfG).

Discretionary acts of administrative bodies face less scrutiny in court than nondiscretionary acts. The Federal Code of Administrative Court Procedure (VwGO) states in accordance with the "doctrine of discretion-related wrongs" (*Ermessensfehlerlehre*)[46] that judicial review of discretion is limited to a short list of mistakes (§ 114 Sentence 1 VwGO). The administrative court[47] is limited to reviewing whether the authority has entirely ignored its discretion, has overstepped it, or exercised its discretion in contravention of the purpose underlying its discretionary powers.

[4] Principle of Proportionality

The principle of proportionality has a long history in German administrative law. Around 1900, it had already developed into a legal standard to limit police action, a then-broadly construed term that covered all administrative authorities with interventionist competences. In a famous metaphor, Professor Fritz Fleiner explained in 1911 that proportionality requires that the police "not shoot at sparrows with cannons."[48] In the early Federal Republic of Germany, proportionality remained an administrative law principle. Only by the late 1950s, the Federal Constitutional Court began to transform proportionality into a principle of fundamental rights adjudication[49] and, eventually, into a universal constitutional principle[50] that is recognized in many jurisdictions around the globe.[51] Today, the administrative courts apply proportionality as a four-step test to weigh ends and means of a particular administrative action. The first step focuses on the legitimacy of the pursued goal, the second step examines the suitability of the means applied. The third step enquires into the necessity of the action and considers alternative, but less invasive means of "equal effectiveness." The fourth and final step controls proportionality *strictu sensu* (balancing) and weighs all affected legal interests against one another.[52]

[D] Legal Categories of Administrative Action

Administrative action could be systematized into different legal categories. On the one hand, there are categories of administrative action of a general nature such as regulations, administrative directives and ordinances (*see infra* §3.02[D][1]–[3]). On

---

46. Maurer/Waldhoff, *supra* note 20, pp. 152 et seq.
47. For details on the special administrative court system in Germany, *see infra* §3.02[G].
48. Fritz Fleiner, *Institutionen des deutschen Verwaltungsrechts* (1911), p. 323.
49. BVerfGE 7, 377.
50. BVerfGE 16, 194, 201 et seq.; BVerfGE 55, 72, 88.
51. Johannes Saurer, *Die Globalisierung des Verhältnismäßigkeitsgrundsatzes*, Der Staat 51 (2012), pp. 3 et seq.
52. On the components of proportionality Aharon Barak, *Proportionality* (2012), p. 433 f.

the other hand, there are categories of administrative action in individual and concrete cases including administrative acts, but also administrative contracts and simple administrative action (*see infra* §3.02[D][4]–[6]).

[1]   Regulations

Based upon preexisting statutory enactments, regulations are norms issued by the Federal Government and other executive authorities. Like parliamentary statutes, regulations are binding norms vis-à-vis citizens, enterprises and the courts. For example, the Federal Code on Road Traffic (*Straßenverkehrsgesetz, StVG*)[53] authorizes the Federal Ministry of Transportation to issue a detailing statutory regulation (§ 6 I StVG). Accordingly, the Federal Ministry enacted the Federal Regulation on Road Traffic (*Straßenverkehrsordnung, StVO*)[54] which contains the bulk of concrete road traffic rules.

The legal framework for regulations is set out in the Basic Law (Article 80 GG).[55] On the one hand, Article 80 I GG acknowledges the practical need of the modern state to relieve the legislature from having to draft every rule necessary to govern the modern administrative state.[56] Thus, Article 80 I GG allows for the delegation of normative power to the executive in all areas covered by federal legislation. On the other hand, Article 80 I GG counters the risk that overly broad regulatory powers of the executive pose to parliamentary democracy and *Rechtsstaat*[57] by establishing strict conditions for delegation.[58] As a formal restraint, every delegation must be authorized by federal statute (Article 80 I 1 GG). As a substantive restraint, the delegating statute must address content, purpose and scope (*Inhalt, Zweck und Ausmaß*) of the normative powers conferred (Article 80 I 2 GG). The Federal Constitutional Court interpreted Article 80 I 2 GG relatively strictly in the first two decades under the Basic Law,[59] but subsequently began to soften its strict stance. Since the 1970s, statutory enactments for federal regulations have been held invalid in only a few cases.

[2]   Administrative Directives

Administrative directives (*allgemeine Verwaltungsvorschriften*) are intraadministrative rules. The head of an administrative authority may issue such rules with binding force within the administrative entity. Administrative directives serve a variety of functions. They aim at unifying administrative processes, reduce complexity, ensure equality in the implementation of statutes, interpret general legal terms or harmonize the exercise of discretion.

---

53. BGBl. 2003 I, 310; BGBl. 2017 I, 3202.
54. BGBl. 2013 I, 367; BGBl. 2017 I, 3549.
55. *See infra* §3.02[E][2].
56. On the historical course of expansion of administrative tasks *see infra* §3.01[D].
57. BVerfGE 1, 14, 59 et seq.
58. *See,* e.g., Susan Rose-Ackerman, *American Administrative Law Under Siege: Is Germany a Model?*, Harvard Law Review 107 (1994), pp. 1279, 1288, 1301.
59. BVerfGE 1, 14; 71, 75; 10, 251; 19, 370; 23, 208.

As an exception to the rule, the Federal Administrative Court classifies certain administrative directives (*normkonkretisierende Verwaltungsvorschriften*) as legally binding vis-à-vis citizens, enterprises and courts, because these directives meet a particular set of legal standards including a specific statutory authorization and public participation in the rulemaking process.[60]

[3]   Ordinances

Ordinances (*Satzungen*) contain the general rules applicable to corporations organized under public law (*öffentlich-rechtliche Körperschaften*). Through the organizational form of the public corporation, the legislature entrusts certain segments of society with autonomy to perform specific tasks in the public interest. Ordinances are legally binding only on the members of such public entities. These corporations enjoy the status of genuine legal persons under public law (*see supra* §3.02[B][1]). Consequently, these corporations follow the principle of democratic self-organization of their membership. Examples include the municipalities with the self-organization of the residents of a certain territory (*see infra* §3.03[C]), the universities with their bodies of self-organization and self-government, and the professional chambers (*Berufsständische Kammern*) in the area of independent professions (*Freie Berufe*). Professional chambers vested with self-organizational powers include the Chamber of Pharmacists (*Apothekerkammer*), the German Medical Association (*Bundesärztekammer*) or the Chamber of Lawyers (*Bundesrechtsanwaltskammer*). Within the corporations under public law, only the main administrative body that directly represents the incorporated members (*Hauptverwaltungsorgan*) has the authority to issue ordinances, e.g., the senate in universities and the municipal assembly in municipalities (*see infra* §3.03[C][4]).

[4]   Administrative Acts

As indicated above, the administrative act is the most significant example of the doctrinal legacy of 19th-century administrative law scholarship in modern administrative law (*see supra* §3.01[A]). The historical concept of Otto Mayer has been largely perpetuated in administrative law scholarship in the Weimar Republic and in the Federal Republic of Germany.[61] Eventually, this concept served as basis for the legal definition in Section 35 Sentence 1 of the Administrative Procedure Act of 1976 (VwVfG) which established the administrative act as an authoritative administrative measure under public law to decide individual cases with the intention to produce external legal effects vis-à-vis the citizen or enterprise. Section 35 Sentence 2 addresses a specific type of administrative act that is the "general order" (*Allgemeinverfügung*).

---

60. BVerwGE 72, 300, 320; BVerwGE 110, 216, 218.
61. Walter Jellinek, *Verwaltungsrecht* (2nd ed. 1929), pp. 237–238; Ernst Forsthoff, *Lehrbuch des Verwaltungsrechts I* (10th ed. 1970), pp. 205–206.

The VwVfG acknowledges the characteristic legal stability of the administrative act by distinguishing between unlawful and invalid administrative acts. Only administrative acts that meet the conditions of invalidity as set out in Section 44 VwVfG remain without effect (§ 43 III VwVfG). Invalidity is considered an exception to the principle that an act of state power is entitled to the presumption of validity.[62] Section 44 II VwVfG contains a limited number of explicit cases of invalidity, e.g., if a written or electronic administrative act does not display the issuing authority (No. 1) and if an administrative act requires an action that would be unlawful under criminal law (No. 5). The general clause of Section 44 I VwVfG provides that an administrative act is invalid in case of a particularly serious and obvious violation of the law. The Federal Administrative Court, however, has interpreted this clause very narrowly.[63]

In contrast, "merely" unlawful administrative acts remain legally effective and evolve into administrative finality (*Bestandskraft*) if they are not challenged within the one-month time limit for judicial review as set out in the Federal Code of Administrative Court Procedure (§ 70 VwGO, § 74 VwGO).

Under conditions provided by Sections 48 and 49 VwVfG, the administrative authority may annul the administrative act. The administrative decision to annul the administrative act is an administrative act itself. According to Section 48 I VwVfG, the administrative authority has discretion to withdraw an unlawful administrative act. The application of this norm must resolve the tension that arises between the principle of legality, which would favor withdrawal, and the principle of protection of legitimate interests, which may provide an argument against withdrawal. The provisions in Section 48 II to IV VwVfG intend to resolve this tension: Section 48 II to IV VwVfG provide a series of objections that an affected citizen may raise in such scenarios. For example, Section 48 II VwVfG concerns administrative acts granting payments of money: The withdrawal is prohibited, if the beneficiary has reasonably relied on the stability of the administrative act and if her reliance deserves protection in relation to the public interest to withdraw the act. Section 48 IV VwVfG sets an absolute time limit of one year for the administrative authority to decide upon the withdrawal.

Section 49 VwVfG concerns the revocation of an administrative act that was initially lawful. The administrative authority is also granted discretion, but (due to the initial lawfulness) the protection of legitimate interests of the affected citizens and enterprises is even stronger than under Section 48 VwVfG. The revocation of an administrative act that is beneficial to the individual is limited to the constellations enumerated in Section 49 II and III VwVfG. There is also an absolute time limit of one year to decide upon the revocation (§ 49 II 2 and III 2 VwVfG refer to § 48 IV VwVfG).

Section 49a I VwVfG contains an additional provision that enables the administration to combine the decision on the annulment with another decision to reclaim public money that a citizen or enterprise has unlawfully received. This provision is particularly important for the effective return of unlawfully paid state subsidies. Such repayments are often required as a consequence of violations of the strict rules of EU

---

62. BVerwG, NVwZ 2000, 1039, 1040.
63. BVerwG, NJW 1985, 2658; NVwZ 1992, 564, 565; NVwZ 2000, 1039, 1040.

law on state aid which permits Member-States to pay subsidies only under exceptional circumstances (Articles 107 et seq. TFEU).

Another important legal feature is the "enforcement function" of the administrative act. An administrative authority is entitled to issue its own writ of enforcement. The conditions for the enforcement of administrative legal acts are detailed in the Federal Statute on Administrative Enforcement (*Verwaltungsvollstreckungsgesetz, VwVG*)[64] and in corresponding *Länder* statutes.

[5] *Administrative Contracts*

In addition to the administrative act, the Administrative Procedure Act (VwVfG) also provides for administrative action on the basis of the so-called administrative contract (§§ 54 et seq. VwVfG).

The VwVfG allows for two kinds of administrative contracts: First, administrative contracts may be concluded between various administrative authorities (so-called *koordinationsrechtlicher Vertrag*). Second, administrative contracts may be concluded between the administration and private individuals (so-called *subordinationsrechtlicher Vertrag*). The latter type of administrative contract is evidence that the modern administrative state transcends the traditional hierarchical relationship between state and individual. Thus, the administrative contract is concluded between the state and the individual as coequal actors.

The legal framework of Sections 54 et seq. VwVfG provides for cooperative administrative action through administrative contracts and also addresses certain concerns vis-à-vis the contracting administration. The concerns addressed include, among others, the structural inequality of the contracting parties and the potential for selling out sovereign rights.[65] For these and other reasons, administrative contracts must meet rather strict formal and substantive requirements. According to Section 57 VwVfG administrative contracts generally must be concluded in writing. Section 59 II VwVG contains special grounds for the invalidity for administrative contracts between the state and the citizen, such as the so-called prohibition of coupling (*Kopplungsverbot*, § 59 II No. 4 VwVfG) according to which administrative contracts that are not materially related to the agreed service are null and void.[66] Section 59 I VwVfG contains a general clause on invalidity of administrative contracts that refers broadly to reasons for invalidity under the German Civil Code (§ 134 BGB), but is interpreted narrowly to cover only specific violations of the law.[67] The proximity to contracts under civil law is also visible in Section 62 VwVfG which provides for supplementary application of the Civil Code to administrative contracts.

Given the equal status of both parties to the contract, the contracting administrative authority is prohibited from sanctioning contract violations by way of an

---

64. BGBl. 2017 I, 2094.
65. For the historic disapproval of Otto Mayer of the administrative contract *see id., Zur Lehre vom öffentlichrechtlichen Vertrage*, AöR 3 (1888), pp. 3, 23–24, 41–42.
66. BVerwGE 111, 162.
67. *See* Higher Administrative Court of North Rhine Westphalia, NVwZ 1992, 988, 989.

administrative act. Rather, administration and individual must pursue their claims in (administrative) court proceedings.[68] Areas of administrative law in which the administrative contract is frequently used in practice include social security administration,[69] public construction law,[70] and environmental law.[71]

[6]   Simple Administrative Action

The category of the "simple administrative action" is not included in the VwVfG. Rather, it emerged in the jurisprudence of the administrative courts and in administrative law scholarship. The category encompasses activities of the bureaucracy that do not qualify as "administrative acts" because the formal criteria in Section 35 Sentence 1 VwVfG are not entirely met. Examples include warnings of administrative authorities to the general public concerning potentially contaminated food[72] or the health risks related of "e-cigarettes,"[73] the publication of violations of food law standards of a restaurant[74] and video surveillance by the police.[75] Notwithstanding the formal legal status, such activities can still have adverse effects. Thus, citizens and enterprises can seek judicial review of "simple administrative actions" in the administrative courts, particularly with the action for a declaratory judgment, Section 43 I VwGO (*Feststellungsklage*).

[E]   Administrative Procedure

[1]   Types of Administrative Procedure

The Administrative Procedure Act (*Verwaltungsverfahrensgesetz*, VwVfG) allows for different types of administrative procedure. The standard administrative procedure is set out in the second part of the VwVfG (§§ 9–34 VwVfG). It applies to the administrative act and the administrative contract (§ 9 VwVfG) and is not subject to formal requirements (§ 10 VwVfG).

Departing from the principle that standard administrative procedure need not observe formal requirements, Sections 63–71 VwVfG provide rules for the "formal administrative procedure," which are applicable in cases in which a statute other than the VwVfG requires them. However, there are but a few instances in which the formal rules apply, for example in cases under the Federal Mining Act (*Bundesberggesetz*, BBergG) and in certain areas of agricultural law.[76]

---

68. *Supra* note 68; BVerwG, Decision of May 10, 2005, 4 B 24/05, juris.
69. Wolfgang Spellbrink, *Sozialrecht durch Verträge?* NZS 2010, pp. 649 et seq.
70. *Supra* note 70.
71. *See* for a dispute on contractual land conservation BVerwG, NVwZ 2007, 1187.
72. BVerwGE 87, 37; BVerfGE 105, 252.
73. BVerwG, NVwZ-RR 2015, 425.
74. Higher Administrative Court of Baden-Württemberg, NVwZ 2013, 1022, 1023.
75. BVerwG, NVwZ 2012, 757, 758.
76. For these examples *see* Michael Sachs & Manuel Kamp, in: VwVfG-Commentary (Stelkens/Bonk/Sachs eds., 9th ed. 2018), § 63, at 39–44.

Another specific type of procedure is the "procedure concerning the single authority" according to Section 71a–71e VwVfG. It was introduced to the VwVfG in 2008[77] and serves the purpose of transposing the EU Services Directive,[78] e.g., in the area of the law of professional chambers.

Sections 72–78 VwVfG contain rules for plan approval procedures. These provisions apply as a supplement whenever a sectoral statute establishes a planning approval procedure. Plan approval procedures apply, for example, to the building and modernization of public infrastructure concerning highways of federal relevance under the Federal Highway Act (*Bundesfernstraßengesetz*), to railroads under the General Railroad Act (*Allgemeines Eisenbahngesetz*), to airports under the Federal Air Traffic Act (*Luftverkehrsgesetz*), and to gridlines for long-distance electricity transportation under the Federal Energy Industry Act (*Energiewirtschaftsgesetz*). Providing for both participation of the public and consultation with public authorities, the procedure leads to the rejection or confirmation of the original plan approval decision in the form of an administrative act.

The VwGO requires as a standard prerequisite for judicial (administrative court) review of an administrative act that the plaintiff first challenge the approval/disapproval embodied in that administrative act in internal administrative appellate procedures (§ 68 VwGO). This administrative appeal procedure generally consists of two steps: First, the administrative entity that originally issued the challenged decision leading to an administrative act reconsiders this decision. Second, if the decision is upheld, the administrative entity ranking above the authority that issued the original administrative act will reconsider the case and will render the final decision upon the appeal. If this decision turns out to be negative for the individual person (legal or natural), it may be challenged in the administrative court. However, the scope and significance of internal administrative appeals procedures varies considerably among the German states. Some *Länder* have limited such internal administrative procedures to a few fields of application while others have even largely abolished them. In such a case (without internal administrative review), a person affected by an administrative act can challenge it directly in the administrative court.

[2] Procedural Rights

The Administrative Procedure Act contains a number of procedural rights. For example, prior to issuing an administrative act affecting the rights of a person, that person has the right to be heard, which extends to factual and essential legal aspects of the case (§ 28 VwVfG).[79]

Furthermore, Section 29 VwVfG contains a very narrowly construed right to access the file. The right to access is limited to the immediate parties to the case and only applies to information that is necessary to pursue their immediate legal claims and

---

77. BGBl. 2008 I, 2418.
78. Directive 2006/123/EC.
79. Maurer/Waldhoff, *supra* note 20, pp. 544 et seq.

defenses. Access to information under Section 29 VwVfG is further limited by countervailing privacy and confidentiality rights which include business and trade secrets of other parties to the administrative proceedings (Section 30 VwVfG).

During the past twenty-five years, however, the scope of access to information has been dramatically widened beyond Section 29 VwVfG. This is due to the constantly increasing recognition of informational rights in German administrative law. At the federal level, the Freedom of Information Act (*Informationsfreiheitsgesetz, IFG*)[80] of 2006 established the right of every person to access any information stored by the federal government and federal administrative entities (§ 1 IFG). The IFG provides several exceptions, in particular in favor of conflicting privacy rights/confidentiality interests and for the protection of the public interest, such as national security. However, courts have construed the exceptions rather narrowly. Most of the *Länder* have enacted similar laws, e.g., the Freedom of Information Act Nordrhein-Westfalen.[81] There is now also a vast body of data protection law that emerged outside the VwVfG including the Federal Data Protection Act (*Bundesdatenschutzgesetz*)[82] and corresponding state statutes, such as the Data Protection Act Nordrhein-Westfalen (*Datenschutzgesetz NRW*).[83]

While the aforementioned right to be heard (§ 28 VwVfG) obligates the administration to communicate with affected citizens before an administrative act (§ 35 VwVfG) is issued, the right to a reasoned decision in Section 39 VwVfG requires communication after the issuance.

The legal consequences of infringements of procedural rights are one of the most controversially discussed areas of German administrative law. According to the view embodied in Sections 45 and 46 VwVfG procedural rights merely serve an auxiliary function which is to realize substantive legal rights and guarantees. Thus, procedural infringements should not be sanctioned in their own right, but only in conjunction with violations of substantive law. Section 45 VwVfG provides the administration with broadly construed opportunities to rectify procedural mistakes by subsequently fulfilling the procedural requirement it ignored beforehand. For example, violations of the right to be heard or the right to a reasoned decision can be cured even after the particular legal act is challenged in court in the first and even in the second instance (§ 45 II VwVfG). According to Section 46 VwVfG a violation of procedural rules is irrelevant if "it is obvious that the infringement did not have an impact on the merits of the decision." Further undermining procedural rights, Section 44a VwGO provides in principle that challenges in court against procedural acts of the administration can only be brought simultaneously with admissible challenges to the administrative decision on the merits. There are serious doubts whether this traditional pattern of sanctions for procedural mistakes is compatible with EU law which generally places great emphasis on procedural rights. Particularly in the field of environmental law, the European Court

---

80. BGBl. 2005 I, 2722; BGBl. 2013 I, 3154.
81. GV. NRW 2001, 806; GV. NRW 2014, 622.
82. BGBl. 2003 I, 66; BGBl. 2017 I, 3618.
83. GV. NRW 2000, 542; GV. NRW 2016, 1052.

of Justice has called for significant adjustments to German law regarding the consequences of violations of procedural rights.[84]

[3]   E-Government and Digitalization

Administrative procedural law must respond to fundamental changes in information
technology and digitalization in society and economy. From the perspective of the
administration, digitalization is a challenge that questions established patterns of
organizational procedures within the administration. However, digitalization yields
considerable efficiency gains and savings potential regarding administrative costs,
especially in the course procedures of mass administration processes (e.g., social
security, administration of taxes and fees, local administration). On the other hand,
digitalization entails special requirements concerning data protection.[85] All forms of
digitalized administration are covered by what is generally termed "E-Government." In
2013, a federal statute on E-Government (*E-Government-Gesetz*) was enacted which
induced digitalization-related changes in more than twenty-five different statutes and
regulations.[86]

Section 3a I VwVfG enables the administration to use electronic communication
as far as the recipients have "established access" to such communication channels. A
distinction applies between communication of the administration with businesses, in
which an implied declaration of consent through regular usage of the medium "email"
suffices, and communication with citizens, in which explicit consensus is required.[87]
Section 3a II VwVfG contains significantly stricter safety measures regarding the
replacement of the requirement of written form through electronic form. Section 35a
VwVfG addresses digitalization even beyond electronic communication as it stipulates
that administrative acts may be issued in full through automated facilities. However,
administrative acts that are subject to discretion must still be issued in the traditional
form.

[F]   State Liability

The law of state liability is perhaps the most fragmented and least clearly arranged area
of general administrative law. In an effort to codify state liability comprehensively the
federal legislature enacted in 1981 the Federal Act on State Liability.[88] However,
finding that the requisite legislative competence was lacking, the Federal Constitutional Court annulled the Act.[89] Even though this legislative power was subsequently

---

84. ECJ, Judgment of November 7, 2013, C-72/12, ECLI:EU:C:2013:712; ECJ, Judgment of October
    15, 2015, C-137/14.
85. BVerfGE 65, 1; 120, 274.
86. BGBl. 2013 I, 2749.
87. Berthold Kastner, in: VwVfG-Commentary (Fehling/Kastner/Störmer eds., 4th ed. 2016), § 3a,
    at 8 et seq.
88. BGBl. 1981 I, 553.
89. BVerfGE 61, 149.

added to the constitutional list of federal legislative competences in 1994 (Article 74 I No. 25 GG),[90] comprehensive legislation is still missing.

Thus, the central legal basis for individual claims for financial compensation of state wrongs is still the so-called *Amtshaftungsanspruch* according to Section 839 BGB which applies in conjunction with Article 34 GG. A successful claim to compensation requires, *inter alia*, that the breach of an official duty by a civil servant caused harm to the plaintiff. In addition, the claim is fault-based and requires negligence or intent on the part of the civil servant. The *Amtshaftungsanspruch* does not include liability for unlawful parliamentary statutes and flawed court judgments. The exclusion of liability for acts of legislatures and courts has caused clashes with EU law prompting the European Court of Justice to require far-reaching adjustments to the German state liability systems in cases in which the implementation of EU law is at stake.[91]

Emanating from rules of customary law, natural and legal persons also are entitled to compensation in cases in which the state, whether unlawfully or lawfully, takes private property (*enteignender/enteignungsgleicher Eingriff*, Article 14 GG). As with the *Amtshaftungsanspruch*, claims for compensation are adjudicated in civil law courts rather than administrative tribunals (*see also infra* §3.02[G]). Finally, there is a claim to restitution that is based by analogy on the unjust enrichment provisions of the German Civil Code (Sections 812 et seq. BGB) or derived from the requirement of *Rechtsstaat* and/or fundamental constitutional rights.

[G]   Judicial Review

The rules of judicial review of administrative action are codified in the Federal Code of Administrative Court Procedure (VwGO). The VwGO establishes an administrative court system that is entirely separated from the ordinary courts which decide private law and criminal law cases. The administrative court system consists of three levels with state courts on the first two levels and the Federal Administrative Court on the third level. At first instance there are the administrative courts that are part of the state (*Länder*) judiciary. According to the geographical size and the number of citizens, the number of courts varies between a single administrative court in Hamburg, Berlin or Saarland and seven administrative courts in the state of Bavaria. The second instance – the appellate level – consists of higher administrative courts that stand on top of the state administrative judiciary. With the exception of the common higher administrative court for Berlin and Brandenburg, each *Land* has one higher administrative court. The Federal Administrative Court is located in Leipzig. Regularly, it is the court of third instance and exercises review on questions of law only. However, in very rare cases, the Federal Administrative Court acts simultaneously as court of first and last instance. In such cases, the court addresses both facts and legal questions, e.g., in certain constellations of legal challenges against federal infrastructure projects.

---

90. BGBl. 1994 I, 3146.
91. ECJ, Judgment of November 19, 1991, Joined Cases C-6/90 and C-9/90, ECR 1991 I-5357 (Francovich); ECJ, Judgment of September 30, 2003, Case C-224/01, ECR 2003 I-10239 (Köbler).

According to Section 40 I VwGO, administrative law courts are competent to decide upon all controversies of public law that do not arise between institutions of constitutional law and are not assigned to another jurisdiction. Section 40 II VwGO provides an important example for such an assignment: The core legal claims in the area of state liability (*see supra* §3.02[F]) are referred to the ordinary courts. The VwGO provides for an enumerated set of actions that allow individuals to raise particular legal claims before the administrative courts. Varying among the German states, actions before administrative courts could be directed either against the administrative authority which has issued the controversial legal act or against the legal entity behind that administrative authority (*Rechtsträgerprinzip*, § 78 VwGO).

The correct choice from the enumerated set of actions depends largely on whether the administrative measure at stake qualifies as an administrative act. For example, Section 42 I Alt. 1 VwGO provides the action for annulment of an administrative act (*Anfechtungsklage*), Section 42 I Alt. 2 VwGO the action for the issuance of an administrative act (*Verpflichtungsklage*). The choice between the two will depend upon whether the administrative act at stake has negative or positive effects on the affected individual. Negative legal effects of administrative actions that do not qualify as administrative acts – simple administrative action (*see supra* §3.02[D][6])) – can be challenged with an action for a declaratory judgment, Section 43 I VwGO (*Feststellungsklage*). Claims for positive administrative actions that have not the legal quality of administrative acts can be pursued by a general action for performance (*allgemeine Leistungsklage*, *see* Section 43 II VwGO). The declaratory judgment action of Section 43 I VwGO also covers legal challenges against statutory regulations at the federal level. Statutory regulations of state authorities can be challenged on the basis of Section 47 VwGO. Moreover, there are legal instruments of interim relief, *see* Section 80 V VwGO, Section 123 VwGO and Section 47 VI VwGO.

The standing requirement of Section 42 II VwGO is a cornerstone of the entire German administrative justice system. As a precondition for substantive judicial review on the merits, Section 42 II VwGO requires the possibility of the violation or the mistaken interpretation of plaintiff's subjective-public right.[92] Section 42 II VwGO applies directly to both actions set out in Section 42 I VwGO (*Anfechtungsklage*, *Verpflichtungsklage*). However, the requirement is seen as a statutory expression of a constitutional decision for a system of individualized judicial review that is included in the fundamental right to effective judicial review in Article 19 IV GG.[93] Thus, Section 42 II VwGO applies directly or by analogy to the action for a declaratory judgment (§ 43 I VwGO) and the general action for performance (*allgemeine Leistungsklage*). Over the past two decades, significant exemptions to the requirement of Section 42 II VwGO evolved, particularly as regards collective standing rights of nongovernmental organizations in the area of environmental sector.

---

92. On the doctrinal origins *see supra* §3.01[A].
93. *Schmidt-Aßmann*, *supra* note 21, p. 213.

§3.03   SPECIAL AREAS OF ADMINISTRATIVE LAW

[A]   Law of the Police

In the German legal system, the function of the police force is twofold. For one, there is the repressive function in which the police investigate criminal activity and provide support for prosecution authorities. This function is largely regulated in the Criminal Procedure Act (*Strafprozessordnung*) and eventually addressed before the ordinary courts. Second, there is the preventive function, which aims at protecting the public of dangers to public safety and public order. It is this second, preventive function that is subject to the administrative law of the police and may lead to in administrative court proceedings.

The law of the police is the oldest layer of modern German administrative law. The terminological and doctrinal foundations can be traced back to the 19th century (*see supra* §3.01[A]; §3.02[C][4]). The mandate of administrative authorities to protect the public of imminent dangers to public safety and public order already existed in the early jurisprudence of the Prussian Superior Administrative Court in the 1880s.[94] During the Weimar Republic, Prussia (the largest of the German *Länder* at that time) codified the law of the police in the Prussian Code on Police Administration of 1931 (*Preußisches Polizeiverwaltungsgesetz*).[95] This statute already distinguished conceptually between a "general clause" and specific authorizations for preventive police action and became the model for the police codes of the *Länder* of the Federal Republic of Germany after World War II.

As a reaction to the centralization of police forces under the dictatorship of National Socialism (1933–1945), the Basic Law of 1949 opted for the decentralization of police forces. Almost all police competences were delegated to the *Länder* (Articles 30, 70 GG). All states share the organizational principle to distinguish between uniformed police forces operating at the street level and the police bureaucracy. As a rule, the default competence for preventative action is allocated to the police bureaucracy, but this competence shifts to the uniformed police forces in cases of imminent danger. However, there are also important organizational differences between the *Länder*. While some, such as Baden-Württemberg, have incorporated the distinction between the police bureaucracy and the uniformed police forces into a single police code and embrace a broad understanding of the term "police" (*Polizeigesetz BW*),[96] others have established two separate codes and different terminology. For example, the state of North Rhine–Westphalia has two different statutes for the law of the uniformed police forces (*Polizeigesetz NRW*)[97] and for the bureaucratic apparatus of the police (*Ordnungsbehördengesetz NRW*).[98]

---

94. Prussian Superior Administrative Court, Judgment of June 14, 1882 (Kreuzberg-case); reprinted *DVBl.* 1985, p. 219.
95. Preuß. GS (*Preußisches Gesetzblatt*) 1931, 77.
96. GBl. BW 1992, 1; GBl. BW 2017, 631.
97. GV. NRW. 2003, 441; GV. NRW. 2017, 806.
98. GV. NW. 1980, 528; GV. NRW. 2016, 1062.

However, over time, police powers at the federal level have become increasingly important. In the 1990s, a new entity, the Federal Police (*Bundespolizei*) vested with genuine police powers was founded to substitute the former Federal Border Protection Guard (*Bundesgrenzschutz*).[99] In addition, the competences of the Federal Criminal Police Office (*Bundeskriminalamt, BKA*) have been constantly extended, for example through the expansion of investigative powers in the Federal Statute on the Protection from Dangers of International Terrorism (*Gesetz zur Abwehr von Gefahren des internationalen Terrorismus durch das Bundeskriminalamt*).[100] This expansion was subsequently challenged in the Federal Constitutional Court, and plaintiffs were in part successful.[101] In addition, there are secret services, such as the Federal Office for the Protection of the Constitution (*Bundesverfassungsschutz*) and the Federal Intelligence Service (*Bundesnachrichtendienst*), which carry out certain police duties. Both services are empowered, *inter alia*, to retrieve information through telecommunication surveillance for the purpose of crime prevention.[102]

Following the Prussian Code on Police Administration of 1931 (*see* above), the police codes at the state level distinguish between a "general clause" and specific authorizations for preventative police action. Each general clause grants discretion to the police authorities to take the necessary actions to protect the public from dangers to public safety (*Öffentliche Sicherheit*) and the public order (*Öffentliche Ordnung*). In practice, police authorities and courts mostly invoke "public safety," a concept that has been shaped by many court decisions. Most importantly, public safety includes the "entirety of the legal order," which means that the breach of any legal norm of the constitution, of a statute, a regulation or an ordinance has the potential for triggering preventative action of the police. In addition, public safety covers individual basic rights, such as personal liberties and property rights. In contrast to "public safety," the authority to act in response to threats to the "public order" is of only little relevance. "Public order" has been defined as encompassing "the total of all the (mostly unwritten) rules whose observation is considered to be essential for a fruitful coexistence in terms of dominant social and ethical views."[103] Because "public order" refers to rules of morality, which tend to be difficult to define in today's pluralistic society, the concept is only rarely used as a basis for police action.[104]

In addition to a "general clause," each state police code includes a detailed list authorizing specific instances of police action for preventative purposes. This type of police action includes summoning a person to the police office for informational purposes, searching homes or offices, banning a person posing a danger to the public from a certain area, temporarily arresting such a person and seizing dangerous items. However, the list of specific authorizations is constantly evolving thus reflecting the

---

99. Federal Police Code, BGBl. 1994, I 2978; BGBl. 2017 I, 1066.
100. BGBl. 2008 I, 3083.
101. *see* BVerfGE 141, 220.
102. *see* Sections 8 ff. Code of the Federal Office for the Protection of the Constitution, BGBl. I 1990, 2954, 2970; BGBl. I 2017, 2097, 2128; Sections 3 ff. Code of the Federal Intelligence Service, BGBl. 1990 I, 2954, 2979; BGBl. 2017 I, 2097, 2129.
103. Gerhard Robbers, *An Introduction to German Law* (6th ed. 2017), p. 79.
104. Robbers, *supra* note 103, p. 79.

ever-changing sources of dangers to public safety. In particular, the advent of internet activities and digitalization prompted the adoption of additional authorizations of effective police action. These amendments to the *Länder* police statutes include the authorization of online searches, automated screening of license-plates, the surveillance of mobile communication and preventative data-storage. The Federal Constitutional Court has critically examined and revised many of the new data retrieving instruments on the ground that they violate privacy rights.[105]

Typically, the state police codes distinguish between three categories of danger attributed to a private individual. The individual can first be categorized as so-called *Handlungsstörer* (the person that caused the threat or the disturbance, e.g., § 6 I PolG BW); second, as *Zustandsstörer* (owner or possessor of an object whose condition threatens or disturbs the public safety or order, e.g., § 7 PolG BW) or, third, as *Nichtstörer im polizeilichen Notstand* (nondisturber in a state of emergency under specific requirements, e.g., § 9 PolG BW). If the police action is lawful, only the latter (nondisturber) is granted a compensation claim against the police to remedy financial losses or damages (*see*, e.g., § 55 PolG BW).

If the addressee of a police order disobeys it, the police may take coercive measures. Such measures include administrative penalties, detention, substitute performance and immediate coercion. The state police codes contain specific provisions which permit the use of firearms as a last-resort remedy.

[B]   *Public Construction Law*

Public construction law encompasses planning law concerning land use for construction purposes on the one hand (*Bauplanungsrecht*) and the building regulations on matters of building permissions, building-related aspects of public safety and administrative instruments to enforce the law on the other (*Bauordnungsrecht*).

The main legal source for planning law concerning land use for construction purposes – that is also referred to as "zoning law" – is the Federal Building Code (*Baugesetzbuch – BauGB*).[106] It provides for a decentralized concept of planning in which the municipalities are the key planning authorities. According to Section 1 II BauGB, there are two types of municipal land-use plans: The preparatory land-use plan (*Flächennutzungsplan*) and the legally binding land-use plan (*Bebauungsplan*). For both types of plans, Section 1 VI BauGB stipulates a broad range of planning goals that the planning municipality is supposed to weigh against one another. Relevant factors in this balancing process are, among others, the housing needs of the population, social and cultural needs of the population, environmental protection including the protection of natural resources and the promotion of renewable energies, economic interests, the need for infrastructure for traffic or utilities and demands of the military.

The preparatory land-use plan encompasses the entire municipal territory. It outlines the types of land-uses based on the goals of and needs for urban development

---

105. BVerfGE 120, 274 (online search); BVerfGE 120, 378 (automated car-plate screening).
106. *Supra* note 54.

(Section 5 I BauGB). The preparatory land-use plan is not classified as one of the conventional legal types of administrative action but rather considered a legal form sui generis. Accordingly, it generally has no binding effects vis-à-vis citizens.

The legally binding land-use plan is issued by the municipal assembly in the form of an ordinance (Section 10 I BauGB). The possible content of the plan is regulated in Section 9 BauGB and in the federal land-use regulation (*Baunutzungsverordnung*),[107] issued by the Federal Ministry of Building Construction. The regulation requires the planning authority to choose from a list of categories of land-use areas (e.g., purely residential areas, general residential areas, mixed use areas, commercial areas, industrial areas). For each area, the regulation provides a standardized set of regular and exceptional types of land use. The land-use plan can also set limits for the height of buildings, as well as the number of floors and can prescribe particular building features that improve energy efficiency and facilitate the use of solar energy.

If a qualified binding land-use plan[108] exists, the competent authority approves of the application for a construction permit if the conditions of the plan and further relevant requirements are met. In exceptional cases, the authority is entitled to allow for dispenses from the conditions of the plan (§ 31 BauGB). In areas without a qualified binding land-use plan, a distinction is made between the inner zone of a municipality (*Innenbereich, § 34 BauGB*) and the undeveloped outlying areas (*Außenbereich, § 35 BauGB*). In the inner zone, a particular important prerequisite for the approval of the application is whether the surrounding area is in fact equivalent to one of the standardized categories of land-use areas under the federal land-use regulation. If that is not the case, the building authority examines, whether the projected building fits into the framework of buildings that already exists in the neighborhood.

In contrast to the inner zone of a municipality, construction projects in outlying areas are generally prohibited, unless they are listed as permissible under Section 35 BauGB, do not conflict with the public interest, and proper development is ensured. Permissible projects under § 35 I BauGB relate to, *inter alia*, agriculture or forestry, the supply of electricity, gas, telecommunications services, and to the generation of renewable energies. Public interest reservations that would still bar the approval of these projects arise in cases of inconsistencies with a preparatory land-use plan (§ 35 III 1 No. 1 BauGB), harmful impacts on the environment (§ 35 III 1 No. 3 BauGB) or violations of the law of natural resources (§ 35 III 1 No. 1 BauGB) (*see infra* §3.02[D][1]).

An important part of construction law is regulated in statutes at the *Länder* level. The state building regulations include the law of building permits, requirements designed to prevent building-related dangers to public safety and authorizations for administrative oversight. The building regulations of the sixteen German states are harmonized to some degree on the basis of the so-called model building regulation – an informal arrangement between all state governments.

---

107. BGBl. 2017 I, 3786.
108. Such a plan must include certain minimum designations, e.g., on type and extent of the use for construction, *see* § 30 I BauGB.

Since the 1990s, state legislatures increasingly favor the deregulation of construction. Today, many state building regulations exempt particular projects from the requirement of a building permit in an attempt to expedite and facilitate construction projects, decrease bureaucratic costs and improve investments conditions. A typical example of such an exempted project would be a single-family home that was built without a permit and but fully complies with the legally binding land-use plan.

The construction of industrial buildings and private homes is increasingly affected by the law regulating energy efficiency. For example, the Federal Energy Saving Act (*Energieeinsparungsgesetz*)[109] and the Federal Energy Saving Regulation (*Energieeinsparverordnung*)[110] set detailed standards for building insulation and require, among other things, that every new building be equipped with solar-thermal panels generating energy for warm water and heating systems. On the European level, the EU directive on the energy performance of buildings requires that all EU Member-States "shall ensure that by 31 December 2020, all new buildings are nearly zero energy buildings."[111]

[C]   Local Administration Law

[1]   *Municipal Autonomy*

Under the German Constitution (Article 28 II 1 GG), municipalities enjoy administrative autonomy (*kommunale Selbstverwaltung*) to regulate all local matters in their own responsibility. The Federal Constitutional Court defined "local matters" as "those needs and interests that are rooted in the local community or that have a specific connection thereto."[112] Municipalities act as legal persons under public law and are part of "indirect" state administration as outlined above (*see supra* §3.02[B][1]). The guarantee of administrative autonomy extends to autonomy concerning the personnel of the municipality, the organization of the local administration, the planning authority over the local territory, financial autonomy and the authority to issue ordinances as general norms on municipal matters.

As the caveat "within the scope of the law" in Article 28 II 1 GG indicates, federal and state legislation may curtail the autonomy of local authorities. Limiting the scope of legislative interference with local autonomy, however, the Federal Constitutional Court has held that at least the core of local administrative powers must remain with the municipalities.[113] Article 28 II 2 GG extends the right to municipal autonomy to the counties (*Landkreise*).

---

109. BGBl. 2005 I, 2684; BGBl. 2013 I, 2197.
110. BGBl. 2007 I, 1519; BGBl. 2015 I, 178.
111. Directive 2010/31/EU, Art. 9 Sec. 1 lit (a).
112. BVerfGE 79, 127, 151.
113. *Ibid.*

[2]   *Constitution of Municipalities*

Article 28 I 1 GG determines the organizational structure of municipalities to the effect that there must be "municipal assemblies" at the local level in order to provide additional legitimacy to the performance of local administrative tasks. Accordingly, in all German states that are not city-states (Berlin, Hamburg, Bremen), the citizens elect representatives to municipal assemblies. These representatives act on an honorary basis. The number of representatives per assembly varies from a single-digit number in the smallest municipalities (less than 1,000 residents) to almost one hundred in big cities such as Cologne, Dortmund or Munich. The term of office varies between the *Länder* but amounts to five years on average. According to Article 28 I 3 GG, citizens of other EU countries have the right to vote and be elected to office in municipal and county-wide elections.

Details on the constitution of municipalities are set out separately for each of the *Länder* in the respective codes for the municipalities (*Gemeindeordnung*). Historically, the German *Länder* established very different models of "municipal constitutions." Since the 1980s, key features of municipal constitutions are converging. Most importantly, all *Länder* introduced the direct election of the mayor by the citizens. His or her term of office varies considerably ranging from five years in North Rhine Westphalia to ten years in the Saarland. Every state provides in one way or another for the direct participation of citizens in municipal decision-making. At the initiative of the municipal assembly or based on a minimum number of citizens (*Bürgerbegehren*), certain issues of municipal politics can be made the subject of a referendum (*Bürgerentscheid*). In practice, these referenda often concern costly municipal infrastructure projects such as a new local convention center, or organizational questions, such as a merger with another municipality. The state codes applying to municipalities regulate the allocation of functions and powers between the municipal assembly and the mayor. Typically, the assembly decides on issues of major importance, while the mayor remains in charge of deciding issues of day-to-day-administration.

The state codes for the municipalities grant a specific legal status to the residents of the municipalities which is independent of the status as German or EU citizen. Thus, citizens of Brazil, Turkey or the United States who are residents of a particular municipality are legally entitled to access to municipal institutions (*öffentliche Einrichtungen*) such as town halls, libraries or sports facilities.

[3]   *Municipal Ordinances*

In all states, the competence to issue ordinances (*Satzungen*) – which are general rules binding on all residents of the municipality (*see supra* §3.02[D][3]) – is reserved to the municipal assemblies. The assemblies may not delegate this competence to the mayor. Ordinances can regulate all aspects of the municipal action. For example, ordinances set out the rules for annual municipal budget plans as well as binding land-use plans (*see supra* §3.03[B]). They also stipulate obligations of the residents to use and to pay for goods and services provided by municipal infrastructure, such as utilities for water supply and sewage water disposal. (*Anschluss- und Benutzungszwang*). Despite the constitutional guarantee of municipal autonomy in Article 28 II GG, the content of ordinances depends heavily on the federal and state legislation. The Federal Constitutional Court has held that interferences of a municipal ordinance with fundamental rights are permissible only if they are authorized by a specific enabling statutory enactment.[114]

[4]   Oversight

As integral parts of the state administration, the municipalities are under oversight of superior administrative levels and, eventually, the state government. The degree of oversight depends on the type of administrative task to be carried out. If an administrative task falls into the sphere of optional or mandatory municipal self-government (*freiwillige oder pflichtige Selbstverwaltungsangelegenheiten*), oversight is limited to controlling whether the administrative action stayed within the applicable legal bounds. Not surprisingly, in cases of administrative tasks which the municipality performs under the direction of the state government (*Auftragsangelegenheiten*), the overseeing state authority not only controls compliance with the law, but also monitors the ways in which the municipality executes the task it assumed.[115]

[D]   Environmental Law

As a prerequisite for the emergence of modern environmental law, a federal legislative competence for legislation on "waste disposal, air pollution control and noise control" (*Abfallbeseitigung, Luftreinhaltung, Lärmbekämpfung*) was added to the Federal Constitution in 1972.[116] The new competence supplemented and strengthened the preexisting federal competences for legislation on nature conservation (*Naturschutz*) and water resources (*Wasserhaushalt*).[117] Accordingly, from the 1970s to the present, the key German environmental law statutes were enacted as federal law.

[1]   Key Statutes

The most important statute of modern environmental law – the Federal Emissions Control Act (*Bundes-Immissionsschutzgesetz, BImSchG*)[118] – was enacted in 1974. The BImSchG addresses air pollution through the regulation of harmful effects of private and commercial facilities on air quality. Regulations under the BImSchG cover a broad

---

114. BVerfGE 97, 332.
115. For terminology and further reading Maurer/Waldhoff, *supra* note 20.
116. Article 74 No. 24 GG, BGBl. 1972, I 593; today Art. 74 I No. 24 GG.
117. Article 75 No. 3, No. 4 GG, BGBl. 1949, 1; today Art. 74 I No. 29, No. 32 GG; in both areas there is the option of variant legislation at the state level, Art. 72 III 1 No. 2, No. 6 GG.
118. BGBl. 1974 I, 721; BGBl. 2017 I, 2771.

range of facilities and other things, including animal farms, wind energy facilities, gas or coal-fired power plants and even lawn mowers as well as wood stoves. Facilities with emissions exceeding certain quantitative thresholds require a specific emission permit (§ 4 BImSchG). The detailed standards for these thresholds are set out in the 4th statutory regulation under the BImSchG which is only one of more than thirty-five federal regulations and administrative directives issued under the BImSchG.

While the BImSchG is dedicated to the protection of the environmental medium "air," the protection of water and soil is at the center of the Federal Act on Water Resources (*Wasserhaushaltsgesetz*)[119] and the Federal Soil Protection Act (*Bundes-Bodenschutzgesetz*).[120] The Federal Nature Conservation Act (*Bundesnaturs-chutzgesetz*)[121] is the core statute for land conservation and the protection of endangered species. In addition, there are statutes which focus on particular substances, such as the Federal Waste Management Act (*Kreislaufwirtschaftsgesetz*)[122] and the Federal Chemicals Act (*Chemikaliengesetz*).[123] In the area of climate change regulation the federal government has issued the Climate Action Plan 2050 which sets forth the principles and goals of the government's climate policy.[124] Some *Länder* have already gone beyond the planning stage and have enacted comprehensive legislation, e.g., the Climate Protection Act North Rhine Westphalia (*Klimaschutzgesetz NRW*).[125]

[2] Europeanization

Across all fields of German environmental law, the influence of EU environmental law is very strong. For example, various EU directives on air quality[126] have required adjustments to domestic air pollutant regulation thereby emphasizing the importance of strict air pollution standards for the protection of individual rights.[127] The EU-wide trading scheme for CO2-emission certificates[128] applies to many facilities with permits under the BImSchG and partially preempts national standards (*see* § 5 II BImSchG). EU law pursues the paradigm of "integrated environmental protection" thus stressing the interdependence of various environmental media (water, air, soil)[129] and challenging the traditional single media-oriented approach of German environmental law.

---

119. BGBl. 2009 I, 2585; BGBl. 2017 I, 277.
120. BGBl. 1998 I, 502; BGBl. 2017 I, 34.
121. BGBl. 2009 I, 2542; BGBl. 2017 I, 3434.
122. BGBl. 2012 I, 212; BGBl. 2017 I, 2808.
123. BGBl. 2013 I, 3498, 3991; BGBl. 2017 I, 2774.
124. www.bmu.de/fileadmin/Daten_BMU/Pools/Broschueren/klimaschutzplan_2050_en_bf.pdf (visited April 5, 2018).
125. GV. NRW. 2013, 29.
126. Directive 80/779/EEC; Council Directive 82/884/EEC; Council Directive 96/62/EC.
127. ECJ, Judgment of May 30, 1991, Case C-361/88, ECR 1991, I-2567; ECJ, Judgment of May 30, 1991, Case C-59/89, ECR 1991, I-2607; ECJ, Judgment of July 25, 2008, Case C-237/07, ECR 2008, I-6221 (Janecek).
128. Directive 2003/87/EC.
129. Directive 96/61/EC.

[3]   Proceduralization

The ongoing proceduralization of German environmental law (*Prozeduralisierung*) is closely related to Europeanization. The European directive on environmental impact assessments (EIA directive) of 1985[130] injected the idea of "environmental protection through procedure" into German environmental law. In 1990, a federal law implemented the EIA directive (*Umweltverträglichkeitsprüfungs-Gesetz*).[131] That law incorporated environmental impact assessments into the preexisting administrative procedures for permits or plan approvals.

The 1990 European directive on environmental information[132] introduced the instrument of environmental informational rights to German law. The directive strengthened informational rights as tools of transparency and public control over the administration of environmental matters. The German legislature implemented the directive in 1994 by enacting the Federal Environmental Information Act (*Umweltinformationsgesetz* – UIG).[133] Because the German legislature repeatedly failed to fully implement the terms and spirit of the directive, the Act was successfully challenged in several cases before the European Court of Justice (*see supra* §3.02[D][3]). Over the years, however, the concept of environmental informational rights met with greater acceptance in Germany and, eventually, the UIG even served as a model for the dramatic expansion of informational rights in the Freedom of Information Act (IFG) (*see supra* §3.02[E][2]).

[4]   Access to Justice in Matters of Environmental Law

A standard problem of environmental law is the representation of environmental interests in the courts. Frequently, infringements of environmental legal goods (air, water, soil, landscapes, plants) cannot be addressed by the judiciary, because there is no single plaintiff, like an owner of property or a tenant, who suffers individual damage and would thus have standing to sue in the courts.[134] In German environmental law, the problem is exacerbated by the strict standing requirement of Section 42 II VwGO (*see supra* §3.02[G]). As an exception to Section 42 II VwGO[135] the Federal Administrative Court has acknowledged the role of environmental NGOs as "attorneys of nature" (*"Anwälte der Natur"*)[136] in nature conservation law disputes. A significant set of standing rights for environmental NGOs is provided in § 64 BNatSchG (*see supra* §3.03[D][1]).

---

130. Directive 85/337/EEC.
131. BGBl. 1990 I, 205; BGBl. 2010 I, 94; BGBl. 2017 I, 3370.
132. Directive 90/313/EEC.
133. BGBl. 1994 I, 1490; BGBl. 2017 I, 2808.
134. *See* the classic Christopher D. Stone, *Should Trees Have Standing? – Towards Legal Rights for Natural* Objects, Southern California Law Review 45 (1972), pp. 450 et seq.
135. The text of § 42 II VwGO acknowledges the possibility of a statutory exception.
136. BVerwG, NVwZ 1998, 279, 280.

In 2006, the Federal Code on Access to Justice in Environmental Matters (*Umwelt-Rechtsbehelfsgesetz, UmwRG*) was enacted[137] to implement EU legislation related to the Aarhus Convention of 1998,[138] a treaty under international environmental law.[139] This legislation strengthened the judicial role of environmental NGOs. The limited standing of NGOs to sue was extended to actions against certain permits under the Federal Emissions Control Act (*BImSchG*) and to actions against a range of infrastructure projects that require an environmental impact assessment (§ 1 and § 2 UmwRG). However, the specifics of the German implementation legislation gave cause for legal disputes over the extent to which some elements of the traditionally restrictive approach to standing (*see supra* §3.02[G]) could be preserved. The ECJ decided in two landmark decisions[140] against the tradition-bound approach of the German legislature and required several amendments to the UmwRG.[141]

[E]   Regulatory Law

Over the past twenty-five years, regulatory law has emerged as an entirely new field of administrative law. Under the influence of EU law, important service sectors have been substantively or formally privatized since the 1990s. Substantive privatization occurred, for example, in the postal services and telecommunication sectors. As pointed out above (*see supra* §3.02[B][1]), the railroad sector was only formally privatized, leading to the formation of the Deutsche Bahn AG, a stock company which is wholly state-owned.

However, even in cases of substantive privatization, the state did not entirely withdraw from these sectors. Rather, the state changed its role from direct provider to that of a guarantor of public infrastructure (*see supra* §3.01[D]). Consequently, for many sectors of the economy, regulatory legislation has was enacted which obligates private economic actors not only to adhere the rules of the market, but also to comply with certain service standards in the interest of the public good. For example, the universal services concept of Sections 78 et seq. of the Federal Telecommunications Code requires that (mobile) telecommunication services be provided at affordable price even to sparsely populated areas.[142] According to Section 2 No. 5 of the statutory regulation of the federal government on universal services in the postal sector (*Post-Universaldienstleistungsverordnung*),[143] postal services must be provided to households every work day.

Regulatory law now also features an interesting institutional dimension. Established by federal statute in 2005[144] and employing some 2,500 staff members, the

---

137. BGBl. 2006 I, 2816.
138. Directive 2003/4/EC; Directive 2003/35/EC.
139. *See* www.unece.org/env/pp/introduction.html (visited April 5, 2018).
140. ECJ, Judgment of November 7, 2013, Case C-72/12, ECLI:EU:C:2013:712; ECJ, Judgment of October 15, 2015, Case C-137/14, ECLI:EU:C:2015:683.
141. BGBl. 2015 I, 2009; BGBl. 2017 I, 1298.
142. BGBl. 2004 I, 1190; BGBl. 2017 I, 3618.
143. BGBl. 1999 I, 2418; BGBl. 2005 I, 1970.
144. *See supra* note 32.

Federal Net Agency (*Bundesnetzagentur*) has nationwide jurisdiction to regulate the fields of electricity, gas, telecommunication, postal services and railroads.

The organizational structure and the competences of this central administrative authority, as well as the ministerial oversight and judicial review of its decisions differ sharply in many respects from traditional institutions of German administrative law. The Federal Net Agency has administrative boards, i.e., collective decision-making bodies, whereas traditional bureaucracy is embedded in a strict hierarchical order of individual office holders. In several legal settings, particularly in the telecommunication sector, both ministerial oversight and judicial review of the agency's decisions on the merits are significantly reduced. Despite legal challenges on the grounds of a potential violation of the fundamental right to effective judicial review (Article 19 IV GG), the Federal Administrative Court has confirmed the extended "regulatory discretion" of the agency.[145]

SELECTED BIBLIOGRAPHY

[A]   General Administrative Law

[1]   Compendia

Peter Friedrich Bultmann, Klaus Joachim Grigoleit Christoph Gusy et al., *Allgemeines Verwaltungsrecht – Festschrift für Ulrich Battis*, 2014.
Wolfgang Hoffmann-Riem, Eberhard Schmidt-Aßmann & Andreas Voßkuhle (ed.), *Grundlagen des Verwaltungsrechts I* (2nd ed. 2012).
Wolfgang Hoffmann-Riem, Eberhard Schmidt-Aßmann & Andreas Voßkuhle (ed.), *Grundlagen des Verwaltungsrechts II* (2nd ed. 2012).
Wolfgang Hoffmann-Riem, Eberhard Schmidt-Aßmann & Andreas Voßkuhle (ed.), *Grundlagen des Verwaltungsrechts III* (2009).

[2]   Textbooks & Treatises

Hans Peter Bull & Veith Mehde, *Allgemeines Verwaltungsrecht mit Verwaltungslehre* (9th ed. 2015).
Dirk Ehlers & Hermann Pünder (ed.), *Allgemeines Verwaltungsrecht* (15th ed. 2016).
Wilfried Erbguth, *Allgemeines Verwaltungsrecht* (8th ed. 2016).
Friedhelm Hufen & Thorsten Siegel, *Fehler im Verwaltungsverfahren* (6th ed. 2018).
Hartmut Maurer & Christian Waldhoff, *Allgemeines Verwaltungsrecht* (19th ed. 2017).
Fritz Ossenbühl & Matthias Cornils, *Staatshaftungsrecht* (6th ed. 2013).
Gerhard Robbers, *An Introduction to German Law* (6th ed. 2017), pp. 67–110.
Wolf-Rüdiger Schenke, *Verwaltungsprozessrecht* (15th ed. 2017).
Thomas von Danwitz, *Europäisches Verwaltungsrecht*, 2008.

---

145. BVerwGE 130, 39; 131, 41, 48; *see also* BVerfG, NVwZ 2012, 694.

[3]   *Commentaries*

Michael Fehling, Berthold Kastner & Rainer Störmer, *Verwaltungsverfahrensgesetz* (4th ed. 2016).

Ferdinand O. Kopp & Ulrich Ramsauer, *Verwaltungsverfahrensgesetz* (18th ed. 2017).

Paul Stelkens, Heinz-Joachim Bonk & Michael Sachs, *Verwaltungsverfahrensgesetz* (8th ed. 2018).

Ferdinand O. Kopp & Wolf-Rüdiger Schenke, *Verwaltungsgerichtsordnung* (23rd ed. 2017).

Helge Sodan & Jan Ziekow, *Verwaltungsgerichtsordnung* (4th ed. 2014).

[B]   Special Areas of Administrative Law

[1]   *Compendia*

Dirk Ehlers, Michael Fehling & Hermann Pünder, *Besonderes Verwaltungsrecht* (ed.), 3 vols. (2nd ed. 2012/2013).

Friedrich Schoch (ed.), *Besonderes Verwaltungsrecht* (15th ed. 2013).

Wilfried Erbguth, Thomas Mann & Mathias Schubert, *Besonderes Verwaltungsrecht* (12th ed. 2015).

[2]   *Treatises*

[a]   *Police and Regulatory Law*

Bill Drews, Gerhard Wacke, Klaus Vogel & Wolfgang Martens, *Gefahrenabwehr* (9th ed. 1986).

Volkmar Götz & Max-Emanuel Geis, *Allgemeines Polizei- und Ordnungsrecht* (16th ed. 2017).

Christoph Gusy, *Polizeirecht* (10th ed. 2017).

Wolf-Rüdiger Schenke, *Polizei- und Ordnungsrecht* (10th ed. 2018).

Hans Lisken, Erhard Denninger & Frederik Rachor (ed.), *Handbuch des Polizeirechts* (5th ed. 2012).

[b]   *Public Construction Law*

Klaus Finkelnburg, Karsten-Michael Ortloff & Martin Kment, *Öffentliches Baurecht*, vol. I: *Bauplanungsrecht* (7th ed. 2017).

Klaus Finkelnburg, Karsten-Michael Ortloff & Christian-W. Otto, *Öffentliches Baurecht*, vol. II: *Bauordnungsrecht, Nachbarschutz, Rechtsschutz* (7th ed. 2018).

Frank Stollmann & Guy Beaucamp, Öffentliches Baurecht (11th ed. 2017).

Michael Brenner, *Öffentliches Baurecht* (4th ed. 2014).

Stefan Muckel & Markus Ogorek, *Öffentliches Baurecht* (2nd ed. 2014).

[c]   *Local Administration Law*

Martin Burgi, *Kommunalrecht* (5th ed. 2015).
Klaus Lange, *Kommunalrecht* (2013).

[d]   *Environmental Law*

Wilfried Erbguth & Sabine Schlacke, *Umweltrecht* (6th ed. 2016).
Michael Kloepfer, *Umweltrecht* (4th ed. 2016).
Reiner Schmidt, Wolfgang Kahl & Klaus Ferdinand Gärditz (ed.), *Einführung in das Umweltrecht* (10th ed. 2017).

[e]   *Regulatory Law*

Michael Fehling & Matthias Ruffert (ed.), *Regulierungsrecht*, 2010.
Josef Ruthig & Stefan Storr, *Öffentliches Wirtschaftsrecht* (4th ed. 2015), pp. 258–327.

CHAPTER 4

Commercial Law

Johannes Köndgen & Georg Borges

TABLE OF CONTENTS

§4.01   GENERAL FOUNDATIONS

[A]   Definition and Scope of Commercial Law

[1]   The Traditional Approach: Commercial Law as Mercantile Law

Germany as well as France, Spain, the Netherlands, and many other countries have a legal system that has developed commercial law as a body of law distinct from general private (civil) law. Such legal systems invariably face the question: What is commercial about commercial law? The question seems anything but rhetorical since we know of mature legal systems that have never developed a separate branch of commercial law and yet have seen commerce prosper.

Students of comparative law take it for granted that the world's commercial law systems may be classified globally under one of two different paradigms. We find systems – commonly labelled "subjective" – which center on the people who practice commerce (commerce being the generic term for economic activity related to the production and the distribution of goods). Under this "subjective paradigm," the core of commercial law is the *law of merchants*. Its substance is *status law* stipulating the criteria for becoming a merchant and defining the rights and duties attached to his position. By contrast, the "objective" paradigm is *transaction-based*. From this perspective, some legal transactions are deemed commercial per se, no matter who carries them out. Commercial law, then, is for the major part a special branch of the law of contracts.

From its early origins, German commercial law has embraced a subjective approach. By all accounts, this choice has not been the result of a deliberate policy decision. At best, it may be explained on historical grounds. The subjective approach in Germany dates back to the first commercial law codification by a major German State – in Chapter 8 of the Prussian General Land Law (*Allgemeines Landrecht* – ALR), in 1794. It is fair to say that this piece of legislation has had a formative influence on the commercial law tradition in Germany and particularly on the codifications that followed (*infra* §4.02[A]). The definition of merchant adopted by the ALR epitomized the traditional meaning of the term – buying and reselling goods for money; it included manufacturers, yet omitted artisans and peasants. No doubt, this subjective approach was a perfect match for the social structure prevailing at the time. By the end of the 18th century, Prussia was a society still stratified by "estates"; its law was, in Maine's terms, status law. In the absence of an industrial working class, there were basically only two classes: the land-owning aristocracy on one side, the mass of artisans and dependent peasants on the other. However, by the time work on the ALR started, the politics of mercantilism originating in 17th-century France had trickled into Prussia, boosting the rise of a new class of merchants as part of the upcoming "third estate." Given such a change in the socioeconomic environment, the law of commerce seemed bound to develop as the status law of merchants.

Surprisingly, however, the subjective approach has survived the complete overthrow of the old social order in the wake of the industrial revolution. Later codifications have only incrementally enlarged the key concept of the merchant (for details, *see infra* §4.04[A]). What makes up the German Commercial Code (*Handelsgesetzbuch* – HGB) of 1897 is still mercantile law, with a minor part devoted to commercial transactions.

[2] *From Mercantile Law to Enterprise Transactions Law*

In contemporary commercial law theory there has been widespread dissatisfaction with the subjective approach in general and with the legal definition of merchant, as originally adopted by the HGB, in particular. Consequently, most of recent commercial law scholarship has focused on overcoming inconsistencies and extending the concept to "quasimercantile" activities not previously encompassed.

In response to this critique, the German legislator has, to some degree, adopted a proposition put forward by Professor Karsten Schmidt that advocates a systematic application of commercial law rules to all commercial enterprises. In a complete overhaul of the traditional notion of "merchant," the new approach makes the concept of "enterprise" a key element of the definition of a merchant. The Reform of Commercial Law Act (*Handelsrechtsreformgesetz 1998*) thus broadened the definition of a merchant so that it now includes all enterprises, with partial exceptions for agricultural and small businesses; *infra* §4.04[A][2]). Still, professionals such as lawyers, accountants, business consultants, or dentists remain, in general, outside the scope of commercial law (*infra* §4.04[A][2][a]).

Apart from this holdover of the traditional view of commercial law as mercantile law, an important shortfall of the new approach is the fact that it equates commercial law with "enterprise transaction law." Consequently, it would have to include enterprise-to-enterprise transactions as well as enterprise-to-consumer transactions. But this would be neither a correct statement of what the law is, nor would it be sound policy. First, some of the Code law on commercial transactions applies only where both parties act in their roles as merchants (so-called bilateral commercial transactions, *see infra*, §4.04[C]). Even as parties to a "unilateral commercial transaction" the Code treats consumers no differently than a merchant party. In other words (and in sharp contrast to the U.S. Uniform Commercial Code), consumer law is beyond the ambit of the German Commercial Code. Second, it is almost generally accepted today that business transactions are governed by different policies from those applicable to consumer transactions. As the late Professor Ludwig Raiser has observed, in our time the great divide is between enterprise-to-enterprise transactions and consumer transactions. The first group is governed by what may be termed either commercial, or enterprise or business law; the second is the domain of consumer law. Of rather marginal importance remains, by contrast, the "civil" law of contracts with both parties acting as "ordinary citizens."

[B]   The Duality of Commercial Law and Civil Law

Traditional commercial law doctrine has it that commercial law, rather than being distinct from general civil law, is a special province of the latter, the idea being one of two concentric circles. This conception is evidenced in the legislative technique chosen by the drafters of the HGB. Many of its provisions are supplementary, i.e., they presuppose the existence of civil law rules that the HGB then either specifies, modifies or displaces. For instance, the HGB provisions relating to commercial agency presuppose the general law of agency, and the law of commercial sales presupposes the civil law of sales. The law of commercial transactions in general cannot be fully understood without the German Civil Code's (*Bürgerliches Gesetzbuch* – BGB) provisions relating to legal capacity, contractual consent, mistake, misrepresentation, etc. Moreover, the same kind of transaction, e.g., a sales contract, may involve quite different layers of the law: In addition to the general rules of the BGB, the transaction will be governed by commercial law if one party to the transaction is a merchant, by consumer law if one party is a consumer, leaving as a group without additional rules transactions between "ordinary citizens" including enterprises that are not merchants, i.e., members of the learned professions (*see infra* §4.04[A][2][a]). For these reasons, the modern German law of commercial transactions presents itself as a hodge-podge with elements of civil law, commercial law, business law specific to certain transactions, and consumer law.

In any case, it is the concept of the merchant (or of the enterprise, for that matter) that marks the threshold separating commercial from civil law. By definition, nonmerchants (nonenterprises) cannot be directly subject to commercial law rules, but may be affected by them if they are a party to a contract with a merchant (*unilateral commercial transactions*). Thus, ordinary citizens may expect compliance with the "mercantile" standard of care (§ 347 HGB) when dealing with a merchant; by the same token they may benefit from the higher statutory interest rate imposed on a merchant's outstanding debt (§ 352 II HGB).

[C] The Sources of Commercial Law

[1] Statutory Law

Like other legal systems that recognize the existence of commercial law as a separate body, Germany has formalized this "distinctiveness" through a special statute, the Commercial Code (*Handelsgesetzbuch* – HGB) of 1897. As will be seen (*infra* §4.02[A] and [B]), the HGB is, notwithstanding its designation as a "code," anything but an all-inclusive codification of commercial law. Unlike the French *Code de Commerce* or the *Uniform Commercial Code* in the United States, it does not even cover all of the core areas. Among other fields, banking transactions and insurance are not part of the HGB, but are addressed by other statutes.

No matter whether such omissions are due to historical coincidence or the result of conscious policy-making, the effect has been the disintegration of the statutory basis of commercial law into a variety of statutes enacted at different times. These are often poorly coordinated. For convenience, only the most important areas are listed below; some others will be addressed in the chapter on "commercial transactions" (§4.04[C]).

[a] Insurance

Insurance law has long evolved into a separate discipline. Insurance contracts are the subject of the Insurance Contracts Act (*Versicherungsvertragsgesetz* – VVG) of 1908, which was fundamentally reformed and reenacted in 2007.

The supervision of insurance companies is regulated in the Supervision of Insurance Companies Act (*Versicherungsaufsichtsgesetz* – VAG) of 1901 which has been significantly overhauled in recent years in order to implement various EU directives. In this way, the Solvency-II Directive, as amended by the Omnibus-II Directive, was implemented in 2016 through significant amendments to the VAG. On the European level, the European Insurance and Occupational Pensions Authority has been supervising insurance companies since 2010. The supervision of insurance companies follows a three-pillar model (capital requirements, verification, and publication).

[b]   Banking Law

The same model also governs banking law, which is regulated outside the HGB. The EU legislature has paid significant attention to banking law in recent years (*see also* §4.04[C][2][a]). In order to implement the EU Payment Services Directive, the law of payment transactions was introduced by §§ 675 (c) et seq. BGB in 2009. These provisions were last amended in 2017 (effective as of January 13, 2018) to implement the Second Payment Services Directive. The 1998 Banking Act (*Kreditwesengesetz* – KWG) contains supervisory requirements relating to banking transactions and, since 2009, the KWG has been supplemented by the Payment Services Supervision Act (*Zahlungsdiensteaufsichtsgesetz* – ZAG) which was itself reenacted in 2017.

[c]   Competition Law

Competition Law has also evolved into a separate discipline. The Unfair Competition Act (*Gesetz über den unlauteren Wettbewerb* – UWG) of 2004, which was significantly amended, at first in 2008, with the implementation of the UCP-Directive 2005/29/EG and then, a second time, in 2015. Along with the 1957 Antitrust Act (*Gesetz gegen Wettbewerbsbeschränkungen* – GWB), which was the subject of significant reforms in 2006, 2007, 2009, 2012, 2013, 2015, 2016, and 2017, it is part of a novel subdiscipline of commercial law, i.e., "competition law."

[d]   Negotiable Instruments

The law relating to negotiable instruments is, strictly speaking, not commercial law at all, because checks and bills of exchange may also be written by nonmerchants (only the drawee of a check is, by necessity, a bank). Even so, for all practical purposes, checks and bills of exchange have been part of the banking business, which has been a prime subject of commercial law for a long time. Joining most other industrial countries, in the early 1930s Germany implemented, with some minor idiosyncratic variations, the uniform law for checks and bills of exchange proposed by the Geneva Conventions of 1930/1931 (Checks Act or *Scheckgesetz* of 1933; Bills of Exchange Act (*Wechselgesetz*) of 1933). Today, the practical importance of checks and bills of exchange has been greatly diminished by the numerous cashless payment methods now available (*see infra*, §4.05[B]). The introduction of a Europe-wide Payment Area (SEPA) has also contributed significantly to this development.

[2]   *Usage of Trade*

By tradition, a fundamental concern of commercial law has been to ensure the unhampered development and performance of mercantile transactions. Regulation primarily serves the goal of transaction cost reduction. Thus, with regulation at a minimum, commercial law is intentionally fragmentary. For cost reasons, it would not be practical to fill this regulatory vacuum with the contracting parties' individual stipulations in all instances. Consequently, there is a need for an intermediate layer of law to bridge the gap between the rules of commercial law and the parties' individual agreements. In the commercial law as it has developed throughout the centuries (*see,* as the most notable example, § 1-205(2) of the *Uniform Commercial Code* in the United States), this function has been performed by the usage that the merchants themselves have adopted. This phenomenon is not peculiar only to commercial transactions. "Civil" contract-making is also often based on the mores, customs, and other shared practices of a local or regional community or trade. The differences between general private and commercial law are a matter of degree. Usage of trade primarily affects the formation of contracts and the construction of contractual agreements and declarations. If transactions in a particular trade are almost invariably executed using a set of standardized terms, those terms may become the basis of the agreement by virtue of usage of trade (e.g., *Incoterms; Uniform Customs and Practices for Documentary Credits* (UCP) promulgated by the International Chamber of Commerce, Paris).

In court, evidence of the usage of trade in question may be established through expert testimony that is mostly provided by the local chamber of commerce, and occasionally by trade or professional associations.

[3]   Lex Mercatoria

In Germany, like in many other countries, the existence and the legal quality of the so-called *lex mercatoria* is controversial. Many authors advocate the idea of a *lex mercatoria* as an independent body of law, distinct from any source of national law. The prevailing view, however, seems to be that the *lex mercatoria* cannot be regarded as a legal system independent of national law. Thus, German courts are reluctant to recognize a transnational *lex mercatoria* as a separate source of law. Even if the parties have agreed to submit their dispute to the *lex mercatoria*, German courts will apply the rules of the national law that applies according to conflict-of-laws rules and contemplate the application of *lex mercatoria* only to the extent provided for by (domestic) conflict rules. This is also true of the *UNIDROIT Principles of International Commercial Contracts* and other "restatements" of contract law such as the *Principles of European Contract Law*.

The position is completely different in arbitration. Arbitration tribunals may decide the case applying *lex mercatoria* instead of national law if – and only if – empowered to do so by the parties.

[4]   *Standard Form Contracts*

To students of legal theory, calling standard form contracts or other general business conditions a "source of law" would be anathema. In their view, standard form contracts, even those widely used, do not make law; they result simply from their author's freedom of contract. Here again, commercial law takes a different perspective. With modern communication technology proliferating, business between merchants is more and more conducted in writing (nowadays increasingly in electronic form).

The use of general business terms promotes the standardization of the ways of doing business. Accordingly, it is fair to say that standard terms and standard form contracts have, to a certain extent, displaced usage of trade in its function as a pioneer of commercial law making. Indeed, most modern business transactions – finance leasing, franchising, or factoring, to name but a few – would not exist were it not in the form of standardized contracts. German commercial law, while not formally accepting standard form contracts as a source of law, accepts widely used standardized terms as legal bases of commercial transactions. German courts have frequently held that widely accepted standard terms were implicitly incorporated into contracts between merchants. If, despite this fact, contract law is reluctant unconditionally to accept law making by economically powerful private parties, it is for quite different reasons. The law suspects such parties, especially in their dealing with consumers, of imposing their standardized terms by means of superior bargaining power. For commercial transactions, namely between large-scale enterprises, this is not really a valid concern, at least not in the same way as for consumer transactions. While here, too, situations of disparate bargaining power may arise, merchants negotiating a contract are usually well informed and tend to be on a more equal footing. Therefore, German law provides for less stringent standards of judicial review of general contract terms and conditions between business entities (*Unternehmer* pursuant to § 14 BGB) than in cases involving consumers (§ 310 I 1 BGB). For example, in purely commercial transactions, there is no "blacklist" of clauses generally considered unfair and thus held void per se.

§4.02   THE GERMAN COMMERCIAL CODE

[A]   Historical Background

In its early origins in the 16th and 17th centuries, commercial law in Germany existed in the form of a variety of municipal laws of kingdoms, counties, towns, and other local or regional entities. In the 19th century, German commercial law became a major force in the legal and political unification process as well as a pacesetter for the growth of general civil law, in particular, of the law of contracts. As early as 1834, the constitution of the German Customs Union (*Zollverein*) foreshadowed the later political union of the German states, which at the time were loosely confederated under the *Deutscher Bund* of 1815. In 1848, the law of negotiable instruments took the lead when a uniform Regulation on Bills of Exchange (*Allgemeine Deutsche Wechselordnung*) was passed by the National Assembly (*Nationalversammlung*) in Frankfurt to replace no less than fifty-six different state laws through state by state enactment. In addition, a comprehensive codification of the commercial law was envisaged. In 1861, the *Bundestag* (the parliament of the German Confederation) passed the General German Commercial Code (*Allgemeines deutsches Handelsgesetzbuch* – ADHGB); the Code also came into force by way of state by state enactment. A few years later (1869), the ADHGB, along with the Regulation on Bills of Exchange, was adopted and promulgated as a federal law by the North German Confederation (*Norddeutscher Bund*), the immediate constitutional predecessor to the German Empire (*Deutsches Reich*). In 1871, the ADHGB became the law for the *Reich* by way of constitutional fiat and was to survive for almost thirty years.

Due to the fact that the two confederations that preceded the German Empire, as well as the Empire itself, originally lacked legislative power in general civil law matters, the ADHGB did not merely deal with what is commonly understood as commercial law; instead, it had to create the legal infrastructure for a meaningful ordering of commercial transactions more generally. Accordingly, the ADHGB contained detailed provisions with regard to general civil law matters, e.g., the formation of contracts or the principles of agency. The ADHGB's concept of "commerciality" adopted the "subjective" standard from the Prussian General Land Law (*supra* §4.01[A][1]), but also incorporated some "objective" elements from the French *Code de Commerce* by adding some "absolute commercial transactions" that could also be entered into by nonmerchants. Furthermore, the ADHGB codified large parts of German company law, including the law of stock corporations (*Aktiengesellschaften*).

Although legal historians consider the ADHGB a fine piece of legislation, its days were numbered when parliament started reordering most of commercial company law in separate statutes, such as the Limited Liability Companies Act (*Gesetz betreffend die Gesellschaften mit beschränkter Haftung* – GmbHG) of 1892. In addition, in 1873, the federal parliament was granted comprehensive legislative jurisdiction in civil law matters by constitutional amendment. This initiated the work on a federal Civil Code. In 1896–1897, these legislative activities culminated in the promulgation of the German Civil Code – the BGB – and a new and *leaner* (i.e., stripped of civil law matters) Commercial Code – the HGB. Both Codes went into effect on January 1, 1900.

[B]   Design and Basic Contents

With the HGB, German commercial law returned to an orthodox "subjective" concept. Yet, the Code extended the key concept of the merchant – which by tradition had been attached to the trading of goods and some transactions ancillary to buying and selling – to include the carrying on of any business activity in a commercial manner. This revision later served as the doctrinal basis for reconstructing the "mercantile" commercial law as "enterprise law" (*supra* §4.01[A][2]).

The HGB is composed of five "books." The first book, under the subtitle "commercial activities," defines the concept of the merchant (§§ 1–6), outlines the law of the commercial register (§§ 8–16), regulates the use of trade names (§§ 17–24), and contains provisions about the merchant's auxiliaries, both employed and self-employed. The second book deals with business associations with special emphasis on commercial partnerships (*see infra* Chapter 5).

The third book is of recent origin. Since 1985, it constitutes the "fundamental law" for commercial book-keeping and accounting.

The fourth book is devoted to commercial transactions. Its choice of transaction types seems selective at best and arbitrary at worst. Its provisions are often fragmentary. While there is adequate coverage of the carriage and storage of goods (warehousing) and of commercial agency, the HGB is silent on banking, secured transactions, and commercial leases. Oddly, the provisions on commercial sales consist of just ten sections. The concluding fifth book of the HGB deals with maritime law, covering such subjects as the carriage of goods by sea, the law of shipping companies, and maritime insurance.

[C]   Evaluation

The HGB, which is more than 100 years old, has enjoyed remarkable longevity. Moreover, it has undergone little revision during its existence. The most fundamental reforms were the regulation of stock companies in a separate statute (i.e., *Aktiengesetz* of 1937, as amended by *Aktiengesetz* of 1965), the implementation of the EU law on book-keeping and accounting in 1985 and the Commercial Law Reform Act of 1998 (*supra* §4.01[A][2]).

One might think that the HGB, a latecomer among European commercial law codifications, breathes the modern spirit of the industrial age and is a piece of superbly drafted legislation. Neither would be true. Rather than epitomizing the spirit of the industrial age and of modern entrepreneurship, the HGB reflects the stuffy milieu of middle class tradesmen in a preindustrial society. With regard to the technical qualities of the HGB, there is almost general agreement that it lacks the excellence of the carefully drafted BGB. As has been pointed out before (*supra* §4.01[A][2]), the HGB fell short of providing an appropriate definition of the concept of merchant. Above all, the rather arbitrary choice of the transactions that are covered by it and the total neglect of important commercial transactions such as banking are unsatisfactory.

Ironically, the long survival of the HGB is primarily attributable to its continuous loss of practical importance. For quite some time, issues that might be expected to fall under the commercial code have evolved outside the HGB under the heading of enterprise law (*Unternehmensrecht*), consumer law (*Verbraucherrecht*), or capital market law (*Kapitalmarktrecht*). Since the Commercial Law Reform Act of 1998 made no attempt to integrate modern forms of business into the HGB, the coverage of the HGB continues to become less and less relevant.

The German HGB has had little influence on other jurisdictions' commercial legislation. In Austria, the German Nazi government put the HGB into force after the country's annexation in 1938, and it seems the Austrians did not care to rid themselves of this legacy after having regained their autonomy. In Turkey, a German-Jewish émigré carrying a copy of the HGB in his luggage helped to reform the Turkish

Commercial Code in the 1930s and 1940s, but the HGB did not have a lasting influence in that country. Outside Europe, the HGB served as a model for the Japanese Commercial Code. The Korean Commercial Code, which is based on the Japanese model, still shows many similarities with the HGB, despite the growing influence of American law.

§4.03 FUNDAMENTAL PRINCIPLES AND POLICIES OF COMMERCIAL LAW

The fundamental principles and policies that govern commercial law seem to be part of the common core of the legal systems of the Western world. Hence, we can be brief on this point, highlighting but a few typical rules illustrative of such principles and policies.

[A] Accountability

A merchant is a professional player in the market, pursuing his competitive advantage. He is, perhaps, better suited than others to judge what is commercially viable and what is not. Therefore, the policy of commercial law is to let him take his risks, but also to have him bear the consequences of his errors or bad judgment. Numerous rules designed to protect nonmerchants, especially consumers, from their inexperience, their ignorance, or indeed their irrationality, do not apply to merchants. Merchants may, e.g., provide a surety by virtue of an oral agreement (§ 350 HGB) while nonmerchants can do so only in writing (§ 766 BGB). Generally, merchants are bound by the more stringent standards of care of a "reasonable merchant" (§ 347 HGB). As a buyer of defective goods, they forfeit their remedies for breach of warranty if they fail to inspect the goods on delivery and to notify the seller of any nonconformity within a reasonable time (§ 377 HGB). If they make contracts on the basis of the other party's standard form, they may seek a remedy against unconscionable terms in court, yet the threshold for finding the term unconscionable is higher than it would be for nonmerchants (§ 310 BGB). Similarly, under the case law, excessive (but not usurious) interest rates may render a consumer loan null and void, whereas a merchant borrower's remedy is restricted to truly exceptional cases.

[B] Transactional Simplicity and Expediency

To maximize utility, merchants are bound to minimize the costs of their business transactions. This goal is best served if commercial transactions are executed smoothly and quickly. Therefore, commercial law seeks to keep cumbersome and time-consuming formalities to a minimum. For example, the scope of rules requiring transactions in writing (*Schriftform*) is reduced (§ 350 HGB). A merchant dealing in services is deemed to have accepted an offer if he remains silent (§ 362 HGB). An important institution of commercial law that promotes speed and simplicity of trans-actions is the commercial confirmation letter (*kaufmännisches Bestätigungsschreiben*).

If the merchant receives a commercial confirmation letter from his counterparty stating the outcome of their bargaining, he will be bound to the contract as stated in that document even where it departs from what has in fact been agreed upon, unless he remonstrates instantly. Generally, the time allowed for communicating a notice, protest, etc. to the other party is kept shorter under the HGB than under the general provisions of civil law. To simplify the making of contracts by a general agent, the HGB positively defines a commercial general agent's scope of authority (*Prokura*) vis-à-vis third parties, regardless of the internal arrangements between principal and agent (§ 50 I HGB).

[C]   Commercial Good Faith, Reliance on External Manifestations

In commercial relationships, the companion principles of good faith and justifiable reliance on external manifestations of intent are paramount. Facilitating the smooth and expeditious conduct of business transactions, they support the operation of the policy discussed above. Under German law, "good faith" governs commercial as well as ordinary civil law transactions (§ 242 BGB). Yet, there is a distinctly commercial application of the principle. Thus, the parties to a long-term commercial contract may be obligated to renegotiate if their relationship has gone awry. Furthermore, the HGB affords greater protection to a good faith purchaser of movables when the seller is a merchant (§ 366 HGB as compared to § 932 BGB).

Also distinctly commercial is the principle that a merchant's external manifestations of intent – especially those in written form – may be generally relied upon. There is an irrebuttable presumption of justifiable reliance if a merchant's declaration is entered into a public record, in particular the commercial register (*see infra* §4.04[B]), unless the parties relying upon it positively know that the record is false. Similarly, negotiable instruments serve to protect the holder in due course against defenses not apparent from the document. Another example is the reliance on a trade name publicly used by a merchant. Case law treats any person or partnership holding itself out under a trade name as a merchant, even if the firm was not entered into the commercial register. In a similar vein, the purchaser of a firm who continues to use the firm's trade name is held liable for the debts the firm had incurred at the time the business was transferred (§ 25 HGB).

§4.04   SELECTED TOPICS OF COMMERCIAL LAW

[A]   The Concept of the Merchant

[1]   *Historical Origins: The Merchant as a Professional Buyer and Seller of Goods*

Under a subjective system of commercial law, the concept of the merchant is obviously of primary importance. It is fair to say that this concept has been a centerpiece of all commercial law reform. Since the late 18th century, it has been as much the subject of recurrent legislative amendment as it has preoccupied the students of commercial law. To be sure, the vicissitudes of the concept of the merchant were not just an offspring of ivory tower conceptualism. Its ideological underpinnings are as obvious as its social and economic implications. As has been said earlier (*supra* §4.01[A][1]), the definition of the merchant as a professional buyer and seller of goods dates back to the Prussian General Land Law (*Allgemeines Landrecht* – ALR), enacted in 1794 when the idea of mercantilism had gained some influence in Prussia. It established merchants as a new social class of people owning substantial amounts of capital and at the same time enjoying a good deal of freedom in ordering their business affairs. Both these characteristic attributes marked a sharp status division between merchants and artisans who, by their social organization in guilds, were far from free entrepreneurs. Agriculture, on the other hand, was held firmly in the hands of the aristocracy that took great pains to separate itself from the "third estate."

[2]   The New Definition by the HGB (1998) and Some of Its Oddities

The HGB establishes three distinctive criteria by which a businessman may be found to be a merchant. The lodestar is that of a person carrying on a commercial activity (*infra* [a] and [b]). Business companies qualify as merchants by virtue of their legal form alone [c].

[a]   Commercial Business Activity (Handelsgewerbe)

Under § 1 I HGB "any person carrying on a commercial business activity is a merchant." The criterion of a "commercial business activity" (*Handelsgewerbe*) is defined in § 1 II HGB. According to this definition, any business activity (*Gewerbebetrieb*) is a commercial business activity, except those that do not require a commercial business operation.

Only business people (*Gewerbetreibende*) can be merchants. This criterion excludes the learned professions (*freie Berufe*). Accordingly, a doctor, an architect, a law firm, or, for that matter, an association of chartered public accountants cannot qualify for the status of a merchant unless they choose to organize themselves as a business company (*infra* [b]).

The requirement of a commercial business operation (*Erfordernis kaufmännischer Einrichtungen*) distinguishes merchants from small businesses. Elements of a commercial setting are the turnover, employees, bookkeeping, bank financing, acting through agents, and the like.

A far-reaching exception by tradition exists for agriculture (§ 3 I HGB). Farmers, fishermen, timber businesses, even large farms that employ industrial techniques of production and are professionally managed, are not merchants under § 1 HGB. Yet, they have an option to register as such (*infra* [b]).

[b]   Merchants by Option (Kannkaufmann)

Any person doing business, except members of the learned professions, has the option of becoming a merchant by registering the business in the commercial register (*infra* [B]) (§§ 2, 3 HGB). This is also true for small associations (§ 105 II HGB).

[c]   Business Associations (Formkaufmann)

Business associations (*Handelsgesellschaften*) such as a general partnership (*Offene Handelsgesellschaft* – OHG), a limited liability company (*Gesellschaft mit beschränkter Haftung* – GmbH) or a stock company (*Aktiengesellschaft* – AG) are merchants by virtue (*Formkaufmann*) of their legal form alone (§ 6 HGB). By choosing the legal form of a company (typically a GmbH) for their business, professionals such as doctors or lawyers have the choice of doing business under the legal form of a merchant. In the long run, this may undermine and indeed thwart the HGB's policy to keep the professions beyond the reach of commercial law.

[d]   Merchants by Appearance (Scheinkaufmann)

Finally, the law treats those holding themselves out as engaging in a commercial activity – be it by registering as a merchant (§ 5 HGB), by carrying a trade name, or by any other behavior deemed commercial – as merchants ("merchant by appearance").

[B]   The Commercial Register

The "commercial register" (*Handelsregister*) is a time-honored institution in Germany, dating back to the medieval guild rolls. While some sort of commercial register has been established by almost every continental legal system over time, Germany, from a comparative perspective, may be said to have enlarged its functions and strengthened its efficacy to a very high degree. For the most part, this can be attributed to the fact (already pointed out above at §4.01[A][1]) that German commercial law has evolved as the status law of merchants.

[1]   Functions

Generally speaking, the primary function of the commercial register is to provide information. Legally speaking, the register is crucial for establishing commercial "publicity" (*Publizität*).

[a]   Disclosure of Relevant Facts

To achieve this goal, a wide range of legally relevant commercial facts is covered by registration. The register collects and publicizes information not only about merchants, but also about commercial partnerships and companies. Among the commercially relevant facts, three categories stand out.

First, the register identifies a merchant (or a company, for that matter) by its trade name (*Firma*). The carrying of trade names is governed by strict rules (§§ 18–24 HGB) which guarantee that a trade name is *true* (i.e., not misleading) and *unambiguous*. Before the reform of 1998, the rules were rigid, requiring that a merchant's trade name be his civil name, with an option to add a word descriptive of his business ("Karl Müller, Drugstore"). Today, any description in words (whether pronounceable symbols – symbols that are generally understood as having an articulable meaning – such as @ – may be used is contentious) may be used as long as the description identifies the merchant in such a manner that he can be unambiguously identified (§ 18 HGB). In addition, the trade name must indicate the legal form of the business. Single (natural) persons add the term "registered merchant" (*eingetragener Kaufmann* – e.K.), partnerships and companies the legal form of organization (e.g., OHG or GmbH). Together with the trade name, the place of business (*Niederlassung*) must be registered (§ 29 HGB). In addition, any branch (*Zweigniederlassung*) of German or foreign merchants is registered separately (§§ 13 et seq. HGB).

Second, since merchants frequently do not, and companies cannot, act in person when making contracts, the commercial register lists any person who holds special statutory authority to act on behalf of the merchant (or the company), e.g., particular agents and representatives, or corporate officers.

Third, those dealing with a firm (be it an individual merchant, a partnership, or a company) need to know who is personally liable – and to what extent – for the debts incurred by the firm. As individual merchants and the members of a partnership are exposed to unlimited personal liability, the commercial register only has to specify the maximum liability incurred by a limited partner and the chartered capital stock of a company.

[b] Supervision of Reporting

For the commercial register to perform its function effectively, the relevant facts need to be reported in a timely and conclusive manner. Accordingly, a "rule of thumb" provides that everything that may be registered is also subject to a statutory obligation to be reported. Noncompliance with that obligation is subject to a fine.

The register shall provide reliable information. Therefore, any reported information is verified before it is published in the register. This verification concerns the compliance with formal requirements, such as the existence of signatures of a person with authority to act on behalf of the merchant, but also the legal basis of an entry, e.g., the validity of a company's articles of incorporation.

[c] Reliance on the Commercial Register

The commercial register is more than just a database that could be set up by a private organization as well. Documenting a relevant fact through the register may have two distinct legal effects. First, in some cases, the register does not merely provide evidence of a legally relevant fact or event; the very act of registration also legally validates an act or event. Thus, the registration of a person doing business "in a commercial manner" is merely evidentiary; but persons engaged in agriculture or small businesses obtain the status of a merchant by the very fact of enrolling in the register. If the merchant gives authority to an agent to act on his behalf, registration of this event is evidentiary only; but for a company to come into existence both as a body corporate and as a merchant, registration is constitutive.

Second and even more important, the commercial register creates a basis for reliance (§ 15 HGB); it does so, however, in a way that is somewhat unusual and difficult to understand. Of course one may rely on publicized information that is true. Furthermore, according to the principle of "negative publicity" (*negative Publizität*), facts that must be, but in fact are not registered may be assumed not to exist by those relying on their nonexistence in good faith. Note that "good faith" is not contingent on whether the relying party has in fact inspected the register; instead, constructive reliance is sufficient. But how about information that is duly registered yet false? Such information may also be relied upon in good faith ("positive publicity" – *positive Publizität*). Of course, in order to keep a wholly unsuspecting party from becoming a victim of false registration, a person cannot be held liable unless he also had a hand in the registration proceedings, even if unwittingly.

[2]   Organization and Administration

The commercial register is a public register. That implies that it is addressed and open to the general public. Basically, disclosure (*Publizität*) is achieved by publication of the facts registered (§ 10 HGB). Since January 2007, the commercial register has been kept electronically. The publication of a fact registered is complete when the entries are made accessible to the public. Subsequently, any person has the unrestricted right to inspect the register or to make online inquiries (§§ 9, 9a HGB). To grant easy and speedy access to the registers, a central register that collects information from all commercial registers is available online. The commercial register is administered by public authorities. Although administering such registers would appear to be a task of an all administrative agency, the task is assigned to the local courts (*Amtsgerichte*), resulting in a decentralized system of (essentially local) commercial registers.

[C]   Commercial Transactions

[1]   General Remarks

Under a subjective system of commercial law there can be no such thing as transactions that are commercial solely by virtue of their specific subject matter. Nor can there be, under the regime of freedom of contract, a closed number of transactions in which only merchants may engage. The HGB's solution to this problem is a principle (§ 343 HGB) according to which any transaction is considered commercial if one party, and in some instances both parties, are merchants. Furthermore, the transaction in question must be part of the merchant's business (This is presumed according to § 344 HGB). In terms of the parties' reciprocal contractual rights and duties, though, this classification does not mean all that much. Basically, the provisions of the general civil law (if any) apply to such transactions. Commercial law merely contributes some status-related provisions, e.g., special exceptions from the form requirements, a statute of limitations generally shorter than for ordinary citizens, and special rules relating to the formation of contracts through a representative or agent. Only for a small number of transactions – commercial sales, carriage and storage of goods – does the HGB detail the conditions of the contract. The bulk of commercial transactions are, however, governed by standardized general business conditions.

[2]   An Overview of Special Transactions

The law of commercial sales is merely supplementary to the sales law provisions of the BGB. Its policy is to strengthen, as between merchants, the position of the seller in relation to the buyer. Provisions to that effect include the seller's statutory right to have the goods that the buyer refuses to accept stored at a public warehouse at the buyer's expense or to resell them in a commercially reasonable manner (in the case of perishable goods, without prior notification) (§ 373 HGB). Furthermore, the HGB imposes an obligation on the buyer to inspect the goods upon delivery and to instantly notify the seller in case of nonconformity (§ 377 HGB). Otherwise, the buyer may lose his warranty claims.

[a]   Banking and Financial Services

Banking is, of course, of great importance for commerce as well as for consumers. Most German banks are chartered as so-called universal banks, allowing them to offer the full range of financial services (except insurance). The BGB only provides a statutory basis for banking transactions between banks and their customers in some areas. Sections 675c–676c BGB, which are based on the Second European Payment Services Directive, contain provisions governing payment services. Sections 488 et seq. BGB refer to loans in general, and in particular (§§ 491 et seq. BGB) to consumer credit, implementing the EU Consumer Credit Directive of 2008 and the Mortgage Credit Directive 2014. The law of checks and bills of exchange is contained in specific acts (*supra* §4.01[C]).

   As the EU continuously enacts directives relating to banking, an ever increasing body of German banking law today is based on EU directives. This is most obvious in the case of the supervision of banks that is governed by the KWG and the ZAG (*supra* §4.01[C][1][b]).

   Important sources of private banking law are the General Banking Conditions (*Allgemeine Geschäftsbedingungen der Banken*) published by the German Bankers' Association (revised version as of January 2018) which is almost uniformly applied to bank-customer relationships. The payment system between banks is operated on the basis of interbank agreements; as between bank and customer, §§ 675c et seq. BGB apply.

The securities business is, again, conducted on the basis of general business conditions, supplemented by statutory sales law (as for the trading of securities) or commercial agency law (securities brokerage). Here, EU legislation continuously broadens the regulatory framework. Among the most important directives on capital market law was the Directive on Markets in Financial Instruments of April 21, 2004 (MiFiD I-Directive), which was replaced by the MiFiD II-Directive of May 5, 2014. An additional tool used by the European legislature is a regulation aimed at preventing the manipulation and abuse of financial markets through insider knowledge: the Regulation 596/2014 on Market Abuse (the Market Abuse Regulation) was published on June 12, 2014 and entered into force on July 3, 2016.

Investment funds are comprehensively regulated, primarily on the basis of EU law. The Capital Investment Act (*Kapitalanlagegesetzbuch* – KAGB) of 2013, which replaced existing legislation, accommodates the provisions of the law on investment funds and implements the Directive 2011/61/EU on Alternative Investment Fund Managers (the so-called AIF Directive) as well as the Directive 2009/65/EU on the coordination of laws, regulations and administrative provisions relating to undertakings for collective investment in transferable securities (the so-called UCITS V Directive) into German law. The KAGB was amended in 2016 to implement the provisions of Directive 2014/91/EU (the so-called UCITS VI Directive) into German law. The Securities Custody Act of 1937 (as most recently amended in 2016) codifies the legal framework for custodian banks. Banks are allowed to exercise the voting rights arising out of shares they have under custody for their customers, provided the banks possess the pertinent power of attorney.

[b]   Carriage of Goods

The Code provisions relating to the carriage of goods used to cover only a very small part of the relevant law, leaving transportation law to a jumble of special statutes, regulations, and general business conditions. In 1998, the law was restructured by the Transport Law Reform Act (*Transportrechtsreformgesetz*). It is now codified in the new §§ 407–475h HGB. The law of shipment is now subject to fairly detailed statutory rules (§§ 407–452 HGB), modelled on the CMR (*Convention relative au contrat de transport international de marchandises par route*). The first part (§§ 407–451h HGB) contains general rules that apply to any means of transportation. The second part on multimodal transportation covers international carriage using different means of transportation. Multimodal transportation is subject to the general rules (§§ 407 et seq. HGB) unless international conventions apply (*infra* §4.05[B]). In addition, the General German Shipment Conditions (*Allgemeine Deutsche Spediteurbedingungen*) of 1926 (revised as of May 2017) are an important source of law. Even if not stipulated expressly, they may become the basis of an agreement as part of commercial custom. Since the carriage of goods is, by its nature, frequently cross-border business, a web of international conventions often displaces purely domestic law (*see infra* §4.05[B]).

[D] Commercial Agents and Other Representatives

In dealing with third parties, a merchant (or company) depends on persons acting for him (or it). The HGB provides for a variety of forms of agency (understood broadly). Such agents, representatives, or intermediaries may be classified according to whether they act on behalf of, or only for the account of, their principal.

[1] "Commercial Authority"

To begin with the first group, a merchant, like any other citizen, may authorize a third party to enter into binding agreements on his behalf. What is peculiar to "commercial authority" is that, in order to facilitate reliance on the part of the principal's business partner, its scope is defined by law. Thus, commercial authority may be general in scope. Such special specific statutory authority is termed *Prokura* (a word of Italian origin) if the agent (*Prokurist*) is granted the power to act in all matters generally related to a business, including litigation (§ 49 HGB). A much less comprehensive type of authority exists under the term *Handlungsvollmacht*; this is statutory and general only insofar as *a presumption* exists to the effect that the agent may act in all matters related to the principal's business. But this presumption does not cover the agent's entering into especially risky transactions, i.e., issuing bills of exchange, selling or encumbering real property, taking loans, and litigation (§ 54 HGB). Agents having *Prokura* or *Handlungsvollmacht* normally belong to the principal's personnel or, when acting for a company, are corporate officers. In contrast, a sales agent (*Handelsvertreter*) is self-employed. They are a merchant in his or her own right. It is their business either to act as a middleman recruiting customers for the principal or to enter into binding agreements on behalf of the principal (§ 84 HGB).

[2] Commission Agency

Regarding the second group of intermediaries – those acting only for the principal's account – the form most widely used is agency for a commission (*Kommissionsgeschäft* – §§ 383 et seq. HGB). A commission agent (*Kommissionär*) is a dealer, again a merchant, who makes it his business to buy or sell goods in his own name but for the account of another (*Kommittent*).

[E] Accounting and Financial Reporting

[1] General Remarks

When Germany implemented the European directives on accounting and financial reporting in 1986 – as set out in the fourth, seventh, and eighth company law directives of the European Union – it had to abandon much of its own tradition. Not only had the former law been rather sketchy; it had also been based on the policy of liberally allowing "hidden" reserves not to appear on the balance sheet. Thus, it had also impaired the primary goal of accounting and financial reporting, namely to achieve effective protection for both the owners (shareholders) and creditors of an enterprise. While the new law does not go all the way to adopting the Anglo-American philosophy of "true and fair view," it certainly means an improvement on all counts. Even in its present shape, however, the German system, unlike its Anglo-American counterpart, remains less exclusively focused on capital markets (i.e., shareholders and other investors). It is designed to report with equal accuracy to creditors and even to tax authorities.

[2]   *Financial Accounting*

German law distinguishes financial accounting from tax accounting. Financial accounting is governed by the third "book" (§§ 238 through 342e) of the HGB containing provisions on the preparation of the annual financial statements (§§ 238–289 HGB), the auditing of the annual financial statements (§§ 316–324 HGB), and the filing with the commercial register of the annual statements and additional documents. The legal requirements vary according to the legal form and the economic size of the enterprise: Sections 238–263 HGB contain general rules applicable to all merchants; additional rules for companies are found in §§ 264 et seq. HGB. In addition to the statutory provisions, mandatory rules of accounting exist as Generally Accepted (German) Accounting Principles (*Grundsätze ordnungsmäßiger Buchführung* – GoB). They contain principles and rules that have been developed in practice. Section 238 HGB requires accounting in accordance with the GoB, the most important of which are now codified in the HGB. The legal status of the noncodified rules may be described as usages of trade or customary law. The German courts will decide on the existence and the content of (noncodified) generally accepted accounting principles and will take into account recommendations published by professional associations such as the Institute of Certified Business Auditors (*Institut der Wirtschaftsprüfer*). As an exception, in the field of consolidated accounts for a group of enterprises (*Konzernrechnungslegung*), the principles recommended by the German Accounting Standards Committee are presumed to be in accordance with the GoB (§ 342 II HGB). Thus, a merchant following the recommended principles may rely on this presumption.

The HGB contains additional financial reporting requirements for consolidated groups of companies (*Konzerne*). Section 290 HGB obligates the parent company to prepare consolidated financial statements for the group. The companies have the option of preparing the statement according to the International Financial Reporting Standards (IFRS). Since 2015, it is no longer possible to prepare the statements according to the American General Accepted Accounting Principles (GAAP). In 2014, the EU substantially amended the law relating to Annual Accounts. The implementation of the Amendment of the Annual Accounts Directive and the amendment of the Annual Accounts Regulation led to significant changes to the provisions of the HGB relating to Annual Accounts (§§ 264–342e HGB).

[F]   Commercial Courts and Commercial Arbitration

Germany does not have separate commercial courts. Yet, there are "chambers for commercial matters" (*Kammer fur Handelssachen*) as separate divisions of the higher courts of first instance (*Landgerichte*). The bench of such chambers is composed of a presiding professional judge and two honorary lay judges ("commercial judges") recruited from respected members of the business community (merchants, company board members, etc.). Apart from this difference, they hear cases under the same rules of procedure as a court of general civil law jurisdiction. Parties may choose to have their dispute tried by a chamber for commercial matters or by a chamber of general jurisdiction; but access to the chambers for commercial matters is commonly requested due to their expertise in commercial practice and their understanding of what is deemed fair and reasonable among merchants.

As in any other Western country, arbitration plays an increasingly important role when it comes to settling commercial disputes – especially if the stakes are high. Since 1997, German arbitration law, §§ 1025 et seq. of the Code on Civil Procedure, – (*Zivilprozessordnung* – ZPO) is based on the UNCITRAL Model Law on International Commercial Arbitration. Generally, commercial parties are free to submit their disputes to a court of arbitration (§§ 1029–1031 ZPO) by written agreement (§ 1031 ZPO). The agreement may be part of a standard form contract. Among merchants, arbitration clauses in standard contracts are upheld by German courts. Arbitration agreements in consumer contracts, however, are subject to specific form requirements (§ 1031 V ZPO) and other restrictions.

In cross-border disputes, tribunals based in Germany and proceedings under the German rules of arbitration were traditionally not very popular in the international business community. By adopting the UNCITRAL Model Law, the arbitration law reform of 1997, Germany aimed to promote itself as a forum for arbitration in international disputes. The changes to the legislation were widely hailed and no doubt served to strengthen Germany's position as an arbitration forum. In 2015, the Deutsche Anwaltsverein working group on "civil procedural law" submitted proposals for necessary changes to §§ 1025 et seq. of the ZPO in order to further strengthen the international acceptance of German arbitration procedure.

§4.05   CROSS-BORDER ASPECTS

[A]   International Commercial Law (Conflict of Laws)

Commerce has never stopped at national borders, nor has commercial law. In the absence of an applicable uniform law (*infra* [B]), the applicable law will be determined by reference to the provisions of the Rome I Regulation (Rome I). This Regulation, which entered into force on December 17, 2009, is directly applicable and binding in (nearly) all EU Member States (*see* Article 288 II AEUV). Rome I replaced the previous conflict-of-laws rules set out in the former Articles 27 et seq. of the Introductory Law to the Civil Code (Einführungsgesetz zum Bürgerlichen Gesetzbuch – EGBGB. Rome I is *loi uniforme* (Article 2 Rome I) and its provisions are applicable, independent of any connection of the contract with a Member State.

As was the case with the EGBGB, Rome I contains the principle (as set out in its Article 3 I) that the law governing the contract may be chosen by the parties. Particularly in business transactions, it is common practice to set out the chosen law in standard contract terms and conditions.

If the parties have not chosen the applicable law, that law will be determined according to Article 4 Rome I, unless the special provisions of Articles 5–8 Rome I apply. For example, Section 1(a) provides that a contract for the sale of goods shall be governed by the law of the country where the seller has his habitual residence.

[B]   International Law Harmonization Through Uniform Laws and Uniform Business Conditions

In recent years, international organizations – most notably the United Nations Commission for International Trade Law (UNCITRAL) – have produced an ever-growing body of worldwide uniform commercial law. Supplementing these legislative efforts, there are ongoing efforts by various agencies, both private and public, to draft uniform business conditions. To what extent the Principles of International Commercial Contracts promulgated by UNIDROIT (Edition 1: 1994, Edition 2: 2004, Edition 3: 2010, Edition 4: 2016) will have a significant impact on business practice remains to be seen.

Germany has faithfully incorporated most of the proposed uniform commercial laws into domestic legislation. To begin with, the most comprehensive project, the (Vienna) UN Convention on Contracts for the International Sale of Goods (CISG) of 1980, was adopted in 1989 and came into effect in 1991. In practice, the CISG has come to be the "fundamental law" of international commercial sales. It may be displaced in favor of domestic sales law by the parties' express choice or even implicitly, e.g., by their referring to the BGB. On the other hand, a general choice of "German law" will be deemed to include the CISG.

Among the numerous uniform laws relating to the carriage of goods and/or persons, Germany has ratified (to name only the most important ones) the *Convention relative au contrat de transport international de marchandises par route* (CMR) (1956, adopted in 1962) relating to cross-border carriage of goods by road, the *Convention international concernant le transport par chemin de fer* (COTIF) (1980, adopted in 1985) relating to cross-border carriage by rail, and the Warsaw Convention Relating to the International Carriage by Air (1929/1955, adopted in 1958) as well as the supplementary Guadalajara Convention (1961, adopted in 1963). Germany has also signed the Convention for the Unification of Certain Rules for International Carriage by Air of 1999 (Montreal Convention).

The Hague Rules relating to carriage by sea (1924) have been an integral part of the HGB since 1937/1940 and the supplementary Hague Visby Rules (1968) since 1986, although Germany has never ratified the relevant international conventions. Yet, yielding to vehement opposition by the sea carrier industry, Germany has not yet ratified, and most probably never will ratify, the UN Convention on Multimodal (Combined) Transport (MT Convention) of 1980.

Among the international general business conditions widely used in cross-border commercial transactions are, most notably, the Incoterms drafted by the International Chamber of Commerce (ICC) in 1936. The Incoterms were revised in 1990 and 2000 and, most recently, in 2010.

For the cross-border banking business, the Uniform Customs and Practices for Documentary Credits (UCP), first promulgated by the ICC in 1933, revised in 1993 (UCP 500) and again in 2006 (UCP 600), are of similar importance.

When executing international electronic credit transfers, banks today usually do so through the S.W.I.F.T. system (Society for Worldwide Interbank Financial Telecommunication). Within the European Union, the T.A.R.G.E.T. (Trans-European Automated Real-time Gross Settlement Express Transfer) system used to be the most important tool for international payments. In 2007, this system was replaced by the T.A.R.G.E.T. 2 which, since then, has been the leading mechanism for transmitting large-value cross-border payments within the European Union.

[C]   Commercial Law Harmonization by the European Union

The legislative activity of the European Union has brought about important changes in many areas of civil and commercial law. Regarding the latter, a path breaking reform was the harmonization of the rules of accounting and financial reporting (*supra* §4.04[E]).

Even more important are the many EU directives on consumer law that affect contracts between merchants and consumers, starting with the Consumer Credits Directive in 1986. The Directive on Unfair Terms in Consumer Contracts of 1993 had a much smaller impact on German law, since it was, to some extent, modelled on the German Standard Term Contracts Act of 1976 (AGBG). As part of the reform of the law of obligations, the provisions of the AGBG were incorporated into the Civil Code (§§ 305 et seq. BGB). Upon entering into force on January 1, 2002, these provisions implemented the terms of the Directive on Unfair Terms in Consumer Contracts. The Directive on the Sale of Consumer Goods of 1999 triggered a major German reform of the law of obligations.

In electronic transactions between merchants and consumers ("b2c" – e-commerce), the Distance Marketing Directive of 1997 and the Directive on the Distance Marketing of Consumer Financial Services of 2002 are of fundamental importance. European consumer law was substantially consolidated by the Consumer Law Directive of 2011 which, amongst other things, incorporated the provisions of and repealed the Distance Marketing Directive. An additional, fundamental legal basis for electronic transactions is the E-Commerce Directive of 2000, whose terms are also applicable to merchants. Since the reform of the law of obligations in 2001, the German legislature has incorporated European consumer law, previously contained in separate special laws, into the Civil Code.

Note that the respective rules apply also to contracts between German consumers and foreign suppliers of goods or services if the contract is made via a website that targets the German market (*see* Article 6 I lit. b) Rome I). General rules for electronic commerce are the subject of the Directive on Electronic Commerce of 2001 which introduced the so-called country of origin principle as an important new foundation of cross-border electronic commerce.

In the classic areas of commercial law, there is the Directive Relating to Self-Employed Commercial Agents of 1986. European legislation has also become a major source of legislation in the field of banking transactions. The Directive Relating to the Public Offering of Securities (1989) became domestic law through the 1990 Sales Prospectus Act (*Verkaufsprospektgesetz*), which was replaced by the Sales Prospectus Act (*Wertpapierprospektgesetz*) in 2005. Finally, the Investment Services Directive of 1993 was implemented by the 1994 Securities Trade Act (*Wertpapierhandelsgesetz* – WpHG). The Directive on Cross-Border Credit Transfers of 1997 has been implemented in the BGB (*supra* §4.04[C][2][a]).

SELECTED BIBLIOGRAPHY

Commercial Code (Handelsgesetzbuch) in English

Thomas Rittler, *Handelsgesetzbuch (HGB) – German Commercial Code* (4th ed. 2017).

Commentaries

Adolf Baumbach & Klaus Hopt, *Handelsgesetzbuch* (38th ed. 2018, by Klaus J. Hopt and Hanno Merkt).
Carsten Ebenroth, Karlheinz Boujong & Detlev Joost (eds.), *Handelsgesetzbuch* (2001).
Christian Zwirner (ed.), *Bilanzrichtlinie-Umsetzungsgesetz: BilRUG* (2016).
Claus-Wilhelm Canaris, Mathias Habersack & Carsten Schäfer (eds.), *STAUB Handelsgesetzbuch* (5th ed. 2015).
Eckhard Flohr & Ulf Wauschkuhn (eds.), *Vertriebsrecht* (2nd ed. 2018).
Harald Wiedmann, Hans-Joachim Böcking & Marius Gros (eds.), *Bilanzrecht, Kommentar zu den §§ 238 bis 342e HGB* (3rd ed. 2014).
Hartmut Oetker (ed.), *Handelsgesetzbuch: HGB* (5th ed. 2017).
Heymann, *Handelsgesetzbuch* (Nobert Horn ed., 2nd ed. 1995 *et seq.*).
Ingo Koller, Peter Kindler, Wulf Henning Roth & Winfried Morck (eds.), *Handelsgesetzbuch: HGB* (8th ed. 2015).
Münchener Kommentar zum Handelsgesetzbuch (Karsten Schmidt ed., 2016 *et seq.*).
Stefan Kröll, Loukas Mistelis & Pilar Perales Viscasillas (eds.), *UN Convention on Contracts for the International Sale of Goods (CISG)* (2nd ed. 2018).
Thomas Heidel & Alexander Schall (eds.), *Handelsgesetzbuch: HGB* (2nd ed. 2015).

Handbooks and Treatises

Claus-Wilhelm Canaris, *Handelsrecht* (24th ed. 2006).
Holger Fleischer & Frauke Wedemann (eds.), *Handelsrecht einschließlich Bilanzrecht* (9th ed. 2015).
Karsten Schmidt, *Handelsrecht* (6th ed. 2014).

On Special Commercial Transactions

Herbert Schimansky, Hermann-Josef Bunte & Hans-Jürgen Lwowski (eds.): *Bankrechts-Handbuch* (2 vols., 5th ed. 2017).
Hans-Peter Schwintowski, *Bankrecht* (5th ed. 2018).
Ingo Koller, *Transportrecht Kommentar* (9th ed. 2016).
Marius Mann (ed.), *Commercial Contracts in Germany* (2015).
Martin Tonner & Thomas Krüger (eds), *Bankrecht* (2nd ed. 2016).
Michael Martinek, Franz-Jörg Semler & Eckhard Flohr, *Handbuch des Vertriebsrechts* (4th ed. 2016).
Norbert Horn (ed.), *German Banking Law and Practice in International Perspective* (1999).

Accounting and Financial Disclosure

Bernhard Großfeld, *Bilanzrecht* (4th ed. 2005).
Brigitte Knobbe-Keuk, *Bilanz-und Unternehmenssteuerrecht* (9th ed. 1993).
Christian Dowe, *Accounting*, in: Robert Amann (ed.), *German Tax Guide* (2001), Chapter 12.
Gunter Wöhe, *Die Handels-und Steuerbilanz* (6th ed. 2010).
Günter Wöhe & Heinz Kußmaul (ed.), *Grundzüge der Buchführung und Bilanztechnik* (10th ed. 2018).
Herbert Brönner, Peter Bareis, Klaus Hahn, Torsten Maurer, Jens Poll & Uwe Schramm (eds), *Die Bilanz nach Handels- und Steuerrecht* (11th ed. 2016).
Jörg Baetge, Hans-Jürgen Kirsch & Stefan Thiele, *Bilanzen* (14th ed. 2017).
Jörg-Markus Hitz, Richard Werner& Jochen Zimmermann (eds.), *Buchführung und Bilanzierung nach IFRS und HGB* (3rd ed. 2015).
Klaus Tipke & Joachim Lang, *Steuerrecht* (22nd ed. 2015).
Robert Winnefeld (ed.), *Bilanz-Handbuch* (5th ed. 2015).

CHAPTER 5

The Law of Business Associations

Rolf Sethe

TABLE OF CONTENTS

§5.01   INTRODUCTION

[A]   Survey of Corporate Forms

[1]   Corporations, Partnerships and Mixed Forms

The aim of this chapter is not to describe the law of associations in general, but to concentrate on business associations. They occur in two different types: corporations and partnerships. German business law provides for three forms of corporations: the stock company (*Aktiengesellschaft* – AG), the public limited partnership by shares (*Kommanditgesellschaft auf Aktien* – KGaA), and the limited liability company (*Gesellschaft mit beschränkter Haftung* – GmbH). In practice, the limited liability company is predominant. In 2016, there were 1,186,598 limited liability companies, 15,453 stock companies and 293 public limited partnerships by shares in Germany. Since 2008 the law provides for the entrepreneurial company (*Unternehmergesellschaft (haftungsbeschränkt) – UG (haftungsbeschränkt)*) which is a subtype of a limited liability company with a share capital that falls short of the regular minimum share capital. The German legislator wanted to establish a domestic alternative to the rising number of incoming British limited liability companies founded with £1. In 2016, there were 115,644 UG and 8,891 UG & Co. KG in Germany.

Civil law and commercial law provide for five forms of partnerships: the partnership under the Civil Code (*BGB-Gesellschaft*), the non-trading partnership under the Partnership Act 1994 (*Partnerschaftsgesellschaft*), the general partnership (*offene Handelsgesellschaft* – OHG), the limited partnership (*Kommanditgesellschaft* – KG) and the "dormant" partnership (*stille Gesellschaft*). In 2016, there were about 24,215 general partnerships and 257,681 limited partnerships (including GmbH & Co KG).

Other types of associations such as the incorporated association (*eingetragener Verein*), the "unincorporated" association (*nicht eingetragener Verein*), the foundation under the Civil Code (*Stiftung*), the shipping company (*Reederei*) and the registered cooperative (*Genossenschaft*), are not covered here because they are of little or no practical importance to business. As the scope of this article is limited to German law, supranational business associations (e.g., Societas Europaea, European Economic Interest Grouping) are excluded as well.

Finally, it should be noted that under German company law, there are no general restrictions on mixing corporate forms. On the one hand, shareholders may give the company an individual structure which differs more or less from the respective form's standard legal model. On the other hand, mixed corporate forms may emerge from mixing basic types by means of one company's participation in another. The most common example is that of the limited liability company & Co. (GmbH & Co. KG): it is a limited partnership (KG) in which a limited liability company (GmbH) participates as the sole personally liable partner. However, a vast amount of court decisions have turned the GmbH & Co. KG almost into a business association in its own right. The same considerations apply *mutatis mutandis* respectively to the UG and the UG & Co. KG.

[2] The Characteristics of Corporations and Partnerships

Both corporations and partnerships may acquire rights and obligations and can sue or can be sued. But in contrast to corporations, partnerships only have partial legal personality. A consequence of the legal personality of corporations is that the corporation itself is the owner of its assets, whereas a partnership is not able to own assets: all assets belong to the partners in joint ownership (*Gesamthandsgemeinschaft*, § 719 BGB). The principle of joint ownership means that two or more persons hold property not in distinct shares but jointly, each having an identical interest in the undivided whole. An asset may be transferred only with the consent of all partners, which can be given either in the partnership contract (e.g., by authorizing the management to make such transactions) or in a general meeting of the partners.

A corporation's credit is the fixed share capital, whereas partnerships do not have fixed amounts of capital (with the exception of the limited partnership, *see infra* §5.03[C][2]). Instead, the partners are personally, jointly and severally liable to the partnership's creditors for any debts of the partnership to the full extent of their private assets. All business associations have a contractual basis to complement the statutory law and to adapt it to the needs of the partners and the members of the corporation respectively. Even the one-person limited liability company (*Ein-Personen-GmbH*) or the one-person stock company (*Ein-Personen-AG*) is deemed to be based on a contract.

The agreement of incorporation for corporations is called "memorandum of association" (*Satzung*). It is the fundamental document, which contains not only the constitution and powers of the company but also the necessary internal regulations, such as the amount of capital or the number of directors. Thus, German law does not differentiate between "memorandum of association" and "articles of association." It provides for one document only. However, separate contractual agreements among groups of shareholders or all shareholders (e.g., agreements binding the parties in the exercise of their membership rights) are often used.

The partnership agreement and the memorandum of association of a limited liability company are by and large governed by the principle of freedom of contract. In contrast, the law of stock corporations leaves little room for the individual structuring of a corporation (*cf.* § 23 V AktG).

[B] The Law of Capital Markets

In industrialized countries' legal systems, corporate law is generally closely linked with the law of capital markets (securities regulation). In Germany, only stock corporations and limited partnerships by shares may list shares (equity) to the country's regulated capital markets whereas all business associations may list bonds (*Anleihen*) or profit participation certificates (*Genussscheine*).

Until the 1990s, capital market law in Germany had not only been practically restricted to stock exchange law but, at the same time, had lacked any consistent regulatory model. In part, this may be attributed to the fact that capital markets themselves were underdeveloped for many decades. Beginning in the 1950s and in

Germany's post-war economy, private savings, if any, were put into low-risk investments. Accordingly, corporate finance was obtained either by self-financing or by borrowing capital.

In the mid-1960s it became obvious that industrial growth without the development of a capital market system of corporate finance was not feasible. At the same time, holders of large amounts of capital were looking for investments offering better returns than those from savings accounts. However, such a market was not generated by the stock corporation. Instead, investors were attracted by new types of investments offered by companies neither organized as stock corporations nor subject to any existing capital market regulation. This led to the birth of the "grey" capital market, which was not subject to statutory regulation. The "grey" market was governed by some judge-made law providing only a minimum of investor protection. This was partly achieved by adapting company law applicable to the investment company to capital market needs, and partly by creating pre-contractual obligations of those participating in the distribution of investments (especially by introducing special disclosure requirements and a quasi-contractual liability regime).

Both competing national and international financial markets as well as the implementation of EU company, banking and capital market harmonization directives in German law have led to a modernization of the country's regulated capital market. Simultaneously, the efforts to live up to international standards of securities regulation have introduced into Germany's capital market laws a variety of legal norms, thereby not only affecting the stock companies' behavior in capital markets but also the companies' organization. This is most obvious with respect to the Securities Trading Act (*Wertpapierhandelsgesetz 1993*) that, *inter alia*, provided for increased disclosure obligations for listed stock companies, such as intermediate (accounting) and immediate disclosure requirements (ad hoc publicity), obligations to report and disclose directors' dealings and major investments or disinvestments in the capital stock of a listed company. The modernization of capital market law is also visible in the imposition of an obligation to publish a prospectus for securities, which are offered to the German public for the first time (*Wertpapier-Verkaufsprospektgesetz 1990*). In order to regulate the "grey" market in 2004 a similar obligation was imposed on the public distribution of any securities other than shares that grant a participation in the profits of a business association or of fiduciary assets. In addition, since 2012 investment advisors and investment brokers of "grey" market's products have to be registered and to abide by investor protection obligations when selling such products. In 2002, the German Securities Acquisition and Takeover Act (*Wertpapiererwerbs- und Übernahmegesetz*) came into force. It provides for special procedural rules and disclosure obligations during takeover bids as well as for a mandatory bid if the bidder has gained control of the target company (i.e., 30% of the voting rights). During the last decade a growing part of the national capital market legislation has been substituted by EU regulations that are self-executing (*cf.* Article 288 II TFEU) such as the Market Abuse Regulation EU No. 596/2014 and the Prospectus Regulation (EU) No. 2017/1129.

§5.02   CORPORATIONS

[A]   The Stock Company

[1]   The Two Types of Stock Companies and the Applicable Law

The Stock Company Act of 1965 (*Aktiengesetz* – AktG), as amended on May 10, 2016, is the legal basis for the stock company and the public limited partnership by shares (*see infra* §5.02[B]). The AktG has been amended several times since 1965, mainly to implement the EU company law harmonization directives. However, the principal objectives of the amendments between 1994 and 2016 were deregulation and modernization: Several sections that had proved to be inadequate or too onerous for small companies were simplified, the notional no-par-value share was introduced and a Corporate Governance Codex was adopted. The administration of a listed stock company is required to declare to what extent the company observes the Codex and, where necessary, to explain why the company does not comply with certain provisions of the Codex (§ 161 AktG). Listed stock companies that fall within the scope of Co-determination Acts (*see infra* §5.02[D]) must meet a gender ratio of at least 30% of each sex in the supervisory board (§ 96 II, III AktG). Stock companies that are either listed or co-determined are under the obligation to take all necessary measures to reach such a ratio within the board of directors, among the top executives who support the board of directors and within the supervisory board (§§ 76 IV, 111 V AktG) by defining a target quota to be reached within the following five years.

In matters not specifically addressed by the AktG, the laws generally applicable to associations also apply to stock companies. For example, §§ 238 et seq. of the Commercial Code of 1897 (*Handelsgesetzbuch* – HGB) provide for most of the regulations relating to commercial records and accounting requirements. Also, pursuant to § 31 BGB, stock companies are vicariously liable for any wrongful acts of their directors and other senior members of management. In addition, a company can be held liable for its employees' misconduct under the general rules of the Civil Code (§§ 278, 831 BGB).

[2]   The Legal Nature of the Stock Company

The stock company (*Aktiengesellschaft*) is a corporation with a fixed capital stock (§§ 6, 7 AktG) divided into transferable shares (§ 1 II AktG). Shareholders are not personally liable for the company's obligations (§§ 1 I 2, 54 I AktG). The stock company, a legal person pursuant to § 1 I 1 of the AktG, has an incorporated organization. Regardless of the actual purpose of the enterprise, the stock company is always deemed to be a commercial company (§ 3 I AktG). Consequently, all provisions of the HGB dealing with merchants apply (§ 6 HGB), even if the company serves a non-profit purpose.

[3]   The Incorporation of the Stock Company

The stock company becomes a legal entity upon registration in the commercial register (§ 41 I 1 AktG). To qualify for registration, five requirements have to be fulfilled:

(i)   The memorandum of association is drawn up by one (or more) founder(s) in notarized form (§§ 2, 23 I AktG). Section 23 II-IV AktG sets out minimum content requirements for the document. Further stipulations are possible, but may only differ from the AktG if the law explicitly allows for deviations (§ 23 V AktG). Because such exceptions are rare, German stock company law is rather strict in comparison with other legal systems.

(ii) The founders have to subscribe for all shares (§§ 2, 28, 29 AktG) and pay in the amount of capital that is determined in the memorandum of association. Section 36a I AktG requires the company to call up at least 25% of the issue price of a share and the entire premium, where shares are issued for an amount higher than the nominal value. A shareholder may not set off a contribution and the company may not waive the obligation to pay the shares (§ 66 I AktG) or to repay a contribution (§ 66 II AktG). Contributions in kind must be verified by independent auditors to determine whether they are equal to the amount stated in the memorandum (§§ 27, 33 III-V, 34, 35 AktG). Section 33a AktG provides for an exception with regard to certain financial instruments or assets with a market value. Such contributions must be fully performed (§ 36a II AktG).

(iii) The founders elect the first auditors and the supervisory board (*Aufsichtsrat*, § 30 I-III AktG) which in turn appoints the board of directors (*Vorstand*, § 30 IV AktG). The founders, the supervisory board, the board of directors, and the first auditors are subject to special civil and criminal liability rules in all respects relating to the correct incorporation of the company (§§ 46 et seq. AktG).

(iv) The founders deliver a written incorporation report that the supervisory board and the board of directors check as to whether all conditions for proper incorporation have been met (§§ 32 et seq. AktG). In special cases, e.g., if one of the founders is a member of the supervisory board, the court must appoint independent auditors to verify the report.

(v)   The founders, the supervisory board and the board of directors apply to the local commercial register for registration and submit all data and documents specified in § 37 IV AktG. The registrar verifies whether the above-mentioned conditions have been met. If this is not the case, the application for registration is rejected (§ 38 AktG). Otherwise the court registers the company in the commercial register, Section B. Registration contains the name and purpose of the company, its registered office (which has to be in Germany, *cf.* § 5 AktG), the date of the memorandum of association (including the date of subsequent changes), the nominal stock capital and the signatures of the directors (§ 39 AktG). The content of the commercial register is deemed to be correct with regard to third parties acting in good faith (§ 15 I, III HGB). The registration is effective immediately. Once registered, a court may declare the incorporation void only on grounds of severe errors (§§ 262 I no. 5, 275 AktG).

A company may operate to a limited extent even before its registration. However, in that case, persons acting on behalf of the company are jointly and severally liable for the obligations and debts incurred prior to the incorporation (§ 41 I AktG).

[4]   *Shares*

The shareholder's right of membership is incorporated in the share. The shareholder acquires membership in the company either as a founder, by subscribing for shares, or by a transfer or transmission of shares subsequent to the incorporation.

In addition to conferring membership, shares carry a second function. They represent a part of the total share capital of the company. According to § 7 AktG, the minimum share capital (*Grundkapital*) is €50,000. It is divided either into shares with a nominal value or in no-par-value shares (proportional shares). The minimum value of a share with a nominal value or of a proportion of a no-par-value share is €1 (§ 8 II, III AktG).

The third function of a share is its use as a security. Membership in the company is represented by a written document (share certificate) that can be transferred within or outside the stock market. Bearer shares, issued only after full payment of the contribution (§ 10 II AktG), are transferred by agreement and delivery of the certificates (§ 929 BGB), whereas registered shares are transferred by agreement, endorsement of the certificates and delivery (§ 68 AktG; §§ 12, 13 Wechselgesetz). The memorandum may require the company's consent to a transfer of a registered share (§ 68 II AktG: *vinkulierte Namensaktie*), to be granted by the board of directors.

In order to prevent money laundering a company may only issue bearer shares if a transfer of ownership leaves a paper trail. Therefore bearer shares are only permitted for listed stock companies or for companies that register their shares in a central securities depository (§ 10 II AktG).

The memorandum may provide for different classes of shares. The most common use of this option is to create preferred shares (*Vorzugsaktien*) without voting rights (§§ 12 I 2, 139 et seq. AktG).

[5]   *Capital Increase and Other Forms of Financing the Company*

As previously stated (*see supra* §5.02[A][3]), the amount of share capital has to be determined in the memorandum of association. The share capital may be increased according to business fluctuations. Capital increases may take four different forms: capital increase against contributions (*Kapitalerhöhung gegen Einlagen*), conditional capital increase (*Bedingte Kapitalerhöhung*), authorized capital (*Genehmigtes Kapital*) and capital increase from the company's funds (*Kapitalerhöhung aus Gesellschaftsmitteln*).

[a]   The Capital Increase Against Contributions

A capital increase against contributions requires a special resolution of the general meeting of shareholders (*Hauptversammlung*) by a qualified majority of at least three-fourth of the share capital represented at the meeting. The memorandum of association may require a larger or a smaller majority (§ 182 I 1, 2 AktG). If different classes of shares were issued, a majority of each class of shareholders has to consent (§ 182 II AktG). If contributions in kind are made, the principles described for the incorporation apply (§ 183 AktG). A capital increase against contributions may only be performed by the issue of new shares, not by an increase of the nominal value of already existing shares or the proportion of no-par-value shares (§ 182 I 4 AktG). The board of directors and the chairman of the supervisory board apply for entry of the resolution in the commercial register; if contributions in kind are made, an auditor's report on the contributions must be attached (§ 184 I AktG), unless the exception with regard to certain financial instruments or assets with a market value applies (§§ 183a, 33a AktG). Subsequently, the subscription for new shares takes place. The pay-in conditions correspond to those prescribed for incorporation (*see supra* §5.02[A][3]). The board of directors and the chairman of the supervisory board certify the fulfillment of these conditions to the commercial register (§ 188 AktG).

A share capital increase is valid and takes legal effect as soon as it has been registered (§ 189 AktG). The new shares may then be issued (§ 191 AktG). To protect the proportionate interests of shareholders, the AktG provides for pre-emptive rights (*Bezugsrecht*), i.e., new shares must first be offered to existing shareholders in proportion to their shareholdings (§ 186 AktG). The offer must be published and must then remain open for at least fourteen days (§ 186 I AktG). Pre-emptive rights may be wholly or partly excluded by a special resolution of the general meeting (§ 186 III AktG). The exclusion has to be expressly announced in the agenda of the general meeting deciding on the issue. Moreover, the board of directors has to deliver a written report setting forth the grounds for the exclusion. A shareholder doubting that the resolution is based on reasonable grounds can contest the resolution in court and may obtain a judgment declaring it void.

In practice, indirect forms of subscription and pre-emptive rights are common. To effect the increase of capital, all shares are subscribed for and paid in by a bank or a consortium of banks with an obligation to offer the shares to the existing shareholders before selling them on the open market (§ 186 V AktG).

[b]   The Conditional Capital Increase

A second form of capital increase is the conditional capital increase (§§ 192 et seq. AktG). It is permitted only to grant a conversion to the owners of convertible bonds (*Wandelschuldverschreibungen*), to prepare the merger or acquisition of several enterprises, and to grant pre-emptive rights to employees or options to board members of the company or affiliated companies (§ 192 II AktG). All other pre-conditions resemble those just explained with respect to a capital increase against contributions. The share capital increase takes effect as soon as the new shares are issued (§ 200 AktG). The board of directors annually reports to the commercial register the amount of shares issued throughout the financial year (§ 201 AktG).

[c]   The Authorized Capital

The third form of capital increase is the authorized capital (§§ 202 et seq. AktG). The board of directors may be authorized for a maximum period of five years (starting from the day of the registration of the resolution in the commercial register) to issue a certain amount of new shares against contributions. The authorization may be granted either in the memorandum of association or by a subsequent amendment to it, requiring a special resolution of the general meeting of shareholders by a qualified majority of at least three-fourth of the share capital represented at the meeting. The memorandum may prescribe a higher majority (§ 202 II AktG). Each different class of shares needs the consent of the required majority (§§ 202 II, 182 II AktG). The board of directors may decide to use the authorization wholly or in part. It may issue the new shares only with the consent of the supervisory board (§ 202 III AktG). The issue of new shares is performed in the same manner as in the case of a capital increase against contributions (*see supra* §5.02[A][5][a]).

[d]   The Capital Increase from the Company's Funds

The fourth form of capital increase is called capital increase from the company's funds (§§ 207 et seq. AktG). The general meeting of shareholders may convert all or part of the "share premium account" (i.e., capital-surplus) or the "revaluation reserve" (i.e., retained-earnings) into share capital. A special resolution is required according to the modes described above. The conversion must not exceed 10% of the previously existing capital stock; a higher percentage is only permissible if the memorandum of association so provides (§ 208 I AktG). Such a capital increase must be based on a properly audited and certified balance sheet of recent date (§§ 208, 209 AktG). The share capital increase is effective as soon as it has been registered (§ 211 AktG). The new shares may then be issued (§ 191 AktG). Each shareholder has a mandatory pre-emptive right on the new shares of his or her class of shares (§ 212 AktG).

[e]   Convertible Bonds, Debentures and Participating Bonds

With the approval by a special resolution of the general assembly, the company may issue convertible bonds, debentures and participating bonds (§ 221 AktG). In contrast, ordinary credit financing without the issuing of securities requires only a decision of the board of directors. It does not require the consent of the general meeting.

[6]   The Capital Reduction

[a]   Legal Basis

The amount of share capital fixed in the memorandum may be reduced. However, it may not be dropped below the minimum stock capital of €50,000 unless it is combined with a parallel capital increase against contributions in cash (§ 228 I AktG).

A capital reduction may serve several different purposes: High losses leading to a balance deficit may require the company to reduce its share capital; by adjusting the capital figures to the actual level of assets, financial soundness is restored. Further objectives may be the distribution of committed assets of the company among the shareholders or the establishment of a free reserve.

Capital reductions may take one of three different forms: ordinary capital reduction, simplified capital reduction, and capital reduction by redemption of shares. The ordinary capital reduction and the capital reduction by redemption of shares may serve all three purposes described above, whereas the simplified capital reduction is available only for the restoration of financial soundness or the establishment of a free reserve (§ 229 I AktG). All forms of capital reduction require a special resolution of the general meeting of shareholders by a qualified majority of at least three-fourth of the share capital represented. The memorandum may prescribe a higher majority and/or further requirements (§§ 222 I, 229 III, 237 II AktG). The purpose of the reduction must be stated in the resolution.

[b]   The Ordinary Capital Reduction

The ordinary capital reduction is effected by a reduction of the total share capital and – in the case of a company having shares with a nominal value – by a reduction of the nominal value of the shares. This is not possible where the nominal value of shares is already set at the legal minimum of €1. A capital reduction would then take the form of a consolidation of shares (§ 222 IV AktG). The ordinary capital reduction is effective as soon as it has been registered (§ 224 AktG). The company must secure payment to all creditors who cannot demand immediate consideration of their claims, on the condition that they apply for the security within six months after registration of the reduction. Payments to shareholders may only be made after the expiry of this six months period (§ 225 AktG).

[c]   The Simplified Capital Reduction

The simplified capital reduction may only be executed to compensate for a deterioration of the value of assets, to cover losses or to transfer value into the capital reserve. Thus, it is only permissible if certain other (reserve) funds have been used to cover the losses (§ 229 II AktG). The procedure for a simplified capital reduction resembles, for the most part, that of an ordinary capital reduction with one exception: as previously stated, assets remain untouched and payments to shareholders are forbidden (§ 230

AktG). Creditors are therefore less endangered. Their interests are properly secured by a limitation of the distribution of dividends to shareholders (§ 233 AktG).

[d] The Capital Reduction by Redemption of Shares

In contrast to other forms of reduction, which concern all shareholders, the capital reduction by redemption of shares is a cancellation of the rights of individual shareholders. A capital reduction by redemption of shares can be executed in two ways: either by redemption subsequent to the company's purchase of shares or by compulsory redemption. The latter is only permissible if it is provided for in the original memorandum of association or a subsequent amendment thereof. The rules governing ordinary capital reductions are applicable in general, but the requirements for, and the method of, execution of the redemption must be set down either in the memorandum or in a special resolution (§ 237 II AktG).

[7] *Membership and Minority Protection*

The legal position of the shareholders may be looked at from two different perspectives: on the one hand, a shareholder has property rights, on the other hand, he or she has administrative rights.

[a] Property Rights

Shareholders have a right to dividends (§ 58 IV AktG), pre-emptive rights (*see supra* §5.02[A][5][a]) and a right to participate in the distribution of assets after liquidation of the company (§ 271 AktG).

[b] Administrative Rights

Shareholders have individual administrative rights. The most important of these is the right to vote (§§ 12 I, 134 AktG), which is exercised in the general meeting of shareholders. A shareholder may be represented by the use of a written proxy (§ 134 III AktG). It is a special feature of German stock company and capital market law not to encourage proxy contests. As a corollary, a large percentage of voting rights in publicly-held companies are exercised on the basis of a proxy voting power for deposited shares held by banks (*Depotstimmrecht*) (§ 135 AktG), whereas proxy voting using shareholder associations is less common. Since most shareholder-depositors refrain from instructing the depositary on how to exercise the voting rights, banks often have a significant influence on the company.

The right to vote implies the right to attend the general meeting (§ 118 I AktG) or, if the memorandum provides for, not to attend the meeting but to exercise the shareholder rights by electronic means. It also requires adequate information as a solid basis for decisions. Complementing a variety of ordinary and extraordinary disclosure and reporting obligations, the board of directors has a special duty to inform share-holders, upon request, about all matters concerning the company, its interests and its policy (§ 131 I, II AktG). Only in certain specific cases (§ 131 III AktG) may the board of directors refuse to inform the shareholder, e.g., in order to avoid damage to the company. Lastly, the shareholder has the right to contest the validity of a resolution of the general meeting (§ 245 AktG), e.g., on grounds of violation of the law or of the memorandum of association (§ 243 AktG).

In addition to these individual rights, shareholders have collective administrative rights in the form of minority rights. A minority representing 5% of the share capital (or a lesser percentage if the memorandum provides for) may request a general meeting (§ 122 I AktG). Similarly, a minority representing 5% of the share capital or €500,000 par value may request that additional items be put on the agenda of the general meeting (§ 122 II AktG). The same minority may also, under certain circumstances, contest the validity of a resolution not to declare a dividend in order to retain profits (§ 254 II AktG) or request the court to order a special examination of an impermissible undervaluation (§ 258 AktG). Some other minority rights are worth mentioning: a company may waive or restrict its damage claims against founders (§ 50 AktG), members of the board of directors (§ 93 IV AktG), or the supervisory board (§ 116 AktG) for breach of duties, unless a minority of shareholders representing 10% of the share capital opposes the resolution. Such a minority may also request that the company enforces its damage claims (§ 147 AktG). A separate discharge of each member of the board of directors or of the supervisory board can be requested by a minority representing €1 million par value or 10% of the share capital (§ 120 I AktG). The same minority may seek the removal of a member of the supervisory board who was not elected but appointed according to a special provision in the memorandum of association (§ 103 III AktG). A minority of 5% or €500,000 par value may, under certain circumstances, petition the court to replace the annual auditor (§ 318 III HGB). A minority of 1% or €100,000 par value can ask for the judicial appointment of special auditors (§ 142 II AktG).

[c]   The Shareholders' Duties and Liabilities

Original shareholders are obligated to pay in their contributions (*see supra* §5.02[A][3]). Shareholders are not personally liable to creditors of the company (§ 54 I AktG). However, shareholders who received unlawful payments by the company are required to reimburse such amount; creditors may claim this amount directly from the shareholder if the company is not able or willing to meet its obligations (§ 62 AktG).

Like any other member of the company, a shareholder is liable for any damages if, by taking advantage of his influence upon the company, he intentionally induces a member of the board of directors or of the supervisory board to act to the detriment of the company or its shareholders (§ 117 AktG). In exceptional cases an individual shareholder may be liable for the debts of the company. The courts have pierced the corporate veil (*Durchgriffshaftung*) if an obvious undercapitalization works to the disadvantage of creditors, and if the company's and the shareholders' private assets have been commingled.

[8] *The Administration*

The stock company has three required organs: the general meeting (*Hauptversammlung*), the supervisory board (*Aufsichtsrat*), and the board of directors (*Vorstand*).

[a] *The General Meeting of the Shareholders*

The general meeting is the assembly of all shareholders. It has to be called at least once a year (§ 175 I AktG). In addition, it must be convened in cases provided for either by the memorandum of association or by law, e.g., if a minority so demands (*see supra* §5.02[A][7][b]) or when it becomes necessary for the welfare of the company (§ 121 I AktG).

The general meeting's competence is not comprehensive but limited to questions assigned to it by law or by the memorandum of association, such as the election of the members of the supervisory board and the auditors (§ 119 I no. 1, no. 7 AktG), the appropriation of accumulated earnings (§§ 119 I no. 2, 174 AktG), the discharge of the members of the board of directors and of the supervisory board members (§§ 119 I no. 3, 120 AktG), the appointment of annual auditors (§ 119 I no. 4 AktG), the amendment to the memorandum of association (§§ 119 I no. 5, 179 et seq. AktG), changes in the capital basis (§ 119 I no. 6, *see supra* §5.02[A][5]), certain decisions relating to the law of "affiliated companies" (§§ 291 et seq. AktG), conversions and fusions (i.e., amalgamations and mergers as regulated by the Law Regulating the Conversion of Companies – *Umwandlungsgesetz* – of 1994), the total transfer of assets (§ 179a I AktG), and the dissolution of the company (§§ 119 I no. 8, 262 I no. 2 AktG).

At the time of writing this chapter, the general meeting of a stock company does not have the competence to decide on the remuneration of the board of directors or the supervisory board (so-called say on pay); nor is any decision of the shareholders, should the topic be on the agenda, binding (*cf.* § 120 IV AktG). § 120 IV AktG will be modified when the "EU-Directive 2017/828 of 17 May 2017 as regards the encouragement of long-term shareholder engagement" will be implemented into German law (expected for summer 2019).

[b] *The Supervisory Board*

The supervisory board is an independent organ elected by the general meeting for a maximum period of four years (§ 102 AktG). If provided in the memorandum of association, some members of the supervisory board may be appointed by certain shareholders (§ 101 II AktG). The board consists of at least three members. The memorandum may set a higher number. The maximum number is determined in relation to the amount of share capital (§ 95 AktG). A company with a share capital of more than €10 million may have a supervisory board of twenty-one members (there are special requirements for companies falling within the scope of the Co-determination Acts, *see infra* §5.02[D]). Only natural persons with full legal capacity may become board members. The memorandum may prescribe additional personal requirements such as age, nationality or special professional qualifications (§ 100 IV AktG). The accumulation of memberships in supervisory boards of different companies is limited to ten (§ 100 II no. 1 AktG). Certain overlaps in capacity are prohibited. Thus, for example, a person serving on the board of directors of a subsidiary company may not be a member of the supervisory board of the parent company (§ 100 II no. 2 AktG).

The supervisory board appoints and supervises the board of directors. Supervision extends to all activities of the board of directors and pertains to both the legality and the commercial soundness of these activities. In order to ensure proper supervision, the board of directors must report regularly on its activities (at least four times a year, § 90 AktG). If necessary, the board of directors must inform the chairman of the supervisory board of any important developments in the company or its subsidiaries. The supervisory board may call a general meeting if the welfare of the company requires it (§ 111 III AktG). In addition, the board must give its consent before certain decisions can be taken (§ 111 IV 2 AktG).

[c]   The Board of Directors

The company's management and representative organ is the board of directors. Its members are elected by the supervisory board. The board of directors may consist of one or more persons (§ 76 II AktG). A company with a share capital of more than €3 million must have at least two directors, unless the memorandum of association provides otherwise. Only natural persons with full legal capacity may be board members (§ 76 III AktG). Persons convicted of certain offenses (e.g., in relation to bankruptcy) may not be appointed (§ 76 III AktG). The appointment is for a maximum period of five years (§ 84 I AktG) and is renewable. The same applies to the employment contract between the appointed persons and the company. It is one of the subject matters of such a contract to fix the remuneration and other terms of employment of board members. The law provides for special stipulations concerning the financial compensation of directors, such as salaries, profit-sharing, expense allowances, retirement, and pension plans (cf. § 87 AktG). The supervisory board may dismiss a member of the board of directors for cause (§ 84 III AktG), e.g., following a vote of no confidence of shareholders at a general meeting.

The management of the company is the sole responsibility of the board (§ 76 I AktG). As a corollary, the board is not subject to any instructions from the general meeting (§ 119 II AktG). It represents the company in and out of court (§ 78 I AktG). The powers of the board to represent the company with regard to third parties are unlimited and may not be limited through special provisions of the memorandum. The ultra-vires doctrine does not apply in Germany.

In contrast, the internal powers of the board may be limited by the declared purpose of the company, the memorandum of association, the supervisory board and by certain resolutions of the general meeting. The most important limitation is that the memorandum or the supervisory board may require certain decisions or transactions to be undertaken only with the consent of the supervisory board (§ 111 IV AktG). In addition, members of the board of directors have fiduciary duties toward the company that may limit the board's internal competence.

When managing the corporation, board members must apply the care of a diligent and prudent manager (§ 93 I AktG). Members of the board of directors who fail to fulfill their duties are jointly and severally liable for any damages caused to the company (§ 93 II, III AktG). The supervisory board enforces such a claim, but under certain conditions creditors have this right as well (§ 93 V AktG).

[9] The Law of Affiliated Companies

[a] Structure of the German Law of Affiliated Companies

Sections 291 et seq. AktG regulate affiliated companies by establishing a system of responsibilities and liabilities for the controlling company. This system is built on the definitions of "dependency" (*Abhängigkeit*, §§ 15, 17 AktG) of one company on another and of the group of companies (§§ 15, 18 AktG), the dependent company being under the unitary management of the controlling company. The law of affiliated companies provides primarily for the protection of creditors and of minority shareholders of the dependent company. The law covers two forms of control: control on the basis of an agreement between two companies (§§ 291 et seq. AktG – *Vertragskonzern* or "contractual group"), and control based on the *de facto* exercise of management power without such an agreement (§§ 311 et seq. AktG – *faktischer Konzern* or "*de facto* group").

[b] Contractual Groups

In cases of control on the basis of an agreement, the controlling company is entitled to give instructions to the board of directors of the dependent company (§ 308 I AktG). In turn, the board of directors of the dependent company is authorized to follow those instructions, even if they work to the disadvantage of their own company (§ 308 II AktG). While the agreement gives the dominating firm the right to place the dependent firm under its management, the directors of the controlling enterprise are liable for any damages caused to the affiliated company as a result of their instructions (§§ 308, 309 II AktG). The controlling company is liable for any annual deficit of the affiliated company (§ 302 AktG).

In addition to the obligations and liabilities of the members of the board of directors, the interests of minority shareholders are taken into account through heightened requirements as to the conclusion, amendment or termination of a contract of domination or a contract to transfer profits (§§ 293–299 AktG). If such agreements are concluded, outside shareholders have the option, guaranteed by an appropriate recurring compensation payment, to remain in the company (§ 304 AktG) or to leave it with an adequate indemnity for the takeover (§ 305 AktG). Because of the disadvantages for minority shareholders of the controlling company arising from these obligations, § 293 II AktG requires the consent of the shareholders' meeting of the dominating company for the conclusion of such an agreement.

[c]   De facto Groups

When drafting the Stock Company Act of 1965, it was the legislature's intention to prohibit all other forms of active control of another company. The draft therefore required that the exercise of group management power is permissible only after the conclusion of a contract of domination. Yet, it turned out to be impossible to reach this goal and to ban the non-contractual exercise of management power in a group. Instead, the law provided for strict liability of the *de facto* dominating company. However, this regulation demonstrates all the problems arising from compromises diluting the original legislative concept.

The law provides that the dependent company must not be subject to instructions or measures that would have a disadvantageous effect on the dependent company (§ 311 I AktG), unless it is compensated immediately or at the end of the fiscal year (§ 311 II AktG). If the disadvantage is not compensated by the controlling company, the dependent company and its shareholders are entitled to claim damages from the controlling company and its management (§ 317 AktG). In order not to make this system of compensation ineffective right from the outset, the law provides for increased disclosure and verification of dependency relationships: the dependent company's board of directors must deliver a report on the relationships with affiliated companies (§§ 312 et seq. AktG – *Abhängigkeitsbericht*). If the disadvantageous measures are not indicated in the report, the dependent company's board of directors is liable to the company as well as to its shareholders for any damages caused (§ 318 AktG).

It is doubtful whether the legislature did succeed in putting the dependent company in the same position as if it were independent. Thus, the legal arrangements for *de facto* groups in stock corporation law are widely regarded as being in need of reform.

[10]   Dissolution and Liquidation

Section 262 AktG lists the causes of a dissolution of the company: the expiration of the period determined in the memorandum of association, a special resolution of the general meeting of shareholders by a qualified majority of at least three-fourth of the share capital represented at the meeting, the opening of bankruptcy proceedings and a final court decision declaring the memorandum of association unlawful (§ 399 FamFG). On request of a competent agency of the federal state in which the corporation has its seat, a court may dissolve a company if it endangers public welfare (§ 396 AktG). In case of a total lack of funds, certain public authorities (e.g., the tax office) may request that the court dissolve the company (§ 394 FamFG). The dissolution has to be entered into the commercial register (§ 263 AktG).

Following the dissolution, liquidation takes place unless bankruptcy proceedings have already been initiated. Usually, the directors are appointed liquidators. They complete current transactions, collect outstanding claims, liquidate the assets and settle the company's liabilities. The liquidators give public notice of the dissolution and request creditors to register their claims against the company (§ 267 AktG). One year after the public announcement of the liquidation, the liquidators may distribute the remaining assets to the shareholders in proportion to no-par-value shares to the capital stock or – in the case of shares with a nominal value – in proportion to the par value of their shares (§ 272 I AktG). The company is terminated and loses its legal capacity when the liquidators have distributed all assets and have reported this fact to the commercial register (§§ 273 AktG, 6 II, 31 II HGB).

[B]   The Public Limited Partnership by Shares

The public limited partnership by shares (*Kommanditgesellschaft auf Aktien* – KGaA) is a combination of a limited partnership (*Kommanditgesellschaft*, – KG) and a stock company (§ 278 AktG). Like the stock company, it is a corporation with a fixed capital stock divided into transferable shares. In contrast to the stock company, however, there are two groups of members: the general partners (*Komplementäre*) and the shareholders (*Kommanditaktionäre*). The general partners have the power to direct the company's business. At the same time they are subject to unlimited liability towards creditors of the company, whereas the shareholders are not personally liable for the company's debts (§§ 278 III, 1, 54 I AktG). This legal model can be altered. The courts have recognized the possibility that a corporation may participate as a general partner (GmbH & Co. KGaA or AG & Co. KGaA).

Section 278 II AktG provides that the law of general partnerships (§§ 105 et seq. HGB) applies to the general partners, including their rights and duties with regard to shareholders (*see infra* §5.03[C][2]). All other matters (e.g., the rights and duties of the shareholders) are regulated in the same manner as for stock companies (§ 278 III AktG). Because the public limited partnership by shares is rarely used in practice, this survey of the law of business associations omits a more detailed description of it.

[C]   The Limited Liability Company

[1]   Introduction

[a]   The Applicable Law

The limited liability company or private limited company (*Gesellschaft mit beschränkter Haftung*) is governed by the Limited Liability Company Act (*Gesetz betreffend die Gesellschaften mit beschränkter Haftung* – GmbHG) of April 20, 1892, as amended on July 17, 2017. The limited liability company is a German invention without any precedent in history. The objective was to fill a gap between the existing types of associations, the stock company on the one hand and the partnership on the other hand. Other countries have adopted this model and enacted laws similar to the German provisions. The Limited Liability Company Act does not regulate all questions that arise in connection with the limited liability company. Some rules can also be found in the Stock Company Act or the Commercial Code. Since the limited liability company is a commercial association within the meaning of the Commercial Code (§§ 13 III GmbHG, 6 HGB), its rules referring to commercial associations apply to the limited liability company as well. Beyond that, other statutory provisions affect the law of the limited liability company, especially the Law Regulating the Conversion of Companies (*Umwandlungsgesetz* of 1994) and the several Co-determination Acts (*see infra* §5.02[D]).

The statutory law of *Gesellschaften mit beschränkter Haftung* has not changed much throughout the last century. Apart from several small reforms to the GmbHG which were enacted to implement EU directives into German, law the first major amendment was the Act of July 4, 1980, which came into force on January 1, 1981. The Amendment of 1980 increased the minimum share capital from DM 20,000 to DM 50,000. It allowed the incorporation of limited liability companies by a single shareholder ("One-person GmbH"; § 1 GmbHG). Last but not least, it adapted statutory law to judge-made law by introducing special rules for the preservation of share capital (§§ 32a, 32b GmbHG). The second major amendment was the Act of October 23, 2008 (MoMiG). Among other things, it allows the drawing up of a memorandum of association without a notarized form if certain requirements are fulfilled and provides for the establishment of the Unternehmergesellschaft (haftungsbeschränkt) (*see supra* §5.01[A][1]) which is a sub-type of the GmbH. The Act modified the case law regarding the circumvention of the rules on contributions in kind. It introduced the possibility of a bona fide acquisition of a share and allowed cash pooling. The above mentioned §§ 32a, 32b GmbHG and the managing director's insolvency filing obligation were transferred from the GmbHG into to the insolvency act.

The internal organization of the GmbH may, to a large extent, be structured as to suit the particular needs of its shareholders. However, the courts, being more flexible than the legislature in adapting the law to practical experience, have developed several doctrines to limit both the freedom to form the articles and the exercise of rights conferred on individual shareholders by the memorandum of association. As in general corporate law, jurisprudence and scholarship have taken the leading role in the further development of the law of the limited liability company.

[b]   Some Characteristics of the GmbH

There is no statutory definition of the limited liability company. However, it can be defined as a company with legal capacity and a capital stock to which one or more shareholders contribute without being personally liable for the company's debts.

The formation of a limited liability company, including the contribution to the capital stock subscribed to by its shareholders, is less formalistic than that of a stock company. The same applies to the internal organizational structure of the GmbH. The company has only two legally required organs, i.e., the "meeting of shareholders" (*Gesellschafterversammlung*) and managing director(s) (*Geschäftsführer*). If not required by the Co-determination Acts (*see infra* §5.02[D]), the establishment of a supervisory board is not mandatory. From the outset, the GmbH may be formed as a one-person limited liability company.

Since the limited liability company is a legal entity, only the company's assets are available to satisfy its creditors (§ 13 II GmbHG). Another characteristic of the GmbH is its flexible structure: although it is neither a smaller version of the stock company nor a special case of a partnership, the memorandum of association may be shaped in a fashion that makes the limited liability company resemble either of these two models. Nevertheless, the statutory law of the limited liability company is guided by the concept of a personally structured corporation, i.e., a company based on the shareholders' close association with the common enterprise.

The procedure for joining and leaving the limited liability company resembles the law of partnerships more closely than the law of the stock company. However, contrary to the membership rights in a partnership, the shares of a GmbH are *ipso iure* transferable and inheritable (§ 15 I GmbHG), unless provided otherwise in the company's memorandum of association. Yet, in order to restrict the negotiability of limited liability shares, the transfer of such shares must be in notarized form (§ 15 III, IV GmbHG). Thus, a GmbH is not a corporate legal form suited to invite members of the public to subscribe to its shares. Accordingly, the GmbH has no access to the public capital markets (unless it issues debentures or bonds).

The limited liability company must have a minimum capital stock of €25,000 (§ 5 I GmbHG). However, only €12,500 have to be paid in prior to the company's registration; if the company is founded as a one-person-company, the founder has to provide security for any cash subscription not entirely paid in (§ 7 II GmbHG). To assure the contribution and preservation of the committed capital, the GmbHG provides a broad range of safeguards such as prohibitions against release, deferment and set-off (§ 19 II GmbHG) and safeguarding rules on contributions in kind (§§ 5 IV, 7 III, 19 IV, V GmbHG).

The law provides for the Unternehmergesellschaft (haftungsbeschränkt) [UG (haftungsbeschränkt)], if the founders want to establish a corporation with a smaller amount of minimum capital (§ 5a GmbHG). It suffices if the UG holds capital ranging between €1 and €24,999. If the capital is increased to €25,000 the UG is converted *ipso iure* into a GmbH (§ 5a V GmbHG). In order to protect creditors, contributions in kind are forbidden and the UG has to transfer 25 % of the net income of a year to the capital reserve. This reserve may only be used to cover losses or to carry out a capital increase from the company's funds (*Kapitalerhöhung aus Gesellschaftsmitteln*) which is the usual way to convert the UG into a GmbH. Apart from these peculiarities, all other provisions of the GmbHG apply to the UG.

The limited liability company and the UG can be established for any legitimate purpose, commercial or otherwise. However, enterprises in special branches of business, e.g., banks and insurance companies, may not be organized as limited liability companies or a UG. Whatever purpose the GmbH or UG pursue, they are always considered a commercial enterprise (*Handelsgesellschaft*) within the meaning of the Commercial Code (§§ 13 III GmbHG, 6 HGB).

[c]   *Appearance and Significance*

Since the introduction of the limited liability company, the number of corporations organized as GmbHs has grown steadily. Today, the limited liability company is the most widely used corporate form in Germany (*see supra* §5.01[A][1]). Due to its flexible structure, the GmbH serves the purposes of small or medium-sized corporations and family-held companies as well as those of big business enterprises (e.g., Robert Bosch GmbH).

The limited liability company and the UG are frequently used in combination with a commercial partnership in the form of a so-called "GmbH & Co. KG" resp. "UG & Co. KG." This kind of company is a limited partnership in which a limited liability company rather than a natural person occupies the position of the general partner. Since the limited liability company is liable for the debts of the partnership, the "GmbH & Co. KG" and the "UG & Co. KG" are, as a matter of fact, partnerships with limited liability. The shareholders of the GmbH/of the UG and the special partners in the limited partnership are usually the same persons. A large number of limited liability companies and UG are organized as one-person companies. About one third of all limited liability companies are dominated by another corporation.

[2]   The Incorporation of the Limited Liability Company

[a]   *Overview*

The incorporation of a limited liability company is governed by statutory law. It requires a contract (memorandum of association) between the founders in notarized form (§ 2 I GmbHG). The notarized form is dispensable if there are fewer than four founders and only one managing director and if the founders use the standardized memorandum of association provided for by the law (§ 2 Ia GmbHG). The capital must be fully subscribed upon formation of the company. Once at least one quarter of each share has been paid and further capital requirements have been met (§ 7 II GmbHG), the managing directors can apply for registration in the commercial register (§ 7 I GmbHG). Upon registration, the limited liability company acquires legal personality (*cf.* § 11 I GmbHG).

[b]   *The Founders*

The limited liability company may be formed by one or more founders. The founders and the subsequent shareholders may be natural or legal persons. Even general partnerships, limited partnerships or partnerships under the Civil Code can be founders. In contrast to many other countries, there is no limitation on the number of shareholders in Germany.

[c]   Contents of the Memorandum of Association and Its Amendments

The memorandum of association (*Gesellschaftsvertrag*) must state at least the company's firm name and registered office, the objectives of the enterprise, the amount of the share capital and the amount of each shareholder's contribution as well as any other obligation put upon the shareholders (§ 3 GmbHG):

– The company's firm name may either indicate the company's purpose or the name of a shareholder or any imaginative term or a combination of these variants. It must have a distinctive character and must not be misleading or confusing (§§ 18, 30 HGB). Moreover, it has to be clear that the name used is the name of the company, not of a sole trader. If a limited liability company succeeds the business of a sole trader or a partnership, the previous name can be taken over. In any case, the name must include the addition "with limited liability" ("*mit beschränkter Haftung*") or the abbreviation "GmbH" as a warning to creditors of the limit upon shareholders' liability (§ 4 GmbHG). The same applies *mutatis mutandis* to the UG ("*haftungsbeschränkt*") (§ 5a I GmbHG). A German subsidiary of a foreign company may comprise the name of the foreign parent company and the words "*Deutsche*" or other reference to Germany.
– The registered office must be determined in the memorandum of association. A change of the registered office within Germany is effected by an amendment to the memorandum of association and its entry in the commercial register.
– The share capital (*Stammkapital*) amounts to at least €25,000 (§ 5 I GmbHG). There is no limit on the maximum amount. The important function of the share capital is that of a liability basis in order to protect creditors. The level of share capital can be altered only by the strict procedure of an amendment to the memorandum of association.

The company's internal organization as well as the shareholders' rights and duties may be structured by the shareholders in the memorandum. In practice, the memorandum usually sets out supplementary and detailed rules referring to shareholders' accessory rights and obligations (e.g., the right to benefits in kind, purchase rights or non-competition clauses), the obligation to make an additional contribution, representation and management of the company, shareholders' meetings and resolutions, preference rights of individual shareholders, the transfer of shares, the distribution of net profits and a supervisory or advisory board.

An amendment to the memorandum of association requires a special resolution of the shareholders' meeting by a qualified majority of at least three-fourth of the share capital represented at the meeting (§ 53 I GmbHG). Amendments to the memorandum of association must be notarized (§ 53 II GmbHG) and registered in the commercial register (§ 54 GmbHG).

[d]   *The Share Capital Contributions*

There are strict rules to ensure that the limited liability company obtains the required share capital (§§ 7, 9, 19 GmbHG). Each founder subscribes to one or more shares on which a capital contributions has to be submitted (§ 14 GmbHG). The sum of the share capital contributions must correspond to the amount of the initial share capital (§ 5 III 2 GmbHG).

Shareholders' contributions may be paid in cash (*Bargründung*) or be made in kind (*Sachgründung*). A shareholder may not set off a contribution (§ 19 II 2 GmbHG). The company may not waive a shareholder's obligation to contribute (§ 19 II 1 GmbHG).

Transferable assets may constitute payments in kind (e.g., land, buildings, know-how, business, patents, copyrights or trademarks). If subscriptions are paid in kind, stricter provisions apply. The memorandum of association must clearly specify the items to be contributed by the shareholder and state their value. The founders have to produce a report (*Sachgründungsbericht*) in which they substantiate whether the value of contributions is equivalent to the amount stated in the memorandum. If a business is transferred as payment, the balance sheets of its last two financial years must be added to the report (§ 5 IV GmbHG). If the value of the consideration in kind is less than the value stated in the memorandum, the respective shareholder is liable to pay the difference (§ 9 GmbHG).

[e]   *The Application for Registration*

In order to apply for registration, the entire share capital must be subscribed to by the founders. At least 25% of the nominal value of each share capital contribution in cash must be paid in; contributions in kind must be submitted in full (§ 7 III GmbHG). In the aggregate, the contributed share capital must amount to at least €12,500 (§ 7 II GmbHG). Managing directors must be elected by a resolution of the founders, unless they are already appointed by the memorandum of association (§ 6 III 2 GmbHG).

Managers have to submit the application for registration and certain documents (e.g., the memorandum of association, the signatures of the managing directors and their power of representation, a list of shareholders and their subscriptions, a domestic address of the company) to the commercial register (§ 8 GmbHG). The registrar ensures that the application for registration complies with statutory provisions (§ 9c GmbHG). He or she verifies the admissibility of the company's name by requesting that the Chamber of Industry and Commerce (*Industrie- und Handelskammer*) reviews the proposed name (§§ 6, 18 HGB, 380 FamFG). The registrar examines, in particular, the memorandum of association, the directors' appointment and the properly effected minimum capitalization. In the case of contributions in kind, the registrar reviews the valuation of these subscriptions.

[f]   Defective Incorporation

Once registered, a court may declare the incorporation void only on grounds of grave error (§ 75 GmbHG), e.g., if the articles of association do not contain any provisions regarding the amount of the share capital or regarding the object of the company, or if the provisions set out in the articles of association on the object of the company are null and void.

[g]   The Pre-incorporation Status of the GmbH

There are several steps on the way to incorporation of a limited liability company. Prior to the conclusion of the memorandum of association, the potential founders form either a partnership under the Civil Code or a general partnership (*Vorgründungsgesell-schaft*), depending on whether or not the intended company will run a commercial business as defined by §§ 1–3 of the Commercial Code (*Handelsgesetzbuch* – HGB). The partners are personally liable for the debts incurred during this period.

For the period between the adoption of the memorandum of association and the registration in the commercial register, the limited liability company is called "pre-incorporation company" (*Vorgesellschaft*). The legal nature of this *Vorgesellschaft* is a particular form of partnership. Its objective is to obtain the registration of the limited liability company. Thus, the rules of the limited liability company apply to this partnership as long as these rules do not require legal personality. However, persons acting on behalf of the company before registration are personally, jointly and severally, liable to creditors (§ 11 II GmbHG). In addition, the founders are liable to the full extent of their subscribed shares. The rights and obligations of the pre-incorporation company pass on to the limited liability company by universal succession. Hence, the liability of persons acting for the *Vorgesellschaft* ends upon registration. Consequently, the liability of founders and the liability under § 11 II GmbHG are of importance only in cases where an incorporation is ultimately not obtained.

In addition to these rules, there are special provisions for the protection of creditors and of the public, such as the liability of founders in cases of a breach of their duties (*cf.* § 9a GmbHG).

*[3]   **Shares***

[a]   Shares Versus Share Capital Contributions

When describing the legal position of the shareholders, the GmbHG uses two slightly different terms: "share" (*Geschäftsanteil*) means the sum of the rights and duties inherent in the position of a shareholder; it represents the membership in the company. For each share the member must submit a "share capital contribution" (*Stammeinlage*) (§ 14 GmbHG).

Rights and obligations are determined, first, by the memorandum of association and, second, by statutory law. Statutory law does not provide for a share certificate or a share register, but the individual shareholder may obtain a share certificate. This certificate is merely a documentary proof. It is not a security and thus not transferable as such.

As previously described (*see supra* §5.02[A][7][a]) with regard to the stock company, there are two kinds of rights inherent in a share: property rights (e.g., right to dividend, § 29 GmbHG) and administrative rights (e.g., voting rights in the shareholders' meeting as well as information and minority rights, §§ 48, 51a, 51b GmbHG). Beyond these statutory rights, the memorandum of association may allocate preferred shares as long as these shares comply with statutory law. Preferred shares carry preferential rights, e.g., the right to receive a fixed rate of dividend or a preferential dividend (§ 29 III 2 GmbHG), the right to appoint one or all managing directors or members of an optional supervisory board, the right to be appointed as managing director or a priority for the repayment of capital in the event of winding-up. The preferential rights attached to preferred shares must be distinguished from special privileges granted to shareholders individually.

[b]   The Transfer of Shares

Shares (but not share certificates) are transferable and inheritable (§ 15 I GmbHG). German civil law distinguishes between the actual contract transferring the property in the share and the underlying contract creating the obligation to do so. Thus two contracts are necessary for the proper and effective transfer of shares. Both need to be notarized (§ 15 III, IV GmbHG). Upon completion of the transfer, the title to the share and the rights and duties connected to it pass to the transferee. § 16 III 1 GmbHG provides for the possibility of a bona fide acquisition of a share if the transferor is (wrongfully) registered in the list of shareholders; the true owner can only raise a limited number of objections (§ 16 III 2–4 GmbHG).

In practice, the memorandum of association often provides that the transfer must be approved by a certain shareholder or at the shareholders' meeting (§ 15 V GmbHG). It is also permitted to exclude the right to transfer the shares. The memorandum of association may provide for a right of first refusal in favor of existing shareholders or may define standards for the qualification of potential shareholders. Thus, it is possible to control the shareholders' composition and in so doing so to stabilize the influence of a family or group of founders on the company. After any transfer or amendment of a share, the managing directors must file a list of all shareholders and the amount of their shares with the commercial register (§ 40 GmbHG).

[4]   Share Capital Maintenance, Capital Increase and Capital Reduction

[a]   Share Capital Maintenance

The provisions to guarantee the payment of the share capital contributions (§§ 7, 9, 19 GmbHG) are complemented by provisions to ensure the maintenance of the share capital and by provisions to protect creditors (*principle of the effective maintenance of the share capital*). The company may neither repay a share capital contribution nor distribute the company's assets to the shareholders (§ 30 I GmbHG), if such a payment or distribution endangers the amount of share capital fixed in the memorandum of association. Shareholders receiving payments contrary to § 30 GmbHG in bad faith are required to refund the amount (§ 31 I GmbHG). In the event that a refund cannot be obtained, all shareholders are liable in proportion to their shares (§ 31 III GmbHG). Loans given to a company instead of equity capital are considered to be subordinated loans in the case of a bankruptcy of the company (§ 39 I no. 5, IV, V InsO).

Pursuant to § 33 GmbHG, the limited liability company may acquire its own shares only if the entire contributions have been paid in and if the payment to purchase the shares does not endanger the amount of the share capital or the capital reserve.

[b] The Capital Increase of Share Capital Against Contributions

The share capital can be increased only by an amendment to the memorandum of association and allotment of new shares to each existing shareholder and/or new shareholders (§ 55 II GmbHG). The statutory law on capital increase (§§ 55 et seq. GmbHG) generally refers to the rules of the incorporation (*see supra* §5.02[C][2][c] and §5.02[C][4][a]). To preserve the ownership structure of companies, new shares must first be offered to existing shareholders in proportion to the nominal value of their share capital (pre-emptive right or *Bezugsrecht*). Pre-emption rights may (similar to the provisions of the stock company, *see supra* §5.02[A][5][a]) be wholly or partly excluded by a special resolution of the shareholders' meeting. A share capital increase is valid and takes legal effect as soon as it has been registered (§ 57 GmbHG).

[c] The Capital Increase from the Company's Funds

By special resolution, the shareholders' meeting may convert (parts of) the "share premium account" (i.e., capital surplus) or the "revaluation reserve" (i.e., retained earnings) into share capital (§§ 57c et seq. GmbHG). Such capital increase must be based on a properly audited and certified recent balance sheet of recent date (§§ 57e, 57f GmbHG). The share capital increase is effective as soon as it has been registered (§ 54 III GmbHG). Each shareholder has a mandatory pre-emptive right to the new shares (§ 57j GmbHG).

[d] Reduction of Share Capital

The amount of share capital fixed in the memorandum may be reduced. However, it may not fall below the minimum stock capital of €25,000, unless it is combined with a parallel capital increase against contributions in cash (§ 58a IV GmbHG). The reduction of capital is effected by an amendment to the memorandum of association. Capital reduction may take two different forms, the ordinary capital reduction (§ 58 GmbHG) and the simplified capital reduction (§§ 58a et seq. GmbHG):

The ordinary capital reduction may serve the purposes of restoration of financial soundness, the distribution of committed assets of the company among the shareholders, or the establishment of a free reserve. The managing directors must publicly announce the capital reduction. Creditors opposing the capital reduction can demand immediate payment of their claims or apply for a security respectively. One year after the public announcement, the managing directors apply to the local commercial register for registration of the reduction and have to affirm that the rights of all creditors opposing the capital reduction have been met. The capital reduction is effective as soon as it has been registered (§ 54 III GmbHG).

In contrast to the ordinary capital reduction, the simplified capital reduction is allowed for the restoration of financial soundness only (§ 58a GmbHG) or for the establishment of a free capital reserve, so long as it does not exceed 10% of the share capital (§ 58b II GmbHG). It is only permissible if certain other (reserve) funds have been used to cover losses (§ 58a II GmbHG). The procedure for a simplified capital reduction resembles, for the most part, that of an ordinary capital reduction but with one important exception: as previously stated, assets remain untouched and payments to shareholders are forbidden (§ 58b GmbHG). Creditors are thus less endangered and may not apply for a security.

[5]   *The Membership*

The shareholder acquires membership in the company either as a founder, by subscribing to a share, or by a transfer or acquisition of shares subsequent to the incorporation (e.g., purchase or devolution by inheritance). In the case of a transfer or acquisition of shares subsequent to the incorporation, the new shareholder may only exercise the relevant rights if he or she was previously registered in the list of shareholders transmitted to the commercial register (§§ 16 I 1, 40 GmbHG) or if this registration is made immediately after the exercise of the right (§ 16 I 2 GmbHG). Transferee and transferor are jointly and severally liable for any overdue contributions at the time of notification (§ 16 II GmbHG).

In the event of the death of a shareholder, the heir or the heirs are entitled to the share of the deceased shareholder. If several heirs inherit the share, it belongs to them in joint ownership until partition occurs according to the last will of the deceased or to statutory provisions.

The memorandum of association may provide for the redemption of shares (*Einziehung* or *Amortisation*) by shareholders' resolution (§ 34 GmbHG). Compulsory redemption requires that the provisions in the memorandum of association precisely stipulate the conditions for the redemption. Its effect is that the redeemed share accrues to the remaining shareholders. The memorandum of association usually provides that a withdrawing shareholder (or his heir or heirs) receives a lump-sum payment corresponding to the value of the share at the moment of his withdrawal.

Although the GmbHG only mentions redemption as a cause for termination of the membership, case law and scholars hold that a shareholder may terminate his or her membership for cause, e.g., a shareholder is not bound to tolerate neither a total change of the company's objectives nor a takeover of the company by another enterprise without his or her consent. In practice, memoranda of association often stipulate that a shareholder may terminate his or her membership without cause.

[6] The Administration of the Company

The statutory organs of the company are the managing director(s) and the meeting of shareholders. The extent of the organs' power depends on the memorandum of association.

[a] Management

The company must have one or more managing directors. In contrast to the general partnership or the limited partnership, managing directors do not need to be share-holders of the company (§ 6 III GmbHG). Only natural persons with full legal capacity can be appointed (§ 6 II 1 GmbHG). Persons convicted of certain offenses (e.g., in relation to bankruptcy) may not be appointed (§ 6 II 2 GmbHG). In practice, most managing directors of limited liability companies are shareholders rather than third parties. The managing directors jointly represent the company in and out of court (§ 35 I 1 GmbHG). The law provides that the directors manage the business jointly (*Gesamtvertretung*), but the memorandum of association may grant managing direc-tors the right to act alone (*Einzelvertretung*) (§ 35 II 1 GmbHG). Shareholders can impose internal restrictions on the ability to act on behalf of the company (§ 37 I GmbHG). However, such limitations are not effective against third parties (§ 37 II GmbHG).

Managing directors are obligated to ensure that proper accounting records are kept (§ 41 GmbHG) and they have to submit the financial statements to the sharehold-ers' meeting (§ 42a GmbHG). They are required to call a shareholders' meeting at least once a year. Furthermore, they must provide information on the company's affairs to shareholders. In the case of bankruptcy, managing directors are required to file a petition for the commencement of bankruptcy proceedings (§ 15a InsO).

Managing directors are nominated by the memorandum of association (§ 6 III 2 GmbHG) or appointed by a resolution passed in the shareholders' meeting (§§ 6 III 2, 46 no. 5 GmbHG). The memorandum of association may set out special requirements with regard to the appointment of managing directors (e.g., additional standards regarding the qualifications of managing directors, age limits). If the company has a supervisory board pursuant to the Co-determination Acts (*see infra* §5.02[D]), it is that board that is responsible for the appointment of the management.

Unless otherwise provided in the memorandum, managing directors are subject to instructions from the shareholders' meeting (§ 37 I GmbHG). Thus, a majority of shareholders can determine the business of the company. Therefore the limited liability company is considered the most appropriate corporate legal form of a subsidiary.

As previously stated, there are two legal relationships between the company and the managing directors: first, a corporate law relationship through their appointment or dismissal and, second, a relationship governed by labor law in relation to their employment contracts. The dismissal of a managing director requires a resolution of the shareholders' meeting (§§ 38 I, 46 no. 5 GmbHG). In practice, the memorandum of association often provides that managing directors may only be dismissed for good and sufficient cause (§ 38 II GmbHG).

Managing directors are responsible to the company for the diligent performance of their duties and are liable for any damages caused (§ 43 GmbHG), unless they acted upon instruction of the shareholders' meeting. Managing directors have fiduciary duties toward the company. Thus, for example, they are forbidden to divert corporate business opportunities for their personal benefit.

Managing directors are liable to third parties only in specific circumstances: first, during the pre-incorporation period; second, in cases of general tort liability for negligence and fraud; and third, in cases in which they breach certain duties associated with the negotiation and conclusion of a contract between the company and third parties (pre-contractual liability or *culpa in contrahendo*).

Recently, courts decided several cases on the issue of general liability of directors for tax fraud and similar misconduct under criminal law. These courts held that such personal liability does apply to directors in the exercise of their functions. Thus, the corporate veil does not protect managers in criminal or tax law proceedings.

Apart from the managing directors, other officers (especially agents within the meaning of the Commercial Code) may be entitled to act on the company's behalf.

[b]   Shareholders' Meeting

By statutory law, the shareholders' meeting is the most important organ. It must be called by the management at least once a year. When calling it, at least one week's written notice must be given (§ 51 I GmbHG). As pointed out previously (*see supra* §5.02[C][6][a]), the shareholders' meeting appoints, supervises, and dismisses the managing directors (§ 46 no. 5 GmbHG). It decides on amendments to the memorandum of association (§ 53 GmbHG), on the approval of annual financial statements, and on the distribution of profits (§ 46 no. 1 GmbHG).

The resolutions need to be passed by a majority of votes cast unless the memorandum of association provides otherwise (§ 47 I GmbHG). Decisions on the basic legal structure or on the purpose of the company, on an amendment to the memorandum of association, on a capital increase or reduction, on an amalgamation or a merger, on a conversion into a stock company or a public limited partnership by shares (regulated by the Conversion Act 1994) and on the dissolution of the company have to be passed by a qualified majority of three quarters of the votes (§§ 53, 60 I no. 2 GmbHG).

The shareholders' resolutions do not need to be notarized, unless the resolution alters the memorandum of association (§ 53 II GmbHG). It is possible to assent to certain decisions by written agreements outside the shareholders' meeting (§ 48 II GmbHG). In the case of a one-person GmbH, resolutions are passed by drawing up and signing minutes (§ 48 III GmbHG).

Each Euro of a share entitles a shareholder to one vote (§ 47 II GmbHG), unless otherwise provided in the memorandum of association (e.g., multiple voting rights). Shareholders may not vote in the resolution on their own discharge from a liability claim or on legal transactions relating to them (§ 47 IV GmbHG). A shareholder may be represented at the meeting by use of a proxy in text form (§ 47 III GmbHG).

There are no specific statutory provisions relating to errors and defects in shareholders' resolutions. The prevailing opinion is that the provisions of §§ 241 et seq. AktG should apply *mutatis mutandis*. Thus, every opposing shareholder may contest the resolution in court, in order to obtain a judgment declaring it void or invalid.

[c] *Supervision of the Management by Supervisory or Advisory Boards*

There is no statutory obligation for a GmbH to set up a supervisory board (*Aufsichtsrat*), unless the Co-determination Acts apply (*see infra* §5.02[D]). In the latter case, the supervisory board of a limited liability company has the same authority as the supervisory board of a stock company.

Nonetheless, a company may establish a supervisory board by a specific provision to this effect in the memorandum of association. In case of an optional supervisory board, the law governing stock companies applies *mutatis mutandis* (§ 52 GmbHG).

Another possibility is the creation of an advisory board (*Beirat*). The shareholders are free to decide which functions are given to this board. In practice, advisory boards can be found particularly in family companies where members come from different branches of the family.

[7] **Liability of the Company and the Shareholders**

From the creditor's perspective, the most important question is who is liable for debts? The company as a legal entity? Its managing directors, or its shareholders? The concept of a corporate veil implies that in principle, only the assets of the company are available to satisfy claims of company's creditors. Once the limited liability company is registered in the commercial register, shareholders are not personally liable for the company's debts (§ 13 II GmbHG). However, there are some exceptions to this rule:

– If a shareholder fails to pay in his or her entire subscription and it cannot be recovered from him or her, then the remaining shareholders are liable for the difference (§ 24 GmbHG).
– The shareholders have to put up additional capital if the memorandum of association so provides (§§ 26 et seq. GmbHG).
– A shareholder-manager may be personally liable to creditors who would not have entered in a contract with the company if a petition in bankruptcy would have been filed in due time (§ 823 II BGB or § 64 GmbHG).
– According to case law, the shareholders may be personally liable if they act *contra bonos mores*, thereby depriving the company of the assets necessary to repay its debts and causing its insolvency (*existenzvernichtender Eingriff*).

– In case of severe abuse of the corporate veil, i.e., commingling of private and company assets or obvious undercapitalization, courts will "pierce" the corporate veil and hold a shareholder personally liable (*Durchgriffshaftung*). The same applies to cases in which the dominant shareholder has exercised his/her management power over a GmbH in an abusive way to the detriment of the company's capital.

– Based on the principle of *culpa in contrahendo* ("pre-contractual liability"), a shareholder-manager is liable to a company's creditor if he or she, while acting for the company, has personally obtained and betrayed the creditors' trust by false representations.

– Finally, the courts have held that a shareholder-manager may be held personally liable if he or she failed to prevent damage to third parties while internally organizing the company.

[8]   Accounting

The provisions of the Commercial Code (§§ 264 et seq. HGB) about annual financial reporting are applicable to the limited liability company as well. Managing directors draw up the annual balance sheet (*Bilanz*), the statement of revenues and losses (*Gewinn- und Verlustrechnung*) and the annual report (*Anhang*) of the company. They must submit properly audited and certified accounts and the annual report to the shareholders without undue delay (§ 42a GmbHG). If the limited liability company is a "small corporation" within the meaning of § 267 HGB, there is no obligation to get the annual financial statements audited by an independent certified public accountant (§ 316 I HGB); the annual financial statements have to be published according to the §§ 325 et seq. HGB). Shareholders adopt the annual financial statements (§ 46 no. 1 GmbHG) and decide about the distribution of profits.

[9]   Dissolution and Liquidation

§ 60 et seq. GmbHG set forth the causes of the (compulsory) dissolution and the requirements of liquidation. Both dissolution and liquidation are regulated in a similar manner as for stock companies (*see supra* §5.02[A][10]).

[D]   Co-determination

In order to secure a certain participation and influence of the employees in a company, German law provides for three different forms of co-determination (*Mitbestimmung*) in the supervisory board of a company:

[1]   The Co-determination Act of 1976

The Co-determination Act (*Mitbestimmungsgesetz* – MitbestG) of 1976, as amended on April 24, 2015, applies to all corporations (stock companies, limited liability companies, public limited partnerships by shares and registered cooperatives) which are not regulated by the Coal and Steel Co-determination Act of 1951 (*see infra* §5.02[D][2]) and which employ more than 2,000 employees, including the employees of affiliated companies (§ 5 MitbestG). The law provides that employees elect 50% of the supervisory board members (§ 7 MitbestG). The board consists of twelve, sixteen, or twenty members depending on the number of employees of the company (i.e., less than 10,000, between 10,000 and 20,000 or more than 20,000). The chairperson, usually appointed by the shareholders, has two votes (§ 29 II MitbestG), whereas all other members of the board have a single vote.

Furthermore, the employees elect one member (*Arbeitsdirektor*) of the board of directors of a stock company, and one managing director of a limited liability company respectively (§ 33 MitbestG). In public limited partnerships by shares, there is no *Arbeitsdirektor* because the management of this type of corporation is personally, jointly and severally, liable for the company's debts.

[2]   The Co-determination with Regard to Coal and Steel Companies

The Coal and Steel Co-determination Act of 1951 (*Montanmitbestimmungsgesetz* – MontanMitbestG), as amended on April 24, 2015, applies to stock companies or limited liability companies of the coal and steel industries which employ more than 1,000 employees (§ 1 II MontanMitbestG). The supervisory board has eleven, fifteen or twenty-one members depending on the total share capital (§§ 4, 9 MontanMitbestG). Shareholders and employees elect 50% of the members, who in turn elect the chairperson. Because of the parity the members of the supervisory board have to agree on a neutral person as a chairperson. In addition to this, employees also elect one director (*Arbeitsdirektor*; § 13 MontanMitbestG).

The Co-determination of coal and steel workers supplementary Act of 1956 (*Montanmitbestimmungsergänzungsgesetz* – MontanMitbestGErgG), as amended on April 24, 2015, covers companies that are not affected by the Coal and Steel Co-determination Act of 1951 but which control one or more companies in which the MontanMitbestG applies (e.g., groups, holding companies of mining companies). Its supervisory board consists of fifteen or twenty-one members depending on the total share capital (§ 5 MontanMitbestGErgG), with 50% shareholder representatives, 50% employee representatives and one additional member. The employees also elect one director (*Arbeitsdirektor)* (*cf.* § 13 MontanMitbestGErgG).

[3]   The Employees' Representation and Co-determination Act of 1952

In companies which are not subject to the above two Acts (*see supra* §5.02[D][1] and [2]) and which employ more than 500 persons, one third of the supervisory board members must be employee representatives, *see* § 4 of the Act on the one-third participation of employees in the Supervisory Board of 2004 (*Drittelbeteiligungsgesetz* – DrittelbG), as amended on April 24, 2015.

§5.03   PARTNERSHIPS

[A]   In General

German law provides for several different kinds of partnership, which may be divided into two general categories: (i) commercial partnerships (i.e., general partnerships, limited partnerships and "dormant" partnerships) which carry on commercial activities as defined by §§ 1 et seq. of the Commercial Code; (ii) non-commercial partnerships (i.e., partnerships under the Civil Code and non-trading partnerships under the Partnership Act of 1994) which serve all other purposes. Sections 705 et seq. BGB apply to non-commercial partnerships. Commercial partnerships are governed by §§ 105 et seq. HGB; the rules generally applicable to associations (mainly §§ 705 et seq. BGB) govern particular matters on which the Commercial Code does not provide specific provisions.

[B]   Non-commercial Partnerships

[1]   *Partnership under the Civil Code*

The partnership under the Civil Code (*BGB-Gesellschaft*) is the basic form of all partnerships. Thus, its law serves to supplement the more specific provisions governing the other legal forms of partnerships (*see infra* §5.03[B][2] and §5.03[C]).

[a]   *The Partnership Agreement and Its Contents*

The partnership under the Civil Code is established by a contract between partners (§ 705 BGB) who can be natural or legal persons. A notarized contract is only necessary if real property is contributed (§§ 311b II, 925 BGB). The partners must agree on a common purpose pursued by the partnership, such as building and construction (so-called *Arbeitsgemeinschaft* – ARGE) or an underwriting syndicate (*Emissionskonsortium*). Any legal common purpose except the operation of a commercial business is permitted. If several partners operate a commercial business they automatically (§ 123 II HGB) qualify as a general partnership (OHG).

Partners are free to decide which matters shall be regulated by the partnership agreement (principle of freedom of contract). The agreement may be amended by unanimous decision, unless the partners have agreed on majority voting in advance. However, this rule is only applicable to operations in the ordinary course of business or to those decisions explicitly mentioned in the partnership contract. Unlike partnerships operating a commercial business (*see infra* §5.03[C]), a partnership under the Civil Code may be structured and operated as a purely internal partnership. In respect to his or her relationships both to the partnership and to the individual partners, each partner is bound by a general duty of loyalty.

Subject to the specifications in the partnership agreement, partners may make contributions in cash, in kind or by rendering personal services (§§ 705, 706 III BGB). In the absence of any agreement to the contrary, the law provides for equal contributions (§ 706 BGB). A subsequent increase of the original contribution is only permissible with the consent of all partners (§ 707 BGB).

[b]   Legal Nature, Liability and Assets

The partnership has only a partial legal personality and, hence, no corporate organization. The partners are personally, jointly and severally, liable to the partnership's creditors. As the partners' liability is accessory to the partnership's liability, each partner may be sued directly for the full amount in dispute (by analogy with § 128 HGB). The personal liability of the partners may be excluded only by a formal agreement with the creditors.

The assets belong to the partners in joint ownership (*Gesamthandsgemeinschaft*, § 719 BGB). The principle of joint ownership means the holding of property by two or more persons not in distinct shares but jointly, each having an identical interest in the undivided whole. An asset may be transferred only with the consent of all partners which can be given either in the partnership agreement (e.g., by authorizing the management to dispose of assets) or in a general meeting of the partners.

[c]   Management

The law provides that partners manage the business jointly (*Gesamtgeschäftsführung*, § 709 BGB), but the partners may agree to entrust one or more partners with the management of the partnership (*Einzelgeschäftsführung, cf.* § 710 BGB). Third persons may not be managers. The partners agree on the scope of authority of the management. If the partnership contract does not provide otherwise, the authority to manage the business is combined with the authority to represent the partners (*Vertretung*, § 714 BGB).

The partners representing the partnership act in the name of and for the account of all partners. The power to represent the partners in joint matters of the partnership may be restricted. While the personal liability of the partners may be eliminated by agreement with the creditors, it can neither be excluded by limiting a partner's power of representation nor by the partnership agreement. Partners acting beyond their power of representation are liable to the creditors (§§ 177, 179 BGB).

[d]   The Distribution of Profits and Losses

Profits and losses are distributed in proportion to the number of partners (§ 722 BGB), unless otherwise agreed upon by the partners (e.g., a distribution proportionally to the amount of each partner's contribution).

[e]   The Dissolution

Sections 723 et seq. BGB set forth the causes of a dissolution of the partnership: notice of termination by a partner, death of a partner, bankruptcy proceedings against a partner or a dissolution on grounds provided for in the partnership agreement. Following the dissolution, liquidation takes place (§§ 730 et seq. BGB). The partners complete current transactions, collect outstanding claims, liquidate the assets and satisfy the obligations. If there is a surplus, the contributions are repaid (§ 733 II BGB). The remaining assets are divided among the partners equally or in proportion to their contributions (§ 734 BGB). If the company's assets are insufficient to cover the debts and to reimburse the capital contributions, the shareholders are liable for the shortfall (§ 735 BGB).

[2]   The Non-trading Partnership under the Partnership Act of 1994

Professionals such as doctors, architects, or interpreters are not subject to § 1 HGB. They are therefore prevented from using commercial partnerships as a form of business association. For a long time, the canons of professional ethics did not allow incorporation either. As a consequence, professionals relied on the partnership concept of the Civil Code. This form of association has several major disadvantages: unlimited liability, the lack of legal personality, and the lack of a firm name.

To improve the situation, the legislature enacted the Non-Trading Partnership Act of 1994 (*Partnerschaftsgesellschaftsgesetz* – PartGG), as amended on December 22, 2015. A partnership (*Partnerschaftsgesellschaft*) under this Act may have a common firm name (§ 2 I PartGG). The partners are still personally, jointly and severally liable to the partnership's creditors (§ 8 I PartGG). However, the partners may limit liability for wrongful acts in a way that only the partner rendering a service to the third party and acting negligently or wrongfully may be held liable (§ 8 II PartGG). The partners may limit or exclude their liability for damages caused by their professional malpractice if the partnership maintains a professional liability insurance prescribed by law for this purpose (§ 8 III, IV PartGG).

A non-trading partnership is established by a written contract between the partners. In particular matters for which neither the Partnership Act 1994 nor the partnership agreement provides specific provisions, the law generally applicable to partnerships or commercial partnerships applies (§§ 1 IV, 6 III, 7 II, III, 8 I, 9 I, 10 II PartGG).

[C] Commercial Partnerships

[1] *The General Partnership*

[a] *The Partnership Agreement and Its Contents*

The general partnership (*offene Handelsgesellschaft* – OHG) is established by a contract between the partners (§ 105 III HGB, § 705 BGB). A notarized contract is necessary only if real property is contributed (§§ 311b II, 925 BGB). The partners must agree on the operation of a commercial business under a common firm name (§ 105 I HGB). With regard to the content of partnership agreements and the contributions to be made, § 105 III HGB refers to the law of partnerships under the Civil Code (*see supra* §5.03[B][1]). The partners must apply to the local commercial register for registration (§§ 106, 107 HGB). If the partnership starts to conduct business before registration, the partnership is deemed to be effective immediately with regard to third parties (§ 123 II HGB).

Similar to a partnerships formed under the Civil Code, partners of a general partnership have a duty of loyalty both to the partnership and to their partners. The duty of loyalty is complemented by each partner's right of equal treatment.

[b] *Legal Nature, Liability and Assets*

A general partnership has only partial legal personality but it can have rights and obligations, acquire ownership and other rights in real property, and it can sue and can be sued in its own name (§ 124 I HGB).

Issues concerning the liability of the partners and their joint ownership are governed by the principles applicable to partnerships under the Civil Code (*see supra* §5.03[B][1][b]). As the partners' liability is accessory to the partnership's liability, each partner may be sued directly for the full amount (§ 128 HGB). While the personal liability of the partners may be excluded by agreement with the creditors, it can neither be excluded by limiting a partner's power of representation (§ 126 II HGB; *see infra* §5.03[C][1][c]) nor by the partnership agreement.

A partner who has been held liable by a creditor may demand reimbursement from the partnership (§ 110 HGB). If the partnership cannot fulfill this obligation, the partner has a right to compensation against the other partners (§ 426 I 1 BGB). Liability to third parties is also imposed upon partners newly joining the partnership. The liability extends even to the partnership's obligations incurred prior to entry of the new partner (§ 130 HGB). Partners withdrawing from the partnership may be held liable for obligations incurred prior to their withdrawal if the claim becomes due within five years after their withdrawal (§ 160 HGB).

[c]   Management

The law provides that the management is carried out jointly by the partners (§ 114 I HGB), but here, too, the partners may appoint one or more from their midst to assume the management of the partnership (§§ 114 II, 115 HGB). Third persons may not be managers.

Each managing partner may represent the partnership in and out of court (§ 126 I HGB). His or her powers to represent the partnership with regard to third parties are unlimited and cannot be restricted through special provisions in the partnership contract (§ 126 II HGB).

In contrast, the powers of managing partners may be limited internally. Managing partners who do not observe such internal limitations are liable for any damages caused to the partnership. A managing partner may be dismissed for cause by final court decision (§§ 117, 127 HGB).

[d]   Other Provisions

The distribution of profits and losses, dissolution, and liquidation are all carried out according to the principles as set out in regard to the partnership under the Civil Code (*see supra* §5.03[B][1][d]–[e]). However, a commercial partnership is not dissolved in the case of a notice of termination by a partner, the death of a partner or bankruptcy proceeding against a partner (§ 131 III HGB). The Commercial Code allows for dissolution of the partnership by court decision on petition by a partner alleging and proving good cause (§ 133 HGB). Membership in a partnership may be acquired by inheritance or succession if the partnership contract so provides (§ 139 HGB).

[2]   The Limited Partnership

In contrast to a general partnership, the limited partnership (*Kommanditgesellschaft*) consists of two different groups of partners: the general partners (*persönlich haftende Gesellschafter* or *Komplementäre*) and the limited partners (*Kommanditisten*). The liability of a limited partner vis-à-vis the partnership's creditors is limited to the specific amount of his or her actually paid-in contribution (§§ 161 I, 171 et seq. HGB). Once the entire contribution has been submitted, the liability of the limited partner to third parties is pre-empted (§ 171 I HGB). To the extent the contribution has been repaid to the limited partner, it is deemed, with respect to creditors, never to have been made in the first place (§ 172 IV HGB). As previously stated for general partnerships, the liability of general partners is unlimited. In fact, most limited partnerships today are a GmbH & Co. KG or a UG & Co. KG, where the general partner is a limited liability company or a *Unternehmergesellschaft* (*see supra* §5.01[A][1] and §5.02[C][1][c]). As a result, only the corporate entity acting as general partner is fully liable.

All other principles governing the general partnership also apply to the limited partnership with one exception: a limited partner may not represent the partnership with regard to third parties (§ 170 HGB).

[3] The Dormant Partnership

The "dormant" partnership (*stille Gesellschaft*) is a partnership between a commercial enterprise (i.e., a corporation, a partnership or a sole trader) and the "dormant" partner who contributes a certain amount of money to the enterprise (§ 230 HGB). The dormant partnership therefore resembles the limited partnership. The main difference is that the partnership agreement has legal effect only internally, i.e., between the enterprise and the dormant partner, but not vis-à-vis third parties which may not even know of the existence of a partnership. Business activities are conducted only by the enterprise. This difference has several consequences: The partnership is not registered in the commercial register. The assets only belong to the enterprise and the principle of joint ownership does not apply. The dormant partner is not liable to the enterprise's creditors. The dormant partnership resembles a loan with participation in the profit, because the dormant partner's remuneration is paid out of the enterprise's profits. The dormant partner bears losses only if explicitly provided in the dormant partnership contract (§ 231 II HGB).

SELECTED BIBLIOGRAPHY

[A] Legal Texts

https://www.gesetze-im-internet.de/Teilliste_translations.html.

[B] Handbooks, Commentaries and Monographs

[1] General

Werner Flume, *Allgemeiner Teil des Bürgerlichen Rechts*, Vol. I/I: *Die Personengesell-schaft* (1977); Vol. II/2: *Die juristische Person* (1983).
Barbara Grunewald, *Gesellschaftsrecht* (10th ed. 2017).
Jens Koch, *Gesellschaftsrecht* (10th ed. 2017).
Friedrich Kübler & Heinz-Dieter Assmann, *Gesellschaftsrecht* (6th ed. 2006).
Münchener Kommentar zum Bürgerlichen Gesetzbuch (Kurt Rebmann & Franz J. Säcker eds, 8th ed. 2018).
Thomas Raiser & Rüdiger Veil, *Recht der Kapitalgesellschaften* (6th ed. 2015).
Karsten Schmidt, *Gesellschaftsrecht* (5th ed. to be published 2018).
Herbert Wiedemann, *Gesellschaftsrecht*, Vol. I (1980), Vol. II (2004).
Christine Windbichler, *Gesellschaftsrecht* (24th ed. 2017).

[2] Law of Capital Markets

Heinz-Dieter Assmann & Rolf Schütze, *Handbuch des Kapitalanlagerechts* (4th ed. 2015).
Petra Buck-Heeb, *Kapitalmarktrecht* (9th ed. 2017).

Siegfried Kümpel & Arne Wittig, *Bank- und Kapitalmarktrecht* (4th ed. 2011).
Katja Langenbucher, *Aktien- und Kapitalmarktrecht* (4th ed. 2018).
Markus Lenenbach, *Kapitalmarktrecht* (2nd. ed. 2010).

[3]   Stock Company Law

Tobias Bürgers & Torsten Körber, *Aktiengesetz* (4th. ed. 2017).
Großkommentar *Aktiengesetz* (Heribert Hirte, Peter O. Mülbert & Markus Roth eds, 5th
    ed. 2017).
Uwe Hüffer & Jens Koch, *Aktiengesetz* (13th ed. 2018).
Kölner Kommentar zum Aktiengesetz (Wolfgang Zöllner & Ulrich Noack eds, 3rd ed.
    2012).
Reinhard Marsch-Barner & Frank A. Schäfer eds, *Handbuch börsennotierte AG* (4th ed.
    2017).
Münchener Handbuch des Gesellschaftsrechts, Aktiengesellschaft, Vol. 4 (Michael
    Hoffmann-Becking ed, 4th ed. 2015).
Münchener Kommentar zum Aktiengesetz (Wulf Goette & Mathias Habersack eds, 4th
    ed. 2016).
Karsten Schmidt & Marcus Lutter eds, *Aktiengesetz* (3rd. ed. 2015).
Gerald Spindler & Eberhard Stilz eds, *Kommentar zum Aktiengesetz* (3rd ed. 2015).

[4]   Limited Liability Company

Adolf Baumbach & Götz Hueck, *GmbH-Gesetz* (21th ed. 2017).
Malte Hesselmann, Bert Tillmann & Thomas Müller-Thuns, *Handbuch GmbH & Co. KG*
    (21st ed. 2016).
Marcus Lutter & Peter Hommelhoff, *GmbH-Gesetz* (19th ed. 2016).
Lutz Michalski et al., *Kommentar zum Gesetz betreffend die Gesellschaften mit bes-
    chränkter Haftung* (3rd ed. 2017).
Münchener Handbuch des Gesellschaftsrechts, Gesellschaft mit beschränkter Haftung
    (Hans-Joachim Priester, Dieter Mayer & Hartmut Wicke eds, 5th ed. 2018).
Münchener Kommentar zum GmbHG (Holger Fleischer & Wulf Goette eds, 3rd ed.
    2018).
Heinz Rowedder & Christian Schmidt-Leithoff, *Gesetz betreffend die Gesellschaften mit
    beschränkter Haftung* (6th ed. 2017).
Franz Scholz, *Kommentar zum GmbH-Gesetz* (12th ed. 2018).
Peter Ulmer, Mathias Habersack & Marc Löbbe eds, GmbHG (2nd ed. 2013).

[5]   Partnerships

Adolf Baumbach & Klaus J. Hopt, *Handelsgesetzbuch* (38th ed. 2018).
Carsten Thomas Ebenroth, Karlheinz Boujong, Detlev Joost & Lutz Strohn eds,
    Handelsgesetzbuch (3rd ed. 2014).
Großkommentar HGB (Hermann Staub et al. eds, 5th ed. 2008).

Handbuch des Sozietätsrechts (Martin Henssler & Michael Streck eds, 2nd ed. 2011).

Martin Henssler, *Partnerschaftsgesellschaftsgesetz* (3rd ed. 2018).

Münchener Handbuch des Gesellschaftsrechts. BGB-Gesellschaft, offene Handelsgesellschaft, Partnerschaftsgesellschaft, Partenreederei, EWIV, Vol. 1 (Hans Gummert & Lutz Weipert eds, 4th ed. 2014).

Münchener Handbuch des Gesellschaftsrechts. Kommanditgesellschaft, Stille Gesellschaft, Vol. 2 (Hans Gummert & Lutz Weipert eds, 4th ed. 2014).

Münchener Kommentar zum HGB (Karsten Schmidt ed., 4th ed. 2012).

Peter Ulmer & Carsten Schäfer, *Gesellschaft bürgerlichen Rechts und Partnerschaftsgesellschaft* (7th ed. 2017).

[6] *Accounting and Financial Disclosure*

Bernhard Großfeld & Claus Luttermann *Bilanzrecht* (4th ed. 2005).

Dirk Hachmeister, Holger Kahle, Sebastian Mock & Matthias Schüppen eds, *Bilanzrecht* (2018).

Münchener Kommentar zum Bilanzrecht (Joachim Hennrichs, Joachim Kleindiek & Christoph Watrin eds, loose-leaf 2014).

Harald Wiedmann, Hans-Joachim Böcking & Marius Gros eds, *Bilanzrecht* (3rd ed. 2014).

Günter Wöhe & Sebastian Mock, *Die Handels- und Steuerbilanz* (7th ed. 2018).

Chapter 6

Contract Law

Wolfgang Wurmnest[*]

TABLE OF CONTENTS

---

[*]   I want to thank Michael Friedman for the linguistic review of this text and Ulrich Magnus, Gerhard Wagner, Merlin Gömann, Maximilian Kübler-Wachendorff and Benedikt Wössner for valuable comments on an earlier version of this chapter. The usual disclaimer applies.

§6.01   INTRODUCTION

[A]   General Concept

Contract law is the body of rules dealing with obligations deriving from a mutual agreement between the parties. Those obligations need to be distinguished from obligations arising by law (*gesetzliche Schuldverhältnisse*), specifically the law of *negotiorum gestio* (§§ 677–687 German Civil Code, Bürgerliches Gesetzbuch – BGB), the law of tort (§§ 823–853 BGB) and the law of unjust enrichment (§§ 812–822 BGB). A contractual obligation is generally enforceable. One of the rare exceptions applies to obligations from gambling and betting contracts (§ 762 BGB).

In addition, under German law, contractual obligations must be distinguished from issues relating to rights in rem. This entails the peculiarity that from a doctrinal viewpoint a single transaction will usually involve two contracts: one creating an obligation (*schuldrechtlicher Vertrag*) and a second one transferring the right in rem (*dinglicher Vertrag*) which serves to fulfil the obligation. If, e.g., the parties agree on the sale of a movable good, both the buyer's right to claim the good and the seller's obligation to hand it over as well as to procure ownership result from the 'obligation contract'. Thus far, German law largely corresponds to other legal systems. But, in contrast to other legal systems, the parties have to conclude an additional in rem 'transfer contract' to perform the sale contract, as the change of possession of the good does not in itself suffice to transfer the property to the buyer. Oftentimes, both contracts are concluded impliedly in one single transaction. Nonetheless, it is important to stress that the legal consequences of the 'obligation contract' and the 'transfer contract' have to be assessed separately (*Trennungsprinzip*), and just because one of these contracts is void does not necessarily mean that the other one is void, too (*Abstraktionsprinzip*). For details, *see* the chapter on property law.

[B]   Sources

[1]   BGB

The main source for German contract law is the *Bürgerliches Gesetzbuch* (BGB). The BGB in its original version came into force on 1 January 1900. Since then, it has undergone several significant reforms, although its general structure has remained stable. A major reform took place in 2001 with the Act to Modernise the Law of Obligations (*Schuldrechtsmodernisierungsgesetz*).[1] In addition, over the last years the

---

1. *Gesetz zur Modernisierung des Schuldrechts of 26 November 2001*, BGBl. I 2001, 3138. An English translation of the modernised rules is available at the German Law Archive:

legislature has substantially reformed more specific fields of contract law, such as the rules for tenancy contracts[2] and contracts for work.[3]

[2] **Acquis Communautaire**

Germany is member to the European Union (EU), which enacts legislation in the field of private law. The body of law it generates is termed *'acquis communautaire'* or simply *'acquis'*. The EU has adopted numerous directives on contract law, mainly to protect consumers against various unfair business practices.[4]

Up to the *Schuldrechtsmodernisierung*, rules from consumer law directives were encased in special statutes (like the Unfair Contract Terms Act[5] or the Distance Contracts Act[6]). The consequence was a fragmentation of the law. A turning point was reached with Directive 1999/44/EC on certain aspects of the sale of consumer goods and associated guarantees, which touched upon the area of sales law. The German legislature decided to incorporate this directive into the BGB (the so-called *'Große Lösung'*)[7] in order to ensure that this codification would remain the primary source for contract lawyers.[8] It further used the European stimulus to significantly overhaul the general rules for breach of contract – a project that originated in the late 1970s.[9] Following the decision to transpose Directive 1999/44/EC into the BGB, all other (then existing) statutes in the field of contract law (although not all consumer protection

---

http://germanlawarchive.iuscomp.org/?p = 632. On this reform, *see* the contributions to Wolfgang Ernst & Reinhard Zimmermann (eds), *Zivilrechtswissenschaft und Schuldrechtsreform* (2001). For a recent assessment of the reform, *see* the contributions to Markus Artz, Beate Gsell & Stephan Lorenz (eds), *Zehn Jahre Schuldrechtsmodernisierung* (2014).

2. *Gesetz zur Neugliederung, Vereinfachung und Reform des Mietrechts (Mietrechtsreformgesetz) of 19 June 2001*, BGBl. I 2001, 1149.
3. *Gesetz zur Reform des Bauvertragsrechts, zur Änderung der kaufrechtlichen Mängelhaftung, zur Stärkung des zivilprozessualen Rechtsschutzes und zum maschinellen Siegel im Grundbuch- und Schiffsregisterverfahren of 28 April 2017*, BGBl. I 2017, 969.
4. For an overview *see* Martin Schmidt-Kessel, 'Verbraucherschutzrecht in der EU', in: Martin Gebauer & Christoph Teichmann (eds), *Europäisches Privat- und Unternehmensrecht, Enzyklopädie Europarecht*, vol. VI (2016), § 4 nos. 205 et seq. Important Directives include: *Directive 93/13/EEC of the Council of 5 April 1993 on unfair terms in consumer contracts*, O.J. L 95, 29; *Directive 2008/48/EC of the European Parliament and of the Council of 23 April 2008 on credit agreements for consumers and repealing Council Directive 87/102/EEC*, O.J. L 133, 66.
5. *Gesetz zur Regelung des Rechts der Allgemeinen Geschäftsbedingungen (AGB-Gesetz) of 9 December 1976*, BGBl. I 1976, 3317 (Directive 93/13/EEC was later transposed into that statute).
6. *Gesetz über Fernabsatzverträge und andere Fragen des Verbraucherrechts sowie zur Umstellung von Vorschriften auf Euro of 27 June 2000*, BGBl. I 2000, 897. This Act transposed *Directive 97/7/EC of the European Parliament and of the Council of 20 May 1997 on the protection of consumers in respect of distance contracts*, O.J. L 144, 19 and *Directive 98/27/EC of the European Parliament and of the Council of 19 May 1998 on injunctions for the protection of consumers' interests*, O.J. L 166, 51.
7. Herta Däubler-Gmelin, 'Die Entscheidung für die so genannte Große Lösung bei der Schuldrechtsreform: Zum Entwurf eines Gesetzes zur Modernisierung des Schuldrechts', *Neue Juristische Wochenschrift* 2001, 2281 et seq.
8. On the functions of a codification *see* Jürgen Basedow, 'Das BGB im künftigen europäischen Privatrecht: Der hybride Kodex', *Archiv für die civilistische Praxis* 200 (2000), 445, 467 et seq.
9. On the process leading to the reform Reinhard Zimmermann, 'Consumer Contract Law and General Contract Law: The German Experience', *Current Legal Problems* 58 (2005), 415 et seq.

rules of the *acquis*) were similarly incorporated[10] to ensure that this codification systematically presents the main rules on all commonly encountered contracts. As a side effect, the BGB turned from a rather static codification into a 'permanent construction site' on which 'two architects [are working]: one in Berlin and one in Brussels/Strasbourg'.[11] The German legislature has to amend the BGB at regular intervals to transpose new or revised directives. In addition, judgments rendered by the Court of Justice of the European Union on matters of EU law can make it necessary to align wordings in the BGB with the Court's rulings.

[3]   Additional Sources

Besides the BGB, there are additional sources that might need to be considered when drafting a contract or resolving a contractual dispute under German law. The General Act on Equal Treatment (*Allgemeines Gleichbehandlungsgesetz*)[12] safeguards the principle of equal treatment regardless of gender, race or ethnic origin, mainly regarding employment, social benefits and access to and supply of goods and services offered to the public (for details, *see* chapter on employment law).

In the commercial context, the Commercial Code (*Handelsgesetzbuch*) sets forth additional rules supplanting or complementing the rules of the BGB. Both codifications must thus be read together.

Finally, the fundamental rights enshrined in the German Constitution (*Grundgesetz* (GG), literally 'Basic Law') may deploy an effect on contractual stipulations via the general clauses of the BGB, such as § 138 BGB (public policy) or § 242 BGB (good faith). For instance, the Federal Constitutional Court (*Bundesverfassungsgericht*) ruled that a surety agreement that had been concluded between a bank and the adult daughter of a debtor was void because the bank asked the virtually destitute daughter to sign it 'for the files'. The Court held that the bank had unlawfully exploited its bargaining position and declared that courts must interpret the general clauses

---

10. For a detailed analysis *see* Thomas Pfeiffer, 'Die Integration von "Nebengesetzen" in das BGB', in: Wolfgang Ernst & Reinhard Zimmermann (eds), *Zivilrechtswissenschaft und Schuldrechtsreform* (2001), pp. 481 et seq.
11. Wulf-Henning Roth, 'Europäischer Verbraucherschutz und BGB', *Juristenzeitung* 2001, 475, 488: 'Wir werden uns an die Vorstellung gewöhnen müssen, dass das deutsche Privatrecht aufgrund des gemeinschaftsrechtlichen Harmonisierungsprozesses eine permanente *Baustelle* sein wird, bei der zwei Architekten – einer in Berlin und einer in Brüssel/Straßburg – am Werke sind'.
12. *Gesetz zur Umsetzung europäischer Richtlinien zur Verwirklichung des Grundsatzes der Gleichbehandlung of 14 August 2006*, BGBl. I 2006, 1897. This Act transposed the following EU directives: *Directive 2000/43/EC of the Council of 29 June 2000 implementing the principle of equal treatment between persons irrespective of racial or ethnic origin*, O.J. L 180, 22; *Directive 2000/78/EC of the Council of 27 November 2000 establishing a general framework for equal treatment in employment and occupation*, O.J. L 303, 16; *Directive 2002/73/EC of the European Parliament and of the Council of 23 September 2002 amending Council Directive 76/207/EEC on the implementation of the principle of equal treatment for men and women as regards access to employment, vocational training and promotion, and working conditions*, O.J. L 269, 15; *Directive 2004/113/EC of the Council of 13 December 2004 implementing the principle of equal treatment between men and women in the access to and supply of goods and services*, O.J. L 373, 37.

contained in the BGB in a way as to safeguard the principle of freedom of contract, which is protected by the Constitution as part of the general freedom of action (Article 2 I GG).[13] Despite this and other important rulings, all things considered, the impact of the case law of the Federal Constitutional Court on contract law is limited.

[C] Contract Law and the Structure of the BGB

The draftsmen of the BGB employed a regulatory technique based on the idea that all rules capable of generalisation should be assembled in parts containing general principles, followed by more specific parts. Although this approach is laudable from a systematic perspective, it has the consequence that foreign contract lawyers (at least from jurisdictions that were not significantly influenced by the German approach) face difficulties in coming to grips with German contract law, given that the relevant provisions are spread among different parts of the BGB.

Book I (§§ 1–240 BGB) contains the General Part of the BGB, i.e., rules that are of relevance for all other books in the Code. It bears the stamp of the Pandectists, who, in the 19th century, systematically developed general rules from the earlier case law.[14] Following this line of 'abstractivism', the legislature codified all rules of general application in Book I.[15] In other national codifications, these rules are enshrined in the more specific field of contract law. For example Book I lays down rules on the capacity to contract (§§ 104–113 BGB), mistake and undue influence (§§ 119–123 BGB), nullity of legal transactions for infringements of form requirements, illegality and public policy (§§ 125, 134, 138 BGB), as well as the formation (§§ 145–156 BCB) and interpretation of contracts (§§ 133, 157 BGB). In addition, the rules on agency (§§ 164–181 BGB) are situated in the General Part, as well as the definitions of 'consumer' and 'entrepreneur' (§§ 13, 14 BGB), which are vital for determining the scope of consumer contract law.

The bulk of contract law rules are assembled in Book II (§§ 241–853 BGB), entitled 'Law of Obligations'. An obligation is the right of the creditor to claim performance from the debtor as flowing from a contract or a legal relationship (§ 241 I BGB). Book II first supplies the rules pertaining to all forms of obligations (the so-called 'General Law of Obligations', *Allgemeines Schuldrecht*), including obligations *ex lege*, e.g., the law of damages (§§ 249–254 BGB). The remainder of Book II contains rules for specific contractual regimes (and for obligations *ex lege*) and is therefore termed 'Special Law of Obligations' (*Besonderes Schuldrecht*). The rules on special contractual regimes concern subjects such as contracts for the transfer of property (e.g., sale, barter, donation), contracts for the use of property (e.g., rent, leasehold, loan) and contracts for the provision of certain services (e.g., work, general services, travel).

---

13. BVerfGE 89, 214.
14. On the development of general rules by legal scholars *see* Mathias Schmoeckel, in: Mathias Schmoeckel, Joachim Rückert & Reinhard Zimmermann (eds), *Historisch-kritischer Kommentar zum BGB*, vol. I (2003), Vor § 1 BGB part III nos. 14 et seq.
15. On the historical background Reinhard Zimmermann, *The Law of Obligations* (1996), 30–31.

The regulatory technique employed by the German legislature (which of course also has an impact on the structure of university curricula) also explains why 'contract law' (*Vertragsrecht*) – unlike in other jurisdictions – is not a common title for legal texts in Germany.[16] Many books dealing (in part) with contract law issues present them along the structure of the BGB. In this vein, textbooks cover the 'General Part of the BGB',[17] the 'General'[18] or 'Special Part'[19] of the law of obligations or more broadly 'contractual obligations'.[20]

[D]   How to Find the Law?

The provisions of the BGB and the other main sources of German contract law can be found online in several legal databases. Some of them are freely accessible,[21] while others have to be paid for.[22] There are various translations of the BGB (or parts of it) into English. Given the high frequency of legal reforms over the last years, however, many translations are at least partly outdated. The most frequently updated translation, one following a rather literal translation approach, seems to be the online publication of the Federal Ministry of Justice and Consumer Protection (*Bundesministerium der Justiz und für Verbraucherschutz*)[23] – although even this translation is not always fully up to date. Case law on German private law is published in various law

---

16. A laudable exception is Hein Kötz, *Vertragsrecht* (2nd ed. 2012).
17. Burkhard Boemke & Bernhard Ulrici, *BGB Allgemeiner Teil* (2nd ed. 2014); Reinhard Bork, *Allgemeiner Teil des Bürgerlichen Gesetzbuchs* (4th ed. 2016); Hans Brox & Wolf-Dietrich Walker, *Allgemeiner Teil des BGB* (41st ed. 2017); Florian Faust, *Bürgerliches Gesetzbuch Allgemeiner Teil* (6th ed. 2018); Dieter Medicus & Jens Petersen, *Allgemeiner Teil des BGB* (11th ed. 2016); Haimo Schack, *BGB – Allgemeiner Teil* (15th ed. 2016); Manfred Wolf & Jörg Neuner, *Allgemeiner Teil des Bürgerlichen Rechts* (11th ed. 2016).
18. Hans Brox & Wolf-Dietrich Walker, *Allgemeines Schuldrecht* (42nd ed. 2018); Christian Förster, *Schuldrecht Allgemeiner Teil* (3nd ed. 2015); Karl Larenz, *Lehrbuch des Schuldrechts, I. Band: Allgemeiner Teil* (14th ed. 1987); Dirk Looschelders, *Schuldrecht: Allgemeiner Teil* (15th ed. 2017); Dieter Medicus & Stephan Lorenz, *Schuldrecht I: Allgemeiner Teil* (21st ed. 2015); Peter Schlechtriem & Martin Schmidt-Kessel, *Schuldrecht: Allgemeiner Teil* (6th ed. 2005); Frank Weiler, *Schuldrecht Allgemeiner Teil* (4th ed. 2017).
19. Hans Brox & Wolf-Dietrich Walker, *Besonderes Schuldrecht* (42nd ed. 2018); Christian Förster, *Schuldrecht: Besonderer Teil* (2nd ed. 2016); Karl Larenz, *Lehrbuch des Schuldrechts, II. Band: Besonderer Teil, 1. Halbband* (13th ed. 1986); Karl Larenz & Claus-Wilhelm Canaris, *Lehrbuch des Schuldrechts, II. Band: Besonderer Teil, 2. Halbband* (13th ed. 1994); Dieter Medicus & Stephan Lorenz, *Schuldrecht II: Besonderer Teil* (17th ed. 2014); Dirk Looschelders, *Schuldrecht: Besonderer Teil* (13th ed. 2018); Peter Schlechtriem, *Schuldrecht: Besonderer Teil* (6th ed. 2003).
20. Books on *Vertragliche Schuldverhältnisse* usually focus on the special contractual regimes and do not treat the rules contained in the General Part, *see* Jürgen Oechsler, *Vertragliche Schuldverhältnisse* (2nd ed. 2017); Hartmut Oetker & Felix Maultzsch, *Vertragliche Schuldverhältnisse* (4th ed. 2013); Klaus Tonner, *Schuldrecht: Vertragliche Schuldverhältnisse* (4th ed. 2016).
21. Examples include the webpages http://www.gesetze-im-internet.de, https://openjur.de and https://dejure.org.
22. The most commonly used databases, which also contain court judgments and journal publications, are beck-online (www.beck-online.de) and juris (www.juris.de).
23. http://www.gesetze-im-internet.de/englisch_bgb.

journals and may be accessed via fee-based databases.[24] For some years, the judgments of the Federal Supreme Court (*Bundesgerichtshof*, BGH) are published on its website,[25] and some German states have developed freely accessible databases for decisions of their local courts.[26]

In addition, there is a vast body of literature on German contract law in all shape and sizes. As it was already mentioned, many textbooks develop the law of contract based on the different parts of the BGB.[27] Other textbooks or handbooks deal with special issues of contract law, for instance general terms and conditions.[28] For more specific information on a particular problem, advice should always be taken from a commentary, explaining every single black letter rule. Commentaries take account of both the case law and doctrinal ideas developed by scholars, and they exist in various types: some are written for time-pressed practitioners who quickly need information on basic issues. Others explore the law in great detail by analysing (and referencing) the case law and scholarly opinions. Amongst others, the latter category includes the *Münchener Kommentar zum BGB*, the *Staudinger* and the *Beck-online.GROSSKOMMENTAR* (the latter is accessible only via a fee-based database).

§6.02   BASIC FEATURES OF GERMAN CONTRACT LAW

[A]   Freedom of Contract

[1]   Principle

Freedom of contract is of paramount importance for German law.[29] Not only does this maxim allow for the development of a private order based on the needs of the parties, 'it is also an indispensable feature of a free economy: it makes private enterprise possible and encourages the responsible construction of economic relationships. Freedom of contract is thus of central significance for the whole of the private law'.[30]

---

24. The major databases are beck-online (www.beck-online.de) and juris (www.juris.de).
25. http://www.bundesgerichtshof.de/DE/Entscheidungen/EntscheidungenBGH/entscheidungen BGH_node.html.
26. Two examples are https://www.justiz.nrw.de and www.justizportal-bw.de.
27. These include the majority of textbooks cited in n. 17–19.
28. Martin Schwab, *AGB-Recht* (2nd ed. 2014); Markus Stoffels, *AGB-Recht* (3rd ed. 2015). There are also larger treatises such as Manfred Wolf, Walter F. Lindacher & Thomas Pfeiffer (eds), *AGB-Recht: Kommentar* (6th ed. 2013); Peter Ulmer, Hans Erich Brandner & Horst-Diether Hensen, *AGB-Recht: Kommentar* (12th ed. 2016).
29. On the justification for this maxim *see* Claus-Wilhelm Canaris & Hans Christoph Grigoleit, 'Interpretation of Contracts', in: Arthur Hartkamp et al. (eds), *Towards a European Civil Code* (4th ed. 2011), pp. 587, 589.
30. Hans G. Leser, 'Contract: Capacity, Formation and Freedom of Contract', in: Norbert Horn, Hans G. Leser & Hein Kötz (eds), *German Private and Commercial Law: An Introduction* (1982), pp. 71, 84.

It therefore does not come as a surprise that this maxim is accepted in all EU Member States[31] and counts among the foundations of European private law.[32]

The maxim has various facets. First, it protects the freedom of each party to choose whether and with whom a contract shall be concluded (*Abschlussfreiheit*). Second, the parties are free to shape the content of the agreement and may thus even create contracts not regulated in the BGB or elsewhere (*Inhaltsfreiheit*). Third, the parties may generally also agree on the form of the contract (*Formfreiheit*).

[2]   Limits to Contractual Freedom

As with all other jurisdictions, German law does not grant unlimited freedom of contract. Although the BGB was drafted at a time that is often described as a 'high time of economic liberalism', its draftsmen set forth various boundaries, which over the years have constantly broadened to protect weaker contracting parties.[33]

[a]   Obligation to Contract (Kontrahierungszwang)

The freedom of each party to decide freely with whom a contract is concluded (*Abschlussfreiheit*) is restricted in various ways. First, the legislature has imposed a legal obligation to contract under certain circumstances so as to ensure access to important goods,[34] e.g., in the area of transport law (§ 22 *Personenbeförderungsgesetz*, § 10 *Allgemeines Eisenbahngesetz*) or energy supply (§ 18 *Energiewirtschaftsgesetz*). Protection against firms with a high degree of market power is furthermore ensured by the rules of competition (antitrust) law, which under certain circumstances grant-dependent firms the right to demand delivery of essential commercial goods or services (e.g., under §§ 19 II no. 4, 20 *Gesetz gegen Wettbewerbsbeschränkungen*).

In addition to these special statutory duties, there is a general obligation to contract. The legal foundation and prerequisites of this obligation are subject to debate. Originally, the Imperial Court (*Reichsgericht*), i.e., the Supreme Court for civil and

---

31. *See* Notes to Art. 1:102 of the Principles of European Contract Law, *Parts I & II* (2000), pp. 99 et seq.
32. Peter-Christian Müller-Graff, 'Allgemeines Gemeinschaftsprivatrecht', in: Martin Gebauer & Christoph Teichmann (eds), *Europäisches Privat- und Unternehmensrecht, Enzyklopädie Europarecht*, vol. VI (2016), § 2 nos. 78 et seq.
33. Basil Markesinis, Werner Lorenz & Gerhard Dannemann, *The German Law of Obligations*, vol. I: *The Law of Contracts and Restitution* (1997), 28. The view that the 19th century was dominated by a very 'formal' conception of contract and that the 'materialisation' of German contract law is a tendency only of the 20th century has recently been softened in connection with evidence that issues of social justice were of much greater concern at the time the BGB was drafted than commonly assumed, *see* Tilman Repgen, *Die soziale Aufgabe des Privatrechts: Eine Grundfrage in Wissenschaft und Kodifikation am Ende des 19. Jahrhunderts* (2001), 490 et seq.; Phillip Hellwege, *Allgemeine Geschäftsbedingungen, einseitig gestellte Vertragsbedingungen und die allgemeine Rechtsgeschäftslehre* (2010), 5 et seq.
34. *See* the overview by Reinhard Bork, in: *J. v. Staudingers Kommentar zum Bürgerlichen Gesetzbuch, Allgemeiner Teil 4b* (revised ed. 2015), Vor §§ 145–156 BGB no. 17; Jan Busche, in: *Münchener Kommentar zum Bürgerlichen Gesetzbuch*, vol. I (7th ed. 2015), Vor § 145 BGB nos. 14 et seq.

commercial matters of the German Reich, derived such a rule from § 826 BGB (a general tort law provision);[35] yet, its adequacy as a basis to create an obligation to contract is in dispute.[36] The prevailing understanding of the rule holds that a party who offers goods or services to the public acts contra *bonos mores* if he – without an objective basis – refuses to conclude a contract with a buyer who cannot otherwise procure the desired goods or services. In such a situation, the buyer is entitled to compensatory relief such that he is put in the position he would have been in but for the wrongful conduct (§ 249 I BGB). Thus, conclusion of the contract is mandatory.[37] The Imperial Court, however, imposed this obligation, in principle, only on firms holding a monopoly position.[38] This approach was basically adopted by the Federal Court (BGH),[39] which also – at least implicitly – limited the scope of application to important goods and services.[40] Beyond this context, it is disputed under which circumstances an obligation to contract will arise. Some authors argue for a lowering of the (monopoly) threshold so as to reach suppliers holding merely a strong market position,[41] whereas other authors would even go so far as extending the duty to contract to persons supplying everyday goods and services.[42]

In recent times, there has been a recurrent debate surrounding cases of discrimination where an individual has been denied entrance to an establishment (e.g., a nightclub, a restaurant or a hotel) because of his ethnicity.[43] Can the individual being discriminated against sue for admission to the establishment or is he limited to claim for damages? Some authors see a compensatory claim in tort (and potentially the filing of criminal charges) as a reasonable and effective sanction.[44] Others, however, find

---

35. RGZ 132, 273, 276; RGZ 133, 388, 392; RGZ 155, 257, 284; concurring Hein Kötz, *Vertragsrecht* (2nd ed. 2012), no. 29; Peter Schlechtriem & Martin Schmidt-Kessel, *Schuldrecht Allgemeiner Teil* (6th ed. 2005), no. 56.
36. Many scholars argue that the obligation to contract is rather a '*quasinegatorischer Unterlassungsanspruch*' (like § 1004 BGB) since the discriminated person wants to prevent future damages rather than obtain compensation for already existing damage, *see* Jan Busche, *Privatautonomie und Kontrahierungszwang* (1999), 230 et seq.; Reinhard Bork, *Allgemeiner Teil des Bürgerlichen Gesetzbuchs* (4th ed. 2016), no. 672; *see also* Tilmann Bezzenberger, 'Ethnische Diskriminierung, Gleichheit und Sittenordnung im bürgerlichen Recht', *Archiv für die civilistische Praxis* 196 (1996), 395, 428. Both approaches (§§ 826, 249 BGB und § 1004 BGB) rest on shaky ground, *see* Jörg Neuner, 'Diskriminierungsschutz durch Privatrecht', *Juristenzeitung* 2003, 57, 61.
37. Hein Kötz, *Vertragsrecht* (2nd ed. 2012), no. 29.
38. RGZ 48, 114, 127; RGZ 132, 273, 276; RGZ 155, 257, 284.
39. BGH, *Neue Zeitschrift für Verwaltungsrecht* 1994, 1240, 1241.
40. RGZ 48, 122, 127; RGZ 99, 107, 109; *see also* Wolfgang Kilian, 'Kontrahierungszwang und Zivilrechtssystem', *Archiv für die civilistische Praxis* 180 (1980), 47, 58. The Bundesgerichtshof left this issue open, *cf.* BGH, *Neue Juristische Wochenschrift* 1990, 761, 763.
41. Hein Kötz, *Vertragsrecht* (2nd ed. 2012), no. 29.
42. Franz Bydlinski, 'Zu den dogmatischen Grundfragen des Kontrahierungszwangs', *Archiv für die civilistische Praxis* 180 (1980), 1, 37 ('*Normalbedarf*').
43. *See* Dieter Martiny, 'Ausländerdiskriminierung und Vertragsschluss', *Zeitschrift für Europäisches Privatrecht* 2001, 563, 578 et seq.
44. Franz Bydlinski, 'Zu den dogmatischen Grundfragen des Kontrahierungszwangs', *Archiv für die civilistische Praxis* 180 (1980) 1, 13, 44 et seq.; Dieter Medicus & Stephan Lorenz, *Schuldrecht I: Allgemeiner Teil* (21st ed. 2015), no. 80.

that an obligation to contract is justified given the blatant injury to human dignity; while a court ruling on this matter may not – as a practical matter – allow the injured party to secure entry on the desired occasion, the affirmation of such an obligation would at least foreclose future instances of wrongful conduct.[45] This latter view is persuasive, leading to the conclusion that an obligation to contract may also exist in the context of blatant discriminatory treatment. This would not unduly interfere with contractual freedom,[46] since protection from discrimination is already embedded in the existing private law regime, namely as an aspect of freedom of action guaranteed to any potential victim of discriminatory treatment. But this is not to say that every act of discrimination based on one's origin must give way to an obligation to contract. If, for instance, a Bavarian is unwilling to sell his car to a man from Berlin because he does not like 'Prussians', the buyer from Berlin will have to turn elsewhere to fill his needs.

In recent times, courts have derived a right against (future) discriminatory treatment from the terms of the Equal Treatment Act (*Allgemeine Gleichbehandlungs-gesetz* – AGG), where its prerequisites were met.[47] In a case where a teenager was denied entrance to a club on account of his skin colour, the Stuttgart Court of Appeals not only awarded the claimant damages but also prospectively prohibited the club from denying the teen entry based on his colour.[48]

[b]   Mandatory Rules

The principle that the parties may shape the content of the contract (*Inhaltsfreiheit*) finds its limits in mandatory rules. These are provisions from which parties may not deviate by agreement. Since 1900, the German legislature has steadily increased the number of mandatory rules, namely in the areas of consumer law, tenancy law, employment law and insurance contract law so as to protect the weaker party to the contract.

Mandatory rules also limit the parties' freedom to agree on the contract's form. If a certain form is mandatory, the parties must comply with this requirement; otherwise their contract is void (§ 125, 1 BGB) except where the law exceptionally provides for a method to cure an infringement. To ensure that unduly severe form requirements do not hinder consumers from exercising their rights, § 309 no. 13b and c BGB further declares that standard contract clauses in consumer contracts – except contracts that are recorded before a notary – are void, insofar as notices or declarations are conditioned on a stricter form than text form (i.e., handwritten, typed or via email) or if special requirements for receipt apply.

---

45. Dirk Looschelders, *Schuldrecht: Allgemeiner Teil* (15th ed. 2017), § 6 nos. 119 et seq.
46. On this debate in relation to the enactment of the AGG Eduard Picker, 'Antidiskriminierung als Zivilrechtsprogramm?', *Juristenzeitung* 2003, 540, 543 et seq.
47. Whether the obligation to contract flows from the AGG or from the general rules (e.g., § 826 BGB) is disputed, *see* Jan Busche, in: *Münchener Kommentar zum Bürgerlichen Gesetzbuch*, vol. I (7th ed. 2015), Vor § 145 BGB no. 17 (with further references).
48. OLG Stuttgart, *Neue Juristische Wochenschrift* 2012, 1085.

[B]   Specific Performance

It is a general principle of German law that, in cases of non-performance of a contractual obligation, the creditor can seek specific performance from the debtor provided that performance is still possible. If this is the case, it does not matter whether the debtor has to deliver goods, keep his shop open at certain times or personally perform a service.[49] The creditor can go to court and demand a so-called *Leistungsurteil* requiring the debtor to perform in kind. This stands in sharp contrast to the Anglo-Saxon approach, under which specific performance of a non-monetary obligation is subject to many restrictions and is rather seen as an exception.[50]

The differences between German law and the common law should, however, not be overstated. Even though the right to claim specific performance has been described as the 'backbone of the obligation' (*Rückgrat der Obligation*),[51] a glimpse at the law in action reveals that, even in Germany, claims for damages are the rule and claims for specific performance the exception. First, whenever a creditor can be fully compensated by a sum of money (i.e., in cases where he can readily secure the promised good or service elsewhere), he will hardly seek performance from a reluctant debtor and will instead limit his claim to damages.[52] Second, even if he seeks specific performance, a closer look at the rules on enforcement reveals that it is only in limited circumstances that such a judgment may be executed. Under §§ 887, 888 Code of Civil Procedure (*Zivilprozessordnung* – ZPO), one has to distinguish between acts that can be performed by another person (*vertretbare Handlungen*) and acts that have to be performed by the debtor (*unvertretbare Handlungen*). The former are enforced by substituting another person for the debtor at the cost of the original debtor (§ 887 ZPO). The creditor's act of securing substitute service effectively releases the original debtor from his obligation to perform the contractual obligation, since he now has to pay a certain sum to the creditor that covers the cost of the substitute. The latter can, in principle, be enforced by certain coercive means such as a fine (*Zwangsgeld*) or even imprisonment (*Zwangshaft*) (§ 888 I ZPO), but to protect the debtor's personal freedom the legislature has exempted the enforcement of judgments concerning the provision of a service that the debtor has to provide in person (§ 888 III ZPO). In such a case, the creditor is effectively limited to a claim for damages.[53] The German procedural enforcement system thus further levels the differences to common law jurisdictions with regard to the outcome of a dispute. However, from a conceptual point of view, significant

---

49. Konrad Zweigert & Hein Kötz, *Einführung in die Rechtsvergleichung* (3rd ed. 1996), 469.
50. For details on English law *see* Edwin Peel, *The Law of Contract* (14th ed. 2015), nos. 21–016 et seq.
51. Konrad Zweigert & Hein Kötz, *Einführung in die Rechtsvergleichung* (3rd ed. 1996), 469.
52. *Ibid.*, 482.
53. Jens Kleinschmidt, 'Specific Performance', in: Jürgen Basedow, Klaus J. Hopt & Reinhard Zimmermann (eds), *The Max Planck Encyclopedia of European Private Law* (2012), vol. II, pp. 1581, 1582 et seq.

differences remain since under German law the creditor can always sue for performance in kind, whereas English law, e.g., leaves it at the discretion of the court to decide whether specific performance is granted or not.[54]

[C]   Interpretation of Contracts

At the end of the 19th century, there were competing views on how to interpret declarations of intent. Put simply (the actual lines of arguments were much more nuanced), the proponents of a subjective approach argued that the aim of interpretation must be an inquiry into the true will of the person making the statement (*Willenstheorie*), while adherents of the objective approach argued that, in principle, it is the objective meaning of a declaration that matters (*Erklärungstheorie*).[55] The BGB did not bring this controversy to an end since two different rules on interpretation were incorporated, both of which can be traced back to the French Civil Code:[56] While § 133 BGB refers to the true intention as a yardstick for interpreting declarations of intent, § 157 BGB demands that contracts be interpreted objectively, in good faith, and with regard to common usage. Nowadays, however, it is settled case law that these two rules of interpretation need to be combined when assessing whether a contract has been formed and what content it ought to have.[57] These two general provisions are flanked by the *contra proferentem* rule that applies to standard contract terms, § 305c II BGB.

As a starting point, declarations leading to the contract must – from a doctrinal point of view – be interpreted in a way as to reflect the true will of the declarators. That is why under German law, a stipulation may be given a meaning differing from the common understanding of an expression. As far as the true intentions of the parties do match, but the parties nonetheless use an expression different from common usage, the courts will construe the contract according to the intended meaning (*falsa demonstratio non nocet*).[58] Thus, if a buyer buys *Haakjöringsköd* (Norwegian for shark meat) from the seller, but both parties understand this expression as meaning whale meat,

---

54. Jens Kleinschmidt, 'Specific Performance', in: Jürgen Basedow, Klaus J. Hopt & Reinhard Zimmermann (eds), *The Max Planck Encyclopedia of European Private Law* (2012), vol. II, pp. 1581, 1583. For details *see* Edwin Peel, *The Law of Contract* (14th ed. 2015), nos. 21–029 et seq.
55. For details *see* Stefan Vogenauer, in: Mathias Schmoeckel, Joachim Rückert & Reinhard Zimmermann (eds), *Historisch-kritischer Kommentar zum BGB*, vol. I (2003), §§ 133, 157 BGB nos. 34 et seq.
56. § 133 BGB was inspired by Art. 1156 CC (now Art. 1188 CC), and a precursor of § 157 BGB was modelled after Art. 1135 CC (now Art. 1194 CC), *see* Stefan Vogenauer, in: Mathias Schmoeckel, Joachim Rückert & Reinhard Zimmermann (eds), *Historisch-kritischer Kommentar zum BGB*, vol. I (2003), §§ 133, 157 BGB nos. 18, 24, 38.
57. It is important to note that the German rules of interpretation differ in detail with regard to, on the one hand, declarations of will that have to be received by another party (*empfangsbedürftige Willenserklärungen*) and, on the other hand, declarations of will that are valid without receipt by another party (*nicht-empfangsbedürftige Willenserklärungen*). Moreover, peculiarities apply in special situations, e.g., when declarations must comply with certain formal requirements.
58. Claus-Wilhelm Canaris & Hans Christoph Grigoleit, 'Interpretation of Contracts', in: Arthur Hartkamp et al. (eds), *Towards a European Civil Code* (4th ed. 2011), pp. 587, 598; Jörg Neuner, 'Vertragsauslegung – Vertragsergänzung – Vertragskorrektur', in: *Festschrift für Claus-Wilhelm Canaris*, vol. I (2007), pp. 901, 908.

they have concluded a contract on the latter.[59] But in practice, such a subjective approach to interpretation is rather the exception given that the true will is often difficult to ascertain. That is why declarations in the context of contract formation are usually to be interpreted from the position of a neutral bystander taking the perspective of the recipient of the declaration (*objektiver Empfängerhorizont*) to protect legitimate expectations.[60] Hence, a contractual stipulation can be given a meaning that corresponds to the true intention of only one of the parties. If, e.g., only the seller understood *Haakjöringsköd* as referring to whale meat, whereas the buyer understood it to mean shark meat, and this meaning is the common understanding in the fish trade, a contract on shark meat would have been concluded. A different issue is whether the seller can rescind the contract based on mistake (*infra* §6.04[D]).

In the event the parties have not formed a will on certain issues related to their contractual arrangement, so that the contract contains a 'gap', courts will usually fill this gap by applying the code's default rules (*ius dispositivum, dispositives Recht*),[61] as far as these rules are compatible with the interests of the parties in the case at hand. If there are no such rules or if they do not fit because the contract concerns an atypical scenario, courts may resort to completive (constructive) interpretation (*ergänzende Vertragsauslegung*), which – under certain circumstances – enables a court to fill the gap with a hypothetical rule that reasonable parties would have agreed on if they had thought about the issue at the time of contracting. Such a gap-filling procedure is, however, not always possible as there are many instances in which no rule that both parties would have agreed on can be conceived. A completive (constructive) interpretation can thus only be applied in exceptional cases and courts must avoid substituting their own conception of contractual justice for the parties' will.[62] A commonly cited example for the application of this interpretational rule is a contract between two physicians from different towns who contractually swap their practices. If, after some months, one of the doctors returns to his home town and opens up a practice in close vicinity to his old place of work (meaning that many of his former patients will likely want to be treated by him and not by the 'new' doctor in town – which, of course, runs counter to the economic purpose of the contract), his contractual partner can in principle only stop him from doing business there if the contract contains a non-compete clause. If the contract does not contain such a prohibition, a temporary limitation of two or three years can nevertheless be read into the contract under German law by resorting to completive interpretation, as there is no default rule of law on this issue and the parties would most likely have intended such a provision if they had thought about the problem.[63]

---

59. This example is based on RGZ 99, 147, 148.
60. Jörg Neuner, 'Vertragsauslegung – Vertragsergänzung – Vertragskorrektur', in: *Festschrift für Claus-Wilhelm Canaris*, vol. I (2007), pp. 901, 908 et seq.
61. BGHZ 158, 201, 206 (with further references).
62. Reinhard Bork, *Allgemeiner Teil des Bürgerlichen Gesetzbuchs* (4th ed. 2016), no. 537; Claus-Wilhelm Canaris & Hans Christoph Grigoleit, 'Interpretation of Contracts', in: Arthur Hartkamp et al. (eds), *Towards a European Civil Code* (4th ed. 2011), pp. 587, 595 et seq.; Dieter Medicus & Jens Petersen, *Allgemeiner Teil des BGB* (11th ed. 2016), no. 344.
63. BGHZ 16, 71, 76; Reinhard Bork, *Allgemeiner Teil des Bürgerlichen Gesetzbuchs* (4th ed. 2016), no. 538; Karl Larenz, 'Ergänzende Vertragsauslegung und dispositives Recht', *Neue Juristische*

When interpreting a contract, German courts are in principle not limited to the 'four corners of the contract' and may also take into account prior communication and negotiations between the parties.[64] Parties to an international commercial transaction, therefore, often include 'entire agreement clauses' in their contracts which aim to prevent courts from looking at material other than the written agreement to determine its meaning.[65]

[D]   Concurrence of Liability

Unlike in French law, where the principle of *non-cumul des actions* prohibits concurrent claims to a large extent,[66] German law allows a claimant to base its claim on different grounds. Thus, claims representing concurrent liability, e.g., contractual claims and tort claims, are frequently observed.[67]

[E]   The Blurred Line Between Contract and Tort Law

A peculiarity of German law is the rather blurred line between contract and tort law. Over the years, courts have expanded the field of contract law considerably. This development was in part an attempt to counterbalance the narrow scope of German tort law. For instance, the draftsmen of the BGB had designed a rather perfunctory rule on vicarious liability. It differs considerably from similar rules in other jurisdictions as it defines the liability of the principal (or master) very narrowly.[68] § 831 BGB holds the principal liable for unlawful damage wrongfully caused by his auxiliary (*Verrichtungsgehilfe*) if the principal did not exercise the necessary care in selecting, training or supervising the auxiliary (for details see the chapter on tort law). Thus, if the principal did not act negligently himself, he is not liable and the damaged person can seek damages only from the employee, who often does not have the means to pay for the damage caused. The second facet of tort law leading the courts to a wide interpretation of contract law is the fact that pure economic loss can be recovered only where the tortfeasor caused damage to his victim intentionally and acted against *bonos mores* (§ 826 BGB).[69]

Wochenschrift 1963, 737, 738 et seq.; the completive (constructive) interpretation as applied by the German courts is rejected by Jörg Neuner, 'Vertragsauslegung – Vertragsergänzung – Vertragskorrektur', in: *Festschrift für Claus-Wilhelm Canaris*, vol. I (2007), pp. 901, 918 et seq.

64. *See*, e.g., BGH, *Neue Juristische Wochenschrift* 1999, 3191.
65. Such a clause will however not completely isolate the contract from its legal context, *see* Giuditta Cordero-Moss, *International Commercial Contracts* (2014), 91 et seq.
66. For details *see* Konstanze Brieskorn, *Vertragshaftung und responsabilité contractuelle* (2010), 218 et seq.
67. For details *see* Basil Markesinis, Werner Lorenz & Gerhard Dannemann, *The German Law of Obligations*, vol. I: *The Law of Contracts and Restitution* (1997), 43 et seq.
68. *See* Gerhard Wagner, 'Vicarious Liability', in: Arthur Hartkamp et al. (eds), *Towards a European Civil Code* (4th ed. 2011), pp. 903, 907–914; Konrad Zweigert & Hein Kötz, *Einführung in die Rechtsvergleichung* (3rd ed. 1996), 632–649.
69. Basil Markesinis, Werner Lorenz & Gerhard Dannemann, *The German Law of Obligations*, vol. I: *The Law of Contracts and Restitution* (1997), 276.

[1] Pre-contractual Liability

Facing the shortcomings of German tort law, courts have, *inter alia*,[70] enlarged the reach of contractual liability. One move in this regard was to expand the doctrine of *culpa in contrahendo*[71] to cover tort-related situations.[72] Back in 1911, the Imperial Court had to decide on the liability of a warehouse owner for damages caused by his sales person to a potential customer. The customer had entered the warehouse to buy linoleum floor covering. When the sales person showed him the product, he moved some rolls of linoleum without exercising the necessary care. These rolls fell on the customer and injured him. The Court held the shop owner liable under the doctrine of *culpa in contrahendo* (now codified in §§ 311 II, 241 II, 280 I BGB). As the accident prevented the customer from contracting with the shop-owner, contractual liability could not be properly claimed. But as the shop-owner had intentionally opened his premises to customers and thus paved the way for concluding contracts (today: § 311 II BGB), the Imperial Court expanded the rules of contractual liability to such pre-contractual situations. This expansion allowed the Court to apply § 278, 1 BGB, under which the fault of a person who is employed to perform an obligation (*Erfül-lungsgehilfe*) can be attributed to the debtor (*respondeat superior*) irrespective of whether the debtor was answerable to the breach of contract himself or not. Expanding contractual liability thus effectively closed the gaps in German tort law left by § 831 BGB. Today, the doctrine of *culpa in contrahendo* has developed into a general doctrine. It has various fields of application. Courts have even turned it into a basis for liability to recover reliance loss (*Vertrauensschaden*) in those cases where a party has signalled to the other side that a contract will certainly be concluded but later breaks off negotiations without a proper reason.[73]

[2] Contracts with Protective Effects Toward Third Parties

The concept of *culpa in contrahendo* is difficult to apply if the person suffering damage had no intention at all to enter into a contractual relationship with the seller. To overcome the perceived gaps in tort law, scholars and courts have developed the concept of 'contracts with protective effects toward third parties' (*Vertrag mit*

---

70. For other attempts to circumvent the application of § 831 BGB *see* Gerhard Wagner, 'Vicarious Liability', in: Arthur Hartkamp et al. (eds), *Towards a European Civil Code* (4th ed. 2011), pp. 903, 911–912.
71. This doctrine was to a large extent shaped by Rudolph von Jhering, 'Culpa in contrahendo oder Schadensersatz bei nichtigen oder nicht zur Perfection gelangten Verträgen', *Jahrbücher für die Dogmatik des heutigen römischen und deutschen Privatrechts* 4 (1861), 1–112.
72. Basil Markesinis, Werner Lorenz & Gerhard Dannemann, *The German Law of Obligations*, vol. I: *The Law of Contracts and Restitution* (1997), 265.
73. BGH, *Neue Juristische Wochenschrift* 1975, 1774. However, in the majority of cases no compensation was awarded due to the particular underlying circumstances, *see* BGH, *Neue Juristische Wochenschrift* 1967, 2199; BGH, *Neue Juristische Wochenschrift* 1970, 1840, 1841; BGH, *Neue Juristische Wochenschrift* 1996, 1884, 1885; BGHZ 71, 386, 395. For details *see* Basil Markesinis, Werner Lorenz & Gerhard Dannemann, *The German Law of Obligations*, vol. I: *The Law of Contracts and Restitution* (1997), 69.

Schutzwirkung zugunsten Dritter).[74] This concept, which today is based on a comple-tive (constructive) interpretation of the contract under the principle of good faith (§ 242 BGB),[75] extends duties of protection to a non-party to the contract, conferring contrac-tual protection to this third person. A first line of cases concerned claims against a landlord for personal damages sustained by family members or other persons who were in close relation to the tenant.[76] Later, courts extended this doctrine to damages caused to property and – more importantly – to pure economic loss.[77]

It is important to note that only duties of protection are extended to a third party, so that the third party cannot claim performance from the debtor. Nonetheless, this concept relaxes the general principle of privity of contract, i.e., that a contract is a bond between the parties. To be able to distinguish contractual liability from tort-based liability, courts have developed four requirements which have to be met for extending the protective scope of a contract to cover a non-contracting party. They take into account the interests of all parties involved (debtor, creditor and third party):

- The third person must have been exposed to the contractual obligation of the debtor in a similar manner as the creditor (*Leistungsnähe*).[78]
- The creditor must have an interest in extending the protective scope of the contract to the third party. This is assumed whenever the creditor is respon-sible for the wellbeing (*Wohl und Wehe*) of the third party, as is the case in family relationships[79] or because of duties resulting from work contracts.[80] Courts have, however, expanded the protective scope of a contract beyond such relationships.[81] Nowadays, it suffices that there is merely an unspecified interest in protecting a third party.[82]
- The debtor must be able to foresee, at the time of contracting, which persons may in fact qualify as third-party beneficiaries of his duties of protection. Yet, it is not necessary that he knows the identity of these people. It suffices that the group of included third parties can be assessed abstractly.[83]

---

74. Wolfgang Fikentscher & Andreas Heinemann, *Schuldrecht Allgemeiner und Besonderer Teil* (11th ed. 2017), no. 305; Holger Sutschet, *Der Schutzanspruch zugunsten Dritter: Unter Berücksichtigung der Pflichtenlehre des Kommissionsentwurfs* (1999), 21 et seq.
75. BGH, *Neue Juristische Wochenschrift* 2004, 3035, 3036; BGH, *Neue Juristische Wochenschrift* 2016, 3432, 3433. The foundation of this principle, originally based on § 328 BGB, is subject to debate, *see* Andreas Zenner, 'Der Vertrag mit Schutzwirkung zu Gunsten Dritter: Ein Institut im Lichte seiner Rechtsgrundlage', *Neue Juristische Wochenschrift* 2009, 1030 et seq.
76. RGZ 102, 231, 232; RGZ 160, 153, 155.
77. BGHZ 49, 350, 355 (damage to property); BGHZ 69, 82, 89 (non-pecuniary loss). On this development Holger Sutschet, *Der Schutzanspruch zugunsten Dritter: Unter Berücksichtigung der Pflichtenlehre des Kommissionsentwurfs* (1999), 23 et seq.
78. BGHZ 133, 168, 173; BGH, *Neue Juristische Wochenschrift* 2010, 3152, 3153.
79. BGHZ 66, 51, 57 (family relationship).
80. BGH, *Neue Juristische Wochenschrift* 1969, 269, 272; BGH, *Neue Juristische Wochenschrift* 1977, 2208, 2209.
81. BGH, *Neue Juristische Wochenschrift* 1965, 1955, 1956 et seq.; BGH, *Neue Juristische Wochen-schrift* 1984, 355, 356.
82. BGH, *Neue Juristische Wochenschrift* 1996, 2927, 2928 et seq.; BGH, *Neue Juristische Wochen-schrift* 2001, 3115, 3116.
83. BGH, *Neue Juristische Wochenschrift* 1968, 885, 887; BGH, *Neue Juristische Wochenschrift* 1984, 355.

- Lastly, the third party must be worthy of protection (*schutzwürdig*). This can be assumed if this party has no equivalent claim of its own against the debtor, i.e., a claim that is based on the same prerequisites.[84]

Based on the concept of contracts with protective effect for third parties, it is, e.g., possible to grant employees who have been harmed by a dangerous substance (which was bought by their employer) a direct contractual claim against the seller. Similarly, a landlord whose auxiliary negligently injured the child of his tenant is liable for that damage under the law of contract and does not have the possibility to exculpate himself, as it would be possible under tort law. A borderline case is the following scenario: A doctor implants a contraceptive device that turns out to be ineffective due to the doctor's negligence. Subsequently, the patient engages in a sexual relationship that results in a child. The BGH ruled that the patient's lover had a claim to relief regarding child support payments since the requirements of a contract with protective effects toward third parties were satisfied.[85]

[3]   Combinations: The Lettuce Leaf Case

The extension of a contract's protective scope may also be combined with the doctrine of *culpa in contrahendo*, as can be demonstrated by the lettuce leaf case:[86] A potential buyer entered a self-service grocery store accompanied by her 14 year old daughter, who slipped on a leaf of lettuce on the floor and injured herself. The BGH held that the obligation arising from the legal relationship between the parent and store, i.e., the obligation resulting from the *culpa in contrahendo* situation, generates a protective effect for the daughter, so that she could raise a contractual claim for damages against the supermarket. Other jurisdictions would clearly have applied tort law (vicarious liability) to such a scenario.

§6.03   CONTRACT FORMATION

[A]   Consensus of the Parties

The formation of a contract requires a meeting of minds of the (two or more) parties. Such a consensus is usually reached when one party makes an offer (*Angebot*) to the other side, which then accepts it (*Annahme*). The CISG (Articles 14 et seq. CISG) and many other jurisdictions provide similar rules.[87] The division of the contracting phase into 'offer' and 'acceptance' is a useful theoretical tool for analysing the parties' agreement – even though the contract-making process is often 'more disorderly [than

---

84. BGH, *Neue Juristische Wochenschrift* 1996, 2927, 2929; BGH, *Neue Juristische Wochenschrift* 2016, 3432, 3433.
85. BGH, *Neue Juristische Wochenschrift* 2007, 989, 991; for details *see* Juliana Mörsdorf-Schulte, 'Vermögensschutz beim One-Night-Stand?', *Neue Juristische Wochenschrift* 2007, 964 et seq.
86. BGHZ 66, 51, 58.
87. For a comparative overview *see* Jessica Schmidt, *Der Vertragsschluss* (2013), 130 et seq.

suggested by these categories]'.[88] The rules for contract formation are laid down in §§ 145 et seq. BGB. As offer and acceptance are declarations of intent, one must read these provisions together with the general rules on such declarations (§§ 104–144 BGB).

[B]   Offer

[1]   Essential Content

An offer is a promise to contract by which the offeror wants to be bound. As any declaration of intent, it can be declared expressly (*ausdrücklich*) or impliedly (*konkludent*). To be valid, the promise must be sufficiently precise and complete regarding the essential components of the contract (*essentialia negotii*). The essential stipulations must at least be ascertainable, so that an acceptance can be declared by just saying 'yes' or 'I agree'[89] – otherwise a contract cannot be formed.[90] What kind of stipulations are deemed essential varies according to the contract type proposed. In a sales contract, at least the price and the item that is put up for sale must be ascertainable.[91] That does not mean that the parties have to fix the price themselves immediately. It is also possible to conclude a contract and agree that one of the parties (§ 315 BGB) or a third person (§ 317 BGB), e.g., an expert, will fix the price for them. To avoid over-formalism, the law provides further exceptions to the rule of completeness. If a client hops into a taxi and instructs the driver to drive him to the airport, a contract is formed if the latter does so despite the parties not having addressed the price for this service. Where a person regularly carries out an obligation for remuneration, the parties are deemed to have tacitly agreed on a price. The customer thus has to pay either the regular tariff or – if no such tariff exists – the 'usual' remuneration. Such rules exist, e.g., with regard to service contracts (§ 612 BGB) or contracts for work (§ 632 BGB).

[2]   Distinguishing Invitations to Treat

An offer must be distinguished from a mere invitation to treat (*invitatio ad offerendum*). Simple postings of goods for sale on a website,[92] advertising in newspapers or on websites[93] or the sending of advertising material (catalogues, etc.)[94] are usually not regarded as offers given that the seller normally still wants to have the last word on

---

88. Arthur Taylor von Mehren, 'The Formation of Contracts', in: idem (ed.), *International Encyclopedia of Comparative Law*, vol. VII/1 (2008), no. 9–112; Basil Markesinis, Hannes Unberath & Angus Johnston, *The German Law of Contract: A Comparative Treatise* (2nd ed. 2006), 57.
89. Basil Markesinis, Hannes Unberath & Angus Johnston, *The German Law of Contract: A Comparative Treatise* (2nd ed. 2006), 59.
90. Arthur Taylor von Mehren, 'The Formation of Contracts', in: idem (ed.), *International Encyclopedia of Comparative Law*, vol. VII/1 (2008), no. 9–60.
91. Helmut Köhler, *BGB: Allgemeiner Teil* (40th ed. 2016), § 8 no. 8; Dieter Medicus & Stephan Lorenz, *Schuldrecht I: Allgemeiner Teil* (21st ed. 2015), no. 210.
92. BGH, *Neue Juristische Wochenschrift* 2005, 976; BGH, *Neue Juristische Wochenschrift* 2005, 3567, 3568; Heinrich Dörner, 'Rechtsgeschäfte im Internet', *Archiv für die civilistische Praxis* 202 (2002), 363, 377 et seq.
93. BGH, *Neue Juristische Wochenschrift* 2012, 2268, 2269.

conclusion of a contract. He might not want to contract with certain potential customers (e.g., with persons that had not made timely payments on previous purchases) and might have to check whether he is actually still able to sell the product (since it may already be sold out at the time the request of a potential buyer reaches him). Whether placing goods on shelves in a supermarket constitutes a binding offer or a mere invitation to contract is still subject to debate. It is argued that such displays should be treated as mere invitations given that the seller would want to reserve the right to contract; among other reasons the seller may wish to retain the possibility of avoiding sales *en gros* to single customers. Thus, in a supermarket a contract should be deemed to be concluded only when the customer puts the chosen goods on the counter and the cashier accepts this offer on behalf of the market.[95] Things are different with regard to the purchase of fuel at a self-service station. Here, the contract is concluded already when the customer puts the fuel into his tank, since in this case both parties have an interest in concluding the agreement at this early point (the seller having already handed over the product and the buyer – as he cannot return it – wanting to keep the fuel irrespective of whether the seller would eventually want to contract with him or not).[96]

[3]   *Mental Reservations and Lack of Seriousness*

A mental reservation that is not communicated to the other party does not render an offer void, unless the other side was aware of this (hidden) reservation (§ 116 BGB). A declaration that is obviously unserious is void, even if the other side understood it as serious offer and accepts it (§ 118 BGB). In the latter case, the offeror may, however, be liable for any damage resulting from reliance on the validity of the unserious declaration (§ 122 I BGB).

[4]   *Communicating the Offer*

An offer becomes effective when it reaches (*zugehen*) its addressee (§ 130 I 1 BGB). From this moment on, the declaration becomes binding (§ 145 BGB) and thus can be accepted to form a contract. § 130 I 1 BGB states a general principle, although, from its

---

94. BGH, *Neue Juristische Wochenschrift* 2009, 1337, 1338 (catalogue of a telecommunication provider); Jessica Schmidt, *Der Vertragsschluss* (2013), 204.
95. Concurring Gerhard Dietrich, 'Der Kauf im Selbstbedienungsladen', *Der Betrieb* 1972, 957, 958; Jan Busche, in: *Münchener Kommentar zum Bürgerlichen Gesetzbuch*, vol. I (7th ed. 2015), § 145 BGB no. 12; Basil Markesinis, Hannes Unberath & Angus Johnston, *The German Law of Contract: A Comparative Treatise* (2nd ed. 2006), 63; Manfred Wolf & Jörg Neuner, *Allgemeiner Teil des Bürgerlichen Rechts* (11th ed. 2016), § 37 no. 7; Jessica Schmidt, *Der Vertragsschluss* (2013), 219; contra Reinhard Bork, in: *J. v. Staudingers Kommentar zum Bürgerlichen Gesetzbuch, Allgemeiner Teil 4b* (revised ed. 2015), § 145 BGB no. 7; Götz Schulze, 'Rechtsfragen des Selbstbedienungskaufs – zur Abgrenzung von Qualifikations- und Identitätsaliud beim Stückkauf über vertauschte Ware', *Archiv für die civilistische Praxis* 201 (2001), 232, 235 (display of goods is an offer by the seller that is accepted by the customer at the cashier's desk).
96. BGH, *Neue Juristische Wochenschrift* 2011, 2871.

wording, it deals with declarations addressed to absent persons.[97] At the latest, an offer reaches the addressee when he takes notice of it. But even prior to that point in time, an offer can be legally deemed to have reached its recipient and therefore become effective. This is the case when it has been conveyed to the addressee's sphere of influence (letter box, email inbox, voicemail, etc) and a sufficient amount of time has elapsed such that it would have been possible under usual circumstances to take notice of the offer.[98]

[5]   Irrevocability of an Offer

German law does not in principle allow the offeror to revoke an offer after it has become binding. This approach stands in sharp contrast to common law, which generally allows the withdrawal of the offer at any time prior to acceptance by the addressee.[99] The drafters of the BGB justified this binding effect with the needs of commerce and the necessity of legal certainty,[100] but they carved out important exceptions: First, it is possible to revoke the offer before it has become binding, i.e., before it has reached its addressee. Hence, if the revocation reaches the addressee prior to or at the same time as the offer (§ 130 I 2 BGB), the latter does not become binding as it was validly revoked. Second, the offeror is free to exclude the irrevocability of his offer (§ 145 BGB). In the commercial world, such a revocable offer can be expressed through wordings such as 'Angebot freibleibend' (offer may change) or 'Angebot ohne Obligo' (offer without commitment). Depending on the circumstances of the particular case,[101] these declarations may also be qualified as mere invitations to treat.[102]

[6]   Expiry of an Offer

If the offer was not revoked on time, it expires if it is explicitly rejected by the addressee or at least not accepted in due time (§ 146 BGB). In principle, the offeror is free to fix the timeframe in which his offer must be accepted (§ 148 BGB). If he has not done so, two scenarios are to be distinguished: First, offers made to a person present in the same physical setting or via direct means of communication, such as the telephone, must be accepted immediately (§ 147 I BGB). Second, offers made to a person not present in the same place, e.g., via letters, fax or email, are binding up to the time at which the offeror may usually expect to receive an answer (§ 147 II BGB).

---

97. Manfred Wolf & Jörg Neuner, *Allgemeiner Teil des Bürgerlichen Rechts* (11th ed. 2016), § 33 no. 10.
98. BGH, *Neue Juristische Wochenschrift* 2004, 1320; BGHZ 137, 205, 208; Hein Kötz, *Vertragsrecht* (2nd ed. 2012), no. 94.
99. Edwin Peel, *The Law of Contract* (14th ed. 2015), no. 2–058.
100. Benno Mugdan, *Die gesammten Materialien zum Bürgerlichen Gesetzbuch für das Deutsche Reich*, vol. I (1899), 443.
101. *See* BGH, *Neue Juristische Wochenschrift* 1984, 1885 et seq. ('*freibleibend entsprechend unserer Verfügbarkeit*' in a charter contract for an airplane was qualified as an offer).
102. Basil Markesinis, Hannes Unberath & Angus Johnston, *The German Law of Contract: A Comparative Treatise* (2nd ed. 2006), 64 et seq. The Imperial Court has regarded such declarations as mere invitations to treat, *see* RGZ 105, 8, 12.

In the event the offeror dies after voicing his offer (or loses his capacity to contract), the offer does not become void *ipso iure* (§ 130 II BGB). Yet whether a contract can still be concluded through a declaration of acceptance conveyed to the heirs (or the legal representative) of the offeror is a different issue. § 153 BGB states that the contract can be concluded unless a 'different intention' of the offeror can be inferred. The latter can be assumed, e.g., if the offer related to a service that only the offeror could provide or the purchase of a good that only the deceased needed.[103] For instance, if a craftsman had offered to repair the roof of a house and his heirs do not want (or are not qualified) to carry on his business, no contract can be concluded. By contrast, if a shopkeeper has offered goods to a customer before dying, the latter can usually accept the offer with the shopkeeper's heirs if there is no ascertainable intention to the contrary on the part of the offeror.

[C]   Acceptance

[1]   *Express and Implied Acceptance*

A contract is concluded if the addressee accepts the offer expressly or impliedly. The declaration of acceptance must match the offer and has to be declared before the offer expires. Any late acceptance or an acceptance modifying the offer is a counteroffer (§ 150 BGB) which must in turn be accepted by the original offeror to produce a contract.

Like an offer, a declaration of acceptance must in principle reach the addressee (§ 130 I 1 BGB) to form a contract, although there are exceptions. § 151, 1 BGB relieves the acceptor from transmitting the acceptance to the offeror if this is commonly not expected or the offeror has explicitly waived the requirement. This provision does not, however, relieve the addressee from accepting the offer at least impliedly.[104]

[2]   *Contracting by Remaining Silent*

If the addressee remains silent and also does not accept the offer impliedly (e.g., by carrying out the works the offeror asked him to do), no contract is concluded as mere silence does not carry any declaration of intent – neither of acceptance nor of refusal.[105] There are, however, some exceptions to this general rule.

The parties may agree that silence is to have a certain meaning.[106] If, e.g., the addressee conveys to the offeror that he wants to sleep on the offer for a night and that the contract should be deemed concluded in the event he does not contact him before noon the next day – and the offeror agrees with this understanding – then a contract is

---

103. Hein Kötz, *Vertragsrecht* (2nd ed. 2012), no. 109.
104. Reinhard Bork, *Allgemeiner Teil des Bürgerlichen Gesetzbuchs* (4th ed. 2016), no. 749; Florian Faust, *Bürgerliches Gesetzbuch Allgemeiner Teil* (6th ed. 2018), § 3 no. 18.
105. Ernst A. Kramer, 'Schweigen als Annahme eines Antrags', *Jura* 1984, 235, 238; Jens Petersen, 'Schweigen im Rechtsverkehr', *Jura* 2003, 687.
106. Manfred Wolf & Jörg Neuner, *Allgemeiner Teil des Bürgerlichen Rechts* (11th ed. 2016), § 31 no. 14.

concluded after the deadline has passed if the addressee has remained silent. However, if the offeror asks a client whether he wants to buy an object and adds that he will deem silence as acceptance, a contract will not be concluded even if the addressee does not reject the offer as there was no agreement between the parties on the meaning of silence.

In exceptional cases, the default rules of the BGB attribute a specific meaning to the addressee's silence. Sometimes, silence is defined as rejection. If, e.g., the contractual partner of a child older than seven but younger than eighteen asks the child's parents to approve the contract, § 108 II 2 BGB stipulates that silence of the legal representatives for more than two weeks is tantamount to rejecting the request. A similar rule can be found in § 415 II 2 BGB on the assumption of a debt. But silence may also be deemed an acceptance. If a person hands over a good to another person and asks the recipient if he wants to accept it as a donation, silence is deemed as acceptance (§ 516 II 2 BGB) since it is presumed that an addressee who does not want to conclude a donation contract will expressly indicate so.

In the commercial world, a failure to object can more easily result in a contract. First, § 362 I HGB states that a merchant whose profession is to provide services (i.e., a carrier or a freight forwarder) must reply immediately to an offer reaching him for the provision of his usual services. Otherwise, his silence is considered an acceptance by law, thus creating a contractual relationship.[107] This rule is, however, limited to cases in which the addressee already has a business relationship with the offeror or cases where the addressee proposed carrying out business with the offeror.

Second, silence following the receipt of a commercial confirmation letter (*kaufmännisches Bestätigungsschreiben*) in the aftermath of contractual negotiations may serve to modify the contract already concluded. If parties to a B2B transaction have negotiated and agreed on a contract, one party often summarises the results of the oral negotiations and might even add some minor points or its standard terms to complete the agreement. If such a confirmation is sent to the other side in a timely manner following the negotiations, the addressee must immediately (i.e., without undue delay) object to it if he believes the letter does not state what was agreed upon.[108] If he remains silent, a contract is concluded on the terms of the confirmation letter.[109] This rule protects legal communication in B2B-settings given that in the commercial world contracts are often concluded after very brief negotiations. The sender and recipient must therefore be merchants or persons participating in business in a similar manner.[110] Courts, will also apply this rule in instances where negotiators agree in principle on the content of a contract without themselves concluding an

---

107. For more details *see* Claus-Wilhelm Canaris, *Handelsrecht* (24th ed. 2006), § 23 nos. 1 et seq.
108. Claus-Wilhelm Canaris, *Handelsrecht* (24th ed. 2006), § 23 nos. 1 et seq.; Tobias Lettl, 'Das kaufmännische Bestätigungsschreiben', *Juristische Schulung* 2008, 849, 850 et seq.
109. BGHZ 7, 187, 189; BGHZ 11, 1, 3; Ludwig Raiser, *Das Recht der Allgemeinen Geschäftsbedingungen* (1935), 193.
110. BGHZ 40, 42, 44; Jan Busche, in: *Münchener Kommentar zum Bürgerlichen Gesetzbuch*, vol. I (7th ed. 2015), § 147 BGB no. 16; Tobias Lettl, 'Das kaufmännische Bestätigungsschreiben', *Juristische Schulung* 2008, 849, 850 et seq.

agreement;[111] in such situations it may be the case that one party was represented by a negotiator that had no signature power, and the other side consequently sends a letter to the principal summarising the arrangement.[112] In this case, too, silence will amount to the conclusion of a contract even though strictly speaking the letter referring to the negotiations is merely an offer.[113]

It is important to note, however, that a confirmation letter may result in a contract or alter the content agreed upon only if the sender could reasonably assume that the recipient would silently approve the letter's content. This is clearly not the case if the sender intentionally misstates the results of the negotiations, e.g., by making up an order.[114] As it is often difficult to establish whether the sender wilfully misstated the results of the negotiation or whether he simply misunderstood or merely completed what was negotiated, courts have developed a second limitation:[115] no contract is concluded if the confirmation deviates significantly from what was originally agreed upon, because in that case the sender cannot reasonably expect that the silent recipient agrees with the significant alteration.[116] This is often the case when the sender adds his standard terms.[117] A third limitation concerns the scenario that both parties have sent confirmation letters to each other containing different terms. Although the views are divided on this matter, it is submitted that no objection is necessary in this constellation as it is obvious to each sender that the other side does not approve of the diverging terms.[118] That does, however, not necessarily mean that no contract was produced. It only means that it was not concluded based on one of the confirmation letters.[119]

[D]   Battle of Forms

In the commercial world, it is commonplace that both parties contract on the basis of their respective standard terms. In many transactions, these terms are, however, not expressly discussed in the course of the negotiations. That often leads to a scenario in which the buyer makes an offer using a form containing his terms and conditions and the seller accepts it through a letter or similar communication including his own standard terms. Standard terms usually differ, e.g., with regard to limitations of liability or prescription periods, because each side acts in a self-favouring manner. In practice, given that there is an agreement on the contract's essential points, none of the

---

111. BGHZ 7, 187, 189; BGH, *Neue Juristische Wochenschrift Rechtsprechungs-Report Zivilrecht* 2001, 680.
112. BGH, *Neue Juristische Wochenschrift* 1964, 1951, 1952; Jens Petersen, 'Schweigen im Rechtsverkehr', *Jura* 2003, 687, 691 et seq.
113. Karsten Schmidt, *Handelsrecht: Unternehmensrecht I* (6th ed. 2014), § 19 no. 94.
114. RGZ 95, 48, 51.
115. Hein Kötz, *Vertragsrecht* (2nd ed. 2012), no. 120.
116. BGHZ 40, 42, 44; BGHZ 61, 282, 286; BGHZ 93, 338, 343; BGH, *Neue Juristische Wochenschrift* 1994, 1288; BGH, *Neue Juristische Wochenschrift Rechtsprechungs-Report Zivilrecht* 2001, 680, 681.
117. BGHZ 61, 282, 286 et seq.; Karsten Schmidt, *Handelsrecht: Unternehmensrecht I* (6th ed. 2014), § 19 no. 111.
118. The BGH makes an exception when the discrepancy is not significant, *see* BGH, *Neue Juristische Wochenschrift* 1966, 1070, 1071.
119. Karsten Schmidt, *Handelsrecht: Unternehmensrecht I* (6th ed. 2014), § 19 no. 117.

contracting parties will pay much attention to the standard terms of the other side while executing the contract. It is, thus, accepted that a contract was concluded under these circumstances, but the question nevertheless arises: What are the terms of this agreement? The traditional view argues that the terms of the party 'firing the last shot' must apply (*Theorie des letzten Worts*). Following this reasoning, since a contract may only be formed if offer and acceptance match, an acceptance joined by the introduction of different standard terms constitutes a counteroffer (§ 150 II BGB) which needs to be accepted by the original offeror at least implicitly by shipping or accepting the shipped goods. Whereas German courts first followed this traditional approach,[120] they later slowly backed away from its application.[121] In 1985 the BGH finally shifted to the knock-out rule in cases where the parties insisted on contracting solely on the basis of their own standard terms.[122] Under this rule, which is since long supported by scholars,[123] opposing standard terms are considered not included in the contract given that there is no agreement of the parties on these stipulations – unlike on the contract as such. Gaps left by the rules 'knocked-out' under this reasoning must be filled by applying default rules. This approach relies on a holistic view of the contract and finds some support in the codified law on standard terms, namely in § 306 II BGB. Although the BGH never explicitly discarded the last-shot rule, it no longer plays a role in practice given that most parties' standard terms will now include defence clauses (*Abwehrklauseln*) specifying the non-acceptance of a contractual partner's general terms.[124]

[E]   Agency

The German law of agency (*Stellvertretung*) and authority (*Vollmacht*) is laid down in §§ 164–181 BGB. These provisions distinguish between two legal relationships, the first being a grant of authority enabling an agent to bind his principal in relation to a third party (external relation) and the second being a legal relationship between agent and principal, e.g., resulting from an employment or mandate contract, that itself forms the basis of authority (internal relation).[125] Both relationships are in principle independent, with the result that the end of the underlying (internal) legal relationship may not

---

120. BGHZ 18, 212, 216; BGH, *Neue Juristische Wochenschrift* 1963, 1248.
121. Before embracing the knockout-rule explicitly, the BGH argued that the standard terms of the counteroffer were not accepted implicitly by the other side through the execution of the contract and that the principle of good faith (§ 242 BGB) barred the parties from claiming that no contract had been concluded at all, *see* BGHZ 61, 282, 286–289. On this argument Oleg de Lousanoff, 'Neues zur Wirksamkeit des Eigentumsvorbehaltes bei kollidierenden Allgemeinen Geschäftsbedingungen', *Neue Juristische Wochenschrift* 1985, 2921, 2924.
122. BGH, *Neue Juristische Wochenschrift* 1985, 1838, 1839.
123. Peter Ulmer & Harry Schmidt, 'Nachträglicher „einseitiger' Eigentumsvorbehalt', *Juristische Schulung* 1984, 18, 20 (with further references).
124. Giesela Rühl, 'The Battle of the Forms: Comparative and Economic Observations', *University of Pennsylvania Journal of International Law* 24 (2003), 189, 203 et seq.
125. This approach can be traced back to Paul Laband, 'Die Stellvertretung bei dem Abschluß von Rechtsgeschäften nach dem allgem. Deutsch. Handelsgesetzbuch', *Zeitschrift für das gesamte Handelsrecht und Wirtschaftsrecht* 10 (1866), 183–241, *see* Wolfram Müller-Freienfels, *Stellvertretungsregelungen in Einheit und Vielfalt* (1982), 94 et seq.

trigger the end of the agent's (external) authority to bind the principal and vice versa.

To bind the principal, the agent himself must form and declare the intent to conclude the contract. If he simply delivers the declaration of his principal, e.g., a written offer, he is not an agent but a mere messenger (*Bote*).[126]

Moreover, the agent must clearly state that he acts on behalf of the principal, unless it is apparent from the circumstances that he wants to contract for another person (*Offenkundigkeitsprinzip*, § 164 I 2 BGB).[127] This is, e.g., the case when the cashier in a supermarket accepts the offer of a customer. If it is not apparent that the agent intended to act for the principal and he has not explicitly stated so, he is himself bound by the contract (§ 164 II BGB). Thus, the BGB provides for direct representation (*unmittelbare Stellvertretung*) only and does not recognise indirect representation in the sense that the agent could bind a 'hidden principal'.[128]

Finally, the agent must have acted within the scope of his powers (*Vertretungs-macht*) to bind the principal (§ 164 I 1 BGB). The power to bind another person contractually may flow from three sources: (i) It can be granted through statutory provisions (*gesetzliche Vertretungsmacht*). For example parents are the legal represen-tatives of their minor children (§§ 1626 I, 1629 BGB) and can conclude contracts on their behalf. Likewise, corporations act through their legal representatives, such as the managing director (*Geschäftsführer*) of a limited company (*Gesellschaft mit beschränk-ter Haftung*, § 35 I 1 GmbHG), and in bankruptcy cases the trustee can conclude contracts for the estate. (ii) Power can also flow from a *Vollmacht*, i.e., an act by which the principal confers authority to his agent (§ 166 II BGB) (*rechtsgeschäftliche Vertre-tungsmacht*). This form of authority to the agent is granted by virtue of a declaration of the principal vis-à-vis the agent or to the contracting partner or by public announce-ment (§ 167 I BGB). The distinction between statutory and contractual authority is not as sharp as it may seem at first sight. This is best illustrated by the granting of a *Prokura* (a very powerful form of authority for commercial transactions): although this is a unilateral act of the owner of a commercial establishment, its limits are prescribed by statute to protect commercial transactions in general (§§ 48–50 HGB). (iii) Finally, the power to bind another person may flow from situations of good faith reliance (*Rechtsscheinsprinzip*). If, e.g., a person pretends to be an agent and through the

---

126. For details *see* Manfred Wolf & Jörg Neuner, *Allgemeiner Teil des Bürgerlichen Rechts* (11th ed. 2016), § 49 nos. 13 et seq. On the foundations of this approach Volker Beuthien, 'Zur Theorie der Stellvertretung im Bürgerlichen Recht', in: *Festschrift für Dieter Medicus* (1999), pp. 1 et seq.

127. On the function of this principle Dorothee Einsele, 'Inhalt, Schranken und Bedeutung des Offenkundigkeitsprinzips – unter besonderer Berücksichtigung des Geschäfts für den, den es angeht, der fiduziarischen Treuhand sowie der dinglichen Surrogation', *Juristenzeitung* 1990, 1005, 1006.

128. An exception applies to everyday cash transactions as in these cases the contracting party generally does not need nor want to know whether the agent himself or the principal is to be bound by the contract ('*Geschäft für den, den es angeht*'), *see* Basil Markesinis, Hannes Unberath & Angus Johnston, *The German Law of Contract: A Comparative Treatise* (2nd ed. 2006), 111.

negligence of the principal it seems that he indeed acts under his authority, the agent can bind the principal (*Anscheinsvollmacht*).[129]

If the agent had no power to conclude the contract on behalf of the principal or acted outside of his powers, he must pursuant to § 179 I BGB at the choice of the contracting partner either fulfil the contract or compensate him for any damage caused.

[F]   No Consideration

German law does not require consideration for an offer to become binding. There is no real equivalent to the Anglo-American doctrine of consideration. That does not mean, however, that German law leaves the offeror unprotected. For instance, the drafters of the BGB have laid down certain formal requirements for important transactions that are intended to protect one or even both parties against overly hasty decisions. Moreover, it always ought to be carefully evaluated whether a declaration really amounts to a binding offer or simply to a promise on a goodwill basis (*Gefälligkeitsverhältnis*), the latter of which may not produce any legal obligations.

§6.04   VALIDITY AND AVOIDANCE OF THE CONTRACT

[A]   Protection of Minors and Persons with Mental Disturbances

Contracts can only be concluded by persons with the legal capacity to do so. As a general rule, anyone can enter into a contract. Exceptions protect persons whose judgment might be impaired such that it would not appear reasonable to bind them to their declarations.

Minors under the age of seven thus cannot conclude contracts at all. As they cannot voice a valid declaration of intent (§§ 104 no. 1, 105 I BGB), they must be represented by their legal representative(s), usually their parents (§§ 1626 I, 1629 BGB). Children older than seven but younger than eighteen have a limited capacity to contract (§§ 2, 106 BGB). They cannot conclude contracts without the consent of their legal representative(s), unless a transaction does not cause any legal disadvantage to them (§ 107 BGB) or the contract was effected by the minor with means knowingly ceded to him by his representative(s) or (with approval of the representative(s)) by a third party with the purpose of concluding the type of transaction at stake (§ 110 BGB).

Persons older than eighteen years (§ 2 BGB) generally have unlimited legal capacity. However, they may lack capacity, when a permanent mental condition impairs them in the exercise of their free will (§§ 104 No. 2, 105 I BGB) (e.g., because of an advanced state of Alzheimer's disease) or they voice declarations of intent in a state of unconsciousness or temporary mental disturbance (e.g., in a state of drug inebriation) (§ 105 II BGB). Given that persons with lasting impairments would not be able to participate in social life at all under such a strict rule as they would need the

---

129. BGHZ 102, 60, 64; Florian Faust, *Bürgerliches Gesetzbuch Allgemeiner Teil* (6th ed. 2018), § 26 no. 38.

consent of their legal representative for every single legal transaction, the legislature has introduced an exception for low-value contracts pertaining to everyday transactions (§ 105a BGB). Such contracts (e.g., on the acquisition of tickets for local public transport or for a cinema visit) are valid as soon as performance has been effected.[130]

[B] Formal Requirements

There is no general rule requiring that contracts assume a certain form. Thus, they can be validly concluded even without uttering a single word, i.e., by declaring offer and acceptance impliedly (*supra* §6.03[C][1]). It is a different matter when the parties have agreed that certain declarations must adhere to a particular form (written form, electronic form, text format and so on). A declaration not adhering to this form is void (§ 125, 2 BGB), unless the parties have agreed otherwise.

To protect the parties from hasty decisions and to secure evidence that a contract was concluded, the legislature has further provided statutory exceptions to the principle that contracts can be formed without abiding by a certain form. For example contracts on the purchase of real estate (§ 311b I 1 BGB) or the donor's promise to enter into a donation agreement that shall not be effected immediately (§ 518 I 1 BGB) must be recorded by a notary public. A surety contract must be in writing (§ 766, 1 BGB) unless it is a commercial transaction (*Handelsgeschäft*) for the surety (*Bürge*) (§ 350 HGB). Over the last decades, new formal requirements have been introduced. In this respect, the so-called text format (§ 126b BGB), requiring a declaration on a reproducible medium (fax, email, etc.), has become more important, e.g., in the field of consumer law. If statutory form requirements are not met, the declaration and thus the overall contract are void (§ 125, 1 BGB). Sometimes, however, the law provides remedies to mitigate this result. An oral or written contract involving real estate becomes valid when conveyance (*Auflassung*) has been declared and the buyer has been recorded in the land register (§ 311b I 2 BGB). The same holds true if a donation promise is not registered by a notary but later nevertheless effected (§ 518 II BGB) or if a surety has fulfilled a surety contract that was not concluded in writing (§ 766, 3 BGB).

[C] Illegality (§ 134 BGB) and Public Policy (§ 138 BGB)

Contracts that violate a statutory prohibition (e.g., a rule of criminal or regulatory law) are void, unless the violated provision does not imply this legal consequence (§ 134 BGB). This rule aims to ensure that essential standards of justice laid down in other fields of law cannot be circumvented by contractual stipulations. Where the statutory prohibition in question is directed against the content or the purpose of the contract

---

130. For details *see* Bernhard Ulrici, 'Alltagsgeschäfte volljähriger Geschäftsunfähiger', *Jura* 2003, 520, 521.

(sale of drugs, violation of competition rules etc.), the contract is null and void.[131] But not all infringements of statutory rules lead to this result. If the parties, for instance, merely violate rules regulating the modalities of a contract, such as the opening hours for a shop, the contract is not void as these rules do not imply this harsh consequence.[132]

Further, contracts that contravene *bonos mores* are void (§ 138 BGB). Whereas § 138 I BGB lays down the general clause stipulating this rule, § 138 II BGB names usury (*Wucher*) as one example of a contract violating public policy. Under German law, a finding of usury demands more than a grossly disproportionate price for a good or service and must thus be distinguished from the concept of *laesio enormis* as known as in other jurisdictions.[133] In essence, to qualify for usury one party needs to exploit a predicament, the inexperience, the lack of judgment or a considerable weakness of the other side, this being in addition to a disproportionate price.

[D]   Defects of Intention (Mistake, Deceit, Duress)

A defect of intention (*Willensmangel*) occurs if the objective meaning of a declaration and the true intention of the declarant do not match. Subject to narrow exceptions (§§ 117 I, 118 BGB), such a declaration is not void *ipso iure*. To set it aside, the person that has made the declaration has to avoid it through rescission (*Anfechtung*). For this purpose, he must declare within certain time limits (§§ 121, 124 BGB) that he does not want to be bound by his declaration (§ 143 I BGB). In addition, there must be a ground for avoidance (*Anfechtungsgrund*). To protect the reasonable expectations of the addressee of the declaration, the drafters of the BGB have limited these grounds to certain forms of mistake, deceit and duress (§§ 119, 120, 123 BGB). A successfully rescinded declaration is deemed to be void *ex tunc* (§ 142 I BGB), so that no contract was formed from the outset. Consequently, contracts already performed need to be rewound according to the rules of unjust enrichment (§§ 812–822 BGB): delivered goods have to be returned and a remuneration paid has to be refunded.

The grounds for avoidance for mistake are laid down in §§ 119, 120 BGB. § 119 I BGB allows avoidance in cases of an *Erklärungsirrtum* ('error of expression') or an *Inhaltsirrtum* ('error of meaning'). The former concerns scenarios in which the declarant erroneously used an incorrect word or signal and did not realise his mistake (slip of tong, crossing the wrong box on a form, typing errors, etc.). The latter covers

---

131. A detailed overview is given by Christian Armbrüster, in: *Münchener Kommentar zum Bürgerlichen Gesetzbuch*, vol. I (7th ed. 2015), § 134 BGB nos. 50 et seq.; Rolf Sack & Maximilian Seibel, in: *J. v. Staudingers Kommentar zum Bürgerlichen Gesetzbuch, Gesetzliches Verbot, Verfügungsverbot, Sittenwidrigkeit* (revised ed. 2017), § 134 BGB nos. 195 et seq.
132. Burkhard Boemke & Bernhard Ulrici, *BGB Allgemeiner Teil* (2nd ed. 2014), § 11 no. 18; Florian Faust, *Bürgerliches Gesetzbuch Allgemeiner Teil* (6th ed. 2018), § 9 no. 2.
133. Basil Markesinis, Hannes Unberath & Angus Johnston, *The German Law of Contract: A Comparative Treatise* (2nd ed. 2006), 249. On the concept of laesio enormis *see* Christoph Becker, *Die Lehre von der laesio enormis in der Sicht der heutigen Wucherproblematik* (1993); Thomas Finkenauer, 'Laesio Enormis', in: Jürgen Basedow, Klaus J. Hopt & Reinhard Zimmermann (eds), *The Max Planck Encyclopedia of European Private Law* (2012), vol. II, pp. 1029 et seq.

scenarios in which a word or sign was correctly used as intended, but the declarant erred with regard to its true meaning. § 120 BGB extends the right to rescind to cases in which a declaration was wrongfully communicated by a third party acting as messenger. Finally, § 119 II BGB allows avoidance in exceptional cases in which erroneous assumptions have been made in respect of certain characteristics of the goods or persons that are regarded as important in the context of the contract. For instance, if the buyer of a piece of land erroneously thinks that construction is permitted on the land, he can in principle rescind the contract if it turns out that the property is located in an area reserved for agriculture. § 119 II BGB thus concerns errors relating to the decision-making process preceding the declaration. This rule is an exception to the general principle that simple motivational mistakes leading to the conclusion of a contract (*Motivirrtümer*), e.g., mere errors on the profitableness of a deal, do not allow for avoidance. Avoidance based on §§ 119, 120 BGB must be declared immediately – i.e., without undue delay – after the error has been detected (§ 121 I 1 BGB). In any case, the right to rescind the contract expires ten years after the declaration was made (§ 121 II BGB). Where a contract has been successfully avoided, the contesting party must compensate the other side for the damage resulting from his reliance on the validity of the contract (§ 122 I BGB).

§ 123 I BGB allows a person to avoid a declaration of intention induced by deceit or unlawful duress. In the case of deceit, avoidance has to be declared within one year of its discovery by the person entitled to avoid; as to duress, avoidance must be effected within one year from the time the unlawful duress ends (§ 124 I, II BGB). If more than ten years have passed since the declaration was made, avoidance is excluded (§ 124 III BGB) in any event.

[E] Scrutiny of Standard Terms

[1] Historical Development and Design of the Law

Standard contract terms have found wide use since the industrial revolution even though their origins can be traced back much further in time. As a consequence, the courts have recurrently confronted such terms. Relying on the general rules on contract formation, courts assessed the circumstances under which standard terms were incorporated into the contract. Moreover, special rules of construction emerged, and over time German courts developed more sophisticated tools to police the content of standard terms.[134] The latter development was hailed by *Ludwig Raiser* as a 'page of glory in German jurisprudence' (*Ruhmesblatt der deutschen Rechtsprechung*).[135] Whereas the beginning of the 20th century saw the Imperial Court strike out an unjust clause on application of § 138 BGB – in a case where a monopolist exploited a predicament faced by his contractual partner – the Federal Supreme Court later widened court control by making the principle of good faith (§ 242 BGB) the yardstick

---

134. *See* the examples cited by Phillip Hellwege, *Allgemeine Geschäftsbedingungen, einseitig gestellte Vertragsbedingungen und die allgemeine Rechtsgeschäftslehre* (2010), 2 et seq.
135. Ludwig Raiser, 'Vertragsfreiheit heute', *Juristenzeitung* 1958, 1, 7.

for review. In 1976, the German legislature enacted the Standard Contract Terms Act (AGBG),[136] which adopted many of the prohibitions shaped to that point by case law. The transposition of the Unfair Contracts Terms Directive 93/13/EEC[137] brought only few changes. Since the *Schuldrechtsmodernisierung*, which again only slightly modified the law, the rules for policing standard terms have been embodied in §§ 305–310 BGB. § 310 BGB defines the scope of application of the different rules (not all rules apply to all types of contracts and contractual parties) and exempts certain fields of law from scrutiny.

The history of the law of standard terms explains why Germany – unlike other jurisdictions and unlike Directive 93/13/EEC – does not limit court control over standard terms to B2C contracts. The principle of good faith and other rules German courts had relied on to police standard terms were of a general nature, and many of the cases in which courts disallowed unfair terms concerned commercial transactions. Indeed, the very first case in which the Imperial Court rejected an unfair term concerned a contract between a ship owner and the operator of the Kiel Canal (*Nord-Ostsee-Kanal*).[138] When enacting the AGBG, the German legislature cast this case law into statutory form but made clear that B2B-contracts ought to be subject to more lenient oversight than clauses in B2C contracts. In recent times, numerous voices have criticised the courts' alleged tendency to scrutinise standard terms in B2B contracts too strictly.[139] They fear that Germany will fall back in the competition of jurisdictions[140] and that parties are being forced to evade German courts by relying on arbitration[141] and (where possible) choice-of-law clauses pointing to a jurisdiction with a more lenient system, such as Switzerland.[142]

[2]   Incorporation of Standard Terms and Their Interpretation

§ 305 I BGB defines standard terms as contractual stipulations that (i) have been pre-formulated for use in a multitude of contracts, (ii) are introduced by one party

---

136. *Gesetz zur Regelung des Rechts der Allgemeinen Geschäftsbedingungen (AGB-Gesetz) of 9 December 1976*, BGBl. I 1976, 3317.
137. *Directive 93/13/EEC of the Council of 5 April 1993 on unfair terms in consumer contracts*, O.J. L 95, 29.
138. RGZ 62, 264, 266.
139. Klaus-Peter Berger, 'Für eine Reform des AGB-Rechts im Unternehmerverkehr', *Neue Juristische Wochenschrift* 2010, 465 et seq.; Lars Leuschner, 'Reformvorschläge für die AGB-Kontrolle im unternehmerischen Rechtsverkehr', ZIP – *Zeitschrift für Wirtschaftsrecht* 2015, 1045 et seq. For an overview *see* Hartmut Oetker, 'AGB-Kontrolle im Zivil- und Arbeitsrecht', *Archiv für die civilistische Praxis* 212 (2012), 202, 229 et seq.; Wolfgang Wurmnest, 'Kautelarpraxis und AGB-Recht', *Rabels Zeitschrift für ausländisches und internationales Privatrecht* 82 (2018), 346, 378 et seq.
140. Jörg Kondring, 'Flucht vor dem deutschen AGB-Recht in Inlandsverträgen', *Recht der Internationalen Wirtschaft* 2010, 184 et seq.; contra Friedrich Graf v. Westphalen, 'Wider einen Reformbedarf beim AGB-Recht im Unternehmerverkehr', *Neue Juristische Wochenschrift* 2009, 2977 et seq.; idem, 'AGB-Kontrolle – kein Standortnachteil', *Betriebs-Berater* 2013, 1357 et seq.
141. Thomas Pfeiffer, 'Die Abwahl des deutschen AGB-Rechts in Inlandsfällen bei Vereinbarung eines Schiedsverfahrens', *Neue Juristische Wochenschrift* 2012, 1169 et seq.
142. Thomas Pfeiffer, 'Flucht ins schweizerische Recht? – Zu den AGB-rechtlichen Folgen der Wahl schweizerischen Rechts', in: *Festschrift für Friedrich Graf v. Westphalen* (2010), pp. 555 et seq.

unilaterally and (iii) have not been negotiated individually between the parties. § 310 III BGB widens these requirements with regard to consumer contacts, as e.g., also clauses that are pre-formulated for single use only can be scrutinised (§ 310 III no. 2 BGB).

§ 305 II BGB sets forth a special incorporation regime for standard terms that takes precedence over the general rules on contract formation. This regime does not apply if standard terms are used against an entrepreneur or a public entity (§ 310 I 1 BGB). Pursuant to § 305 II no. 1 BGB, the user of standard terms must expressly draw the contractual partner's attention to the standard terms or, where this is too onerous, must put up a clearly visible notice at the place of contracting. § 305 II no. 2 BGB further specifies that the other side must have an opportunity to take notice of the standard terms. In the field of transport law and in the utility sector a relaxed incorporation test applies (§ 305a BGB), reflecting that these terms are often approved by an authority and announced to the public in advance. Even if the user of the standard terms has complied with these requirements (or with those laid down in §§ 145 ff. BGB outside the field of consumer contracts), clauses that are 'surprising' from the standpoint of a contracting partner's legitimate expectations are not incorporated into the contract (§ 305c I BGB). A term can be deemed surprising not only when it significantly alters the content of the contract (e.g., by setting forth a payment obligation in the event of a consensual termination of a rental contract)[143] but also when it is placed in an unusual position within the body of standard terms.[144]

When interpreting standard terms, the *contra proferentem* rule applies: Any doubt as to the interpretation of standard terms must be decided against their author (§ 305c II BGB). This rule also applies if terms were used against an entrepreneur or a public entity, as can be inferred from § 310 I BGB.[145] Historically, in many jurisdictions this rule was one of the first to limit the substantive scope of unfair clauses as courts construed the clauses in favour of the contractual partner when possible.[146]

[3]   *Fairness Test*

Standard terms incorporated into a contract can be reviewed on the basis of §§ 307–309 BGB. In accordance with Directive 93/13/EEC, German law sets forth a general provision (§ 307 BGB) flanked by non-exhaustive lists of contractual clauses that are regularly (§ 309 BGB) or at least usually null and void (§ 308 BGB). These lists are intended to guide the courts and enhance legal certainty. Whereas the general clause applies to all contracts covered by the law of standard terms, most of the prohibitions in the non-exhaustive lists (except § 308 no. 1a, 1b BGB) are limited to B2C contracts (§ 310 I BGB) even so there is a certain spill over effect on B2B contracts. In practice,

---

143. OLG Karlsruhe, *Neue Juristische Wochenschrift Rechtsprechungs-Report Zivilrecht* 2000, 1538, 1539.
144. BGHZ 84, 109, 113.
145. BGH, *Neue Juristische Wochenschrift Rechtsprechungs-Report Zivilrecht* 2012, 1261.
146. Kevin Kosche, *Contra proferentem und das Transparenzgebot im Common Law und Civil Law* (2011), 68 et seq.

the fairness test under the general provision of § 307 BGB is of much greater importance than the non-exhaustive lists given that their prohibitions are well known and predominantly avoided by lawyers drafting standard contracts.

The fairness test is subject to a number of qualifications. First, only terms that deviate from (or supplement) statutory provisions are subject to full scrutiny (§ 307 III 1 BGB). If a term simply reproduces the law in plain and comprehensible language, it is not open to a fairness test since 'ordinary' courts should not have the power to indirectly review statutory provisions. Second, German law does not allow courts to review actual contractual stipulations which, by their very nature, cannot be regulated by default rules but must be determined by the parties in exercise of their party autonomy.[147] Therefore, the terms that describe the essential performance (*Leistungs-beschreibungen*) cannot be reviewed on the basis of §§ 307–309 BGB. The same applies to the price because courts cannot and must not evaluate 'whether the deal is a good or a bad one'.[148] Clauses altering the price or performance are, however, not exempt from scrutiny.[149]

§ 307 I 1 BGB stipulates that terms unreasonably disadvantaging the other party contrary to the requirement of good faith are void. Such an unreasonable disadvantage can be assumed if the term deviates from essential principles of the default rules in the BGB or other statutes (§ 307 II no. 1 BGB) or if it limits the essential rights or duties of the parties under the contract so as to jeopardise its purpose (§ 307 II no. 2 BGB). In addition, § 307 I 2 BGB specifies that courts can strike out clauses on the basis that they are non-transparent, i.e., not worded in plain and comprehensible language.

The 'black list' (§ 309 BGB) prohibits, for instance, price increases on short notice in contracts for the delivery of goods or for the provision of services where performance has to be rendered up to four months after the contract was concluded, though this is limited to contracts that cannot be classified as contracts of continuing obligation (*Dauerschuldverhältnisse*) (no. 1). Other prohibitions limit the possibility of the user including in his standard terms certain unfair penalties (no. 6) or liability limitation clauses (no. 7). The 'grey list' (§ 308 BGB) concerns, *inter alia*, terms granting their user an additional and unreasonably long timeframe to perform (no. 1), the right to terminate the contract without any reason (no. 3), or the right to modify performance in an unreasonable manner (no. 4).

Unfair standard terms are void and the gap has to be filled by applying default rules found in the law (§ 306 II BGB). The remainder of the contract continues to be valid unless it creates an unreasonable hardship for one party (§ 306 I, III BGB).

---

147. Thomas Pfeiffer, in: Manfred Wolf, Walter F. Lindacher & Thomas Pfeiffer (eds), *AGB-Recht – Kommentar* (6th ed. 2013), § 307 BGB no. 288.
148. Basil Markesinis, Hannes Unberath & Angus Johnston, *The German Law of Contract: A Comparative Treatise* (2nd ed. 2006), 175.
149. For details *see* Michael Coester, in: *J. v. Staudingers Kommentar zum Bürgerlichen Gesetzbuch, Recht der Allgemeinen Geschäftsbedingungen* (revised ed. 2013), § 307 BGB nos. 275 et seq.; Andreas Fuchs, in: Peter Ulmer, Hans Erich Brandner & Horst-Diether Hensen (eds), *AGB-Recht: Kommentar* (12th ed. 2016), § 307 BGB nos. 18 et seq.; Wolfgang Wurmnest, in: *Münchener Kommentar zum Bürgerlichen Gesetzbuch*, vol. II (7th ed. 2016), § 307 BGB nos. 12 et seq.

§6.05 PERFORMANCE AND OTHER FORMS OF EXTINGUISHING AN OBLIGATION

[A] Performance

A contractual obligation expires if the performance is rendered by the debtor to the creditor as promised (§ 362 I BGB) or (with the creditor's approval) to a third party for the purpose of performing the contract (§ 362 II BGB) (*Erfüllung*). The parties may stipulate the modalities of performance in their agreement. In case they have not done so, the BGB provides default rules, e.g., regarding the place and time of performance (§§ 269, 271 BGB) or partial performance (§ 266 BGB).

In the event that a personal performance was agreed upon, the debtor is the only person that can perform the contract (§ 267 I 1 BGB). In other cases, a third party may step in to perform the obligation even without the debtor's consent (§ 267 I 2 BGB). However, where the debtor objects to performance by a third party, the creditor may choose to (but is not required to) reject the performance (§ 267 II BGB). The person to whom the obligation must be effected is the creditor if not agreed otherwise. An exception applies if the creditor is no longer entitled to receive the performance, e.g., because he is insolvent (§ 80 I InsO). Likewise, performance made towards persons lacking capacity or towards minors does not extinguish the obligation unless the legal representative has given his consent.[150]

Even though the extinction of an obligation usually requires that the promised obligation has been effected, performance can also be assumed if the creditor accepts another type of performance in lieu of the agreed performance (*Leistung an Erfüllungs statt*, § 364 I BGB). This can, e.g., be assumed if the seller of a new car accepts the buyer's old car in lieu of a part of the agreed purchase price.[151] It is a different situation when a new obligation towards the creditor is assumed, as it often occurs in the commercial world in order to facilitate or to secure payment. Handing over a cheque or a promissory note does not (unless otherwise agreed upon) lead to the extinction of the creditor's claim. Performance of this claim can be assumed only if the creditor receives the promised obligation by cashing the cheque or promissory note.[152]

[B] Set-Off

[1] *Concept and Effect*

Two parties owing each other obligations of the same kind, such as money, can be discharged of their obligations by an off-setting of one party's claim to performance against that of the other party (§§ 387, 389 BGB). A set-off has to be declared by one

---

150. Dirk Looschelders, *Schuldrecht: Allgemeiner Teil* (15th ed. 2017), no. 346.
151. BGHZ 46, 338, 342.
152. Hein Kötz, *Vertragsrecht* (2nd ed. 2012), no. 855; Dirk Looschelders, *Schuldrecht: Allgemeiner Teil* (15th ed. 2017), no. 368; Dieter Medicus & Stephan Lorenz, *Schuldrecht I: Allgemeiner Teil* (21st ed. 2015), no. 276.

party to the other party as it does not arise *ex lege* (§ 388, 1 BGB). The notice is not subject to special formal requirements and can also be declared outside judicial proceedings, as, under German law, set off is a matter of substantive law. It leads to an extinguishing of the mutual obligations to the extent that they correspond to each other (§ 389 BGB). This applies retroactively so that discharge operates as of the moment when the two obligations could have been set-off for the first time.[153] Consequently, a contractual penalty clause that seemed to have been triggered already might fall away upon set-off of the underlying claim.[154]

The function of set-off is twofold: On the one hand, the party declaring set-off can discharge himself from an existing contractual obligation. On the other hand, the party declaring set-off can enforce the claim he has against the other party (cross-claim), e.g., in cases where the contractual partner does not currently have the means to pay the debt.[155]

[2]   Requirements for Set-Off

As far as not agreed otherwise by the parties, set-off requires that the claim and the cross-claim are mutual and of the same kind (§ 387 BGB), e.g., monetary claims. Mutual claims for money in different currencies are, however, not considered to be of the same kind, such that a claim in Euros may not be set-off against a claim in USD (unless agreed otherwise).[156] Due to the enforcement effect of set-off, the cross-claim that the person declaring set-off has against the other party must be enforceable (§ 387 BGB), i.e., the claim must exist and be due. Moreover, the other side must not have a defence against the cross-claim (§ 390), such as the defence of the other side's non-performance (§ 320 I BGB). An exception applies to claims that are time-barred. § 215 BGB provides that a set-off is not excluded when the cross-claim was not time-barred at the time when the set-off could first have been declared. Whether the person declaring set-off has a defence against the claim of the other party is of no relevance as a debtor is always free to perform even though he could refuse to do so.[157]

In certain situations, set-off is excluded by law. In order to avoid self-administered justice, a set-off may not be effected for a tort that was deliberately committed (§ 393 BGB) (otherwise a creditor may be encouraged to beat up a recalcitrant debtor and then off-set the debtor's claim for damages with the claim he

---

153. For a critical view *see* Peter Bydlinski, 'Die Aufrechnung mit verjährten Forderungen: Wirklich kein Änderungsbedarf?', *Archiv für die civilistische Praxis* 196 (1996), 276, 281 et seq.; Reinhard Zimmermann, 'Die Aufrechnung: Eine rechtsvergleichende Skizze zum Europäischen Vertragsrecht', in: *Festschrift für Dieter Medicus* (1999), pp. 707, 723 et seq.
154. Ingeborg Schwenzer, 'The Law of Contracts' in: Werner F. Ebke & Mathew W. Finkin (eds), *Introduction to German Law* (1996), pp. 173, 187.
155. Dirk Looschelders, *Schuldrecht: Allgemeiner Teil* (15th ed. 2017), no. 373; Dieter Medicus & Stephan Lorenz, *Schuldrecht I: Allgemeiner Teil* (21st ed. 2015), no. 293.
156. Martin Schlüter, in: *Münchener Kommentar zum Bürgerlichen Gesetzbuch*, vol. II (7th ed. 2016), § 387 BGB no. 32.
157. Dirk Looschelders, *Schuldrecht: Allgemeiner Teil* (15th ed. 2017), no. 378.

has against the debtor).[158] Moreover, restrictions apply to claims that are seized (§ 392 BGB) or that are not subject to attachment (§ 394, 1 BGB), such as minimum wages.

In addition, the parties can agree by contract to exclude the right to set-off, although standard terms to this effect are subject to restrictions. § 309 no. 3 BGB prohibits clauses that deprive a consumer of the right to set off a claim that is uncontested or that has been ascertained by a court whose decision has become final. The BGH has held that this prohibition applies *cum grano salis* also to B2B contracts.[159]

[C]   Release

An obligation is extinguished in full or in part through a valid release (*Verzicht*). Whereas in some jurisdictions, a release is conceptualised as being of a unilateral nature (such that the creditor may extinguish the debtor's obligation without the consent of the latter), the drafters of the BGB codified a contractual concept (§ 397 BGB) as the release was seen as *actus contrarius* to the creation of the obligation.[160] A valid release thus requires offer and acceptance, as does an agreement by which creditor and debtor concur that there is no obligation (§ 397 II BGB). The contractual foundation of the concept of release has been severely criticised by scholars, who point out that a defence or a property right can be relinquished either contractually or unilaterally. Given that the relinquishment of a defence or a property right is a mechanism comparable to a release concerning an obligation, the inconsistency resulting therefrom should be brought to an end by granting a right to unilateral release.[161]

[D]   Other Forms

An obligation can be extinguished if the debtor deposits the owed sum, valuables, securities or other documents for the benefit of the creditor with a public authority (§ 372 BGB), such as a court, provided that the debtor gives up his right to reclaim the deposited things (§ 378 BGB). Deposits of this nature are open to the debtor if the creditor cannot be identified with certainty or if the creditor is in default of acceptance (§ 372 BGB). In the latter case, the debtor may also auction or sell the objects not capable of being deposited pursuant to the rules set forth in §§ 383–386 BGB (*Selbsthilfeverkauf*).

---

158. Hein Kötz, *Vertragsrecht* (2nd ed. 2012), no. 875.
159. BGHZ 92, 312, 316.
160. On the historical origins *see* Jens Kleinschmidt, 'Release', in: Jürgen Basedow, Klaus J. Hopt & Reinhard Zimmermann (eds), *The Max Planck Encyclopedia of European Private Law* (2012), vol. II, pp. 1446, 1447.
161. Jens Kleinschmidt, *Der Verzicht im Schuldrecht: Vertragsprinzip und einseitiges Rechtsgeschäft im deutschen und US-amerikanischen Recht* (2004), 262 et seq.; Reinhard Zimmermann, 'Vertrag und Versprechen: Deutsches Recht und Principles of European Contract Law im Vergleich', in: *Festschrift für Andreas Heldrich* (2005), pp. 467, 483 et seq.

§6.06   THE GENERAL SYSTEM OF CONTRACTUAL REMEDIES

[A]   Introduction

As a general term for all sorts of scenarios concerning the non-performance of a contractual obligation, German lawyers coined the expression *Leistungsstörungen* (irregularities in the performance of a contract). Since the *Schuldrechtsmodernisierung* there are three general remedies: Performance *in specie* of the primary duty (*supra* §6.02[B]), damages (§§ 280–283 BGB and other rules) and termination of the contract (§§ 314, 323–325, 326 V, 346–348).[162] Recovering expenses occurred in reliance on the debtor's promise to perform (§ 284 BGB) may be grouped into the category of 'damages'. Regarding the remedy of termination, it is important to understand that German law distinguishes between *Kündigung* for what are termed contracts of continuing obligations (*Dauerschuldverhältnisse*), e.g., contracts for rent or work and *Rücktritt* for all other contracts, e.g., sales contracts. In addition, consumers may revoke certain contracts (§§ 355–361 BGB and other rules). In exceptional cases, a party may demand adaption or termination of a contract based on the doctrine of the 'foundation of the transaction', i.e., a variant of frustration (§ 313 BGB). These general rules are complemented (and sometimes supplanted) by the rules laid down in the specific part of the law of obligations dealing with specific contractual regimes (*see infra* §6.07), such that both sets of rules still have to be read together when assessing claims for breach of contract.

From an Anglo-American perspective, the German breach of contract rules contain some particularities. The first stems from the fact that under German law – unlike under common law – performance *in specie* (of non-monetary obligations) can be enforced if the creditor so demands. This difference also affects remedies for breach of contract. *Markesinis, Unberath & Johnson* remark in this respect that under German law the parties 'should at least make one attempt to keep the contract alive [before they are entitled to seek satisfaction elsewhere]. Hence, granting the debtor a period of grace (*Nachfrist*) becomes a *Leitmotiv* of the German approach to "breach". This also ties in well with the German (indeed continental European) predilection to protect the debtor'.[163] The second major difference is that, under German law, a debtor is only liable for damages if he is responsible for the breach of contract, which is to say that he has acted with fault, as far as it is not provided otherwise (§ 276 I 1 BGB). This general principle differs from the Anglo-American system that regards contractual promises as guarantees such that any failure to perform triggers damages claims to the extent that the breach cannot be excused.[164]

---

162. Basil Markesinis, Hannes Unberath & Angus Johnston, *The German Law of Contract: A Comparative Treatise* (2nd ed. 2006), 386.
163. *Ibid.*, 381.
164. *Ibid.*, 380 et seq.; Konrad Zweigert & Hein Kötz, *Einführung in die Rechtsvergleichung* (3rd ed. 1996), 501 et seq.

[B] The Right to Specific Performance and Exclusions of This Right

[1] Specific Performance

The right to specific performance may concern the contract's main obligation, such as the delivery of the purchased good or the payment of the remuneration for a service rendered. It may also relate to auxiliary obligations, i.e., obligations that complement or secure the performance of the main obligation, such as packaging the sold good.[165] A special form of performance *in specie* is the right to claim *Nacherfüllung*, i.e., the cure of defective performance rendered earlier. If the contractual partner has tried and failed to perform his obligation because this first attempt did not comport with the standards agreed to, the creditor may demand that the debtor cure the defect. This right exists in sale contracts (§§ 437 No. 1, 439 BGB) and in contracts for work (§§ 634 no. 1, 635 BGB). It protects the debtors by granting them a second chance to perform the contract and thus a chance to secure full payment.[166]

[2] Impossibility of Performance

[a] General Rule

The creditor's claim for performance *in specie* is excluded if performance is impossible for the debtor or any other person (§ 275 I BGB). This rule applies to all types of impossibility regardless of timing and modality.[167] It does not matter whether performance was impossible at the time the contract was concluded ('initial impossibility') or whether impossibility arose after that time ('subsequent impossibility'). It is also irrelevant whether the impossibility to perform is confined to the person of the debtor ('subjective impossibility') or whether performance is impossible for all individuals ('objective impossibility').[168] In all of these cases, the debtor is released from his obligation to perform the contract, irrespective of whether or not he is answerable for the circumstances leading to impossibility.

§ 275 I BGB also applies to claims for cure of defective performance (*Nacherfüllung*). For example, if it turns out that a sold second-hand car had been involved in an accident, it is impossible for the seller to cure this defect, provided that the car was sold as accident-free. It is a different situation if interpretation of the contract reveals that the seller is allowed to deliver another car similar to the car initially sold. In such a scenario, the seller would be able to perform his obligation. This example plainly shows that impossibility always has to be measured against the precise content of the contract.

---

165. Dirk Looschelders, *Schuldrecht: Allgemeiner Teil* (15th ed. 2017), no. 12.
166. Hein Kötz, *Vertragsrecht* (2nd ed. 2012), no. 762.
167. Claus-Wilhelm Canaris, 'Die Reform des Rechts der Leistungsstörungen', *Juristenzeitung* 2001, 499.
168. Reinhard Zimmermann, 'Remedies for Non-Performance: The revised German law of obligations, viewed against the background of the Principles of European Contract Law', *Edinburgh Law Review* 6 (2002), 271, 280 et seq.

[b]   Practical Impossibility

Sometimes, performing the obligation may not be impossible but come at the price of unreasonable efforts or expenses. § 275 II BGB allows the debtor to refuse performance whenever performing would require an effort grossly disproportionate to the creditor's interest in obtaining the performance. Scholars speak of 'practical impossibility' (*praktische Unmöglichkeit*) when referring to such a situation. In assessing proportionality, the principle of good faith and the content of the obligation must be taken into account. It also matters whether the debtor is responsible for the impediment or not. The classic textbook example of 'practical impossibility' hypothesises a previously sold ring of little value that – prior to be received by the buyer – has fallen into a deep lake at no fault of the seller.[169] As the seller could drain the lake and recover the ring, § 275 I BGB does not apply. Under the assumption that the ring is of little value to the creditor (buyer) in comparison to the costly efforts the debtor (seller) would incur in order to deliver the ring, the law allows the seller to refuse performance in this case. Given that § 275 II BGB is a defence of the seller, it is up to him to invoke the unreasonableness of performance or to overcome the impediment and perform the contract.

To understand the scope of § 275 II BGB, it is important to note that this rule does not protect the debtor from economic risks associated with commercial transactions inherent to the contract concluded. A builder having promised to construct a house for a fixed price, for instance, cannot rely on § 275 II BGB if it turns out that building the house is much more onerous and costly because the ground is swampy.[170] Also, cases of 'economic impossibility' (*wirtschaftliche Unmöglichkeit*) in which a change of circumstances causes a strong imbalance between performance and counter-performance causing economic hardship to the debtor, do not qualify as cases of 'practical impossibility'. In those cases, the interest of the creditor to obtain performance is usually very strong and outweighs the costs to be incurred by the debtor when performing the contract. Cases of such economic hardship due to a change of circumstances following the conclusion of a contract might in exceptional cases be remedied under the doctrine of the 'foundation of the transaction', i.e., the German equivalent of frustration (*infra* §6.06[E]).[171]

[c]   Moral Impossibility

Finally, § 275 III BGB gives the debtor a defence when he has to render a service in person and it would be unreasonable to expect him to perform. The textbook case of

---

169. This example was already cited close to a century ago by Philipp Heck, *Grundriß des Schuldrechts* (1929), 89.
170. A similar example is given by Hein Kötz, *Vertragsrecht* (2nd ed. 2012), no. 811.
171. Claus-Wilhelm Canaris, 'Die Reform des Rechts der Leistungsstörungen', *Juristenzeitung* 2001, 499, 501; Reinhard Zimmermann, 'Remedies for Non-Performance: The revised German law of obligations, viewed against the background of the Principles of European Contract Law', *Edinburgh Law Review* 6 (2002), 271, 282.

such a 'moral' or 'personal impossibility' (*persönliche Unmöglichkeit*) is a singer who refuses to perform a concert after having learned that a close family member has died or become severely ill.[172]

[d]   Rights of the Creditor

In the event the debtor is released from performing the obligation, § 275 IV BGB specifies the rights of the creditor. He can claim damages if the debtor is answerable for the subsequent impediment leading to the impossibility (§§ 280 I, III, 283 BGB) or (in a case of initial impossibility) if he knew or ought to have known that it would be impossible to fulfil the obligation he has entered into (§ 311a II BGB). Alternatively, he can claim reimbursement of frustrated expenses that were made (in vain) in reliance on the debtor's promise to perform (§ 284 BGB) (*infra* §6.06[F][6]).

In addition, under § 285 I BGB, the creditor may claim the substitute (*commodum*) the debtor received in lieu of what he was supposed to deliver to the creditor. If, e.g., the object to be delivered under the contract was destroyed, the debtor might have acquired a claim against an insurer. The debtor has to cede this claim to the creditor.

With regard to reciprocal contracts, § 326 I 1 BGB stipulates that a debtor who is released from fulfilling his contractual duties in accordance with § 275 I-III BGB cannot claim counter-performance (i.e., payment) from the creditor. Hence, the creditor is also relieved of his payment obligations and need not pay. If the creditor has already paid the debtor, he may reclaim the money pursuant to §§ 326 IV, 346 et seq. BGB. Matters are different if the creditor of the performance is solely or predominately responsible for the impossibility (§ 326 II 1 BGB). In this case, he is deemed unworthy of protection and must pay the price without receiving performance. If, e.g., a tenant has negligently burned down the house, § 275 I BGB releases the landlord from the obligation to grant the tenant use of the house. He is, however, still entitled to claim the rent pursuant to § 326 II 1 BGB because the tenant is responsible for causing impossibility.[173] Similarly, the creditor is not released from paying the price if he was in delay of accepting the performance when the harm occurred (§ 326 II 1 BGB). Breach of his own obligations thus justifies that the creditor bears the risk of having to pay the price without receiving the promised good or service.[174] Further, the creditor has to pay the price if he claims the substitute item under § 285 BGB (§ 326 III 1 BGB). There are further exceptions, e.g., in sales law, when the risk has passed onto the buyer.

---

172. Dirk Looschelders, *Schuldrecht: Allgemeiner Teil* (15th ed. 2017), no. 441; Reinhard Zimmermann, 'Remedies for Non-Performance: The revised German law of obligations, viewed against the background of the Principles of European Contract Law', *Edinburgh Law Review* 6 (2002), 271, 285.
173. Hein Kötz, *Vertragsrecht* (2nd ed. 2012), no. 828.
174. Hartmut Oetker & Felix Maultzsch, *Vertragliche Schuldverhältnisse* (4th ed. 2013), § 2 no. 376.

[C]   Termination

[1]   Overview

A contract can be terminated (the German lawyer speaks of *Rücktritt*) if a right to termination has been contractually agreed upon or if the statutory rules laid down in §§ 323–326 BGB apply. Termination allows one contractual partner to be discharged from his own obligations towards the other side, with the consequence that both parties are released from their duties to perform and have to return whatever they have received in performance of the contract so far (§§ 346–348 BGB). That is why the statutory rules on termination concern merely mutual contracts, i.e., contracts in which one party promises performance in exchange for receiving a performance from the other party in return. For gratuitous (non-reciprocal) contracts, the BGB provides special rules that may release a person from his duty to perform. A donor, e.g., is entitled to revoke the donation under specific circumstances (*infra* §6.07[C]).

The law of termination has to strike a balance between the interests of the debtor and those of the creditor. The debtor, on the one hand, will generally want to fulfil the contract and earn the remuneration (if the deal is beneficial to him), whereas the creditor, on the other hand, may want to pull out immediately in order to obtain the promised good or service elsewhere.[175] The CISG limits the right to terminate a contract to cases of fundamental breach (Article 49 I a, 64 I a, 25 CISG), whilst English law limits termination to breaches of obligations forming the basis of the contract.[176] Unless the parties have agreed otherwise, German law allows termination for all forms of breaches provided that the other side has been granted a second chance to perform (§ 323 I BGB). Nevertheless, there are exceptions to the 'second chance rule' whenever the interest of the creditor in immediate termination outweighs the interest of the debtor in fulfilling the contract (§§ 323 II, 324 BGB). Exceptions apply to trivial breaches of contract (§ 323 V 2 BGB) and where the creditor's interest in terminating the contract is unworthy of protection (§ 323 VI BGB). The right to terminate a contract does not depend on any fault of the debtor nor does it preclude the creditor from claiming damages (§ 325 BGB). A special termination regime exists for continuing obligations, which can only be terminated by a *Kündigung* (not: *Rücktritt*).

[2]   The Requirements for Termination

The general requirements for terminating a mutual contract are laid down in §§ 323, 324 BGB. These rules were modelled on the rules for damages (§§ 281, 282 BGB) to

---

175. For a comparative analysis *see* Axel Flessner, 'Befreiung vom Vertrag wegen Nichterfüllung', *Zeitschrift für Europäisches Privatrecht* 1997, 255 et seq.; Hein Kötz, *Europäisches Vertragsrecht* (2nd ed. 2015), 320 et seq.
176. Jan M. Smits, *Contract Law: A Comparative Introduction* (2nd ed. 2017), 231.

avoid circumvention of the prerequisites for termination by claiming damages in lieu of performance.[177]

[a]   Late Performance and Improper Performance

§ 323 I BGB treats two different forms of breaches. The first is what is termed late performance (the sold good was not delivered or the promised work was not finished on time). The second form is a performance of the debtor that does not comply with the contractual obligation (the delivered good or the promised work is non-conforming). The latter category is often referred to as an improper performance (*Schlechtleistung*).

If the debtor did not perform at all or improperly, the creditor may terminate the contract if performance was due (§ 323 I BGB) and the debtor could not raise any defences against it (e.g., flowing from § 275 BGB or § 320 I 1 BGB). Exceptionally, the creditor may terminate the contract before performance is due should it be obvious that the requirements for termination will be met (§ 323 IV BGB). Termination further requires the – 'unsuccessful' – expiration of a reasonable period of time to perform the contractual obligation or cure the improper performance which the creditor must have set the debtor (§ 323 I BGB). What length of time is to be considered reasonable depends on the circumstances of each case. If the deadline set is too short, the creditor may nonetheless terminate the contract after a reasonable period has lapsed.[178] Fixing such a period does not require that the creditor informs the debtor of his intention to terminate the contract should performance not be forthcoming, as long as it is clear from the wording that such a consequence is not excluded. In addition, setting a precise date for effecting performance is not necessary. Demanding performance 'within a reasonable time' or 'promptly' is enough to set the grace period.[179] A warning (*Abmahnung*) must be given in lieu of setting a grace period for effecting performance when the latter is not feasible (§ 323 III BGB).

Setting a grace period is dispensable when the debtor has unequivocally and definitively refused to perform (§ 323 II no. 1 BGB). In this case, it would be a pure formality to grant the debtor a second chance.[180] Moreover, the creditor may terminate a contract without prior warning where a specified date or a certain time frame was fixed in the contract and the debtor was aware that timely performance was essential to the creditor (§ 323 II no. 2 BGB). Finally § 323 II no. 3 BGB provides a clause covering situations in which special circumstances justify terminating the contract without providing for an additional period to cure performance. Further exemptions apply to specific contracts (§§ 440, 636 BGB).

---

177. Reinhard Zimmermann, 'Remedies for Non-Performance: The revised German law of obliga- tions, viewed against the background of the Principles of European Contract Law', *Edinburgh Law Review* 6 (2002), 271, 304 et seq.
178. BGH, *Neue Juristische Wochenschrift* 1982, 1279, 1280; BGH, *Neue Juristische Wochenschrift* 1985, 2640.
179. BGH, *Neue Juristische Wochenschrift* 2015, 2564, 2565; BGH, *Neue Juristische Wochenschrift* 2016, 3654 et seq.
180. BGH, *Neue Juristische Wochenschrift* 2012, 3714, 3716.

In cases of improper performance, § 323 V 2 BGB excludes termination for trivial breaches, e.g., the delivery of a good with a very minor defect. Termination is also excluded if the creditor was responsible for the circumstance that would otherwise entitle him to terminate the contract or if such a circumstance for which the debtor is not responsible occurs at a time when the creditor is in default of acceptance (§ 323 VI BGB).

[b]   *Infringement of Protective Duties*

§ 324 BGB covers infringements of ancillary duties as defined by § 241 II BGB. Such duties relate to a creditor's general rights and interests and do not affect the performance as such.[181] A debtor breaching such duties enables the creditor to terminate the contract (without setting a reasonable period to perform) if the breach was so severe that one could not reasonably expect the creditor to accept performance. A seller's driver insulting the buyer severely or handing out drugs to the buyer's children are examples of cases in which the creditor may terminate the contract based on § 324 BGB.[182]

[3]   **Mechanism and Legal Consequences of Termination**

To terminate a contract, one party must expressly or impliedly communicate to the other side that the contract is to be terminated and that restitution is to be made for performances to the extent they have been effected (e.g., 'I terminate the agreement' or 'I want my money back')[183] (§ 349 BGB). Consequently, both parties are relieved from their initial duties. However, unlike other legal systems, German law does not eradicate the entire contract in cases of termination.[184] Instead, a *Rücktritt* transforms the contract into a winding-up relationship (*Rückgewährschuldverhältnis*)[185] governed by §§ 346–348 BGB.

§ 346 I BGB provides that the parties have to return what they have received from the other side, including benefits from use and enjoyment (§§ 99, 100 BGB). Thus, the buyer of a defective car has to return it to the seller and restore title to him (as far as the parties did not agree on a retention of title, meaning that the property did not pass to the buyer before termination was declared); in return, the seller has to refund the purchase price, from which he may deduct a certain sum depending on the kilometres

---

181. Reinhard Zimmermann, 'Remedies for Non-Performance: The revised German law of obligations, viewed against the background of the Principles of European Contract Law', *Edinburgh Law Review* 6 (2002), 271, 305.

182. Hein Kötz, *Vertragsrecht* (2nd ed. 2012), no. 972.

183. Wolfgang Fikentscher & Andreas Heinemann, *Schuldrecht Allgemeiner und Besonderer Teil* (11th ed. 2017), no. 535.

184. For a comparative assessment *see* Michael Sonnentag, *Das Rückgewährschuldverhältnis* (2016), 65 et seq.

185. BGH, *Neue Juristische Wochenschrift* 2008, 911; BGH, *Neue Juristische Wochenschrift* 2010, 2426, 2427; Reinhard Zimmermann, 'Remedies for Non-Performance: The revised German law of obligations, viewed against the background of the Principles of European Contract Law', *Edinburgh Law Review* 6 (2002), 271, 306.

driven by the buyer.[186] Restitution has to be effected concurrently (*'Zug um Zug'*, § 348 BGB).

Where restitution in kind is impossible, § 346 II BGB allows the debtor to claim compensation equal to the value of performance instead of the performance itself (*Wertersatz*). This is the case, for instance, whenever a service was rendered, the sold good was consumed or processed, or the good has deteriorated or was destroyed. However, § 346 III BGB excludes compensation for the value where the defect permitting termination was discovered only in the course of processing the good (§ 346 III no. 1) or where the creditor was responsible for the destruction or loss of the good (§ 346 III no. 2). The same applies if the good was destroyed or has deteriorated in the sphere of the person terminating the contract, provided that this person exercised the level of care that he usually employs in his own affairs (*diligentia quam in suis*) (§ 346 III no. 3 BGB). Effectively, this means that a purchaser of a used car that was destroyed in a serious accident may reclaim the full purchase price after terminating the contract if he discovers that the car had been involved in previous accidents despite having been sold as 'accident-free'. If the buyer did not cause the accident intentionally or by grossly negligent conduct, he only has to return the car 'as it is' and does not have to compensate the seller for the value of his performance (*mortuus redhibetur*[187]). This rule, which reallocates the risk of accidental deterioration back to the seller, is based on the idea that the party in breach of contract has to bear the risk of accidental loss or deterioration in cases where neither party is responsible for the loss or deterioration.[188]

[4] *Special Rules for Continuing Obligations* (Dauerschuldverhältnisse)

A special form of termination applies to continuing obligations (*Dauerschuldverhält-nisse*), i.e., contracts requiring more than one act of performance over a certain period of time. Such a continuing performance is typical for partnership, rental, employment or service contracts. These contracts can be terminated *pro futuro* only, which makes it unnecessary to codify a special restitution regime (i.e., as laid down in §§ 346–348 BGB). The German lawyer uses a different legal term for this form of termination (*Kündigung* instead of *Rücktritt*). Put simply, there are two types of *Kündigungen*: For some contracts, such as rental contracts for housing premises, the law provides for the possibility of terminating the contract by giving notice within a certain period of time, and the tenant (unlike the landlord) does not even need to state any grounds for termination (*ordentliche Kündigung*). In addition, the law grants the parties an extraordinary right to terminate the contract if certain events occur that justify a unilateral withdrawal from the contract (*außerordentliche Kündigung*). In some cases

---

186. On the calculation of use benefits (*Gebrauchsvorteile*) for cars *see* Reinhard Gaier, in: *Münchener Kommentar zum Bürgerlichen Gesetzbuch*, vol. II (7th ed. 2016), § 346 BGB no. 27.
187. On this aspect *see* Gerhard Wagner, '*Mortuus Redhibetur* im neuen Schuldrecht?', in: *Festschrift für Ulrich Huber* (2006), pp. 591, 592 et seq.
188. Reinhard Zimmermann, 'Remedies for Non-Performance: The revised German law of obliga-tions, viewed against the background of the Principles of European Contract Law', *Edinburgh Law Review* 6 (2002), 271, 308.

this type of *Kündigung* becomes effective after a certain time has lapsed (*außerordentliche fristgebundene Kündigung*), whereas in other cases it can be excised with immediate effect (*fristlose außerordentliche Kündigung*). An example for a termination with immediate effect is the right to terminate a continuing obligation for a compelling reason (*Kündigung aus wichtigem Grund*), e.g. because the other side manifestly breached the contract even after a warning had been given (§ 314 BGB). For details on the termination of rental contracts for housing premises *see infra* §6.07[D][3].

[D]   Revocation

German consumer law allows consumers (§ 13 BGB) to revoke certain contracts concluded with an entrepreneur (§ 14 BGB).[189] This right is essentially based on rules of European origin (*see* §6.01[B][2]). Revocation must be communicated to the entrepreneur (§ 355 I 2 BGB) within certain deadlines. The right is not bound to any reasons (unlike termination or rescission). Thus, even where an entrepreneur has rendered performance in full conformity with the terms agreed upon, the contract may be revoked by the consumer solely based on a determination that he does not want to keep the goods or use the service. Under German law, revoking a contract is generally permissible in situations in which the legislature considered the consumer typically unable of assessing the full risks of the contract when concluding it.[190] Such a right exists for off-premise contracts (§ 312b BGB), distance contracts (§ 312c BGB), time-share contracts (§ 481 BGB), contracts on long-term holiday products (§ 481a BGB), consumer loan contracts (§ 491 BGB), financial assistance contracts (§ 506 BGB), instalment supply contracts (§ 510 BGB) and also for distance teaching contracts (§ 4 Distance Teaching Act). The general rules concerning revocation and the legal consequences (restitution of what was received, costs of sending back goods etc.) are set out in §§ 355–361 BGB. It is important to note that revoking a consumer contract extends to certain contracts closely tied to it, such as consumer loan contracts brokered by the contractual partner (§ 358 BGB).

[E]   Contract Adaptation Based on the Doctrine of the 'Foundation of the Transaction'

The German version of the doctrine of frustration, which has a much broader scope and different legal consequences than its common law counterpart, was essentially developed by the courts in the aftermath of World War I in order to cope with the fundamental economic changes being witnessed at that time, particularly rampant inflation. Although first seen as a variant of impossibility,[191] courts later embraced the

---

189. On the historical development of consumer contract law *see* Reinhard Zimmermann, 'Consumer Contract Law and General Contract Law: The German Experience', *Current Legal Problems* 58 (2005), 415, 417 et seq.
190. On the *raison d'être* of the right to revoke a contract Horst Eidenmüller, 'Die Rechtfertigung von Widerrufsrechten', *Archiv für die civilistische Praxis* 201 (2010), 67 et seq.
191. RGZ 88, 71, 75 et seq.; RGZ 94, 46, 47.

doctrine of 'disturbances relating to the foundations of the transaction' (*Störung der Geschäftsgrundlage*)[192] shaped by *Paul Oertmann*,[193] based on the principle of good faith (§ 242 BGB). The *Schuldrechtsmodernisierung* has cast these principles in statutory form (§ 313 BGB) without intending major changes, meaning that the bulk of the old case law still stands.

The requirements and legal consequences of this doctrine can be summarised as follows: If the circumstances forming the foundation of the transaction change significantly after the contract was entered into and the parties – assuming they had foreseen these changes – would not have concluded the contract at all or only under different terms, the aggrieved party may demand adaptation of the contract, provided that it cannot reasonably be expected that it continue to be bound by the unmodified agreement (§ 313 I BGB). Such a judge-made adaptation of the contract is also permissible if assumptions shared by both parties forming the basis of the transaction turn out to be false (§ 313 II BGB). Should adaptation of the contract be impossible or unreasonable, the disadvantaged party may terminate the agreement (§ 313 III BGB). When assessing whether adapting the obligation (or even terminating the contract) is justified, the allocation of contractual risks must be taken into account. Changes relating to a risk assumed by one party in the contract do not entitle this party to rely on the doctrine of the foundation of the transaction.[194]

The German variant of the doctrine of frustration essentially covers two narrow groups of cases: The first one concerns a serious alteration of the balance between performance and counter-performance, such as caused by a drastic rise in prices due to economic shocks or hyperinflation, given that one cannot expect the disadvantaged party to perform or accept performance at such economically unreasonable terms.[195] The second one concerns situations in which the common purpose of the contract is frustrated. The classic example is modelled on *Krell v. Henry*:[196] If a party leases a balcony or room at a very high price for a very short period (a day, an afternoon or the like) to see a coronation-event that ultimately does not take place because the (future) king is taken ill that day, a German lawyer would seek to remedy the situation by applying § 313 BGB.[197] However, this scenario is exceptional. Usually, the risk of reselling a good or making use of a rented item of property is allocated to the buyer or lessee through the agreement entered into by the parties.[198]

---

192. The landmark ruling was RGZ 103, 328, 332 et seq.
193. Paul Oertmann, *Die Geschäftsgrundlage: Ein neuer Rechtsbegriff* (1921). As to this doctrine, its precursors, and its development, *see* Basil Markesinis, Hannes Unberath & Angus Johnston, *The German Law of Contract: A Comparative Treatise* (2nd ed. 2006), 320 et seq.; Rudolf Meyer-Pritzel, in: Mathias Schmoeckel, Joachim Rückert & Reinhard Zimmermann (eds), *Historisch-kritischer Kommentar zum BGB*, vol. II/2 (2007), §§ 313–314 BGB nos. 4 et seq.
194. BGH, *Neue Juristische Wochenschrift* 1978, 2390, 2391; BGH, *Neue Juristische Wochenschrift* 2000, 1714, 1716.
195. BGH, *Wertpapiermitteilungen* 1978, 322, 323.
196. [1903] 2 KB 740.
197. Dieter Medicus & Stephan Lorenz, *Schuldrecht I: Allgemeiner Teil* (21st ed. 2015), no. 565.
198. BGH, *Neue Juristische Wochenschrift* 1984, 1746, 1747 (regarding the risk that the buyer will be able to resell the purchased object); BGH, *Neue Juristische Wochenschrift* 2000, 1714, 1716 (regarding the risk that the lessee will be able to make profitable use of the rented shop space).

[F]   Damages

[1]   Overview

The *Grundnorm* (basic standard) for damages for breach of contract is laid down in §
280 I BGB. It enshrines the core requirements applicable to all claims for damages for
any breach of contract, including the 'fault principle' (some modifications apply to
claims under § 311a II BGB). This general rule is complemented by §§ 281–283, 286
BGB, (mostly) setting forth additional requirements for particular types of breaches,
particularly to preserve the debtor's right to cure. In cases of late or improper
performance, §§ 280 I, III, 281 BGB make claims for damages in lieu of performance
contingent upon fixing a period for performance for the debtor (so he gets a second
chance to perform) unless the interest of the creditor in claiming damages without prior
warning prevails (similar to § 323 BGB). Admittedly, making the right to claim
damages contingent on a prior warning does not make sense in all cases. It would be
a purely formalistic exercise to demand that the creditor set a period for performance
where performance is impossible. For this reason, damages may be claimed immediately in such a situation (§§ 280 I, III, 283 BGB, § 311a II BGB). Claiming damages for
delay in performance requires that the debtor be in default (§§ 280 II, 286 BGB). A
further qualification added to § 280 I BGB is supplied by § 284 BGB, which allows the
creditor to claim (instead of damages) reimbursement of expenses made in reliance on
the debtor's promise to perform the contract.

From the foregoing, it becomes clear that three main types of damages claims
have to be distinguished:[199]

- First, damages in lieu of performance (*Schadensersatz statt der Leistung*), i.e.,
  claims that either replace or supplement the performance of the debtor. This
  category covers damages in cases of late or improper performance (§§ 280,
  281), damages for breach of a protective duty (§§ 280, 282), and damages
  occurring from an initial (§ 311a II BGB) or subsequent (§§ 280, 283 BGB)
  impossibility.
- Secondly, damages for delayed performance (*Schadensersatz wegen
  Verzögerung der Leistung* (§§ 280, 286 BGB).
- Thirdly, (simple) damages alongside performance (*Schadensersatz wegen
  Pflichtverletzung neben der Leistung*) (§ 280 BGB).

The aforementioned rules only stipulate the prerequisites for claims for damages.
The law of damages (*quantum*) itself, which is explained in more detail in the chapter
on tort law, is contained in §§ 249–254 BGB.

---

199. Basil Markesinis, Hannes Unberath & Angus Johnston, *The German Law of Contract: A
     Comparative Treatise* (2nd ed. 2006), 441; Reinhard Zimmermann, 'Remedies for Non-
     Performance: The Revised German Law of Obligations, Viewed Against the Background of the
     Principles of European Contract Law', *Edinburgh Law Review* 6 (2002), 271, 288.

[2] The General Requirements for Damages Claims

§ 280 I BGB states the basic requirements for damages claims. Put simply, this rule sets forth four basic requirements.

[a] Obligation

Every contractual claim for damages requires the existence of an obligation between the debtor and the creditor. Such an obligation need not necessarily be a contract between the parties but may also come into existence if the parties have such a close relationship to each other that duties of protection (§ 241 II BGB) arise. Examples of such a close relationship without a prior contract include the commencement of negotiations or the opening of business premises to customers (§ 311 II BGB).[200] Therefore, § 280 I BGB is also relevant for claims under the doctrine of *culpa in contrahendo* (*supra* §6.02[E][1]). It also applies to contracts having a protective effect towards a third party (*supra* §6.02[E][2]).

[b] Breach of Duty

A claim for damages further requires the breach of a duty (*Pflichtverletzung*). Although the German term carries a connotation of blameworthy behaviour, this is actually not implied. A breach of duty simply means that the debtor has not done what he was supposed to do (or not do) under the contract (§ 241 I BGB) or that he breached a duty of care (§ 241 II BGB). The reasons behind the breach are of no relevance.[201]

[c] 'Fault Principle'

A person is liable for damages only if he is answerable for the breach of duty (*Vertretenmüssen*). The negative formulation of § 280 I 2 BGB ('This is not the case if the debtor is not answerable for the breach of duty') indicates that the existence of this requirement is presumed, and it is up to the debtor to prove he is not answerable for the breach.[202] Even though *Vertretenmüssen* is not identical with fault (*Verschulden*), the latter is the starting point, as § 276 I BGB specifies that the debtor is liable for all forms of fault, i.e., intentional acts and negligence, unless provided otherwise. It is important to note that § 276 II BGB defines negligence objectively: A person acts negligently if he infringes the standard of care that applies to members of his trade and profession. Thus, it does not matter whether an individual debtor is subjectively capable of doing

---

200. In addition, § 280 I BGB applies to a breach of obligation arising by law.
201. Dieter Medicus & Stephan Lorenz, *Schuldrecht I: Allgemeiner Teil* (21st ed. 2015), no. 327.
202. Peter Schlechtriem & Martin Schmidt-Kessel, *Schuldrecht Allgemeiner Teil* (6th ed. 2005), nos. 589 et seq.; Oliver Brand, *Schadensersatzrecht* (2nd ed. 2015), § 11 no. 13.

what he promised. All that matters is what a member of his business community could and would have done.[203]

If the debtor makes use of another person (*Erfüllungsgehilfe*) to perform his duties under the contract, the fault of this auxiliary is imputed to the debtor without granting him a chance of exculpation (§ 278 BGB) (*supra* §6.02[E][1]).

The yardstick for measuring whether the debtor is answerable for the breach can be altered by agreement. The parties are free (within the boundary set forth in § 276 III BGB) to contract for a stricter or more lenient liability regime (when this is done by general contract terms, further limitations apply). Exceptionally, the law may vary the standard of liability. A stricter standard may, for instance, be inferred from the content of the contract when the debtor gives a guarantee with regard to the quality of a good or service or assumes the risk of procuring a certain good (§ 276 I BGB). In addition, should the debtor have to pay a sum of money, financial impediments will not excuse non-performance. In this regard, the debtor is strictly liable to have the funds necessary to effectuate performance at his disposal.[204] In turn, the law occasionally relaxes the standard of liability; this is the case regarding donors, e.g., as they do not receive (material) remuneration for their donation (*see infra* §6.07[C]).

[d]   *Damage*

The law of damages is laid down in §§ 249–254 BGB.[205] The provisions rest upon the general principle that the victim of a wrong is to be compensated to the full extent for the loss incurred (*Totalreparation*). § 249 I BGB requires the wrongdoer to restore the victim to the situation he hypothetically would have been in but for the breach. This means that the debtor owes restitution in kind (*Naturalrestitution*). But restitution in kind is not the only form of compensation provided for by law. As far as damage claims concern personal injuries or damaged property, the creditor can claim either compensation in kind or a sum of money (§ 249 II BGB). In addition, monetary compensation has to be paid whenever restitution in kind is not effected within a certain period (§ 250 BGB) or when it would be either impossible or an insufficient means of compensating the debtor (§ 251 BGB). Reading the German rules on the law of damages, one could get the impression that money claims are the exception and restitution in kind is the general rule. However, as for breaches of contract, this is not the case. Damages in lieu of performance and damages for delay in performance are necessarily monetary claims given that they replace or complement the primary remedy (performance *in specie*). Also, in cases of simple damages, the creditor will regularly seek monetary relief.[206]

---

203. Basil Markesinis, Hannes Unberath & Angus Johnston, *The German Law of Contract: A Comparative Treatise* (2nd ed. 2006), 448.
204. Dieter Medicus, "'Geld muß man haben': Unvermögen und Schuldnerverzug bei Geldmangel', *Archiv für die civilistische Praxis* 188 (1988), 489 et seq.; Hein Kötz, *Vertragsrecht* (2nd ed. 2012), no. 1095.
205. On the law of damages, *see* Oliver Brand, *Schadensersatzrecht* (2nd ed. 2015).
206. Basil Markesinis, Hannes Unberath & Angus Johnston, *The German Law of Contract: A Comparative Treatise* (2nd ed. 2006), 442.

Under German law, lost profits also have to be compensated (§ 252 BGB). This rule is complemented by § 376 II HGB. It states that the creditor of a commercial sales transaction can claim compensation for the difference in the price agreed upon and the (achievable) market price at the time and place delivery was due (*abstrakte Schadens-berechnung*) if the parties agreed upon a fixed delivery date (*Fixhandelskauf*). Contributory negligence on the part of the creditor can mitigate his claim for damages (§ 254 BGB).

While punitive damages U.S. style are alien to German law, contractual penalty clauses are permissible (§§ 336–345 BGB). Nevertheless, a judge has the power to reduce the sum agreed upon to a reasonable amount in the event the penalty is disproportionally high (§ 343 BGB). Moreover, penalty clauses in standard terms are subject to certain restrictions (*supra* §6.04[E][3]).

[3] Damages for Delay in Performance (§§ 280, 286 BGB)

Damages for a delay in performance (*Schadensersatz wegen Verzögerung der Leistung*) concern cases in which the creditor wants to hold on to the performance *in specie* but seeks compensation for lost profits or expenses suffered due to late performance. If, e.g., the contractor of a turnkey contract regarding an office building were to hand over the keys to the premises some weeks later than agreed upon, the employer would be entitled to claim compensation for expenses incurred in leasing a different office space for the time he was unable to use the contracted premises. Damages for delay are recoverable if the requirements of § 280 I BGB and § 286 BGB are met (§ 280 II BGB).[207] Besides the general requirements discussed above, most notably that the debtor is answerable for the breach (§§ 280 I 2, 286 IV BGB), the debtor must be in a state of *mora debitoris* (*Schuldnerverzug*). The creditor's claim for performance must have been due and free of defences. In addition, the creditor must have sent a *Mahnung* (a special notice) to the debtor (§ 286 I BGB) and the debtor must still not have performed.[208]

In certain cases, a notice is not necessary to put the debtor in default. Requiring such a warning would be a pure formality whenever the debtor unequivocally and definitely refuses performance (§ 286 II no. 3 BGB). More importantly, the debtor needs no 'reminder' when the performance date can be determined merely based on the calendar (1 February 2017, calendar week no. 5) or by reference to the calendar in conjunction with a certain event (fourteen days after delivery) (§ 286 II nos. 1, 2 BGB). Regarding obligations to pay money, the debtor is, at the latest, in default when he fails to cover the debt within thirty days of receiving an invoice or an equivalent demand for payment. A debtor who is a consumer can only be deemed in default after this period has lapsed if he was informed about this consequence in the invoice or demand for payment (§ 286 III BGB). These exceptions to the requirement of a *Mahnung* allow

---

207. For a critical assessment of these rules in a comparative and European perspective Eva Lein, *Die Verzögerung der Leistung im europäischen Vertragsrecht* (2015), 484 et seq.
208. Dieter Medicus & Stephan Lorenz, *Schuldrecht I: Allgemeiner Teil* (21st ed. 2015), nos. 463 et seq.

skilled contract drafters to ensure damage claims for late performance without prior warning.[209]

The creditor of a monetary claim for which the debtor is in default may claim additional interest. Notwithstanding a creditor's right to seek a higher rate of interest (§ 288 III BGB), the rate of interest is statutorily fixed at 9 percentage points above the current 'base rate'[210] for transactions not involving consumers and at 5 percentage points above this rate for all other transactions (§ 288 I, II BGB). A creditor may also claim a lump sum of €40 compensating expenses that typically accrue in cases of late payment. However, this sum is set off against a subsequent claim for damages (§ 288 V BGB).[211]

In addition to the consequences just mentioned, *mora debitoris* also alters the general liability standard of the debtor (§ 287 BGB). Most importantly, the debtor can no longer invoke certain limitations of liability as he is liable for all forms of negligence. Moreover, he is also answerable for his performance becoming impossible regardless of fault, unless the damage would have occurred even if the debtor had performed in a timely manner.

[4] Damages in Lieu of Performance

Damages in lieu of performance grant the creditor an equivalent in money which substitutes for the debtor's promise to perform.[212] Thus, his interest in receiving performance (*Erfüllungsinteresse*) must be satisfied. That is to say, the debtor must place the creditor in a position similar to the one he would hypothetically have been in, had the debtor performed properly.[213] The prerequisites to be met for this claim vary according to the breach at stake.

[a] Late or Defective Performance (§§ 280, 281 BGB)

If the debtor does not perform timely (the good was not delivered) or performs in a manner incompatible with the contract (the goods delivered had defects as to quality necessitating repair), the creditor may claim damages provided that the requirements of § 280 I BGB and § 281 BGB are met (§ 280 III BGB). This claim's main aim is to

---

209. Stefan Grundmann, 'Der Schadensersatzanspruch aus Vertrag', *Archiv für die civilistische Praxis* 204 (2004), 569, 603.
210. The 'base rate' as defined by § 247 I BGB is 3,62% but is adapted twice a year by the German *Bundesbank* based on European parameters set forth by the European Central Bank. The current rate is published in the *Bundesanzeiger* and on the website of the German *Bundesbank* (https://www.bundesbank.de). As of 1 January 2018 the base rate is fixed at -0.88%.
211. For details *see* Tim W. Dornis, 'Die Entschädigungspauschale für Beitreibungsaufwand – Neujustierung von Kompensation und Prävention im europäischen und deutschen Verzugsrecht?', *Wertpapiermitteilungen* 2014, 677 et seq.
212. Claus-Wilhelm Canaris, 'Die Reform des Rechts der Leistungsstörungen', *Juristenzeitung* 2001, 499, 512.
213. Basil Markesinis, Hannes Unberath & Angus Johnston, *The German Law of Contract: A Comparative Treatise* (2nd ed. 2006), 451.

recover expenses incurred in procuring a substitute performance at a higher price.[214] In addition to performance having been due, the creditor must have set the debtor a reasonable period to perform or cure any defects. The creditor may only claim damages if this period has lapsed without cure coming forward. When claiming damages in lieu of performance, the creditor loses his right to claim specific performance (§ 281 IV BGB) so as to avoid double recovery.

The law states two exceptions to the general rule of giving the debtor a second chance to perform: Setting a period is dispensable whenever the debtor unequivocally and definitely refuses to perform or special circumstances justify a claim for damages without prior warning (§ 281 II BGB). Further exemptions are laid down in §§ 440, 636 BGB for sale and work contracts. Given that the rule of setting a reasonable period as well as the exceptions to this rule, the latter being laid down in § 281 II BGB, correspond with § 323 II BGB (which sets forth an additional exception for *Fixgeschäfte*), the principles discussed above apply (*supra* §6.06[C][2][a]).

[b]   Impossibility (§§ 280, 283 BGB, § 311a II BGB)

In the event of impossibility (§ 275 I-III BGB) it makes no sense to provide the debtor with a second chance to perform. Therefore, the creditor is entitled to claim damages without fixing a period of grace. This rule applies regardless of whether the impossibility arises prior or subsequent to having entered into the contract. In addition, the drafters of the *Schuldrechtsmodernisierung* based both types of liability on the 'fault principle', thus avoiding arbitrary results as it is often only a matter of seconds whether the facts making performance impossible arise before or after the contract's formation.[215]

However, the liability standards set out in §§ 280, 283 BGB (subsequent impossibility) and § 311a II BGB (initial impossibility) are not entirely congruent. The point of reference for the 'fault principle' differs in the two scenarios: In cases of subsequent impossibility, the 'fault' of the debtor relates to the impediment to performance, i.e., usually a lack of diligence in procuring or safeguarding an object. This does not work for cases of initial impediments to performance as a prospective debtor is under no duty towards a prospective creditor to anticipate impediments or to apply care in guarding an object before the conclusion of a contract.[216] Against this backdrop, the draftsmen of the *Schuldrechtsmodernisierung* decided that claims for damages in lieu of performance are permissible if the requirements set forth in § 280 I

---

214. Reinhard Zimmermann, 'Remedies for Non-Performance: The Revised German Law of Obligations, Viewed Against the Background of the Principles of European Contract Law', *Edinburgh Law Review* 6 (2002), 271, 290.
215. Claus-Wilhelm Canaris, 'Die Reform des Rechts der Leistungsstörungen', *Juristenzeitung* 2001, 499, 506; Reinhard Zimmermann, *The New German Law of Obligations: Historical and Comparative Perspectives* (2005), 64.
216. Basil Markesinis, Hannes Unberath & Angus Johnston, *The German Law of Contract: A Comparative Treatise* (2nd ed. 2006), 458; Reinhard Zimmermann, 'Remedies for Non-Performance: The Revised German Law of Obligations, Viewed Against the Background of the Principles of European Contract Law', *Edinburgh Law Review* 6 (2002), 271, 299.

BGB are met, as § 283 BGB refers back to the *Grundnorm* without introducing additional requirements. Thus, a person is answerable for the breach if responsible for the impediment leading to impossibility. In turn, damages for initial impossibility require that the debtor knew or should have known that performance was impossible (but not that he was responsible for causing impossibility). Analogous to the interpretation of § 280 I 2 BGB, the prerequisite that the debtor is answerable can be presumed (but the presumption can be rebutted) given the negative formulation found in § 311a II 2 BGB ('This is not the case...').[217]

§ 311a II BGB also covers damages in lieu of performance when the defect of a delivered good cannot be remedied. A person selling a second-hand car as being accident-free even though it was not, for instance, is liable for damages only if he knew or should have known of the defect (however, his knowledge is presumed pursuant to § 311a II 2 BGB).[218]

[c]   *Breach of Protective Duties (§§ 280, 282 BGB)*

A claim for damages under §§ 280, 282 BGB in lieu of performance covers breaches of ancillary duties (§ 241 II BGB) relating to the creditor's general rights and interests. The requirements set forth in § 282 BGB correspond with those in § 324 BGB (apart from the 'fault' criterion). This claim for damages concerns scenarios in which the main performance itself was proper, though made under circumstances detrimental to the creditor. In such a case, the creditor may claim damages in lieu of performance if one cannot reasonably expect him to accept performance. Such cases are rare.[219] The textbook example is a painter who, though painting in an orderly manner, regularly damages household furniture severely with his ladder over the course of his long-lasting assignment.[220] Here, the creditor may terminate the contract (§ 324 BGB), engage another painter to finish the job and claim damages from the original painter for any additional costs incurred.[221]

[5]   *Damages Alongside Performance (§ 280 BGB)*

Claims for damages alongside performance under § 280 BGB, also called 'simple damages' (*einfacher Schadensersatz*)[222] cover the infringement of ancillary duties as defined in § 241 II BGB, i.e., duties not relating to the main performance. Such claims relate to situations where the harmed party seeks damages alongside (and not instead

217. Hans Brox & Wolf-Dietrich Walker, *Allgemeines Schuldrecht* (42nd ed. 2018), § 22 no. 69.
218. Hein Kötz, *Vertragsrecht* (2nd ed. 2012), nos. 1184 et seq.
219. Wolfgang Ernst, in: *Münchener Kommentar zum Bürgerlichen Gesetzbuch*, vol. II (7th ed. 2016), § 282 BGB no. 2.
220. Regierungsbegründung, BT-Drs. 14/6040, 141 (regarding § 282 BGB).
221. Claus-Wilhelm Canaris, *Schuldrechtsmodernisierung 2002* (2002), 682.
222. Reinhard Zimmermann, *The New German Law of Obligations: Historical and Comparative Perspectives* (2005), 111.

of) performance.[223] Thus, a supermarket customer slipping on a leaf of lettuce can claim damages for breach of contract (besides claims under the law of tort). Should he slip prior to the conclusion of a contract, the doctrine of *culpa in contrahendo* (§§ 280 I, 311 II, 241 II BGB, *supra* §6.02[E][1]) enables him to claim damages. Should the accident occur after the conclusion of a contract, §§ 280 I, 241 II BGB apply. In addition, § 280 I BGB may cover cases in which the debtor has breached a duty of performance, such as a bank giving incorrect advice to a client where financial losses result.[224]

[6] Expenses Made in Reliance of the Debtor's Promise (§ 284 BGB)

Proof of damages can be difficult sometimes, especially with regard to lost profits. For this reason, § 284 BGB allows the creditor – instead of claiming damages – to recover expenses incurred in vain in reliance on the debtor's promise to perform.

[G] Other Remedies

In addition to the principal remedies highlighted so far, the BGB provides additional ones that cannot comprehensively be treated in this context. For example, in some situations a buyer may have the right to reduce the price in sale and work contracts (§ 441 BGB and § 638 BGB, respectively). There are also rules on *mora creditoris* (§§ 293–304 BGB) which, however, do not entitle the debtor to sue the creditor for breach of contract.

§6.07 SPECIAL CONTRACTUAL REGIMES

[A] Overview

Already upon its initial creation, the draftsmen of the BGB included various sets of rules in the law of obligations concerning specific contracts that were commonly encountered at the time. This set of rules was constantly supplemented, as new types of contracts developed by practising lawyers had to be codified, European directives had to be transposed, and the protection of weaker parties had to be enhanced. Today, the most important rules in the BGB concern the following contracts:[225]

- Sale (including consumer sale) and barter contracts (*Kauf* and *Tausch*), §§ 433–480 BGB.
- Timeshare contracts, contracts on long-term holiday products, brokerage contracts, exchange system contracts (*Teilzeit-Wohnrechte-Verträge, Verträge*

---

223. Hans Brox & Wolf-Dietrich Walker, *Allgemeines Schuldrecht* (41st ed. 2017), § 2 nos. 11 et seq.; Hein Kötz, *Vertragsrecht* (2nd ed. 2012), nos. 1026 et seq.
224. Hein Kötz, *Vertragsrecht* (2nd ed. 2012), no. 1028.
225. A similar list was provided by Ingeborg Schwenzer, 'The Law of Contracts', in: Werner F. Ebke & Mathew W. Finkin (eds), *Introduction to German Law* (1996), pp. 173, 191.

über langfristige Urlaubsprodukte, Vermittlungsverträge, Tauschsystemverträge), §§ 481–487 BGB.
- Consumer loan contracts, finance assistance contracts, and instalment supply contracts (*Darlehen, Finanzierungshilfen* and *Ratenlieferung für Verbraucherverträge*), §§ 488–515 BGB.
- Donation (*Schenkung*), §§ 516–534 BGB.
- Rent and usufructuary lease (*Miete* and *Pacht*), §§ 535–597 BGB.
- Gratuitous loan for use (*Leihe*), §§ 598–606 BGB.
- Service and treatment contracts (*Dienstvertrag* and *Behandlungsvertrag*), §§ 611–630h BGB.
- Contracts for work and similar contracts, especially package travel contracts (*Werkvertrag, Reisevertrag*), §§ 631–651y BGB.
- Brokerage contracts (*Mäklervertrag*), §§ 652–655e BGB.
- Promises of a reward (*Auslobung*), §§ 657–661a BGB.
- Mandate, management of the affairs of another, payment services (*Auftrag, Geschäftsbesorgung, Zahlungsdienste*), §§ 662–676c BGB.
- Deposit (*Verwahrung*), §§ 688–700 BGB.
- Partnership (*Gesellschaft*), §§ 705–740 BGB.
- Suretyship (*Bürgschaft*), §§ 765–778 BGB.
- Settlement (*Vergleich*), § 779 BGB.
- Acknowledgment of debt (*Schuldanerkenntnis, Schuldversprechen*), §§ 780–782 BGB.
- Orders (*Anweisung*), §§ 783–792 BGB.
- Bearer bonds (*Schuldverschreibung auf den Inhaber*), §§ 793–808 BGB.

[B]   Contract of Sale

[1]   Structure of the Law

Under a contract of sale, the seller has to deliver a thing to the buyer and transfer the title to him in exchange for payment of the purchase price (§ 433 BGB). Since the *Schuldrechtsmodernisierung* implemented Directive 1999/44/EC, the rules on sales law distinguishes between sales transactions in general (§§ 433–453 BGB) and consumer sales (§§ 474–479 BGB). The rules on consumer sales have to be read together with the general rules on consumer protection applicable to specific types of sales (§§ 312–312k BGB). The law of sales is also important for barter contracts (§ 480 BGB).

[2]   General Rules

[a]   Obligations of the Parties

The general rules apply to all types of sales contracts, including contracts for the purchase of real estate, goods, aggregate of goods (e.g., a collection of paintings), rights (e.g., claims, shares, rights to a name or patents), as well as aggregates of all these categories (e.g., a business), irrespective of the parties to the contract. The seller has to hand over the thing – that must be free from defects as to quality and title – to the buyer and procure ownership to him (§ 433 I BGB). The seller may have additional obligations, such as packing fragile goods in a secure fashion or providing directions for use when selling a machine.[226] The buyer has to pay the purchase price and accept the thing (§ 433 II BGB). Unless agreed otherwise, the buyer has to bear the cost of shipping the purchased things to a place other than the place of performance (§ 448 I BGB) and – in the case of a sale of land – the cost of recording the contract with a notary public (§ 448 II BGB).

The ownership of the sold thing does not pass to the buyer *ipso iure* when the sale contract is concluded or performed. Rather, the parties have to agree on transferring property to the buyer (which is in principle a separate contract, *supra* §6.01[A]) and the buyer must receive some form of possession over the good. Movables, e.g., must usually be handed over to the buyer (§ 929, 1 BGB). In sales of real estate, the buyer has to be recorded in the land register (§§ 873, 925 BGB) and similar rules apply with regard to registered ships and ships under construction. Even though the 'obligation contract' and the 'transfer contract' are independent from each other, § 449 I BGB allows the linking of both transactions by an agreement so as to ensure that the seller retains the title to goods handed over to the buyer up until the full purchase price has been paid (*Eigentumsvorbehalt*).

The parties may agree on the place where the seller must deliver the goods. This place of performance is of importance because the risk of the good being lost or destroyed passes to the buyer when it is handed over to him (§ 446, 1 BGB). Usually, the seller has to provide the goods at his place of business unless the parties have stipulated otherwise or it can be inferred from the nature of the obligation that the place of performance is elsewhere (§ 269 I BGB). In cases where the good is to be shipped elsewhere, e.g., to the place of business of the buyer, the fact that the seller has borne the cost of shipment alone does not suffice to alter the place of performance (§ 269 III BGB). Thus, if a good is shipped, the risk usually passes when the good is handed over to the first carrier (§ 447 I BGB) unless it is agreed upon otherwise. The situation is different in consumer sales contracts (*see infra* §6.07[B][3]).

[b] *Breach of Contract*

Upon the execution of a contract, all forms of impairments discussed in the section on breach of contract may occur, and the buyer and the seller will have the general remedies discussed above. The law of sales, however, provides some additional rules for breaches relating to defects as to quality and title (*Sachmängel, Rechtsmängel*, §§ 434–445b, 453 BGB). These rules must be read together with the general rules in order to assess remedies available for a breach of contract.

---

226. Wolfgang Fikentscher & Andreas Heinemann, *Schuldrecht Allgemeiner und Besonderer Teil* (11th ed. 2017), no. 811.

As a general principle, the purchased object must be free from defects as to quality and title at the time the risk passes to the buyer. Defects as to title concern the existence of any third-party rights in relation to the purchased object that have not been specified in the contract (§ 435 BGB). What is to be considered as a defect in quality can be inferred from § 434 BGB. The parties may choose to define the quality standards that the purchased object must conform to (*Beschaffenheitsvereinbarung*), § 434 I 1 BGB. This can be done explicitly (by specifying the standards in the contract) or impliedly (e.g., when the seller puts a sign on the car for sale stating certain technical information regarding the car, such as the mileage).[227] If the parties have failed to agree on a standard, the good is free of defects if suitable for the contractually intended use (§ 434 I 2 no. 1 BGB) or for the customary use the buyer can reasonably expect (§ 434 I 2 no. 2 BGB). A defect may also be assumed when the good does not demonstrate the special characteristics claimed in public statements made by the seller or the producer (which can also be the importer, *see* § 4 II ProdHaftG) or an auxiliary unless the seller was not aware of the statement (§ 434 I 3 BGB). Thus, if a watch producer advertises his products as being 'absolutely waterproof', a watch taking on water is defective even if the seller has not mentioned this characteristic when concluding the contract (as far as the seller could be aware of the advertising campaign). If a purchased good needs to be assembled, a defect can be assumed if the assembly instructions are defective (§ 434 II 2 BGB) or if the seller or his auxiliaries have assembled it improperly (§ 434 II 1 BGB). Finally, a defect is assumed even when the seller delivers an object different from that agreed on (or a lesser amount) (§ 434 III BGB).

In cases of defects, the buyer's remedies are listed in § 437 BGB, a rule referring partly to the general system of remedies but also to other rules of the sales law complementing the general rules. First, the buyer must in principle ask for cure of the defect either by remedying the defect (*Nacherfüllung*), e.g., by repairing the object (*Nachbesserung*) or by delivering another object free of defects (*Nachlieferung*) (§§ 437 no. 1, 439 BGB). This remedy – which is based on the idea that the seller should get a second chance to perform as agreed upon – does not require fault on the side of the seller. If performance is impossible or not rendered in time, the buyer is also entitled to reduce the price (§§ 437 No. 2, 441 BGB) or to terminate the contract (§§ 437 no. 2, 440, 323, 326 V BGB). Finally, the buyer may claim damages according to the general rules (§§ 437 no. 3, 440, 280, 281, 283, 311a BGB) or, alternatively, reimbursement of expenses that he reasonably incurred in expectation of performance (§§ 437 no. 3, 284 BGB).

A buyer knowing of the defect – mere doubts are insufficient – at the time of contract formation has no remedy against the seller (§ 442 I 1 BGB).[228] If the buyer was grossly negligent in overlooking the defect when the contract was formed, his rights are abrogated unless the seller acted fraudulently (§ 442 I 2 BGB). In addition, a seller

---

227. BGH, *Neue Juristische Wochenschrift* 1975, 1693, 1695; Kurt Reinking & Christoph Eggert, *Der Autokauf: Rechtsfragen beim Kauf neuer und gebrauchter Kraftfahrzeuge sowie beim Leasing* (13th ed. 2017), no. 2782.
228. Annemarie Matusche-Beckmann, in: *J. von Staudingers Kommentar zum Bürgerlichen Gesetzbuch, Kaufrecht* (revised ed. 2014), § 442 BGB no. 12.

having guaranteed that the object comports with certain standards is liable for any deviances from that standard as in such cases even a limitation of liability would be void (§ 444 BGB).[229] The formation of the contract being the relevant point in time, the buyer does not forfeit his remedial rights should he gain knowledge of the defect in the timeframe between signing the contract and accepting delivery. This is true even if he accepts the object without notifying the seller of the defect – unless one can construe the delivery of the defective good and the unconditional acceptance as an alteration of the original contract.[230]

It is important to note that buyers in general do not have to inspect the goods and to give timely notice of defects to maintain their claims regarding defects as to quality, unlike merchants who are under such an obligation (§ 377 HGB).

[3]   *Consumer Sale Contracts*

Special mandatory rules, which alter the general rules, govern contracts concluded between a 'consumer' (§ 13 BGB) and an 'entrepreneur' (§ 14 BGB) on the sale of movables (§ 474 BGB).[231] These rules, which transpose the European Directive 1999/44/EC (*supra* §6.01[B][2]), also apply when the consumer sale is accompanied by a service to be effected by the seller (§ 474 I 2 BGB), e.g., assembling the purchased item. Due to space limitations, only two important rules can be outlined here.

First, § 475 II BGB alters the general rule enshrined in § 447 I BGB that the risk of accidental loss or deterioration passes to the buyer when the good is handed over to the first carrier. In consumer sales, the risk passes only at that time if the buyer instructed the carrier to ship the good to him and the seller had not named this carrier previously. In commonly encountered consumer sales, these conditions are rarely met. If, e.g., the consumer shops online and agrees with the seller on delivery to his place of residence, the seller usually chooses the carrier himself or has specified certain potential carriers on his website from which the buyer can select one. In both cases, the risk does not shift to the buyer until receipt. Thus, if the good does not arrive, the seller has no claim for the purchase price against the consumer (§ 326 I 1 BGB).

Second, § 477 BGB contains an important rule on the burden of proof. Remedies for defective goods apply only if the product was defective at the time the risk passed to the buyer (§ 434 I 1 BGB), i.e., usually when it was delivered to him (§ 446, 1 BGB). Generally, the buyer has to prove that the object was defective upon delivery and must refute that his improper handling of the object caused the defect, should the other side plead this.[232] § 477 BGB, however, shifts the burden of proof: Where an object's defect manifests itself within six months after the date of the risk passed to the buyer, the defect is presumed to have existed at the time the risk passed (allowing the buyer to exercise his remedies), unless such a presumption is incompatible with the nature of

---

229. Ingo Saenger, in: *Bürgerliches Gesetzbuch: Handkommentar* (9th ed. 2017), § 442 BGB no. 6.
230. *Ibid.*, § 442 BGB no. 4.
231. These rules do not cover public auctions of used goods which the consumer may attend in person, § 474 II BGB.
232. Ingo Saenger, in: *Bürgerliches Gesetzbuch: Handkommentar* (9th ed. 2017), § 476 BGB no. 1.

the object or the defect. The ECJ has clarified that the consumer is required neither to prove which circumstances produced the defective state nor that the defect can be attributed to the seller.[233] Thus, if the consumer bought a second-hand car whose automatic transmission no longer works properly after five months, it is presumed that the car was defective at the time of delivery (unless the seller can prove that the defect resulted from the buyer's driving habits).[234]

[4]   International Sales

Germany is party to the CISG. Within its scope, the provisions of the BGB and HGB are applicable only as far as the Convention leaves a gap to be filled by national law, provided that German law applies at all. Parties also often refer to the INCOTERMS of the ICC to allocate the duties, costs and risks associated with an international sales contract, including shipment and insurance.

[C]   Donation

Under a donation contract, a donor uses his own assets to enrich a contractual partner without receiving money or any other kind of payment in exchange (§ 516 I BGB). Donations immediately executed (even without a proper prior agreement, § 516 II BGB) do not have to be recorded (*Handschenkungen*). Things are different if the donation shall be executed after the donation contract was formed. In this case, the donor's promise (*Schenkungsversprechen*) has to be recorded by a notary public to form a valid donation contract (§ 518 I 1 BGB). Consideration is not necessary to bind the promisor because under German law the form requirement protects the promisor sufficiently. If the donor, however, executes the donation contract even though it was concluded in a non-appropriate form, he knowingly and wilfully diminishes his assets and thus needs no additional warning. Therefore, the defect as to form is remedied (§ 518 II BGB).[235]

Given that the donor does not receive a (material) remuneration in exchange for the gift, the law provides many rules in his favour. The donor can choose not to fulfil his promise as far as performing would render him in a position in which he could not care for himself reasonably or could not fulfil statutory maintenance obligations towards other persons, e.g., his family (§ 519 I BGB). Subject to certain restrictions, impoverishment also entitles the donor to reclaim the gift from the donee in accord with the rules of unjust enrichment (§§ 528, 529 BGB). Moreover, his liability towards the donee is relaxed: Generally, a donor is liable only for intentional acts or those done with gross negligence (§ 521 BGB). Regarding defects as to quality or title, the donor's liability is even limited to situations in which he fraudulently conceals the defect (§§

---

233. Case C-497/13, *Faber v. Autobedrijf Hazet Ochten BV*, ECLI:EU:C:2015:357, para. 75.
234. BGH, *Neue Juristische Wochenschrift* 2017, 1093, 1099. In this case, the BGH relaxed its older case law (*see* BGH, *Neue Juristische Wochenschrift* 2004, 2299, 2300) to implement the ECJ's *Faber* ruling.
235. Dirk Looschelders, *Schuldrecht: Besonderer Teil* (13th ed. 2018), no. 312.

523 I, 524 I BGB). The donor may also be entitled to revoke his donation for gross ingratitude on the part of the donee (§§ 530–534 BGB).

[D] Contract of Rent

[1] Structure of the Law

Under a contract of rent, use of an item of property, be it a car, a flat, a collection of things, or a piece of land, is granted to another person for a specified period of time in return for a remuneration (§ 535 BGB). Within the relevant part of the BGB, the first section lists general rules on all forms of lease agreements (§§ 535–548 BGB), the second part lays down special rules on residential property (§§ 549–577a BGB) and the last part supplies rules on renting of other property, such as office space or ships (§§ 578–580a BGB). If the use of the rented property includes a right to exploit its yields, German law classifies the contract as a *Pachtvertrag* (usufructory lease). As this type of contract is a variant of the rental contract, the section dealing with usufructory leases is attached to the sections on contracts of rent (§§ 581–584b BGB). As far as these rules do not provide otherwise, the rules of rental contracts also apply to usufructory leases (§ 581 II BGB). Additional rules for usufructory leases of real property are laid down in §§ 585–597 BGB.

With regard to the lease of residential property, additional statutes are of practical importance, such as the regulation on the calculation of heating costs (*Verordnung über Heizkostenabrechnung*)[236] and the regulation on operating costs (*Betriebskostenverordnung*).[237] These regulations contain rules on the distribution of costs for warm water, heating, the calculation of overhead, and charges associated with a building. In addition, there are public law rules allowing authorities to take measures against the alienation of residential property so as to avoid or overcome housing shortages occurring in larger cities.

[2] General Rules

[a] Obligations of the Parties

Under the general rules on rental contracts, the lessor has to grant the lessee possession over the property (§ 535 I 1 BGB). In addition, the property must be in a condition suitable for the contractually agreed upon use, and the lessor has to bear the cost of maintaining the property during the rental period (§ 535 I 2, 3 BGB). The latter obligation is – as most rules in the first part of the law of contracts of rent – not mandatory, which means parties may deviate from it. This is frequently done in

---

236. *Verordnung über die verbrauchsabhängige Abrechnung der Heiz- und Warmwasserkosten (Verordnung über Heizkostenabrechnung – HeizkostenV) of 5 October 2009 (Neubekanntmachung),* BGBl. I 2009, 3250.
237. *Verordnung über die Aufstellung von Betriebskosten (Betriebskostenverordnung – BetrKV) of 25 November 2003,* BGBl. I 2003, 2346 (as amended).

contracts for the lease of real estate. The parties often agree that the lessee shall bear the obligation of repairing normal wear and tear (*Schönheitsreparaturen*). Such an agreement contained in a standard term is valid as far as the lessee only has to undertake repairs or painting the rooms when the necessity to do so actually arises.[238] Finally, the lessor may have additional duties, such as ensuring that the premises are supplied with water and electricity. He also has to respect duties of protection (§ 241 II BGB), e.g., warning the lessee about dangers, such as the risk of break-ins.[239]

The lessee is obliged to pay the rent agreed upon (§ 535 II BGB). Even though this usually means money, this is not mandatorily so as services such as upkeep of the house or garden can be owed to the lessor as well.[240] At the end of the rental period, the lessee has to return the property (§ 546 I BGB). Whether or not he can actually use the leased object does not affect the right of the lessor to claim the rent. Thus, a lessee must pay the rent even if he has taken ill and is unable to drive a leased car.

The lessee is limited to using the rented property as agreed upon in the contract and is not liable for any deterioration of it brought about by use in conformity with the contract (§ 538 BGB). Without prior permission of the lessor, the lessee is not entitled to sublet the property to a third party (§ 540 I 1 BGB). If the lessor denies the request for permission, the lessee may terminate (*kündigen*) the contract within the statutory notice period unless there is something significant about the third party that entitles the lessor to deny the request. The latter is the case if, e.g., a landlord running a business in his building has rented out some space to another business. The landlord is entitled to withhold his permission for a sublease if the tenant intends to sublet the office space to a business that is a competitor of the landlord.[241] If the lessee sublets the property without the permission of the lessor, the latter can terminate the contract immediately (§ 543 II 1 no. 2 BGB). In the event the lessee gained profits from subletting the property, the lessor may not skim off these profits despite the unlawful behaviour of his contractual partner (unless agreed otherwise).[242]

[b]   Breach of Contract

Thus far, the system of remedies for breaches of contracts of rent has not been fully aligned with the general rules on remedies as was done in sales law.[243] The general

---

238. For details *see*: Wolfgang Wurmnest, in: *Münchener Kommentar zum Bürgerlichen Gesetzbuch*, vol. II (7th ed. 2016), § 307 BGB nos. 114 et seq.

239. OLG Hamburg, *Neue Juristische Wochenschrift Rechtsprechungs-Report Zivilrecht* 1988, 1481; Dirk Looschelders, *Schuldrecht: Besonderer Teil* (13th ed. 2018), no. 406.

240. Wolfgang Fikentscher & Andreas Heinemann, *Schuldrecht Allgemeiner und Besonderer Teil* (11th ed. 2017), no. 1012.

241. OLG Nürnberg, *Neue Zeitschrift für Miet- und Wohnungsrecht* 2007, 567; Hans-Jürgen Bieber, in: *Münchener Kommentar zum Bürgerlichen Gesetzbuch*, vol. IV (7th ed. 2016), § 540 BGB no. 20.

242. BGH, *Neue Juristische Wochenschrift* 1996, 838 et seq.

243. For a detailed proposal on the synchronisation of the rules on rental contracts with the general rules on *Leistungsstörungen see* Karl Riesenhuber, 'Mietrechtsgewährleistung im System des Allgemeinen Leistungsstörungsrechts: Ansätze zu einer Integration', *Zeitschrift für die gesamte Privatrechtswissenschaft* 2016, 448 et seq.

system has been altered to some extent by special rules on rental contracts. Distinguishing between the applicability of these special rules and the general rules on remedies for breach of contract may sometimes turn out to be a difficult task. Moreover, it has to be noted that a contract of rent is a continuing obligation (*Dauerschuldverhältnis*). Consequently, termination is effected by a *Kündigung* and not by a *Rücktritt* (*supra* §6.06[C][4]). Although not comprehensive, the following overview focuses on some important remedies of the lessee.[244]

Where a defect regarding the quality or title of the property is identified upon its handover to the lessee or during its period of rent, and where this defect precludes or significantly limits the item's use as envisioned in the contract, the lessee is exempted from paying rent or has to pay only a reduced rent to the extent the defect is not negligible (§ 536 I BGB). This remedy does not require fault on the side of the lessor and must not even be declared by the lessee (unlike in the law of sales). Of course, the lessee has to notify the lessor about defects arising during the rental period to enable him to cure them (§ 536c I 1 BGB).

With regard to claims for damages, the lessor is subject to a type of guaranteed liability with regard to defects that existed at the time of the conclusion of the contract (§ 536a I BGB). He is liable for any damages caused by such defects irrespective of fault (unlike under the general rules). This strict liability aims to protect the lessee.[245] Damages can also be claimed for defects arising during the rental period due to a circumstance for which the lessor is responsible or if the lessor is in default (§ 286 BGB) of curing a defect (§ 536a I BGB). § 536b, 1 BGB excludes claims under §§ 536, 536a BGB where the lessee knows of the defect at the time the contract was concluded (unless he informs the lessor when accepting the leased object that he wants to maintain these rights); the lessee does, however, in any case retain the right to demand from the lessor to cure the defect.[246]

Each party may terminate the contract extraordinarily (with immediate notice) (*außerordentliche Kündigung*) for a compelling reason (§ 543 I 1 BGB). A serious breach of a contractual obligation by one of the parties entitles the other party to exercise this right under certain conditions. Besides the already mentioned sublease without permission (§ 543 II 1 no. 2 BGB), the lessor may terminate the contract if the lessee is in default on two successive dates with the payment of the rent or parts thereof, provided that the amount is significant (§ 543 II 1 no. 3 BGB). The lessee may terminate the contract if the lessor does not grant him the use of the leased item of property or in the event he is deprived of it (§ 543 II 1 no. 1 BGB).

---

244. For a detailed analysis *see* Peter Derleder, 'Mängelrechte des Wohnraummieters nach Miet- und Schuldrechtsreform', *Neue Zeitschrift für Miet- und Wohnungsrecht* 2002, 676 et seq.; Volker Emmerich, 'Neues Mietrecht und Schuldrechtsmodernisierung', *Neue Zeitschrift für Miet- und Wohnungsrecht* 2002, 362 et seq.; Barbara Dauner-Lieb & Wolfgang Dötsch, 'Aufwendungsersatz für eine Mängelbeseitigung durch den Mieter: Alte Fragen in neuem Gewand?', *Neue Zeitschrift für Miet- und Wohnungsrecht* 2004, 641 et seq.
245. Dirk Looschelders, *Schuldrecht: Besonderer Teil* (13th ed. 2018), no. 421.
246. Marcus Bieder, in: *beck-online.GROSSKOMMENTAR BGB* (1 April 2018), § 536b BGB no. 36.

[c]   Ending the Agreement

If the parties have agreed on an indefinite lease period, the lease ends when one party lawfully terminates the contract (§ 542 I BGB). Leases for a definite period end at the point of time agreed upon unless the contract is terminated earlier or the parties agree on a renewal (§ 542 II BGB).

[3]   Special Rules for Housing Premises

For lease contracts concerning residential property, the general rules apply only as far as §§ 549–577a BGB do not provide otherwise (§ 549 I BGB). The framework for the lease of housing premises has been changed significantly since 1900.[247] Over the years, the legislature limited the circumstances under which a landlord may terminate the contract and evict the tenant so as to grant the lessee a greater degree of housing security. The legislature has also introduced various rules protecting tenants from rents considered 'too high'. In more recent times, the tenant's power to terminate a rental contract within a reasonable time has been strengthened to respond to increased mobility needs. Tenants may have to move for job purposes or – in the case of an elderly person – to a retirement home. In addition, rules on the modernisation of dwellings were incorporated in the BGB, *inter alia*, as an attempt to lower heating emissions. As far as these rules protect the tenant, they are mandatory. The most important rules will be sketched in the following discussion.

Lease agreements for residential property for a period longer than one year must be entered into in writing (§ 550, 1 BGB). This rule aims to ensure that buyers of land learn about such agreements given that § 566 BGB enshrines the rule whereby 'sale does not break lease' (*Kauf bricht nicht Miete*). Under this maxim, the buyer of residential property steps into the shoes of the seller and becomes party to all the rental contracts in place at the time of sale.

Landlords often demand a security deposit in case the tenant damages the premises. Pursuant to § 551 I BGB, the maximum amount of the deposit is limited to three times the monthly rent. The provision also supplies rules on the administration of the money.

To facilitate the subletting of rooms by tenants to third parties, § 553 BGB allows the tenant to demand from the landlord approval to sublet a part of the rented space to a third party if the tenant has a legitimate interest in doing so. Examples of such an interest are a tenant who, because of a decrease in income, wishes to sublease a room to cover part of the rent, or a tenant who wants to bring a person in need of care into the apartment.[248] The landlord can deny approval only if the sublease would

---

247. Volker Emmerich, in: *J. v. Staudingers Kommentar zum Bürgerlichen Gesetzbuch, Mietrecht 1: Allgemeine Vorschriften; Wohnraummiete* (revised ed. 2018), Vor § 535 BGB nos. 1 et seq.
248. Hans-Jürgen Bieber, in: *Münchener Kommentar zum Bürgerlichen Gesetzbuch*, vol. IV (7th ed. 2016), § 553 BGB no. 7.

overcrowd the premises or if there is something significant about the person to be taken in that would make it unreasonable for him to accept the sublease.[249]

Another subchapter deals with the payment of rent and specifies to what extent the operating costs associated with a building can be passed onto the tenant (§§ 556–556c BGB). In addition, the BGB contains various rules on rent control. In areas with tight housing markets, which are defined by ordinance, rules limit the amount of rent demandable by the landlord at the initiation of a lease agreement (§§ 556d–556g BGB) to avoid sharp rises in the general level of rent in these areas. Outside these areas, the amount of rent can be freely negotiated when concluding the contract. The BGB, however, contains various rules limiting the grounds for rent increases during the lease period (§§ 557–561 BGB).

For contracts concluded for an indefinite period of time, the legislature introduced an 'ordinary' right to terminate the contract (*ordentliche Kündigung*), this sitting alongside with the 'extraordinary' termination right which can be exercised in case certain events occur (*see* §6.07[D][2][b]). To protect the tenant, the termination rights are asymmetric: This means that the tenant can terminate the contract within a certain notice period (usually three months, but longer periods may apply) without stating a reason (§ 573c I 1 BGB), with immediate effect for certain breaches of contract by the landlord (§§ 543, 569 BGB) or within the statutory notice period in certain cases in which the landlord denies the tenant to sublet the premises (§ 540 I BGB). The landlord's right to terminate the contract, by contrast, is much more restricted. He can, for instance, terminate the contract if the tenant has given him a reason to do so (e.g., by significantly disturbing the neighbours) or if the landlord needs the premises for himself or a family member or if the tenant has breached the contract significantly (§§ 569, 573 BGB).

[E]   Contracts for Services

A service contract obliges the service provider to perform a service in exchange for remuneration (§ 611 I BGB). The BGB distinguishes this type of contract from a contract for work by looking at the obligation to be performed: A service provider has to provide the service and is remunerated regardless of whether the service achieves the intended results, whereas a contract for work obliges the contractor to produce a certain work, i.e., a certain result. Whether a contract has to be interpreted as a contract for a service or a contract for work depends to a large extent on the content of the contract (what the parties have agreed upon) and which party is to bear the risk of the activity agreed upon not producing the intended outcome.[250]

The provisions of the BGB on the law of service contracts address a wide range of services, which were deeply reformed and supplemented over the years. § 611 BGB and related rules cover service contracts concluded by certain freelance professionals

---

249. Volker Emmerich, in: *J. von Staudingers Kommentar zum Bürgerlichen Gesetzbuch, Mietrecht 1: Allgemeine Vorschriften; Wohnraummiete* (revised ed. 2018), § 553 BGB nos. 13–14.
250. Dirk Looschelders, *Schuldrecht: Besonderer Teil* (13th ed. 2018), nos. 541 et seq.; Hein Kötz, *Vertragsrecht* (2nd ed. 2012), no. 647.

(lawyers, accountants, tax advisors, commercial agents, etc.) with their customers. Employment contracts are dealt with in § 611a BGB, but this field of law is dominated by many rules outside the BGB protecting employees (*see* chapter on employment law). A special form of service contract is the 'treatment contract' (*Behandlungsvertrag*) entered into by a doctor and a patient, which was incorporated into the BGB in 2013 (§§ 630a–h BGB).[251] Essentially, these provisions codify the rules on medical malpractice that have been developed by the courts over the years.[252]

[F]   Contracts for Work and Related Contracts

[1]   Stucture of the Law

Under a contract for work, the contractor (*Werkunternehmer*) promises to produce a certain result (the work) in exchange for a remuneration, paid by the employer (*Besteller*). In April 2017, the German legislature enacted a major reform of the rules on these contracts, which entered into force on 1 January 2018.[253] The revision overhauled the existing structure of the law significantly, as rules on consumer protection were implemented and different variants of contracts for work were codified. The section on contracts for work is divided into three parts: The first part deals with contracts for work, including construction contracts, in general (§§ 631–650o BGB); the second part sets forth special rules for contracts with architects and engineers (§§ 650p–650t BGB); and the third part lays down rules for real estate development contracts (*Bauträgervertrag*, § 650u–650v BGB). For reasons of space, the following overview focuses on selected general rules for contracts for work and on construction contracts.

[2]   General Rules for Contracts for Work

§§ 631–650 BGB are applicable to contracts for work of any kind. These rules specify the mutual obligations of the parties. The contractor has to produce the promised work and the employer has to pay the remuneration agreed upon (§ 631 I BGB).[254] The object of the contract may concern the production or modification of an object or any other

---

251. *Gesetz zur Verbesserung der Rechte von Patientinnen und Patienten of 20 February 2013*, BGBl. I 2013, 277.
252. Gerhard Wagner, in: *Münchener Kommentar zum Bürgerlichen Gesetzbuch*, vol. IV (7th ed. 2016), Vor § 630a BGB no. 8.
253. *Gesetz zur Reform des Bauvertragsrechts, zur Änderung der kaufrechtlichen Mängelhaftung, zur Stärkung des zivilprozessualen Rechtsschutzes und zum maschinellen Siegel im Grundbuch- und Schiffsregisterverfahren of 28 April 2017*, BGBl. I 2017, 969. For details, *see* Jochen Glöckner, 'BGB-Novelle zur Reform des Bauvertragsrechts als Grundlage effektiven Verbraucherschutzes', *Verbraucher und Recht* 2016, 123 et seq. (part 1), 163 et seq. (part 2) (on the proposed bill); Gerd Motzke, 'Der Reformgesetzgeber am Webstuhl des Architekten- und Ingenieurrechts', *Neue Zeitschrift für Baurecht und Vergaberecht* 2017, 251 et seq. The reform's scope is criticised by Martin Illmer, 'Warum nur Bauverträge?', *Zeitschrift für Rechtspolitik* 2017, 122 et seq.
254. For an implied setting of remuneration, *see supra* §6.03[B][1].

result that may be achieved by a service (§ 631 II BGB). Contracts for work concern, e.g., the construction of a building, the cutting of hair, performance of a concert or the transportation of a person. However, if the promisor undertakes to produce a movable object and deliver the same to the employer, this so-called *Werklieferungsvertrag* is governed by sales law (§ 650 BGB).

If the work conforms to the standards agreed upon by the parties, the employer has to approve the work (*Abnahme*, § 640 I 1 BGB). Approval can be declared expressly or impliedly, e.g., by paying for the service rendered despite obvious defects. To ensure a timely approval, it is assumed as a matter of law after the lapse of a reasonable period set by the contractor in the event the employer is unable to point to any defect in the work to justify withholding approval (§ 640 II BGB). The same should apply if the employer names only a very minor defect.[255] Upon *Abnahme*, the remuneration becomes due (§ 641 BGB), unless the parties have agreed otherwise. The contractor may, however, demand partial payment (*Abschlagszahlung*) beforehand pursuant to § 632a BGB. If the nature of the work excludes an *Abnahme*, as in the case of a concert or transportation service, completing the work triggers the legal consequences associated with an approval by the employer (§ 646 BGB).[256]

The structure of the remedial system for contracts for work is similar to that of sales law. §§ 633–639 BGB supplement the general rules discussed above (*supra* §6.06) with regard to defective performance, i.e., defects as to quality and title (*Sachmängel, Rechtsmängel*).

Under the law of work contracts, the contractor has to produce the work free of defects (§ 633 I BGB). The parties may define the standards the work has to comply with (§ 633 II 1 BGB), which is regularly done in larger transactions such as construction contracts. In the absence of such an agreement, the work is free of any defects if suitable for the contractually intended use (§ 633 II 2 no. 1 BGB) or for the customary use that the employer may expect (§ 633 II 2 no. 2 BGB). Finally, a contractor producing a different work or a lesser amount than agreed upon also presents a defect as to quality (§ 633 II 3 BGB).

Where the work is defective under § 633 BGB, the remedies of the employer are listed in § 634 BGB. This provision is structured similarly to § 437. It links the special rules in the law of contracts for work with the general rules for breach of contract described above. As in sales law, the employer can ask the contractor to cure the defect by repairing it or producing a new work (§§ 634 no. 1, 635 BGB) irrespective of the issue whether the contractor acted with 'fault' or not. If the contractor fails to cure the defect within a reasonable grace period, set by the employer, the latter may cure the defect himself (or ask a third person to do so) and charge the contractor for expenses incurred in doing so (§§ 634 no. 2, 637 BGB). The employer may – if the general conditions are met (§§ 634 no. 3, 636, 323, 326 V BGB) – also terminate the contract, which usually requires the setting and lapse of a grace period. In addition, the employer

---

255. Ralf Leinemann, 'Das neue Bauvertragsrecht und seine praktischen Folgen', *Neue Juristische Wochenschrift* 2017, 3113, 3114; Tobias Breitling, 'Abnahme und Zustandsfeststellung nach neuem Recht', *Neue Zeitschrift für Baurecht und Vergaberecht*, 2017, 393 et seq.
256. Hein Kötz, *Vertragsrecht* (2nd ed. 2012), no. 683.

may demand a price reduction should he want to keep the work as it is (§§ 634 no. 3, 638 BGB). Finally, the employer is entitled to claim damages in accord with the general rules (§§ 634 no. 4, 636, 280, 281, 283, 311a BGB) or, alternatively, reimbursement of expenses incurred in the expectation of performance (§§ 634 no. 4, 284 BGB).

Irrespective of an existing defect, the employer may terminate (*kündigen*) the contract at any time before the contractor finishes the work without reason (§ 648, 1 BGB). In this case, the employer has to pay the agreed-upon remuneration but may deduct the contractor's saved expenses or the sum of money the contractor acquired or could have acquired from making use of his labour resources in another way (§ 648, 2 BGB). In addition, either party has the right to terminate the contract for a compelling reason (§ 648a BGB). This usually requires a prior warning and the setting of a reasonable period of time to allow the contractual partner to cure the breach, unless such a warning can be dispensed with pursuant to §§ 648a III, 314 II, 323 II nos. 1, 2 BGB.[257]

[3]   (Consumer) Construction Contracts

Construction contracts concern the construction, restoration, demolition or reconstruction of a building (§ 650a I BGB). As these contracts often involve high stakes and pose special problems, e.g., concerning changes to the work the constructor is to carry out, the German legislature decided to codify special rules for this important type of contract, namely §§ 650a–650h BGB. They contain, e.g., a mechanism which enables the parties to modify the remuneration after the conclusion of the contract in cases (i) where the employer demands changes to the work to be carried out or (ii) if such changes are necessary to reach the purpose of the contract (§ 650b BGB). If the parties do not reach an agreement on the modification of the price within thirty days, the employer can order the contractor to effect the changes necessary to reach the purpose of the contract, provided that he communicates these changes in text form. Consequently, he has to bear the additional costs (§ 650b II 1, 650c BGB). In the event that the employer merely wants to modify the work even though changes are not necessary to reach the purpose of the building contract, the contractor is obliged to effect these changes only if doing so is reasonable for him (§ 650b II 2 BGB).[258]

The parties to construction contracts often incorporate (at least parts of) the General Conditions for Construction Works (*Vergabe und Vertragsordnung für Bauleistungen, Teil B: Allgemeine Vertragsbedingungen für die Ausführung von Bauleistungen* = VOB/B) into their contract. This set of boilerplate provisions was drafted by an institution composed of representatives of public bodies that often commission building works, representatives of the construction business, and technical experts. These

---

257. Ralf Leinemann, 'Das neue Bauvertragsrecht und seine praktischen Folgen', *Neue Juristische Wochenschrift* 2017, 3113, 3114.
258. For details, *see* Klaus Englert & Florian Englert, 'Die 'Zumutbarkeit' der Befolgung von Anordnungen nach dem neuen Bauvertragsrecht', *Neue Zeitschrift für Baurecht und Vergaberecht* 2017, 579 et seq.

General Conditions build upon the general rules of the BGB and adapt them to the needs of construction contracts.

§§ 650i–650n BGB provide special rules for consumer construction contracts. For the most part, these rules are mandatory (§ 650o BGB). It is important to note that, by definition, not all contracts concluded between a consumer and an entrepreneur on construction works qualify as consumer contracts. § 650i I BGB defines these contracts as agreements on the construction of a new building or the reconstruction of an existing one. Under a consumer construction contract, the contractor (entrepreneur) has, *inter alia*, to provide detailed information about the work to be carried out (§ 650j BGB), and the law restricts his ability to demand partial payments (§ 650m BGB). The consumer is entitled to revoke the contract within fourteen days after its conclusion unless the contract was recorded by a notary public (§§ 650l, 355 BGB).

[G]   Suretyship and Guarantee

Rules on securities are regulated primarily in the BGB's part on property law (*see* chapter on property law). A security interest of practical importance that is dealt with in the law of obligations is the suretyship contract (*Bürgschaft*). A suretyship is concluded between the surety (*Bürge*) and a creditor to secure a debt of the principal debtor (*Hauptschuldner*), § 765 I BGB. To be valid, the contract must be concluded in writing (§ 766, 1 BGB) – unless the surety is a merchant who concludes the suretyship for commercial purposes (§ 350 HGB). Irrespective of this, fulfilment of the contractual obligation by the surety remedies any defect in form and validates the surety contract (§ 766, 3 BGB). Suretyship is premised on the main debt, even though it is a distinct contract. The term of art used in German legal doctrine is that of *Akzessorietät* (accessory relationship) between the suretyship and the main debt. The principal debt determines the liability of the surety (§ 767 I 1 BGB). If the main debt does not exist, either because the main debtor rescinded the main contract or the contract is void for other reasons, the creditor cannot demand payment under the suretyship. Similarly, where the principal debtor paid up part of his debt, the liability of the surety diminishes accordingly. The principle of *Akzessorietät* also explains why the surety can raise certain defences against the creditor even if the main debtor has waived them (§ 768 BGB).

As the surety is only a substitute and not a joint debtor, the drafters of the BGB gave him special defences of his own, which he can raise against the creditor as long as he has not waived them by agreement. If the main debtor would be entitled to rescind the contract (but does not do so), the guarantor can refuse to satisfy the creditor (§ 770 I BGB). The same holds true when the creditor could obtain satisfaction by off-setting his claim with a claim he has against the main debtor (§ 770 II BGB) or – within certain limitations – where the creditor has not tried to seek satisfaction from the main debtor (§§ 771, 773 BGB).

Given that the accessory principle can make it difficult for the creditor to receive prompt payment from the surety, parties may therefore have resort to another type of security interest, the guarantee (*Garantievertrag*), which is not expressly regulated in the BGB. This security interest is independent from the main debt. Where a bank provides such a guarantee for a commercial transaction, it is often a 'guarantee on first demand' (*Garantie auf erstes Anfordern*), which is not only independent of the secured debt but must also be honoured immediately upon the creditor's request. Objections of the guarantor with regard to the main debt are usually excluded, apart from claims of an abuse of law.

SELECTED BIBLIOGRAPHY

Burkhard Boemke & Bernhard Ulrici, *BGB Allgemeiner Teil*, 2nd ed. 2014.

Reinhard Bork, *Allgemeiner Teil des Bürgerlichen Gesetzbuchs*, 4th ed. 2016.

Hans Brox & Wolf-Dietrich Walker, *Allgemeiner Teil des BGB*, 41st ed. 2017.

Hans Brox & Wolf-Dietrich Walker, *Allgemeines Schuldrecht*, 42nd ed. 2018.

Hans Brox & Wolf-Dietrich Walker, *Besonderes Schuldrecht*, 42nd ed. 2018.

Claus-Wilhelm Canaris, *Handelsrecht*, 24th ed. 2006.

Florian Faust, *Bürgerliches Gesetzbuch Allgemeiner Teil*, 6th ed. 2018.

Wolfgang Fikentscher & Andreas Heinemann, *Schuldrecht Allgemeiner und Besonderer Teil*, 11th ed. 2017.

Hein Kötz, *Vertragsrecht*, 2nd ed. 2012.

Karl Larenz, *Lehrbuch des Schuldrechts, I. Band: Allgemeiner Teil*, 14th ed. 1987.

Karl Larenz, *Lehrbuch des Schuldrechts, II. Band: Besonderer Teil, 1. Halbband*, 13th ed. 1986.

Karl Larenz & Claus-Wilhelm Canaris, *Lehrbuch des Schuldrechts, II. Band: Besonderer Teil, 2. Halbband*, 13th ed. 1994.

Dirk Looschelders, *Schuldrecht: Allgemeiner Teil*, 15th ed. 2017.

Dirk Looschelders, *Schuldrecht: Besonderer Teil*, 13th ed. 2018.

Basil Markesinis, Hannes Unberath & Angus Johnston, *The German Law of Contract: A Comparative Treatise*, 2nd ed. 2006.

Dieter Medicus & Stephan Lorenz, *Schuldrecht I: Allgemeiner Teil*, 21st ed. 2015.

Dieter Medicus & Stephan Lorenz, *Schuldrecht II: Besonderer Teil*, 17th ed. 2014.

Jürgen Oechsler, *Vertragliche Schuldverhältnisse*, 2nd ed. 2017.

Hartmut Oetker & Felix Maultzsch, *Vertragliche Schuldverhältnisse*, 4th ed. 2013.

Dietrich Reinicke & Klaus Tiedtke, *Kaufrecht*, 8th ed. 2009.

Peter Schlechtriem & Martin Schmidt-Kessel, *Schuldrecht: Allgemeiner Teil*, 6th ed. 2005.

Peter Schlechtriem, *Schuldrecht: Besonderer Teil* (6th ed. 2003).

Karsten Schmidt, *Handelsrecht: Unternehmensrecht I*, 6th ed. 2014.

Manfred Wolf & Jörg Neuner, *Allgemeiner Teil des Bürgerlichen Rechts*, 11th ed. 2016.

Reinhard Zimmermann, *The New German Law of Obligations: Historical and Comparative Perspectives*, 2005.

CHAPTER 7
The Law of Torts

Harald Koch

TABLE OF CONTENTS

§7.01   GENERAL INTRODUCTION

[A]   System, Notion and Policies of Tort Law

The German law of torts is a set of rules that is part of the private law of obligations (Second Book of the Civil Code, *Bürgerliches Gesetzbuch* – BGB). For this reason, it shares certain features with the law of contract, especially with regard to the available damages. Yet, rather than presuming a contractual relationship, tort law creates obligations "*ex lege*" of the tortfeasor towards the victim (*gesetzliches Schuldverhältnis*). Thus, it is clearly distinguished from, and independent of, contract law with regard to the elements of liability.

The term "torts" is unknown in German Law. Instead, the BGB speaks of "unlawful acts" (*unerlaubte Handlungen*) in the heading of the respective subchapter (title 25 of the Second Book of the BGB). While there are no fundamental differences between various tort actions (like in the common law system) the BGB is not based on a single general rule of tort liability either (as are the French influenced codes). Instead, a century ago, the legislator decided in favor of a semi-general clause of non-contractual liability protecting certain legal interests, either under fault (*infra* §7.02, §7.03) or strict liability principles (*infra* §7.04).

The objectives and functions attributed to tort law in Germany have changed over time. Originally, its primary purpose was to compensate the victim. More recently, this individualistic notion has been supplemented by a regulatory function of tort liability. Today, especially in certain areas, tort law aims, at least in part, at controlling and preventing certain behavior and seeks to deter wrongdoing.

It is widely agreed that the general function of tort law is the protection of the individual's sphere of rights against unlawful intrusion. But as soon as one seeks to determine its function more specifically, one has to distinguish between the various rights protected and interests concerned. In accident cases, the primary objective is to provide for the victim's compensation. Where rights of privacy or of the personality are violated, tort law is primarily concerned with providing satisfaction and ensuring a lasting settlement of the conflict rather than with compensation in the sense of restoration of a former economic status. In cases of injury to economic and commercial interests, prevention and deterrence, and thus, regulatory functions are additional goals of tort liability; they coexist with, and supplement, merely compensatory aims.

[B]   Relevance of Tort Law

Tort law cannot, however, exist in splendid dogmatic isolation. Under modern welfare state conditions, tort law in the area of personal injuries is closely connected and overlapping with third party insurance and social security compensation systems. Hence, the practical relevance of tort law has dramatically shifted from the original level of victim compensation by tortfeasors to a complex structure of risk distribution, granting benefits under insurance schemes, combined with subrogation, recovery, and recourse. Even in the area of property loss, widespread, sometimes even mandatory, third party insurance (as in automobile accident cases) has displaced and replaced original tort law to a considerable extent.[1] In these fields, tort law plays a minor practical role only. The bulk of financial consequences of personal injuries in Germany are covered by public insurance or workmen's compensation and long-term disability pension schemes. Most of them are funded by bilateral contributions of employers and employees. Up to a certain level of income, these first party insurance schemes are mandatory and often supplemented by additional coverage through the employer or under privately bought policies.

As a result, accident victims in Germany, in particular at the work place or on the road, do not have to rely on tort law for compensation alone. Rather, they are widely protected either by first party insurance or, in case the accident results in property damage, by third party insurance covering the liability of the wrongdoer. In many circumstances, they can even sue the liability insurer directly (direct action).

Most social security and insurance statutes provide for subrogation of the insured's claim against the tortfeasor so that it is the insurer who relies on tort law when seeking indemnification from the wrongdoer or his liability insurer. That is why tort law in Germany has sometimes been referred to merely as "the law of recourse conditions."[2]

In contrast, the area of non-patrimonial wrongs – e.g., pain and suffering, violation of privacy, and defamation – is marked by more traditional concepts of tort liability, although the calculation of damages in these cases cannot be prescribed in exact and objective terms. Also, recent legislative reform has extended the actionability

---

1. Ulrich Magnus, *Compensation for Personal Injuries in a Comparative Perspective* in: 39 Washburn L.J. (2000) 347 at 359.
2. Hein Kötz & Gerhard Wagner, *Deliktsrecht* (12th ed. 2013) no. 47.

of non-pecuniary losses to include strict liability claims as well.[3] This makes recovery of damages for pain and suffering available to accident victims who rely on strict liability causes of action; such actions, not fault-based rules, are now the usual bases for recovery in accident cases.

[C]   Classification, Sources and General Principles of German Tort Law

German tort law can roughly be divided into three types of torts.[4] They are essentially characterized by the requisite degree of fault respectively.

The basic principle and most common category is traditional fault liability. Within this category, a further distinction has to be made. The fundamental provisions of § 823 I and § 823 II BGB can be fulfilled intentionally as well as negligently, whereas § 826 BGB requires intentional wrongdoing.

The second category of tort liability is based on a rebuttable presumption of fault by the wrongdoer. Sections 831, 832, 833 II, 834, 836–838 BGB are part of that category.

The final category is strict liability, i.e., liability without fault. This approach differs from the general thrust of the (fault-based) liability rules in the German Civil Code but has gained increasing importance over the last few decades. Strict liability can occur under a variety of provisions, many of which are located in special statutes outside of the Civil Code in special statutes. It may also coexist with other forms of liability. For example liability for defective products may arise under the fault-based rules of the Civil Code (§§ 823 et seq.) as well as under the strict liability rules of the Product Liability Act likewise.

The sources of German tort law are primarily statutory,[5] supplemented by case law consisting mainly of decisions of the German Supreme Court (*Bundesgerichtshof*).[6] As already mentioned, the general rules of tort liability can be found in §§ 823 et seq. BGB. Yet, in a number of special areas, the legislator has provided special rules, often based on strict liability, particularly in cases of special risks (rail and road traffic, air transport, use of nuclear energy, pharmaceutical products, and environmental hazards, cf. *infra* §7.04).

In some areas of practical concern, where traditional provisions were regarded as inadequate, the courts have interpreted them creatively and have even established a body of case law which sometimes considerably exceeds the statutory rules. This is particularly true for defamation and privacy violations and for medical malpractice and

---

3. Ulrich Magnus & Joerg Fedtke, *Non-pecuniary Loss under German Law*, in: Damages for Non-pecuniary Loss in Comparative Perspective (W.V. Horton Rogers, 2001) pp. 108 et seq. *See also* Basil S. Markesinis & Hannes Unberath, *The German Law of Torts* (4th ed. 2002) pp. 917et seq.
4. Product liability is an exception – or potential fourth category – because it may be based on any of these three categories, depending on the circumstances of the case.
5. English translation of secs 823 et seq. in Markesinis & Unberath, *The German Law of Torts, supra* at pp. 14 et seq.
6. Markesinis & Unberath, *supra* in Sections B. of each chapter provide for a vast amount of case analyses (151!), standing for a case law approach within a civil (statute) law system.

defective product cases where the courts have created novel liability rules that are usually tougher on defendants than the statutory provisions.

All in all, the German compensation regime for injured parties can be described as a four-track-system: traditional fault-based liability, statutory strict liability, social insurance and private insurance. Among these, tort liability is based on the principle already expressed by *O. W. Holmes*[7] that the victim of an accident has to bear its own loss unless someone else can be held responsible for it. This requires the showing of a particular reason explaining why the loss should be shifted to the defendant. Among these reasons, fault and the creation of a specific risk are prominent. Under the regime of the BGB, fault was and still is the traditional basis for imposing liability (*infra* §7.02) though in practice, strict liability rules play an enormously important role today as well.

[D]   Private International and European Tort Law

In an era of increasing cross border contacts, international torts have become a common experience: traffic accidents as well as product defects, offensive media publications or environmental damages often have a foreign element in that the parties are from different countries or the tortious conduct originates in one country while the damage occurs in another. In such cases, the applicable national law has to be determined.

In Germany, cross-border torts are primarily governed by the relevant European Regulation (Rome II).[8] As an exception, violations of privacy or personality rights (Article 1(2)) are still governed by German national conflicts law (EGBGB Article 40). As a general rule, both German and European conflict rules provide that the law of the place of the wrong applies – which in most instances is the place where the damage occurs (Article 4(1) Rome II). Only in the rare cases when the place of the torfeasor's conduct differs from the place of the resulting damage, then German conflicts law and Rome II diverge: Under German law, it is the place of the tortious act that matters, regardless of where the damage occurs. This literal meaning of "place of the wrong," however, is only relevant in the exceptional areas mentioned above. In addition, where the case is clearly more closely connected to another country (e.g., by the parties' common residence or a pre-existing contract between them), that law applies (Article 4(2) and (3) Rome II).

Still, some other, more special points connecting the case to a certain country are provided for in special areas of tort law like products liability, unfair competition, environmental damage, violation of intellectual property, and industrial action (Articles 5–9 Rome II).

---

7. *The Common Law*, 1851, 50: "Sound policy lets losses lie where they fall, except where a special reason can be shown for interference".
8. Regulation No. 864/2007 on the Law Applicable to Non-Contractual Obligations, O.J. 31-7.2007, L 199 p. 40. – Cf. Ulrich Magnus & Peter Mankowski, *Rome II-Regulation – Commentary* (European Commentaries in Private International Law, 2018); Andrew Dickinson, *The Rome II-Regulation: The Law Applicable to Non-Contractual Obligations* (2010).

As business and private activities may expose anyone to tort liability, different standards of liability in different countries can have an influence on the decision of where to act. Thus, these differences may impair the freedom of cross-border movement. Since this freedom is one of the fundamental liberties within the European Union (EU), there have been a number of efforts to harmonize the tort laws of the EU Member States. These efforts have left their mark in German tort law. In areas like product liability and environmental damage, the EU has issued Directives under Article 288(3) TFEU (Treaty on the Functioning of the European Union) These Directives provide harmonized rules but leave their implementation and the regulation of many details to the legislation of the Member States. The German statutes on products liability, environmental liability, and data protection are examples of statutory tort provisions induced by European directives.

In addition, there are efforts generally to harmonize private law in Europe, often with a view ultimately to arrive at a European civil code.[9] These efforts have been extended to tort law as well. Since the 1990s, the European Group on Tort Law,[10] among others, has prepared comparative reports on different elements of tort liability in order to formulate common and convincing solutions in the form of general principles that can serve as a blueprint for a harmonized European regime.

§7.02   TORT LIABILITY BASED ON FAULT

The first category of tort actions is based on fault. Here, the specific reason for charging the wrongdoer with liability is the negligent or even intentional violation of the victim's legal rights.

[A]   Violation of Certain Protected Interests (§§ 823 I, 824 BGB)

The cause of action most often invoked in German law is provided in § 823 I BGB:

> A person who, in violation of the law, deliberately or negligently, causes harm to the life, person, health, liberty, property, or other right of another person must compensate that person for any damage arising there from.

Furthermore, in cases of bodily injury, the victim has a right to demand compensation from the tortfeasor for the pain suffered.[11] The enumeration of specific rights and protected interests in § 823 I BGB is crucial for German tort law because, in order to make a claim, the victim has to prove violation of a right mentioned in this provision. This may be easy enough regarding "life, person, health, liberty, property,"

---

9. Resolutions of the European Parliament of 1989, 1994 and 2001, text in *Zeitschrift für Europäisches Privatrecht* (ZEuP) 2002, 635, Christian von Bar, ZEuP 2002, 629. *See also* Ewoud Hondius et al., *Towards a European Civil Code* (2004).
10. Cf. Jaap Spier & O.A. Haazen, *The European Group on Tort Law*, ZEuP 1999, 469; European Group on Tort Law (ed.), *Principles of European Tort Law* Text and Commentary (2005) and Christian von Bar, *The Common European Law of Torts*, Vol. 1, 1998, Vol. 2, 2000.
11. § 253 II BGB, §§ 249–253 deal with the detailed problems of damages in general, including contractual damages.

but what is an "other right" in this context? It is not any other legal position. Rather, the exclusive enumeration shows that only so-called absolute rights are protected, meaning rights that must be respected by everyone and that can be enforced against everyone. In consequence, merely contractual rights are not protected by § 823 I BGB since they exist only in relation to the other contracting party. They are so-called relative rights and, thus, can be enforced only through claims based on contract.

[1] Protected Rights

(a) The provision expressly mentions life, person (body), health, liberty and property as examples for absolute rights protected.
Life: A wrongful death action under German law by the victim's dependants exists only if they would have been entitled to support (§§ 844, 845 BGB), there is no obligation to compensate the surviving relatives or heirs. Only if bodily injury after some time has resulted in the victim's death, then his or her own damage claims having arisen (like medical bills or damages for pain and suffering) may devolve on the heirs.
Person, health: The physical integrity of a person is protected so that personal injury including infliction of pain engenders liability. Even medical treatment (operation, injections etc.) is, prima facie, regarded as an invasion of this right though it is normally justified by consent or by its therapeutical intent and the exercise of due diligence. Unintended pregnancy because of failure of a sterilization (wrongful life) results in physician's liability for child mainte-nance.[12] Mere mental strain, however, as a result of bad news and the like are not considered physical injury unless they have a clear pathological impact (e.g., nervous breakdown).[13]
Liberty is infringed if a person's freedom of movement is severely restricted either physically or by threats or persecution.
Property is confined to legal ownership and does not encompass financial assets in general. Pure economic loss is outside the scope of § 823 I BGB proper. But it can be a violation of property rights if an owner is prevented from using his belongings (e.g., a vehicle).
(b) Section 823 I BGB extends the scope of protection beyond the list of these explicitly mentioned rights by including *other rights*. These *other rights* include, e.g., all limited rights in rem (e.g., a security interest) as well as industrial property rights, e.g., patents, trademarks and copyrights.
Two such *other rights* are particularly frequently invoked. One is the right of an established business enterprise, which is important because of the com-mercial interests involved. The other is the general right to an individual's protection of personality (*Allgemeines Persönlichkeitsrecht*) which is occa-sionally violated by the yellow press and other mass media and thus becomes

---

12. Entscheidungen des Bundesgerichtshofs in Zivilsachen (BGHZ) 76,249; BGHZ 129,178. For "wrongful birth" of a handicapped child after incorrect consultation *see* BGHZ 86, 240.
13. BGHZ 56, 163.

a matter of public interest from time to time. The right of an established and operated business (*Recht am eingerichteten and ausgeübten Gewerbebetrieb*) was created by the courts when it turned out that the protection against harm caused in economic competition could not sufficiently be dealt with by means of unfair competition, trademark, copyright or patent law. Today, anyone who runs a business as well as any self-employed person can sue another person for wrongfully and culpably causing damage to this business under § 823 I BGB, provided that the defendant's conduct was aimed at the business (business-connected). An action under § 823 I BGB does not lie in cases of only indirect causation of damage. If a cable is ruptured by a bulldozer during road construction leading to the interruption of energy supply for a plant, the damage occurring is not covered because the harm was not specifically directed at the business (it affected all potential users of power). Due to the fact that the right to an established business is subsidiary and severely circumscribed, its practical importance has recently decreased. Furthermore, it had turned out that this right, in most instances, ultimately protects merely pecuniary interests. This is in conflict with the general principle that financial assets as such are not protected by § 823 I BGB.

The legislature deliberately refrained from implementing a right to an individual's personality and privacy. Especially defamation cases and personal data as well as digital information were thought to be sufficiently protected under § 823 II BGB[14] in conjunction with respective penal code provisions or the rules in media laws. Yet, the development of mass media like the press, broadcasting or television soon revealed the shortcomings of the protection of the right to personality solely under § 823 II BGB. Hence, the Federal Supreme Court (*Bundesgerichtshof*, BGH) drew on Articles 1 and 2 of the German Constitution (protecting human dignity and personal freedom) and recognized a right to personality and privacy as *another right* under § 823 (1) BGB. In several leading cases, the court protected the plaintiffs against invasions of their privacy, their right to be left alone, against defamation, and against the commercialization of their personal rights,[15] by granting an action for damages. Even though constitutional issues arguably demanded the recognition of new rights to be protected by tort law, § 823 I BGB is not applicable if a more special statute governs the violation of this right. Yet, there may be considerable differences between the protection of rights under § 823 I BGB and under such special statutes.

Under § 823 (1) BGB, the wrongfulness of the violation of personality rights is usually subject to an extensive balancing of the plaintiff's and the defendant's interests.

Also, there is no presumption of wrongfulness so that it must be positively established by the plaintiff. In this process, several areas of law can come into

---

14. Granting damages for breach of statutes protecting the victim (Schutzgesetze, see *infra* sub II).
15. Cf. Basil S. Markesinis & Hannes Unberath, *The German Law of Torts – A Comparative Treatise*, (4th ed. 2002) pp. 70–79; BGH Neue Juristische Wochenzeitschrift (NJW) 2005, p. 215.

play, e.g., constitutional law, criminal law and civil law. This results in a case-by-case analysis requiring special consideration of the particular circumstances.

[2] Conduct and Causation

The violation of a right mentioned in § 823 I BGB can either be caused by the wrongdoer's positive act or, if he had a legal duty to act (i.e., to protect the victim), result from an omission. Apart from the special duties to act imposed by statute, German courts, especially the Federal Supreme Court, have played an important role in the development of such general duties. Most importantly, duties of care, to protect victims against certain kinds of harm, are imposed on everyone who creates or maintains a source of danger.[16]

There must be a causal connection between the violation of the victim's rights and the corresponding damage. Such a connection must not only exist concerning the harm as such but also with regard the specific damages. Thus, a causal connection has to be examined twice in a tort claim under § 823 I BGB: the defendant's conduct must be the cause of the victim's injury, and the victim's injury must have led to the damages claimed.

The requisite causal link between the defendant's conduct and the plaintiff's damage is not simply a factual question; the *but for*-test alone is not sufficient. Of course, if the plaintiff would not have been injured but for the act of the defendant, the defendant's act is normally considered the cause-in-fact of the harm suffered by the plaintiff. Yet, beyond that, the question of causation in German law, as well as in most other laws, is infused with value judgments designed filter out distant events considered not to be responsible for the damage., e.g., because they are too remote. Thus, German courts and writers have developed several theories to narrow the excessively wide scope of the cause-in-fact test. Earlier on, it was said that only *adequate causation* could trigger liability. This test was essentially based on probability and foreseeability: a victim's harm would only be attributable to the defendant, if, according to everyday experience, his conduct significantly increased the probability of the injury. Yet, this *adequacy theory (Adäquanztheorie)* eliminates only highly improbable scenarios. It was soon considered insufficient as a limitation of causal attribution in many cases. It is now complemented by the *protective scope of the rule theory (Schutzzweck der Norm)* which provides that damage can be only recovered if it is within the scope of protection of the rule that has been violated. In addition, courts have more recently considered the respective spheres of risk when assessing a causal link between conduct and damage.[17]

---

16. Cf. with regard to roads, buildings, children's playgrounds, public swimming pools or cemeteries: BGH Neue Juristische Wochenschrift (NJW) 1975, 533; 1978, 1626; 1977, 1965; 1988, 1392; 1980, 1159; 1982, 1144; 1977, 1392.
17. In one of the cases, the plaintiff operated a pig farm under tight conditions (a large number of pigs were crammed into a small area). The defendant's car crashed into a nearby street corner (some 50 m away) with a loud bang. The noise caused a panic among the pigs which resulted in many deaths among them. The Federal Supreme Court rejected the pig owner's claim because he had created the risk that had materialized in the first place when he operated his farm under

Considerations involving the violated rule's scope of protection and the respective spheres of risk are, of course, quite different from the original cause-in-fact analysis. They clearly demonstrate that, today, causation is not so much a logical test as it is a policy issue.

[3]   Unlawfulness

The defendant's conduct must have been unlawful. In German law, a violation of the rights expressly named in § 823 I BGB is presumed to be unlawful so that it is up to the defendant to justify his conduct, e.g., by asserting a special privilege, e.g., self-defense, necessity, use of force in defense of property, or the victim's consent. The latter plays a significant role in medical malpractice cases. Here, the patient's consent provides a valid defense only if the chances of success as well as the risks of the treatment had been properly explained to the patient (informed consent).

[4]   Fault

The defendant's conduct, i.e., the violation of a legally protected absolute right, must have been culpable, that is intentional or negligent. Intent is usually judged by examining the wrongdoer's attitude towards the consequences of his act. Thus, a person's conduct is intentional with respect to an injury if that person desires to cause the injury and knows about the consequences of his conduct; it is also sufficient, however, if the person is substantially certain that the injury will occur and accepts it as inevitable. Negligence is defined by § 276 I BGB as not applying the level of care required for social interaction (*die im Verkehr erforderliche Sorgfalt außer Acht lassen*). Hence, the evaluation is objective. The standard is the care exercised by a reasonably prudent member of the relevant social group in the respective situation, regardless of individual knowledge, capacity or experience.

[5]   Harm Caused by Children (§ 828 BGB)

Damages caused by children are of great importance, in particular in accidents related to traffic, playing, and sports.

Under certain circumstances, no liability is imposed on children who cannot be held responsible for harm caused by them as they are not yet able to realize the harmful consequences of their behavior. § 828 II BGB exempts children from liability for accidents, provided that they are not yet 10 years old – unless a child between 7 and 10

---

conditions that made pigs extremely sensible to noise. BGHZ 115, 84: for a comparative review of this decision *see* Shaw/Quickenborne/ Abeltshauser in 1 *European Review of Private Law* (1993) 241.

has acted intentionally. The same privilege applies to children's contributory negligence.[18] Children between 10 and 18 years are only exempt from liability if they did not have the necessary understanding to realize their responsibility (§ 828 III BGB)

[B]   Violation of Protective Statutes (§ 823 II BGB)

Since § 823 I BGB does not cover anything except life, physical integrity, health and freedom as well as the absolute rights mentioned above, further tort law provisions step in to fill existing gaps so that no important interest will ultimately remain unprotected. One of these gap-filling provisions is § 823 II BGB, stating that:

> The same obligation [as in § 823 I BGB, i.e., to compensate for harm caused] is placed upon a person who violates a statute intended for the protection of others. If, according to the provisions of the statute, a violation is possible even without fault, the duty to compensate arises only in the event of fault.

Thus, § 823 II BGB gives a plaintiff the opportunity to bring a tort action based on the infringement of a specific protective statute even in cases not involving interests specifically protected under § 823 I BGB. Section 823 II is particularly important because it allows compensation even for pure economic loss.

Most problems concerning (potential) actions under § 823 II BGB therefore deal with the question whether a specific statute has a *protective purpose* in the sense of this provision. Any legal norm may qualify as a protective statute in this sense, including criminal law provisions (like fraud), administrative regulations, city ordinances and even collective labor agreements as well as unwritten norms, e.g., customary law. But the rule must aim at the protection of individual interests, and the injured person must belong to the class of persons which the rule intends to protect.

[C]   Intentional and Unconscionable Injury (§ 826 BGB)

Under § 826 BGB a person is liable if he or she intentionally causes harm to another in a way that is contrary to public policy. Section 826 BGB opens up the opportunity to establish a cause of action even where the requirements laid down in § 823 I BGB are not met and even if no protective statute in the sense of § 823 II BGB has been violated. Section 826 BGB also protects even purely economic interests. Yet, in contrast to § 823 BGB, negligence alone does not suffice to make § 826 BGB applicable. The requirement of intentional conduct heavily limits the applicability of § 826 BGB, clearly shows its narrow scope, and indicates the lack of opportunity to develop this rule much further.

The wide scope of the term "contrary to public policy" (unconscionable, *contra bonos mores*) constitutes a second problem within that section. This blanket notion can also be found in the general part of the BGB (§ 138) as well as in other statutes (e.g., the Unfair Competition Act). It refers, implicitly, to case law, traditionally a secondary

---

18. Cf. Hein Kötz & Gerhard Wagner, *Deliktsrecht*, at no. 43 et seq. As to similar preceding legislation in France and Belgium *see* Christian von Bar, *The Common European Law of Torts,* pp. 84 et seq.

source in the civil law tradition. The meaning of *public policy* in this and other contexts can be gleaned mainly from situations to which the provision has been applied: inducing a contracting party to breach the contract; delaying a debtor's filing for bankruptcy in order to satisfy one's debts at the expense of other creditors; or abusing a formal legal position solely in order to harm someone else.[19]

§7.03   TORT LIABILITY UNDER A PRESUMPTION OF FAULT

[A]   Liability for Third Persons (§§ 831, 832 BGB)

Regarding civil liability for third persons, § 831 BGB is the most important cause of action. Thus it can serve as a general example for the whole category. Section 831 I BGB reads as follows:

> Anyone who employs another person to do any work is liable for the injury unlawfully caused to a third party in the performance of this work.

> No liability shall arise if the employer has exercised the necessary care in the selection of the employee; and where he has to supply tools or equipment or to supervise the work, provided he has exercised reasonable care as regards such supply or supervision, or if the injury would have arisen notwithstanding the exercise of such care.

The underlying idea of the previously mentioned tort provisions (§ 823 I, § 823 II and § 826 BGB) was that the injured party can bring an action against the primary tortfeasor himself. In a sense, § 831 BGB establishes liability based on the wrongdoing of another. Still, as the second clause makes it clear, it ultimately holds the principal liable for the harm caused by his agent because of the principal's failure to select a competent person or to supervise him or her carefully. In that sense, liability is not – strictly speaking – vicarious. Instead, it is liability for the principal's own fault which is then presumed.

[1]   Employees

The most common kind is the liability of an employer for the harm caused by his employees committed within the scope of their duties. The employer is blamed for not having selected and supervised his employee carefully enough.

§ 831 BGB requires the victim to establish that the person whose conduct leads to the damage was indeed a *Verrichtungsgehilfe*, roughly the equivalent of an employee. Established in the 19th century, this concept underwent considerable changes throughout the 20th century. A person qualifies as employee when he or she is dependent on the instructions of the principal. Although this does not necessarily require permanent and paid employment, it is required that the principal have the authority to determine the scope and duration of the employee's tasks and to restrict or terminate them as he

---

19. As e.g., cf. Walter van Gerven, Jeremy Lever & Pierre Larouche, *Tort Law – Common Law of Europe Case Books* (2000), pp. 231 et seq.

finds necessary. Thus, a partner in a general partnership is not an employee while the lawyer commissioned and instructed by his client for a specific task can be an agent in the sense of § 831 BGB.

[2]   Torts in the Course of Employment

In order to hold the employer liable for harm caused by his agent, § 831 I BGB requires that the conduct of the employee has occurred within the scope of the employment. It is not enough that the person causing the harm did so merely on occasion of the employment so that his or her wrongful act was not substantially connected to the task he or she was entrusted with. Rather, the injurious conduct must fall within the range of conduct which the accomplishment of his or her tasks entails.[20]

[3]   Burden of Proof

The significance of § 831 I BGB lies in the shift of the burden of proof regarding fault. In an action brought under § 831 BGB, the plaintiff has the burden of proving that the defendant's employee caused wrongful damage to one of his rights protected by tort law. But it is presumed that the principal acted culpably with regard to the selection and supervision of his employees as well as with regard to the causal connection between his fault and the damage caused. Thus, it rests with the defendant (principal) to rebut this presumption. Under the assumption that the employer was not at fault, he can rely on the defense set out in § 831 I 2 BGB stating that the principal is not liable if he has exercised the necessary care in selecting and supervising the agent, or if the damage would have arisen anyway.

Among the policies underlying this shift of the burden of proof is the idea that the primary person responsible should be the employer, not the employee, although the latter may very well be liable him- or herself under any of the above mentioned tort provisions. Yet, it is made easier to sue the employer because he is more likely to have the financial means to compensate the victim as well as to carry insurance. In certain cases, however, the employer can seek recourse against the employee although that generally requires that the employee have acted intentionally.

Similar principles of liability and burden of proof apply to parents breaching their duty to supervise their child if the child has injured a third party (§ 832 BGB). Again, the parents are not answerable for the child's fault; rather, they are blamed for their own breach of the duty to supervise the child.

[B]   Liability for Animals and Buildings (§§ 833–838 BGB)

The position of victims is strengthened by a presumption of fault in other cases as well. Liability of an owner or keeper of an animal as well as that of an owner or keeper of a

---

20. Van Gerven, Lever & Larouche, *Tort Law*, at p. 512.

building is also based on a rebuttable presumption of fault. The victim only has to show that the defendant was in charge of the animal or building and that the harm he suffered was the realization of a risk typically associated with that source of danger. If the defendant wants to escape liability, he has to rebut the presumption of fault.

§7.04   STRICT LIABILITY

Liability without fault is based on the risk the defendant created, i.e., he is responsible for a source of danger that may lead to injury. In Germany, the rise of risk-based liability has its origins in the rise of industrial enterprises in the late 19th century. Originally, strict liability was a narrow and clear exception to the fault principle. Instead of raising duties of care owed by modern industrial and other business actors to a level virtually impossible to attain, the German legislature introduced, in part already before the BGB's enactment in 1900, statutory liability based on risks then perceived as extremely high: railroads (Act of 1871), road traffic (Act of 1909) and air traffic (Act of 1929). Although there is no general provision on strict liability in German civil law, the common rationale underlying these statutes (and others, cf. *infra*) is that (at least the financial) consequences of certain risks should be borne by those who control and take advantage of them.[21]

[A]   Railroads, Road Traffic, and Energy Facilities

Originally, it was the exceptional character of strict liability that gave rise to the statutes in these and other areas. Imposing strict liability is still regarded as a domain of the legislature rather than the courts. Liability without fault was first imposed on the operators of accident-prone traffic vehicles:

(1) The keeper (*Halter*) of a motor vehicle is liable for damage caused by its operation under § 7 of the *Road Traffic Act* (*Strassenverkehrsgesetz, StVG*). If he was also the driver, then he may be liable under general BGB tort rules (§§ 823 et seq.) as well. It is characteristic of German tort law that plaintiffs can plead claims under both fault-based and risk-based liability regimes in the same case; each claim is treated independently so that both forms of liability can coexist.[22] Where the plaintiff has such a choice, he will of course primarily rely on the cause of action most beneficial to him although that may require some judgment. For example under the strict liability statute, he does not have to show the defendant's fault – but he can only sue the *keeper* of the vehicle (or his liability insurer according to the direct action provision of the *Pflichtversicherungsgesetz*, Mandatory Insurance Act). If he wants to hold the

---

21. Basil S. Markesinis & Hannes Unberath, *German Law of Torts*, at p. 717; Hein Kötz & Gerhard Wagner, *Deliktsrecht*, nos. 498 et seq.; Van Gerven, Lever & Larouche, *Tort Law*, at pp. 545 et seq.
22. Cf. Van Gerven, Lever & Larouche, at p. 542.

driver liable, the action must be based on § 823 I BGB and, hence, fault must be established.[23]

(2) Another special act, the *Public Liability Act* (*Haftpflichtgesetz*), imposes strict liability on operators of railway installations (including trams and suspension railways), of cables and of conduits and pipes for the transmission of energy. Also, under the Air Traffic Act (*Luftverkehrsgesetz*), keepers of aircraft are strictly liable for damages caused to persons other than passengers by accidents resulting from the operation of an aircraft. A strict liability regime is imposed on operators of nuclear power plants for *nuclear events* and on those in possession of radioactive material under the Nuclear Energy Act (*Atomgesetz*). Finally, the Water Resources Act (*Wasserhaushaltsgesetz*) imposes strict liability for the discharge of harmful substances into water.

Despite certain differences between these statutes regarding the precise degree of responsibility – e.g., the Air Traffic Act also provides for liability for force majeure and inevitable events while the Public Liability Act does not – all these statutes have in common that liability is not based on notions of fault or unlawfulness but on the exceptional risk connected with the covered activities.[24] As a counterbalance to the strictness of liability, the majority of these statutes provide for maximum liability caps.

[B]   Product Liability

[1]   *Development*

a) A manufacturer's liability for defective products was known in German law long before "product liability" became a distinctive concept and branch of law; it was part of general tort law, hence claims could be made under the same conditions as under any other tort action. Consequently, the *Reichsgericht* (Imperial Court) held the manufacturer of a fruit gatherer's ladder liable for its negligently defective construction.[25] It was only in the 1960s that the courts – under the strong influence of both academic scholarship and comparative considerations[26] – began to recognize that liability for defective products could not simply be mastered through traditional tort law instruments but required a special regime of liability. Initially, the courts devised special rules reversing the burden of proof, then they extended the protected interests beyond the traditional restrictions to "life, health, property," raised the duties of care and broadened the concept of defectiveness, and finally extended the group of potential defendants. The policy question underlying this whole development

---

23. Before the most recent tort law reform in 2002, another difference between the two causes of action was that damages for pain and suffering could be claimed only in fault-based actions, not under a strict liability approach. The law has since been amended to allow the latter as well (§ 11 s. 2 StVG).
24. Van Gerven, Lever & Larouche, at p. 547.
25. RG LZ 1915 Sp. 1025.
26. Cf. Konrad Zweigert & Hein Kötz, *Introduction into Comparative Law* (3rd ed. 1998), p. 424.

was who should bear the ultimate burden of industrial and technological development, mass production and distribution that is socially and economically useful but the risks of which are often borne by those injured as consumers, users, or bystanders?

In the wake of the Thalidomide tragedy in the 1960s, the German legislature in 1976 enacted a special Statute on Pharmaceuticals (*Arzneimittelgesetz*) in 1976 that provided for strict liability of drug companies which put defective pharmaceutical products into circulation. The regulation of this specific sector is regarded as the forerunner of the EU Product Liability Directive.

b) The 1985 EEC Product Liability Directive and its implementation into national law are characteristic for another trend in the development of German product liability law. Its most important features are the emphasis on consumer protection and the adoption of the strict liability principle. Yet, bar and bench have been very hesitant to apply the new law. As a result, there was no radical shift in the practice of product liability. Thus, the traditional national regime based on the rules of the BGB continues to coexist with the harmonized European products liability law, and in practice, the former is much more frequently invoked than the latter.

c) The traditional German approach to product liability was based on the general tort cause of action (§ 823 I BGB). Among the prerequisites of traditional tort (as well as contract) liability, negligence is often the most critical one because it is often difficult for victims to plead and prove fault on behalf of the manufacturer. As this difficulty is often insurmountable – in many situations victims cannot determine the ultimate cause of the defect – the German Supreme Court some forty years ago relieved the victim from having to prove the manufacturer's fault.[27] Today, it is the defendant who has the burden of proof for his innocence.

In 1990, the statute implementing the EU Product Liability Directive into German law (Product Liability Act)[28] took effect. In that statute, the negligence rule was abandoned as a matter of principle. Under the statute, the manufacturer (and others in the chain of distribution, *see* below) are liable for having put the defective product into circulation regardless of fault.

[2]   Parties: Consumer, Bystander, Producer, Agent

(a) As the basis of product liability in Germany is tort, it is not only the buyer who has a cause of action in case of product defects. Instead, everyone who suffers damage resulting from the product's defect can bring a claim, including the innocent bystander. This is the rule under general tort provisions of the BGB.

---

27. BGHZ 51, 91 ("chicken pest case").
28. Statute on Liability for Defective Products, Product Liability Act (Gesetz über die Haftung für fehlerhafte Produkte). *See* Joachim Zekoll, *The German Products Liability Act*, Am.J.Comp.L. 37 (1989), pp. 809 et seq.

Under the Product Liability Act, there are two limitations regarding property damage: only damage to *another* thing (not the product itself) is covered; and only property for private use is protected so that property used for business purposes is excluded from the special statute's scope altogether.

(b) Under German law, it is primarily – but not only – the manufacturer who is liable for product defects. Again, this is due to the general tort principle which imposes liability on the person responsible for the damage caused to health or property by negligent conduct. In the first place, this is the manufacturer, including the producer of the defective component. Other members in the chain of distribution will usually not be liable in tort since they cannot be blamed for unlawful conduct. Yet, in cases involving insufficient instruction, others may be liable as well, especially a dealer who may be under a special duty to provide the product with instruction for correct application and use.[29] The Product Liability Act also contains a special provision (§ 4) extending liability to "quasi-producers"; they include any person who presents himself as the product's manufacturer; anybody putting his name or trademark on the product; anybody who imported the product into the European Community; and each supplier of a product the manufacturer of which cannot be identified.

(c) As mentioned, the principal (usually the employer) can be held liable for wrongs committed by his agents (usually his employees) under § 831 BGB. According to general tort principles, the manufacturer could plead careful selection and supervision of his employees as a defense. However, German courts have accepted that plea extremely rarely in product liability cases. Instead, they have been very demanding as far as proof of perfect organization and supervision of the production is concerned. Thus, it has been said that "proof of producer's innocence for his employees' fault is dead."[30] The Product Liability Act being based on strict liability, of course, eliminates any such defense in the first place.

[3]   Conditions of Liability under § 823 I BGB and the Product Liability Act

(a) The concept of product liability in Germany originally rested on the producer's general tortious conduct (§ 823 BGB). The tort basis of product liability is clearly established in the Product Liability Act of 1989 (in force 1990) as well. Yet, if there is a direct contractual relationship between the manufacturer and the victim, liability can also be based on breach of contract. In that event, the victim can choose between, and even combine, tort and contract claims since there is no "*non-cumul*" rule in German law. The two causes of action may

---

29. BGHZ 47, 316.
30. Uwe Diederichsen, Neue Juristische Wochenschrift 1978, 1281, 1287.

differ, however, with regard to the interests protected, to the statute of limitations, and various other details.

(b) The concept of "defect" under general tort law (§ 823 BGB) has been subdivided in a tripartite fashion: design defects, manufacturing defects, and insufficient instruction and monitoring. Under the 1990 Product Liability Act, these categories are not distinguished although they are still considered useful for analytical purposes. The statute provides a broad definition of "defect" that comprises all three categories and focuses on lack of safety. Its § 3 provides:

> A product is defective when it does not provide the safety which a person is entitled to expect, taking all circumstances into account, including (a) the presentation of the product, (b) the use to which it could reasonably be expected that the product would be put, (c) the time when the product was put into circulation.

This definition clearly has to be distinguished from the contractual understanding of fitness of goods. The latter pertains to the value of the good, the economic interest to use and consume it. In contrast, the definition of a defect under the Product Liability Act purports to protect the user (and bystander) in their physical integrity. It contains a number of criteria pertaining to safety expectations that can be inferred from generally recognized standards, ranging from the external appearance of the product to the reasonable expectations of the user and the manufacturer. These criteria are objective. They are not determined by the individual consumer's or manufacturer's ideas of the product's qualities. What ultimately counts is the use of the product that can be *reasonably anticipated* by the manufacturer.

(c) Under general tort law as well as under the Product Liability Act (§ 1 IV), the plaintiff has to prove the defective condition of the product, the damage, the causal nexus between defect and damage and the attribution of the defective product to the defendant.

The defendant has the burden of proof for certain defenses he wants to raise, e.g., that he did not put the product into circulation; that the product did not have the defect, yet, when put into circulation; that the manufacturer did not produce the product for sale or other distribution in the course of his business; that the product complied with mandatory regulations at the time of distribution; that the product's defect could not be discovered according to the state of the art at the time it was put into circulation; and in the case of a component part manufacturer, that the defect is due to the design of the complete product or to instructions of its producer or assembler.

(d) The general tort provisions of the BGB (§§ 823 I et seq.) provide for damages in case of physical harm to persons and property only. Recovery for pure economic loss is possible only in cases of violation of statutory rules that are especially intended to protect individual interests of the plaintiff (§ 823 II), *supra* sub §7.02[B]). In product liability situations, this provision comes into play in cases of public safety regulations (e.g., safety rules for automobiles, food and drugs or appliances[31]). In the Product Liability Act, there is another restriction as to the type of injury concerned: as mentioned, property damage is covered only if it affects an item other than the product itself and if the damaged property is intended for private use and was in fact mainly used or consumed in that fashion (§ 1 I 2).

Whereas the original version of the Product Liability Act did not provide for non-pecuniary damages ("pain and suffering"), it does so since 2002: A *"billige Entschädigung in Geld"* (fair and reasonable money compensation) may be asked for under § 8 Sentence 2 Product Liability Act in case of personal injury as well.

[4] *Major Defenses*

The major affirmative defenses under both, general tort law and the Product Liability Act, constitute a fairly long list. The manufacturer can plead that he did not introduce the product into "the stream of distribution" (§ 1 II No. 1 Product Liability Act), e.g., the product had not yet left the production site or was wrongfully sold under the manufacturer's trademark (counterfeit merchandise). He can argue that the product was not defective when put onto the market; if the producer shows a high probability that a defect did not exist when it left his sphere of control, he will be discharged. He can defend by showing that the product was not produced or distributed in the course of the producer's business and not for a commercial purpose (§ 1 II No. 3 Product Liability Act). He can say that the defect was due to compliance of the product with mandatory public regulations (§ 1 II No. 4 Product Liability Act). Under German law, the producer can also raise the state of the art defense: general tort law does not hold him liable if he could not know or discover the defect for lack of fault, and the Product Liability Act expressly provides for this defense (§ 1 II No. 5). If a "development defect" is realized later, however, the manufacturer has to take the necessary steps to prevent further damage, i.e., he is under a duty to monitor, warn, and possibly even to recall the product. Special rules pertaining to development risks apply in the area of genetic engineering: If the product defect is due to genetic engineering activities, the producer will even be liable for "development risks" since they are typical for genetic technology.[32]

In case of component part problems, the manufacturer can also argue that the defect is attributable to the design or instructions of the (main) product into which the component has been fitted (§ 1 III Product Liability Act).

Personal negligence on behalf of the consumer normally reduces, but may also completely eliminate the victim's claim. The degree of reduction depends on the ratio

---

31. *Straßenverkers-Zulassungsordnung*, StVZO (automobiles), *Arzneimittelgesetz*, AMG (drugs), *Lebensmittel- und Bedarfsgegenständegesetz*, LMBG (food, tobacco and cosmetic products, other consumer requisites), *Medizingeräteverordnung*, MedGV (medical-technical equipment), *Gerätesicherheitsgesetz*, GSG (technical appliances), *Produktsicherheitsgesetz*, ProdSG (product safety and CE-labelling). – As to a more complete list of those protection statutes *see* Otto Palandt & Hartwig Sprau, *Bürgerliches Gesetzbuch*, (76th ed. 2017)), § 823 marginal n. 203.

32. Section 32 Gentechnikgesetz, *Genetic Engineering Act.*

between the defendant's and plaintiff's contribution to the harm (*see* § 6 I Product Liability Act, § 254 BGB).

Finally, the defendant may invoke the statute of limitations running three years from the time when the victim first became aware, or should have become aware, of the damage, the defect, and the producer's identity. In addition, the Product Liability Act (but not general tort law) provides a statute of repose under which claims cannot be brought more than ten years after the product was put into circulation, even if the injury occurs later (§ 13).

[C]   Environmental Liability

Environmental damage is rarely compensated under general tort law (§ 823 I BGB) since the necessary conditions, in particular negligence, are not often met or are at least difficult to prove. As a result, strict liability according to a patchwork of special statutes[33] is very important for environmental protection. The Water Management Act (*Wasserhaushaltsgesetz*) mentioned before (*supra* §7.04[A][2]) provides for such liability of polluters. Air pollution by gas, smoke or other agents as well as noise is merely covered in part by § 906 BGB and in part by § 14 of the Federal Pollution Control Act (*Bundesimmisionsschutzgesetz*) because under these rules, only land owners may be entitled to an "adequate" compensation, and only if their rights are "substantially" impaired by the pollution, provided injunctive relief is not available.

The more recent Environmental Liability Act 1991 (*Umwelthaftungsgesetz*, UmweltHG) provides for claims by everyone who suffers damages to the classically protected interests (life, health, property) if the damage is caused by "environmental impact" (*Umwelteinwirkungen*), i.e., pollution of soil, air and water. The operators of certain industrial installations listed in an annex to the statute are liable regardless of fault if the installation discharges harmful substances (including shocks, odours, pressure, radiation, heat) and could typically cause the injury: it is then presumed that the damage involved in the case has been caused by the installation. The presumption can only be rebutted by proof of operation in accordance with applicable regulations and without any disturbance of operations (*Störung des Betriebs*, § 6 UmweltHG). Liability is imposed in cases of nuisance as well as damages caused by lawful and normal operation; the state-of-the-art defense is not available.

Yet, the problem of "ecological damage" in the sense of damage to the environment itself (i.e., beyond individually protected interests), e.g., damage to nature or biodiversity, lies beyond the scope of the statute. In addition, the German environmental liability regime is not fit to provide compensation for gradually arising (chronic) harm which accumulates over time. Given the immense economic and ecologic interests at stake and the wide-ranging effects across national borders, it is generally agreed that a broad European and international liability regime is required.[34] The only (special) environmental liability concept that also covers damages caused by gradual

---

33. Markesinis & Unberath, *The German Law of Torts,* at p. 747.
34. Van Gerven, Lever & Larouche, *Tort Law,* p. 685.

contamination is contained in the Nuclear Energy Act, section 25(1) and the Paris Convention on Nuclear Third Party Liability (which widely harmonizes national European laws on compensation for damages resulting from nuclear accidents to the public).[35] Under these provisions the nuclear power plant operator is strictly liable for damages caused by "a nuclear incident," defined as "any occurrence ..." and thus covering gradual contamination over time as well.

§7.05   RELIEF AVAILABLE IN TORT CASES

[A]   Compensation

[1]   Restitution in Kind and Monetary Compensation

The extent and kind of damages available under German law are generally addressed in the general part of the law of obligations (§§ 249–254 BGB); these rules apply to all damage claims, regardless of whether they arise from tort, contract, or another source. They are then supplemented by several more specific provisions in the subchapter on tort liability, pertaining to personal injury (§§ 842–846 BGB) and property damage (§§ 848–851 BGB). As a result, the determination of available tort damages must always rely on a combination of both, the general and the specific rules.

The general rules on liability draw a distinction between two basic methods: repair of the damage in kind (§ 249 BGB) and compensatory damages in monetary form (§ 251 BGB). The basic principle in the German law of damages is compensation in the sense of *restitutio ad integrum*, i.e., the tortfeasor should actually put the victim in the position in which he or she would be if the injurious act had never occurred (§ 249 I BGB). Yet, the tortfeasor himself is rarely capable of restoring the *status quo ante*, and even if he is, it is rarely acceptable for the victim to have the tortfeasor treat his injuries or repair his damaged property. Thus, the victim can ask for monetary compensation instead, i.e., for the sum necessary to repair the damage incurred. In a similar vein, if repairing the damage in kind is possible but would impose a disproportionate burden on the defendant, he has the right to compensate the victim with money (§ 251 II) BGB. In practice, financial compensation is the overwhelming rule.

The plaintiff may claim damages for medical treatment, loss of earnings, repair bills, and other expenses. This includes lost profits (§ 252 BGB). The latter provision is supplemented by the special (tort) rules of § 842 and § 843 BGB. They provide that the duty to compensate the victim includes damages "which the act causes to his earnings or prosperity" (§ 842 BGB) as well as damages resulting from the fact that "the earning capacity of the injured person is destroyed or impaired" (§ 843 BGB).

In principle, the loss suffered by the plaintiff must be precisely quantified, itemized and, if the defendant contests the amount, proven. Yet, if the precise amount of damages cannot be determined given the available methods of proof, § 287 I of the

---

35. Gesetz über die friedliche Verwendung der Kernenergie v. 23.12.1959, BGBl I 814; (Paris) Convention on Third Party Liability in the Field of Nuclear Energy of July 29, 1960, (German) text in BGBl 1985 II 963.

German Code of Civil Procedure (*Zivilprozessordnung*, ZPO) allows the court to determine the damages "according to its free conviction in consideration of all circumstances."

[2]   Non-pecuniary Harm

The most controversial provision in this area of law is the recently amended provision contained in § 253 BGB. As always, § 253 I BGB still states that non-pecuniary damages are allowed only in cases provided by statute. Formerly, this was the case only under the general rules of tort law (§ 847 BGB old version) but not under the strict liability rules of special statutes and not for damages resulting from breach of contract. As of 2002, however, § 253 II BGB provides a general cause of action for pain and suffering damages in all cases involving harm to body, health, liberty or sexual self-determination. This action is no longer restricted to cases arising under the tort provisions of the BGB but includes strict liability actions and breach of contract claims as well.

As a result, the legislature established several provisions in various strict liability statutes granting the injured individual compensation for pain and suffering. Examples include § 8 Product Liability Act, § 11 of the Road Traffic Act and § 87 II of the Pharmaceutical Products Act.

Under German law, awards for pain and suffering are limited to compensation for the elements of injury which cannot be specified and precisely calculated. In order to determine the amount of financial compensation in these cases, the courts are given wide discretion (cf. also § 287 ZPO). Usually, they take into consideration both, the situation (and suffering) of the victim and the conduct and position of the wrongdoer.

Punitive damages are not allowed and the enforcement of foreign punitive damage awards has been rejected by the Federal Supreme Court as a violation of German public policy. It is true, however, that in setting the amount of damages for non-pecuniary harm, especially for pain and suffering or for violations of personality rights (*supra* §7.02[A][1][b]), courts may consider the need for prevention and deterrence. Thus, certain regulatory elements may occasionally play a role in the German law of damages. Still, punishment itself continues to be regarded as incompatible with the functions of German tort law and as belonging to the realm of criminal sanctions.

[3]   Contributory Negligence and Joint Tortfeasors

§ 254 BGB supplies a general provision on contributory negligence. It provides for a reduction of the defendant's liability to the extent that the plaintiff's conduct contributed to the harm. Additionally, § 254 BGB frequently overlaps with similar provisions in various strict liability statutes, e.g., § 9 of the Road Traffic Act or § 6 of the Product Liability Act.

Joint tortfeasors are jointly and severally liable (§ 840 I BGB).

[B] Injunctive and Declaratory Relief

(1) German tort law can provide the basis for a prohibitory or mandatory *injunction* designed to counter the immediate threat of injury. Injunctions are considered special procedural devices supplementing the protection provided by other remedies, e.g., damage awards. Injunctive relief is expressly provided for in some articles of the BGB, and while these provisions are part of substantive tort law, defendants can still be enjoined from committing unlawful acts regardless of fault. For example injunctive relief is expressly allowed for the protection of property rights (§ 1004 BGB) and the right of possession (§ 862 I 2 BGB) as well as the protection of one's name (§ 12 BGB). In addition, several other statutes (especially in the area of unfair trade law and intellectual property law) provide for injunctive relief against imminent infringements. In the Unfair Terms and Conditions Act (*Unterlassungsklagegesetz, UKlaG*),[36] injunctive relief is especially granted to EU-wide "qualified institutions" like consumer agencies, associations or chambers of commerce if consumer or data protection laws have been violated. Monetary compensation, however, cannot be demanded by such institutions under the UKlaG. Finally, German courts will, in appropriate cases, grant injunctions for the protection of all the rights listed in §§ 823 et seq. BGB by way of analogy to § 1004 BGB.

(2) If tort law provides a cause of action for damages or injunctive relief, the plaintiff cannot bring an action for declaratory judgment instead. Procedural economy requires that declaratory relief can be granted only if other remedies are not available (principle of subsidiarity, cf. § 256 Code of Civil Procedure). In tort cases, declaratory actions are often filed if the exact amount of damages cannot yet be determined but some legal action is necessary to toll the statute of limitations. Declaratory relief can also be sought if the dispute is limited to the issue of liability while the amount of damages is not contested.

§7.06 PROCEDURAL ENVIRONMENT

Given the traditional and rather rigid distinction between substance and procedure in German law, the impact of the procedural environment on the tort system has long been underestimated. Today, the bench and bar as well as legal academics widely agree on the necessity to include procedural factors in any analysis of tort law that aims at a description of its functions and an assessment of its actual performance. In particular, comparative perspectives on tort law have highlighted the importance of the procedural environment:

---

36. UKlaG 27.08.2002, BGBl I 3422.

(1) In the modern German civil justice system, there is no lay participation in the sense of trial by jury or decision making by lay judges. All tort cases are decided by professional judges only, usually sitting alone at the trial level and in panels of three (or more) at the appellate level. Appeals on issues of both fact and law are widely available in all but the most trivial cases.

(2) German damage awards tend to be relatively modest. This is due to a combination of several, mainly procedural, factors of which the lack of trial by lay jury is just one. In principle, damages must be precisely specified and, if disputed, proven; this prevents wildly overstated claims. In addition, the more inquisitorial method of fact gathering and the lack of Anglo-American style pre-trial discovery makes it difficult for plaintiffs to put together a truly powerful case.

(3) Too many or frivolous tort suits are not a major concern. This is, again, mainly due to certain features of the procedural and social environment. Most importantly, the German fee system strongly discourages spurious or inflated claims. Contingency fee arrangements are not allowed, and under the "European rule" of costs, the loser not only has to pay the court fees and his own attorney but the opponent's lawyer's fees as well. As a result, a defeat will cost the plaintiff dearly since he has to pay for both his and his opponent's counsel. In addition, the important role of public and private insurance (*see supra* §7.05[A][1]) in the German tort system diminishes the incentives to litigate accident claims as most of a victim's loss will already be covered by some form of insurance. As a result, accident victims in Germany have a rather modest "claims consciousness" and sue in tort more rarely than, e.g., tort victims in the United States.

(4) Mass tort suits used to be virtually unknown in Germany. In recent years, they have become somewhat more frequent in response to mass accidents, e.g., aircraft crashes, drug and other product defects, oil spills or securities fraud. Still, most of such cases do not lead to mass litigation, mainly because the law of civil procedure does not allow class or group actions.[37] Traditional procedural instruments for consolidating claims, e.g., joinder, common representation of a number of plaintiffs or fiduciary assignments of claims to a trustee, have occasionally been used in tort cases. Yet, since they require active "opting-in" by every member of the claimant group, even these strategies are rarely employed. In special areas like consumer and securities fraud, however, recent legislation has provided for simplified assignment of claims for collective and hence more efficient enforcement.[38]

---

37. Harald Koch, *Mass Torts in German Law*, in: Erik. Jayme (ed.), German National Reports in Civil Law Matters for the 14th Congress of Comparative Law in Athens 1994 (1994), 67 at 77.

38. Under the Legal Services Act (*Rechtsdienstleistungsgesetz*) § 2 II, § 8 IV consumer claims may be assigned to consumer associations or consumer centers who then collect these claims in a fiduciary capacity. Cf. Eva Kocher, in Marina Tamm & Klaus Tonner, *Verbraucherrecht*, 2nd ed. 2016, § 24 at nos. 46, 47.

SELECTED BIBLIOGRAPHY

Gert Brüggemeier, *Common Principles of Tort Law: A Pre-Statement of Law* (London 2004).

Cees van Dam, *European Tort Law* (2nd ed. Oxford 2013).

Walter van Gerven, Jeremy Lever & Pierre Larouche, *Tort law – Common Law of Europe Case Book* (2000).

Harald Koch, *Complex Damages and Their Settlement: Liability Principles, Procedural Economy or Law's Retreat*, 6th International Liability Forum Munich 2002 (2002), pp. 26 et seq.

Harald Koch, *Mass Torts Damage in Europe: Aggregation of Claims, Effective Enforcement and Adequate Representation*, in: Willem H. van Boom & Gerhard Wagner, *Mass Torts in Europe: Cases and Reflections* (Berlin, Boston 2014), pp. 157 et seq.

Hein Kötz & Gerhard Wagner, *Deliktsrecht* (12th ed. München 2013).

Helmut Koziol (ed.), *Unification of Tort Law: Wrongfulness* (The Hague, London, Boston 1998).

Helmut Koziol (ed.), *Unification of Tort Law: Causation* (The Hague, London, Boston 2000).

Ulrich Magnus, *Compensation for Personal Injuries in a Comparative Perspective*, Washburn L. J. 39 (2000) pp. 347 et seq.

Ulrich Magnus (ed.), *Unification of Tort Law: Damages* (The Hague, London, Boston 2001).

Basil S. Markesinis & Hannes Unberath, *A Comparative Introduction to the German Law of Torts* (4th ed. Oxford, Portland 2002).

Jaap Spier (ed.), *The Limits of Liability: Keeping the Floodgates Shut* (1996).

Gerald Spindler & Oliver Rieckers, *Tort Law in Germany* (Alphen NL 2011).

Gerhard Wagner, *Comparative Tort Law*, in: Mathias Reimann & Reinhard Zimmermann (eds), *The Oxford Handbook of Comparative Law* (Oxford 2008).

Joachim Zekoll, *The German Products Liability Act*, Am. J. Comp. L. 37 (1989), pp. 809 et seq.

CHAPTER 8

Property Law (*Sachenrecht*)

Jürgen Kohler

TABLE OF CONTENTS

§8.01   TERM AND POSITION IN THE LAW

The term *Sachenrecht*, which literally means "law of things," is best translated as the law of property or of rights in rem. This part of private law is concerned with those rights which a person has in direct relation to a *Sache*, i.e., "thing." According to § 90 of the German Civil Code (*Bürgerliches Gesetzbuch* – BGB), the term "thing" covers any substantive inanimate object (§ 90 BGB), i.e., both movables and land; in effect, animals are included (§ 90a BGB). Therefore, *Sachenrecht* does not pertain to intellectual property rights, e.g., patents, trademarks or copyright.

Since *Sachenrecht* is intended and designated to identify and define the entirety of rights which establish an immediate link between a person and a material object, its very definition indicates the elementary and clear distinction which German civil law makes between *Sachenrecht* and *Schuldrecht*, i.e., the law of obligations. The latter (§§ 241–853 BGB) deals with interpersonal legal relations in terms of rights and duties between legal entities. It is concerned with enforceable imperatives to a person's will to act, desist, or tolerate. An obligation, accordingly, establishes a claim against the debtor but does not provide legal links with an object, even though a change of legal position of a person vis-à-vis an object may be the ultimate goal of the obligatory relationship. Consequently, the law of obligations only deals with the question of personal relationships and liabilities. *Sachenrecht*, by contrast, primarily focuses on the right, total or partial, to a material object, a "thing" (*Sache*); attendant interpersonal rights ensuing from a violation of a person's right vested in an object are of secondary concern.

The legislative material on the history of the Civil Code succinctly explains the aforesaid characteristics of *Sachenrecht* in contrast to the law of obligations:

> *Sachenrecht* occupies an independent position in the system of the Code. It excludes itself from the law of obligations [...]. Its independence is mainly based on the difference between the right in rem (*dingliches Recht*) and the right *ad personam* (*persönliches Recht*). For whilst the law of obligations [...] is only concerned with legal relations between persons amongst themselves and therefore deals with personal rights only, [...], it is the task of *Sachenrecht* to regulate relations between a person and a thing, i.e., the rights in rem. [...] The obligatory right establishes a claim for performance against the debtor. The right in rem takes hold of the very thing, i.e., either as property or as a limited right, depending on whether the will of the titleholder with regard to the thing is to be decisive in all respects or only in certain aspects; the claim which it generates is not limited in the direction of a certain person. The term right in rem, as a general rule, means that it is of absolute legal effect. Insofar as it puts the thing under the authority of the titleholder, it excludes any interference from a third party; it can therefore act against anyone whose acts violate it [...]. The essence of rights in rem lies in the immediate power of a person over a thing [...]. It is decisive that the right can be exercised without another person's will, that there is no need for the existence of a debtor.[1]

In accordance with this definition, *Sachenrecht* covers a wider field than only the right of property as such. In addition, it covers possession (*Besitz*) and also limited rights in rem, mainly rights of use and various kinds of security interests.

§8.02 SOURCES OF THE LAW OF RIGHTS IN REM

The main body of *Sachenrecht* is contained in the third book of the Civil Code, from §§ 854–1296 BGB, with §§ 90–103 BGB providing definitions of related basic legal terminology, such as "thing" (*Sache*), "component" (*Bestandteil; Zubehör; Inventar*) and "fruits" (*Früchte*). There are also several important statutes outside the Civil Code that deal with special aspects of rights in rem, such as the *Wohnungseigentumsgesetz*[2] (Condominium Act) and the *Erbbaurechtsgesetz*[3] (Building Lease Act). Rights in land used for agriculture or forestry are dealt with by the *Grundstücksverkehrsgesetz*[4] (Land

---

1. Benno Mugdan, *Die gesammten Materialien zum Bürgerlichen Gesetzbuch für das Deutsche Reich*, vol. III, *Sachenrecht* (1899, reprint 1979).
2. *Gesetz über das Wohnungseigentum und das Dauerwohnrecht*, March 15, 1951, BGBl. I, p. 175, correction at p. 209, last *amendment* by Law of December 5, 2014, BGBl. I 2014, p. 1962.
3. *Erbbaurechtsgesetz (ErbbauRG;* formerly *Verordnung über das Erbbaurecht*, January 15, 1919, RGBl.1919, p. 72, correction at p. 123), *last amendment* by Law of October 1, 2013, BGBl. I 2013, p. 3719.
4. *Gesetz über Maßnahmen zur Verbesserung der Agrarstruktur und zur Sicherung land-und forstwirtschaftlicher Betriebe*, July 28, 1961, BGBl. I 1961, p. 1091, correction at p. 1652, 2000, *last amendment* by Law of December 17, 2008, BGBl. I 2008, p. 2586.

Transfer Act) and the *Pachtkreditgesetz*[5] (Lease Credit Act), rights in registered ships are addressed by the *Schiffsregistergesetz*[6] (Ship Register Act). The Civil Code's chapter on *Sachenrecht* is concerned with matters of substantive law only; it does not deal with procedural questions. The latter arise particularly with respect to registration of rights in land, which is governed by the *Grundbuchordnung*[7] (Land Register Act).[8]

§8.03   PRINCIPLES OF *SACHENRECHT*

[A]   Distinction among Objects

The Code's provisions on *Sachen* (things) draw a clear distinction between movable property (*bewegliche Sachen*) and immovables (*Grundstücke*). This distinction is relevant with respect to the modes of acquisition and the types of rights in rem available. Although the distinction does not have any theoretical effect as to the quality of property rights in private law, it does have practical implications due to the impact of public law, especially zoning and environmental laws on land.

According to § 93 BGB, there cannot be any separate or distinct rights in integral components (*wesentliche Bestandteile*) of a thing which are joined in such a way that one component part cannot be separated from the other without destroying or essentially altering it. § 94 BGB extends this rule to all things – including buildings – that are firmly attached to land when stating that these objects are to be considered integral components of the land unless the integration is intended to be of limited duration (§ 95 BGB). In effect, this rule amalgamates the ownership of land with the buildings erected on it, thus making certain movables integral parts of land subject to all legal dispositions concerning the site.[9]

[B]   Absolute Effect

As is explained in the legislative history of the Civil Code,[10] it is characteristic of rights in rem, the subject matter *of Sachenrecht*, to be "absolute." Here, "absoluteness" means that these rights bear legal effect vis-à-vis anyone who interferes with the thing concerned, be it in fact, i.e., by depriving the titleholder of his possession or trespassing against his possession, or in law by means of legal transactions affecting the legal position of the object. This is the main difference between rights in rem and obligatory

---

5. *Pachtkreditgesetz*, August 5, 1951, BGBl. I 1951, p. 494, *last amendment* by Law of November 8, 1985, BGBl. I 1985, p. 2065.
6. *Gesetz über Rechte an eingetragenen Schiffen und Schiffsbauwerken*, November 15, 1940, RGBl. I 1940, p. 1499, *last amendment* by Law of January 21, 2013, BGBl. I 2013, p. 91.
7. *Grundbuchordnung*, August 5, 1935, RGBl. I 1935, p. 1073, *last amendment* by Law of June 1, 2017, BGBl. I 2017, p. 1396.
8. As to procedural matters with regard to agricultural and forestry land, *see Gesetz über das gerichtliche Verfahren in Landwirtschaftssachen*, July 21, 1953, BGBl. I 1953, p. 667, *last amendment* by Law of July 23, 2013, BGBl. I 2013, p. 2586. With regard to registered ships, *see* the *Schiffsregistergesetz*, *supra* note 6.
9. For the effects of an *Erbbaurecht*, *see infra* sub §8.06[B][2][a].
10. *See* Mugdan, *supra* note 1.

rights. The latter bind only the parties privy to the contractual or other relationship; they do not, in principle, offer a defense against a third party to whom the property of the thing in question – i.e., the object of the obligation – was transferred first, even though this transaction may violate another person's prior obligatory right to obtain property of that object. In contrast to an obligatory right, a right in rem is "absolute" in the sense that such a right is assertable with respect to the object in relation to any other person. In principle, this rule also applies in the case of a non-titleholder attempting to transfer title to a third person; an exception is only made in the case of bona fide acquisition (*see infra* sub §8.03[F]).

[C]   Numerus Clausus of Rights In Rem

The absolute legal effect of rights in rem against all third parties poses a risk to the general public since the aforesaid principle may interfere with the ability to acquire property and other rights pertaining to objects unimpeded by rights in rem held by third parties. Thus, in order to enable third parties to assess the scope of possible risks arising from other persons' absolute rights, it is imperative for a legal system to define the types of rights which are recognized by law as having such an effect upon third parties. The Civil Code meets this requirement by limiting the number of rights in rem exclusively to those provided in the Code and in specific legislation, and by describing and largely also prescribing the contents of these rights by law. The freedom to develop new types of rights and to define their contents by means of consensus which is, in principle, characteristic for the law of obligations, does not pertain to *Sachenrecht*. Variations which do not fall within the categories of rights in terms provided by the Code or specific legislation are considered void. This rule is known as the principle of *numerus clausus* of rights in rem.

[D]   Disclosure and Agreement

In order to enable the public to calculate the risk caused by the absolute effect of rights in rem, the law requires, in principle, that the existence of any of these rights be made visible to third parties. Such disclosure of rights in rem is directly integrated into the legal act of transferring or establishing a right in rem. With movables, disclosure of the existence of a right in rem under the legal authority of an identifiable person is required and therefore also safeguarded since the actual handing over of the thing is an indispensable prerequisite for transfer of legal title. With land, the law ensures such disclosure by making the entry of the change in legal position into the land register (*Grundbuch*) an essential legal prerequisite for effecting such a change of rights.

In a legal system based on individual freedom, the transfer of title and the establishment of secondary rights in rem require an element of consent in addition to making provision for visibility of transfer or establishment of such rights. The Civil Code meets this additional requirement by making the transfer or the creation of a right in rem dependent on an agreement between the present and the future titleholder. This agreement merely contains the consensus on establishing or transferring the title or right in rem for or to the recipient.[11] This agreement, contractual by nature, is known as *dinglicher Vertrag*, which may be translated as "property rights contract." Therefore, all in all, the creation or transfer of a right in rem requires both elements – the aforesaid agreement, and the element of publicity, with the latter being transfer of possession in case of movables or entry into the land register with rights in real estate.

[E]   The Principle of Abstraction (Independence of *Sachenrecht* from the Law of Obligations)

The independent position assigned to *Sachenrecht* in the system of private law makes it imperative for legislation to interpret and design legal acts concerning object-related transactions independent of legal acts which apply to other parts of the legal system, namely the law of obligations.[12]

This basic position has, rightly or wrongly, led to the phenomenon peculiar to German law which is known as *Abstraktionsprinzip* – literally, the principle of abstraction. According to this principle, transactions concerning rights in rem are abstract, in the sense of being legally independent in terms of performance and its validity, from any underlying obligation which may bind the parties concerned to perform the transaction in question.[13] Thus, the transfer of title (*Verfügung*) may well be entirely valid even if the underlying (obligatory) relationship (*Verpflichtung*), e.g., a contract of sale, is not. The rules on the establishment of rights in rem are designed to put this principle into effect. They do so by making the existence and validity of any title transfer or title establishment dependent solely on the two elements discussed above – transfer of possession (for movables) or entry into a public register (for land), and a corresponding agreement between the titleholder and the acquiring party on the actual transfer or establishment of title. The latter agreement, while being contractual itself, must be strictly distinguished from the underlying contractual promise of one party privy to an obligatory relation to effectuate the transfer of title – namely the promise of the seller to pass property of the object of the sale (*Kaufvertrag*) –and the other party's – i.e., as for the example given here, the buyer's – promise to pay for the thing. In other words, the rules of *Sachenrecht* consider contractual promises of an obligatory nature to be neither a requirement for the establishment or transfer of a right in rem, nor to be sufficient for the establishment or transfer of such rights.

While an underlying obligation is not a prerequisite for the existence and validity of a legal act in rem, an obligation is necessary to make the transaction in rem permanent. An underlying obligation is required as *causa*, i.e., the legal ground for maintaining the transaction in the future. The absence of such an underlying *causa* gives rise to a quasi-contractual, however merely obligatory claim for restitution. This

---

11. This agreement must be distinguished from (and may not be confused with) the "obligatory agreement" (*schuldrechtlicher Vertrag*) containing the (mere) promise to perform a transfer of title or to grant a secondary right in rem. For details, *see infra* sub §8.03[E].
12. Mugdan, *supra* note 1, at p. 4.
13. This also applies to other transactions concerning legal rights established by law outside of *Sachenrecht*, such as immaterial rights or the assignment of claims (§§ 398, 413 BGB).

claim is based on § 812 I 1 BGB, which reads: "A person who receives something by means of someone else's performance or at someone else's expense without justifying cause is bound to restitute the object received to that person." In other words, a right in rem passes under rules established solely by *Sachenrecht*, but the acquisition of title, though valid, lacks permanent stability unless there is a legally valid underlying obligation which induces and supports the transfer.

The principle of abstraction, which is virtually unique to German law, is designed to ease and secure acquisition by means of separating the transfer of title from any occurrence that may impede the validity of the underlying obligation. In addition, it makes it more likely for possession and property to be united in the same hands. Also, in the case of the acquirer's bankruptcy, or when enforcing a judgment against him, his creditors will find that their debtor's possession usually implies property rights which they can seize to satisfy their claims. Notably, this effect on creditors works to the detriment of a party who had transferred property to the debtor, for such a party's claim of restitution under the law of unjust enrichment is not privileged in the case of the recipient's bankruptcy or an enforcement of a judgment against him.

[F]   Bona Fide Acquisition from a Non-titleholder

In principle, the transfer of rights in rem or the establishment of limited rights in rem requires a contractual agreement between the current titleholder and the acquirer on the establishment or transfer of a right in rem. Any such agreement with regard to property or other rights in rem attempted by a person who acts as transferor while not holding legal title is invalid. The true titleholder can thus claim the object directly from the transferee (§ 985 BGB). However, this rule is in conflict with the objective to facilitate transactions, which the law also favors, as is illustrated by the aforementioned principles of *numerus clausus* and abstraction as well as the freedom of alienation.[14] Therefore, the law recognizes circumstances under which a person may acquire a right in rem from a non-titleholder bona fide. In general,[15] the prerequisites of a bona fide acquisition are as follows:

First, for obvious reasons the third party whose acquisition is to be protected must be bona fide. In the case of movables, a person is presumed to have acquired the thing *mala fide* if he knew that the transferor did not have a right in rem or failed to know due to gross negligence (§ 932 II BGB). With respect to rights in real estate, a person cannot acquire title if he knew that the transferor did not have a right in rem (§ 892 BGB).

Second, the third party's good faith in the transferor's right in rem must be based on objective criteria. In case of movables, the criterion used is the transferor's possession (*Besitz*) or, at least, his power to induce the immediate possessor to transfer possession. With real estate, the objective feature which serves as base for protection of bona fide acquisition is the entry in the land register which indicates the transferor

---

14. For details of the latter, *see infra* sub §8.03[G].
15. For details concerning bona fide acquisition of rights in movables and in real estate, *see infra* sub §8.05[A][1] and [B][1].

as being the titleholder, albeit wrongly. However, bona fide acquisition of rights in real estate can be prevented by entering a notice which indicates protest (*Widerspruch*) against the accuracy of the land register.

Finally, the aforesaid basis for the acquirer's good faith in the transferor's legal authority to establish or transfer title must have been caused by a voluntary act of the true titleholder. As for movables, this is the case if the titleholder has granted possession to a person who later enters into an agreement with a third party on title transfer while pretending to be the true titleholder, thus proving himself to be untrustworthy. By contrast, according to § 935 BGB there can be no bona fide acquisition if the object in question was stolen, lost, or got out of the titleholder's hands in any other way. However, this exception to bona fide acquisitions does not apply with respect to money or negotiable instruments payable to bearer; due to their purpose to serve unimpeded circulation, in these cases safeguarding the validity of transactions is paramount. With respect to rights in real estate, there is no correspond-ing general rule to limit the scope of bona fide acquisition with regard to absence of the true titleholder's responsibility for the existence of a false entry in the land register, which serves as the base for protecting bona fide acquirers. In principle, such a rule is deemed unnecessary due to the accuracy of the state-run registration process in operation for rights in real estate; however, the rule applies in very exceptional cases where the land register was falsified under duress.[16] An acquisition bona fide is valid even if the transaction was gratuitous. In this case, the "principle of abstraction" is carried to its extreme, because *Sachenrecht* still disregards the obligation underlying the transaction as far as the acquisition of title is concerned. However, under the law of unjust enrichment (§ 816 I 2 BGB) there is an obligation to restitute the title to the original titleholder. In effect, therefore, the bona fide acquisition of title is only temporary.

The titleholder who finds himself permanently expropriated as a result of a bona fide non-gratuitous acquisition will normally have a claim for damages against the transferor, either for breach of contract (§§ 280 I and III, 283 BGB) or arising from delictual liability (§ 823 BGB). In addition, the former titleholder has a claim under the law of unjust enrichment, irrespective of negligence, against the transferor for any proceeds received in exchange for the property or any other right in rem (§ 816 I 1 BGB).

[G]   Freedom of Alienation

In principle, the freedom of the bearer of a title in rem to transfer title cannot be infringed upon by means of private agreement or unilateral private act, such as a will. § 137 sentence 1 BGB renders any agreement or unilateral act contrary to the freedom to transfer title void. Hence there is no need for rules against perpetuities with regard to long-term limitations to the freedom of alienation. Again, the purpose is to facilitate and secure transactions.

---

16. BGHZ 7, 64.

However, such limiting agreements or acts are valid as contractual obligations, i.e., between the parties to the agreement only, though not with respect to third parties (§ 137 sentence 2 BGB). Although the actual transfer of title is unaffected, the law recognizes that breach of an agreement on abstaining from transfer of title may give rise to a claim for damages or contractual penalty between the contracting parties. There are, however, indirect means to limit the freedom of alienation even with effect to third parties. The transfer of title to movable property may be subject to a condition of abstention from any further transfer of title; if and when this condition is violated § 158 II BGB automatically induces reversion of title to the previous titleholder. As to land, a similar result can be achieved if the parties agree on a contractual claim for a retransfer of title, the fulfillment of which can be secured *inter omnes* by means of a *Vormerkung*.[17] Under § 2113 BGB, a similar effect can be created with regard to testate succession.

§8.04   FACT AND RIGHT: POSSESSION (*BESITZ*)

The distinction between fact and right is a basic feature of *Sachenrecht*. While property is the all-embracing right in rem, and while there are limited rights in rem derived from property rights, possession (§§ 854–872 BGB) is essentially different in that it is a mere fact with legal consequences attached. Possession (*Besitz*) is characterized by mere physical, not necessarily legal, control over a "thing" (§ 854 BGB). Possession is normally established by acquiring immediate power over an object, either de facto or by means of an agreement if the object can be brought under the possessor's control without hindrance (§ 854 BGB).

This principle is modified in two ways. First, if a person[18] is in control of a thing on behalf of another person – to whom he renders services in his household or business subject to his directions – only that other person is considered to be the possessor (§ 855 BGB) even though that person may, for the time being, be unable to exercise immediate control over the thing. Second, if a person[19] possesses a thing as a usufructuary, pledgee, lessee, tenant, depositary, or in any similar legal relation subject to which he is entitled or obliged to be in possession for a limited time vis-à-vis another person, that other person is also considered to have (indirect) possession (§ 868 BGB) regardless of his actual power of control.

Possession as such is legally protected by claims (*Ansprüche*) against infringements through dispossession (§§ 861, 1007 BGB) or interference (§ 862 BGB). In addition, the possessor may physically defend his position against attempts to dispossess him or interfere with his possession (§ 859 BGB). However, these rights only exist in cases of unlawful dispossession or interference (§§ 859, 863 BGB). Unlawful dispossession or interference (*verbotene Eigenmacht*) is defined as depriving the possessor of his possession or infringing upon his possession without the possessor's

---

17. *See infra* sub §8.05[B][1].
18. Commonly described (though not by the BGB itself) as *Besitzdiener* ("possessory servant").
19. The technical term (defined and used by the BGB itself) is *mittelbarer Besitzer* ("indirect possessor").

consent or other legal authorization (§ 858 BGB). However, although the aforementioned rights arise from possession, possession as such does not grant a right to use the thing or to acquire its fruit, nor does it provide a sufficient defense against the rightful owner's claim for restitution or damages. A right to use the thing or to acquire its fruit or to defend possession vis-à-vis the owner's claim for restitution may arise from an underlying contractual obligation or a right in rem. Thus possession, as a matter of mere fact, must be distinguished from the existence of an underlying legal right which makes the de-facto position of the possessor lawful.

§8.05   ESTABLISHING, TRANSFERRING AND ABANDONING RIGHTS IN REM

In principle, establishing, transferring, and abandoning rights in rem by means of a legal transaction follow the same pattern. As mentioned, these legal acts require two elements:

(a) An act which makes the change in legal position visible to the public; and
(b) consent as to the change in legal position between the titleholder and the acquiring party. In exceptional cases, consent is not required. For example the titleholder may abandon a right or establish a limited right in his own property by a unilateral act manifesting his intent to do so.

It must again be borne in mind that the consent at issue here pertains only to the change of legal rights in rem. Contractual consent with regard to the underlying obligation to perform such a transaction is a different matter. Such an underlying – obligatory – agreement is irrelevant as regards the existence and validity of such a transaction; it is of importance only as *causa* for the change in real rights, i.e., for the question whether the transaction in rem is permanent or whether there is an obligation to revert it (§ 812 I 1 BGB).

[A]   Movables

[1]   Acquisition by Means of Transaction

§§ 929–935 BGB deal with the transfer of movable property. As a general rule, there is only one way to transfer title to movables. According to § 929 sentence 1 BGB, transfer of movable property requires the owner of the thing to hand it over physically to the acquiring party and both parties to agree on the transfer of property.

There are three modifications to this basic rule. They all concern the physical transfer of the object. First, if the purchaser is already in possession, mere agreement on the passing of property suffices to transfer title (§ 929 sentence 2 BGB).This may be the case, for instance, if the purchaser is already in possession as a lessee. Second, if the owner is in possession of the thing, the act of handing the object over to the purchaser can be substituted by an agreement between the owner and the purchaser providing that the purchaser shall only have "indirect possession" (*mittelbarer Besitz*) (§ 930 BGB) as defined in § 868 BGB. This abstract concept is a mode of transferring property by maintaining the transferor's prior position as the immediate possessor, e.g., under a lease or deposit agreement. Third, if a third party is in possession of the thing, handing over the object can be replaced by assigning the owner's right to claim the object from that third party to the purchaser (§ 931 BGB). This method is viable, e.g., if the object to be transferred has been leased to a third party.

If the transferring party is not the owner, property can nevertheless be transferred, thus expropriating the true owner. Evidently, a third party transfer is valid if the owner agrees to it, either before or after the transaction (§ 185 BGB). The same is true if the transferor is empowered by statute to carry out valid transactions in rem. Thus, for instance, the trustee in bankruptcy is empowered by law to transfer title to the debtor's property even though the debtor in bankruptcy continues to be its owner (§ 80 I InsO[20]).

§§ 932–934 BGB, however, also provide for bona fide acquisition of property from a non-owner. The purchaser is not in good faith if he knows or, due to gross negligence, ignores the fact that the thing in question is not owned by the transferor (§ 932 II BGB). Systematically, the rules on bona fide acquisitions are arranged according to the way the thing has been handed over. The underlying principle is that a bona fide acquisition depends not only on the purchaser's good faith but also on the transferor's ability to transfer possession or to cause it to be transferred. In case of a transaction by a non-owner in accordance with §§ 929, 930 BGB, title does not pass until the thing is actually handed over to the purchaser (§ 933 BGB). With transactions subject to §§ 929, 931 BGB, title can only be acquired bona fide if the assigned claim constitutes indirect possession (§ 868 BGB)[21] or if the third party duly hands over the thing to the purchaser (§ 934 BGB).

Even under these circumstances, a bona fide acquisition is precluded if the thing in question was stolen, lost, or got out of the owner's immediate possession against his will or in any other way (§ 935 I BGB). The key idea is that bona fide acquisition does not only require the purchaser to be worthy of protection, which can be derived from his good faith based on objective circumstances, but also that the losing party, i.e., the true owner, bears some measure of responsibility for his loss of title. However, with regard to money and negotiable instruments the law protects the bona fide recipient even if the owner is not responsible for his loss of possession, with the rationale for this rule being that money and negotiable instruments are meant to circulate as freely as possible (§ 935 II BGB).[22]

---

20. *Insolvenzordnung* (Insolvency Act), October 5, 1994, BGBl. I 1994, p. 2866, *last amendment* by Law of June 23, 2017, BGBl. I 2017, p. 1693.
21. *See supra* sub §8.04.
22. For gratuitous purchases and for the liability of the transferring party, *see supra* sub §8.03[F].

[2]   Acquisition by Law

Movable property can also be acquired by provision of the law irrespective of the existence of an agreement on property transfer. There are several ways to acquire title *ex lege*. It occurs, e.g., after a person has possessed a thing for ten years bona fide, which is the case if he has erroneously, yet unknowingly considered himself to be the owner (§§ 937–945 BGB).

Likewise, it was noted earlier[23] that things may be connected with each other in such a way that they cannot be separated without destroying or changing the character of one of them. Such a commixture of things can lead to joint ownership, unless one thing can be considered to be the dominant object (§§ 947, 948 BGB) in which case ownership of the entire thing is vested in the owner of the dominant object. Where goods are processed, the person in charge of processing – i.e., in commercial production, the employer and not the employee – acquires property unless the value resulting from processing is considerably lower than the price of the materials involved (§ 950 BGB). If an owner loses his rights through commixture or processing (§§ 947–950 BGB), the party acquiring these rights has to compensate the previous owner of the thing in accordance with the law of unjust enrichment (§ 951 BGB).

After separation, products and parts of a thing belong to the owner of that thing. However, if a person is entitled to acquire title to such products or parts on grounds of a right in rem, e.g., a usufructuary, or otherwise based on the owner's permission, which is usually granted in a land lease, that person takes precedent over the owner in acquiring ownership (§§ 953–957 BGB).

Title may also be acquired in a thing not owned by anyone (§§ 958–964 BGB). In addition, those who find lost property acquire title if they have observed the rules concerning the handling of lost property and if the owner has not reclaimed his lost property within six months after the object found had been surrendered to the local lost property office (§§ 969–984 BGB).

[B]   Land

[1]   Acquisition by Means of Transaction

All changes of rights in land, any transfer and encumbrance of such rights are subject to a uniform principle of law which is stated in § 873 BGB. These legal acts require an agreement on the change in the right in rem between the present titleholder and the acquiring party,[24] plus an entry of the change of legal position in the land register, with the latter not merely being a declaratory act but an essential condition for the actual

---

23. *See supra* sub §8.03[A].
24. Specific requirements apply to the form of agreement (*Auflassung*) on the transfer of property in real estate (§ 925 BGB).

change in legal position. The modalities for effecting the entry of the change of legal position in the land register (*Grundbuch*) are prescribed by the *Grundbuchordnung*.[25] As is the case with rights in movable goods, establishing and transferring rights in land does not depend on an underlying obligatory contract as far as the existence and validity of these legal acts are concerned. The underlying obligation is only relevant with regard to the exclusion of a claim (§ 812 I 1 BGB) for restitution or abandonment of the right in land so acquired.

A transaction initiated by a non-titleholder can cause a change of legal position to the detriment of the true titleholder if the land register does not record the legal position in rem correctly. In this rare case, §§ 892, 893 BGB make provision for a bona fide purchaser to acquire rights in the land as recorded. A purchaser is bona fide if he does not know of the incorrectness of the land register entry.

In the case of a false entry in the land register, the true titleholder may demand that the person wrongly registered agrees to correct it (§ 894 BGB, *Grundbuchberichtigungsanspruch*) in order to prevent any future bona fide acquisition. To avoid any transactions disadvantageous to the true titleholder before the land register has been corrected, the true titleholder can file a protest notice (*Widerspruch*) and can have it recorded in the land register (§ 899 BGB). This entry requires either the consent of the falsely registered titleholder or a temporary injunction by a court (*einstweilige Verfügung* – §§ 935, 940 ZPO[26]). A protest notice effectively prevents subsequent bona fide acquisitions (§ 892 BGB).

The land registration system delays transactions concerning land and makes them dependent on bureaucratic acts the timing of which the parties cannot influence and cannot predict with sufficient precision. This poses a risk in cases of bankruptcy because the system makes it practically impossible to carry out simultaneous performance of reciprocal obligations. In addition, the *Abstraktionsprinzip* poses the risk that the seller of land might transfer it to a third party even if the buyer has already paid the price. In order to safeguard against these risks, all rights as to the change in legal position can be secured by means of a *Vormerkung*, ("priority notice") entered into the land register (§§ 883–888 BGB). A *Vormerkung* will be entered either with the transferring party's consent or based on a temporary injunction (§ 885 BGB). The *Vormerkung* renders void any legal disposition of the right in land which would prevent the performance of the promisor's duty to fulfill his obligation (§ 883 II BGB). In the case of insolvency, a *Vormerkung* prevents the trustee in bankruptcy from refusing to fulfill an obligation entered into by the debtor prior to bankruptcy (§ 106 InsO). Because the *Vormerkung* thus protects the purchaser from any risks resulting from the debtor's insolvency, the purchaser can provide payment as soon as the *Vormerkung* has been recorded in the land register, even if the passing of the title or the right in rem as such has not yet been effected by means of entry in the land register.

---

25. *See supra* note 7.
26. *Zivilprozessordnung* (Code of Civil Procedure), as published on December 5, 2005, BGBl. I 2005, 3202, *last amendment* by Law of July 5, 2017 (BGBl. I 2017, 2208).

[2]   Acquisition by Law

In practice, the most common form of acquisition by law involves movables used for building purposes. According to § 946 BGB in conjunction with §§ 93–95 BGB, title to movable property passes to the owner of the land if the movables are made an integral part of a building permanently connected to the land. Thus,[27] the person who holds the title to the land also becomes owner of the building. Those who lose their rights as a result of this rule are entitled to compensation in accordance with the law of unjust enrichment (§ 951 BGB).

§8.06   PROPERTY AS THE PRINCIPAL RIGHT IN REM: CONTENTS AND CONSEQUENCES

[A]   Property as an All-Embracing Right In Rem

Property is the all-embracing right in rem. Being a right, it is different from possession (§§ 854–872 BGB) which is merely factual in nature, characterized by physical control over a thing.[28] Being all-embracing, the essence of property is succinctly described by § 903 BGB as the right to dispose of a thing at will and to exclude others from any interference, legal restrictions or third party rights notwithstanding. Property rights can be used actively, allowing the owner to use the property in certain ways, and in a defensive mode, which applies if and when others interfere with them.

[B]   Active Use

The owner may use his property de facto, namely by possessing and making use of it, by taking any natural or legal "fruit," such as interest. The owner acquires property of all natural "fruit" (§ 953 BGB) unless he has granted the right to take "fruit" to a third party. Since the owner's power to enter into legal transactions concerning his property cannot be limited by contract (§ 137 sentence 1 BGB),[29] the owner may transfer property or establish limited rights in rem at will.

[C]   Protection Against Infringements

The law also grants the owner the right to defend his property against various kinds of infringements.

---

27. See supra sub §8.05[A][2].
28. For details of possession (Besitz), see supra sub §8.04.
29. See supra sub §8.03[G].

[1]   De Facto Infringements

De facto infringements can be of various kinds and may therefore require different legal responses. If possession of the thing is withheld from its owner, § 985 BGB (which is derived from the *rei vindicatio* of Roman law) grants the owner the right to be put in possession. However, this right is excluded or limited by § 986 BGB if the possessor has a right to possess the thing vis-à-vis the owner. Such a right may be based on a limited right in rem or on a contract, such as a lease.

If possession is interfered with by noise or physical pollution, the owner may demand that the person who causes the nuisance desist (§ 1004 I BGB). The owner may also sue the person to prevent him from causing future interferences. The defendant may, however, refuse to comply based on the argument that the owner is bound by agreement or law to tolerate the interference (§ 1004 II BGB). Such defenses are often raised in disputes between neighbors. In such cases, courts will take into account the nature and gravity of the disturbance, the location of the property, and the availability of reasonable means to limit the interference (§ 906 I and II 1 BGB). Similarly, emissions caused by business establishments operating within the limits of a state license may not be forbidden by a neighboring land owner (§ 14 sentence 1 BIm-SchG[30]). However, if the owner is required by law to tolerate certain infringements of his rights, he may nevertheless be entitled to compensation (§ 906 II 2 BGB, § 14 sentence 2 BImSchG).

If the owner's right of possession is violated, and in cases of physical damage to or legal interference with the object, compensation based on infringement of property may be claimed in accordance with the law of torts, though only if the defendant acted intentionally or negligently (§ 823 I BGB). However, if the damage was inflicted by an unlawful possessor, as a rule compensation may be claimed only if either the possessor had been sued for repossession at the time of damage (§ 989 BGB), or else if he was in bad faith (§ 932 II BGB) as to his right to possess at the time of damage (§ 990 BGB). In all cases, the owner is also entitled to damages in the case of criminal interference with property (§ 823 II BGB). Such cases include, e.g., theft, § 242 StGB (*Straf-gesetzbuch*, Criminal Code), or physical damage to property, §§ 303–305a StGB. The owner may claim either restitution or monetary compensation (§§ 249–253 BGB).

[2]   Violation by Legal Acts

Violations of property by means of legal acts may take several forms. Attempts by an unauthorized person to transfer title to property or to establish a limited right in rem are, as a rule, rendered void, since the law requires that the actual owner and the acquiring person agree on the transfer. Since these transactions have no legal effect, the true titleholder can be put into possession of his property under § 985 BGB. If the entry in the land register is incorrect due to a transaction caused by a non-titleholder, the

---

30. *Bundes-Immissionsschutzgesetz* (Federal Emission Control Act), as published on May 17, 2013, BGBl. I 2013, p. 1274, *last amendment* by Law of May 29, 2017 (BGBl. I 2017, p. 1298).

owner is entitled to a correction of the records (§ 894 BGB). However, the defenses mentioned in cases of legal transactions entered into by an unauthorized person are not available if the owner agrees to the transaction (§ 185 BGB), or if the third party has acquired bona fide rights under the rules set out for the particular transaction.[31]

In the latter case, the owner is merely entitled to compensation under the law of contract (§ 280 I BGB), if applicable, the law of torts (§ 823 I and II, possibly also § 826 BGB), or within the limits of the aforementioned rights established vis-à-vis unlawful possessors (§§ 989, 990, 992 BGB). The owner may also claim the proceeds from the unlawful transferee, namely under the law of unjust enrichment (§ 816 I 1 BGB) or on grounds of *unberechtigte Geschäftsführung ohne Auftrag* (illicit agency without specific authorization), § 687 II BGB. The bona fide purchaser is bound to retransfer property only in the case of gratuitous acquisition (§ 816 I 2 BGB).

Moreover, the owner can prevent the enforcement of a judgment against his property by the creditor of another person. The problem can arise if the judgment creditor's debtor possesses the owner's property. In such a case the owner may demand that the property in question be released from execution (§ 771 ZPO). Similarly, if the owner's property is seized in the course of the possessor's bankruptcy, the owner can claim release from the trustee (§ 47 InsO).

§8.07 LIMITED RIGHTS IN REM

Limited rights in rem – *beschränkte dingliche Rechte* – are special rights derived from property. They are limited and special in that these rights grant only specific legal powers to the titleholder. Though limited as to their content when compared to property as the all-embracing right, these rights are nevertheless rights in rem. This is the case because it is characteristic for them to bear legal effect vis-à-vis any third party. Furthermore, they remain attached to the object whenever the property title related to this object is transferred to a third person. This feature distinguishes limited rights in rem from contracts such as leases or loan agreements which do not automatically[32] have legal effect in relation to a new owner.[33]

Limited rights in rem can be categorized according to the particular benefit they create: the right to seize the object for security purposes, the right of use, and the right of purchase.

---

31. *See supra* sub §8.05[A][1] (concerning movable goods) and §8.05[B][1] (concerning property and rights in land).
32. With respect to lease agreements, however, *see* § 566 I BGB, which states: "If [title to] space leased for accommodation is transferred to a third party after the lessee has been put into possession, the purchaser takes over the lessor's position with regard to the rights and duties resulting from the lease for the duration of his ownership."
33. These contracts may, however, give the possessor a defense against the new owner's *rei vindicatio*, thus retaining possession vis-à-vis the new owner. *See* § 986 II BGB: "The possessor of a thing the ownership of which has been passed in accordance with § 93 BGB may defend himself vis-à-vis the new owner by means of the same defense which he was entitled to raise against the assigned claim". As for the meaning of § 931 BGB, *see supra* sub §8.05[A][1].

[A]   Security Rights

The written law[34] provides several types of security rights. As for these, the distinction between immovable and movable property is essential.

[1]   Hypothek *(Mortgage) and* Grundschuld

With respect to land, the Civil Code establishes *Hypothek* (§§ 1113–1190 BGB) and *Grundschuld* (§§ 1191–1198 BGB) which are of great importance in practice. In addition, though less significant, there is the *Rentenschuld* (§§ 1199–1203 BGB), a particular type of *Grundschuld* which often serves to secure private pension payments. It shares this purpose with the *Reallast* (§§ 1105–1112 BGB), which, unlike the *Rentenschuld*, is not limited to payments in regular instalments but also covers services to be rendered at regular intervals.[35]

Hypothek and *Grundschuld* are created and transferred in accordance with the general rules on rights in land, i.e., by agreement and corresponding entry into the land register (§ 873 BGB).[36] Unless excluded by the parties concerned, the land register office will issue a transferable *Hypothek* or *Grundschuld* document (*Hypothekenbrief* or *Grundschuldbrief*). Except in rare cases (§ 848 ZPO), *Hypothek* and *Grundschuld* are not established *ex lege* since the law usually avoids the creation of rights in rem outside the land register in order to maintain correctness of the land register. However, the law may provide a contractual right to a *Hypothek*, namely as a security to the benefit of building contractors (§ 650e BGB). A *Hypothek* can also be acquired by enforcing a judgment (§ 867 ZPO).

It is the purpose of both a *Hypothek* and in practice usually also a *Grundschuld* to secure a claim for money, be it a loan or any other. The security provided by a *Hypothek* and a *Grundschuld* is three-fold. First and foremost, these rights allow their holders (*Hypothekar* or *Grundschuldgläubiger*) to initiate the sale of the pledged land (§ 1147 BGB) if the debtor fails to make his payments. The sale claimed under § 1147 BGB is carried out in accordance with the procedures stated in the *Zwangsversteigerungsgesetz* (*ZVG; Forced Sale Act*).[37] Second, in relation to third parties, a *Hypothek* or *Grundschuld* established prior to a third party's right takes priority (§§ 10 I no. 4, 44 ZVG). Finally, in the case of the landowner's bankruptcy, *Hypothek* and *Grundschuld* allow for separate proceedings and revenue distribution outside of insolvency proceedings (*abgesonderte Befriedigung*, § 49 InsO).

The legal role of *Hypothek* and *Grundschuld* is similar to that of a mortgage. However, with these two rights being rights in rem, as such they do not encompass the claim for (re-)payment of the credit itself. A credit – i.e., a claim for payment, usually

---

34. For important types of securities accepted and developed *praeter legem, see infra* sub §8.08.
35. Due to lesser importance and for reasons of space, this article does not consider *Rentenschuld* and *Reallast* in detail.
36. *See supra* sub §8.05[B][1].
37. *Gesetz über die Zwangsversteigerung und die Zwangsverwaltung,* May 20, 1898, RGBl. I 1896, p. 713, *last amendment* by Law of May 24, 2016, BGBl. I 2016, p. 1217.

but not necessarily a loan – is granted subject to a contract obligating the debtor in persona to pay money, in the case of a loan to repay capital and, if bargained for, interest. The obligatory – usually contractual – rights and remedies concerning payment are to be distinguished from securing that payment, be it a loan or any other claim for money. Security is provided by granting a right in rem. Hence the person bound in rem under the terms of *Hypothek* or *Grundschuld* need not be identical with the person liable for payment under the terms of the law of obligations.

Although identical in principle, *Hypothek* and *Grundschuld* differ in terms of purpose and function. The *Hypothek* as such invariably secures a debt and cannot exist without it. Even though the *Grundschuld* usually also serves as a security for a monetary debt – in which case it is called *Sicherungsgrundschuld* (§ 1192 Ia BGB) –, it is not a legal requirement of a *Grundschuld* as such to secure a debt; therefore, in principle, the *Grundschuld* can stand alone. The contrast between § 1113 BGB for the *Hypothek* and § 1191 BGB for the *Grundschuld* illustrates both the common elements and the differences. Both statutory provisions define *Hypothek* and *Grundschuld* respectively as an encumbrance of the land which grants the titleholder a right to payment from the land, i.e., by foreclosing on the land (§ 1147 BGB). However, only § 1113 BGB provides that this right is granted in consideration of, and is thus legally dependent on, a personal, i.e., obligatory claim of the holder of a *Hypothek*.

As a consequence, a *Hypothek* cannot be transferred without the personal claim it secures. It is only the personal claim that can be assigned (§§ 398, 1154 BGB), with the *Hypothek* following suit automatically (§ 1154 BGB). The total or partial absence of a secured personal debt automatically transforms the *Hypothek* into a right of the owner of the land (§§ 1163, 1177 BGB), thus in effect keeping the *Hypothek* in existence. This direct legal tie between the personal claim and the *Hypothek* securing it is known as the *Akzessoritätsprinzip*, which can be translated as "principle of accessory relationship."

A *Grundschuld*, by contrast, is valid irrespective of the existence of a personal debt (§ 1192 BGB). It is tied to the underlying obligation it secures, if any, only indirectly, i.e., by means of a fiduciary agreement (*Sicherungsvertrag; Sicherungszweckabrede*). This agreement links personal obligatory debt and *Grundschuld* by limiting the right of foreclosure to the debtor's default and by granting the land owner the right to have the *Grundschuld* extinguished or transferred to him when the need for security has ceased. The independence of the *Grundschuld* as a right in rem from the obligation which it secures is technically known as the "principle of abstraction" (*Abstraktionsprinzip*).[38]

[2]   Pfandrecht *(Pledge)*

The *Pfandrecht*, pledge, is a security interest in moveable property (§§ 1204–1258 BGB) or rights (§§ 1273–1296 BGB) which resembles the *Hypothek* in terms of both purpose

---

38. This case of "*Abstraktionsprinzip*" may not be confused with the same term used to describe the independence of transfer of title in rem from the existence and validity of an obligation to perform a transfer of title in rem; for the latter, *see supra* sub §8.03[E].

and legal construction. A *Pfandrecht* is defined in § 1204 BGB as an encumbrance of movables to secure the titleholder's monetary claim by granting him the right to satisfy his claim by selling the property according to the rules set forth in §§ 1233–1247 BGB. The *Pfandrecht*, like the *Hypothek*, is "accessory" (*akzessorisch*). Hence the pledge follows the assignment of the monetary claim it secures (§ 1250 BGB), and it expires automatically when the claim has been paid (§ 1250 BGB).

A *Pfandrecht* can be established contractually by means of a pledge agreement between the owner and the pledgee, with the transfer of possession of the thing to be pledged to the pledgee being an additional requirement (§§ 1205–1206 BGB). The existence of a debt to be secured is a third prerequisite for creating a *Pfandrecht* (§ 1204 BGB). In some cases a *Pfandrecht* is directly established by law. It has the same legal effect as pledges created by agreement (§ 1257 BGB). A *Pfandrecht* exists *ex lege* for the benefit of landlords (§ 562 BGB) and contractors (§ 647 BGB) regarding movables brought onto the rented premises or into the contractor's possession. There are other cases of *Pfandrecht ex lege*, particularly in certain commercial contracts, as defined in the Commercial Code (*Handelsgesetzbuch*),[39] which also provides for rights of retention having legal effects similar to those of a *Pfandrecht*. In accordance with § 804 ZPO, a *Pfandrecht* may also result from the enforcement of a money judgment against a debtor.

Due to its character as a right in rem, the main effect of a *Pfandrecht* is its enforceability against any owner of the pledged object. This right only ceases if there has been a bona fide purchase (§ 936 BGB), which is unlikely to happen since the pledgee is in possession of the pledged thing. Also, if the object in question is subject to judgment enforcement, the titleholder may claim his right to preferential distribution of the proceeds (*vorzugsweise Befriedigung*) under § 805 ZPO. Finally, in the case of the owner being subject to insolvency proceedings, a *Pfandrecht* entitles the holder to pursue his right to sell the pledged object and to claim priority to revenue from the sale outside insolvency proceedings (§ 50 InsO).

A *Pfandrecht* is rarely found in commercial and banking practice because of the cumbersome procedures required to establish it.[40] §§ 1205–1206 BGB require the owner to pass possession, in whole or in part, to the pledgee. A *Pfandrecht* levied upon a right is awkward due to the legal requirement to disclose the existence of a *Pfandrecht* to the third party debtor (§ 1280 BGB). In addition, the "accessory" nature of a *Pfandrecht* renders it impractical for long-term business relations with changing claims for money and varying credit levels. For these reasons, the predominant model of security rights in movables has developed outside of the Code.[41]

---

39. *Handelsgesetzbuch* (HGB), May 10, 1897, RGBl. 1897, p. 219; *last amendment* by Law of July, 5, 2017 (BGBl. I 2017, 2208).
40. *See supra* sub §8.05[A][1].
41. *See infra* sub §8.08.

[B]   Right of Use

[1]   Niessbrauch *(Usufruct)*

Niessbrauch (§§ 1030–1089 BGB), i.e., *usufruct*, grants a comprehensive right of use, be it land, movables, or rights. In practical effect, *Niessbrauch* resembles a lease (*Miete* and *Pacht*, §§ 535–597 BGB). Both are marked by complex regulations of rights and duties concerning the use of the object and of its fruit. § 100 BGB defines the term "fruit" (*Nutzung*) of a thing as comprising both its "products" (*Früchte*, § 99 I BGB), i.e., its natural fruit plus all other gain obtained from the thing in accordance with its intended use, and all advantages brought about by its use (*Gebrauchsvorteile*). However, being a right in rem, *Niessbrauch* differs from a lease in that the right to use and acquire fruit is, by definition, safe against a transfer of property.[42] In the case of lease of land and buildings this is achieved only indirectly, i.e., by means of the purchaser's succession to the lease (§ 566 BGB) and, with leases of movables, by means of maintaining the contractual right of possession vis-à-vis the new owner (§ 986 II BGB).

A *Niessbrauch* concerning movables is acquired like property, the difference being that the relevant agreement pertains to the establishment of a *Niessbrauch* instead of property transfer (§ 1032 BGB). *Niessbrauch* concerning land is subject to the general rules concerning the acquisition of rights in land.[43] The *Niessbrauch* as such cannot be transferred to a third person, though the rights to use and take fruit which are derived from the *Niessbrauch* can be transferred (§ 1059 BGB). The *Niessbrauch* ends when the beneficiary is deceased (§ 1061 BGB), thus avoiding permanent separation of ownership from the right to use the object and to benefit from its fruit.

[2]   Right of Use as to Land

With respect to land, there are several types of rights in rem which grant limited, specific kinds of use.

[a]   Erbbaurecht *(Building Lease)*

The *Erbbaurecht* covers the right to build, keep and own a building on another person's land (§ 1 ErbbauRG[44]). An *Erbbaurecht* may be gratuitous. In practice, however, it is usually based on a contract which makes provision for payment. For the purchaser, the advantage in acquiring merely an *Erbbaurecht* rather than real property lies in saving capital otherwise required for the land purchase. The landowner sees his advantage in maintaining the security of land property while gaining a flow of income from the land.

---

42. With movables, there is the risk of losing the usufruct in the case of bona fide purchase of property (§ 936 BGB), but only if the titleholder is not in possession.
43. *See supra* §8.05[B][1].
44. *See supra* §8.02.

An *Erbbaurecht* serves purposes similar to a lease, but as a right in rem it is protected against any transfer of the land. Its main advantages over a lease are twofold. First, the building erected or purchased under an *Erbbaurecht* is the property of the holder of the *Erbbaurecht* (§ 95 I sentence 2 BGB), thus making an exception from the rule that property in the land is by law extended to buildings erected upon it (§§ 93, 94, 946 BGB).[45] Second, the *Erbbaurecht* is treated like land; thus it can be the object of a *Hypothek*, a *Grundschuld*, or – to secure the remuneration of the land owner by means of payment due from the holder of the *Erbbaurecht* – a *Reallast*.[46] This is an indispensable prerequisite for financing building projects.

The establishment of an *Erbbaurecht* follows the general principles governing the acquisition of rights in land.[47] The same applies to its transfer. A transfer can, by agreement, be made subject to the land owner's consent which, however, may only be refused for valid reasons (§§ 5–7 ErbbauRG). An *Erbbaurecht* is also hereditary. It may be perpetual, but normally there is a contractual limit on its duration, often ninety-nine years.

[b]   Dienstbarkeit *(Easement)*

A *Dienstbarkeit*, i.e., an easement or servitude, can exist with respect to land only. Its acquisition follows the general rules for the acquisition of rights in land.[48] There are two types, the *Grunddienstbarkeit* (§§ 1018–1029 BGB), i.e., real servitude, and the *beschränkte persönliche Dienstbarkeit* (§§ 1090–1093 BGB), i.e., a restricted personal easement. Both make land, irrespective of present ownership, available for the holder's use in some particular respect, which is to be defined by individual agreement and entered into the land register. In most cases, a *Dienstbarkeit* concerns a right of way, a right to maintain a cable or a pipeline, water rights, or limitations as to the way the site may be used by the owner. Even certain restraints on commercial use of land can be secured by a *Dienstbarkeit*. The two types of *Dienstbarkeit* differ in that the *Grunddienstbarkeit* serves to the benefit of another – usually an adjacent – site, whereas the *beschränkte persönliche Dienstbarkeit* grants a right to an individual person as such.

[C]   *Vorkaufsrecht* (Right of Pre-emption)

A *dingliches Vorkaufsrecht* (§§ 1094–1104 BGB) grants a person an option to purchase with respect to a piece of land, but only if the land in question is being sold to a third party. The *Vorkaufsrecht* can be established under the regular rules pertaining to rights in land.[49] The *Vorkaufsrecht* entitles its holder to substitute for the third party buyer under the same conditions bargained for by the seller and the third party buyer (§ 1098 I BGB in conjunction with §§ 504–514 BGB). In relation to the third party purchaser,

---

45. For the latter, *see supra* sub §8.05[B][2].
46. For *Reallast, see supra* sub §8.07[A][1].
47. *See supra* sub §8.05[B][1].
48. *See supra* sub §8.05[B][1].
49. *See supra* sub §8.05[B][1].

who may have acquired title to the property in the meantime, the *Vorkaufsrecht* has the effect of a *Vormerkung*[50] (§ 1098 II BGB). This legal effect, which may be granted to any present or future owner of a particular piece of land vis-à-vis any present or future owner of another piece of land, makes the *Vorkaufsrecht* in rem different from a *Vorkaufsrecht* of merely obligatory nature (§§ 504–514 BGB).

§8.08   SECURITIES *PRAETER LEGEM*

With the exception of securities in land, where the *Grundschuld* serves as the type most frequently used, the security rights provided by the Civil Code have not gained great practical significance in commercial and banking circles. Merchants and banks have developed security interests outside the provisions of the BGB largely by using property titles as objects and means of security.

[A]   *Sicherungsübereignung*

As for loans, *Pfandrecht* (the right of pledge, as designed in §§ 1204–1296 BGB) fails to meet practical needs both with respect to things and rights. The legal requirement to transfer possession of the thing to be pledged in order to establish a *Pfandrecht* (§§ 1205, 1206 BGB) as a security for a creditor is highly impractical, and so is the legal requirement to disclose the establishment of a *Pfandrecht* levied upon a debtor's claim against a third party to that third party debtor (§ 1280 BGB). In addition, the legal dependency of the pledge on the existence of a claim to be secured is disadvantageous in cases of long-term credit relations with varying levels of credit. Furthermore, the rigid and cumbersome rules governing the sale of pledged property (§§ 1233–1246 BGB) are an obstacle to achieving market prices.[51]

In practice, these drawbacks have led to widespread avoidance of pledges in favor of transfers of property title of movable goods (*Sicherungsübereignung*, i.e., security transfer). § 929 sentence 1 BGB in conjunction with § 930 BGB allows the debtor to transfer his title for the purpose of securing his debt without actually transferring possession by entering into a contractual agreement to retain physical custody for a limited period of time on behalf of the creditor as the new owner. Likewise, with claims serving as security, the right of assignment allows the passing of title to the creditor by means of a simple contractual agreement (§ 398 BGB), without disclosure of this legal act to the third party debtor (*Sicherungsabtretung* or *Sicherungszession*, i.e., security assignment). Both *Sicherungsübereignung* and *Sicherungsabtretung* may be agreed upon even before the debtor has acquired the object to be transferred or assigned, taking immediate effect as soon as the debtor acquires the object in the future.

The security effect of a *Sicherungsübereignung* – and similarly, that of a *Sicherungsabtretung* – is three-fold. First, being the new owner or the new creditor

---

50. *See supra* sub §8.05[B][1].
51. For detail concerning pledge of movable goods and rights, *see supra* sub §8.07[A][2].

vis-à-vis the third party debtor, he can sell the object or enforce the claim against the third party debtor if his debtor fails to pay. Second, in the case of his debtor's insolvency, the creditor can seek preferential treatment of his security by means of selling the object or by proceeding directly against the third party debtor. However, in the context of insolvency proceedings both the sale of movables and the enforcement of a claim against third party debtors needs to be carried out by the trustee (§§ 50 I, 51 No 1 InsO in conjunction with § 166 InsO; *abgesonderte Befriedigung*). Third, if a third party seeks to enforce a judgment against the debtor, the creditor can invoke his security rights to halt the proceedings (§ 771 ZPO).

A fiduciary contract (*Sicherungsvertrag*) ties the transfer of title to its sole purpose to provide security for debts. This contractual agreement must be distinguished both from the debt – in banking, it is usually derived from a loan – which is to be secured, and from the actual transfer of the object, which is carried out subject to the rules of property transfer or of assignment of rights. Hence, in essence there are three contractual agreements of different content – the loan (*Darlehen*) or any other monetary obligation, the agreement on transferring property (*Sicherungsübereignung*) or on assigning a claim against a third party (*Sicherungsabtretung*), and the fiduciary contract (*Sicherungsvertrag*) – although these may be stipulated in the same document. Of these, the Sicherungsvertrag mainly serves to define the rights of creditor and debtor with respect to the security interest in the property or assigned claim against the third party debtor. Usually, the *Sicherungsvertrag* contains the following provisions:

The debtor promises and transfers to his creditor certain movable goods or certain rights – in particular, claims – against his debtors, acting in accordance with §§ 929, 930 BGB in the first case and in accordance with § 398 BGB in the latter case. Such transactions may – and usually will – cover specified clusters of goods or rights, including goods or rights to be acquired by the debtor in the future. Transfer of title to the debtor's creditor may serve as security for a single debt but also for several current and all future debts arising from the business relationship between creditor and debtor (current account clause or *Kontokorrentklausel*). However, debts of companies affiliated with the creditor are not to be secured (*Konzernklausel* or group of affiliated company clause). As long as the debtor is not in default, the creditor promises not to make use of his title gained, be it either as a result of transfer of property subject to §§ 929, 930 BGB or following from the assignment of his debtor's claim against a third party debtor based on § 398 BGB. However, due to the merely obligatory nature of this promise, any acts in violation of this promise will be valid in relation to third parties.

After full payment of the debt the creditor is bound to transfer the title back to the debtor. This may be effected by means of an express condition (§ 158 II BGB) added to the title transaction, stating that the title reverts automatically as soon as the debt has been fully paid. This legal modality is usually not accepted by creditors who, as a rule, only accept obligatory duties to restitute title. By contrast, if the debtor defaults, the creditor may sell the object or execute the right assigned to him vis-à-vis the third party debtor. However, any revenue in excess of the outstanding debt is to be returned to the debtor.

While the credit relationship and the ensuing security rights are pending, the rights of the debtor to deal with the property or claim against third party debtor are largely identical to those he would have if he were still holding title. Therefore, for instance, it is agreed upon that movables must be serviced and insured at the debtor's expense for the duration of the security agreement. Moreover, the debtor may sell movables in the course of ordinary business. He may claim payment from his debtors despite the security assignment. Since the creditor, being the real titleholder, consents to such legal acts of his debtor in advance in the security agreement, any such transaction carried out by the debtor is valid (§ 185 I BGB) irrespective of good faith on behalf of third parties. The debtor may also process movables in the course of production. However, usually there are provisions concerning proceeds from the sale or processing of goods, i.e., a stipulation that when the property has passed to a third party the claim for money against that person arising from the sale will automatically be assigned as a surrogate security. In the case of processing, the newly manufactured object is made the creditor's property, either by anticipated transfer of title in accordance with §§ 929, 930 BGB or, more frequently, by contractually defining the creditor as being the manufacturer (processing clause or *Verarbeitungsklausel*) under the provisions of § 950 BGB.[52]

[B]   *Eigentumsvorbehalt*

While the aforesaid types of securities were developed *praeter legem*, the law explicitly grants sellers the right to retain title, i.e., to negotiate an *Eigentumsvorbehalt*. The legal significance of this term is set out in § 449 BGB. With respect to the passing of title, *Eigentumsvorbehalt* means that title passes only subject to the condition (§ 158 I BGB) that the buyer has fully paid the purchase price. The security for the seller lies in his right to cancel the sales contract (*Rücktritt*, § 346 BGB) if the buyer fails to meet his obligation under the general rules of default (*Verzug*, § 323 BGB), and to regain possession of the sold object (§§ 985, 346 I BGB). Money already received must be repaid, usually with interest (§§ 346 I BGB). In cases of long-term and complex business relations, the *Eigentumsvorbehalt* may be extended (*erweiterter Eigentums-vorbehalt*) to cover payments due from all sales performed (current account clause or *Kontokorrentklausel*). As previously noted, however, the extension to debts of companies affiliated with the creditor – the *Konzernklausel* – is considered void (§ 449 III BGB). In the case of the buyer's insolvency, the seller may reclaim his property if the trustee fails to pay the price (§ 47 InsO), and judgment execution by a third party affecting property retained under *Eigentumsvorbehalt* can be prevented (§ 771 ZPO).

    Even before full payment, considerable administrative powers usually pass to the buyer. In this respect, *Eigentumsvorbehalt* does not differ much from security transfer of property[53] and security assignment of monetary claims. The right to transfer property in the ordinary course of business is granted to commercial buyers (§ 185 I BGB), but the seller acquires the right to the proceeds on grounds of an anticipatory assignment of claims resulting from the sale (*verlängerter Eigentumsvorbehalt*). The

---

52. *See supra* sub §8.05[B][2].
53. *See supra* sub §8.08[1].

buyer may process the object, but the seller is made owner of the new product either by defining him as the processor (§ 950 BGB) or by an anticipated security transfer of property rights (§§ 929, 930 BGB) in the new object.

[C]   Conflicts

Conflicts between security interests of sellers and loan creditors, and among members of either of these two groups, are inevitable. Such conflicts often concern anticipatory assignments of claims against third parties, or else they arise with regard to products newly created by processing a thing which had originally been subject to a security agreement. In principle, precedence in time of the security agreements is decisive. Since business relationships with banks tend to be long-term, in effect this rule tends to favor lenders. In order to correct this result, a bank security extending to proceeds which violates a seller's legitimate security interests is considered void as being *contra bonos mores* (§ 138 I BGB). Banks can avoid this effect by waiving their right to such surrogate security assignments. In return, however, sellers are bound to ensure that the value of their security does not exceed the credit to be secured by more than about 20%, for failing to observe such a limit renders this assignment void as being *contra bonos mores* (§ 138 I BGB) since excessive security unduly restricts the buyer's freedom to do business. However, it is assumed that the security agreement between seller and buyer tacitly implies a claim of the buyer against the seller to yield securities in excess of the aforesaid limit, thus safeguarding the security agreement from being invalid on grounds of § 138 I BGB. The excess is then at the disposal of unsecured creditors or of other creditors expecting to be secured, particularly banks.

The result and purpose of this rather complex legal design may be described as follows: There is a tendency to enable security holders to maintain their security in whatever may become of the object in the debtor's sphere; but security holders must limit the scope of their security in accordance with the amount of credit extended, thus allowing unsecured creditors to obtain some security as well.

§8.09   DEVELOPMENTS *EXTRA LEGEM* BETWEEN *SCHULDRECHT* (OBLIGATION) AND *SACHENRECHT* (RIGHTS IN REM)

The clear distinction between contractual rights and rights in rem is blurred by the fact that some rights rooted in the law of obligations have developed into quasi-rights in rem.

[A]   Leases of Immovables

This observation applies to leases of land and buildings or parts thereof, i.e., accommodation and premises. § 566 BGB stipulates that any new owner of leased land or a leased building or part thereof enters into his preceding owner's contractual rights and duties as lessor vis-à-vis the lessee if the lessee had been in possession before title to the land, building or part thereof passed from the previous to the new owner. Such an extension of a contractual obligation to third parties contravenes the principle of the law of obligations, because in essence obligations establish merely relative, i.e., interpersonal legal relations between the parties privy to the obligation in question. In effect, the rule established in § 566 BGB enables lessees to defend themselves (§ 986 BGB) against the new owner's right to demand possession based on the *rei vindicatio* (§ 985 BGB)[54] by granting lessees a contractual right to possession which bears effect against whoever the owner of the land or building may be. As a consequence, the owner's obligation brings forth an "absolute" effect by extending its legal validity in relation to a third party, which usually applies to rights in rem only.

[B]   *Anwartschaftsrecht*

Furthermore, legal doctrine and jurisdiction have recognized certain rights in rem that can develop during an extended process in performing a contractual obligation. If a transaction has been carried out to the point where the transferor of title has done everything required for the transfer so that performing its completion lies solely in the hands of the transferee, the latter has acquired a position *quasi* in rem. His position has developed from a mere expectation of a future acquisition based on a contractual obligation to a legally guaranteed and therefore currently secure expectancy of an imminent acquisition of a right in rem. The German term for such a position is *Anwartschaftsrecht*, which can roughly be translated as "prospective entitlement safeguarded by law."

There are three cases in which an *Anwartschaftsrecht* may exist. First, and of foremost importance in practice, the situation arises where goods have been delivered under retention of title as defined in § 449 BGB, i.e., when the passing of property is made dependent on full payment of the purchase price.[55] In this case, since all requirements for transfer of property as defined in § 929 sentence 1 BGB have been fulfilled, the buyer in possession acquires property automatically if and when he has met the aforesaid condition by paying the price (§§ 158 I, 161 I and III BGB), which is entirely in his hands. Second, the passing of title to land is sufficiently secure after the agreement on the transfer of property (§§ 873, 925 BGB)[56] has been made, in conjunction either with the entry of a *Vormerkung* (§§ 883 II, 888 I)[57] or else with the purchaser filing his application for entering his right into the land register (§ 17 GBO). Third, acquisition of rights is also guaranteed with regard to a *Hypothek* after it has been agreed upon and recorded in the land register and, unless precluded by the parties,[58] the corresponding document (*Hypothekenbrief*) has been passed on to the creditor, but before the loan has been paid to the debtor; for granting the loan automatically leads to establishing the *Hypothek* in the hands of the creditor.)

---

54. *See supra* sub §8.06[C][1].
55. *See supra* sub §8.08[B].
56. *See supra* sub §8.05[B][1].
57. *See supra* sub §8.05[B][1].
58. *See supra* sub §8.07[A][1].

These legal positions are of lesser status than, but similar in nature to, the full rights in rem which they lead to. Therefore, their content is characterized as being a *wesensgleiches Minus*, i.e., a "minor right, though similar in legal nature." Thus, they are treated like in rem rights in most legal aspects. In particular, this means that these positions, unlike the underlying obligations, are rights protected by the law of torts under § 823 I BGB. Infringing these rights can give rise to a claim for damages *inter omnes*. In addition, under § 985 BGB there is a right to claim possession against unlawful third party possessors. Furthermore, an *Anwartschaftsrecht* can be transferred as such, following the rules applicable to transferring the rights in rem which they precede, with the full right eventually being established directly in the hands of the transferee. Thus, an *Anwartschaftsrecht* widens the scope of collateral available to creditors.

[C]   Final Observations

By and large, German property law is a fairly stable, if not static, field of law, at least when compared with other areas of private law. Its principles and rules are essentially clear, consistent, practically workable, and generally accepted. Yet, as the developments in the field of security rights, especially those outside of the Civil Code, and the recognition of *Anwartschaftsrechte* have demonstrated, *Sachenrecht* can also be quite dynamic and responsive to changing societal and economic needs.

SELECTED BIBLIOGRAPHY

Fritz Baur & Rolf Stürner, *Lehrbuch des Sachenrechts* (18th ed. 2009).
Wolfgang Brehm & Christian Berger, *Sachenrecht* (3rd ed. 2014).
Peter Bülow, *Recht der Kreditsicherheiten* (8th ed. 2012).
Walter Gerhardt, *Immobiliarsachenrecht* (5th ed. 2001).
Walter Gerhardt, *Mobiliarsachenrecht* (5th ed. 2000).
Philipp Heck, *Grundriß des Sachenrechts* (1930, reprint 1970).
Klaus Müller & Urs Gruber, *Sachenrecht* (5th ed. 2016).
Hanns Prütting, *Sachenrecht* (36th ed. 2017).
Dietrich Reinicke & Klaus Tiedtke, *Kredtitsicherung* (6th ed. 2012).
Jan Schapp & Wolfgang Schur, *Sachenrecht* (4th ed. 2010).
Klaus Schreiber, *Sachenrecht* (6th ed. 2015).
Rolf Serick, *Eigentumsvorbehalt und Sicherungsübertragung*, vols 1–6 (1963–1987).
Klaus Tiedtke, *Gutgläubiger Erwerb im bürgerlichen Recht, im Handels- und Wertpapierrecht sowie in der Zwangsvollstreckung* (1985, reprint 2014).
Klaus Vieweg & Almuth Werner, *Sachenrecht* (7th ed. 2015).
Hansjörg Weber & Jörg-Andreas Weber, *Kreditsicherungsrecht* (9th ed. 2012).
Ralph Weber, Sachenrecht (2nd ed. 2016).
Marina Wellenhofer, *Sachenrecht* (32nd ed. 2017).
Harm-Peter Westermann, *Schwerpunkte BGB – Sachenrecht* (12th ed. 2012).
Harry Westermann, Karl-Heinz Gursky & Dieter Eickmann, *Sachenrecht* (8th ed. 2011).

Hans Josef Wieling, *Sachenrecht*, vol. 1: *Sachen, Besitz und Rechte an beweglichen Sachen* (2nd ed. 2006).

Hans Josef Wieling, *Sachenrecht* (5th ed. 2007).

Jan Wilhelm, *Sachenrecht* (5th ed. 2016).

Martin Wolff & Ludwig Raiser, *Lehrbuch des Sachenrechts* (10th ed. 1957).

Rainer Wörlen & Axel Kokemoor, *Sachenrecht* (10th ed. 2017).

CHAPTER 9

Family Law

Dieter Martiny

TABLE OF CONTENTS

§9.01   INTRODUCTION

For some decades now, enormous changes have been occurring in German society and German family structures, and this has been reflected in the development of family law. Though many provisions of the Civil Code of 1896 are still in force, their present content is different in many respects from the law originally enacted. As a consequence of altered views on the role of spouses, the Equal Rights Act of 1957 was passed, leading to equality of the sexes in marriage law; the old paternalistic pattern is no longer a model for the legislature. Living together unmarried is increasingly tolerated. The Illegitimacy Act of 1969 for the most part called for the equal treatment of legitimate and illegitimate children. Today, at least one in three marriages ends in divorce, a phenomenon which has become more or less socially accepted. In 1976, the principle of fault was abandoned in divorce law. Other law reforms have reshaped adoption, parental custody and custody of persons of full age. After Germany's reunification, another reform of the law of parent and child took place (1997), further reforms were undertaken regarding the formation of marriage (1998), child mainte-nance, maintenance after divorce (2008) and pension rights adjustment (2009). In 2017 same-sex marriage was introduced. On the other hand, achieving consensus in a pluralistic society is increasingly difficult and is not made easier by continuous change in society.

§9.02 THE SOURCES OF GERMAN FAMILY LAW

[A] Constitution

The Basic Law (*Grundgesetz – GG*) of 1949 established equality between men and women (Article 3 II GG). A transitional provision made it clear that all statutes not in conformity with this principle would cease to be valid as of 31 March 1953 (Article 117 I GG). From then on, the courts struck down an increasing number of family law provisions on the ground that they were unconstitutional. Later, many provisions of substantive family law were re-codified by the Act on Equal Rights of Men and Women in the Field of Civil Law (*Gleichberechtigungsgesetz*) of 18 June 1957. Furthermore, in recent years the decisions of the Federal Constitutional Court (*Bundesverfassungsgericht*) have been influential and have stimulated legal reform especially in the field of parent and child law. The same is true for decisions of the European Court on Human Rights.

Article 6 I of the *Grundgesetz* states that marriage and family shall enjoy the special protection of the State. 'Family' includes the relationship between parents and their children, whether legitimate or illegitimate. This is understood not only as a constitutional 'guarantee of an institution' and the expression of a basic value in the areas of public and private law, but also as a mandate to take action to benefit marriage and the family. Since 'marriage' has traditionally been interpreted as a legal relationship between a man and a woman, the constitutionality of the Act introducing same-sex marriage of 20 July 2017, has been put into question. In principle, according to the Federal Constitutional Court, non-marital cohabitation enjoys protection only under the general freedom of action clause (*allgemeine Handlungsfreiheit*) of Article 2 I GG. The same is true for unregistered homosexual relationships.

According to Article 6 II GG, the care and rearing of children is the parents' natural right and foremost obligation. This is considered to be not only the constitutional basis for the principle that the best interest of the child is paramount, but also a barrier to State intervention.

Article 6 V GG states that illegitimate children are to be provided by legislation with the same opportunities for their development and their place in society as are enjoyed by legitimate children. This constitutional mandate was the basis for the reform measures of 1969 and 1997.

[B] Civil Code

The primary source of German family law is the Fourth Book of the Civil Code (BGB §§ 1297–1921), with its three sections, 'Civil Marriage' (*bürgerliche Ehe*) 'Family Relationships' (*Verwandtschaft*) and 'Guardianship' (*Vormundschaft*). However, judge-made law dominates many areas, e.g., the details of the allocation of custodial rights, non-marital cohabitation and especially the calculation of maintenance.

The former German Democratic Republic had its own Family Code (*Familiengesetzbuch*) of 20 December 1965 (as amended). Since the unification of the two German republics, the West German Civil Code has been applicable both in East and West Germany (Article 8 of the Reunification Treaty; Article 230 of the Introductory Act to the BGB, EGBGB). In principle, all legal relationships created in East Germany under the former Family Code remained valid but, as of 3 October 1990, their effects have been governed by the BGB.

[C]   Other Statutes

There are several special statutes dealing with certain aspects of family law which will be discussed below in their respective contexts. The Act on Registered Life Partnerships (*Lebenspartnerschaftsgesetz* – LPartG) of 16 February 2001 (as amended), enables two persons of the same sex to register their partnership and thereby acquire a legal status similar to a marriage.

As far as civil registration is concerned, the details concerning civil status registers are laid down in the Act on Civil Status (*Personenstandsgesetz* – PStG) of 19 February 2007 (as amended). The competent authority is the local Registrar of Births, Deaths and Marriages (*Standesbeamter*) at the Office for Registration of Personal Status (*Standesamt*) The local Registrar will issue a birth certificate (*Geburtsurkunde*), marriage certificate (*Eheurkunde*) or death certificate (*Sterbeurkunde*).

The official declaration of death of a missing person follows the Act on Missing Persons (*Verschollenheitsgesetz*) of 15 January 1951 (as amended). Such a declaration creates a presumption that the missing person died at the time fixed by an order of the local court (*Amtsgericht*).

Status proceedings (paternity and divorce) and maintenance actions for minor children are regulated by the Family Proceedings Act (Act on Proceedings in Family Matters and in Matters of Non-contentious Jurisdiction; FamFG – *Gesetz über das Verfahren in Familiensachen und in den Angelegenheiten der freiwilligen Gerichtsbarkeit*) of 17 December 2008 (as amended).[1] The local court has special departments for family matters, the family court (*Familiengericht*), and for care proceedings, the care and protection court (*Betreuungsgericht*), § 23b and c Courts Jurisdiction and Organization Code (*Gerichtsverfassungsgesetz;* GVG).

Of particular importance is the Children and Young Persons Assistance Act (KJHG; *Kinder- und Jugendhilfegesetz*) of 11 September 2012 (as amended), which forms Book Eight of the Social Security Code (*Sozialgesetzbuch* – SGB). Under this statute, the State Youth Welfare Office (*Jugendamt*) plays a central role. The Youth Welfare Service (*Jugendhilfe*) provides, among other things, advice on education, adoption and guardianship (§§ 28, 51, 52a et seq. of the Act); it supervises foster parents (§ 44), commits children and young persons into custody (§ 34), participates in court proceedings (§§ 50 et seq.), and acts as legal adviser, legal curator and guardian (§§ 55 et seq.).[2] Another task is the authentication of statements such as an acknowledgement of paternity or a commitment to pay maintenance (§ 59).

---

1. *See infra* Chapter 13, The Law of Civil Procedure.
2. *See infra* sub §9.08[A].

State financial support is often an important determinant of the economic situation of a family and thereby also directly or indirectly affects family law. Beginning with the first child, child benefits (*Kindergeld*) are paid, and needy persons can apply for welfare payments (*Sozialhilfe*). Children can be given maintenance advancement payments (*Unterhaltsvorschuss*).[3] To meet the costs of care, especially in retirement or nursing homes, an obligatory insurance for nursing care of the elderly was introduced by an Act on Nursing Care Insurance of 26 May 1994 (*Pflegeversicherungsgesetz*), which forms Book Eleven of the Social Security Code.

§9.03   LAW OF MARRIAGE

[A]   Marriage

The civil marriage, the only legally recognized form of marriage in Germany, is referred to in § 1353 I BGB as a bond for life. A marriage may be entered into by two persons of the opposite sex or of the same sex. The celebration of a marriage is regulated by the Civil Code (§§ 1303–1312, as amended). A valid marriage requires that the parties have the capacity to marry (*Ehefähigkeit*) and that there is no impediment to the marriage (*Ehehindernis*).

The capacity to enter into legal transactions is a prerequisite to the conclusion of a valid marriage. The minimum age to marry is 18 years, which is also the age of majority (§ 1303 S. 1 BGB). The formerly existing exemption as to a younger marriage age was abolished in 2017 for the purpose of preventing child marriages. In principle, the marriage ceremony (*Eheschließung*) must be performed before the Registrar of Births, Deaths and Marriages (§ 1310 I BGB). A religious ceremony may follow the official ceremony but must not precede it, except in special cases in which both partners are foreigners (Article 13 IV Introductory Act to the BGB).[4] It is only in the case of a major defect that an earnestly intended marriage ceremony will fail to result in a marriage. Thus, for instance, a ceremony before a person who is not a registrar is said to result in a non-existent marriage (*Nichtehe*). Such a situation must be distinguished from one which involves an annullable marriage (*aufhebbare Ehe*), in which an annulment of the marriage cannot be asserted for legal purposes until it has been declared by a court (§ 1313 BGB).

In the case of an action for annulment of marriage (*Aufhebung der Ehe*), the annulment, like a divorce, only operates *ex nunc*, i.e., from the date of the judgment (§ 1313 BGB). Grounds for annulment are, for instance, formal defects in the celebration of marriage, a marriage with a minor over 16 years (§ 1314 I no. 1 BGB), the mental disorder of a party (§ 1314 II no. 1 BGB), bigamy (§ 1306 BGB), a marriage between persons related in the direct line of affinity, and a marriage between a brother and a sister (§ 1307 BGB). Other grounds for an annulment are lack of consent of the legal representative, mistake as to the significance of the ceremony or the identity of the

---

3. *See infra* sub §9.09[B].
4. *See infra* Chapter 12, Private International Law.

other party, mistake as to personal qualities, deceit or threat (§ 1314 BGB). A sham marriage is also a ground for annulment (§ 1314 II no. 5 BGB). The pecuniary consequences are in some cases the same as those of a divorce (§ 1318 I BGB). A child of such a marriage remains legitimate (*cf.* § 1592 no. 1 BGB). Annulment is rare in practice. The former nullity of marriage no longer exists.

[B]   Effects of Marriage

[1]   In General

The spouses are mutually obliged to live in conjugal community (§ 1353 I BGB). Today, however, there is no fixed legal model for marriage, and the parties are free to decide who will be gainfully employed, who will work inside the home, or whether both spouses will share these responsibilities (*cf.* § 1356 BGB). Each spouse is entitled to enter into transactions for the appropriate provision of the necessities of life for the family. Within these limits, each spouse possesses a 'power of the key' (*Schlüsselgewalt*), a special kind of statutory authority. The resulting obligations bind both spouses (§ 1357 BGB).

However, if the spouses are separated or if one of them wants to live separately, either spouse may plead severe hardship and apply for exclusive possession of the matrimonial home on this ground (§ 1361b BGB). Separation is only a factual situation; judicial or legal separation as a precondition to divorce or as an alternative to divorce does not exist under German law. Today there is also a special Protection against Violence Act (*Gewaltschutzgesetz* – GewSchG) of 11 December 2001. The statute allows spouses and cohabitants to have a violent partner removed from the common household. The non-violent spouse or cohabitant can obtain a temporary order vesting them with sole right to use the home.

[2]   Name

German law used to follow the traditional rule that spouses have a joint family name. According to the Family Names (Amendment) Act (*Familiennamensrechtsgesetz*) of 12 December 1993, spouses are to have a common 'matrimonial name' (*Ehename*), which they are free to determine by agreement. They may choose either the original birth name of one of them or the surname the husband or wife uses at the time of the declaration on the determination of the matrimonial name. Names not so chosen may be added to or placed in front of the chosen name, unless the name is already a double name. If the name of a spouse is a double name, only one element of the name may be added. However, in the absence of such an agreement, the spouses will continue to use the names they had before their marriage (§ 1355 I BGB). Declarations as to the use of a matrimonial name may be made at the marriage ceremony or at a later time.

[C]   Non-marital Cohabitation

Despite growing social acceptance of unmarried cohabitation, there are no statutory rules dealing with it. However, the majority of the approximately 2.8 million unmarried couples (2015) living together are younger couples in a 'trial marriage' that often leads to a formal marriage. Approximately 33% of such relationships result in children; only a minority perceives cohabitation as an alternative to marriage.

During cohabitation and after the breakdown of the relationship, there is no statutory maintenance duty. The only exception is the care for a common child (§ 1615l BGB). Compensation for services cannot normally be claimed by a partner (*Lebens-gefährte*) after cessation of cohabitation. There are no special rules dealing with property; the general rules of civil law apply. All property, real or personal, owned by one of the parties remains personal property of this party. Property acquired by the parties with joint resources and funds shall be considered joint property only if there is an appropriate agreement. However, in the case of major transactions, such as the construction of a common family home, a compensation claim based on the statutory rules of partnership law (§§ 705 et seq. BGB) or the rules on unjust enrichment (§ 812 I 2 BGB) may be made. This example shows that, despite a certain tendency to treat non-marital cohabitation and marriage legally alike, this is not the case in all respects. The success or failure of compensation claims depends on the special circumstances of each case.

[D]   Same-Sex Partnerships

The Act on Registered Life Partnerships enabled two persons of the same sex to register their partnership. The consequence of such a registration (*Eintragung*) is a legal status similar to marriage. The principal obligations of the partner (*Lebenspartner*) are basically the same as under marriage law. Following the 2017 introduction of same-sex marriage, a life partnership may be transformed into a marriage upon a declaration of the partners (§ 20a LPartG). However, as of 1 October 2017, it is no longer possible to enter into a life partnership (Article 3 III Act introducing same-sex marriage).

[E]   Engagement to Marry

A seriously expressed promise to marry (*Verlöbnis*) is regarded as a contract, but is nevertheless unenforceable (§ 1297 BGB). The only consequences for breaching an engagement are a duty to compensate the other engaged person and his or her parents for any expenses incurred in expectation of marriage (§ 1298 BGB) and a claim for the return of engagement presents (§ 1301 BGB).

§9.04   MATRIMONIAL PROPERTY

[A]   Legal Regime

Under German law, there exists a statutory matrimonial property regime as well as a choice between various contractual matrimonial property regimes. The statutory matrimonial regime was created by the Equality Act of 1957. Despite its misleading designation of 'community of accrued gains' (*Zugewinngemeinschaft*), it prescribes a separation of property subject to an *equalization* of the accrued gains (*Zugewinnausgleich*) after the marriage has come to an end. Marriage has no impact upon the property previously owned by the spouses; assets acquired after the marriage become the sole property of the acquiring spouse. In principle, each spouse owns and administers his or her property independently. However, in order to secure the common household and the material existence of the family, a spouse can only dispose of household objects and the whole of his or her assets with the consent of the other (§§ 1365–1369 BGB). Most married couples live under the statutory matrimonial property regime.

On termination of the statutory matrimonial property regime, the gains that accrued during the marriage are *equalized*. Different rules apply according to whether the regime is terminated by reason of death or by divorce. If one of the spouses dies, the surviving spouse's statutory share of the deceased's estate is usually increased by an additional quarter of the estate, irrespective of an actual increase in assets (§ 1371 BGB).[5]

In the case of a divorce, the increase in the value of the assets during the marriage is divided equally between the two spouses. The decisive factor is the amount by which the value of the assets owned by a spouse at the end of the matrimonial regime exceeds their value at the beginning of marriage. Some assets acquired by a spouse as a gift or by succession are exempted (§ 1374 II BGB). In principle, however, it is assumed that the accrued gains are due to the efforts of both spouses and they are therefore divided equally. The spouse with the higher accrued gains is obliged to pay one-half of the excess to the partner with the smaller increase (§ 1378 BGB). There is also some protection of the equalization claim from detrimental transactions such as wasting assets during the marriage (§ 1375 BGB).

In the former German Democratic Republic, the statutory matrimonial property regime was a 'community of property and assets' (*Eigentums- und Vermögensgemeinschaft*). All the wealth accumulated through normal income during the marriage belonged jointly to the spouses (§ 13 I Family Code). Property already owned at the time of the marriage remained the sole property of the respective spouse. Items which one spouse inherited or received as a gift during marriage, as well as smaller personal belongings, remained the property of that spouse. In 1990, this system of matrimonial property was automatically transformed into the regime of a community of accrued gains. The common property which each spouse had owned under the community of

---

5. *See infra* Chapter 10, The Law of Succession.

property and assets was then converted into co-ownership with equal fractional shares. Either spouse had the right to declare before October 1992 that the former statutory regime should remain in effect (Article 234 § 4 Introductory Act to the BGB). In that event, community property was transformed into community property under the Civil Code (Article 234 § 4a Introductory Act to the BGB, as amended 1993).

[B]   Contractual Matrimonial Property Regimes

The spouses may choose their matrimonial property regime by means of a prenuptial or postnuptial marriage contract (*Ehevertrag*) entered in person before a notary (§ 1410 BGB). However, the spouses' freedom of choice is restricted. Reference to a foreign matrimonial property regime is not permitted and is not valid if, pursuant to the choice-of-law rules, only German domestic law is applicable (§ 1409 BGB).

If the spouses exclude the statutory matrimonial regime, separation of property (*Gütertrennung*) occurs (§ 1414 BGB). Such an exclusion of the statutory matrimonial regime is effective against third parties only if the marriage contract has been entered in the Register of Matrimonial Property (*Güterrechtsregister*) at the competent local court or if the third party has had notice of it (§§ 1412, 1558 BGB). Under the separate property regime, chosen mainly by self-employed persons, each spouse can manage and dispose of his or her property without restriction, and marriage has no financial consequences other than maintenance obligations.

Another possible matrimonial property regime is community of property (*Gütergemeinschaft*). For purposes of this regime the Civil Code distinguishes between the spouses' joint property (common property; *Gesamtgut*), special property (*Sondergut*) and reserved property (*Vorbehaltsgut*) and provides very detailed rules for these different types of property (§§ 1415 et seq. BGB). No spouse has the right to dispose of assets constituting common property without the consent of the other spouse (§ 1419 I BGB). No spouse has the right to demand the division of common property.

Special property comprises items which cannot be transferred by legal transaction, e.g., a salary or a maintenance claim not subject to attachment. Each spouse manages and disposes of his special property independently but as a component of the common property (§ 1417 III BGB). Reserved property comprises (1) items designated in the marriage contract, (2) assets received by way of gift or succession and designated by the donor as reserved property and (3) property replacing any of these assets (substitutes). Reserved property is managed and disposed of independently by its owner (§ 1418 III BGB).

The matrimonial contract ought to state which spouse is to manage common property. Failing that, both spouses have the right to manage the property jointly (§ 1421 BGB). Dissolution of the community property regime may occur by mutual consent, by death or by divorce. Each spouse, or his or her heirs, becomes owner of one-half of the common property (§§ 1476, 1482 BGB).

§9.05   DIVORCE

[A]   Grounds for Divorce

A marriage can only be dissolved by a judgment of the family court (*Familiengericht*), which is a special division of the local court (*Amtsgericht*). Since the Civil Code follows the doctrine of irretrievable breakdown, there is only one ground for divorce: failure of the marriage (§ 1565 I BGB). A marriage has failed if the community of the spouses no longer exists and if its restoration cannot be expected. Marital fault as such is to play no role in the availability of divorce.

In principle, separation of the spouses for one year is a precondition to divorce. By way of exception, a marriage may be dissolved if the continuation of the marriage would result in 'unbearable hardship' for the petitioner (§ 1565 II BGB).

In order to establish failure of marriage the court has, in principle, to inquire whether the marriage has actually broken down. However, after a separation period of three years, failure is conclusively presumed (§ 1566 III BGB). The court has to grant the divorce except in cases of hardship (§ 1568 BGB). However, the hardship clause (*Härteklausel*) is narrowly defined. It requires special reasons in the interests of common underage children or exceptional, severe hardship for the opposing party which prevails over the interests of the petitioner.

Divorce by mutual consent is possible where the spouses have been living apart for one year (§ 1566 I BGB). In that case, the law provides for an irrefutable presumption of marriage breakdown if the spouses apply concurrently for a divorce, or if one spouse applies for a divorce and the other supports the application. More than two-thirds of the 153,500 divorces granted in Germany in 2017 were pronounced on this basis.

[B]   Legal Consequences of Divorce

In principle, the same family court has jurisdiction over both the divorce as such and over its consequences. At the same time as the family court issues the divorce judgment, it will usually also make a decision concerning the consequences of the divorce. In fact, the parties frequently make an agreement and submit it to the court for approval. In the case of a divorce by mutual consent, such an agreement is a pre-condition to the admissibility of the divorce application (*cf.* § 133 I no. 2 FamFG). The main issues are child custody,[6] maintenance claims,[7] matrimonial property claims[8] and the adjustment of pension rights. Special rules apply to the division of household goods and to the use of the matrimonial home (§ 1568a and § 1568b BGB). The competent court applying these rules is the family court.

---

6. *See infra* sub §9.08[B].
7. *See infra* sub §9.09.
8. *See supra* sub §9.04.

A divorced spouse retains his or her matrimonial name unless he or she declares the intention to revert to his or her pre-marital name. An ex-spouse may also decide to put his or her name by birth (*Geburtsname*) in front of the matrimonial name (§ 1355 V BGB).

[C]   Pension Rights Adjustment

The pension rights adjustment (*Versorgungsausgleich*) aims at compensating a spouse, usually the wife, whose time has been devoted totally or substantially to childcare and housework. At divorce, an equal division takes place of all pension rights accrued by the spouses during the marriage (§ 1587 BGB in conjunction with the Act on Pension Rights Adjustment; VersAusglG – *Versorgungsausgleichsgesetz* of 3 April 2009) (as amended).

Such a pension rights adjustment is independent of the matrimonial property regime of the parties. However, it can be excluded by a prenuptial or postnuptial agreement (*cf.* § 6 VersAusglG). Included in the pension rights adjustment are all expectations or promises of a pension on the grounds of age, disability or incapacity. For these purposes, the marriage is deemed to have ended with the month which precedes the one during which the action for divorce was filed (§ 3 I VersAusglG).

A spouse who has the higher income expectations is subject to the principle of equalization. If the spouse has acquired annuity rights in a statutory social security pension scheme (*gesetzliche Rentenversicherung*) and these exceed the prospective pension rights of the other spouse, the family court will transfer half the difference in value of these pension rights to the pension fund of the other spouse (§ 3 II VersAusglG). Thus, one of the divorced spouses improves his or her pension entitlement at the expense of the other. The administrative details of this so-called splitting follow the rules applicable to social security pension insurance.

There are two kinds of splits: 'internal division' (*interne Teilung*) and for exceptional cases 'external division' (*externe Teilung*). Internal division occurs if both spouses are insured under the same scheme (§ 10 VersAusglG). An external division occurs if there are pension expectancies of the spouses in different schemes and a transfer of value from one scheme to another becomes necessary. In cases of external division, an expectancy is created for the claimant corresponding to a certain compensation value in the other pension scheme (§§ 14 et seq. VersAusglG).

The Family Court must adjust pension entitlements at the same time it enters the divorce decree. However, where the marriage did not last more than three years, a pension rights adjustment only takes place after an application by a spouse (§ 3 III VersAusglG). If there was no earlier adjustment, a claim can arise after divorce. This claim may be one for obligatory compensation (§§ 20 et seq. VersAusglG), payment of a lump sum (§§ 23 et seq. VersAusglG) or for participation in the pension for surviving dependants in the event of death (§§ 25 et seq. VersAusglG).

§9.06   PARENTAGE

[A]   Legitimacy

After the reform of 1997, German law no longer makes a distinction between legitimate (*eheliche*) and illegitimate children (*nichteheliche Kinder*). Literally translated, *nichtehelich* means 'non-marital'. The East German Family Code did not contain special provisions for illegitimate children. Today, in principle, the same rules of the Civil Code are applicable. There are, however, some legal provisions dealing with the situation of 'children whose parents are not married to one another'. A child born after the conclusion of a marriage or within 300 days following the dissolution of the marriage by death is legitimate (§§ 1592, 1593 BGB). However, when the child is born after the commencement of divorce proceedings and a third person acknowledges paternity, then after divorce the other man acknowledging paternity assumes the status of the father (§ 1599 II BGB). In a court proceeding, it is generally presumed that the husband cohabited with the wife at the time of conception (§ 1600d II BGB), which is deemed to have been between the 181st day and the 300th day before the birth of the child (§ 1600d III BGB).

This presumption of paternity can only be rebutted by a special action contesting paternity (*Vaterschaftsanfechtung* – §§ 1599 et seq. BGB). Such actions can only be brought within a certain period of time and by a limited group of persons (i.e., the child, the presumed father, the mother and, in limited cases, also a man who claims to be the biological father). Paternity cannot be contested by the husband more than two years after he has obtained knowledge of the circumstances which indicated the lack of paternity (§ 1600b BGB). The child may contest paternity through his or her legal representative (§ 1600a III BGB). After reaching the age of majority, the child also has two years to contest paternity (§ 1600b III BGB). This period of time begins to run only from the time at which the child obtained knowledge of the circumstances indicating the lack of paternity. It is also possible to clarify paternity independently of contestation proceedings (§ 1598a III BGB).

Children born in wedlock will receive the matrimonial name of the parents.[9] Where there is no common matrimonial name, the parents may, by declaration, decide which of their names will be the child's surname (§ 1617 I BGB).

[B]   Children of Unmarried Parents

While German law treats maternity as a biological question only (§ 1591 BGB), paternity must be determined either by an acknowledgement of paternity (*Vaterschaftsanerkennung*) or by a court decision establishing paternity (*Vaterschaftsfeststellungsurteil* – §§ 1592 et seq. BGB). The acknowledgment of paternity and the declaration of the child's consent must be officially authenticated (§ 1597 BGB). It is irrelevant that the father is married to another woman. However, he may contest the acknowledgment

---

9. *See supra* sub §9.03[B][2].

within two years of learning about the circumstances which militate against his paternity (§ 1600b I BGB). The child and the mother of the child may also contest the acknowledgment (§ 1600 I BGB). Under certain circumstances even a man pretending to be the father may contest the acknowledgment. In the absence of an effective acknowledgment, paternity can be judicially declared upon an action brought by the child, the mother or by the man who asserts paternity (§ 1600d, e BGB). The competent court is the family court.

The man who procreated the child shall be adjudged the father. In a court proceeding, the child is presumed to have been procreated by the man who cohabited with the mother during the period of conception (§ 1600d III 1 BGB). This presumption does not apply if, in view of all the circumstances, substantial doubt as to the paternity remains. Because no restrictions have been placed upon the ways in which paternity can be proven, DNA paternity testing, blood-group examination, serostatistical investigations, methods based on the duration of the pregnancy and other methods are widely used. The legal basis for the duty to submit to such an investigation is found in § 178 FamFG. The period of conception is the same for all children. Where there is no joint custody, the child receives the surname of the person having custody at the time of his or her birth (§ 1617a BGB). This is generally the mother. It is also the mother who decides on the first name of the child. In 2015, there were 257,900 such children given birth by unmarried women, representing nearly 35% of all births in Germany. Many of these children will subsequently acquire the status of children of married parents by virtue of the marriage of their mother and father.

[C]   Artificial Conception and 'Surrogate' Motherhood

Apart from the fact that the use of the semen of the husband in an artificial insemination (homologous insemination) cannot be presumed, this kind of artificial insemination does not present any legal problems. Artificial insemination with the semen of another man (heterologous insemination) is, in principle, also accepted. The resulting child is the husband's legitimate child. A husband who consented to the artificial insemination cannot contest the paternity (§ 1600 IV BGB). A centralized register for children born after artificial insemination – which also spells out the conditions for official, thus non-private, sperm donations – recognizes a child's right to know his or her own genetic origins (§ 10 Act on the Registering of Sperm Donors [*Samenspenderregistergesetz*] of 17 July 2017). On the other hand, the previously existing possibility of designating the sperm donor as the legal father has been abolished (§ 1600d IV BGB).

In vitro fertilization as such is an accepted procedure and is permitted. However, some other modern reproductive techniques are illegal under German law, which tries to prevent any kind of manipulation of human life at an early stage. It is, for instance, an offence to use the semen of a deceased man for fertilization (§ 4 I no. 3 Act on the Protection of Embryos [*Embryonenschutzgesetz*] of 13 December 1990). It is also an offence to perform an artificial insemination with or to transplant a human embryo (a fertilized egg) into a 'surrogate mother' (*Ersatzmutter*), i.e., a woman who is prepared to surrender her child to third parties (§ 11 no. 7 Act on the Protection of Embryos). Surrogacy arrangements are also an offence under §§ 13a et seq. of the Adoption Arrangements Act of 1976 (as amended). There is not, as yet, established case law as to whether the surrogate mother who has given birth to a child, or the 'genetic' mother, is the legal mother, nor as to whether contracts concerning surrogate motherhood are always immoral and void under § 134 and § 138 BGB. There is, however, a broad discussion on a reform of parentage law which could be based on an extended concept of the establishment of parent and child relationships.

[D]   Change of Legal Gender

Recognition of self-determined gender identity is guaranteed by fundamental rights. The Transsexuals Act (*Transsexuellengesetz* – TSG) of 10 September 1980 (as amended) provides two options intended to make it possible for transsexuals to live in their self-determined gender. According to the first, changing of one's first name is allowed without the necessity of prior gender reassignment surgery. It is required only that the person feels that he or she belongs to the other gender; that he or she has felt compelled to live according to these feelings for at least three years; and that it can be assumed with a high degree of probability that the person's self-identification with the other gender will not change (§ 1 I no. 1 TSG). The second procedure is the possibility under the Law of Civil Status (*Personenstandsgesetz* – PStG) of 19 February 2007 (as amended) to recognize the self-determined gender, with the consequence that gender-dependent rights and obligations of the person will be determined by the new gender. If it is not possible to determine the gender of a child, the birth certificate will be issued without specifying a gender (§ 22 III PStG).

§9.07   ADOPTION

By adoption a child acquires the status of a child of the adoptive parent or parents (§ 1754 BGB). Under German law, an adoption is always a 'full adoption' (*Volladoption*). It completely severs the legal relationship between the child and his biological parents and establishes a new one between the child and the adoptive parent. However, the kinship relationship of a spouse whose child is adopted by the other spouse remains unaffected (§§ 1754 et seq. BGB).

Adoption is effected by decree of the family court (§ 1752 I BGB). In 2016, there were 3,980 such decrees. The number is decreasing. An adoption is permissible only if it serves the welfare of the child and it is expected that a parent-child relationship will be created between the adoptive parent and the child (§ 1741 I BGB). When the prospective adoptive parents already have children, an adoption will not be decreed if it would be contrary to the prevailing interests of the natural descendants. Property interests, however, should not be decisive (§ 1745 BGB). As a rule, the adoption decree will not be issued until the prospective adopter has had the child in his care for an appropriate period (§ 1744 BGB), which is usually one year but may be longer.

A married couple may adopt jointly. For such a joint adoption, one of the spouses must be at least 25 years old, and the other at least 21. A sole adopter must be at least 25 years old. A person who adopts a child of his or her spouse must be at least 21 (§ 1743 BGB). These relatively low age requirements are the result of a change in the function of adoption. Its primary purpose is no longer to enable a childless couple to have a child but to give to children, particularly small children, opportunities of growing up with fairly young adoptive parents.

The law requires the personal consent of any child who is older than 14 years. Consent for a younger child is given by his or her legal representative (§ 1746 BGB). A child may be adopted with the consent of his or her parents. Where no other man is to be regarded as the father under § 1592 BGB, a person who can demonstrate that the presumption of conception is fulfilled is deemed to be the father (§ 1747 BGB). In cases of a gross violation of parental duties or indifference to the child's welfare, the consent of the court may be substituted for that of the parent (§ 1748 BGB). The adoption of persons of full age was abolished in the former German Democratic Republic. Under the Civil Code, it is admissible only if the adoption is morally justifiable. This is presumed to be the case especially where a parent-child relationship has already been created, for instance between a child and his or her former foster parents (§ 1767 BGB). Such an adoption follows basically the same rules as those applicable to children. However, its effects do not extend to the relatives of the adopter; similarly, the family relationship between the adopted person and his or her descendants is not affected by the adoption (§ 1770 BGB).

The selection of potential adopters and the placement of children under 18 years rest exclusively with State Youth Welfare Offices and certain legally recognized associations. The details are dealt with in the Adoption Arrangements Act (*Adoptionsvermittlungsgesetz*) of 22 December 2001 (as amended).

§9.08   CHILD CUSTODY

[A]   Parental Custody

While the Civil Code originally recognized and regulated 'parental authority' (*elterliche Gewalt*), today parents have 'parental custody' (*elterliches Sorgerecht*) (§§ 1626 BGB et seq., as amended in 1979 and 1997). This change in terminology reflects the modern principle that the 'best interests' of the child should control and that the increasing ability of the child to act independently has to be taken in account. Although under tort law parental custody is protected as an absolute right against interference from third parties (§§ 823 I, 1632 I BGB), the concept appears to be shaped just as much by the parents' duties towards the child.

Both parents of a child have parental custody. In cases of disagreement concerning educational matters or other issues affecting the child's life, each parent may apply to the family court. However, the court's powers of intervention are limited. It cannot make the decision for the parents, it may only determine which of them is to have the final say (§ 1628 I BGB). In matters of parental custody, the law distinguishes between the personal and the property interests of the child. 'Personal custody' (*Personensorge*) includes the right and the duty to care for the child and to determine his or her education and place of residence. However, the commitment of the child to an institution, which would entail the deprivation of the child's liberty, requires the approval of the family court (§ 1631b BGB). The determination of the first name of the child is also a question of personal custody. Under a special statute, a child of 14 already has complete religious freedom (§ 5 Act Concerning the Religious Education of Children of 1921).

The parents also have to take care of the child's property (*Vermögenssorge* – § 1626 I BGB). The parents may only use income from the child's property for their own support and for the support of siblings when it is not needed for the proper management of the child's property or for the child's maintenance, and if such a use is equitable in view of the assets and income of all the parties involved (§ 1649 II BGB). Particularly important legal transactions concluded in the child's name, such as the sale of real property, require the approval of the family court (§ 1643 BGB).

A child of unmarried parents is in principle placed solely under the parental custody of the mother (§ 1626a III BGB). There can be joint custody only with a common declaration of custody (*Sorgeerklärung*) by the parents (§ 1626a I no. 1 BGB) or when the parents marry each other (§ 1626a I no. 2 BGB) or by virtue of a court decision based on the welfare of the child (§1626a I no. 3 BGB). The father can obtain a court order for sole custody of his child either with consent of the child's mother (§ 1671 II no. 1 BGB) or if his sole custody complies with the welfare of the child (§ 1671 I no. 1 BGB); other cases are when the custody of the mother has been suspended (§ 1678 II BGB) or when the mother has died or has lost her custody right (§ 1680 BGB).

The State Youth Welfare Office can provide advice and support (*Beratung und Unterstützung*). It also can act as the legal adviser (*Beistand* – §§ 1712 et seq. BGB) and in some cases as the legal curator (*Amtspfleger*) for the child. Its task is mainly to promote and protect the rights and interests of the child in relation to paternity and maintenance determinations (§§ 52a et seq. SGB VIII). The reform of legal curatorship – in the past often criticized as unnecessary State interference – as well as the improvement of the legal position of the father of an illegitimate child were the main objectives of the 1997 reform of parent and child law.

If the personal welfare or the property interests of the child are in jeopardy, the family must take the necessary protective steps (§§ 1666 et seq. BGB). As a matter of last resort, the parents may be deprived totally or partially of their parental custody. A detailed catalogue of additional powers held by the Youth Welfare Authorities is contained in the Children and Young Persons Assistance Act of 1998.[10] However, intervention must be limited to what is really necessary.

---

10. *See supra* sub §9.02[C].

[B] Custody after Divorce

Joint custody is also now the rule after divorce. However, on application of one parent the family court must determine which parent is to have custody of the children (§ 1671 BGB). Custody depends solely upon the 'welfare of the child' (*Wohl des Kindes*). When the parents have reached agreement and jointly propose a solution on the issue of custody, the family court will usually accept it. However, it may depart from the agreement when the child's welfare requires it or when the proposal runs counter to the wishes of a child who has reached the age of 14 years. When determining what the welfare of the child requires, the courts are guided by the principles that: (1) the parent to be given custody is usually the one who can offer the best opportunities for the child's development (*Förderungsprinzip*); (2) the stability of the child's situation should be preserved (*Kontinuitätsgrundsatz*); and (3) the separation of siblings is usually undesirable. Most courts grant joint custody only when both parents are willing to cooperate. Detailed statutory regulation of joint custody is still lacking.

[C] Personal Contact

A parent who is not entitled to personal custody nevertheless retains the right to personal contact (*persönlicher Umgang*) with his or her child (§ 1684 I BGB). He or she may also demand information about the personal condition of the child insofar as this is compatible with the child's welfare (§ 1686 BGB). A court order for personal contact may be enforced by a civil fine (*Ordnungsgeld*) against the other parent (§ 89 FamFG). Today, also persons with a 'social-family' relationship (*sozial-familiäre Beziehung*) to the child, i.e., grandparents, brothers and sisters, (former) stepparents and registered partners, have a right of personal contact (§ 1685 BGB). The same is true for a biological father not having the status of a legal father.

In practice the person caring for an illegitimate child, e.g., the mother, decides under what circumstances the father will have contact. If the parents cannot agree on the terms of contact, the father may apply to the family court to determine the scope of contact consistent with the best interest of the child (§ 1684 BGB).

§9.09 MAINTENANCE OBLIGATIONS

[A] Spousal Support

Marriage always entails maintenance obligations. The spouses are mutually obligated to support the family by means of their work or property. Household management, if entrusted to one of the spouses, is in principle regarded as an adequate performance of his or her obligation to contribute to the support of the family (*Familienunterhalt* – § 1360 BGB). If the spouses are separated, either spouse may demand from the other reasonable support, depending upon the living standard, the income and the property situation of the spouses (§ 1361 I BGB).

[B]   Maintenance for Relatives, Particularly for Children

The concept underlying the maintenance provisions of the Civil Code is the solidarity among family generations. Maintenance for children (*Kindesunterhalt*) is only a subcategory of the broad concept of maintenance for relatives (*Verwandtenunterhalt*). Not only do parents have obligations to their children and vice versa, but there are also maintenance obligations between grandparents and grandchildren (§ 1601 BGB). On the other hand, children-in-law and parents-in-law, stepparents and stepchildren (despite their special status in some social security statutes) and siblings are not obligated to support one another. Need (*Bedürftigkeit*) and an ability to pay (*Leistungs-fähigkeit*) are general preconditions to a maintenance obligation. Children are in need when, and for as long as, they cannot support themselves. Parents have an obligation to apply all their means to the maintenance of underage, unmarried children without regard to a child's legitimate or illegitimate status. This is also true for children under 21 years who still live in the parental household and who go to school (§ 1603 BGB). However, according to settled court practice, parents have the right to reserve an adequate amount of money for themselves (*Selbstbehalt*).

Where the child does not live with his or her parents, maintenance must be paid monthly in advance (§ 1612 III BGB). As a rule, a custodial parent fulfils his or her obligation to contribute to the support of an underage, unmarried child by caring for and bringing up the child (§ 1606 III BGB). This 'equal value rule' (*Gleichwertigkeits-grundsatz*) means that if, after separation or divorce, the children live with their mother, her contribution is generally restricted to care (*Betreuungsunterhalt*); only the father has to pay child support (*Barunterhalt*).

Retroactive maintenance payments may be claimed only when the debtor has been ordered by the court to give information on his earnings and assets, or has been given notice of default, or when the maintenance claim is pending in court (§ 1613 I BGB). Future maintenance may not be waived (§ 1614 I BGB). There is no legal age limit for the entitlement to maintenance. Maintenance includes the costs of educating a child, including the costs of a university education, and of training him or her for an occupation (§ 1610 II BGB). Retraining for another occupation, including further tertiary study, may also be claimed in exceptional cases.

Children of unmarried, separated or divorced parents often encounter great difficulties in actually obtaining maintenance payments. These children can obtain a percentage of the 'minimum support' (*Mindestunterhalt*), a standard minimum amount prescribed by federal regulation, instead of an amount calculated on an individual basis (§ 1612a BGB). When calculating maintenance, the courts generally follow the so-called Düsseldorf Table (*Düsseldorfer Tabelle*), originally a maintenance table only for the North Rhine-Westphalian courts in Düsseldorf. This table is adjusted at regular intervals and contains a scale of amounts required to meet the needs of underage children of differing ages. For other calculations the German courts of appeal use their own non-binding maintenance guidelines (*Unterhaltsleitlinien*).

While there is no general 'indexing' of child maintenance, a special adjustment may be made. The percentage by which maintenance payments are to be increased depends on the actual regular amount. For this purpose the claimant may use a simplified court procedure (§§ 249 et seq. FamFG).

If the maintenance debtor fails to pay, a child under the age of 12 is entitled to State benefits under the scheme of the Maintenance Advancement Act (*Unterhaltsvor-schussgesetz* – UVG) of 17 July 2007 (as amended). These benefits are in principle restricted to 72 months, but they can be extended until the child reaches the age of 18. The benefits are only subsidiary, i.e., there is a reimbursement claim against the debtor based on subrogation (*cessio legis*). Such a reimbursement claim can also arise under the general welfare scheme of 'social assistance' (*Sozialhilfe*).

[C]   Maintenance after Divorce

The basic principle is that every divorced spouse must provide for his or her own maintenance. However, there are several instances in which maintenance after divorce (*nachehelicher Unterhalt*) may be claimed. Most important is maintenance for a spouse who is caring for a child of the marriage and who is thus prevented from earning a living. This maintenance claim exists for at least three years after the birth of the child (§ 1570 BGB). Other cases are maintenance for an aged divorced spouse (§ 1571 BGB), maintenance on account of sickness or infirmity (§ 1572 BGB), maintenance until appropriate employment is found (§§ 1573, 1574 BGB) and maintenance in support of further education or retraining (§ 1575 BGB). There is also a general hardship clause (§ 1576 BGB).

Usually the amount of maintenance is adjusted to the standard of living the parties enjoyed during marriage (§ 1578 I BGB). The courts generally apply a formula contained in the *Düsseldorf Table*.[11] Maintenance may be restricted to a transitional period of time in order to enable the recipient to undertake appropriate education or to find suitable gainful employment (§ 1575 BGB). Where the divorced spouse has some (but insufficient) income of his or her own, he or she may demand the difference between that income and full maintenance (§ 1573 II BGB). The maintenance claim of the divorced spouse may be limited in time (§ 1578b II BGB).

Grossly inequitable maintenance claims will be excluded, reduced or limited in time. The pertinent Code section lists eight cases of 'grossly inequitable' claims: (1) short duration of the marriage, (2) living in a new stable relationship, (3) criminal acts against the maintenance debtor or close relatives, (4) wantonly self-induced indigence, (5) wanton disregard for property interests of the maintenance debtor, (6) a gross breach of the duty to contribute to the support of the family, (7) manifestly gross and unilateral misconduct and (8) other 'equally serious reasons' (§ 1579 BGB). The harshness of these exclusionary rules is mitigated to some extent if the claimant carries the responsibility for a child of the marriage. That responsibility must be taken into account and may lead to a certain minimum amount of alimony.

However, if a maintenance debtor's ability to pay is restricted as a result of his or her remarriage, there arises the problem of ranking maintenance creditors. Minor

---

11. *See supra* sub §9.09[B].

children are always ranked first. Parents who are entitled to maintenance for the care of a child, or would be so entitled in the case of a divorce, come next in the order of priority (§ 1609 no. 2 BGB). Every spouse, former spouse, single parent or cohabitant caring for a child occupies the same position. However, former spouses from a long-term marriage are also ranked alongside those who look after children. The entitlement to maintenance ceases on the remarriage or death of the maintenance creditor (§ 1586 BGB). A waiver of maintenance claims is possible; it is not valid, however, when it is grossly unfair due to an unequal bargaining power of the spouses.[12]

[D]   Special Provisions for Unmarried Parents

The mother of an illegitimate child may claim maintenance from the father for a period of six weeks prior to, and eight weeks after, the birth of her child. This maintenance obligation can be extended to three years if the pregnancy or a pregnancy-related illness prevents her from being gainfully employed (§ 1615l II 1 BGB). This obligation can be extended even further. The same applies to the extent that the mother cannot be expected to be engaged in gainful employment by reason of the care or upbringing of the child (§ 1615l II 2 BGB). The obligation to maintain begins as early as four months before the birth and continues for at least three years after the birth (§ 1615l II 3 BGB). It is extended, as long as and to the extent that this is equitable (§ 1615l II 4 BGB). The mother may also claim compensation for expenses in connection with her pregnancy or childbirth (§ 1615l I 2 BGB). This provision is interpreted, however, as not covering payments made by her employer or insurance. If the father cares for the child, he may have a maintenance claim against the mother (§ 1615l IV BGB).

§9.10   GUARDIANSHIP AND OTHER PROTECTIVE MEASURES

[A]   In General

Under the general heading of 'guardianship' (*Vormundschaft*), the Civil Code differentiates between guardianship for minors (*Vormundschaft für Minderjährige*), a special guardianship for persons of full age (*Betreuung Volljähriger*) and curatorship (*Pflegschaft*). In all these cases, the goal is to aid persons who are not able, or are not fully able, to look after their own affairs. While the provisions of the Civil Code on guardianship for minors and for curatorship have remained essentially unchanged, a statute of 12 September 1990, in force since 1 January 1992, has replaced the former interdiction (*Entmündigung*) and guardianship for persons of full age with a modern form of guardianship. This is increasingly important in view of the 'greying' of the German population.

---

12. Decision of the Federal Constitutional Court of 6 February 2001 = BVerfGE 103, 89.

[B]   Guardianship

An underage child is given a guardian (*Vormund*) if he or she is not subject to custody or cannot be represented by parents (§ 1773 BGB). The guardian is appointed by the family court (§ 1774 BGB). The child's parents may nominate a person to become the guardian (§ 1776 BGB). In the absence of a parental nomination, the court will select a suitable person and may appoint an association or the State Youth Welfare Office (§§ 1791a et seq. BGB).[13]

The guardian's tasks are to care for the person and the property of the ward (§ 1793 BGB) and to act as his or her legal representative. The guardian is under the supervision of the family court. He or she may not represent the child in situations which involve the possibility of certain conflicts of interests (*cf.* § 1795 BGB). For some important transactions, such as the acquisition or the alienation of land, and the acceptance of an inheritance, the guardian needs the formal approval of the guardianship court (§§ 1821, 1822 BGB). Guardianship comes to an end upon the lapse of the conditions under which it was established (§ 1882 BGB).

[C]   Care and Protection for Persons of Full Age

A person of full age who is incapable of managing his own affairs as a result of either a mental disease or a physical, mental (*geistig*) or psychological (*seelisch*) disability may be given a 'carer' (*Betreuer*), §§ 1896 et seq. BGB. The carer is appointed ex officio by the care and protection court (*Betreuungsgericht*). However, care for a person of full age (*Betreuung*) is also possible with the consent of the protected person. A carer may be an agent of an approved 'association of carers' (*Vereinsbetreuer*) or an agent of a State authority responsible for the coordination of carers (*Behördenbetreuer*), § 1897 BGB. When a person of full age cannot be cared for sufficiently by one person alone, the court may also appoint an approved association of carers (*Betreuungsverein*) (§ 1900 BGB).

The institution of care and protection for vulnerable adults (*rechtliche Betreuung*) is attempting to facilitate a flexible and sensible reaction to the actual disability, and to restrict the invasion of rights in accordance with the individual case. The carer has to act in the best interest of the person who is under his or her care. To the extent possible, this includes allowing that person to continue to arrange his or her own life according to his or her own ideas and preferences (§ 1901 BGB). Within the individualized scope of responsibilities, the carer has to represent the person placed under the care (§ 1902 BGB) even though, in principle, that person retains the legal capacity to enter into contracts. In this way, a 'double competence' (*Doppelzuständigkeit*) of the carer and the protected person to enter into a contract may exist. Of course, the capacity of the protected person may be affected by the general rules such as those addressing the case of a mental disorder (§ 104 no. 2 BGB).

---

13. *See supra* sub §9.02[C].

The court may order that a prior 'consent' (*Einwilligungsvorbehalt*) of the carer is necessary for certain declarations of intention by the person subject to the care (§ 1903 I BGB). However, this consent requirement does not apply to certain personal affairs, such as marrying or making a will (§ 1903 II BGB). The carer has to examine whether determinations in an existing living will (*Patientenverfügung*) correspond to the current living and treatment situation (§ 1901a I BGB). Medical treatment which involves a risk to life or a serious risk to the health of the person under care requires court approval (§ 1904 BGB). Under very limited circumstances, and only with the approval of the family court, the carer may also consent to sterilization (§ 1905 BGB) or commitment to an institution (§ 1906 BGB). The care for a person of full age ends if the reasons giving rise to the care lapse. It is also possible to restrict the scope of duties of the carer (§ 1908d BGB) if some but not all prerequisites are no longer present.

[D] Curatorship

Curatorship (*Pflegschaft*) is ordered by the family court for purposes of taking care of specific matters in respect of some persons or assets. A 'supplementary curator' (*Ergänzungspfleger*) is needed in affairs which parents or a guardian are actually or legally prevented from managing (§ 1909 BGB). This is particularly true in cases of conflict of interests between the protected person and his legal representative. A curator may be appointed for an absent person whose whereabouts are unknown (*Abwesenheitspfleger*) if the affairs of such a person require management (§ 1911 BGB). Other cases include curatorship for an unborn child and curatorships for persons of unknown identity having legal entitlements.

SELECTED BIBLIOGRAPHY

Nina Dethloff, *Familienrecht* (32nd ed. 2018).
Peter Gerhardt, Bernd von Heintschel-Heinegg & Michael Klein, *Handbuch des Fachanwalts Familienrecht* (11th ed. 2018).
Joachim Gernhuber & Dagmar Coester-Waltjen, *Lehrbuch des Familienrechts* (6th ed. 2010).
Karlheinz Muscheler, *Familienrecht* (4th ed. 2017).
Thomas Rauscher, *Familienrecht* (2nd ed. 2008).
Kai Schulte-Bunert, *Familienrecht* (3rd ed. 2017).
Dieter Schwab, *Familienrecht* (25th ed. 2017).
Dieter Schwab, Peter Gottwald & Saskia Lettmaier, *Family and Succession Law in Germany* (3rd ed. 2017).
Marina Wellenhofer, *Familienrecht* (4th ed. 2017).

CHAPTER 10

The Law of Succession

Dennis Solomon

TABLE OF CONTENTS

§10.01   GENERAL ASPECTS OF THE GERMAN LAW OF SUCCESSION

[A]   Sources of Law

The law of succession (*Erbrecht*) governs the devolution of property (both assets and liabilities) upon the death of an individual. The substantive provisions of the German law of succession are mainly contained in the Fifth Book of the Civil Code (§§ 1922–2385 BGB). However, individual provisions which bear upon the devolution of a decedent's estate can also be found in other parts of the Civil Code, particularly in the sections on family law or the law of property.[1] Further provisions may also be found in other statutes, e.g., §§ 25–27 of the Commercial Code (HGB) governing the heir's liability where he continues the business of the decedent[2] or § 10 of the Act on Registered Life Partnerships (*Lebenspartnerschaftsgesetz*; LPartG) on the inheritance rights between same-sex life-partners.[3] Some of the German *Länder* also have special rules governing the succession to agricultural property.[4]

The choice-of-law provisions with regard to the law of succession are contained in Articles 20–38 of the European Succession Regulation (Regulation No. 650/2012) of July 4, 2012. Furthermore, Germany has ratified the Hague Convention on the Conflicts of Laws relating to the Form of Testamentary Dispositions of October 5, 1961. Supplementary provisions are contained in Articles 25 and 26 of the Introductory Act to the Civil Code (EGBGB).

While some procedural rules relating to the devolution of an estate can be found in the BGB itself (e.g., §§ 2353–2370 BGB on the certificate of inheritance[5]), most are contained in the Act on the Procedure in Family Matters and in Matters of Non-contentious Jurisdiction (FamFG, in particular §§ 342–373). Again, individual

---

1. *See*, e.g., § 1371 BGB on the spouse's share (*infra*, §10.02[B]).
2. *See infra*, §10.09.
3. *Cf. infra*, §10.02[C].
4. The so-called *Höfeordnung* or other provisions of the *Länder*; cf. Art. 64 EGBGB.
5. *See infra*, §10.11.

provisions relating to questions of succession law may also be found in other statutes like the Code of Civil Procedure (ZPO), the Act on the Compulsory Sale of Real Property (ZVG) or the Insolvency Act (InsO). The relevant tax law is contained in the Inheritance Tax Act (ErbStG).

The German Constitution protects the law of succession in Article 14 I GG in two distinct ways: On the one hand, it provides for a so-called institutional guarantee, which means that the objective existence of a law of succession in its essential substance is guaranteed by the Constitution. On the other hand, it protects both the subjective right of the testator to pass on his property upon death and the right of the heir to obtain the estate by way of inheritance.[6] In particular,[7] the Constitution guarantees the principles of private succession, testamentary freedom and succession by the next of kin. In a leading case of 2005, the German Constitutional Court held that the Constitution also grants the decedent's children the right to a minimum share in the estate that is independent of their needs and cannot be excluded by the decedent.[8]

[B] Basic Concepts

The decedent or testator (*Erblasser*) is the person whose property passes to one or more heirs upon his death. Only natural persons can be testators.

Heirs (*Erben*) are the individuals to whom the estate of the decedent passes upon his death by way of universal succession: Pursuant to § 1922 I BGB, upon the death of the decedent, the estate passes as a whole to the heir or heirs. The heir is determined either by the testator by way of testament or contract of inheritance (§§ 1937, 1941 BGB – testamentary heir) or, failing provision by the testator, by statute (§§ 1922–1936 BGB, § 10 LPartG – statutory heir).

As beneficiary under a will, the heir must be distinguished from other persons who acquire rights against the estate under a will. It is only to the heir that title to the estate property automatically passes under § 1922 I BGB. In contrast, the beneficiary of a specific legacy (*Vermächtnisnehmer*, § 1939 BGB) does not automatically become the owner of the object bequeathed but only acquires a personal claim against the heir (§ 2174 BGB). To fulfill his obligation arising from the legacy, the heir must still transfer title according to the relevant rules, e.g., those of property law. Similarly, a statutory heir who has been disinherited but is entitled to a statutory compulsory share (*Pflichtteilsberechtigter*) does not obtain title to the estate (or part of the estate) as such, but only a personal money claim against the heir (§§ 2303, 2317 BGB).

Every natural person living at the time of the decedent's death has the legal capacity to inherit, § 1923 I BGB. This capacity is extended by § 1923 II BGB to those already conceived, but not yet born, at the time of the decedent's death. As the capacity

---

6. Cf. BVerfGE 93, 165.
7. The following principles are discussed in more detail *infra*, §10.01[C].
8. BVerfGE 112, 332; also *see* (with further references), Leipold, *supra*, marg. nos. 72–73. For the rules regarding the statutory forced share *see infra*, §10.06.

to inherit is a specific emanation of legal capacity in general, all entities with legal capacity also have the capacity to inherit. Thus, all legal persons (e.g., corporations) can be heirs, as can partnerships to the extent that the law recognizes their legal capacity.

The devolution of the estate (*Erbschaft, Nachlass*) occurs at the time of death (*Erbfall*). The estate passing to the heir under § 1922 BGB includes both the assets and the liabilities of the decedent (with regard to liabilities, *see* § 1967 I BGB). As a general rule, all real and personal property rights and liabilities are inheritable and devolve on the heir in the same way. In particular, German law does not distinguish between succession to personal and to real property.

[C] Fundamental Principles

The German law of succession is characterized by four basic legal principles. These fundamental principles, which are in part guaranteed under constitutional law, are the principles of private succession (*Privaterbfolge*), testamentary freedom (*Testierfreiheit*), succession by the next of kin (*Familienerbfolge*) and universal succession (*Gesamtrechtsnachfolge*).

According to the principle of private succession, all privately held property is subject to private inheritance when its owner dies, that is, it devolves to other private individuals determined either by the testamentary disposition of the decedent or by statutory provision. The State does not become heir to an estate, as long as the decedent has determined an heir or there are relatives who are eligible as statutory heirs (§ 1936 BGB).

The principle of testamentary freedom allows the testator to freely determine the fate of his property after his death by means of a testamentary disposition. The testator is free to appoint heirs and to assign shares in his estate as he pleases. Furthermore, as a general rule, he is also free at any time to modify or revoke a previously made testament. This freedom is protected by § 2302 BGB, which provides that the testator cannot validly obligate himself to make, not to make, to revoke or not to revoke a will. There are, however, certain limits to the testator's freedom of disposition.[9] One of the most important limits to the testator's freedom is presented by the statutory compulsory share of his spouse, his descendants and his parents: Even though the testator may freely designate anyone as heir to his estate, the law guarantees these relatives a claim in the amount of half their statutory intestate share.[10]

The principle of succession by the next of kin manifests itself in two different ways: First, where the decedent has not disposed of his property by will, the law provides for succession by the decedent's spouse (or registered life partner) and his relatives (priority being determined by order of their different classes) as statutory heirs.[11] Second, even where the decedent has made a will, the statutory compulsory

---

9. Also *see infra*, §10.03[A].
10. *See infra*, §10.06.
11. *See infra*, §10.02.

share guarantees some relatives a certain participation in the value of the estate.[12] In this regard, there is some tension between the principle of testamentary freedom and the principle of succession by the next of kin.[13]

The principle of universal succession, finally, is fundamental to a proper understanding of the German law of succession and denotes one of the main differences to common law systems. As provided in § 1922 I BGB, the property of the decedent passes in its entirety *ipso iure* to the heir or heirs. Thus, upon the death of the decedent, title to any asset of the estate automatically passes to the heir by operation of the law. Succession occurs without the need of any further acts of transfer with regard to individual assets. The principle of universal succession is closely linked with the principle of *ipso iure* acquisition: Succession to the estate requires neither the acceptance of the inheritance by the heir nor the involvement of any court. While § 1922 I BGB only speaks of succession to the "property" of the decedent, § 1967 I BGB makes it clear that the heir is the decedent's successor not only with regard to the assets of the estate, but also with regard to its liabilities. As a consequence of the principle of *ipso iure* acquisition, German law does not generally require administration of the estate by a personal representative.

According to the principle of universal succession, the heir becomes successor to the estate as a whole or, where there are several heirs, to a share in the estate as a whole. This has two important consequences: First, only the successor to the estate as a whole or to a share in the estate is taken to be "heir" under German law. Beneficiaries of a specific legacy, therefore, are *not* heirs and do not automatically become owners of the object bequeathed. Instead, title to such object passes under § 1922 I BGB to the heir who is then obligated to transfer it to the legatee under § 2174 BGB.[14] Second, under § 1922 I BGB co-heirs (*Miterben*) do not become co-owners of individual assets but only of the undivided estate in its entirety (§§ 2032, 2033 BGB). In order to acquire title to individual assets, the individual co-heir must have it transferred to him by the community of co-heirs acting as a whole.[15]

There are some instances where German law stipulates exceptions to the principle of universal succession (*Universalsukzession*) by providing that specific assets may directly pass to individual beneficiaries (*Singularsukzession*). Such instances of "non-probate transfers" are less common in Germany than in U.S. jurisdictions, but still concern important matters such as the inheritance of partnership interests or rights arising out of third party beneficiary contracts (e.g., life insurance contracts).

§10.02 INTESTATE SUCCESSION (*GESETZLICHE ERBFOLGE*)

The rules of intestate succession are laid down in §§ 1924–1936 BGB. They apply whenever the decedent dies without having left a valid will or without having validly

---

12. *See infra*, §10.06.
13. Cf. *supra*, n. 9.
14. Cf. *supra*, §10.01[B].
15. *See*, in more detail, *infra*, §10.08.

disposed of all of his estate. But even where the decedent has left a valid will, the following rules provide the basis on which the statutory compulsory shares of certain relatives of the testator are calculated. The statutory heirs are the decedent's relatives (§§ 1924–1930), his spouse (§ 1931 BGB) or life partner (§ 10 LPartG) and, when there are no other statutory heirs, the State (§ 1936 BGB).

[A]   Succession of the Next of Kin

If there is no surviving spouse, the entire estate passes to the decedent's relatives according to the following rules. If the decedent's spouse is still alive at the time of death, the spouse's share must first be determined pursuant to § 1931 BGB;[16] the remaining part of the estate is then inherited according to the following principles.

The statutory inheritance rights of the next of kin are determined on the basis of a system of classes (*Erbfolge nach Ordnungen, Parentelsystem*). Every class is composed of a common ancestor or pair of common ancestors and their descendants, with classes being counted in the ascending line. *Class one* are the lineal descendants of the decedent (§ 1924 I BGB). Thus, the children, grandchildren and great-grandchildren of the decedent belong to the first class of heirs. *Class two* are the parents of the decedent and their descendants (§ 1925 I BGB), e.g., the decedent's siblings, nieces and nephews. *Class three* are the grandparents of the decedent and their descendants (§ 1926 I BGB). Heirs belonging to the third class are, e.g., the decedent's uncles, aunts and cousins. The higher classes are determined according to the same system (§§ 1928, 1929 BGB), the number of possible classes not being limited.

Parentage is determined according to the respective rules of family law. By statutory reform which entered into force on April 1, 1998 (*Erbrechtsgleichstellungsgesetz*), children born out of wedlock were granted the same legal status as other children; the substitute right of inheritance (*Erbersatzanspruch*) formerly awarded to children born out of wedlock was abolished and replaced by the general legal share of children pursuant to § 1924 I BGB.

With regard to the relationship between *different classes*, § 1930 BGB provides that a relative of the decedent does not become statutory heir if there exists a relative belonging to a lower class. Thus, grandchildren (first class) will exclude the decedent's parents or siblings (second class), and the decedent's nephews (second class) will exclude his grandparents and cousins (third class). Under this system, inheritance rights do not necessarily depend on the degree of relatedness: as has been seen, the decedent's grandchildren or great-grandchildren exclude his parents, even though they are less closely related to the decedent.

With regard to the selection of heirs from among members of the *same class*, the law provides for two different systems: Within the first three classes, succession is determined *per stirpes* (*Erbfolge nach Stämmen*): As for the first class, every child of the decedent creates his own stirps. Every stirps receives the same share. To that effect, § 1924 IV BGB provides that children inherit in equal shares. Within each stirps, the

---

16. *See infra*, §10.02[B].

share goes only to the relative most closely related to the decedent; this relative is held to "represent" those descendants who are related with the decedent through him (§ 1924 II BGB, "system of representation"). If, for example, the decedent is survived by three children and several grandchildren, each of the children inherits one-third of the estate and the grandchildren do not share in the estate. Where one of the decedent's children has pre-deceased him, the child's share is still kept within his stirps: The deceased child's share goes to his children (§ 1924 III BGB) who in turn inherit in equal shares (§ 1924 IV BGB). If, in the example given, one of the decedent's children has already died, his one-third of the estate is divided among his children in equal shares (if he has left two children, they each inherit one-sixth of the estate). The same basic system applies for the second and third class. Within the second class, if both parents are still living, they inherit the estate in equal shares, to the exclusion of the other members of their class (§ 1925 II BGB). If one parent has pre-deceased the decedent, his share does not pass to the surviving parent, but rather to the pre-deceased parent's descendants according to the system provided for in § 1924 BGB (§ 1925 III 1 BGB); this is called "inheritance according to lineage" (*Erbfolge nach Linien*). It is only if the parent does not leave any descendants that his share goes to the surviving parent (§ 1925 III 2 BGB). Where both parents have died, each of the parents' shares passes to that parent's offspring respectively, pursuant to the rule in § 1925 III 1 BGB. Thus, the decedent's half-siblings and their offspring inherit only in the line of the parent with whom they are related. The same principle applies within the third class: If all grandparents are still living, they inherit in equal shares, to the exclusion of the other members of their class (§ 1926 II BGB). When a grandparent has pre-deceased the decedent, his share passes in the first place to that grandparent's descendants, in the second place to the other grandparent or his descendants, or, in the last place, to the other pair of grandparents or their descendants (§ 1926 III, IV BGB).

Example: The decedent has died intestate. She was not married and did not have any children. She is survived by her mother, an uncle, a sister and her daughter, and two nephews, the children of a brother who has already died. Intestate succession is as follows: Mother, sister, niece and nephews are all statutory heirs of the second class (§ 1925 I BGB); therefore, pursuant to § 1930 BGB, they preclude the uncle, who belongs to the third class (§ 1926 I BGB). The mother inherits half of the estate (§ 1925 II BGB), the father's half goes to his offspring (§ 1925 III 1 BGB). The sister inherits half of her father's share (§§ 1924 IV, 1925 III 1 BGB), i.e., one-fourth of the estate; her daughter does not inherit (§§ 1924 II, 1925 III 1 BGB). The pre-deceased brother's share goes to his sons in equal shares (§§ 1924 III, IV, 1925 III 1 BGB); thus, they each inherit one-eighth of the estate.

Starting with the fourth class, succession to the estate is no longer determined *per stirpes* but exclusively according to the degree of relationship: The closest relative within the class becomes the heir. If there are several relatives of the same degree, they inherit per capita, in equal shares (§§ 1928 III, 1929 II BGB). The degree of relationship is determined according to the number of intervening births (§ 1589 sentence 3 BGB).

[B]   The Spouse's Share

The spouse's intestate share is determined pursuant to § 1931 BGB. The Act introducing the Right to Same-Sex Marriage (*Gesetz zur Einführung des Rechts auf Eheschließung für Personen gleichen Geschlechts*), which entered into force on October 1,
2017, has extended the application of the following rules of intestate succession to
same-sex spouses. It has left unaffected the rules regarding the statutory rights of
registered (same-sex) life partners under § 10 LPartG.[17]

The prerequisite for a spouse's right to inherit is the existence of a valid marriage
at the time of the decedent's death. Therefore, a putative spouse does not inherit if, at
the time of death, the marriage has been dissolved by annulment of marriage (*see* §§
1313 et seq. BGB) or divorce (§§ 1564 et seq. BGB). Dissolution by annulment or
divorce as such takes effect only when the corresponding court judgment has become
final. However, § 1933 BGB already precludes the spouse from inheriting if, at the time
of the decedent's death, the conditions for annulment or divorce were fulfilled and the
decedent had already filed the respective petition (or consented to the divorce).[18] The
surviving partner of a non-marital domestic relationship does not have any statutory
right to succeed to the estate (while he or she may, of course, be appointed as heir by
testament).

The surviving spouse's share in the estate depends on two factors, that is, on the
class of relatives that may become entitled to inherit along with the spouse and on the
matrimonial property regime the decedent and his spouse lived under at the time of
death.

With regard to the spouse's share in relation to the decedent's relatives, § 1931 I
1 BGB first grants the spouse a basic share (without taking into account modifications
resulting from the matrimonial property regime) of one-fourth if he inherits together
with relatives of the first class, and a basic share of -half if he inherits together with
relatives of the second class or the decedent's grandparents. If grandparents have
pre-deceased the decedent, any share that would normally pass to their descendants
under § 1926 BGB is instead inherited by the decedent's spouse (§ 1931 I 2 BGB). If
there are neither relatives of the first or second class nor grandparents surviving, the
spouse becomes the sole heir (§ 1931 II BGB).

This basic share may be further modified depending on the matrimonial property
regime the decedent and his spouse lived under at the time of the decedent's death.[19]
If the spouses were living under the contractual property regime of separation of
property (*Gütertrennung*), § 1931 IV BGB modifies the surviving spouse's share where
he inherits together with one or two children of the decedent. As relatives of the first
class, the children preclude any other relatives of the decedent (§§ 1924 I, 1930 BGB)
and inherit in equal shares (§ 1924 IV BGB). Under § 1931 I BGB, the spouse's share
would only be one-fourth, even if there was only one child, who would accordingly

---

17. *See infra*, §10.02[C].
18. § 2077 BGB provides a similar rule where the spouse is the beneficiary of a *testamentary*
    provision of the decedent.
19. Cf. *supra*, Chapter 9.

become heir to the remaining three-fourths. However, § 1931 IV BGB provides that, where the spouse inherits together with one or two children, the spouse and the child or children inherit in equal shares. If there is only one child, the child and the spouse thus each inherit one half of the estate. Where there are *more* than two children, however, the spouse's share is not reduced, but remains one-fourth pursuant to § 1931 I BGB.

In the case of the contractual regime of community property (*Gütergemeinschaft*), the provisions of § 1931 I and II BGB apply without modification. In particular, the spouse's share remains one-fourth, even if he or she inherits together with only one or two children. Provision for the surviving spouse is already taken into consideration by the fact the he or she has an interest in the joint marital property independent of his participation in the decedent's estate by virtue of the law of succession. Normally, the community property regime is terminated when one spouse dies. The decedent's share in the joint property (*Gesamtgut*, § 1416 BGB) – together with any separate (*Sondergut*, § 1417 BGB) or reserved property (*Vorbehaltsgut*, § 1418 BGB), which does not become joint property, but remains property of the individual spouse himself – then falls to his estate and is inherited according to the provisions of the law of succession (§ 1482 BGB), in case of intestate succession according to §§ 1924 et seq. BGB, as set out above. Thus, the surviving spouse keeps his own share in the joint property and may inherit all or part of the dead spouse's share pursuant to § 1931 I, II BGB. As the death of one of the spouses terminates the community property regime, the joint property is then distributed pursuant to §§ 1471–1481 BGB. However, the spouses may provide that after the death of one of them the community will be continued between the surviving spouse and their joint offspring (§ 1483 BGB). In this case, the decedent's share in the joint property does not fall to his estate and the joint ownership is continued between the surviving spouse and those descendants who are called to inherit under the rules of intestate succession. Only the decedent's separate and reserved property is then inherited according to the principles of the law of succession (§ 1483 I 3 BGB).

If the spouses were living under the statutory property regime of community of surplus (*Zugewinngemeinschaft*), which is by far the most common matrimonial property regime, §§ 1931 III, 1371 I BGB provide that the surviving spouse's intestate share (as determined under § 1931 I, II BGB) is increased by one-fourth. Thus, the spouse's share will be one-half in conjunction with heirs of the first class and three-quarters in conjunction with heirs of the second class and grandparents (cf. § 1931 I 1 BGB). The increase of the surviving spouse's intestate share by § 1371 I BGB is intended as a lump-sum substitute for the regular equalization of surplus as it would be calculated pursuant to §§ 1372 et seq. BGB in cases where the community of surplus is terminated for reasons other than the spouse's death (particularly in case of divorce). As a lump-sum substitute, § 1371 I BGB applies regardless of whether the decedent actually had acquired any surplus which he would have had to equalize under §§ 1372 et seq. BGB.[20]

---

20. *See supra*, Chapter 9, Family Law, at Part §9.04.

If the spouse neither becomes heir (e.g., if he has been disinherited by the decedent) nor benefits from a legacy, § 1371 II BGB provides that he can claim equalization of the surplus pursuant to §§ 1373 et seq. BGB. In addition, as a disinherited statutory heir, he can also claim the statutory compulsory share (§ 2303 II BGB) calculated on the basis of his legal share under § 1931 I, II BGB, that is, without the increase provided for by § 1371 I BGB (the so-called small compulsory share). If the spouse disclaims the inheritance, he also does not become heir (§ 1953 I BGB).[21] As a consequence, he is entitled to equalization of the surplus pursuant to §§ 1371 II, 1373 et seq. BGB. However, under general principles, disclaiming the inheritance would also preclude the spouse from claiming the compulsory share. As an exception to the general rule, § 1371 III BGB preserves the spouse's right to the compulsory share. Thus, disclaimer of an inheritance has the same effect with regard to the spouse's rights as a disinheritance under § 1371 II BGB.

The situation is different if the spouse has been appointed as heir or legatee by the decedent, but the benefit bestowed upon him is lower than his compulsory share. In such a case he is entitled to claim compensation for the deficit by way of the supplementary compulsory share (§§ 2305, 2307 I 2 BGB).[22] However, as in such a case the spouse is not entirely disinherited, § 1371 II BGB does not apply and he cannot claim equalization of the surplus pursuant to §§ 1373 et seq. BGB. As a consequence, the amount of the spouse's compulsory share must be calculated on the basis of the *increased* legal share (§§ 1931 I, II, 1371 I BGB; so-called large compulsory share).

[C]   The Registered Life Partner's Share

The legal consequences of a registered life partnership with regard to the law of succession are regulated in § 10 LPartG. Intestate succession of a life partner follows the model of the BGB provisions on the spouse's share, with only minor variations. Thus, § 10 I, II LPartG essentially corresponds to § 1931 I, II BGB, and § 10 III LPartG to § 1933 BGB. The statutory property regime is the same as for spouses (*Zugewinnge-meinschaft*), § 6 LPartG. As a consequence, the principles of § 1371 BGB, as set forth above, also apply with respect to life partners. Section 10 VI LPartG grants the life partner a compulsory share pursuant to the respective provisions of the BGB.[23]

[D]   The State's Right to Succeed to Heirless Property (Escheat)

Pursuant to § 1936 BGB, the State (generally the *Land* where the decedent had his last residence) becomes statutory heir if there exists neither a testamentary nor a statutory heir to the estate. Even the most distant relative precedes the State as legal heir.

---

21. *See infra*, §10.04[A].
22. Cf. *infra*, §10.06.
23. For the succession rights of same-sex *spouses see supra*, §10.02[B].

§10.03 TESTATE SUCCESSION (*GEWILLKÜRTE ERBFOLGE*)

[A] General

The testator can make provisions for the case of his death (*Verfügungen von Todes wegen*) in two basic ways, either by testament (*Testament*, also called *letztwillige Verfügung*, *see* § 1937 BGB) or by a contract of inheritance (*Erbvertrag*, *see* § 1941 BGB).[24] The testament can either be a single will, containing only testamentary provisions by the testator himself (*Einzeltestament*), or a joint will (*gemeinschaftliches Testament*), which may only be made by spouses.

The fundamental principle of testamentary freedom allows the testator to eliminate or modify the statutory right to succession at his discretion. As has been seen,[25] the principle of testamentary freedom is protected by § 2302 BGB, which provides that any contract to make, not to make, to revoke or not to revoke a will is void. The testator's autonomy regarding the establishment of testate succession is further safeguarded by the rule that the testator must make testamentary dispositions personally (§§ 2064, 2274 BGB) and cannot leave the power to appoint an heir to another person (§ 2065 II BGB). Thus, a power of appointment with regard to heirs cannot validly be created under the German law of succession.

While the law recognizes the principle of testamentary freedom, there are also certain limits to this freedom: First, the testator's autonomy to dispose of his estate is limited by the statutory compulsory share of his spouse and close relatives.[26] Second, like any other legal transaction, a testamentary disposition may be invalid because it violates a legal prohibition (§ 134 BGB) or is contrary to morality (§ 138 BGB). Finally, while it is true that under § 2302 BGB the testator cannot validly *obligate* himself to make a certain testamentary disposition, this does not preclude the testator from making a testamentary disposition which is binding under its own terms. This is the case with the contract of inheritance and, in some instances, the joint will.

[B] The Will

[1] Formal and Substantive Validity

The valid execution of a will generally requires that the testator possessed testamentary capacity at the time of execution and that the formal requirements for the making of wills have been observed.

Testamentary capacity is governed by § 2229 BGB. § 2229 I BGB provides that a minor may only make a will if he has reached the age of 16. Before reaching this age, a minor cannot make a will even with the consent of his legal representative (i.e., normally, his parents, §§ 1626, 1629 BGB). On the other hand, once he has reached the

---

24. Thus, somewhat confusingly, the term *"Verfügung von Todes wegen"* refers to both *"letztwillige Verfügung"* and *"Erbvertrag"*.
25. Cf. *supra*, §10.01[C].
26. *See infra*, §10.06.

age of 16, he can make a will without obtaining the consent of his legal representative (§ 2229 II BGB). There are, however, restrictions as to form: in particular, a minor cannot make a holographic will (§§ 2233 I, 2247 IV BGB). Finally, a will cannot validly be made if for certain mental reasons the testator is unable to understand the meaning of the testamentary disposition made and to act in accordance with such understanding (§ 2229 IV BGB).

The will is a unilateral transaction which does not require receipt by another person to become effective. However, there are certain formal requirements which must be observed. With regard to form, German law distinguishes between ordinary wills and emergency wills. The testator may choose between two forms of ordinary wills (§ 2231 BGB): the public will, which is made before a notary (§ 2232 BGB), and the holographic will (§ 2247 BGB). The holographic will must be entirely handwritten and undersigned by the testator personally. Thus, a will which was written on a typewriter or computer does not meet the formal requirements, even if it was signed by the testator. Witnesses are not required for the holographic will. § 2247 II BGB provides that the testator should state the date and place of writing the will. However, if the validity of the will depends on either the date or place of its making, these circumstances may also be established by other means of evidence (§ 2247 V BGB).

In certain emergency situations, particularly where the testator is close to death, the testator may execute the will under relaxed requirements. Such emergency wills may be made before a mayor (§ 2249 BGB) or before three witnesses (§§ 2250, 2251 BGB). An emergency will becomes invalid *ab initio* if the testator is still alive three months after the making of the will (§ 2252 BGB).

As regards substance, a testamentary disposition may be invalid because it violates a legal prohibition (§ 134 BGB[27]) or because it is contrary to morality (§ 138 BGB). Examples of legal prohibitions are the rules contained in the federal and state *"Heimgesetze,"* which seek to prevent unequal treatment and exploitation in care and retirement institutions by restricting residents' ability to perform monetary transactions or to testate in favor of their carers.[28] In general, a transaction is considered to violate good morals if it is repugnant to the sense of propriety of all fair and equitably-minded persons. Nowadays, it is rare for a will to be deemed contrary to morality. A notable if unusual exception was a testamentary disposition made by a former Crown Prince of Prussia that threatened his descendants in the male line with disinheritance, should they enter into a marriage not befitting their (supposed) social status. Taking into account the considerable fortune involved, the *Bundesverfassungs-gericht* declared this undue pressure a violation of the heirs' freedom of marriage not justified by the decedent's testamentary freedom.[29]

---

27. Also *see* §§ 2171 I, 2192 BGB for testamentary legacies and burdens.
28. For further detail, *see* Leipold, *op. cit.*, marg. nos. 241–242a.
29. BVerfGK 3, 112.

[2]   *Testamentary Dispositions and Their Construction*

There are a variety of possible kinds of dispositions which the testator may include in his will. The most important of these are listed in §§ 1937–1940 BGB: The testator may appoint heirs (*Erbeinsetzung*, § 1937 BGB) or may exclude statutory heirs from inheriting (*Enterbung*, § 1938 BGB), he may bequeath individual assets (*Vermächtnis*, § 1939 BGB)[30] or impose a testamentary burden on an heir or a legatee (*Auflage*, § 1940 BGB).[31] Furthermore, he may make provisions with regard to the distribution of the estate (*see*, e.g., §§ 2044, 2048, 2049 BGB)[32] or he may appoint an executor (§ 2197 BGB) who will administer the estate and carry out the provisions of the testator (§§ 2203, 2205 BGB).[33] It is also possible to provide for certain matters of family law by will, e.g. to appoint a guardian for minor children (§ 1777 III BGB). However, it should be noted that the testator is limited in the types of testamentary dispositions he can make. Under the system of enumeration derived from §§ 1937–1940 BGB and other provisions, the testator is only allowed to make dispositions of a kind expressly permitted by law.

If a testamentary disposition is not clear from its terms alone, it requires interpretation. The guiding principle of interpretation is laid down in § 133 BGB, pursuant to which the true intent of the testator must be ascertained without clinging to the literal meaning of the words. The emphasis on the testator's intent is particularly strong in the case of unilateral wills which are not directed at a recipient meriting protection. Therefore, in the interpretation of wills, it is generally considered that the intent of the testator is to be given effect to the greatest extent possible. To that effect, all relevant circumstances, including extrinsic evidence, may be taken into consideration. However, to fulfill the formal requirements for the validity of wills, the result of interpretation must find at least some basis in the text of the will (so-called theory of intimation, *Andeutungstheorie*).

Another important general principle of construction is that of benevolent interpretation, set forth in § 2084 BGB. Under this provision, if a testamentary disposition allows for different ways of interpretation, that interpretation is to be preferred which will allow the disposition to be legally effective. Furthermore, a will may also be subject to supplementary interpretation: If, after the will was made, circumstances have changed in a way not anticipated by the testator, the respective gap in the testator's will may be filled on the basis of the testator's hypothetical intention. To that effect the court must determine what the testator would have provided in his will if he had taken the change of circumstances into account when making the will.

Finally, there are various specific rules of interpretation, which the law has established for a series of typical doubtful cases. With regard to the distinction between heirs and legatees, which is fundamental to the German law of succession,[34] § 2087

---

30. *See infra*, §10.05[A].
31. *See infra*, §10.05[B].
32. *See infra*, §10.08.
33. *See infra*, §10.10.
34. Cf. *supra*,§10.01[B].

BGB provides that a beneficiary who is given the estate in its entirety or a fraction thereof is to be considered heir even if the testator has not used the correct legal terms, whereas a beneficiary who is given individual objects of the estate is normally to be considered a legatee. §§ 2066 et seq. BGB contain rules of construction for certain classes of gifts like gifts to the testator's "relatives," his "children" or "the poor." §§ 2088 et seq. BGB provide supplementary rules for cases where the determination of the individual testamentary heirs' shares may appear doubtful.

[3]   Revocation (Widerruf)

The testator has the right at any time to revoke or modify the will in its entirety or any individual provision contained in it (§ 2253 BGB). Revocation may be made by another testament (§§ 2254, 2258 BGB), by destruction or alteration of the original testament (§ 2255 BGB) or by withdrawal of the testament from official custody (§ 2256 BGB). If revocation is made by testament, the revocation itself may be revoked (e.g., by destruction); in such a case, the original testament is usually revived (§ 2257 BGB).

While, pursuant to § 2302 BGB, the testator cannot validly obligate himself to revoke or not to revoke a certain testamentary disposition, revocation may be limited by way of a contract of inheritance or a joint will.

[4]   Contest (Anfechtung)

As with any other legal transaction, when making a will, the testator may have acted under a mistake or subject to deceit or duress. In such cases, the will may be contested pursuant to §§ 2078–2083 BGB, which contain special provisions modifying or displacing the general rules on the avoidance of legal transactions for mistake (§§ 119 et seq. BGB). As the testator is generally free to revoke a will regardless of whether there has been a mistake, there is no need for the testator himself to formally contest the will.[35] Therefore, contest under §§ 2078–2083 BGB is a remedy provided primarily to potential heirs or legatees who are prejudiced by the mistaken testamentary disposition. Given the testator's right of revocation, contest is possible only after the testator has died. As long as he is still alive, it is up to him to decide whether to revoke the will or not.

§ 2078 BGB provides two basic grounds for challenging a will: mistake or duress. With regard to mistake, under § 2078 I BGB, a testamentary disposition can be contested if the testator was subject to either a mistake of content (*Inhaltsirrtum*) or a mistake of expression (*Erklärungsirrtum*). However, § 2078 II BGB further extends the grounds for challenging a will to any mistaken assumption or expectation with regard to the existence or non-existence of certain circumstances. Thus, in contrast to legal

---

35. Consequently, § 2281 BGB extends the right to contest to the testator himself where he cannot revoke his disposition because he is bound by a contract of inheritance; cf. *infra*, §10.03[D]. As the testator may similarly be bound when he has made a joint will (cf. *infra*, §10.03[C]), it is generally admitted that §§ 2281 et seq. BGB apply to joint wills by analogy; *see*, e.g., Lange & Kuchinke, *supra.*, p. 461 (§ 24 VI 8).

transactions in general, a testamentary disposition may be contested for any mistake in motive on the part of the testator. In addition, pursuant to § 2079 BGB, a will may also be contested if the testator made no provision for a person entitled to a statutory compulsory share and the existence of that person was unknown to the testator when making the will or that person was only born or became entitled to the compulsory share at a later time.

Under the basic rule of § 2080 I BGB, a will may be contested by the person who would directly benefit from its cancellation. Contest must be made to the probate court (*Nachlassgericht*) and is subject to a one-year time limit (§§ 2081, 2082 BGB). If a testamentary disposition has been successfully contested, it is deemed to have been void *ab initio* pursuant to the general rule in § 142 I BGB.

[C] The Joint Will

In §§ 2265–2272 BGB, German law provides for a joint will (*gemeinschaftliches Testament*) which can only be made by spouses (§ 2265 BGB) or life partners (§ 10 IV LPartG).[36] In the first place, the possibility of making a joint will represents a formal privilege with regard to holographic wills:[37] While under § 2247 I BGB each of the spouses would have to write his or her testamentary dispositions entirely by hand, it suffices under § 2267 BGB that only one spouse has written the entire document by hand and both spouses have signed the will. Of course, the spouses may also make a joint public will pursuant to the general rules (§§ 2231 no. 1, 2232 BGB).

In a joint will, each spouse makes testamentary dispositions. In principle, these testamentary dispositions are subject to the same rules as dispositions contained in individual wills. In fact, the only particularity of a joint will may be that the wills of the spouses, rather than being executed in separate documents, are contained in one single document. In such a case, the legal effect of the respective testamentary dispositions remains unchanged. However, the spouses may also make dispositions which are in substance mutually contingent. Such provisions are called interdependent dispositions (*wechselbezügliche Verfügungen*) and are subject to special rules, as set forth in §§ 2270, 2271 BGB.

Pursuant to § 2270 I BGB, testamentary dispositions in a joint will are interdependent if it can be assumed that the disposition of one spouse would not have been made without the disposition of the other. Under an often-quoted formula, this is the case if the dispositions are so closely interconnected that they are meant to "stand or fall together." Whether dispositions in a joint will are of such a nature must be ascertained by interpretation, with the focus being placed upon the intentions of the testators at the time the will was made. For a special case, § 2270 II BGB provides a presumption in favor of interdependency: Unless different intentions of the spouses can be established, those dispositions are deemed interdependent in which the spouses make mutual provision in favor of each other or in which one spouse makes a

---

36. In the following text, reference will only be made to spouses. Pursuant to § 10 IV LPartG, the same principles apply to life partners.
37. Cf. *supra*, §10.03[B][1].

disposition in favor of the other and the latter, for the event of his or her survival, makes a disposition in favor of a person who is related to or otherwise close to the first spouse to die. Pursuant to § 2270 III BGB, only the appointment of an heir, the bestowal of a legacy, the provision of a testamentary burden or the choice of applicable law may be interdependent. Any other testamentary dispositions (e.g., the nomination of an executor or provisions regarding the distribution of an estate) are therefore necessarily unilateral, even if they are contained in a joint will. Consequently, the special rules regarding interdependent dispositions do not apply to such provisions.

The interdependency of testamentary dispositions has two major consequences: In the first place, the invalidity or the revocation of one interdependent disposition automatically results in the invalidity of the corresponding reciprocal disposition (§ 2270 I BGB). In the second place, unilateral revocation of an interdependent disposition by one of the spouses is restricted by § 2271 BGB. During the lifetime of the other spouse, each spouse retains the right to revoke his or her own disposition; however, pursuant to §§ 2271 I, 2296 BGB revocation cannot be made by a new, unilateral testament (as under §§ 2254, 2258 BGB), but only by giving notice (in notarial form) to the other spouse. Upon the death of the other spouse, the right of revocation is normally lost; however, the surviving spouse may revoke his or her own disposition if he or she disclaims the benefit from the pre-deceased spouse's disposition (§ 2271 II 1 BGB). Of course, it is always possible for the spouses to jointly revoke interdependent dispositions in accordance with the general revocation provisions, that is, by the execution of a new joint will (§§ 2254, 2258 BGB), the joint withdrawal from official custody of a public will (§§ 2256, 2272 BGB) or by the destruction of the will by both spouses (§ 2255 BGB).

[D]   The Contract of Inheritance

The testator can also make testamentary dispositions by means of a contract of inheritance (*Erbvertrag*), which is governed by §§ 2274–2302 BGB. The particular purpose of a contract of inheritance lies in the fact that it allows a testator to make binding testamentary dispositions which are generally not subject to revocation.

In contrast to the joint will, the contract of inheritance can be made between any parties. The conditions for entering into it, however, are strictly formalized due to its far-reaching binding effect. In the first place, testamentary dispositions in a contract of inheritance cannot be made by minors, with exceptions being made for spouses and fiancés (§ 2275 BGB). With regard to form, § 2276 I 1 BGB provides that the contract of inheritance must be officially recorded by a notary in the simultaneous presence of both parties to the contract. Thus, in contrast to simple or joint wills, there is no holographic contract of inheritance.

In a contract of inheritance, either one or both of the parties may make testamentary dispositions. The testamentary dispositions may be either unilateral or contractual. By way of unilateral disposition, the parties may make any provision that would be permissible in a simple will. Such unilateral dispositions are governed by the general rules regarding testamentary dispositions (§ 2299 BGB); in particular, they may be revoked in accordance with the general principles on the revocation of wills. Contractual dispositions are such provisions which are meant to be binding on the respective party. Only the appointment of heirs, legacies, testamentary burdens or the choice of applicable law can be made by way of contractual disposition (§ 2278 II BGB).[38] Whether provisions of this kind are meant to be contractual or merely unilateral dispositions depends upon the intention of the parties which must be determined by way of interpretation.

The particular effect of contractual dispositions is set down in § 2289 BGB: Like a simple will (cf. §§ 2254, 2258 BGB), the contract of inheritance revokes any prior testamentary dispositions to the extent that they would impair the rights of the beneficiary under the contract (§ 2289 I 1 BGB). To the same extent, however, the contract of inheritance also invalidates subsequent testaments (§ 2289 I 2 BGB). In principle, the testator can therefore no longer unilaterally revoke contractual provisions by executing a new testament.

Rescission of the contract of inheritance (or of individual contractual dispositions) is possible by way of a new contract between the parties to the original contract (§ 2290 BGB), by a joint will, if the original contract was made between spouses or life partners (§ 2292 BGB), and with regard to testamentary legacies or burdens also by testament with the consent of the other party to the contract (§ 2291 BGB). Unilateral rescission of the contract is possible where the respective party has reserved the right to rescind (§ 2293 BGB), where the beneficiary of a contractual disposition is guilty of serious misconduct (§ 2294 BGB) or where the obligation of counter-performance is cancelled (§ 2295 BGB). Finally, a party to the contract may be entitled to avoid the contract by way of contest pursuant to §§ 2281 et seq., 2078 et seq. BGB.[39]

The binding nature of the contract of inheritance as laid down in § 2289 I 2 BGB protects the beneficiary against testamentary dispositions which would impair his rights under the contract. On the other hand, § 2286 BGB expressly provides that a testator bound under a contract of inheritance retains the right to freely dispose of his property by way of *inter vivos* transactions. This creates the danger that a testator who is unable to avoid his obligations under the contract pursuant to the respective rules (cf. §§ 2290–2297 BGB) instead undermines these obligations by transferring his property *inter vivos*, thus leaving only a reduced estate to be inherited under the contract. In view of this danger, §§ 2287, 2288 BGB protect beneficiaries against certain acts (in particular, gifts) made with the intent to prejudice the contractual beneficiaries' rights.

---

38. Cf. § 2270 III BGB for the joint will, *supra*, §10.03[C].
39. Cf. *supra*, §10.03[B][4].

§10.04 DISCLAIMER OF THE INHERITANCE, RENUNCIATION OF FUTURE RIGHTS OF INHERITANCE AND DISQUALIFICATION TO INHERIT

[A] Disclaimer of the Inheritance

Pursuant to § 1922 I BGB, the estate passes to the heir in its entirety upon the death of the decedent.[40] The transfer of the estate occurs automatically, by operation of law, without the need for an additional act either by a court or by the heir (such as acceptance of the inheritance), regardless of whether the heir has been appointed by will or statutory provision. Upon the passing of the estate, the heir is liable for the debts of the estate (§ 1967 I BGB).[41]

However, the heir retains the right to disclaim the estate (§ 1942 I BGB; *Ausschlagung*). If he disclaims, the estate is considered not to have accrued to the disclaiming heir (§ 1953 I BGB); succession is then determined as if the disclaiming heir had not been alive at the time of the decedent's death (§ 1953 II BGB). While acceptance of the inheritance is not necessary for the estate to pass to the heir, it is still possible for the heir to accept the inheritance. Such acceptance operates to preclude the heir from later disclaiming the inheritance (§ 1943 BGB). The same principles apply to legacies (§§ 2176, 2180 BGB).

The disclaimer is made by way of a unilateral declaration by the heir expressing his intention not to inherit. Pursuant to § 1945 BGB, the declaration must be made to the probate court, either for the record of the court or in notarial form. The time limit for disclaiming the inheritance is six weeks and begins to run when the heir has learned of the decedent's death and of the basis of his inheritance right (e.g., statute or will) (§ 1944 BGB). A disclaimer of the inheritance is possible only after the decedent has died (§ 1946 BGB); the prior renunciation of inheritance rights is governed by the provisions in §§ 2346–2352 BGB.[42]

In principle, the inheritance can only be disclaimed in its entirety (§ 1950 BGB). As an exception to the rule, §§ 1948, 1951 BGB permit a partial disclaimer where the heir can base his inheritance rights on different grounds. If, for example, the heir under a will would also be included among the statutory heirs under §§ 1924 et seq. BGB, he may disclaim the inheritance based on the will and instead inherit as statutory heir (§ 1948 I BGB).

Pursuant to § 1953 I BGB, the disclaimer has retroactive effect. As a consequence, if the heir disclaims the inheritance, any disposition of estate property made by the heir prior to the disclaimer is considered to have been made without title. The passing of title therefore depends on the general rules on good faith purchase (§§ 892, 932 et seq. BGB). In addition, § 1959 II BGB provides that any disposition made by the heir prior to the disclaimer is valid if it could not have been postponed without prejudice to the estate. The liability of the disclaiming heir as against the heir who is called to inherit in

---

40. Cf. *supra*, §10.01[B],[C].
41. *See*, in more detail, *infra*, §10.11.
42. *See infra*, §10.04[B].

his place is governed by the general rules on the unauthorized management of another's affairs (§ 1959 I BGB).

[B]   Renunciation of Future Rights of Inheritance

Statutory heirs may also renounce their statutory right of inheritance by contractual agreement with the decedent during the latter's lifetime (§ 2346 I BGB; *Erbverzicht*). The agreement to renounce future rights of inheritance is usually, but not necessarily, linked to the payment of compensation.

The rules governing the renunciation of future inheritance rights are set forth in §§ 2346–2352 BGB. To be effective, the contract of renunciation requires certification by a notary (§ 2348 BGB). If a statutory heir has validly renounced his right of inheritance, he is treated as if he were not alive at the time of the decedent's death and cannot claim the statutory compulsory share (§ 2346 I 2 BGB).

[C]   Disqualification to Inherit (*Erbunwürdigkeit*)

If the heir committed an act of serious misconduct against the decedent, it can be presumed that it would be contrary to the intent of the decedent to permit the offender to inherit. The testator may, of course, disinherit the offender (§ 1938 BGB), and he may also deprive him of the statutory compulsory share (§§ 2333 et seq. BGB).[43] However, the testator may not become aware of the offense or may not be in a position to react to it. Therefore, § 2339 BGB provides that an heir is disqualified from inheriting in certain cases which are exhaustively enumerated in § 2339 I BGB, e.g., where he willfully and unlawfully killed or tried to kill the decedent (§ 2339 I no. 1 BGB), where he willfully and unlawfully prevented the decedent from making or revoking a will (§ 2339 I no. 2 BGB) or where he induced the decedent to make or revoke a will by way of fraudulent misrepresentations or illegal threats (§ 2339 I no. 3 BGB).

If the requirements of § 2339 BGB are met, disqualification does not occur automatically but must be asserted by way of an action to set aside the acquisition of the estate (§§ 2340, 2342 BGB). The action may be brought after the decedent's death by anyone who would benefit from the disqualification of the heir (§ 2341 BGB). The time limit is one year after the person entitled to bring the action has learned of the grounds of disqualification (§§ 2082, 2340 III BGB). If the heir is declared disqualified, he is considered not to have inherited and the estate passes to those who would have inherited if the disqualified heir had not been alive at the time of the decedent's death (§ 2344 BGB). The action for disqualification is excluded if the decedent has forgiven the offending heir (§ 2343 BGB).

---

43. Cf. *infra*, §10.06.

§10.05   LEGACIES AND TESTAMENTARY BURDENS

[A]   The Legacy (*Vermächtnis*)

The testator may bestow a benefit upon a person without appointing that person as heir by providing for a legacy (*Vermächtnis*; §§ 1939, 2147–2191 BGB). In particular, where specific objects are bequeathed by the testator, the beneficiary is normally held not to become heir but only the beneficiary of a legacy (§ 2087 II BGB). As beneficiary of a legacy, the legatee does not automatically acquire title to the object bequeathed upon the testator's death. Rather, title passes to the heir under the principle of universal succession laid down in § 1922 I BGB. The legatee only obtains a personal claim against the heir[44] to have the item transferred to him (§ 2174 BGB). In that respect, the beneficiary of a legacy is simply a creditor of the estate, whose claim must be satisfied by a corresponding performance on the part of the heir.

Normally, the item bequeathed will be legally a part of the estate. In that case, the heir is obligated under § 2174 BGB to transfer title to the legatee. If the object of the legacy is not part of the estate, the legacy is considered void, unless it can be inferred that the testator meant the legacy to be effective even if the object did not belong to the estate (§ 2169 I BGB). In that case the heir is obligated to procure the item for the beneficiary (§ 2170 I BGB; *Verschaffungsvermächtnis*).

Under the general principle of § 2065 BGB, the testator must himself decide whether a testamentary disposition should be effective and must personally determine the object and the beneficiary of the disposition. However, with regard to legacies, §§ 2151–2156 BGB provide important exceptions to that principle. Thus, for example, the testator may designate a class of potential beneficiaries and leave the choice of beneficiary to the heir or a third party (§ 2151 I BGB), or he may simply bequeath alternative objects from which the heir or a third party is to choose (§ 2154 BGB). Moreover, pursuant to § 2156 BGB, the testator may merely designate the purpose the legacy is meant to serve and leave the determination of the object, time and manner of performance under the legacy to the discretion of the heir or a third party (*Zweckvermächtnis*). However, these provisions do not allow the testator to leave the decision regarding the legacy entirely to the discretion of another person. Thus, the testator must still decide personally on the class of people from among whom the beneficiary is to be chosen and whether a legacy is to be made at all. In the case of § 2156 BGB, the testator must determine the purpose of the legacy with such precision that there is an adequate basis on which the discretion of the other party can be exercised. Testamentary provisions that do not fulfill these requirements are null and void.

The testator may also provide that the legacy is to take effect not immediately upon his death but only upon a certain later date or upon the occurrence of a certain event (cf. § 2177 BGB). In that case, §§ 2162–2163 BGB lay down a rule that resembles the common law "rule against perpetuities": In principle, the legacy becomes void

---

44. Pursuant to § 2147 BGB, the person obligated by a bequest may be either the heir or a legatee, that is, another beneficiary of a legacy. In the following text, reference will only be made to the standard case of the heir being obligated under the bequest.

thirty years after the testator's death, unless the date or the event provided for by the testator has occurred before that time period has lapsed (§ 2162 BGB, with exceptions to that rule being provided in § 2163 BGB).

[B]   The Testamentary Burden (*Auflage*)

If the testator wishes to make a testamentary provision in favor of some person without at the same time providing that person with an enforceable claim, he can accomplish this by means of a testamentary burden (*Auflage*; §§ 1940, 2192–2196 BGB). Pursuant to § 1940 BGB, the testamentary burden obligates the heir (or the beneficiary of a legacy) to provide the performance laid down by the testator but does not entitle the beneficiary of the burden to a corresponding legal claim to that performance. Rather, performance of the burden may be enforced by the heir, a co-heir or any other person who would directly benefit if the person charged with the burden were to fall away (§ 2194 sentence 1 BGB). For example, if a legatee is charged with a burden, the heir (or co-heirs) are entitled to enforce the obligations arising from the burden against the legatee. If performance of the burden is in the public interest, the burden may also be enforced by the competent public authority (§ 2194 sentence 2 BGB).

As the burden does not provide any enforceable rights to the beneficiary, it can be established without the existence of a beneficiary who would be able to enforce the burden. Accordingly, the testator may, for example, burden the heir (or legatee) with the care for a pet or for a grave after the testator's death.

§10.06   THE STATUTORY COMPULSORY SHARE (*PFLICHTTEIL*)

In principle, the testator is free to appoint any person as his heir. The freedom granted to the testator with regard to the appointment of heirs may, however, conflict with legitimate interests of the testator's spouse and close relatives. Therefore, even though the testator is free to appoint the heirs who succeed to his estate under § 1922 I BGB, the law protects the surviving spouse and certain close relatives by granting them a compulsory share (*Pflichtteil*), if they have been (completely or partly) disinherited by the testator (§§ 2303–2338 BGB).[45]

The basic principle is set forth in § 2303 BGB which grants a compulsory share to the decedent's descendants, parents and spouse,[46] if they have been excluded from succession by the decedent's will. Pursuant to § 2309 BGB, however, descendants and parents do not receive a compulsory share if under the rules of intestate succession they would have been excluded from inheriting because of the presence of closer relatives or relatives of a lower class.[47] Thus, parents have no claim to a compulsory share if the testator appoints his children as sole heirs, because children preclude

---

45. For the constitutional guarantee of a forced share *see supra*, §10.01[A], at n. 8.
46. For the spouse's forced share also *see supra*, §10.02[B].
47. Cf. *supra*, §10.02[A].

parents from inheriting under §§ 1924 I, 1925 I, 1930 BGB. § 2303 BGB is supplemented by § 10 VI LPartG which grants a compulsory share also to the decedent's life partner.

The amount of the compulsory share is one-half of the value of the intestate share (§ 2303 I 2 BGB). The persons entitled to a compulsory share do not become successors to the estate, but are only granted a personal money claim against the estate, which arises upon the decedent's death (§ 2317 I BGB). Where such a person is not entirely disinherited by the testator, but appointed as heir with a testamentary share lower than the compulsory share, he may claim a "supplementary" compulsory share (*Zusatzpflichtteil*) under § 2305 BGB. A testator may be tempted to avoid the restrictions imposed by the statutory compulsory share by transferring his property *inter vivos*, thus leaving only a reduced estate from which to calculate the compulsory share under § 2303 I 2 BGB. Therefore, § 2325 BGB grants the right to an augmented compulsory share (*Pflichtteilsergänzungsanspruch*) where the testator had made gifts to third persons within the last ten years before his death.

The right to a compulsory share does not arise where a person is excluded from succession not by the testator's will but for other reasons, e.g., because that person has renounced his right to inherit (§ 2346 I 2 BGB)[48] or is disqualified to inherit under § 2339 BGB (§ 2345 II BGB).[49] § 2339 BGB is supplemented by §§ 2333–2337 BGB which allow the testator to exclude the compulsory share where the respective person is guilty of specific kinds of serious misconduct.

§10.07 PRELIMINARY AND SUBSEQUENT HEIRS

In some cases the testator may wish to preserve the estate as an economic unit and to have an influence on its fate after the time of his death. Such control is not possible if the testator simply appoints an heir, because in that case the heir becomes the owner of the estate without any restrictions and when the heir dies the remainder of the testator's estate is passed on to the former's statutory or testamentary heirs. However, it is possible for the testator to appoint preliminary and subsequent heirs (*Vorerben und Nacherben*) and thereby determine the fate of the inherited property beyond its immediate devolution upon the testator's own death (§§ 2100–2146 BGB).

To that effect, the testator may provide that his estate first passes to one person (the preliminary heir) and then to another (the subsequent heir) (§ 2100 BGB). The testator may condition the succession of the subsequent heir on a specific event (e.g., the death of the preliminary heir) or provide that it will occur at a specific point in time (e.g., "on January 1, 2030"). If the testator appoints a subsequent heir but does not determine when the subsequent heir is to succeed to the estate, it is presumed that the subsequent succession shall occur when the preliminary heir dies (§ 2106 I BGB). The preliminary heir and the subsequent heir consecutively inherit the testator's estate: Upon the death of the testator, his estate first devolves on the preliminary heir. Upon the occurrence of the event or the arrival of the date triggering the succession of the

---

48. *See supra*, §10.04[B].
49. *See supra*, §10.04[C].

subsequent heir, the preliminary heir ceases to be heir and the testator's estate passes to the subsequent heir (§ 2139 BGB). In any event, it must be borne in mind that the subsequent heir is not a successor to the estate of the preliminary heir, but rather succeeds to the estate of the testator. This is true even where the subsequent succession occurs at the time of the preliminary heir's death. In such a case, therefore, succession to the testator's estate and succession to the preliminary heir's own estate must be distinguished: The remainder of the testator's estate passes to the subsequent heir as determined by the testator's will. The preliminary heir's estate is inherited pursuant to the general rules of testate or intestate succession.

The testator may also appoint more than two heirs successively. However, a time limit is set by § 2109 BGB which provides, in principle, that the appointment of a subsequent heir becomes void thirty years after the testator's death, unless the condition for the succession of the subsequent heir has occurred before that period has lapsed.

Upon the death of the testator, the preliminary heir becomes universal successor and thus the owner of the estate property pursuant to § 1922 I BGB. As legal owner of the estate, he is free to dispose of any property belonging to the estate inherited from the testator (§ 2112 BGB). However, §§ 2113–2115 BGB impose restrictions on the preliminary heir's power of disposition in order to protect the reversionary interest of the subsequent heir. Under these rules, the preliminary heir cannot validly enter into certain transactions that are typically detrimental to the interests of the subsequent heir, unless he obtains the latter's consent. In particular, he is not permitted to dispose of real estate, rights in real property or ships or to make gifts (apart from customary gifts) if this would defeat or impair the rights of the subsequent heir (§ 2113 BGB). Further restrictions apply to the cancellation of liens on real property (§ 2114 BGB) and to compulsory orders against the preliminary heir (§ 2115 BGB). Upon the event giving rise to the succession of the subsequent heir, any dispositions made in violation of § 2113 BGB automatically become ineffective. However, the bona fide purchaser who had no knowledge of the limitation of the powers of the preliminary heir is protected in accordance with the general provisions of §§ 892, 932 et seq. BGB (§ 2113 III BGB).

As a principle, the preliminary heir is obligated to administer the decedent's estate with due care, the standard of care being limited to the diligence he usually employs in managing his own affairs (§ 2131 BGB). The relative rights between the preliminary and the subsequent heir with regard to the administration of the preliminary estate are subject to the detailed provisions of §§ 2116 et seq. BGB. In essence, the relationship created by these provisions is comparable to that of a trust with regard to the property of the preliminary estate.

Pursuant to § 2136 BGB, the testator may relieve the preliminary heir of certain restrictions and obligations imposed by §§ 2113 et seq. BGB. This is referred to as "exempted preliminary succession" (*befreite Vorerbschaft*).

§10.08   COMMUNITY OF CO-HEIRS

The relationship between several heirs who are called to inherit concurrently is governed by §§ 2032–2063 BGB on the community of co-heirs (*Miterbengemeinschaft*). Upon the death of the testator the estate passes "as an entirety" (§ 1922 I BGB) to the heirs and becomes their joint property pursuant to § 2032 I BGB. As long as the estate is not partitioned, each co-heir's share exists only as a share in the undivided estate as a whole and does not attach to individual assets of the estate (*Gesamthandsgemein-schaft*, joint ownership). The estate inherited from the decedent thus constitutes a separate estate which is held jointly by the co-heirs and which must be distinguished from the individual property of each co-heir.

As a consequence of the principle of joint ownership, § 2033 BGB provides that a co-heir may dispose of his share in the estate as a whole but not of his share in individual assets of the estate. Individual assets of the estate can only be disposed of by the heirs jointly (§ 2040 BGB). Such joint disposition by the co-heirs does not necessarily require that all of the heirs personally take part in the disposition itself but can also be effected by individual heirs acting in representation of the community of co-heirs or with the authorization of the other co-heirs. If one co-heir sells his share in the estate as a whole, the other co-heirs have a right of pre-emption pursuant to §§ 2034, 2035 BGB.

The administration of the estate is governed by § 2038 BGB. In principle, the estate must be administered by the co-heirs jointly (§ 2038 I 1 BGB), which requires unanimous action by all co-heirs. Each co-heir is obligated to participate in measures which are necessary for the proper administration of the estate (§ 2038 I 2 BGB). Within the limits of § 745 BGB, matters of regular administration may also be decided by a majority vote (§ 2038 II 1 BGB). Measures necessary for the conservation of the estate assets can even be taken by individual co-heirs alone (§ 2038 I 2 BGB).

Joint ownership by the community of co-heirs is terminated by the partition of the estate pursuant to §§ 2042–2057a BGB. In principle, every co-heir has the right to demand partition at any time (§ 2042 I BGB). Partition of the estate is accomplished by the settlement of the estate liabilities (§ 2046 BGB) and the distribution of the remaining estate according to the individual heirs' shares (§ 2047 BGB). The manner of distribution is not determined by law. In principle, the co-heirs must agree on the distribution of the estate assets by way of a settlement contract. The testator may also provide for a certain way of distribution by will (§ 2048 BGB) or may appoint an executor who will decide on the distribution of the estate (§ 2204 BGB).[50]

Pursuant to § 2058 BGB, co-heirs are jointly and severally liable for joint estate debts. Therefore, estate creditors may either bring their claim against the undivided estate by an action against all joint heirs collectively (§ 2059 II BGB) or he may bring his action against an individual heir, who is liable for the full amount of the claim under §§ 2058, 421 BGB but may limit his liability to his share in the estate (§ 2059 I BGB). After partition of the estate, creditors may no longer bring a claim against the undivided

---

50. Cf. *infra*, §10.10.

estate but only against the co-heirs. In that case, liability can no longer be limited to the co-heirs' respective shares in the estate pursuant to § 2059 I BGB, but the amount recoverable from each individual heir may be limited to a fraction of the claim corresponding to the respective heir's share in the estate (§§ 2060–2061 BGB).

§10.09   THE HEIR'S LIABILITY FOR THE DEBTS OF THE ESTATE

Pursuant to § 1967 I BGB, the heir is liable for the debts of the estate.[51] The debts of the estate can be of three kinds: § 1967 II BGB expressly mentions the debts incurred by the decedent (and inherited by the heir) and the obligations incumbent on the heir as such, in particular, obligations arising out of legacies[52] or the statutory compulsory share.[53] In addition, the debts of the estate also comprise the debts incurred by the heir in the administration of the estate. The latter are not only estate debts, but also personal debts of the heir.

Even though § 1967 I BGB generally provides for the liability of the heir, the estate creditors cannot bring an action against the heir as long as the heir has not accepted the inheritance (§ 1958 BGB). Upon acceptance, the heir is liable for the debts of the estate without limitation, that is, both with the inherited assets as well as with his own property. However, the heir has different possibilities to limit his liability:

First of all, as provided by §§ 1970–1974 BGB (supplemented by §§ 433 et seq., 454 et seq. FamFG), the creditors of the estate may be given public notice to present their claims in a so-called *Aufgebotsverfahren* (public notice procedure). Claims which have not been presented within the respective time limit are formally barred by way of a court judgment. As a consequence, the heir may refuse to satisfy the barred claim to the extent the estate is already exhausted by the satisfaction of claims which have not been barred by the notice procedure (§ 1973 BGB). With respect to claims properly presented (and therefore not barred), however, the notice procedure does not bring about a limitation of liability.

Furthermore, the heir may limit his liability to the estate by effecting formal administration of the estate (*Nachlassverwaltung*) or the institution of insolvency proceedings with regard to the estate (*Nachlassinsolvenzverfahren*) (§ 1975 BGB).

Both procedures are instituted by a corresponding court order on application of the heir (or certain other interested parties, in particular estate creditors). As a consequence of such an order, the estate is legally segregated from the heir's personal assets and subject to the exclusive administration and disposition of the estate administrator (*Nachlassverwalter*) or insolvency administrator (*Nachlassinsolvenzverwalter*). The administration of the estate is governed by §§ 1981–1988 BGB, the proceedings on an insolvent estate by § 1980 BGB and §§ 315–331 InsO.

If the estate is insufficient to cover the costs of either the administration or the insolvency proceedings, the heir is entitled to refuse settlement of an estate creditor's claim to the extent that the estate is insufficient to satisfy the claim (§ 1990 I 1 BGB).

---

51. For the liability of co-heirs *see supra*, §10.08.
52. *See supra*, §10.05[A].
53. *See supra*, §10.06.

In that case, he must surrender the estate to the creditor who may then proceed to levy execution (§ 1990 I 2 BGB). Thus, in case of insufficiency of the estate, the heir can limit his liability without the institution of formal proceedings under § 1975 BGB.

The heir may lose his right to limit his liability to the estate with respect to all or only certain creditors of the estate. He loses the right with respect to all creditors if he fails to set up an inventory of the assets and liabilities of the estate within the time period set by the probate court upon application of an estate creditor (§§ 1993 et seq., in particular § 1994 I 2 BGB), or if he intentionally files an incomplete or incorrect inventory (§ 2005 I 1 BGB). The heir loses the right to limit his liability with respect to individual creditors if he fails to provide an affirmation in lieu of an oath (*eidesstattliche Versicherung*) regarding the accuracy of the inventory (§ 2006 III BGB), or if he waives his right to limit his liability with respect to certain creditors.

Special rules apply where a commercial enterprise is part of the estate. If the heir continues the business under the former business name, he is liable without limitation for all business debts incurred by the decedent under §§ 25, 27 I HGB. The heir can avoid unlimited liability by ceasing to carry on the business within three months after he has learned of the devolution of the inheritance or within the time limit for disclaiming the inheritance (§ 27 II HGB). If the heir succeeds the decedent as partner in a general partnership (*Offene Handelsgesellschaft, OHG*), he is generally liable for the debts of the partnership pursuant to § 130 HGB. However, he may have his position converted to that of a limited partner (*Kommanditist*) or withdraw from the partnership pursuant to the provisions of § 139 HGB.

§10.10   THE EXECUTION OF A WILL

In order to ensure that the estate is properly administered and that the testator's will is followed, the testator may appoint an executor (*Testamentsvollstrecker*). The rules governing executorship of an estate are set forth in §§ 2197–2228 BGB.

There is no compulsory administration of a decedent's estate in German law. An executor is only appointed if the testator has so provided in his will (§ 2197 BGB) or in a contract of inheritance (§ 2299 I BGB). In all other cases, the administration of the estate is left to the heirs (unless an administrator is appointed pursuant to §§ 1975 et seq. BGB[54]). While it is for the testator to decide whether there is to be execution of the will at all, he may leave the determination of the person who shall become executor to a third party (§ 2198 BGB) or to the probate court (§ 2200 BGB). It is also possible to appoint several executors (§§ 2197 I, 2224 BGB).

It is the executor's duty to see to it that the testamentary dispositions of the decedent are carried out (§ 2203 BGB), to effect the partition of the estate if there are several heirs (§ 2204 BGB) and to administer the estate (§ 2205 BGB). To that effect, he is entitled to take possession of the estate and to dispose of estate property (§ 2205 sentence 2 BGB). While the estate is subject to the administration by the executor, the power of disposition with regard to estate property is exclusively vested in the

---

54. *See supra,* §10.09.

executor; the heir cannot validly dispose of such property, unless the person acquiring property from the heir is protected by the general rules on bona fide purchase (§ 2211 BGB). The executor may incur liabilities with effect for the estate to the extent necessary for the proper administration of the estate and to the extent that he is entitled to dispose of estate property (§ 2206 BGB). The executor is exclusively competent to bring actions on claims belonging to the estate (§ 2212 BGB), whereas claims against the estate may be brought either against the executor or against the heir (§ 2213 BGB).

The executor must use proper care in the administration of the estate and follow the instructions of the testator (§ 2216 BGB). To a large extent, the relationship between the executor and the heir is subject to the rules on the contract of mandate (§ 2218 I BGB). If the executor intentionally or negligently breaches his duties, he must compensate the heir for the damage arising therefrom (§ 2219 BGB). The executor is entitled to be paid a reasonable compensation unless otherwise provided by the testator (§ 2221 BGB).

In principle, the rights and duties of the executor are subject to modification by the testator (§§ 2207–2209, 2216 II 1 BGB, with limits being imposed by § 2220 BGB). For example, the testator may restrict the executor of the will to the administration of individual assets or to ensuring that a testamentary burden with which a beneficiary under the will has been charged is carried out (cf. § 2223 BGB). In general, two basic kinds of execution are distinguished in German law: On the one hand, the functions of the executor may be limited to such administration as is necessary for the immediate settlement and partition of the estate (so-called *Abwicklungsvollstreckung*). On the other hand, the testator may provide that the administration of the estate by the executor is to extend to a longer period beyond the settlement and partition of the estate as such (so-called *Dauervollstreckung*; *see* § 2209 BGB). The testator may want to order such extended execution if, for example, the estate comprises a business which the heir is too young or too inexperienced to continue. Pursuant to § 2210 BGB, even extended execution ordered under § 2209 BGB normally must end thirty years after the testator's death. In practice, both prototypes of execution may blend, as the testator is free to shape the powers of the executor according to his particular purposes.

In the administration of the estate, the executor is not under the supervision of the probate court. However, the court may remove the executor from office upon application of an interested party for important reasons, particularly for serious misconduct or incompetence (§ 2227 BGB). The executor's office also ends if the administration of the estate is completed, if the executor dies (§ 2225 BGB) or if he terminates his office by giving notice pursuant to § 2226 BGB.

§10.11 THE CERTIFICATE OF INHERITANCE

Pursuant to § 2353 BGB, the heir may apply to the probate court (*Nachlassgericht*) for the issuance of a certificate of inheritance (*Erbschein*). The certificate of inheritance states the identity of the heir and his respective share in the estate (§ 2353 BGB) as well as any limitations to the heir's power of disposition over the estate, which may result from the rules on preliminary and subsequent heirship[55] or from the appointment of an executor[56] (cf. § 352b FamFG). No certificate of inheritance will be issued to beneficiaries of a legacy[57] or the statutory compulsory share,[58] as these do not give rise to rights in rem but only to personal claims against the heir. If it turns out that a certificate of inheritance is inaccurate, the probate court has to revoke the certificate (§ 2361 BGB).

Issuance of a certificate of inheritance is not a prerequisite of succession to the estate, which occurs automatically by operation of law (§ 1922 I BGB). However, the certificate serves as an important means for the heir to prove his right of inheritance. Pursuant to § 2365 BGB, it is presumed that the person identified as heir in the certificate has the right of inheritance stated therein and is not subject to limitations other than those stated. Furthermore, § 2366 BGB protects those who in good faith acquire an item belonging to the estate from the person named as heir in the certificate of inheritance; they obtain title even though the transferor is not the true heir, unless they had knowledge of the inaccuracy of the certificate.

In addition to the certificate of inheritance under German national law (governed by §§ 2353 et seq. BGB, §§ 352 et seq. FamFG), the European Succession Regulation (Regulation No. 650/2012) of July 4, 2012 has introduced a *European* "Certificate of Succession," governed by Articles 62 et seq. of the Regulation. Both certificates may be obtained independently and are subject to their own specific rules.

§10.12   *INTER VIVOS* DONATIVE PROMISES FOR THE EVENT OF THE DONOR'S DEATH

Under German law, in principle, every person is free to enter into *inter vivos* transactions which are to take effect only after that person's death. However, a too liberal application of that principle would create the possibility that the legal provisions on testamentary dispositions (in particular, the formal requirements for wills) could be evaded by way of corresponding *inter vivos* arrangements. Therefore, § 2301 I BGB provides that donative promises which are made under the condition that the donee shall survive the donor (and which are meant to take effect only after the donor's death) shall be governed by the provisions on testamentary dispositions. In particular, such promises must be made in the forms prescribed for wills or contracts of inheritance. An exception is made by § 2301 II BGB if the donor executes the donative promise in his lifetime by transferring the benefit promised; in that case the gift is governed by the provisions on *inter vivos* gifts.

---

55. *See supra*, §10.07.
56. *See supra*, §10.10. The executor may himself be issued a certificate of executorship pursuant to § 2368 BGB.
57. Cf. *supra*, §10.05[A].
58. Cf. *supra*, §10.06.

SELECTED BIBLIOGRAPHY

English

Dieter Schwab, Peter Gottwald & Saskia Lettmaier, *Family and Succession Law in Germany* (3rd ed. 2017).

German: Treatises

Theodor Kipp & Helmut Coing, *Erbrecht* (14th ed. 1990).
Heinrich Lange & Kurt Kuchinke, *Erbrecht* (5th ed. 2001).
Knut Werner Lange, *Erbrecht* (2nd ed. 2017).
Karlheinz Muscheler, *Erbrecht* (2010).

Shorter Textbooks

Hans Brox & Wolf-Dietrich Walker, *Erbrecht* (27th ed. 2016).
Rainer Frank & Tobias Helms, *Erbrecht* (7th ed. 2018).
Dieter Leipold, *Erbrecht* (21st ed. 2016).
Lutz Michalski, *BGB – Erbrecht* (4th ed. 2010).
Dirk Olzen & Dirk Looschelders, *Erbrecht* (5th ed.2017).
Wilfried Schlüter & Anne Röthel, *Erbrecht* (17th ed. 2015).
Matthias Schmoeckel, *Erbrecht* (5th ed. 2018).
Walter Zimmermann, *Erbrecht* (4th ed. 2013).

Handbooks

Manfred Bengel & Wolfgang Reimann (eds), *Handbuch der Testamentsvollstreckung* (6th ed. 2017).
Wolfgang Burandt & Dieter Rojahn (ed.), *Erbrecht* (2nd ed. 2014).
Ottmar Dittmann, Wolfgang Reimann & Manfred Bengel (eds), *Testament und Erbvertrag* (6th ed. 2015).
Günter Esch et al., *Handbuch der Vermögensnachfolge* (7th ed. 2009).
Karl Firsching & Hans Lothar Graf, *Nachlassrecht* (10th ed. 2014).
Klaus-Michael Groll (ed.), *Praxis-Handbuch Erbrechtsberatung* (4th ed. 2015).
Gerrit Langenfeld & Oliver Fröhler, *Testamentsgestaltung* (5th ed. 2015).
Jörg Mayer et al., *Handbuch Pflichtteilsrecht* (4th ed. 2017).
Heinrich Nieder et al., *Handbuch der Testamentsgestaltung* (5th ed. 2015).
Kurt Schellhammer, *Erbrecht nach Anspruchsgrundlagen* (3rd ed. 2010).
Stephan Scherer (ed.), *Münchener Anwaltshandbuch – Erbrecht* (5th ed. 2018).
Gerhard Schlitt & Gabriele Müller, *Handbuch Pflichtteilsrecht* (2nd ed. 2017).
Walter Zimmermann, *Die Testamentsvollstreckung* (4th ed. 2014).

CHAPTER 11

Labor Law

Manfred Weiss

TABLE OF CONTENTS

§11.01   INTRODUCTION

In Germany, labor law is understood as the set of rules applicable to individual employment relationships and to collective relationships between management and labor. As far as the employment relationship is concerned, labor law is only applicable to relationships based on private contract. As a consequence, an important segment of the workforce, that of career public servants, falls outside the scope of ordinary labor law. The relationship between career public servants and the State is not a private contractual relationship but is defined by, and based on, public law. This is why the law of career public servants is considered to be a special aspect of public law. Their rights and duties, as well as their working conditions, are not determined by individual or by collective agreements but by acts passed by the legislative bodies of the Federal Republic and of the *Länder*. Disputes concerning career public servants are not settled by labor courts but by administrative courts. However, the exclusion of career public servants from labor law does not mean that labor law is inapplicable to the public service as a whole. There are not only career public servants, but also blue- and white-collar workers employed in the public service. These public employees are ordinary employees within a regular contractual employment relationship and are therefore covered by labor law.

German labor law consists of rules governing individual contracts (hereinafter "individual labor law") and rules regulating collective bargaining agreements (hereinafter "collective labor law"). Individual labor law addresses the individual employment relationship. It covers the rules on how a labor contract is concluded, what rights and duties the parties have in such a contractual relationship, to what extent the parties can waive these rights and duties by negotiating alternative clauses and, finally, how a labor contract can be terminated. In addition, individual labor law covers all the laws protecting individual employees, thereby setting rather elaborate minimum standards, which the parties to the individual contract cannot fall below.

Collective labor law focuses on the structures of industrial relations. It defines and regulates the rights and duties of the parties involved, and how their activities and agreements affect the individual employment relationship. Collective labor law consists of four main parts: first, the law on collective bargaining, including the law on trade unions and employers' associations; second the law on industrial conflict; third, the law on employee representation by works councils; and fourth, the law on employee representation on the supervisory boards of large companies. It is the third part – concerning employee representation by works councils – where the differences between collective labor law in the private sector and its public sector counterpart are most pronounced. Whereas the Works Constitution Act of 1972, amended in 2001, regulates the private sector, the Federal Staff Representation Act of 1955, amended in 1974, governs the public sector. For present purposes, the differences between the two can be neglected; our focus will be on the Works Constitution Act. In this chapter, I will first outline the sources of German labor law and the system of specialized courts in which this law unfolds. I will then address the institutional arrangements of collective labor law. It would be a misconception to view individual labor law and collective labor law as two separate entities. These bodies of law interact closely, and a realistic assessment of the working conditions in an individual employment relationship requires that collective labor law be examined thoroughly. In other words, the individual employment contract, the protective laws, the collective agreement, the works agreement concluded between works council (*Betriebsrat*) and employer cannot be seen as isolated factors but must be seen as parts of a whole. Finally, I will take a look at four basic aspects of the employment relationship: the notion of the employment relationship, the concept of freedom of contract, the main implications of the employment relationship and the rules on job security. The overall emphasis of this chapter will lie on the institutional arrangements of collective labor law and on the rules on job security; these are the areas in which German labor law differs most from its foreign counterparts.

§11.02 THE SOURCES OF GERMAN LABOR LAW

As in any other Member State of the European Union (EU), the law of this supranational entity ranks highest among all legal sources in German labor law. This priority does not only apply to primary EU law which is spelled out in the Treaty of the European Union (TEU) and the Treaty on the Functioning of the European Union

(TFEU). The so-called secondary EU law consisting of directly applicable Regulations and Directives which must be transposed into national law also takes precedence over conflicting domestic rules. The impact of European labor law on German labor law is on individual labor law. However, since EU law only establishes minimum standards, in most cases German law exceeds this level. An exception to this rule are two recent Directives outlawing discrimination on grounds of race, ethnic origin, religion, sexual orientation, age, and disability which have an enormous effect on German labor law. In this respect German individual labor law now resembles U.S. employment law.

Concerning purely domestic German labor law the Basic Law (*Grundgesetz*) is at the top of the legal order. Indeed, it plays a dominant role in the field of labor law. This is particularly true for collective labor law where legislation is very fragmented. Questions that the legislature did not address must be solved by recourse to the Constitution (Basic Law). For example, all rules on industrial conflict were developed by interpretation of principles set out in the Basic Law (particularly Articles 9 and 12). Furthermore, the Constitution (Basic Law) also plays an important role in individual labor law. A great number of legal provisions concerning contractual relationships originated from the late 19th century. Promulgated in 1900, the German Civil Code (*Bürgerliches Gesetzbuch*) still contains these provisions, but many of them are no longer compatible with the more recent basic principles of constitutional law. These principles are both broad and unspecific, and the courts have often used their powers to shape individual labor law in line with their interpretation of constitutional mandates. More often than not, that interpretation has strengthened the position of employees.

In addition to the pivotal role of constitutional jurisprudence, specific federal legislative acts have also increased the rights of employees. Federal legislation is particularly important because it sets minimum standards for all employees, whether or not they are union members. Since the competence to legislate in the field of labor law lies with the federal legislature, it is almost exclusively federal law that counts. Thus, despite a well-developed German federalism, a homogeneous pattern of labor law evolved throughout Germany. To the extent that state (*Länder*) laws and constitutions conflict with federal law the latter invariably preempts the former. There is one area where differences between the *Länder* play an important role, i.e., staff representation in the public sector. Here the Federal Act on Staff Representation (*Bundespersonalvertretungsgesetz*) only sets a framework which is interpreted differently by the acts on staff representation of the various *Länder*.

Until recently, Germany did not have a statutory minimum wage. This mainly can be explained by the fact that in the Nazi period collective bargaining was destroyed and wage policy exclusively executed by the Government. As a reaction to this development, the trade unions and employers' associations agreed after World War II to make wage policy an exclusive matter for collective bargaining. This historical experience also explains why even the trade unions until recently were against a statutory minimum wage. Their view only changed when they realized that due to the erosion of collective bargaining patterns in a number of sectors decent wage could no longer be guaranteed. The statutory minimum wage has been introduced by a law of 2014, effective since the beginning of 2015. Originally, this minimum wage amounted to €8.50 per hour, in 2017 it has been increased to €8.84.

Because German labor law consists of various legal sources, many of which were enacted at different times and spread over a great number of specific acts, it is difficult even for experts to grasp the whole picture. Nevertheless, all attempts to combine at least the principal rules of individual labor law into one single code have failed.

To an increasing extent, the legislature delegates the power to regulate a specific matter to administrative agencies or other bodies. The Constitution (Basic Law) requires that such a delegation be precisely defined so as to avoid the danger of vesting the respective agency or body with undue legislative powers. For the same reason, fundamental decisions cannot be delegated at all by the legislature.

As already indicated, court decisions play a very important role in the field of labor law. Courts not only interpret the general clauses and general terms of laws, but also fill in the gaps left open by the legislature. According to the Labor Courts Act (*Arbeitsgerichtsgesetz*), the Federal Labor Court has sole power to develop the law further. In fact, in the field of labor law, the Federal Labor Court has become at least as important as the legislature. Not surprisingly, there is fierce debate over the proper role of the labor courts, compared to that of the legislature. The central question of this debate is whether the actual role of the courts, particularly that of the Federal Labor Court, still comports with the principle of separation of legislative and judicial powers required by the Constitution (Basic Law). But given legislative inertia or the frequent inability of the legislature to generate the necessary votes on specific issues, the courts have little choice but to act on behalf of the legislature. Thus, the allocation of power discussion remains largely academic.

The normative part of collective agreements addressing such core matters as hiring, wages and termination, stands in contrast to the obligatory part which deals with other rights and duties between the contracting parties in that it directly affects the individual employment relationship. In other words, if rights laid down in normative clauses of collective agreements are violated, the individual employee, or the employer to whom these clauses apply, has recourse to the court. In principle, however, such clauses cover only union members being employed by an employer who himself is a member of the employers' association which signed the respective collective agreement.

The relation between legislation and the normative part of collective bargaining agreements is rather complicated. If there is a legislative act which stipulates a minimum standard, the collective agreement cannot fall below, but can only rise above, this standard. Nevertheless, there are many exceptions in which the legislature explicitly permits a collective agreement to fall below the minimum level. The reason for such legislative leeway is the realization that parties to a collective agreement know better than the legislature what is appropriate in a specific context. Naturally, if the law does not set a minimum standard but only contains nonbinding regulations, the collective agreement may disregard these regulations. The problem is that it is often not clear whether the legislature intended to set binding or nonbinding standards, and it is left to the courts to decide these cases by interpreting the legislative intent.

The relation between collective agreements and court decisions is even more complicated. The problem arises if the courts are setting standards not simply implicated by existing legislation. This judge-made law sets minimum standards and, in principle, excludes clauses in collective agreements which fall below this standard. But this jurisprudence generally entails more freedom for the contracting parties than does legislation. It is virtually impossible to delineate a general borderline because these are matters decided on a case-by-case basis. If, however, a court decision is held to have created merely an optional rule, the contracting parties are certainly at liberty to negotiate different terms in their collective agreements.

The works council and the employer in the private sector (or staff representation and employer in the public sector) may sign works agreements containing normative clauses, having basically the same effect on the individual employment relationship as normative clauses of collective agreements. There is an important difference though: works agreements always cover the entire workforce, whether or not the workers are union members; collective agreements cover only those who are members of the union which signed the respective collective agreement.

The individual labor contract is still an important source of law even for those covered by protective laws, collective agreements and/or works agreements. The area dominated by the individual contract in these cases is above the minimum level already regulated. Thus, the function of the individual labor contract serves mainly to improve the individual working conditions already guaranteed by other sources.

Custom may only be a source of law if it favors employees. Under certain conditions, privileges voluntarily granted by the employer cannot simply be withdrawn. The mere fact that they were granted for a certain period may nevertheless entitle employees to claim their continuation. Such a claim is then treated as if it were based on individual contract.

§11.03   THE SYSTEM OF SPECIALIZED LABOR COURTS

In Germany, specialized labor courts provide the main forum for conflict resolution, both in individual and collective labor disputes. The legal basis for the structure, jurisdiction, and procedure of today's labor judiciary is primarily the Labor Courts Act of 1953, revised in 1979. The German labor court system has three tiers: Labor courts of first recourse, *Land* labor courts, and on top the Federal Labor Court.

Both the labor courts of first recourse and *Land* labor courts are composed of one or more panels, each with a career judge as chairperson and two lay judges, one with an employer background and one with an employee background. *Land* labor courts, as courts of second instance, have exclusive jurisdiction over appeals against decisions of the labor courts of first recourse. Judgments handed down by a *Land* labor court may, under specific conditions, be appealed to the Federal Labor Court which now comprises ten divisions, called "senates." Each senate consists of three career judges and two lay judges from employer and employee sides. Since the Federal Labor Court is exclusively focusing on questions of law and, consequently, is not passing judgment on the facts of a case, the professional element carries more weight than in both courts below where decisions on facts also are at stake.

At the Federal Labor Court there is also a so-called Large Senate, composed of the Court President, one career judge from each of those senates which are not chaired by the Court President, and six lay judges serving in the Federal Labor Court, three from the employers' side and three from the employees' sides. If one senate of the Federal Labor Court wishes to deviate from a decision handed down by another senate or by the Large Senate itself, the senate wishing to deviate must *refer* the matter to the Large Senate. Furthermore, matters of fundamental importance may be referred to the Large Senate provided this is considered necessary for the development of the labor law system or in order to guarantee uniformity of decisions. The explicit competence to decide matters concerning the development of the labor law system reveals that the Large Senate is, within limits, entrusted with tasks akin to those of the legislature.

Although the Federal Labor Court is in principle the final arbiter in labor law matters, its decisions can be challenged as being unconstitutional. If a party believes that the Federal Labor Court's decision violates the Constitution (Basic Law), it may file a complaint of unconstitutionality with the Federal Constitutional Court, which has discretion to accept this matter for a final decision. This instrument is used with increasing frequency, particularly in areas in which the Federal Labor Court's decisions fundamentally influence industrial relations.

If a matter is governed not only by German law but also by EU law, and if the latter is outcome-determinative for the case, labor courts of first recourse and *Land* labor courts may, and the Federal Labor Court must, refer any doubts as to the interpretation of EU law to the Court of Justice of the European Union (CJEU) in Luxembourg for a so-called preliminary ruling. Due to the principle of supremacy of EU law, the decision of the CJEU is binding on all German labor courts and the Federal Constitutional Court (FCC).

As a rule, the career judges of all labor courts are appointed for life after three years of service until they reach retirement age of 65. They can be recalled only under very narrow circumstances. A transfer to another court – even if this means a promotion – is invalid without the judge's consent. Of course, all career judges have graduated from law school and passed the required exams. In addition, at least in principle, they are already specialized in labor law when they join the court.

Lay judges of the Labor Courts of first instance and of the *Land* Labor Courts are appointed for a term of four years by the Government of the respective *Land* from lists submitted by the trade unions and employers' associations of the respective judicial district. These organizations may nominate whoever they think is capable of serving as a lay judge. In actual practice, the lay judges nominated by the trade unions almost always are trade union officials; on the employer's side they may be employers' association officials, members of the management board of companies, individual employers, or other trusted persons. Lay judges on the Federal Labor Court are supposed to have special insight into labor law and labor matters. This requirement is considered to be met if they have served for at least four years in the same capacity in a Labor Court of First Instance or in a *Land* Labor Court.

Just as career judges, lay judges in the labor court system are independent. They can neither be recalled nor transferred, nor are they bound by instructions. The organizations nominating them are prohibited to exert influence on their performance in court.

In Germany, contrary to many other countries, not only trade unions but also individual employees can, and often will be parties in labor disputes. Trade unions have no means to prevent an employee from going to court. These standing rights correspond with deeply rooted concepts of private autonomy, individual dignity and equal protection.

Every case brought before a Labor Court begins with a conciliation hearing, conducted by the career judge sitting alone. This procedure aims at early settlements and, in fact, most cases end in that way.

Due to the specific skills of career labor judges and the participation of qualified lay judges, the system of labor courts on the whole has proven to be rather successful. It has gained acceptance by parties even in cases in which controversial public debate on the issues involved made such acceptance very unlikely.

§11.04   COLLECTIVE LABOR LAW

[A]   Freedom of Association as a Basis

In Germany the freedom to form an association, to join an association, to remain in an association, and to be active in an association is called "positive freedom of associa-tion." Whereas it is perfectly clear that Article 9, paragraph 3 of the Basic Law protects this aspect of freedom of association, there has been controversy over whether and to what extent the same provision also guards against infringements of the so-called negative freedom of association. The Federal Labor Court has held in the affirmative, thus preventing the trade unions from doing anything that might put pressure on a worker to join or stay in the union. Forbidden are, for example, closed shop agree-ments, shop agency agreements and even agreements which are intended to reserve advantages exclusively for trade union members. Nevertheless, in practice it is quite difficult to decide from which point on the trade union violates the negative freedom of association.

The German Basic Law does not only guarantee the individual's freedom of association but also protects collective industrial organizations that have been set up to guard and promote employment and economic conditions of its members, i.e., the so-called collective freedom of association. It is generally agreed that a constitutional guarantee of the individual's freedom of association would be meaningless if the organization itself did not enjoy this protection as well. This is why Article 9, paragraph 3 of the Basic Law is understood to protect the associations' existence, their organiza-tion, and their activities. But when is the existence of an organization threatened? Must this question be evaluated from a short-term, a medium range, or a long-term perspective? And what are the activities protected by this constitutional guarantee? For a long time, the answers to these questions were the subject of many controversies. In the meantime, the Federal Constitutional Court has held repeatedly that the limits are not drawn too narrowly, for example, by granting unions more leeway in using factory premises to promote their services.

Only those associations that seek to safeguard and improve working conditions fall within the scope of Article 9, paragraph 3 of the Basic Law. The Federal Labor Court has developed a whole range of requirements, such as independence and permanence, that associations must meet if they wish to avail themselves of the protection of Article 9, paragraph 3 and to carry out the activities reserved to associations within the meaning of this provision. Only associations fulfilling these criteria are allowed to participate in collective bargaining and to conclude collective agreements.

[B]   Trade Unions

A characteristic feature of today's union structure in Germany is the fact that different political and ideological wings are amalgamated in one association. This means that within the union movement there is no political or ideological fragmentation (so-called principle of amalgamated unions). The exception to this general pattern – the Christian Unions – has so far played only a marginal role.

The second important characteristic of unions in Germany is the fact that they are organized on an industry or branch basis. This means that a union is open to all employees (including those with management functions) in the industry concerned, no matter which trade or occupation they are engaged in. This again implies that there is only one union for all employees of the branch or industry. Industry or branch in this context should be understood in a very broad sense. Thus, for example, the Metal Workers' Union includes the automobile industry, the electrical industry, the ship-building industry, the machine building industry, as well as the computer industry, to mention just a few. There are unions which do not fit in this industry or branch-based pattern, for example, the Union of Education and Science, which is not open to all employees of a particular establishment but only to those who have specific professions and occupations within the system of education and science. A third feature of German trade unions is that they are highly centralized. The main influence emanates from their national headquarters where they develop concepts, policies and strategies. This high degree of centralization explains why German trade unions espouse macro-perspectives whose focus is not on the individual company but the respective sector of economic activity.

The most important associations of employees in Germany are those unions organized in the German Federation of Trade Unions (DGB). Members of this Federation are not individual employees but unions. In the beginning of the 1990s, the Federation embraced sixteen individual unions. Since then, however, several mergers have taken place with the result that only eight unions remain. According to the standing rules of the DGB, member unions must coordinate their fields of organization. These can be modified only in agreement with the union or unions concerned and with the DGB itself.

The DGB is financially supported by the individual unions. Its primary function is to develop and articulate nonbinding policies. On one hand it acts as spokesperson for the labor movement and, on the other hand, as co-coordinator of the policies of its member unions. If asked to do so, the DGB also mediates interunion disputes. It does not conclude collective agreements. This competence lies with its member unions.

Outside of the DGB in recent years trade unions for powerful groups of employees (air pilots, engine drivers in the railway system, medical doctors, etc.) tried to significantly improve the situation of their members. This led to quite a few strikes and finally to a reaction by the legislature as will be explained in greater detail below (*infra* §11.04[D]).

In Germany the rate of unionization has long remained stable, somewhere between 30% to 40% of the relevant workforce. In recent years, there has been a decline. In the meantime, the rate of unionization has fallen below 20%. However, since the middle of the present decade the decline has come to an end and there is already a slight increase.

The role of trade unions as organizations representing the employees' interests is generally accepted in Germany. Trade unions are not only factually integrated in society but have many institutionalized rights of participation. These rights are not limited to matters of the labor market. Among other things, unions are integrated in boards dealing with educational and cultural matters, in boards of mass media, in institutions involved in economic and social security matters, in the labor court and social security court system. In addition to improving and safeguarding working and economic conditions, unions offer a large variety of services to their membership, such as travel agencies and all kinds of insurance plans.

[C]   Employers' Associations

Like the trade unions, the employers' associations also are amalgamated associations, are organized along branches of activity, and are highly centralized. They also do not engage in micromanagement, but focus on larger policy objectives.

There are, in principle, two associations which employers may join. They usually belong to both, to a national association of a branch of industry at the federal level and to a multiindustry Land association which incorporates all trade associations at the *Land* level. Also like trade unions, employers' associations are typically organized on three levels, locally or within a district, statewide, and on a federal level.

The federal trade associations as well as the multiindustrial Land associations belong to an umbrella organization, the Confederation of German Employers' Associations (BDA). According to its standing rules, the task of the Confederation is to represent the socio-political interests of employers beyond the scope of one Land or one economic sector. Its members are not bound by its policies. Neither the Confederation of Employers' Associations nor the multiindustrial associations participate in collective bargaining. Collective bargaining falls within the exclusive competence of the individual employers' associations. However, the Confederation does make recommendations as to bargaining strategies.

Although the degree of organization among German employers used to be relatively high, it has been rapidly declining over the past ten years. One reason is the economic problems that arose after German reunification, particularly in the territory of the former GDR. Even if German employers' associations cover all types and sizes of enterprises within one and the same organization, the rate of participation of small companies is significantly lower than that of big enterprises.

In the public sector there are two employers' associations, one for the *Länder*, the Association of German *Länder*, and one for the municipalities, the Union of Municipal Employers' Association. The latter is a confederation of member organizations operating within a region of a *Land*.

Collective bargaining is sometimes carried out jointly by the two organizations, and sometimes by the two organizations in cooperation with the Federal Government. The more it turns out, however, that collective bargaining has to do with the allocation of cost burdens between the Federal Republic and the individual Länder on one hand, and municipalities on the other, the more difficult it becomes to maintain this joint bargaining structure. The first signs of erosion have surfaced.

[D]   Collective Bargaining

The main function of trade unions and employers' associations is to engage in collective bargaining. The central legal basis for collective bargaining is the Act on Collective Agreements of 1949, last amended in 2015. That Act designates trade unions as the sole parties to a collective agreement on the employees' side and individual employers or associations of employers on the employers' side.

Collective agreements concluded at the company level between a trade union and a single employer are a rarity in Germany. Collective agreements are generally concluded between a trade union and an employers' association. These agreements may cover a particular geographic region in which an industry operates or they may apply to an industry nationwide. In most industries, the territory of Germany is divided into several regions for collective bargaining purposes. The associations are free to determine the geographic scope of the bargaining unit. In some cases these units are identical with the territory of a *Land*.

Because collective bargaining in Germany occurs at a sectoral level, two effects are almost inevitable. First, the terms of the agreement cannot take account of particular circumstances in individual companies. Thus, the standards tend be vague and ambiguous. Second, since the agreements cover a large number of enterprises and employees, public attention and public pressure is ubiquitous. Consequently, parties to collective agreements are under pressure to act in a responsible manner, which means, among other things, that the minimum standards set out in collective agreements generally will not exceed the abilities of small companies within the respective industry. This is why collective agreements are quite often of only limited relevance for the more prosperous companies.

The ultimate decision on what a trade union will demand in the collective bargaining process typically rests with the Federal Executive Board. In most DGB unions the Federal Executive Board is authorized to make binding decisions not only on the specific demands but also on the conclusion and termination of an agreement. Decisions on the employers' side are made by the Federal Executive Board of the respective employers association. If the negotiations fail, the trade union is entitled to go on strike. In response, and to a much more limited extent, the employers' side may call for a lockout. The rules governing both the right of strike and lockout have been developed exclusively by the Federal Labor Court.

Collective agreements cover practically all areas of the private and the public sector. Until the beginning of the economic crisis in the mid-1970s, collective bargaining concentrated mainly on remuneration and other economic benefits, such as compensatory measures in cases of layoffs. Since the1980s, other issues, including the reduction and flexibility of working hours, job security, and vocational training, have become increasingly important.

Collective bargaining is understood to be the main implication of the guarantee of collective freedom of association as provided in Article 9, paragraph 3 of the Basic Law. But what exactly is negotiable under this provision which entrusts unions and others with the task to "safeguard and improve working and economic conditions"? Does this formula include decisions on investment, pricing, and other matters that traditionally have been within the realm of management only? Because Article 9, paragraph 3 competes with other, fundamental constitutional rights – in particular with the property rights spelled out in Article 14 – there is widespread agreement that the phrase "working and economic conditions" must be interpreted more narrowly. Collective agreements may influence the costs for business decisions by setting standards for remuneration, vacation days, working hours and the like. Collective agreements may also regulate the effects of such decisions, for example, by stipulating the consequences in cases of layoffs. However, basic business decisions, such as investments and plant closings, fall outside the bargaining process and are left to management alone. Even so, borderline questions remain and answers are not always clear-cut.

It is characteristic for collective agreements in Germany to contain provisions with normative, that is direct and mandatory, effects on all employment relationships to which they apply. There are two types of normative provisions: those relating to the individual employment relationship in its strict sense (individual normative provisions), and those transcending the individual employment relationship, such as clauses relating to work organization and the works council system (collective normative provisions).

Individual normative provisions may regulate the content, the conclusion, and the termination of the individual contract of employment. Normative provisions concerning the content of the employment contract may stipulate all terms and conditions of an employment contract, including pay, working hours, job protection, working conditions, and required skills. These content-related provisions can also cover mere corollaries of the employment relationship, such as employee liability or time limits for asserting entitlements. Any individually agreed arrangement which conflicts with an individual normative provision of a collective agreement is null and void in principle. Deviations from the collective agreement are lawful only when the agreement expressly permits them or if they provide more favorable conditions for the employee. The principle of more favorable conditions as such is uncontested. Individual normative provisions are legally binding only if both parties to the individual contract of employment, employee and employer, are members of the respective party to the collective agreement, i.e., if the employee is organized in the contracting union and is employed by an employer who is a member of the contracting employers' association. Most enterprises, however, employ both union and nonunion members. Thus, there are two different legal regimes applicable to the two groups of employees. In principle, the employer could impose working conditions on nonunion members that are below the collectively agreed minimum standards without violating equal treatment rights. In the real world, things are different. If the employer is bound by a collective agreement, the working conditions set out therein are often extended to nonunion members as well by reference clauses in the individual employment contract.

In spite of these reference clauses, the coverage by collective agreements steadily has been reduced in the recent past. There is another possibility to extend the scope of application of collective agreements to nonorganized employers and nonunionized employees, which is the so-called declaration of general binding. However, the law imposes high thresholds for the use of this instrument. General application can be requested only if a minimum of 50% of employees falling within the scope of the collective agreement work for employers with a binding commitment to collective agreements. In addition, the general application of collective agreements can only be enacted by the Government after an agreement of a committee of an equal number of representatives from the employers' and employees' umbrella organizations and if it is in the general public interest.

Amending the Act on Collective Agreements in 2014, the legislature facilitated the declaration of general binding by removing the requirement of 50% and by defining the general public interest in a way which makes it easier to pass such a declaration. Now, the general public interest is to be assumed if the collective agreement has gained main relevance in the sector for which it is made or if the declaration of general binding is necessary to prevent bad economic consequences. Thereby, the legislature has significantly reduced the leeway for the government's decision.

However, in spite of this amendment the number of declarations of general binding has not yet significantly increased. The mechanism still appears to be too complicated. Also, trade unions still seem to hesitate to provide the benefits of collective agreements to nonunionized employees.

Collective normative provisions apply directly and are mandatory to all establishments of an employer who belongs to the contracting employers' association, whether or not the employees are members of the contracting trade union. Consequently, distinctions between union and nonunion members are not to be made. This difference between the applicability of individual normative provisions and collective normative provisions is based on practical considerations. Patterns set by collective normative provisions only operate in practice if they are applied homogeneously. Drawing a distinction between individual normative provisions and collective normative provisions is not always easy but, in light of the different scopes of application, necessary in every single case. In practice this exercise is a source for never-ending controversies.

The Act on Collective Agreements did not address the problem of how to handle several collective agreements treating the same subject and covering the same company. Originally the Federal Labor Court ruled that there can be only one collective agreement on the same subject for a company and resolved the conflict by the principle of specialty. According to this principle, the trade union which is only acting for special professions within a branch of an industry, or for a region within a branch, has priority compared to a trade union acting for the whole branch. However, in 2010 the same court performed a spectacular turnaround and ruled that there can be different collective agreements concluded with different trade unions on the same subject in a company for the simple reason that individual norms only apply to the members of the respective trade union. This new approach was opposed by the DGB unions as well as by the employers' associations. The DGB unions felt threatened by the already mentioned trade unions for specific powerful groups and the employers were afraid of chaos, in particular in view of strike activities. Their unified pressure let to a highly controversial law in 2015, according to which only the collective agreement of the trade union which has the majority of members in the companies is to be applied. The trade unions representing specific professional groups went to the Federal Constitutional Court claiming that this law violates their constitutionally guaranteed freedom of association. In 2017 the Court rejected these claims, at least in principle. The legislature now is required to amend the law again, thereby taking care of the legitimate interests of these minority trade unions and their members. It is safe to say that this task will be difficult to perform.

[E]   The Works Council System

[1]   The Basic Organizational Structure

The venue for employee involvement is the works council in the private sector and the staff council in the public sector. The following account will focus on the private sector. The system of employee involvement is probably the most important characteristic of German labor law. It has implications for practically all aspects of individual and collective labor law.

The legal basis for the works council is the Works Constitution Act of 1972. That Act was significantly amended in 2001 to reflect the radical changes which the organizational structures of companies had undergone through such advents as outsourcing and joint ventures.

Contrary to many other countries, works councils in Germany consist exclusively of employee representatives. Works councils act as counterparts to management. Works council members are elected by secret ballot by all employees who are over 18 years of age. Employees over 18 years of age, who have been employed for at least six months, may be elected for a term of four years; there are no term limits.

Section 1 of the Works Constitution Act, provides for the election of works council members in every establishment with more than five employees over 18 years of age, provided three of them have been employed for at least six months. Nevertheless, many small and medium-sized enterprises (SME) do not have a works council. Only larger companies fully comply with the law. Ultimately, it is up to the employees of the establishment to establish a works council. There is no sanction if they fail to do so, but employees who do not take the initiative relinquish all rights vested in the works council by law. In order to encourage the creation of more such councils in SME, the amendment of 2001 facilitated the election procedure. That change has led to a significant increase of work councils in SME.

As a matter of law, works councils are not affiliated with trade unions. They represent all employees of an establishment. But in spite of the institutional separation between unions and works councils, close links do exist, because the unions succeeded in influencing the composition of works councils. The large majority of works council members are union members.

According to the Works Constitution Act, the size of the works council depends on the number of employees in the establishment. Thus, in establishments with up to 20 employees there is only one council member. Works councils in firms with more than 20 and up to 50 employees are entitled to three members. Companies with more than 7,000 and up to 9,000 employees have 31 works council members. Above this level, the number of works council members increases by two for each additional 3,000 employees.

Since the last amendment of 2001, manual workers and white-collar employees are no longer treated as separate groups. According to a provision also introduced through this amendment, men and women must be represented in the works council according to their proportional rate within the workforce.

If works councils are established in different establishments of a multiplant enterprise, they shall form a company works council. Each works council appoints two of its members to the company works council. The works councils of the individual establishments are not subordinate to the company works council. The company works council is only authorized to deal with matters which either cannot be resolved within the individual establishment or which are delegated to it by an individual works council.

It is up to the company works councils of enterprises belonging to one group of companies to establish a group works council at the level of the parent company. Each company works council would have to appoint two of its members.

The works council may delegate specific functions and rights to subcommittees which play an important role in practice. In enterprises with at least 100 employees, a committee dealing with economic affairs shall be appointed by the works council (or by the company works council in a multiestablishment enterprise). This committee consists of at least three and at most seven members. One of the members of the economic committee has to be a member of the works council in order to establish a communication link. All other members shall be employees of the enterprise, but do not have to be works council members.

According to the 1972 Act, all employees of an establishment should meet four times each year. These so-called works meetings take place during working hours and do not entail any loss of wages. Works meetings must be initiated and chaired by the works council. The works council is supposed to report on its activities. The employer shall be invited to the works meetings. He, or his representative, is entitled to address the works meeting. At least once a year the employer, or his representative, shall report to the works meeting on matters of personnel policy and social affairs in the establishment, as well as on the present and prospective economic situation of the establishment. It is evident that the law attaches great importance to the works meeting as a communication link between works council and its constituency. Nevertheless, in this area the legal prescriptions do not correspond with reality.

Empirical studies show that only in a small proportion of establishments all four works meetings are annually held, and that in quite a few establishments such meetings do not occur at all.

The Works Constitution Act 1972 also introduced a measure of representation for those workers who have not reached the age of majority. The organizational structure, as well as the election procedure, is very much identical to that of the works council, except that the juvenile delegation is not entitled to act directly as a counterpart to management.

According to the Works Constitution Act, executive staff is not covered by works council representation. Members of this group are neither permitted to participate in the election of works council members, nor can they be elected. The definition of this group was very controversial when the Act was promulgated in 1972. The legislature did not actually resolve the conflict but, instead, employed broad and unspecific language, thus forcing the courts to step in with their interpretation. The Courts strictly limited the scope of this group, and a 1989 amendment to the Act codified this jurisprudence. In the same year, an Act on a Representative Body for Executive Staff was passed, providing the legal basis for separate executive staff representation. Representative bodies of executive staff only enjoy information and consultation rights.

[2]   The Link to the Trade Unions

Works councils and trade unions are for historical reasons institutionally separated. Over time, however, trade unions have succeeded in overcoming the institutional pattern of dual representation due to the fact that a great number of works council members are also union members. In addition, the Works Constitution Act grants unions with at least one member in a company the right to become active within that company. Thus in companies without works council, unions may take the initiative and call a works meeting during which the employees may decide whether they wish to establish a works council. Furthermore, if no works meeting has taken place for a certain period, unions may insist on having one. Considering the widespread nonexistence of works councils and the low frequency of works meetings, it is apparent that these initiatives play only a marginal role in practice. More important, then, are the control functions unions assume. The unions are legally empowered to control the works council election procedure. They may even move for the nullification of a works council election by court decision if legal rules were disregarded. If a member of the works council or the works council as such has violated its duties of office, the union may obtain a court decision excluding a works council member from office or dissolving the works council. If the employer violates the duties imposed on him by the Works Constitution Act, unions are entitled to call for the imposition of sanctions by the labor courts. Although works meetings do not take place in public sessions, external union representatives have a right to be present. At the request of at least one-fourth of the works council members, an external official of a union represented in the works council is entitled to participate in the works council meeting. The same rule applies to committee meetings, including meetings of the economic committee. Provided the employer was put on notice, agents of unions that are represented within an establishment must be granted access to the establishment. Works council members are entitled to participate in training courses at the employer's expenses. These courses are supposed to impart the knowledge necessary for works council members to fulfill their task. Because these courses are almost exclusively offered by trade unions, they obviously serve as a powerful tool to bring works council members in line with union positions.

To obtain an accurate picture of the influence of trade unions on works council policy, however, one has to go beyond the formal structure of the works council system. Informally in some branches, and particularly in larger corporations, the unions install so-called trusted representatives inside the establishment. Either appointed by the union or elected by the union members employed in the respective establishment, these "trusted representatives" establish the link of communication between trade union members and trade union administration. In addition, these representatives support, influence, and to some extent even control works council activities. Naturally, their influence varies from establishment to establishment, but often, it is considerable.

[3]   The Legal Position of the Works Council Members

During their term of office, works council members can only be recalled on the basis of a labor court decision, which may either be initiated by a union represented in the establishment or by one-fourth of the employees, or by the employer. An individual works council member may be removed from office, or the works council as a whole may be dissolved, only if the member or the council severely violated the Works Constitution Act or neglected the duties pertaining to the office. Such claims are hardly ever taken to court and are rarely successful. Works council members (as well as members of juvenile delegations) enjoy far reaching protection against dismissals. According to Section 78 of the Works Constitution Act, works council members may neither enjoy privileges nor may they suffer disadvantages as a consequence of holding office. Essentially, this general rule has three specific implications: first, works council members are not entitled to receive additional payments or benefits as a compensation for holding office. Second, it is guaranteed that their remuneration stays in lockstep with the wage increases they would have received had they not joined the works council. Third and perhaps most importantly, members are guaranteed to stay employed in a position that corresponds to their level of occupational skills. One corollary of this occupational standard guarantee is that works council members must not be excluded from further vocational training which other employees may enjoy. All these guarantees apply during the term of office and until one year after it has expired.

Works council members are entitled to be released from their duty to work without loss of pay "to the extent that is necessary for properly carrying out their functions, taking into account the size and nature of the establishment." In other words, the time to be released from work is not fixed, but depends on the circumstances of the particular case. According to the rules developed by the labor courts, the works council members decide what time is necessary to carry out their functions. The employer may refuse to release a works council member from his job duties only in cases of flagrant abuse.

Large enterprises are required to release a certain number of works council members entirely from their ordinary job duties for the full term of their office. The exact number varies with the number of employees, but the rule does not apply at all to firms with less than 200 employees. The possibility of a full release from work duties is one of the most important features of the works constitution in Germany. Its effects are ambiguous. On the one hand, it leads to more professionalism and greater efficiency on the part of works council members. On the other hand, these professional works council members find it difficult, or unattractive, to be reintegrated in the rank and file when their term of office expires. This is why these members often work hard on their reelection and treat their status as a lifetime career. Thus, there is some valid concern that the system fosters a functionary-driven bureaucratic power structure with self-serving interests that distracts from the original tasks.

[4]   The Financial Structure and the Basic Duties

It is the employer who bears all the expenses arising from the activities of the works council. In addition, the employer must provide the necessary accommodation, facilities (including books and periodicals on labor law), and office staff required for meetings, consultations, and day-to-day operation of the works council. The exact scope of the duty to pay works council expenses is subject to many controversies. The Federal Labor Court invokes the principle of proportionality to decide such controversies. It requires that there be a reasonable relationship between the costs on the one hand and the size as well as the financial resources of the company on the other hand.

The employer must provide the works council with all the information, including the files, the works council needs to carry out its tasks properly. Under certain rather limited circumstances, the works council is entitled to call on the advice of experts. The restrictions on this choice are in place because the expenses are borne by the employer. This is why in most cases union officials fulfill the function of providing expert advice to works councils free of charge.

Works councils are required by law to cooperate with the employer in good faith. Consequently, industrial action as a means of conflict resolution is explicitly prohibited. This, of course, does not mean that works council members are not allowed to participate in legal strikes called by a trade union. But according to the prevailing view among labor law scholars, the works council as a representative body must remain neutral even during a lawful strike. Subject to controversy is the question whether, and to what extent, the participation and codetermination rights of the works council are suspended during a strike. At present, uncertainty prevails.

The Works Constitution Act contains a provision which prevents the works council from divulging information that was explicitly classified as secret by the employer. This applies only to information acquired by virtue of holding the office of a works council. The ban on disclosing information applies neither to the exchange of information between members of the works council nor to the communication with other bodies of workers' representation in the company. Not infrequently, this kind of information forms the basis for the decision of a works council on specific matters. On the other hand, the works council must not communicate such facts to its constituency. The resultant lack of transparency can be a source of alienation between the works council and the employees it represents.

[5] The Arbitration Committee

Since strikes and lockouts as means of conflict resolution are only legal in the context of collective bargaining, but are expressly prohibited under the Works Constitution Act, a special dispute settlement body has been created by law. This institution, the arbitration committee, can either be formed as a permanent committee or as an ad hoc committee for each case as necessary. In practice, the permanent committee is never used for fear that this body might be permanently biased in one way or another.

One half of the arbitration committee members are appointed by the employer, the other half by the works council. A neutral president, chosen by both sides, chairs the committee. There rarely is agreement over who this person should be. Absent an agreement, the Labor Court will appoint the president, typically a career labor judge. The total number of arbitration committee members is determined by agreement between the works council and the employer. If an agreement cannot be reached, either side may request the Labor Court to decide the matter. A special procedure regulates the formation and composition of an arbitration committee and expedites the resolution of conflicts. Decisions can be reached within a few days. The costs of the arbitration committee, as all other costs associated with the works constitution, are to be borne by the employer.

In reaching its decision, the arbitration committee must take into account the interests of the establishment and the interests of the employees concerned. Employer and/or works council may appeal to the Labor Court within two weeks of the date of notification of the award. On appeal, the Court may annul, but not rewrite, the decision of the committee only if the arbitration committee exceeded its discretionary powers. If that happens, the works council and the employer may again call on the arbitration committee. However, in practice, appeals are very rare so that, typically, the arbitration committee's first decision becomes final. The law requires that decisions of the arbitration committee be recorded in writing, signed by the chairperson, and forwarded to the employer and the works council. During the deliberations of the committee, outsiders are not admitted. The exclusion of the public is considered necessary to allow for compromises that may be necessary to reach equitable results.

[6]   The Works Council's Rights of Participation

The Works Constitution Act grants the works council an array of specific rights of participation, which include access to information, and the right to be heard, control, and veto rights, and the most important right of all, the right to codetermination. In matters in which this right applies the decision-making process is no longer the prerogative of management. Codetermination in this context means that management cannot make any decisions without the consent of the works council. In the absence of consensus, any unilateral move by management would be illegal. However, codetermination means even more, it gives both sides an equal voice in the decision-making process.

To illustrate the codetermination process, consider the conflict over working short hours. Whether management or the works council wishes to introduce this tool, the parties must first reach agreement on all kinds of specific questions, including whether short-time working should be introduced at all, when it is to begin and when to end, and which groups of employees will be affected. In short, every single relevant aspect is subject to codetermination. If management and the works council cannot agree on these matters, the conflict is referred to the arbitration committee. Its decision is binding on management and the works council. Either party may appeal to the Labor Court, but, as stated before, the court's power to review is very limited.

Participatory rights of the works council are subdivided into three areas, covering social, personnel, and economic matters. Personnel matters include personnel planning and vocational training as well as hiring, transfer, or dismissal of employees. Economic matters are defined as everything concerning the economic policy of management, such as investment, production and marketing. The most difficult questions have arisen in connection with social matters. It is this area in which the works council is vested with the most extensive rights to codetermination. According to Section 87 of the Works Constitution Act, the works council enjoys these rights in the following cases:

(1) matters relating to order within the establishment and conduct of the employees in the establishment;
(2) beginning and termination of daily working hours, including breaks and allocation of working hours over the single days of the week;
(3) temporary reduction or extension of the usual working hours in the establishment;
(4) time, place, and mode of payment of wages and salaries;

(5) establishment of general principles regulating annual vacations, establishment of a vacation schedule, as well as fixing individual employee vacation schedule if employer and employee fail to reach an agreement;

(6) introduction and use of technical devices designed to monitor the employees' conduct or performance;

(7) regulations for the prevention of work accidents and occupational diseases [...];

(8) form, structure, and administration of social services whose scope is limited to the establishment, to the enterprise, or to the group;

(9) assignment and cancellation of rooms, apartments or houses rented to employees in view of their employment relationship, as well as general determination of the conditions of using these facilities;

(10) questions relating to remuneration arrangements, including in particular the establishment of principles of remuneration and the introduction and application of new remuneration methods as well as the modification of existing methods;

(11) determination of piece-rates, premiums and other comparable payments based on results, including money factors;

(12) establishment of principles for the handling of proposals for improvements;

(13) principles on the performance of team-work. [...]

In personnel matters, a right to codetermination exists in only a few areas, for example, as regards the content of guidelines on selection, the content of written questionnaires, and the establishment of general criteria for the evaluation of test results. As far as in-house vocational training is concerned, the works council has a rather strong position as to the appointment of training personnel and selection of employees who are allowed to participate in such programs. The works council also enjoys significant rights of participation concerning the hiring of employees, their dismissal and transfer, even if below the level of codetermination.

In economic matters it is the economic affairs committee which enjoys specific rights under the Works Constitution Act. But the competence of this committee does not go beyond a mere right to information and consultation. The employer may even refuse to hand over information if disclosure to the committee members could endanger business or trade secrets.

More important than the rights of the economic affairs committee are participation rights of works councils in specific economic decisions which may cause substantial disadvantages to the workforce of the establishment or to a significant part of it. According to Section 111 of the Works Constitution Act, the works council enjoys these rights in companies with a minimum of twenty employees with respect to the following decisions: the reduction of operations, partial or total closings, a transfer of the establishment or transfer of essential parts of it, a merger with other establishments or the breaking up of establishments, basic organizational changes, basic changes of the purpose of the establishment, changes affecting the plant facilities, the introduction of new work methods and production processes. Furthermore, a reduction of the workforce is considered tantamount to a reduction of operations. Thus, the case of collective dismissal is, in principle, also included.

In all these cases, management must provide full information in advance in order to enter into negotiations with the works council. "Information in advance" means that it has to be given at an early planning stage. "Full information" means that management must not only disclose its plans but must supply information on all possible alternatives and modifications which were taken into account at any time. This obligation to disclose enables the works council to have some input in the decision making process.

In addition to supplying information, management is required to reach a so-called reconciliation of interests with the works council. This means that management must make an effort to reach an agreement with the works council on whether, and in what manner, the management plans will be carried out. If the parties fail to agree, either side can call on the President of the Land Employment Office for mediation. If this mediation is not successful or does not occur because neither party called for it, either side may take the issue to the arbitration committee. But in this instance, the arbitration committee has no power to issue a binding decision. It can only present a proposal which may or may not be acceptable to the parties Thus, the law provides a procedure for the reconciliation of interests, but if the procedure fails, management has the final say. Ultimately, then, the works council has no legal power to force management in a certain direction.

Regardless of whether management has fulfilled its duties to inform the works council and has tried to reach a reconciliation of interests, the works council is always entitled to enforce a so-called social plan. A social plan means nothing less than a special works agreement to compensate or reduce the disadvantages that employees suffer in the event of a substantial change of the establishment or in cases of insolvency. A social plan is not confined to financial compensation but may include important affirmative measures such as retraining programs and transfer of employees to other establishments of the enterprise. If an agreement on a social plan cannot be reached, either side is entitled to appeal to the arbitration committee which then acts as the final decision-maker. Its decision is binding on both sides. Except in cases of insolvency, which cannot be treated here, there are no minimum or maximum financial limits for a social plan.

In view of high unemployment, trade unions and employers' associations have developed models of social plans that favor job skills improvement and reintegration measure over financial compensation. For example, in 1998 when a large chemical company went out of business, a new enterprise was founded to employ those workers who had neither retired nor found other jobs. The sole object of the new company was employee training geared toward occupational as well as job application skills. In order to reach the goal of finding new jobs within a two-year period at other companies, the parties even agreed to engage an outplacement service which ordinarily is reserved for executive staff only. Similar models in other areas, such as in the banking and transport (railway) sectors, were also successful.

In 1998, the conclusion of such social plans giving reintegration into employment priority over financial compensation gained strong support from the legislature.

According to Sections 254–259 of Part III of the Social Security Code, the Employment Office can sponsor measures provided for in a social plan that aim at the reintegration of employees who would presumably be unable to find a permanent position without such a plan. This solution is available if it can be expected that these persons would otherwise be entitled to other payments from the Employment Office.

[7]   Works Agreements

Employer and works council may conclude so-called works agreements not only in matters in which the works council has a right to codetermination, but in all matters relating to labor-management relations within the establishment. Of course, without codetermination rights for the works council there would be little leverage to induce management to sign such an agreement.

Works agreements must be in writing and signed by both sides. The employer must give the employees the opportunity to familiarize themselves with the text of the agreement by displaying it in a suitable place in the establishment. Just as a collective agreement, a works agreement may establish rights and duties between the concluding parties (employer and works council). Furthermore, it may contain individual normative provisions and collective normative provisions. Such normative clauses have a direct and mandatory effect on the parties to the individual employment relationship. Works agreements may be concluded for a definite or for an indefinite period. Unless otherwise agreed upon, works agreements may be terminated on three months' notice, but the parties remain free to agree on different terms.

Works agreements dealing with remuneration or other working conditions are only permitted if the same matter is not already regulated in a collective agreement. A matter is considered "already regulated" if it is usually regulated in collective agreements in the respective region and industry branch. In other words, an existing collective agreement that covers the region and the industry branch, preempts a works agreement even if the former does not apply to the specific establishment and to the employment relationships within this establishment. As a result, even in establishments where neither the employer is a member of the employers' association nor the employees are union members, remuneration or other working conditions cannot be regulated by works agreements. This rather rigid rule only applies to works agreements on matters in which the works council has no right to codetermination. In these cases the works council has no power to induce the management to sign such an agreement. The reason for excluding such works agreements in cases of already existing collective agreements is to prevent the works council from competing with trade unions. Such a competition is seen as a threat to the collective bargaining system. Should the system of collective agreements break down, then there would be no adequate substitute at plant level where works agreements cannot be enforced by the works council. Thus, in order to safeguard the strength of the collective bargaining system, the status of collective agreements as exclusive means to regulate working conditions was long left untouched.

This general rule notwithstanding, parties to a collective agreement may authorize that works agreements supplement the collective agreement. This may be done by including a so-called opening clause into the collective agreement. In the past, few collective agreements contained opening clauses because the unions feared that this device might destroy the homogeneous standards within the branch of activity and undermine the basis for solidarity within the trade union. In the meantime, however, the trade unions have changed their approach. Nowadays the inclusion of opening clauses into sectoral collective agreements has become the rule. Thereby, the collective agreements have become much more flexible and the collaboration between trade unions and works councils have been intensified significantly.

[F]   Workers' Representation in the Supervisory Board

[1]   Three Different Models

Workers' representation on company boards is understood to be one further step toward changing the power structure in the economic field. The first successes in implementing such change occurred in the coal, iron, and steel industries. After World War II, the enterprises in these areas of industry faced the danger of being totally dismantled by the Allied Forces. To avoid what would have amounted to obliteration, these industries sought the support of the unions. Because the unions had not been affiliated with the Nazi regime, they had an important voice in this context. In order to gain the support of trade unions, the leaders of the coal, iron, and steel industries offered equal representation of employees on the supervisory boards of the companies in exchange. After much controversy, this model featuring strong employees' representative rights was established and confirmed by the legislature in 1951. This historical development explains why until today the representation rules in the coal, iron, and steel industries differ from those applying to other German industrial sectors.

By 1952 the political and economic circumstances had changed: With the danger of dismantlement banned, employers were in no need to enlist the support of the unions and were no longer prepared to make concessions. Not surprisingly, then, the 1952 Works Constitution Act introduced a model of employee representation on the supervisory board which remained far below the level of representation reached in the coal, iron, and steel industries. In the years following the adoption of the Works Constitution Act, the unions undertook great efforts to extend the 1951 model of the coal, iron, and steel industries to all areas of industry. In 1976, these efforts led to a third model which represents a compromise between the previous two. All three different models still exist today and will be discussed below (infra at §11.04[F][3]–[5]).

[2]   The Function of the Supervisory Board

In order to appreciate the impact of employee representation on the supervisory board, it is necessary to understand the general role of this board within the power structure of an enterprise. Under company law, the supervisory board is a company organ which must be present in registered cooperative societies and public limited companies. In the case of private limited companies, it is mandatory only if certain preconditions exist, in all other cases it is optional. The Acts providing employee representation on the supervisory board did not create new institutions. They simply fit employee representation into the traditional corporate framework, modifying only the composition of the governing bodies. The supervisory and management boards, which existed prior to the introduction of employee participation, retained their traditional functions. The only difference is that these boards are no longer composed exclusively of individuals guided by the interest of the owners.

According to the German two boards system of company law, it is exclusively the management board which represents and manages the enterprise. The supervisory board has only two basic functions, to elect the members of the management board, and to supervise the activities of the management board. The members of the management board are elected by majority vote of the supervisory board for a certain period. In order to discharge its monitoring tasks, the supervisory board has extended rights of access to information. At least once a year, the management board must supply the supervisory board with comprehensive information on all basic issues concerning the management of the enterprise. Furthermore, the supervisory board or any member of the supervisory board can request at any time additional information on matters of importance to the enterprise. The management board is statutorily required to meet such a request.

The shareholders' meeting, or even the supervisory board itself, may extend the powers of the supervisory board by majority vote. Either one can establish rules which require the consent of the supervisory board to certain types of managerial decisions. However, even if the supervisory board withholds its consent, the management board may nevertheless effectuate its decision by obtaining approval in the course of a shareholders' meeting. Such approval always remedies a lack of consent on the part of the supervisory board.

The extent of the supervisory board's authority depends on the legal status of the company. As compared with other models of company law, the supervisory board of a public limited company (stock corporation) is in the strongest position. Of course, the authority of even that supervisory board pales in comparison with any management board, because it is the latter that is actually in charge of the company's operations and in a position to employ a staff of experts who prepare its decisions.

[3] The Model of the Coal, Iron, and Steel Industries

This model is based on equal representation of shareholders and employees on the supervisory board, the chairpersonship being reserved for a "neutral" person, elected by majority vote of both, employee representatives and shareholder representatives. The Act on Employee Representation in the Coal, Iron, and Steel Industries of 1951 applies to enterprises that were created as public limited companies (stock corporations) and private limited companies employing more than 1,000 employees.

In general, the supervisory board consists of eleven members. In very large enterprises the number may increase to fifteen or even twenty-one members. Taking the normal case of a supervisory board with eleven members, shareholders and employees each appoint five members.

At least two of the five employee representatives must belong to the workforce of the enterprise. The remaining three employee representatives need not be employed by the enterprise, but may be external representatives. Whereas two of the three external members always are members of the respective unions, the third member (the so-called additional member) must neither be a trade union member nor an employee of the respective enterprise nor have economic interests in the enterprise. After consultation with the unions represented in the enterprise, the works council nominates the employee representative candidates belonging to the workforce of the enterprise by secret ballot. The unions represented in the enterprise propose the candidates for the remaining three seats, and the works council formally nominates these representatives, again by secret ballot. Finally, all nominated representatives must be elected and confirmed by the shareholders' assembly. However, the nominations are binding on the assembly. This election is only a formality which reflects the original structure of the electoral power of the shareholders' assembly.

The neutral chairperson of the supervisory board is nominated by a majority vote of the other members of the supervisory board (shareholder representatives and employee representatives). This nomination is again binding on the shareholders' meeting, which should formally elect and confirm the chairperson. If a majority decision on the supervisory board cannot be obtained, a rather complicated procedure provides alternative means for the nomination of the candidate. Should this procedure fail, it is up to the shareholders to decide. A neutral chairperson is deemed necessary to ensure that the supervisory board can overcome a deadlock between shareholder representatives and employee representatives.

The Act on Employee Representation in the Coal, Iron, and Steel Industries of 1951 does not only provide for employee representation on the supervisory board. It is the only Act that also provides for some employee representation on the management board. The elected representative, the "employee director in charge of personnel and social affairs of the enterprise," is a full member of the management board, who enjoys the same legal status as all other board members. This representative cannot be elected against the majority of votes of the employee representatives on the supervisory board.

In the period after 1951, it turned out that employee representation in enterprises of the coal, iron, and steel industries was not very effective if the representatives did not have access to the supervisory board of the parent company of the group. Several Acts introduced and expanded these representation rights at the level of parent companies. Today, it applies whether coal, iron, and steel activities within a group amount to a share of at least 20% of all activities, or if at least 2,000 employees are employed in those industries. This legal development notwithstanding, the number of companies and groups that are actually subject to the rules of this model is steadily decreasing.

[4]   The Model of 1952

Established by the Works Constitution Act of 1952 and reformulated as "Law on One Third Participation" in 2004 ("Drittelbeteiligungsgesetz"), this model also covers only certain types of enterprises. These are public limited companies (stock corporations), private limited companies, cooperatives, and mutual insurance companies. The Act, prescribing rules on employees' representation, only applies to companies with a supervisory board. While company law requires all public limited companies to establish this board, other enterprises are forced to do so only if additional legal and factual circumstances are present. All enterprises covered by this model must employ at least 500 employees.

According to the Act, one-third of the supervisory board members must be employee representatives. The size of the supervisory board depends on the rules of company law. If only one or two employee representatives can be elected, these representatives must be in the employ of the enterprise. If more than two representatives are up for election, at least two must be employees of the enterprise. The additional representatives may, but do not have to, be elected from external candidates. Works councils as well as groups of one tenth of the employees (or at least 100 employees) of the enterprise are entitled to nominate candidates. Employee representatives are elected by all employees of the enterprise who are over 18 years of age.

[5]   The Model of 1976

Like the other Acts concerning employee representation on the supervisory board, the Codetermination Act of 1976 is applicable to a limited number of types of enterprises with a certain size. It covers public limited companies (stock corporations), partnerships limited by shares, private limited companies, and cooperatives which, in principle, must employ at least 2,000 employees. Under certain circumstances, involving the formation of partnerships, the Act also governs enterprises with less than 2,000 employees. As far as holding companies are concerned, the Codetermination Act 1976 applies to enterprises employing less than 2,000 employees, provided that the holding company and the German group entities employ in the aggregate at least 2,000 persons.

While the Act applied to 481 companies in 1983, that number rose to 728 in 1996. The number of companies and corporate groups with more than 2,000 employees that are not subject to codetermination amounts to about 75. If an enterprise covered by the 1976 Codetermination Act is a holding company, the employees of the subsidiaries participate in the election of the employee representatives to the supervisory board of the holding company. Therefore, the number of subsidiaries which are indirectly covered by the 1976 Codetermination Act is significantly higher than the above mentioned number of directly affected enterprises. However, foreign subsidiaries are not included. In the mid-1980s, some 4.5 million employees worked in enterprises to which the 1976 Act applied. By 1996 that number had risen to 5 million.

In enterprises covered by the 1976 Codetermination Act, the supervisory board consists of an equal number of shareholder representatives and employee representatives. The numbers are as follows: in enterprises with up to 10,000 employees 12 representatives, 6 from each side; in enterprises with more than 10,000 and up to 20,000 employees 16 representatives, 8 from each side; and in enterprises with more than 20,000 employees 20 representatives, 10 from each side. The company statutes may provide for more representatives. A board consisting of 12 members may be enlarged to 16 members, and a board consisting of 16 members may grow to a maximum of 20 members.

On supervisory boards with 12 or 16 members, 2 seats are reserved for trade union representatives, and on supervisory boards with 20 members, there are three such seats. The remaining seats on the employees' side (four, six, or seven, depending on the size of the board) are reserved for the workers and the executive staff of the enterprise. Each group, if represented at all, is guaranteed at least one seat. Although the exact distribution depends on the proportion in which these groups are represented, executive staff is in fact almost always overrepresented.

In holding companies, employees of the holding company, as well as their colleagues employed in their subsidiaries within Germany, may vote and be elected to the supervisory board. For purposes of election to the supervisory board, the employees of all subsidiaries of a group within Germany are considered to be employees of the holding company. It became controversial whether the fact that employees of subsidiaries in other EU Member States are not entitled to vote is in line with EU law, in particular with the employees' right to freedom of movement. By a judgment of July 2017 the CJEU has rejected these doubts.

The procedure for the election of employee representatives is perplexingly complicated. For present purposes, it suffices to sketch its main features. There are two types of elections, direct election by majority vote of all employees of the enterprise, and election by delegates. In enterprises with up to 8,000 employees, direct election is the rule, whereas in enterprises of a larger size, election by delegates is the normal procedure. All employees of the companies, including those who are not union members, elect the trade union representatives. The trade unions represented in the enterprise or in the group may propose candidates but, in contrast to the de facto binding nature of nominations under the coal, iron, and steel model (*supra*, §11.04[D][3]), nominations under the 1976 Codetermination Act are not necessarily successful. Instead, it is the vote of the employees that actually determines who will represent the union on the supervisory board.

The chairperson and the vice-chairperson of the supervisory board are elected by a two-thirds majority of the board members. If an election fails to yield a two-thirds majority, a frequent result, the shareholder representatives elect the chairperson, and the employees elect the vice-chairperson from among their own group. In practice, then, the position of the chairperson is reserved to the shareholders' representatives.

Thus, in contrast to the coal, iron, and steel industries model, which features a neutral chairperson in charge of overcoming deadlocks on the board, the 1976 Codetermination Act favors a shareholder-selected chairperson who has the casting vote.

The vast majority of employee representatives on the supervisory board are members of a trade union. This is not only true for the external representatives but also for those employed in the respective enterprise or group. The number of nonunionized members only amounts to about 3%. Not surprisingly, representatives of executive staff usually do not belong to a trade union.

[6]   The Legal Position of Employee Representatives

Employee and shareholder representatives on the supervisory board are coequals. The law assigns identical rights and obligations to either group. Employee representatives are privy to any information accessible to members of the supervisory board.

As under traditional company law, the members of the supervisory board are free to discuss company matters among themselves. However, they are strictly prohibited from disclosing this information to anyone else. This confidentiality requirement severely hampers the communication between the employee representatives and their constituency which, in turn, fosters alienation and the perception about employee representatives as an elitist, isolated group with limited legitimacy.

The so-called interest of the enterprise is the crucial legal point of reference for the substantive board decisions which both shareholder representatives and employee representatives are called upon to make. While this criterion was formally understood as referring solely to the interests of the capital owners, it is today generally accepted as covering employee interests as well. However, the standard has become so malleable that it is difficult to delineate the permissible scope of the board's activities.

Equal status of employee and shareholder representatives also implies equal remuneration. For the former, this income is considered a threat to neutrality if not a source of corruption. Therefore, the standing rules of the unions require employee representatives on the supervisory board who are trade union members to transfer a high percentage of this income to a union foundation. Of course, this duty does not apply to nonunion members.

Shareholder representatives obviously do not need protection against dismissal or a right to participate in vocational programs in order to become or stay qualified for their job. This is different for employee representatives. If they are employed in the enterprise, protection against dismissal may be just as necessary as for members of the works council. And if employee board members actually are to have an impact on the policy of the supervisory board, they must be highly qualified, particularly in view of the qualifications the shareholders' representatives usually bring to bear as qualified experts in economic and financial affairs. To create a level playing field, it would arguably be appropriate to let employee representatives participate in educational programs without loss of pay. This is not an option, however, due to the principle of equal legal status of employee and shareholder representatives. On the other hand, it is generally agreed that employee representatives ought to be released from their ordinary job duties to participate in supervisory board meetings without loss of pay.

[7]   The Implementation in Practice

Within the relationship between the management board and the supervisory board (*see supra*, at §11.04[F][2]), the position of the latter has been weakened by the redefinition of the criterion "interest of the enterprise" as outlined above (*see supra* at §11.04[F][6]). It has become more difficult to argue that specific measures taken or suggested by the management board do not comport with this rather vague formula. Nevertheless, the supervisory board at least continues to be an important source of information for the employees' representatives. Thus, they have access to all relevant facts which give rise to management activities, to discuss these activities and to present their views. Of course, only the model of the coal, iron, and steel industries actually enables them to overrule the shareholders' bench if the neutral chairperson sides with the employees' representatives

However, to better appreciate the role and influence of employee representation on the supervisory board, the works council system must be considered as well. In practice, at least some of the employee representatives on the supervisory board belong to the workforce of the enterprise and in most cases are also works council members. On the whole, this has strengthened both instruments of participation. In particular, it has promoted communication through informal channels. Because management has an interest to stay on good terms with the works council, it is likewise interested in avoiding conflicts with works council members who are also members of the supervisory board. Thus, before informing the supervisory board, management tends to discuss critical questions with at least the internal employee representatives in informal meetings. These informal communications are most important under the coal, iron, and steel industries model in which the employee director functions as a crucial link. It is primarily these informal structures which make employee representation on the supervisory board effective. This informal communication tends to soften the original position of management and the manner in which it presents questions to the supervisory board. As a result, most decisions on the supervisory board are reached unanimously. Notwithstanding the right of all supervisory board members to deal with all questions arising under its mandate, employee representatives focus primarily on the social aspects of company policies and less on economic and financial strategies that lead to basic management decisions. With little or no expert knowledge in economic and financial matters, employee representatives thus typically concentrate their efforts on preventing or mitigating the immediate negative consequences that basic business decisions would have for the workforce.

§11.05 EMPLOYMENT LAW

[A] The Employment Relationship

[1] The Basic Approach

The employment contract is concluded between employer and employee. The scope of application of labor law depends on the definition of "employee." In principle, all employees, whether fully employed for an indefinite period or hired as so-called atypical workers, enjoy the same legal protection.

Until recently, there was no statutory provision defining "employee" for purposes of labor law. According to the traditional understanding, the elements of personal subordination within a private contract setting determine the employment status. The private contract requirement excludes all involuntary relationships (such as work performed by prisoners), and all relationships based on instruments of public law (such as career public servants and judges).

The concept of "personal subordination" is more difficult to define. For a considerable time, it included all those who acted on orders from their employers, regardless of the remuneration they received. Today, this traditional view no longer corresponds with modern developments. Many highly skilled individuals enjoy so much freedom in deciding how and when they carry out their work that it might be appropriate to conceive of them as self-employed.

Courts have struggled to address these developments but, so far, have failed to provide clear-cut answers. What is clear, however, is that the parties to the individual contract cannot escape the constraints of labor law by merely characterizing their relationship as one that does not involve employment duties. Rather, it is the content of the agreement that determines whether labor law applies. Concerning the "personal subordination" requirement, courts have come to rely on a multipronged test, which does not yield predictable outcomes but, more often than not, confirms the claim of the individual who argued that he or she actually was an employee protected under labor law. The factors employed to reach this conclusion include the following: the enterprise expects the individual on a regular basis to be prepared to accept new work assignments; the individual is not free to refuse assignments; the extent to which the individual is integrated in the organizational structure of the enterprise; the length of time the individual spends in performing work for the enterprise. These and other factors underlie the central, albeit circular, inquiry whether the terms applicable to the individual are sufficiently similar to those applicable to persons whose status as employees is not questioned. Of course, in the absence of a generally accepted understanding of what an employee is in the first place, this approach begs the real question, and leaves much room for the discretion of courts.

By an amendment to the Civil Code in 2016 the law now contains a definition of "employee." However, it does not provide anything new, it simply codifies the definition espoused by case law.

[2]   The "Employee-Like" Relationship

In Germany, the dichotomy between the status self-employment, which falls entirely outside the scope of labor law, and the employee status, which is pervasively regulated by this legal regime, has never been accepted as a satisfactory solution. For this reason, courts developed the concept of the employee-like relationship, a third category designed to provide a measure of labor law protection for those who are self-employed but whose economic situation is closer to that of an employee. The individuals in this group are supposed to be covered by at least some rules and principles of labor law. The criterion applied to identify eligible self-employed persons, which is their "economic dependency" on the employer, proved difficult to apply in practice. The situation improved in 1974 with an amendment to the Act on Collective Agreements. Section 12a of that Act introduced the statutory definition of "employee-like" persons. According to this section, individuals are economically dependent if they work under the following conditions: first, they perform their contractual obligations personally and essentially without the support of employees; secondly, they work predominantly for one person, or receive on average more than half of their total income from one person. The term "person" does not only include a legal person, but also encompasses a group of companies. Thus, the individual who works for different enterprises within a group is considered to work only for one person for purposes of this definition.

As indicated in the previous paragraph, persons who are in an "employee-like" status cannot avail themselves of all protective labor law provisions. Most importantly, the law protecting employees against dismissals does not apply to them. Those privileges that "employee-like" individuals do share with "regular" employees include the following: their working conditions can be regulated by collective agreements; disputes between them and their contractual partners are to be settled by labor courts; minimum standards for annual vacation days and public holidays applicable to regular employees apply to them as well.

[B]   Freedom of Contract as Basic Concept

Originally, freedom of contract was the only principle governing employment relationships. It was up to the parties to decide whether, with whom, and under which conditions they concluded a labor contract. From the perspective of 19th century liberal philosophy, this freedom was a giant step forward and a move away from the constraints of the feudal state. On the other hand, freedom of labor contract without any regulation fostered *Manchester liberalism*. This development enabled owners to exploit the competition for jobs, permit working conditions to deteriorate, and to cause massive impoverishment of the workforce. The attempts to steer against these lopsided developments, by curbing contractual freedom to some extent, mark the beginning of labor law. Indeed, the development of labor law can be seen as an ongoing effort to overcome the imbalances that are inherent in the concept of labor contract freedom. These efforts have led to restraints concerning the conclusion of contracts, their content, and their termination through the employer. Nevertheless, freedom of contract as such has never been questioned; the concept is alive and well and remains one of the central principles of labor law, and one that enjoys constitutional protection. For the most part, the objective of emerging labor law has been to create a greater equilibrium in bargaining power.

[C]   Main Implications of the Employment Relationship

Regardless of their specific employment status, all employees enjoy the protective statutory minimum standards of labor law. A multitude of statutes that provide this protection do not distinguish between part time and full time workers, or between permanent employees and those working for a limited time only. Among other things, these statutes prescribe the minimum duration of paid annual vacation (presently twenty-four working days), the guarantee of full payment of remuneration for six weeks in each case of sickness and numerous minimum standards for health and safety. In addition to these statutes which apply to all employees, there are protective provisions for specific groups, for example, those that apply in case of maternity and disability. Of course, the level of all these statutory minimum standards may be raised in favor of the employees by collective agreements, work agreements and individual employment contracts.

One of the characteristic features of employment relationships in Germany is the principle to integrate all employees in the compulsory social security system. Based on the idea of solidarity within the workforce as a whole, this system dates back to the last third of the 19th century. It includes health insurance, the statutory pension scheme, insurance in case of work accidents, insurance in case of partial or total incapacity to work and unemployment insurance. With the exception of work accidents insurance, which is exclusively financed by employers' contributions, the costs for all the other insurances benefits under this regime are shared equally by employers and employees. Each month, the employer pays the amount as a whole to the social security agencies and deducts the employee's share from his or her paycheck. Naturally, this comprehensive coverage of all employees by the social security system comes with a considerable price tag. For the employee it widens the gap between gross wages and net wages, and for the employer it significantly increases the labor costs. These so-called incidental labor costs have become a source of ongoing controversy over whether and how to reform the social security system. One solution would be a reduction of benefits; another one envisages a shift to a tax-financed model. So far, the political pressure to maintain much of the traditional structure is still fairly strong. However, material changes appear inevitable and are beginning to occur. In the area of pensions, the benefits of the statutory scheme have already been slightly reduced and are concurrently supplemented with a second pillar of state-subsidized private insurance. Furthermore, voluntary company pension schemes as a means of supplementing retirement income have always played a role and, considering the foreseeable further retrenchments of statutory benefits, are likely to become even more important in the future.

[D]   Job Security

[1]   The Cancellation Contract

It is always possible to terminate the labor contract by mutual consent. These so-called cancellation contracts (*Aufhebungsverträge*) must be in writing but need not meet any other requirements. Not even the works council has a right to intervene. Whether or not the freedom to terminate the employment contract should be upheld without restrictions has become a subject of fierce debate. Not infrequently, employees suddenly find themselves in a situation in which they feel they have little choice but to agree to the termination of the employment contract in exchange for financial compensation packages. What may look attractive at first glance, however, often turns out to have been a bad choice given subsequent difficulties in finding a new job and the fact that such compensation tends to result in a reduction of unemployment benefits. There have been attempts to establish a right for employees to revoke the cancellation contract during a "cooling-off" period or, alternatively, to require involvement of the works council prior to the conclusion of the cancellation contract. So far, these efforts have failed and courts have refused to step in.

[2]   Dismissal

Germany has quite an elaborate system of protection against dismissals. There is a general regime covering all employees and one providing special protection for certain groups. For present purposes, it suffices to focus on the general statutory regime.

[a]   The Minimum Term of Notice

The first step of improving job security in Germany was to extend the minimum length of the term of notice. Historically, different rules for manual workers and white-collar evolved. Today, a four week minimum term of notice applies to all employees. The notice period gradually increases over time, from one month after two years of employment to seven months after twenty years. For these notice extensions to begin to accrue, the employee must be at least 25 years of age. During a probation period, which may not exceed six months, the term of notice is only two weeks.

The mandatory minimum terms of notice only apply to individual labor contracts. Collective agreements may provide for shorter terms, because parties to such agreements are supposedly in the best position to judge what is appropriate at a given moment in a given branch and region. Conversely, of course, parties to collective agreements are free to extend the minimum term of notice in favor of employees and, in fact, that is what occurred in most branches. Parties to an individual employment contract are also free to extend notice terms. If they do so, however, the following rule must be observed: the term of notice the employer must observe cannot be shorter than the term the employee shall conform to when he himself gives notice of quitting. On the other hand, the term of notice the employee must respect may be shorter than the term of notice the employer has to comply with.

[b]   Extraordinary Dismissal Without Term of Notice

According to Section 626 of the Civil Code a dismissal without notice is lawful only if "there are reasons which in view of all circumstances of the case, and in evaluating the interests of both parties, make it unacceptable for either party to fulfill the contract until the end of the notice period." This Section covers every employment contract. Reasons justifying an extraordinary dismissal may not only be based on misconduct or incompetence but also on severe economic circumstances, which have nothing to do with the employee's acts or omissions. Because all circumstances of the particular case have to be evaluated, any generalization of what constitutes a justified reason for extraordinary dismissal would be misleading. In order to avoid uncertainty on the part of the employee, Section 626 of the Civil Code requires that notice of this type of dismissal be given within two weeks after the reason for the termination became known. In addition, the dismissing employer has to disclose the reason for the dismissal at the request of the employee.

[c]   The Applicability of the Act on Protection against Dismissal

The Dismissal Protection Act only focuses on dismissals with a term of notice. Until recently it applied to establishments employing more than five employees. In order to give employers an incentive to increase hiring, the Act now applies to firms with more than 10 employees, each of whom must have been employed by the same employer for at least 6 months In determining the number of employees, part-time slots with no more than 20 hours and those with no more than 30 hours count, respectively, as .5 and .75 positions.

[d]   The Concept of Social Justification under the Act on Protection Against Dismissal

As a rule, a dismissal under the Dismissal Protection Act is socially unjustified and therefore unlawful. The Act lists three exceptions which render a dismissal legal: first, reasons that relate to the person of the employee; second, the employee's conduct; and third, economic reasons. When the legality of a dismissal is challenged, the employer bears the burden of proving that the prerequisites for one or more of these exceptions existed at the time the employee received the notice of dismissal.

The first exception justifying a dismissal under the Act – reasons relating to the employee's person – applies to situations in which the employee is unable to perform his or her job duties. The main example for this category is prolonged or recurring illness. However, the economic interest of the employer in dismissing a sick employee must be carefully balanced against the interests of the employee. The factors that must be examined in this respect include the actual impact on the enterprise and on work performance, the impact on other employees, the possibility of a transfer, and the seniority of the employee. A crucial factor is the size of the enterprise. Large enterprises are presumed to cope better than small enterprises with problems created by sick leave. In general, the dismissal is lawful only if an evaluation of all relevant facts reveals that it was necessary as a last resort.

The second exception – reasons relating to the employee's conduct – applies to cases of misconduct. It differs from misconduct giving rise to extraordinary dismissals in that the latter requires a particularly egregious wrongdoing. Since again all circumstances of the individual situation must be taken into account, it would be of little help to list the types of misconduct that may (or may not) warrant dismissal. The application of the third exception – dismissal for economic reasons – may be based on external factors, such as an economic crisis, or on internal, employer-initiated measures, such as the introduction of new technologies. The dismissal is justified if the economic situation renders it virtually impossible for the employer to retain the employee. Again, it is for the employer to show why continued employment is economically unfeasible. However, the decision of whether or not to take particular organizational measures that caused the economic exigency is not subject to judicial control. This decision is the management's prerogative even if the works council is involved.

In cases of economic reasons affecting more than one employee, it is necessary to select those to be dismissed. Until recently, the selection had to be made according to "social aspects." The rationale was that those who would suffer most from the effects of a dismissal should be the last ones to be dismissed. However, the notion "social aspects" was rather nebulous and difficult to apply. To aim at social justice in each individual case may have been laudable but came at the expense of legal certainty and simplicity. To improve predictability and practicability, the legislature replaced the notion of "social aspects" with four exclusive criteria, albeit without indicating their relative weight. These criteria are seniority, age, maintenance duties, and disability. Formerly, the selection process did not have to reflect "social aspects" only if technical, economic, or other relevant reasons made it necessary to keep specific employees. Under the recently amended rules, it is possible to retain certain employees regardless of the four criteria if this is necessary to maintain a balanced composition of the workforce. However, much will depend on how the courts will interpret this formula.

Even if the cause for a dismissal relates to the employee's persona or is premised on economic reasons, the dismissal is still considered to be socially unjustified and therefore void if the employee can be transferred to a comparable job with comparable working conditions, either immediately, after retraining, or after further training. The expenses for retraining must not exceed a reasonable level, taking into account the financial resources of the employer. A dismissal is also void if the employee has agreed to be transferred to an inferior job position. The Federal Labor Court has held that the possibility of transfer to any establishment of the enterprise is subject to court review, irrespective of the reaction of the works council whose role in these matters is outlined immediately below. Even if the employee's conduct were to justify dismissal, the employer must first consider a transfer when the source of misconduct can be eliminated in this way.

[e]   *The Works Council's Role*

The Works Constitution Act, Section 102 I, requires the employer to consult the works council prior to any dismissal, be it for ordinary or extraordinary reasons. Without such consultation, the dismissal is null and void. The employer must provide the works council with all relevant details surrounding the dismissal. This information includes the type of dismissal (with or without term of notice), the reason for the dismissal, the date the dismissal shall take effect, the criteria applied for selection, and the considerations concerning a potential transfer. Thus, the works council is entitled to receive all information necessary to review the legality of the dismissal. It is imperative that the works council be consulted before the dismissal is declared; any violation of this rule cannot be corrected later.

In the case of a dismissal without notice, the works council has three days to agree or to express its reservations in writing. If the works council does not react within this period, its consent is statutorily assumed. But even if the works council expresses its reservations in due time and in due form, they do not prevent the employer from dismissing the employee. Although such reservations have no direct legal effects, they may still prove helpful in subsequent court proceedings where they can serve as a record that can be compared with other cases, particularly those in which the works council did consent to a dismissal. The lack of direct legal effects, furthermore, does not fully capture the role and status of the works council in this context. The employer depends in many ways on the works council's cooperation, and therefore tends to avoid conflicts where possible. Particularly in large enterprises, the position of the works council is in fact often much stronger than it appears under black letter law.

In cases of dismissal with a term of notice, the works council has one week to react; it can agree, it can remain inactive, it can declare its reservation in writing, or it can object to the dismissal in writing. As in dismissal cases without notice, the works council's inaction entails the irrefutable presumption of its consent. Likewise, none of the works council's possible reactions prevents the employer from dismissing the employee. The only reaction which may have some effect is a declaration of objection. Before discussing the effects of that reaction, its legal prerequisites should be stated briefly. These are according to Section 102 III of the Works Constitution Act:

- the employer has not, or not sufficiently, taken account of the criteria for selecting the employees to be dismissed;
- the dismissal violates a guideline on selection by which the relative weight of the criteria for selection can be specified;
- the employee to be dismissed could be transferred to a comparable job within the same establishment or in another establishment of the enterprise immediately after retraining or further training;
- the employee has agreed to be transferred to an inferior job position in the establishment or in another establishment of the enterprise.

The works council can exert a measure of control over the procedure of selecting employees to be dismissed by requesting and partaking in the issuance of so-called guidelines which assign an order of priority to the different selection criteria employed to determine the individuals who may be dismissed. In enterprises with more than 500 employees, the works council does not only have the right to request such guidelines, but may invoke arbitration committee proceedings to impose them should the employer refuse to cooperate. However, such guidelines exist only in a few enterprises. One of the main reasons for the hesitation of works councils to insist on weighted guidelines is their concern that they might be blamed by the workforce for having assumed the responsibility for the conditions of dismissal. Once the works council and the employer have reached an agreement on the criteria and the order of their priority, courts have no choice but to uphold the selection of those employees to be dismissed, unless it resulted from a flagrant misapplication of the guidelines.

The works council's declaration of objection has essentially two legal implications. First, when the employer gives notice of dismissal, it must concurrently transmit the written declaration of objection to the dismissed employee. The declaration can and often does serve as the blueprint of the employee's complaint should he choose to fight the dismissal in court. This explains in part why the frequency of lawsuits in cases in which the works council has declared its objection is significantly higher than in other cases.

Secondly, if the dismissed employee files a legal action against his employer then, in principle, he is entitled to stay employed until the end of the lawsuit. However, the Works Constitution Act, Section 102, enables the employer to avoid this obligation by way of injunctive relief. Among other reasons, the injunction will be issued if the continuation of the employment would impose an "intolerable economic burden" on the employer. Given that litigation over the legality of dismissals can take years, employers often prevail. Consequently, only a small percentage of employees actually succeed in keeping their job until the conclusion of the lawsuit.

[f]   Reinstatement Versus Financial Compensation

The normal remedy for employees who have successfully contested the legality of their dismissal is the right to be reinstated. Nevertheless, the employee is often unable to avail herself of this remedy. The employer may move for, and the court may grant, the dissolution of the contract if "continued fruitful co-operation cannot be expected." The facts necessary to meet this requirement may be established during the lawsuit. If the employer's motion is successful, he must pay appropriate compensation to the employee. The law only prescribes the maximum compensatory awards which range between twelve and eighteen monthly wages, depending on the employee's age and length of employment. It is up to the court to determine the exact amount, taking into account the circumstances of the particular case.

In practice, compensation has over time gradually replaced reinstatement as the primary remedy. What triggered and subsequently precipitated this development was the realization on the part of the employee that, ultimately, she would be unable to prevent the dissolution of the contract despite the unlawfulness of the dismissal. Faced with this prospect, employees shifted their strategy. Rather than fighting the dissolution, they aimed at settling their case in court early, in exchange for compensation that exceeded the legally prescribed limits. Employers, for their part, would find this option attractive, because protracted litigation binds resources and may affect the reputation of the company. These incentives explain why empirical research of the late 1970s and early 1980s found that financial compensation had largely displaced the legislative model of reinstatement.

This incentive structure changed, however. Dissolution despite an unlawful dismissal realistically only constituted a threat to the employee if, during litigation, she was no longer integrated into the company's workforce. Under these circumstances, it was promising for employers to argue that "further fruitful co-operation" would not be possible. In 1985, the Federal Labor Court made it more difficult to invoke this argument. Although it held that the dismissed employee only has a right to continued employment pending the outcome of the lawsuit if the dismissal was obviously illegal, the court decided to assume such obvious illegality in cases in which the Labor Court of First Instance declares the dismissal unlawful. Vested with this decision of the lower court, the dismissed employee is entitled to continue working while the litigation continues in the appellate levels until final judgment.

The new approach introduced a radical change. It is now difficult to convince the Court of the impossibility of fruitful cooperation as long as the employee continues to be employed. Therefore, employees are no longer willing to agree to a compromise on compensation prior to the first judgment. If this decision is in favor of the employee, she has an unrestricted right to be reinstated for the remainder of the lawsuit. The employer, now facing real uncertainty about the final outcome, must examine even more carefully the lawfulness of the dismissal. As a result, unlawful dismissals are becoming less frequent. While they still occur in small and medium sized companies with lack of expert knowledge, they are practically no longer existent in large enterprises where legal departments specialize in employment termination issues. Typically now, if a company wishes to terminate contracts successfully even though the legal requirements for termination are not present, that company will have to offer financial settlements that far exceed the compensation packages employees used to accept prior to the 1985 Federal Labor Court decision. Not surprisingly, the Court's new approach has given rise to much criticism on the part of employers and employers' associations but, so far, this employee-oriented jurisprudence has largely remained in place.

One slight change that did occur recently was introduced through an amendment to the Dismissal Protection Act. In declaring the dismissal for economic reasons, the employer may, but does not have to, offer the employee a compensation whose minimum amount is fixed by law (half a monthly salary for each year of seniority), provided the employee does not fight the dismissal in Court. However, that option is hardly apt to change the incentive structure which characterizes the pattern of job security in Germany since the decision of the Federal Labor Court in 1985.

[E]   Atypical Employment

The traditional employment relationship (full employment for an indefinite period) is less and less the standard pattern. If compared to other countries, however, it still occurs frequently in Germany, particularly in the manufacturing industry. Other forms of employment – so-called atypical employment – are steadily increasing.

[1]   Fixed-Term Contracts

Pursuant to the Act on Part-Time and Fixed-Term Contracts of 2001, parties may agree on fixed-term contracts only under certain conditions. If there is no objective reason for limiting the term, newly hired employees can only be employed with a fixed-term contract for up to two years or for a maximum of three shorter periods which in sum do not exceed two years. For newly founded companies, this period of time is extended to a maximum of four years. The conclusion of such a fixed-term contract, however, is invalid if an employment relationship with the same employer, be it of limited or of unlimited duration, has ever existed before. According to the Act of 2001, this means that it is completely irrelevant how much time has passed since the first employment relationship. However, the Federal Labor Court has modified this rule, forbidding such fixed term contracts only if the former employment occurred within three years before hiring.

For any fixed-term contract beyond the maximum limit as set out above, a specific justification is required. There is an exception for elderly employees. If they are at least 52 years old and were unemployed for at least four months directly before hiring, a fixed-term contract can be concluded for up to a maximum period of five years.

[2]   Part-Time Work

Both part-time work and fixed-term contracts are regulated in the same Act of 2001. The most important innovation in this Act is the employee's right to reduce the agreed working time, the so-called right to part-time work. The right to part-time work applies if only two conditions are fulfilled: First, an employee must have been continuously employed for more than six months. Second, the employer must be employing more than fifteen employees. Smaller firms are exempted from the organizational and administrative burdens resulting from the right to part-time work.

The employee has to request the reduction of his or her work time and to specify the extent of the reduction at least three months in advance. The employee need not give reasons for his or her request. The three-month period is supposed to give the employer sufficient time to provide for organizational adjustments. Voluntary agreements to reduce the work time can still be concluded at any time. The law furthermore stipulates that the employee shall indicate to the employer from when to when the employee would like to work. The employer is obligated to discuss the requested reduction of working time with the employee, explicitly with the aim of reaching an agreement. This demonstrates the legislature's hope that the parties to the employment contract will usually voluntarily agree to reduce the working time. If such an agreement is reached, the employment contract changes accordingly. If no agreement can be reached, the employer nevertheless must grant the requested reduction of working time and must determine the distribution of work time in accordance with the employee's wishes, unless valid "operational reasons" can be advanced against the new work schedule. The Act explicitly states that operational reasons may be present in particular if the reduction of the working time interferes considerably with the organization, the course of work or the safety in the establishment, or if the reduction of working time causes disproportional costs.

In spite of the rather complicated technicalities, the right to part-time work normally does not create problems. Importantly, there is only a right to reduce the agreed working time. There is not yet a corresponding right to return to full time employment. Only if there is a vacancy, the part-timer must be given preference if he or she so wishes. In 2017 an initiative to establish a right to return to full time became very controversial and failed.

[3]   *Marginal Part-Timers*

If the monthly remuneration for any employment is less than 450 Euro, the job is a so-called mini job. Persons employed in a "mini job" are excluded from the statutory systems of social security, irrespective of the number of weekly working hours worked. The employer has to pay only a low rate of social security contributions for any "mini jobber" plus low flat-rate taxes of 2%. The employee performing a "mini job" is neither obligated to pay statutory social security contributions nor to pay taxes for the income resulting from the "mini job." Nor is he or she entitled to benefits from the statutory systems of social security. Although employees have the option to pay into the social security system they rarely, if ever, do so.

This regulation has led to a dramatic increase of "mini-jobs." For the vast majority of them it is the only source of income which means that they need social assistance in addition to make a living. The "mini job" system led to a significant decrease of the unemployment rate. Nevertheless, this system has been sharply criticized, particularly by the trade unions. The effort to reintegrate the "mini jobbers" into the social security system and treat them the same way as all other employees, supported by many groups, has not yet succeeded. However, recently the number of "mini jobs" has been reduced significantly due to the statutory minimum wage. It turned out that "mini jobbers" in most cases did not earn the hourly minimum wage as prescribed by the new law and, consequently, "mini jobs" have now become less attractive for employers. Due to the booming labor market in Germany, this fortunately has not led to an increase of unemployment but to a significant increase of jobs covered by social security.

[4]   Temporary Agency Work

In Germany, temporary employees have a regular contractual relationship with so-called temporary employment agencies. These agencies assume all of the usual employer's duties. Different from a normal employment relationship, both parties agree that the employee will be regularly hired out to a third-party (user), where he or she is to perform work.

There are contractual relationships between agency and user on the one hand, and between agency and temporary employee on the other hand. There is, however, no contractual relationship between temporary employee and the user for whom the employee is working. Hence, the temporary employee receives his wages from the agency. Nevertheless, certain duties as regards work performance are incumbent on the temporary employee vis-á-vis the user; the user also has rights and duties as to the temporary employee. The law aims at an effective control of the operation of temporary work and, at the same time, at a minimum protection of the temporary employees regarding employment conditions and social security. The temporary agency needs a license which only can be granted under strict conditions.

The original legal framework of 1972 has been frequently amended, with the most recent change occurring in 2016.

A crucial element of temporary agency work is the principle of equal treatment with regard to remuneration. In this respect, temporary agency workers are to be treated the same way as comparable employees in the company that makes use of these temporary employment relationships. However, there is a possibility to deviate from this principle by collective agreement, and there is also the possibility of extending the derogation to nonunionized temporary workers by reference clauses in individual employment contracts. Originally, there was no time limit for this deviation. This was changed by a law in 2016 according to which the possibility to derogate from the principle of equal treatment by collective agreement only applies up to nine months of the engagement of the temporary employee. The period can be extended to fifteen months if specific conditions are present.

The fact that an ever increasing number of temporary agency workers receive assignments for an indefinite time, thereby substituting employees in the user company, has been the cause for grave concern in Germany. This development was strongly opposed by the trade unions. Now, the law of 2016 prescribes that the time to be hired-out to a user company is limited to eighteen months. If between two engagements of the same temporary employee with the same user there are not at least six months, the former period is to be fully added in the counting toward the eighteen months limit. The length of assignment in the user company can be extended to a maximum of twenty-four months by way of collective agreement or by agreement between the works council and the employer if this is permitted by a collective agreement. If the maximum period is exceeded, an indefinite employment relationship between the temporary employee and the user company is presumed unless the temporary employee declares within a month that he or she is not interested in such a relationship.

SELECTED BIBLIOGRAPHY

Günter Halbach, Norbert Paland, Rolf Schwedes & Otfried Wlotzke, *Labour Law in Germany: An Overview* (4th ed. 1992).

Thomas Klikauer, *Trade Union shop floor representation in Germany*, Industrial Relations Journal 2004, pp. 2 et seq.

Achim Seifert, *Employment Protection and Employment Promotion as Goals of Collective Bargaining in the Federal Republic of Germany*, The International Journal of Comparative Labour Law and Industrial Relations 1999, pp. 343 et seq.

Manfred Weiss, *Labour Law Reforms in Germany*, in: Tomas Davulis (ed.), Labour Law Reforms in Eastern and Western Europe, Brussels 2017, 83 et seq.

Manfred Weiss, *Workers Participation in the Enterprise in Germany*, in Adalberto Perulli / T. Treu (eds.), Enterprise and Social Rights, Wolters Kluwer 2017, 293 et seq.

Manfred Weiss, *German Trade Unions: Their Role in Collective Bargaining*, in: Joe Carby-Hall / Magdalena Rycak (eds.), Trade Unions and Non-employee Representation in Europe – The Current State of Play and Prospects for the Future, Warsaw 2016, 33 et seq.

Manfred Weiss, *Regulating Temporary Work in Germany*, in: Roger Blanpain / Frank Hendrickx (eds.), Temporary Agency Work in the European Union and The United States, Bulletin of Comparative Labour Relations 82, 2013, Wolters Kluwer, 113 et seq.

Manfred Weiss & Marlene Schmidt, *Labour Law and Industrial Relations in Germany* (4th ed., Wolters Kluwer, 2008).

Manfred Weiss & Marlene Schmidt, *Job Creation Policies in Germany – The Role of Labour Law, Social Security Law and Industrial Relations*, in: Marco Biagi (ed.), Job Creation and Labour Law: From Protection Towards Pro-action (2000), pp. 145 et seq.

Manfred Weiss, *Labour Dispute Settlement by Labour Courts in Germany*, Industrial Law Journal (South Africa) 1994, pp. 1 et seq.

Manfred Weiss, *The Future of the Individual Employment Contract in Germany*, in: Lammy Betten (ed.), The Labour Contract in Transforming Labour Relations (1995), pp. 438 et seq.

Manfred Weiss, *Employment Versus Self-Employment: The Search for a Demarcation Line in Germany*, Industrial Law Journal (South Africa) 1999, pp. 741 et seq.

Manfred Weiss, *Fundamental Rights and Labour Law in Germany*, in: Roger Blanpain (ed.), Labour Law, Human Rights and Social Justice (2001), pp. 187 et seq.

Manfred Weiss, *Modernizing the German Works Council System: A Recent Amendment*, The International Journal of Comparative Labour Law and Industrial Relations 2002, pp. 251 et seq.

Manfred Weiss, *Recent Developments in German and European Labour Law*, in: Walther Müller-Jentsch & Hans-Jörg Weitbrecht (eds.), The Changing Contours of German Industrial Relations (2003), pp. 157 et seq.

Manfred Weiss, *Contract and Industrial Relations: The German Case*, in: Philippe Auvergnon (ed.), La Contractualisation du Droit Social (2003), pp. 163 et seq.

CHAPTER 12

Private International Law

Kurt Siehr

TABLE OF CONTENTS

§12.09   International Arbitration
§12.10   International Judicial Assistance
Selected Bibliography

§12.01   SOURCES AND PRINCIPLES

[A]   *Sources*

German conflict rules are codified in Articles 3–48 of the Introductory Act to the German Civil Code (Einführungsgesetz zum Bürgerlichen Gesetzbuch – EGBGB) of 1896, last amended in 2017, and in some scattered provisions of several other statutes (e.g., Statute on Bills of Exchange). Rules on jurisdiction and enforcement of foreign judgments are supplied by the German Code of Civil Procedure *(Zivilprozeßordnung –– ZPO)* and in the Act on Court Procedure in Family Matters and Non-litigious Matters *(Gesetz über das Verfahren in Familiensachen und in Angelegenheiten der freiwilligen Gerichtsbarkeit* – FamFG).

Several supranational instruments, international treaties, and conventions cover the same matters as German domestic statutes. They take priority over the national provisions on the same subject. The most important instruments are Council Regulation No. 1215/2012 of December 12, 2012 on Jurisdiction and the Recognition and Enforcement of Judgments in Civil and Commercial Matters (Brussels I *bis*), the Lugano Convention of 2007 on Jurisdiction, Recognition and Enforcement of Judgments in Civil and Commercial Matters, Regulation (EC) No. 593/2008 of June 17, 2008 on the Law Applicable to Contractual Obligations (Rome I) and Regulation (EC) No. 864/2007 of July 11, 2007 on the Law Applicable to Non-Contractual Obligations (Rome II). There are several Hague Conventions on these matters, too.

Far from being exhaustive, the statutory and conventional rules have been interpreted, extended, and qualified by both, courts and commentators. Therefore, case law, learned commentaries, treatises, articles, and notes are important and need to be consulted in order to get a correct picture of the development of the law.

[B]   Principles

[1]   Black Letter Rules

Unlike U.S. Conflicts Law, German Private International Law is governed by more or less detailed black letter rules and not by open-ended provisions indicating the considerations which have to be taken into account when deciding what law to apply to a specific case. Courts may qualify some vague rules in special situations, apply evasion clauses and may develop new rules along the lines of existing statutory law. They are, however, not free to change statutory provisions. This is also true for rules on jurisdiction. A German court is not allowed to decline jurisdiction by virtue of the *forum non conveniens* doctrine.

[2]   *Principle of Nationality*

National conflicts law of natural persons, family law and succession law still adhere to the principle of nationality. The respective nationality of persons, spouses, parents, and deceased persons determines their personal status. The principle of nationality also influences several rules on jurisdiction.

There are, however, several exceptions to the principle of nationality. In family law, the principle is equivocal in cases of spouses or parents with different nationalities because, in order to ensure gender equality, a common connecting factor must be chosen. Also, for refugees and persons without any nationality, the law of their habitual residence prevails (Article 5 II EGBGB). Several Hague Conventions and all EU-Regulations prefer habitual residence as connecting factor and therefore replace nationality.

[3]   Renvoi

Especially in family and successions law, German courts are required under Article 4 I EGBGB to accept a *renvoi,* i.e., a referral of foreign conflicts law back into German law *(Rückverweisung)* or into the law of a third State *(Weiterverweisung).* The German concept of *renvoi* differs from the foreign court theory insofar as every foreign reference to German law is considered a reference to German substantive law (Article 4 I 2 EGBGB). Under the Rome Regulation *(infra* §12.02[B][1]–[5]), a *renvoi* is expressly excluded in cases of conflicts of contract laws (Article 20 Rome I), but admitted by Article 34 I of the Successions Regulation of 2012.

[4]   *Public Policy*

If the application of foreign law mandated by German Conflict rules manifestly violates German public policy *(ordre public),* foreign law will not be applied, applied differently or substituted by German domestic law (Article 6 EGBGB). Courts however refrain from invoking this clause. Even less use is made of the public policy clause in civil procedure (§ 328 I no. 4 ZPO, § 109 I no. 4 FamFG).

[5]   *Application of Foreign Law*

German courts, with respect to facts and to law, are not bound by the pleadings of the parties. The courts have to insist on being supplied all material facts relevant for deciding the case and then have to apply the law ex officio. The principle of *iura novit curia* applies by virtue of § 293 ZPO and § 26 FamFG. In order to collect information on foreign law (conflict rules as well as rules of substantive law and court practice) courts may ask universities or Max Planck-Institutes for expert legal opinions.

§12.02   LAW OF CONTRACTS

[A]   Jurisdiction

[1]   General Heads of Jurisdiction

German courts have jurisdiction when supra- or international instruments (especially Regulation No. 1215/2012 and the Lugano Convention) so provide or when German statutes (in particular the Code of Civil Procedure) establish the local jurisdiction of German courts. Regulation No. 1215/2012 and the Lugano Convention (except Articles 2, 11 II, 18 I, 21 II, 24 and 25 of the Regulation and Articles 2, 9 II, 15 II, 18 II, 22 and 23 of the Lugano Convention) apply only if the defendant is domiciled or has his seat in a Member or Contracting State to these instruments. In contracts cases, a person may be sued in German courts if:

- he or one of several defendants is domiciled or has his seat in Germany (Articles 4 and 8 I of the Regulation No. 1215/2012 and Articles 2 and 6 I the Lugano Convention; § 13 ZPO); or
- a contract has to be performed in Germany (Article 7 I of the Regulation No. 1215/2012 and Article 5 I of the Lugano Convention; § 29 ZPO); or
- a dispute arises out of the operation of a branch, agency or other establishment situated in Germany (Article 7 V of the Regulation No. 1215/2012 and Article 5 V of the Lugano Convention; § 21 ZPO).

[2]   Special Heads of Jurisdiction in Favor of Weaker Parties

There are three special types of contractual relations for which Regulation No. 1215/2012 and the Lugano Convention provide special heads of jurisdiction favoring the weaker party: insurance contracts, special types of consumer contracts and labor contracts.

[a]   Insurance Contracts

In cases relating to insurance, German courts have jurisdiction if:

- the defendant-insurer is domiciled or has his seat or a branch, agency or other establishment in Germany (Articles 11 I lit. a, 11 II and 14 of the Regulation No. 1215/2012; Articles 8 I no. 1, 8 II and 11 I of the Lugano Convention); or
- the policy-holder is domiciled in Germany (Article 11 I lit. b Regulation No. 1215/2012 and Article 8 I no. 2 Lugano Convention); or
- the harmful event occurred in Germany in respect of a liability insurance or insurance of immovable property (Article 12 Regulation No. 1215/2012 and Article 10 I of the Lugano Convention).

[b]   *Consumer Contracts*

The Conflict rules on certain consumer contracts (defined in Article 17 Regulation No. 1215/2012 and Article 13 Lugano Convention as sale of goods on instalment credit terms, loans repayable by instalments, credit for financing a sale of goods, certain types of transborder consumer contracts) establish privileges for the consumer in allowing him to sue the other party at the place of his habitual residence (Article 18 I Regulation No. 1215/2012 and Article 14 I Lugano Convention) and protect privilege against forum-selection prior to a legal dispute (Article 19 Regulation No. 1215/2012 and Article 15 Lugano Convention).

[c]   *Labor Contracts*

In labor relations with an employer having his seat or branch in a Member State, under Article 21 Regulation No. 1215/2012, the employee may sue the employer in the following Member States:

- at the employer's domicile (I lit a);
- at the place where the employee habitually carries out his work (I lit. b i);
- at the place where the business which hired the employee is situated if;
- the employee carries out his work in several countries (I lit. b ii).

[3]   *Exclusive and Prorogated Jurisdiction*

Article 24 Regulation No. 1215/2012 and Article 16 Lugano Convention fix certain heads of exclusive jurisdiction regardless of the domicile of the parties:

- in certain proceedings in rem the courts of the Member State in which the property is situated;
- in certain proceedings concerning the constitution, the nullity or dissolution of a company the courts of the Member State in which the company has its seat;
- in certain proceedings requiring the registration in public registers;
- in certain proceedings concerning the registration or validity of patents, trademarks or similar rights the courts of the Member State where the registration or deposit has been applied for;
- in proceedings concerning the enforcement of judgments the courts of the Member State where the judgment has been or is to be enforced.

Under Article 25 Regulation No. 1215/2012 and Article 17 Lugano Convention, the parties of a contract or dispute may agree that a court of a Member State is to have jurisdiction to decide their controversy.

[4]   Jurisdiction under Domestic Rules of Procedure

If Regulation No. 1215/2012 or the Lugano Convention do not apply, jurisdiction may be based on provisions of German domestic law. This is in particular the case when a lawsuit is filed against a person or company having the domicile or seat in the United States.

[B]   Applicable Law

[1]   Vienna Convention on International Sales of Goods

The Vienna Convention on Contracts for the International Sale of Goods (CISG) of 1980 entered into force in Germany on January 1, 1991. It governs contracts if it is applicable and has not been excluded by the parties to the contract.

Based on Article 95 CISG, the United States of America has declared that it will not be bound by Article 1 I (b) of the Convention. Germany has restricted her declaration under Article 95 CISG. German courts will not apply the Convention if, under Article 1 I (b), German conflict rules refer to the law of a State which has made a declaration under Article 95 CISG. Thus, e.g., German courts will apply the New York version of the Uniform Commercial Code when an American seller with his place of business in New York brings a suit in Germany against a purchaser who, at the time of contracting, had his place of business not in a Contracting State (e.g., in the UK).

[2]   Rome I-Regulation

The Rome I Regulation of 2008 almost completely substitutes German national rules on private international law of contracts. The Rome Convention of 1980 on the Law Applicable to Contractual Relations is applicable to states not bound by Rome I, e.g., to Denmark.

[a]   Freedom of Choice

A contract is governed by the law chosen by the parties (Article 3 I 1 Rome I). By their choice, the parties may substitute the law that, in absence of choice, would govern under Article 4 Rome I (i.e., the law of the country with the closest connection), including the mandatory provisions of that legal system. There are, however, limits to party autonomy *(Parteiautonomie)* provided for in the Rome I Regulation:

- If at the time of the choice of law agreement, all elements relevant to the case are connected with one country only, a choice of law-clause shall not prejudice the application of mandatory rules of law of that country which cannot be derogated from (Article 3 III Rome I).
- For contracts for carriage of passengers, only the laws of particular jurisdictions, mentioned in Article 5 II § 2 Rome I, may be chosen.

- In certain consumer contracts, a choice of law-clause shall not deprive the consumer of the protection afforded to him by the mandatory rules of the law of the country in which he has his habitual residence (Article 6 II Rome I).
- In insurance contracts (except those for large risks) party autonomy is limited by virtue of Article 7 III Rome I Regulation.
- In individual employment contracts, a choice of law-clause shall not deprive the employee of the protection afforded to him by the mandatory rules of the law which would be applicable in the absence of choice (Article 8 I Rome I).

Article 46b EGBGB provides for the applicability of non-waivable mandatory rules for certain consumer and timeshare contracts with a close relation to the territory of a Member State or Contacting State (of the European Economic Area).

A valid choice of law clause does not prevent a forum from applying internationally overriding mandatory rules (defined in Article 9 I Rome I) or public policy rules of the law of the forum (Articles 9 II ad 21 Rome I) and from not applying foreign law if its application leads to a result that is manifestly incompatible with overriding mandatory rules of the law of the state where the contractual obligation was performed (Article 9 III Rome I).

[b]   Law Applicable in the Absence of Choice

[i]   Closest Connection

If the law applicable to a contract has not been validly chosen by the parties, the contract shall be governed by the law of the country with which it is most closely connected (Article 4 I Rome I). In order to determine this connection more easily, it is presumed that:

- A contract for the sale of goods shall be governed by the law of the country where the seller has his habitual residence (Article 4 I lit. a Rome I).
- A contract for the provision of services shall be governed by the law of the country where the service provider has his habitual residence (Article 4 I lit. b Rome I).
- A contract relating to a right in rem in immovable property or in a tenancy of immovable property shall be governed by the law of the country where the property is situated (Article 4 lit. c Rome I).
- Notwithstanding Article 4 lit. c, a tenancy of immovable property concluded for temporary private use for a period of no more than six consecutive months shall be governed by the law of the country where the landlord has his habitual residence, provided that the tenant is a natural person and has his habitual residence in the same country (Article 4 I lit. d Rome I).
- A franchise contract shall be governed by the law of the country where the franchisee has his habitual residence (Article 4 I lit. e Rome I).
- A distribution contract shall be governed by the law of the country where the distributor has his habitual residence (Article 4 I lit. f Rome I).

- A contract for the sale of goods by auction shall be governed by the law of the country where the auction takes place, if such a place can be determined (Article 4 I lit. g Rome I).
- A contract concluded within a multilateral system (*see* recital 18 Rome I) which brings together or facilitates the bringing together of multiple third-party buying and selling interests in financial instruments, as defined by Article 4(1), point (17) of Directive 2004/39/EC, in accordance with non-discretionary rules and governed by a single law, shall be governed by that law (Article 4 lit. h Rome I).
- A contract for the carriage of goods shall be governed by the law of the country of habitual residence of the carrier, provided that the place of receipt or the place of delivery or the habitual residence of the consignor are also situated in that country. If those requirements are not met, the law of the country where the place of delivery agreed by the parties is situated shall apply (Article 5 I Rome I).
- A contract for the carriage of passengers shall be governed by the law of the country where the passenger has his habitual residence, provided that either the place of departure or the place of destination are situated in that country. If these requirements are not met, the law of the country where the carrier has his habitual residence shall apply (Article 5 II Rome I).
- A consumer contract not subject to the rules of Article 6 I Rome I is governed by Article 4 I Rome I (Article 6 III Rome I).
- An insurance contract is governed by the law of the country determined by Article 7 Rome I.
- An individual employment contract shall be governed by the law of the country in which or, failing that, from which he habitually performs his work pursuant to the contractual stipulations (Article 8 II Rome I). The law of the habitual place of work continues to apply when an employee temporarily performs his work in another country. If the employee does not habitually carry out his work in any specific country, the law of the country in which the place of business through which he was engaged is situated applies (Article 8 III Rome I).
- For all other contracts (except certain contracts of carriage, consumer contracts, individual employment contracts and insurance contracts), the closest connection is with the country where the party who is to effect the performance which is characteristic of the contract has, at the time of conclusion of the contract, his habitual residence, or, in the case of a corporate entity or unincorporated business association, its central administration, or, in certain situations, its principal place of business (Article 4 II Rome I).
- These presumptions may be rebutted if it appears in the light of all circumstances that the contract is more closely connected with another country (Article 4 III Rome I). If the characteristic performance *(charakteristische Leistung)* cannot be determined, also the law of the closest connection applies (Article 4 IV Rome I).

[ii]   Consumer Contracts

Special rules apply to certain consumer contracts to protect the consumer as the weaker party. For certain consumer contracts, the law governing in the absence of a choice of law clause will not be substituted by the law of a country which is more closely connected. According to Article 6 I Rome I, the law of the country where the consumer has his habitual residence governs:

- if the professional pursues his commercial of professional activities in the country where the consumer has his habitual residence; or
- if by any means, the professional directs such activities to that country or to several countries including that country and the consumer contract falls within the scope of such activities.

In consumer contracts which do not meet any of these conditions (e.g., consumer contracts concluded by a German tourist in a market in Rome) the law chosen by the parties or the law of the country with the closest connection governs (Article 6 III Rome I refers to Articles 3 and 4 Rome I).

Article 6 II Rome I limits party autonomy with respect to the choice of the law of a non-Member State. If the law of such a state has been chosen by the parties and if the contract has close connections to the territory of a Member State (in particular by advertisement in the EU or by the contracting of a consumer habitually resident in a Member State), the mandatory provisions of these consumer directives apply (cp. Article 46b EGBGB).

According to Article 6 IV Rome I the provisions in Article 6 I and II Rome shall not apply:

- to certain contracts for the supply of services;
- to certain contracts of carriage;
- to certain contracts relating to a right in rem in immovable property or a tenancy of immovable property;
- to rights and obligations which constitute a financial instrument;
- to contracts concluded within the type of system falling within the scope of Article 4 I lit. h).

[c]   *Scope of the Applicable Law*

The law applicable under a choice of law clause or, in the absence of such a clause, the law designated by Article 4 Rome I governs:

- the existence and validity of a contract or of any term of a contract (Article 10 I Rome I);
- the formal validity of a contract unless the contract is subject to special provisions (e.g., for certain consumer contracts, contracts the subject of which

are rights in immovable property or to use immovable property) or the *lex loci actus* applies alternatively (Article 11 Rome I);

– the interpretation, performance of a contract, consequences of breach of contract including the assessment of damages (unless governed by procedural law), ways of extinguishing obligations, prescription and limitation of actions and the consequences of nullity of a contract (Article 12 Rome I);

– the burden of proof and presumptions of law (Article 18 I Rome I). Different rules apply for any mode of proof (Article 18 I Rome I).

[d]   Special Rules

Special rules govern matters of formalities, authority of an agent, assignment and subrogation, multiple liability and set-off.

In favorem negotii, the *formal validity* of a contract is governed either by the law governing the material validity of the contract or by the law of the country where it is concluded, i.e., by the *lex loci contractus* (Article 11 I Rome I). A contract concluded *inter absentes* is governed by the law where the offer or the acceptance was dispatched (Article 11 II Rome I). The *lex loci contractus* does not apply to the formal validity of consumer contracts and to certain contracts involving a right in immovable property if the *lex rei sitae* mandatorily requires a special form (Article 11 IV and V Rome I). For consumer contracts, the law of the country where the consumer has his habitual residence governs formalities of the contract.

The law applicable to the authority of an agent (*Vollmacht*) is not explicitly provided for by Rome I. It is excluded from its scope by Article 1 II lit. g Rome I. German law provides a conflicts rule in Article 8 EGBGB. The relation between principal and agent is subject to the same conflicts rules as other contracts. Thus, the agent's authority to bind the principal is governed by the chosen law or, if not chosen, by the law of the country where the agent does business for the principal. Special rules apply to agents who are employees, to long-term agents and to agents dealing with immovable property, to agents selling at auction or doing business at a stock exchange (Article 8 III – VII EGBGB).

Voluntary *assignments* are governed, as to the relationship between assignor and the assignee, by the regular conflicts rules of contract law. As to problems of assignability, the relation to the debtor and discharge, the law governing the underlying right controls (Article 14 Rome I). A subrogation is governed by the law applicable to the relation between the third party and the creditor who received payment from the third party, e.g., due to a guarantee given to the creditor by the third party: Article 15 Rome I.

If the creditor has more than one debtor (so-called *multiple liability*) and one debtor has satisfied the creditor in whole or in part, the law governing the debtor's obligation towards the creditor also governs the debtor's right to claim recourse from the other debtors (Article 16 sent. 1 Rome I).

Set-off, absent an agreement by the parties, is governed by the law applicable to the claim against which the right to set-off is asserted (Article 17 Rome I).

[e]   *General Conflict Rules*

Renvoi is excluded by Article 20 Rome I and a public policy exception is provided by Article 21 Rome I. The vague notion of "habitual residence" is replaced for corporate bodies by the place of their central administration and for natural persons at their principal place of business (Article 19 I and II Rome I).

Article 9 Rome I is of utmost importance when dealing with overriding mandatory provisions of the forum state and of third countries that are not the law governing the contract as a whole. After having defined overriding mandatory provisions which are considered crucial by a country in order to safeguard its public interests, such as its political, social or economic organization in Article 9 I, Article 9 II Rome I states that the Regulation does not restrict the application of such overriding mandatory provisions of the law of the forum. Among overriding mandatory provisions of a third country, not being the law of the forum or the law governing the contract, only those provisions may be given effect which are provisions of the country where the obligations arising out of the contract have to be or have been performed, and only in so far as those overriding mandatory provisions render the performance of the contract unlawful (Article 9 III Rome I). All other overriding mandatory provisions may only be given effect thanks to the substantive law governing the contract.

Example: Greek school teachers are employed by the Republic of Greece in order to teach Greek students in German schools the Greek language. By agreement German courts have jurisdiction and German law applies as law governing. In the Greek financial crises the salary of Greek civil servants is reduced and this reduction is also extended to the Greek teachers in Germany. The teachers bring a lawsuit in Germany against Greece and ask for full payment. Greek law on reduction of payment is not recognized in Germany because it is not the law of a State in which the contracts have to be performed (ECJ C-135/15, *Griechenland ./. Nikiforidis*, ECLI:EU:C:2016:774). However, Member States are free to take these reductions into account when applying the law governing the contracts. This can be done in Germany by termination of the contracts and the offer to renew them at different terms of employment (reduced compensation), so-called *Änderungskündigung*.

[C]   Recognition of Foreign Judgments

Foreign judgments in matters of contract are recognized in Germany if supra- or international instruments or German domestic rules on recognition so provide. Between the Member States of the European Union, the Regulation 1215/2012 (Brussels Ibis) applies and substitutes all other rules. The same applies under the Lugano Convention between the contracting states of the European Union and the members of the European Free Trade Association (EFTA). The German-British Treaty of 1960 on Recognition of Foreign Judgments and every other bilateral treaty on recognition between Member States of the European Union or of the Lugano Convention do not apply insofar as these multilateral instruments take priority (Articles 67 et seq. Regulation 1215/2012 and Articles 64 et seq. of the Lugano Convention). According to

German domestic rules on the recognition of foreign judgments (§ 328 ZPO, §§ 108 et seq. FamFG), foreign decisions are recognized if:

- the foreign court had jurisdiction (according to German standards), except Article 45 III Brussels ibis and Article 35 III Lugano Convention; and
- the defendant has received service of process; and
- the foreign decision does not conflict with a decision previously rendered or recognized in Germany; and
- German legal proceedings between the same parties on the same issue were not initiated before the foreign proceedings became pendent; and
- the foreign decision does not violate German public policy; and
- the foreign forum State guarantees or exercises reciprocity in certain proceedings.

The question whether reciprocity is guaranteed between Germany and a foreign state has to be decided for every type of proceedings separately. No formal guarantee is necessary. It is sufficient that a German judgment of the same type as the decision seeking recognition in Germany has in fact been recognized in the foreign forum state.

In order to enforce a foreign judgment, a German decision on the enforceability of the foreign judgment has to be rendered (§§ 722, 723 ZPO).

§12.03 LAW OF TORTS AND OTHER NON-CONTRACTUAL OBLIGATIONS

[A] Jurisdiction

Under Regulation 1215/2012 (Brussels Ibis) and the Lugano Convention 2007 or, if these instruments do not apply, under German domestic rules on jurisdiction of German courts, an action in tort may be brought before German courts against a person if:

- the defendant is domiciled or residing in Germany (Article 4 I Brussels Ibis and Article 2 I Lugano Convention; § 13 ZPO); or
- the tortious act was committed in Germany (Article 7 II Brussels Ibis and Article 5 III Lugano Convention; § 32 ZPO); or
- the injury took place in Germany (Article 7 II Brussels Ibis and Article 5 III Lugano Convention; § 32 ZPO); or
- the tort was also a criminal offense, criminal proceedings have been initiated in Germany and the criminal court has also decided to deal with the suit for damages (Article 7 III Brussels Ibis and Article 5 IV Lugano Convention); or
- the parties agreed on a choice of jurisdiction-clause conferring jurisdiction on German courts for actions in contract and tort based on a specific relation between the parties (Article 25 Brussels Ibis and Article 23 of the Lugano Convention; § 38 ZPO).

If Brussels Ibis or the Lugano Convention apply, jurisdiction may not be based on provisions of domestic law.

[B]   Applicable Law

Since January 11, 2009 Regulation (EC) No. 864/2007 of the European Parliament and the Council of July 11, 2007 on the law applicable to non-contractual obligations (Rome II) is in force and supplies conflicts rules for most tort obligations and other non-contractual obligations.

[1]   Torts

[a]   Basic Rule

Under Article 4 1 Rome II, tort claims are governed by the law of the country in which the damage occurs irrespective of the country in which the event giving rise to the damage occurred and irrespective of the country or countries in which the indirect consequences of that event occur.

In the tortfeasor and the victim had their habitual residence or seat in the same State, that law applies under the rule of Article 4 II Rome II.

[b]   Special Escape Clause

In order to guarantee equitable results, the special escape clause of Article 4 III Rome II has been enacted. If the law of another country than the chosen one is manifestly more closely connected than the law of the country designated by Article 4 I or II Rome II, the former law governs. A substantially closer connection may, e.g., be based on a preexisting relationship between the parties, such as a contract that is closely connected with the tort in question.

Example: The car of plaintiff P, habitually resident in country A, was inspected by the defendant, the garage-owner D, in country B. The inspection was done incorrectly and one of the front wheels was not sufficiently fastened. In country C, the incorrectly fastened front wheel went off, the car ran into a tree and P got hurt and had expenses in his home country A. Under Article 4 I Rome I, P may sue D for damages under the law of country C where the damage occurred irrespective of the law of country B (where the event giving rise to the damage occurred) and of the law of country A (where indirect consequences of that event occurred). The exception of Article 4 II Rome II does not apply because P and D have their habitual residence in different countries. However, the escape clause of Article 4 III Rome II may be applicable, with a view to the contract between P and D, as D's defective performance caused the traffic accident. The contract is governed by the law of country B because D in county B effected the characteristic performance (Article 4 II Rome I).

[c]   Choice of Law

Under Article 14 Rome II, the parties may choose the law governing in two different situations:

- by an agreement entered into *after* the event giving rise to the damage occurred; or
- where all the parties are pursuing a commercial activity, also by an agreement freely negotiated *before* the event giving rise to the damage occurred.

These agreements are subject to two limitations which may be explained by giving two examples.

Examples: 1. If, in the last example, all elements of the tort are located in county A and the plaintiff and defendant agree that their relation should be governed by the law of country B, they cannot derogate from provisions which, according to the law of country A, cannot be derogated from by agreement, e.g., warranty provisions (Article 14 II Rome II).

2. If in the same case, the parties were commercial actors (P is a logistic company and D runs a garage business) and agreed to submit their relation to the law of a non-Member State (e.g., Swiss law), and if the event giving rise to the damage occurred in a EU Member State, the parties cannot derogate in their agreement from provisions which according to EU law cannot be derogated from by agreement (Article 14 III Rome II).

These limitations are similar to those which, according to Rome I, are also limiting the choice of law in contracts (Article 3 III and IV Rome I).

[d]   Rules Applying to Special Categories of Torts

Articles 5–9 Rome II provide separate rules for five subcategories of tort.

[i]   Article 5: Product Liability

Without prejudice to Article 4 II Rome II (common habitual residence within the same country), the law applicable to a non-contractual obligation arising out of damage caused by a product shall be:

- the law of the country in which the person sustaining the damage has his habitual residence when the damage occurred, if the product was marketed in that country; of failing that;
- the law of the country in which the product was acquired, if the product was marketed in that country; or failing that;
- the law of the country in which the damage occurred, if the product was marketed in that country (Article 5 I sent. 1 Rome II).

Where, however, the defendant could not reasonably foresee the marketing of the product in a country the law of which is applicable under (Article 5 I sent. 1 Rome II), the law of the country governs in which the defendant is habitually resident (Article 5 I sent. 2 Rome II).

An escape clause similar to that of Article 4 III Rome II is added in Article 5 II Rome II.

[ii]   Article 6: Competition Law

The law applicable to a non-contractual obligation arising out of an act of unfair competition or of restricting competition shall be:

- the law of the country where competitive relations or the collective interests of consumers are affected (Article 6 I Rome II); or
- if the act of unfair competition exclusively affects the interests of a specific competitor, Article 4 shall apply (Article 6 II Rome II); or
- in case of a restriction of competition the law of the market that was affected (Article 6 (3) lit. a Rome II) or, if the market of more than one country was affected, Article 6 III lit. b Rome II applies.

The law applicable under Article 6 Rome II cannot be derogated from by an agreement pursuant to Article 14 (Article 6 IV Rome II).

[iii]   Article 7: Environmental Damage

The law applicable to a non-contractual obligation arising out of environmental damage shall be the law determined pursuant to Article 4 I Rome II. However, in an effort to protect the victim, the latter may also base his claim on the law of the country in which the event giving rise to the damage occurred. Thus, the law more favorable to the victim controls.

Example: A farmer in Peru brings a claim against a German electricity company running a power plant emitting a very large quantity of CO_2. According to Article 4 I Rome II, the claim for damages is governed by the law of Peru, as the country where the harm occurred. But the plaintiff may also base his claim on the law of Germany where the event giving rise to the damage occurred (Article 7 Rome II).

[iv]   Article 8: Intellectual Property Rights

For claims arising from an infringement of an intellectual property right, the applicable law just as the underlying principle will be the *lex loci protectionis* (Article 8 I Rome II). If, however, a unitary EU intellectual property right has been infringed, the law, which is not governed by the relevant EU instrument, shall be the law of the country in which the act of infringement was committed (Article 8 II Rome II). The law applicable under Article 8 may not be derogated from by an agreement pursuant to Article 14 (Article 8 III Rome II).

[v]   Article 9: Industrial Action

The law applicable to a non-contractual obligation for damages caused by an industrial action shall be, except for cases like those mentioned in Article 4 II Rome II, the law of the country where the action has been taken.

[e]   *Common Rules*

[i]   Article 15: Scope of the Law Applicable

The law applicable to the tort claim governs all issues of tortious liability including heads of damages, form of compensation, limitation of liability, burden of proof and rules on prescription and limitation (Article 15 Rome II).

[ii]   Article 16: Overriding Mandatory Provisions

Article 16 Rome II provides that nothing in this Regulation shall restrict the application of the provisions of law of the forum in a situation where they are mandatory irrespective of the law otherwise applicable to non-contractual obligations. This is part of the general public-policy clause of Article 26 Rome II.

[iii]   Article 17: Rules of Safety and Conduct

An exception applies with regard to rules relating to the control of conduct. In cases of road accidents, e.g., the rules of the road in force at the place and time of the accident apply (Article 17 Rome II).

[iv]   Article 18: Direct Action of the Victim Against Insurer of Liable Person

Pursuant to Article 18 Rome II, the victim of a tort may directly sue the tortfeasor's insurance company if either the law governing the tort claim or the law governing the insurance contract provides for a direct action of the victim.
      Example: The German victim V of a road traffic accident in Italy may sue the liability insurer of the responsible car driver D, domiciled in Greece if either Italian law as the law of the country where the accident and the injury of V occurred, or Greek law governing the insurance contract of D provides for such a direct action.

[v]   Article 19: Subrogation

Where a third person has to satisfy the obligation of the tortfeasor against the victim of the tort, the law applicable to the duty of the third person decides whether the third person is entitled to exercise against the tortfeasor the rights which the victim had against the tortfeasor under the law governing their relationship (Article 19 Rome II).

[vi]   Article 20: Multiple Liability

If there are several tortfeasors and one tortfeasor satisfies the claim of the victim, the question of that paying debtor's right to demand compensation from the other tortfeasors shall be governed by the law applicable to that tortfeasor's non-contractual relationship with the victim.

[vii]   Article 21: Formal Validity

The form of a unilateral act (e.g., the unilateral choice of the law of the country in which the event giving rise to the damage occurred under Article 7 Rome II) is governed, alternatively, by the law governing the tort or by the law of the country in which the act is performed (Article 21 Rome II).

[viii]   Article 22: Burden of Proof

With respect to proof of facts, two different aspects have to be distinguished according to Article 22: With respect to presumptions of law or the determination of the burden of proof, the law governing the tort applies (Article 22 I Rome II). The proof of an act, however, may be established by any mode of evidence recognized by the law of the forum (Article 22 II Rome II).

[f]   Other General Provisions

[i]   Article 23: Habitual Residence of Corporate or Incorporate Bodies

Article 23 Rome II does not define the habitual residence of physical persons other than for those acting in the course of their respective business (Article 23 II Rome II). With regard to business entities, Article 23 I Rome II fixes the habitual residence of corporate and unincorporated entities at the place of their central administration. If the victim suffered injury in the course of an agency or any other establishment, the place where this branch or establishment is located substitutes for the place of central administration (Article 23 I Rome II).

[ii]   Article 24: Exclusion of Renvoi

Renvoi of the law applicable to a tortious act is excluded.

[iii]   Article 25: States With More Than One Legal System

Member States with different territorial units that operate different rules in respect of non-contractual obligations are not obliged to apply the Rome II Regulation to domestic conflicts between the laws of such jurisdictions (Article 25 II Rome II). If, however, States have different units each of which has its own rules of law in respect to non-contractual obligations, each territorial unit shall be considered as a country for the purposes of identifying the law applicable under this Regulation (Article 25 I Rome II).

Example: While traveling in the United States for pleasure, a person habitually resident in Germany became the victim of a road traffic accident in New Hampshire/United States. His claim against the responsible driver of the car causing the accident is governed not by federal American law, but by the law of New Hampshire (Article 25 I Rome II).

[iv]   Article 26: Public Policy of the Forum

The application of foreign law applicable according to the Rome II Regulation may be refused only if such application is manifestly incompatible with the public policy of the forum.

Examples: A German court may refuse to apply foreign tort law if it provides for compensation that substantially exceed the amount required for appropriate compensation of the injured person (e.g., exemplary or treble damages), or if it obviously serves purposes other than the provisions of appropriate compensation for the injured person (e.g., punitive damages). In all these cases, the compensation is reduced to the amount compatible with the German law of damages.

[v]   Articles 27 and 28: Relation to Community Law and to International Conventions

The Rome II Regulation does not prejudice the application of provisions of Community law which, in relation to particular matters, establish choice of law-rules relating to non-contractual obligations (Article 27 Rome II).

Article 28 I Rome II provides that this Regulation shall not prejudice the application of international conventions to which one or more Member States are parties and which lay down choice of law-rules relating to non-contractual obligations such as, e.g., the Hague Convention of 1971 on Road Traffic Accidents. However, as between Member States, the Rome II Regulation takes priority (Article 28 II Rome II).

[2]   *Unjust Enrichment*

[a]   *Basic Rules*

Unjust enrichment claims may arise in many different situations:

- unjust enrichment because of performance rendered under a non-existing or terminated legal relation is governed by the law governing this relation (Article 10 I Rome II);
- unjust enrichment which cannot be determined by virtue paragraph 1, and provided the concerned parties have their habitual residence in the same country when the unjust enrichment occurred, shall be governed by the law of that country (Article 10 II Rome II);

- unjust enrichment which cannot be located by paragraphs 1 and 2, shall be governed by the law of the country in which the act of unjust enrichment took place (Article 10 III Rome II);
- the law applicable to unjust enrichment is determined a special escape clause of Article 10 IV Rome II if the act of unjust enrichment cannot be fixed on the basis of paragraphs 1–4 of Article 10 Rome II.

Example: A theatre in Germany performed a play written by the English author A and translated by translator B. A and B ask for royalties to be paid by the theatre. Neither is there any relation between the parties (Article 10 I Rome II) nor do they have their habitual residence in the same country (Article 10 II Rome II). Therefore, the claim for royalties based on unjust enrichment must be decided by the law of the country in which the act of unjust enrichment took place (Article 10 III Rome II). This law is German law where the play was performed and this law is identical with the law of the protection as applied under Article 8 I Rome II according to Article 13 Rome II.

[b]   Choice of Law

Article 14 Rome II on choice of law also applies to claims based on unjust enrichment.

[3]   *Agency Without Mandate or Out of Necessity* (Negotiorum Gestio)

[a]   Basic Rules

Article 11 Rome II deals with the law applicable to *negotiorum gestio*, i.e., with claims for damages arising out of an act performed without due authority in connection with affairs of another person. Accordingly, different steps of localizing the applicable law must be distinguished:

- In case of a preexisting relationship between the parties (such as a contract or a tort) which is closely connected with the *negotiorum gestio*, the law governing that relationship applies (Article 11 I Rome II).
- Where there is no such preexisting relationship but the parties have their habitual residence in the same country, the law of the country in which the event that gave rise to the damage occurred applies (Article 11 II Rome II).
- Where the law governing cannot be determined on the basis of paragraphs 1 and 2, the law of the country in which the *negotiorum gestio* was performed shall apply (Article 11 III Rome II).
- A usual escape clause in favor of the law which is manifestly more closely connected is added to the rules mentioned above (Article 11 IV Rome II).

Example: One of the heirs of a deceased person sold part of the estate without being authorized by the other heirs. He may be sued by the other heirs to disgorge the price into the estate to be distributed correctly to all the heirs. This claim may be based on a *negotiorum gestio* of the selling heir. In this case, the applicable law is the one of the country which governs the estate and the relation between the heirs (Article 11 I Rome II).

[b]   Choice of Law

Article 14 Rome II on choice of law (*supra* §12.03[B][1][c] also applies to claims based on *negotiorum gestio.*

[4]   Culpa in Contrahendo

There used to be debate as to whether *culpa in contrahendo* must be qualified as being either contractual or non-contractual. Finally, the qualification as non-contractual prevailed.

[a]   Basic Rules

Accordingly, the applicable law is to be determined according to the following sequence:

- If the obligation arises out of contacts prior to the conclusion of a contract, the law to be applied shall be the law governing the concluded or potentially concluded contract (Article 12 I Rome II).
- Where the law applicable cannot be determined according to Article 12 I Rome II, the law of the country where the damage occurred shall apply (Article 12 II lit. a Rome II).
- When the parties of the dispute have their habitual residence in the same country at the time when the damage occurred, the law of that country shall apply (Article 12 II lit. b Rome II).
- Finally, there is the usual escape clause which makes an exception for the law of the country with which the case has manifestly more close connections (Article 12 II lit. c Rome II).

[b]   Choice of Law

Article 14 Rome II on choice of law (*supra* §12.03[B][1][c] also applies to claims based on *culpa in contrahendo.*

Example: Parties of an international contract of sale had already prepared the final version of their contract (including a choice of English law) and agreed on a specific day for their ultimate signature. Without any reason given, the buyer, based in France, did not show up and later gave notice of not being interested in the merchandise of the German seller anymore. The German seller sues the French party for damages because of culpa in contrahendo. Pursuant to Article 12 I Rome II, the law of the country which would have governed the contract of sale if it had been concluded applies (i.e., English law), rather than German law (*see* § 311 II BGB) as the law of the party bound to supply the characteristic performance (Article 4 I lit. a Rome I). Thus, it is for English law to decide whether there is any obligation on the part of a party to contract negotiations not to pull out at the last moment, without reasonable excuse.

[C]   Recognition of Foreign Judgments

In tort matters and matters of non-contractual obligations, the rules on recognition of foreign judgments apply in the same way as in contractual matters (*supra* §12.02[C]). Thus, Regulation No. 1215/2012 (Brussels Ibis) or the Lugano Convention apply and, if these instruments are not applicable, the German rule of § 328 ZPO governs.

§12.04   LAW OF PROPERTY

[A]   Jurisdiction

The law of property falls within the scope of Regulation 1215/2012 (Brussels Ibis) and the Lugano Convention. Apart from jurisdiction in personam, there is an exclusive jurisdiction in rem for certain matters of immovable property under Article 24 I Regulation 1215/2012 and Article 22 I Lugano Convention. In proceedings over rights in rem in, or tenancies of, immovable property, the courts of the Contracting State in which the property is situated have exclusive jurisdiction regardless of the domicile of plaintiff or defendant. Article 24 I Brussels Ibis and Article 22 I Lugano Convention limit this exclusive jurisdiction in rem by adding another forum for certain tenancies. In proceedings concerning tenancies of immovable property concluded for temporary private use for a maximum period of six consecutive months, the courts of the Member State in which the defendant is domiciled also have jurisdiction, provided that the tenant is a natural person and that the landlord and the tenant are domiciled in the same Member State) or in the same State bound by the Convention (Article 22 I Lugano Convention).

[B]   Applicable Law

The international law of property has not yet been unified in Europe. This part of conflicts law is still national law to be regulated by national legislators or courts. In Germany, Articles 43–46 EGBGB provide the necessary guidance.

[1]   Basic Rule

Matters of property rights are governed by the *lex situs*, i.e., by the law of the country where the piece of property was situated at the time of a certain transaction (Article 43 I EGBGB; English translation of the newly codified provisions in 47 Am.J.Comp.L. 652). If, thereafter, the piece of property is removed to some other country, the right in rem once acquired is preserved as a vested right but cannot be asserted in contradiction to the new *lex situs* (Article 43 II EGBGB).

Examples: 1. Movables stolen in Germany from owner O are sold in Italy to a bona fide purchaser P and title has been validly transferred to him under Article 1153 Codice civile. The buyer P of the object moves to Germany and is sued by the former owner O of the object for return to him. The claim fails because P obtained good title in Italy (then the governing *lex rei sitae*) and, once validly acquired, P keeps title as a vested right so long as he does not transfer it to somebody else.

2. In Germany, the unpaid seller may retain ownership without any formality. If, however, the sold merchandise is exported to Switzerland, where such a clause of retention of ownership has to be registered at the debtor's residence, the German informal security interest cannot be enforced any more unless duly registered in Switzerland, the country of the new *situs*.

Article 43 III EGBGB takes care of a special case of *conflit mobile*. If, e.g., the period of prescription necessary for a transfer of title has not expired before the change of *situs*, the time expired so far will be added to the time necessary under the new *lex situs* for prescription.

Example: A has acquired property of a stolen piece of movable property in Switzerland bona fide and has held it in Zürich for four years without getting any title by prescription (Ersitzung) which requires five years of bona fide possession (Article 728 I ZGB). A moves to Germany having spent four years in Switzerland. In German law, the time period for prescription (Ersitzung) is ten years (§ 937 I BGB). According to Article 43 III EGBGB, A, after six years of bona fide possession, will acquire good title in the stolen object because four years of possession in Switzerland will be added to six years of possession in Germany.

The *lex situs* is subject to the provisions of the special escape clause of Article 46 EGBGB.

[2]   Means of Transportation

According to Article 45 I EGBGB, means of transportation, because of their inherent mobility, are not governed by the respective *lex situs* but by the law of their country of origin. i.e:

- for aircrafts the State of their nationality;
- for ships the State of registration or, if there is no registration, the State of their home port;
- for railway carriages the State granting the original license.

All security interests arising *ex lege* are governed by the law applicable to the claim that is to be secured. The priority among several security interests are governed by the respective state of origin governing under Article 43 I EGBGB. Contractual security interests are governed by the law of the State of origin (Article 43 I EGBGB).

Example: A maritime lien for bunker oil provided by an oil company to a German ship in the port of Piraeus (Greece) is governed by Greek law because the bunker oil was provided in Greece and, insofar, Germen law of registration of the ship does not apply.

[3] Emissions from Real Property

Any claim arising from the adverse effects of emissions from real property is governed by the law applicable to tort claims under Regulation Rome II.

[C] Recognition of Foreign Judgments

The Regulation Brussels Ibis and Lugano Convention apply. Foreign judgments violating the exclusive jurisdiction in rem will not be recognized (Article 45 I lit. e (ii) Brussels Ibis and Article 35 I Lugano Convention). If these instruments do not apply, foreign judgments are recognized under bilateral treaties or under domestic law (§ 328 ZPO).

§12.05 FAMILY LAW AND LAW OF PERSONS

International family law nowadays regulates marriage of heterosexual couples, marriage of homosexual couples, registered partnerships and the relations of parent and child.

International family law has remained untouched by the European Union for a long time. This has changed in recent years. However, according to Article 81 III TFEU, family matters require unanimity of the Member States or enhanced cooperation of cooperating Member States under Articles 326 et seq. TFEU.

[A] Marriage

[1] Celebration of Marriage in Germany

German registrars have jurisdiction to register every marriage performed in Germany (§ 11 I *Personenstandsgesetz* or Personal Status Act).

Whether a person can validly marry someone is determined by the law of the country which he or she is a national of (Article 13 I EGBGB). If that country refers back into German law (as, e.g., the law of the person's domicile), German law applies. If the primarily designated law refers to the law of a third country *(Weiterverweisung)*, that law governs (Article 4 I EGBGB). If a foreign law governing the substantive requirements of marriage does not allow a marriage, German law applies if:

- the engaged person is a German national or is habitually residing in Germany; and
- the engaged person has undertaken all reasonable steps to satisfy the requirements of the governing law; and

445

- the invalidity of the marriage to be entered into is incompatible with the freedom to marry ensured by Article 6 of the German Constitution (*Grundgesetz, GG*), in particular, if a previous marriage has been dissolved in Germany or abroad, the foreign divorce decree is recognized in Germany and such a German or foreign decree is not recognized by the governing law (Article 13 II EGBGB).

Marriages by minors of less than 16 years are null and void. The marriages are voidable if the spouse was more than 16 years of age, but less than 18 years old (Article 13 III EGBGB).

The form of marriage to be celebrated in Germany is governed by German law, i.e., the marriage has to be celebrated before a German registrar (Article 13 IV EGBGB). If, however, foreigners want to marry in Germany, they are allowed to do so before a person duly authorized by the government of the State of which one of the engaged persons is a national (Article 13 IV EGBGB).

[2]   Marriages Celebrated Abroad

Marriages celebrated abroad are recognized in Germany if the marriage is valid according to the national laws of the spouses. If, however, the marriage celebrated abroad is a marriage of a minor spouse of less than 16 years of age at the time of marriage, the marriage is null and void and therefore cannot be recognized in Germany. If the marriage is one of a minor of 16 years of age but less than 18 years of age at the time of marriage, the marriage is avoided by German courts according to § 98 II FamFG. This much debated provision has been added in 2017 to German law in order to fight marriage of minors fleeing from the countries of the Middle East and settling in Germany as asylum seekers or refugees.

A foreign marriage is valid as to form if it is celebrated abroad in accordance with the law of the country where the celebration took place or in accordance with the law governing the validity as to substance (Article 11 I EGBGB).

[B]   Personal Effects of Marriage

Unless governed by special rules (*see infra*), the general effects of marriage between husband and wife are dealt with in Article 14 EGBGB. The general idea of this provision is to determine the governing law, which is or was common to the spouses. In order to realize this goal, a complicated system was introduced. Under Article 14 I EGBGB, the general effects of marriage are governed by:

- the law of the State of which both spouses are nationals (special rules apply to persons being nationals of more than one State) or were nationals if one of them still keeps the former common nationality; otherwise by;
- the law of the State in which both spouses have their habitual residence or had their habitual residence if one of them still resides there; ultimately by;

– the law of the State with which the spouses are mutually most closely connected in some other manner.

[C]   Maintenance

Maintenance is the most important personal effect of marriage and extensively regulated by international and European instruments.

[1]   *Maintenance: Jurisdiction*

In matters of maintenance, Regulation (EC) No. 4/2009 of December 18, 2008 on jurisdiction, applicable law, recognition and enforcement of decisions and cooperation in matters relating to maintenance obligations (Maintenance Regulation) exclusively applies. This Regulation provides four different heads of jurisdiction: general jurisdiction, jurisdiction by choice of court or based on defendant's appearance before the court, subsidiary jurisdiction, forum necessitatis and jurisdiction for provisional measures. Ancillary provisions of Articles 8–13 deal with "Limits of proceedings," "seizing of a court," "examination as to jurisdiction," "examination as to admissibility," "lis pendens," and "related actions."

[a]   *Article 3: General Jurisdiction*

German courts have jurisdiction in matters of maintenance if:

– the defendant is habitually resident in Germany (the same is true under Article 2 I Lugano Convention); or
– the creditor is habitually resident in Germany (the same is true under Article 5 II lit a Lugano Convention),
– German courts have jurisdiction concerning the status of a person (e.g.,divorce jurisdiction according to Brussels IIbis Regulation) and German courts have to decide on matters to maintenance unless status jurisdiction is solely based on the nationality of one of the parties (the same is true under Article 5 II lit. b Lugano Convention);
– German courts have jurisdiction in matters concerning parental responsibility (e.g., jurisdiction according to the Brussels IIbis Regulation or the Hague Convention on Minors of 1996) and German courts also have to decide matters of maintenance unless jurisdiction on parental responsibility is solely based on the nationality of one of the parties (the same is true under Article 5 II lit. c Lugano Convention).

[b]   *Articles 4 and 5: Choice of Court and Appearance of the Defendant*

The parties may agree that the courts of Member States or of states parties to the Lugano Convention have jurisdiction to decide matters of maintenance (Article 4 Maintenance Regulation).

If the claim is brought in the court of a Member State not having jurisdiction under the Regulation, this court shall have jurisdiction thanks to appearance of the defendant (Article 5 Maintenance Regulation).

[c]   *Article 6: Subsidiary Jurisdiction*

If there is no court having jurisdiction pursuant Articles 3–5 and no court of a state party to the Lugano Convention which is not a Member State has jurisdiction pursuant the provisions of that Convention, the courts of the Member State of the common nationality of the parties shall have jurisdiction.

Example: A couple from Lebanon, not yet habitually resident in Germany, applies being admitted as refugees in Germany. The wife asks for maintenance. German courts have jurisdiction pursuant Article 6 because there is no jurisdiction under Articles 3–5 and the parties have a common nationality.

[d]   *Article 7: Forum Necessitatis*

If there is no jurisdiction pursuant Articles 3–6, the claim for maintenance cannot be brought in the Middle East because of warfare and if the case has a sufficient connection with Germany, German courts are *fora* necessitatis.

Example: If the couple in the last example have no common nationality, but she is of Transjordan and he of Lebanon, the maintenance jurisdiction of German courts may be fixed by Article 7 Maintenance Regulation.

[e]   *Article 14: Provisional and Protective Measures*

Assets of the defendant, located in Germany may be seized by protective measures (*einstweilige Anordnung durch dinglichen Arrest*) in Germany although the maintenance proceedings are or will be pending in another Member State (e.g., in Austria where the debtor and the defendant are habitually resident).

[f]   *Lugano Convention 2007*

With respect to state parties of the Lugano Convention, German courts have jurisdiction in maintenance matters either if the defendant has his domicile in Germany (Article 2 I Lugano Convention) or if the maintenance creditor has his domicile in Germany (Article 5 II lit. a Lugano Convention) or German courts are competent to decide matters of status or of parental responsibility (Article 5 II lit. b and c Lugano

Convention). In the two cases mentioned at last, German courts also have jurisdiction to decide the ancillary matter of maintenance.

[2]   Applicable Law

The law applicable to maintenance obligations between spouses is determined by the Hague Protocol of November 23, 2007 on the Law Applicable to Maintenance Obligations (Hague Protocol). The Protocol is declared applicable within the EU by virtue of Article 15 Maintenance Regulation and by virtue of its ratification by the Member States (all Member States except Denmark and the UK have ratified the Hague Protocol). According to the Hague Protocol, the law of the place of habitual residence of the maintenance creditor primarily governs the maintenance claim (Article 3 I of the Hague Protocol) unless the parties have chosen another law (Article 8 Hague Protocol). In the case of spouses or ex-spouses, the law designated by Article 3 shall not apply if one of the parties objects and the law of another state, in particular the state of their last common habitual residence, has a closer connection with the marriage. In such cases, the law of that other state shall apply (Article 5 Hague Protocol).

[3]   Recognition and Enforcement of Foreign Judgments

Maintenance decisions of foreign Member States are governed by Articles 16–43 Maintenance Regulation. A distinction is drawn between such Member States bound by the Hague Protocol of 2007 (Articles 17–22 Maintenance Regulation) and such not bound by the Hague Protocol (Articles 23–38 Maintenance Regulation). For the recognition of decisions rendered by a court of a Member State, the exequatur procedure was abolished (Article 17 Maintenance Regulation) and enforcement in Germany can be refused or suspended under very limited conditions only, not comprising any public policy exception. This is different with respect to decisions given in Member States not bound by the 2007 Hague Protocol (e.g., Denmark). Whether this distinction, based on the law applicable to maintenance claims, makes any sense, shall not be discussed here.

Maintenance decisions of state parties to the Lugano Convention are recognized and enforced according to Articles 32 et seq. Lugano Convention.

Maintenance decisions of countries not being Member States but state parties to the 1973 Hague Convention on the Recognition and Enforcement of Decisions Relating to Maintenance Obligations (e.g., Albania, Andorra, Australia, Norway, Switzerland, Turkey, and Ukraine) are recognized in Germany if the requirements of this 1973 Convention are met.

Maintenance decisions given in all other countries neither being Member States nor state parties to the 1973 Hague Convention (e.g., United States, Canada) are recognized in Germany if these decisions meet the German requirements for recognition set out in §§ 108–110 FamFG.

[D]   Matrimonial Property

Matrimonial property is regulated by the Council Regulation (EU) 2016/1103 of June 24, 2016 implementing enhanced cooperation in the area of jurisdiction, applicable law and the recognition and enforcement of decisions in matters of matrimonial property regimes (Matrimonial Property Regulation = MPR). All EU Member States except Denmark, Estonia, Hungary, Ireland, Latvia, Lithuania, Poland, Rumania, Slovakia, and the UK take part in the cooperation. The Regulation applies in Germany from January 29, 2019 and covers the three main subject matters of international matrimonial property as indicated by its title. Until January 28, 2019, FamFG, Article 15 EGBGB and the statute of 1969 on matrimonial property of expelled people and refugees will continue to apply (*cf.* the 2nd edition for further details).

[1]   Jurisdiction

[a]   Articles 4 and 5: Dependent Jurisdiction

German jurisdiction is given as ancillary jurisdiction in matters:

- of succession if there is German probate jurisdiction (Article 4 MPR); or
- of divorce if there is German divorce jurisdiction (Article 5 I MPR).

[b]   Article 6: Original Jurisdiction

In all cases not covered by Article 4 or 5, German courts have jurisdiction in matters of matrimonial property if, at the time the court was seized:

- the parties had their place of habitual residence in Germany (Article 6 lit. a MPR); or failing that
- one of the parties still resides in Germany where the spouses were last habitually resident (Article 6 lit. b MPR); or failing that
- the respondent is habitually resident in Germany (Article 6 lit. c MPR); or failing that
- the spouses' common nationality is German (Article 6 lit. d MPR).

[c]   Articles 7 and 8: Choice of Court

The parties may agree in writing that the courts of a Member State whose law is applicable pursuant to Article 22 or 26 I lit. a or b MPR or where the conclusion of the marriage took place shall have jurisdiction in matters of matrimonial property (Article 7 MPR). The same is true for jurisdiction by appearance of the defendant (Article 8 MPR).

[d]   *Article 9: Alternative Jurisdiction*

If the marriage in question is not recognized for purposes of matrimonial property proceedings by German private international law, other courts may be competent to seize jurisdiction in matters of matrimonial property (Article 9 MPR).

    Example: A Greek marriage in Germany is celebrated before a Greek-orthodox pope not authorized to do so under Greek state law. According to German private international law (Article 13 IV EGBGB), this marriage is non-existent (*Nicht-Ehe*). In this case, German courts competent according to Article 6 lit. a MPR (at the habitual, residence of the spouses) may decline jurisdiction and the Greek spouses may agree to choose the courts of another Member State or turn to Greek courts competent pursuant to Article 6 lit. d MPR.

[e]   *Article 10: Subsidiary Jurisdiction*

If there is no jurisdiction of any Member State of the Union, but immovable property of one or both spouses is located in Germany, German courts have jurisdiction, however, limited to immovable property located in Germany (Article 10 MPR).

[f]   *Article 11: Forum Necessitatis*

In case there is no Member State jurisdiction by virtue of Articles 4–10 MPR – including the decline of jurisdiction based on Article 9 and the absence of subsidiary jurisdiction by virtue of Article 10 MPR, Member State courts can serve as *fora necessitatis* if matrimonial property proceedings cannot if proceedings cannot reasonably be brought or conducted or would be impossible in a third state with which the case is closely connected. (Article 11 MPR).

    Example: A Syrian couple of refugees applying for asylum in Germany is expected to have their marriage declared null and void (*Aufhebung*) given that the wife was 14 years old at the time of marriage (§ 98 II FamFG). There is no other jurisdiction pursuant to the MPR because neither spouse is habitually resident in Germany and has German nationality. Proceedings cannot be brought before Syrian courts without great difficulty because of the ongoing war. With respect to matrimonial property (return of payment of *mahr* = a sort of dowry) German courts have jurisdiction as *fora necessitatis*.

[g]   *Article 13: Limitation of Proceedings*

Jurisdiction under the MPR is comprehensive and not limited to assets located in the Member State exercising jurisdiction. There are, however, two exceptions.

    If assets are located in a third state and this state is likely not to recognize the decision of another country with respect to these local assets, one of the parties may request the court not to rule on such assets (Article 13 I MPR).

Article 13 II MPR contains an opening clause for exception clauses provided by the national law of the court seized. Because German law does not allow to limit jurisdiction by request of one party, this exception does not apply in Germany.

[2]   *Applicable Law*

[a]   *Law Governing until January 28, 2019*

The matrimonial property regime is governed by the law applicable to the general effects of marriage at the time of marriage (*supra* sub [a]), Article 15 I EGBGB. Contrary to the general effects of marriage, the matrimonial property regime is fixed at the time of marriage and does not change if the spouses change their nationality or habitual residence.

The spouses may make a valid choice of law by a formally valid marriage contract (usually in notarized form). The spouses are not, however, completely free to choose any law they like. By virtue of Article 15 II EGBGB, their choice is restricted to:

- the law of the State of which one of them is a national; or
- the law of the State in which one of them has his habitual residence; or
- for matters involving immovable property, the law of the State where the property is located.

The choice of law may be altered at any time. Spouses should try to fix the law governing their matrimonial property regime in a way that it will coincide with the prospective law governing their succession. According to Article 16 EGBGB, third parties relying bona fide on the applicability of a given matrimonial property regime are protected in their reliance under certain circumstances.

[b]   *MPR: Basic Principles*

The governing law is determined by Articles 20–35 MPR, applicable in the cooperating Member States as of January 29, 2019. The choice of law rules evidence six basic principles:

- *universal application*: the law designated by the MPR shall be applied regardless of whether it is the law of a Member State (Article 20 MPR);
- *unity of assets*: the law applicable governs all assets falling under the MPR-regime no matter where they are located (Article 21 MPR);
- *immutability of the law applicable*: the law to be applied is fixed by party agreement or by virtue of objective conflict rules and does not change in case of a change in the facts underlying the respective connecting factors (Articles 22 and 26 MPR);
- *party autonomy*: the parties are allowed to fix the law to be applied to their regime by a limited choice of law (Article 22 MPR);

- *no renvoi*: a renvoi of the applicable foreign law is not accepted (Article 32 MPR);
- *overriding mandatory and public policy provisions of the forum not excluded*: these kinds of provisions of the forum state are not excluded and may be applied (Articles 30 and 31 MPR).

[c]   *Articles 22–25: Limited Choice of Law*

Choice of law (Articles 22–24 MPR) has to be distinguished from a substantive matrimonial property agreement (Article 25 MPR).

According to Article 22 I MPR the spouses or future spouses may agree at any time to choose for their matrimonial property regime either:

- the law of the State where both spouses or one of them is habitually resident at the time the agreement is concluded; or
- the law of a State of nationality of either spouse at the time the agreement is concluded.

The choice of law clause does not work retroactively (Article 22 II MPR), has to be formally valid (Article 23 MPR) and the consent to this agreement has to meet the requirements set out in Article 24 MPR.

As in most jurisdictions there is more than one regime for matrimonial property, Article 25 MPR provides rules on the formal validity of matrimonial property agreements.

Example: Future spouses (the fiancé is German and has his habitual residence in Germany, the fiancée is Swiss and is habitually resident in Switzerland) choose German law as the law applicable to their matrimonial property relations and coincidentally enter into an agreement in favor of separation of property, as known in German law (§ 1414 BGB) in Switzerland. The choice of German law may be done in writing unless Switzerland lays down additional formal requirements (Article 23 IV MPR). After elimination of Article 15 III EGBGB (abolished by the MPR in 2019) Article 11 EGBGB applies which – just as Article 53 I 1 IPRG of Switzerland – does not stipulate additional formal requirements. But with respect to the agreement of the German regime of separation of property, certification by a notary public is required (§ 1410 BGB) and necessary pursuant to Article 25 II and III MPR. The same would be true if the couple chose Swiss separation of property regime (Article 184 Swiss Civil Code, Article 25 III MPR).

[d]   *Article 26: Applicable Law in the Absence of Any Choice*

In the absence of a choice of law agreement, the law applicable to the matrimonial property regime, according to Article 26 I MPR, shall be the law of the State:

- of the spouses' first common habitual residence after the conclusion of the marriage (except the escape clause of Article 26 III MPR applies); or failing that
- of the spouses' common single nationality at the time of conclusion of the marriage; or failing that
- the law with which both spouses, taking into account all circumstances, have the closest connecting at the time of the conclusion of the marriage.

Article 26 III MPR escape clause leading into the law of one spouse's nationality. If Article 26 I lit. a MPR applies (law of the first common habitual residence), either spouse may choose a different law than the one applicable by virtue of Article 26 I lit. a MPR if he demonstrates that:

- the spouses had their last common habitual residence in that other State for a significantly longer period of time than in the State designated pursuant to Article 26 I lit. a MPR; and
- both spouses had bona fide assumed that the aw of that other State applies in arranging or planning their property relations.

Example: An elderly couple of mixed nationality (the husband is a German, the wife is a Swiss citizen) wants to file for divorce in Germany. The spouses had their first common habitual residence in Switzerland where the husband had a job for two years. After expiration of two years the couple moved to France and lived there for more than thirty years. Following her retirement, the wife (now living in Switzerland) sues her husband (now living in Germany) for divorce according to Article 3 I lit. a Brussels IIbis Regulation, Article 5 I MPR, and assumes that Swiss law applies to their matrimonial property relations. The husband argues that French law will govern the relations because the couple had their last common habitual residence in France, lived there for a considerably longer time than in Switzerland and had relied on French law (which applied pursuant to Articles 54, 55 Swiss IPRG) when planning their property relations. The motion filed by the husband should be admitted under Article 26 III MPR.

Some specific provisions deal with the scope of the law applicable (Article 27 MPR), with the effect in respect of third parties (Article 28 MPR), and adaption of rights in rem (Article 29 MPR).

[3]   *Recognition of Foreign Judgments*

[a]   *Recognition until January 28, 2019*

Until the MPR becomes binding on January 29, 2019, the recognition and enforcement of foreign decisions on matrimonial property law is regulated by §§ 108–110 FamFG unless there are specific international instruments taking priority over these national provisions and providing international standards of recognition and enforcement. With respect to matrimonial property, there are no such international instruments. The Hague Conference has never dealt with the recognition of matrimonial property decisions.

[b]   MPR: Recognition from January 29, 2019

As of January 29, 2019, the MPR is in force in the Member States taking part in the enhanced cooperation with respect to matrimonial property. Pursuant to this instrument, foreign decisions on matrimonial property will be recognized under Articles 36 et seq., MPR. Decisions of third states or Member States not bound by the MPR, are to be recognized pursuant to §§ 108–110 FamFG.

[E]   Divorce

[1]   Jurisdiction

In Germany, only public courts have jurisdiction to dissolve a marriage (Article 17 II EGBGB). Religious courts, consular officers, or private parties (under Islamic or Jewish law) have no power to dissolve a marriage if they are acting in Germany.

[a]   Jurisdiction under European Law

According to Article 3 I of Council Regulation No. 2201/2003 of November 27, 2003 concerning jurisdiction and the recognition and enforcement of judgments in matrimonial matters and the matters of parental responsibility (Brussels IIbis), divorce jurisdiction is vested in German courts if:

– the spouses are habitually resident in Germany; or
– the spouses were last habitually resident in Germany if one of them still resides in Germany; or
– the respondent is habitually resident in Germany; or
– in the event of a joint application, either one of the spouses is habitually resident in Germany; or
– the applicant is habitually resident in Germany if he or she resided in Germany for at least a year prior to the application; or
– the applicant is habitually resident in Germany if he or she resided in Germany for at least six months prior to the application and is a German national; or
– both spouses are German nationals.

These heads of jurisdiction are exclusive if the respondent is habitually resident in a Member State or is a national (with respect to the UK: is a domiciliary) of a Member State (Article 6 Regulation 2201/2003). If a German wife applies for a divorce in Germany and her American husband is habitually resident in New York, German courts have jurisdiction under Article 3 I Regulation 2201/2003 (second but last indent) but also under § 98 I no. 1 FamFG. In this event, jurisdiction provided by the Regulation is not exclusive and hence national heads of jurisdiction are given alternatively.

[b]   Jurisdiction under German Domestic Law

If there is no jurisdiction under Regulation 2201/2003, German domestic law applies (Article 7 I Regulation 2201/2003), i.e., § 98 I FamFG. Under this provision, German courts have jurisdiction in divorce proceedings if:

- at least one spouse is a German national or was a German national at the time of marriage; or
- both spouses have their habitual residence in Germany; or
- one spouse is stateless and habitually resident in Germany; or
- only spouse only has his habitual residence in Germany under the condition that it is not impossible a limine that at German divorce decree will recognized by the law of nationality of any of both spouses.

Under § 98 FamFG, German courts do *not* have divorce jurisdiction only because one of the spouses is domiciled or habitually resident in Germany. Rather, one of the additional four criteria mentioned above must be met. In the United States of America and in some other countries, a divorce decree rendered at the place of habitual residence of the plaintiff will be recognized. Therefore, German courts will assume jurisdiction under § 98 I no. 4 FamFG if one of the spouses is a national of a State which will recognize a German divorce decree.

[c]   Jurisdiction in Collateral Matters of Divorce

Collateral matters are not covered by Article 3 of Brussels IIbis. Jurisdiction for these matters are provided, e.g., by Article 5 MPR or by Articles 8 et seq. Brussels IIbis or by Article 5 II lit. b Lugano Convention.

[2]   Applicable Law

Since June 21, 2012 Council Regulation (EU) No. 1259/2010 of December 20, 2010 implementing enhanced cooperation in the area of the law applicable to divorce and legal separation (Rome III) applies in Germany. At least sixteen Member States (Austria, Belgium, Bulgaria, France, Germany, Greece, Hungary, Italy, Latvia, Lithuania, Luxemburg, Malta, Portugal, Rumania, Slovenia, and Spain) take part in this enhanced cooperation and apply the regulation.

[a]   Basic Principles

Five basic principles of Rome III should first be mentioned:

- The law applicable need not be the law of a Member State. Rome III applies *universally* and irrespectively of whether the designated law is that of a Member State or not (Article 4 Rome III).

- The parties may, however, *choose* the law applicable to their divorce with a restriction to the law of specific countries mentioned in Article 5 III Rome III.
- In the absence of a choice of law clause, the governing law should have a close connection to *either* spouse (Article 8 Rome III).
- A *renvoi* of foreign law governing divorce is *not* accepted (Article 11 Rome III).
- The law of the forum may be applied if the foreign law applicable pursuant to Rome III violates the public policy of the forum or the general principles underling the enhanced cooperation (Articles 10 and 12 Rome III). This includes the equal possibility of both spouses to file for divorce.

[b]   Choice of Law

A choice of the law applicable is restricted to the law of four different jurisdictions mentioned in Article 5 I Rome III:

- the law of habitual residence of the spouses at the time they enter the agreement;
- the law of a former habitual residence of the spouses in the same state if one of the spouses still resides there at the time they enter the agreement;
- the law of nationality of either spouse at the time they enter the agreement;
- the law of the forum.

The consent and substantive validity are to be determined by the law which would govern under this Regulation if the agreement or term were valid (Article 6 I Rome III). Form is governed by Article 7 Rome III.

[c]   Applicable Law in the Absence of a Choice of Law

If the parties did not choose the applicable law, Article 8 Rome III determines the law applicable to divorce proceedings. Four different steps of a common or formerly common connecting factor have to be distinguished. The court must apply the law of the state

- where the spouses are habitually resident at the time the court is seized; or failing that
- where the spouses were last habitually resident, provided that the period of residence did not end more than one year before the court was seized, in so far as one of the spouses still resides in that state at the time the court is seized; or failing that
- of which both spouses are nationals at the time the court is seized; or failing that
- the law of the state where the court is seized.

[d]   Public Policy

Article 10 Rome III provides a special public policy clause. Where the law applicable makes no provision for divorce or does not grant one of the spouses equal access to divorce or legal separation on grounds of gender, the law of the forum applies.

Example: Muslim spouses of Egyptian nationality living in Germany have agreed that their divorce shall be governed by the religious law of Egypt for Muslims. The wife files for divorce before a German court and is faced with Egyptian law, which does not grant equal access to divorce. In this event, Article 10 Rome III calls for the application German law as law of the forum. I prefer a reductory reading of Article 10 Rome III, resulting in a modified application of Egyptian law so as to guarantee equal access of both spouses to divorce.

[e]   Law Applicable in Collateral Matters of Divorce

Collateral matters of divorce proceedings such as, e.g., maintenance, matrimonial property or custody are governed by the law applicable to these matters according to the relevant Regulations, Conventions or national law.

[3]   Recognition of Foreign Judgments

Divorce decrees given by a court of a Member State are recognized according to Articles 21, 22 and 24 et seq. Regulation 2201/2003 (Brussels IIbis). Foreign non-European decrees are submitted to the ministry of justice of the German state where one of the spouses has his or her habitual residence (Article 7 § 1 of Statute of August 11, 1961, on the Revision of Family Law – FamRÄndG). Such exequatur proceedings are, however, not necessary if both spouses, at the time of the rendering the divorce decree, were nationals of the state where the marriage was dissolved (Article 7 § 1 I [3] FamRÄndG). Apart from provisions granting jurisdiction to recognize foreign divorce decrees, the requirements for recognition are governed by §§ 107, 109 FamFG. Unlike under § 328 I No. 5 and II ZPO, reciprocity is not required for the recognition of foreign divorce decrees (§ 109 IV FamFG, Article 7 § 1 I [2] FamRÄndG).

[F]   Registered Partnerships

[1]   Establishment

According to Article 17b I 1 EGBGB, the establishment of a registered partnership is governed by the law of the state where the partnership is registered. In Germany, only same-sex partners were eligible enter into a registered partnership under the Act of February 16, 2001 on Registered Partnerships, and only until October 1, 2017. Partnerships between couples of the same or opposite sex are recognized in Germany if validly registered abroad. This is also true for German couples of opposite sex registered as partners abroad and living abroad because there is no provision holding that Germans can only register if the partners are of the same sex.

If the same partners have been registered in different countries the last registration determines the effects of the registered partnership since that last registration (Article 17b III EGBGB).

[2] Effects

[a] Basic Rule

The law of the state where the partnership is registered governs the general and the patrimonial effects of the registered partnership (Article 17b I 1 EGBGB) unless EU-Regulations or Hague Conventions provide otherwise.

[b] Maintenance

EU Regulation No. 4/2009 on maintenance applies to registered partners likewise because their relation is a "family relationship" within the definition of Article 1 I Maintenance Regulation. The same principles as those mentioned *supra* at [C]. apply.

[c] Property Relations

Council Regulation (EU) 2016/1104 of June 24, 2016 implementing enhanced cooperation in the area of jurisdiction, applicable law and the recognition and enforcement of decisions in matters of property consequences of registered partnerships (Partnership Property Regulation = PPR) will apply from January 29, 2019 in those Member States taking part in the enhanced cooperation in this field. These States are: Austria, Belgium, Bulgaria, Croatia, Cyprus, Czech Republic, Finland, France, Germany, Greece, Italy, Luxemburg, Malta, Netherlands, Portugal, Slovenia, Spain, and Sweden. Ten states do not take part in enhanced cooperation: Ireland and the UK, Denmark, Estonia, Hungary, Latvia, Lithuania, Poland, Romania, and Slovakia.

The PPR is almost identical with the MPR (*supra* at [D]) except two major differences; the partners may choose the law of the state under whose law the registered partnership was created (Article 22 I lit. c PPR) and this law applies in the absence of a choice of law agreement (Article 26 I PPR).

[d] Remaining Effects of Personal Relations

Private international law does not deal with matters of public law as, e.g., the registration of persons as "married," "registered partners," or as "single," the tax exemptions for married persons or pension rights of spouses or registered partners (*Versorgungsausgleich*). It is up to the competent authorities and the law to be applied by them to determine whether a registered partner qualifies as a person of a special status favored by provisions of domestic public law (*see* Article 17b I 2 and 3 EGBGB).

[3]   Termination

The termination of a registered partnership is governed by the law of the State where the partnership has been registered (Article 17b I 1 EGBGB).

[G]   Registered Heterosexual Partners

In Germany, heterosexual partners cannot be registered as partners. This is different in countries like France where heterosexual partners may register as parties to a "*pacte civil de solidarité*" (*PACS*) pursuant to Article 515-1 Code civil. Such a partnership is recognized in Germany and has the consequences mentioned above sub B.

[H]   Marriage of Same-Sex Partners

Since October 1, 2017, same-sex partners may enter marriage with the same consequences as heterosexual partners. According to Article 17b IV EGBGB, the provisions of registered partners apply *mutatis mutandis*. EU Regulations and Hague Conventions on marriage will still apply likewise, given that these instruments do not define "marriage" but leave the interpretation of this term to their respective Member States. For want of unified rules on registered partnership, German courts are very likely to apply the Brussels IIbis Regulation, the Maintenance Regulation, the MPR and the Rome III regulation to same-sex marriages. These issues will soon be regulated in an "amending" bill to the same-sex marriage bill.

[I]   Reputed Spouses, De Facto-Marriages and Cohabitants

There are no specific national, inter- or supranational provisions for reputed spouses, de facto marriages or cohabitants not formally married or registered. If, however, the partners of such unions have reciprocal obligations under foreign law and the question of whether they form a union is to be decided as an incidental question in legal proceedings in Germany, some private law consequences may in fact be acknowledged. Matters are different in public law. Once the registration or formal validity of a marriage is required, a de facto-union cannot meet this requirement.

[J]   Parent and Child

[1]   *Establishment of Parent-Child Relations by Decent*

[a]   *Jurisdiction*

In most cases, parent-child relationships are established by law (e.g., by birth or by recognition by the parent) without necessary adjudication. In these cases, the question of jurisdiction does not arise.

In all other cases, German courts have jurisdiction for establishing a parent-child relationship through a law suit or contesting such a relation if one of the parties is a German national or has his or her habitual residence in Germany (§ 100 FamFG).

[b]   *The Law Applicable*

Descent is governed by the law of the state where the child is habitually resident (Article 19 I 1 EGBGB). Descent from each of the parents can also be established under the national law of the respective parent (Article 19 I 2 EGBGB). If the child's mother is married, descent may be established under the law governing the general effects of marriage under Article 14 I EGBGB (Article 19 I 3 EGBGB). By this alternativity applicable law German legal doctrine leans towards a better law-approach, favoring the valid establishment of a parent-child-relationship. In such cases, a *renvoi* will not be accepted if it would harm the child.

The establishment of descent may be contested under each law governing the establishment and the child may contest it under the law of the state where it is habitually resident (Article 20 EGBGB).

[c]   *Recognition of Foreign Judgments*

Foreign decisions on the establishment of parent-child relations are recognized in Germany pursuant to §§ 108, 109 FamFG.

Up to now, German law prohibits surrogate mothers to give birth to a child in replacement of spouses or partners not being able to give birth to a child themselves. However, foreign court decisions may declare not the surrogate parents but the ordering couple, residents of Germany, to be the parents of the child. Such a decision was recognized in Germany under the condition that at least one spouse of the ordering couple is the natural parent of the child. If, however, the surrogate mother gives birth to a child with no natural relations to the ordering couple, the child has to be given into foster care by the ordering couple with an option to adopt it later on. This being said, the European Court of Human Rights decided that the ECHR requires that states make sure that surrogate children do not have to suffer from the "sins" of the(ir) ordering parents.

[2]   Establishment of Parent-Child Relations by Adoption

With respect to adoption of children, there are no EU regulations, but a well-received Hague Convention adopted in 1993 (*see* below).

[a]   Jurisdiction

According to § 101 FamFG, German courts have jurisdiction in adoption cases if either the adopting persons or the child is German or has his habitual residence in Germany.

[b]   Applicable Law

Adoptions in Germany are governed by the national law of the adopting persons (Article 22 I 1 EGBGB). If the adopting parents are married or registered as partners, the law governing their relationship applies (Article 22 I 2 and 3 EGBGB).

In order to fight international child trafficking, the Hague Conference adopted the Convention of 1993 on Protection of Children and Cooperation in Respect of Intercountry Adoption. This Convention was ratified by Germany and implemented by the so-called Implementation Act of 2001 (*Adoptionsübereinkommens-Ausführungsgesetz*). Pursuant to these instruments, the state parties have to make sure that the state of origin of the child cooperates with the country of adoption and makes sure that the child left the country of origin lawfully in order to be adopted abroad.

[c]   Recognition of Foreign Adoptions

Adoption orders of ninety-seven states parties (all EU Member States are parties and also Canada and the USA) to the Hague Convention of 1993 are recognized pursuant to Articles 23 et seq. Hague Convention. Other orders (e.g., local adoptions not covered by the Hague Convention and orders of Argentina or Japan not being state parties) are recognized under §§ 108, 109 FamFG.

[3]   Hague Convention on the Protection of Children

The Hague Convention of October 19, 1996 on Jurisdiction, applicable Law, Recognition, Enforcement and Cooperation in Respect of Parental Responsibility and Measures for the Protection of Children (Hague CPC) is valid in forty-seven countries (as of 2017). All EU Member States are state parties to this Convention, replacing the old Hague Convention of 1961 on the Protection of Minors. Between Member States of the EU, the Brussels Regulation IIbis applies if the child concerned has his habitual residence in the territory of a Member State and, as concerns recognition and enforcement of judgments in another Member State, even if the child had his habitual residence in a third state (e.g., Switzerland) which is a state party to the Hague CPC (Article 61 Brussels IIbis).

[a] Jurisdiction

Court protection orders in children (equivalent to a person until reaching the age of 18 years) and his property may be issued by German courts under the Hague Convention of 1996 on the Protection of Children (Hague CPC) if:

- the child is habitually resident in Germany (Articles 5 I and 7 Hague CPC); or
- the child is present in Germany if it is a refugee or without any known habitual residence (Article 6 Hague CPC; Article 13 Brussels IIbis);
- divorce proceedings are pending in Germany and the state of the child's foreign habitual residence agrees that measures of protection are taken by German courts (Article 10 Hague CPC) or the parties of divorce proceedings made a choice-of-court agreement in this respect (Article 12 Brussels IIbis);
- the child or its property are situated on German soil, bearing the consequence that Germany may take necessary protection measures (Article 11 Hague CPC); or
- German courts at the place of the child's dwelling or at the place of the property belonging to the child may take provisional measures to protect the person or property (Article 12 Hague CPC);
- If there is no jurisdiction in any Member State under Brussels IIbis, German law applies according to Article 14 Brussels IIbis. Therefore, German courts may, by virtue of § 99 I 1 FamFG, take protective measures for a German child habitually resident in, e.g., Africa.

German authorities may decline jurisdiction in two situations:

- if the authority considers the authority of another contracting state in a better place to assess the best interest of the child and the other state accepts to assume jurisdiction (Article 8 Hague CPC; Article 15 Brussels IIbis); or
- another contacting state asks for jurisdiction and therefore the German court declines to assume jurisdiction (Article 9 Hague CPC).

[b] Applicable Law

The law applicable is exclusively regulated by Articles 15–22 of the Hague CPC in. The law at the child's habitual residence governs any measure of protection (Article 15 I Hague CPC), as well as the attribution and extinction of parental responsibility by operation of law (Article 16 Hague CPC) and the exercise of parental responsibility (Article 17 Hague CPC) even with respect to any transaction of the parents as the child's legal representative (Article 19 Hague CPC).

Renvoi is not accepted (Article 21 Hague CPC) and the law at the child's habitual residence can only be refused to be applied if that law manifestly violates the public policy of the forum state (Article 22 Hague CPC).

[c]   Recognition of Measures Taken by Foreign Authorities

With respect to recognition of measures taken by foreign authorities, a distinction has to be drawn between measures taken by Member States, those taken by contracting states and others taken by states not bound by any convention ratified by Germany.

- Measures taken by EU Member States are recognized under to Articles 21 et seq. Brussels IIbis (Article 61 lit. b Brussels IIbis).
- Measures taken by contracting states of the Hague CPC (e.g., by Norway, Switzerland or Turkey) are recognized pursuant to Articles 23 et seq. Hague CPC).
- Measures taken by states not bound by any Convention with Germany (e.g., Canada, USA) are recognized according to §§ 108 et seq. FamFG.

In all these cases, at least three conditions have to be met for recognition: (1) jurisdiction of the foreign authority (except Article 24 Brussels IIbis); (2) fair hearing, and (3) no violation of German public policy.

[4]   Hague Child Abduction Convention of 1980

The Hague Convention of October 25, 1980 on the Civil Aspects of International Child Abduction (Hague CAC) has been ratified by Germany as well as by other ninety-seven States (all EU Member States are state parties). Within the EU, Regulation Brussels IIbis takes precedence over the Hague CAC (Article 60 lit. e Brussels IIbis).

The Hague CAC is a convention on international legal assistance in matters of child abduction. If a child has been abducted into Germany (the case of main interest for foreign readers) the following procedure has to be followed:

(1) Application for return of the child within a year since abduction addressed to the German central authority (Article 12 Hague CAC):
Bundesamt für Justiz
D 53094 Bonn
Tel.: +49 (228) 99 410 5212
Fax: +49 (228) 99 410 5401
e-mail: int.sorgerecht@bfj.bund.de

(2) The German central authority investigates the whereabouts of the abducted child and helps to initiate return proceedings with the competent court (Article 7 Hague CAC).

(3) The competent court, before deciding the application of return, is not allowed to decide on the merits of custody matters (Article 16 Hague CAC).

(4) A child wrongfully abducted (Article 3 Hague CAC; a certificate of the State of origin as to wrongful removal has to be presented according to Article 15 Hague CAC) has to be returned unless one of the following five conditions are given:

- the application for return has been made after the expiration of one year and the German authorities are convinced that the child is now settled in Germany (Article 12 II Hague CAC); or
- the person having care of the child did not exercise his right at the time of removal (Article 13 I lit. a Hague CAC); or
- the return would create a grave risk to the child exposing him to physical or psychological harm or otherwise place the child in an intolerable situation (Article 13 I lit. b Hague CAC); or
- the child, having attained a sufficient age and degree of maturity, objects against the return and the German court agrees not to return (Article 13 II Hague CAC); or
- a return decision of German courts would violate principles of human rights and fundamental freedoms (Article 20 Hague CAC).

If the return of the wrongfully abducted child has been declined, the German courts have jurisdiction on the merits, may issue protective measures and award exclusive custody rights to the abducting parent. In this respect, the German courts have the "last word." This is different in other Member States of the EU. According to Article 11 VIII Brussels IIbis, the Member State the child was abducted from can enforce its return decision in Germany. Hence the Member State where the child had its last habitual residence prior to the abduction has the "last word."

[5] Maintenance of a Child

Maintenance obligations towards the child and also obligations of the (normally grown up) child towards his elderly parents are regulated by the Maintenance Regulation of the EU, the Lugano Convention, the Hague Convention of 1973 and finally by German private international law (*supra* [C]).

[K] Law of Natural Persons

[1] Capacity

Article 7 I 1 EGBGB provides that the law of nationality governs the question of existence of a person (*Rechtsfähigkeit*) and the capacity to act (*Geschäftsfähigkeit*). Once capacity has been acquired, it is vested with the person even if the newly acquired law of nationality does not recognize his capacity (Article 7 II EGBGB).

[2] Name of Persons

In Germany (as in most of civil-law-countries) the name of a person is an issue of private international law that has remained untouched by the legislation of the EU. Hence, German private international law governs.

In most cases the name of a person is acquired by birth, adoption or marriage and may be altered by adoption or divorce. The law applicable to the acquisition of name is supplied by Article 10 EGBGB. Articles 47 and 48 EGBGB provide additional choice of law and recognition rules following the registration of a name in another EU Member State.

[a]   Principle of Nationality (Article 10 I EGBGB)

According to Article 10 I EGBGB, the law of nationality governs the question which name is attributed to a person.

[b]   Name of Spouses

According to Article 10 II EGBGB, spouses may choose their married name at the time of marriage or afterwards before the civil registrar among:

- the law of nationality of one of the spouses; or
- German law if one of the spouses is habitually resident on Germany.

[c]   Name of Children

According to Article 10 III, the custodian may choose the name of his child and tell the registrar that the name of the child should be the name:

- attributed by the law of nationality of one of the parents; or
- attributed by German law if one of the parents is habitually resident in Germany; or
- attributed by the law of nationality of the person who transfers his name to the child.

[d]   Change of Name

German authorities have jurisdiction to change the name of a person applying for a change of his or her name if that person is German or is habitually resident in Germany (§ 1 Change of Surnames and First Names Act = *Gesetz über die Änderung von Familiennamen und Vornamen*). There must be serious reasons for changing the name (e.g., foreign name hardly to be pronounced correctly in Germany). Changes of name executed in foreign jurisdictions are recognized if they were executed by an authority having jurisdiction according to German law and do not violate German public policy.

[3]   Protection of Adults

The Hague Convention of January 13, 2000 on the International Protection of Adults (Hague PAC) applies in Germany and, as of January 1, 2018, in seven other Member States of the EU (Austria, Czech Republic, Estonia, Finland, France, Latvia, and the UK). Eight Member States (Belgium, Cyprus, Greece, Ireland, Italy Luxemburg, Netherlands, and Poland) are signatory states to the Convention. The remaining twelve Member States (Bulgaria, Croatia, Denmark, Hungary, Lithuania, Malta, Portugal, Romania, Slovakia, Slovenia, Spain, and Sweden) have to date refrained from doing so. Non-European countries did not take part in the Convention.

The Hague PAC is very similar to the Hague Convention of 1996 on the protection of Children (Hague CPC).

[a]   Jurisdiction

German courts and authorities have jurisdiction to take measures of protection of adults if:

- the adult has his habitual residence in Germany (Article 5 I Hague PAC); or
- the adult is a refugee or permanently displaced and present in Germany (Article 6 I Hague PAC); or
- if property of the adult is located in Germany and the measure taken by German authorities are compatible with the measures taken by otherwise competent authorities (Article 9 Hague PAC); or
- in urgent matters, if the adult resides in Germany or has property there. In this event, German authorities may take necessary measures of protection (Article 10 Hague PAC); or
- if the adult resides in Germany, German authorities may take temporary measures of protection, limited to the territory of Germany and compatible with measures taken by the normally competent authorities of other state parties (Article 11 I Hague PAC).

German authorities may:

- take measures of protection granted to German citizens if the regularly competent authorities do not object (Article 7 Hague PAC); or
- decline jurisdiction and ask another state party (mentioned in Article 8 II Hague PAC) to assume jurisdiction based on the assumption that this other jurisdiction is in a better position to take care of the adult (Article 8 I Hague PAC).

[b]   Applicable Law

German authorities apply German law if they are competent according to the Hague PAC (Articles 15 et seq. Hague PAC).

[c]   Recognition of Measures Taken by Foreign Authorities

Foreign decisions on measures of protection are recognized under the condition set out in Articles 22 et seq. Hague PAC. Recognition may be refused if the foreign authority had no jurisdiction or the measures violate German public policy.

[d]   Cooperation

Cooperation is emphasized in modern Hague conventions. The Hague PAC provides detailed rules on international co-operation in matters of protection of adults (Articles 28–37 Hague PAC).

[4]   Declaration of Death

The law of declaration of death is regulated by a special statute, the *Verschollenheitsgesetz* (VerschG = Statute on Missing Persons) of 1957.

According to §§ 12 et seq. VerschG, German courts have jurisdiction to declare person as deceased if either:

– the person is a German citizen; or
– there is need for a declaration of death because, e.g., heirs need to decide on the disposition of the estate of the missing person.

The same applies to decisions on the time of death and whether several persons, e.g., a married couple, died at the same time through a common danger or it rather must be assumed that the elder person passed away first, and the younger spouse followed.

Any decision of German authorities is governed by German law (Article 9 EGBGB).

§12.06   LAW OF SUCCESSION

Since August 17, 2015, the law of succession is determined by virtue of EU Regulation of July 4, 2012 on Jurisdiction, Applicable Law, Recognition and Enforcement of Decisions and Acceptance and Enforcement of Authentic Instruments in Matters of Succession and on the Creation of a European Certificate of Succession (SuccReg). The SuccReg – as every Regulation on matters of private international law – chooses the habitual residence as its primary connecting factor and – preempting fragmentation of the estate – forces all of the property of the deceased under a single law. It is for this reason that the UK and Ireland opted out of the SuccReg.

[A]   Jurisdiction

[1]   *Jurisdiction on Succession as a Whole*

German courts have probate jurisdiction on succession as a whole if:

- the deceased was last habitually resident in Germany at the time of his death (Article 4 SuccReg); or
- the deceased has chosen the German law of succession and the requirements of Articles 5–7 SuccReg are fulfilled; or
- the deceased was a German citizen, had his last habitual residence in a country not being a Member State, left assets in Germany, and the conditions mentioned in Article 10 I lit. a SuccReg are satisfied; or
- the deceased was a foreigner with assets in Germany and had his last habitual residence in Germany no longer than five years ago (Article 10 I lit. b SuccReg); or
- the deceased had his last habitual residence in a third state in which probate proceedings cannot be brought and the conditions of Article 11 SuccReg on *forum necessitatis* are fulfilled.

[2]   *Limited Jurisdiction*

German courts have limited jurisdiction if:

- assets are located in a third state and that state does not recognize foreign probate jurisdiction on immovable assets located in that state (e.g., USA); in that event one of the parties may request not to include the immovable assets in probate proceedings (Article 12 I SuccReg); or
- the deceased was a foreigner with his last habitual residence in a third state (e.g., the USA) and leaves immovable assets in Germany (Article 10 II SuccReg); or
- German law, by virtue of § 352c FamFG, allows for a German certificate of succession but limits it to assets located in Germany (Article 12 II SuccReg).

[B]   Applicable Law

The law specified by the SuccReg applies regardless of whether it is the law of a Member State or of a third state (Article 20 SuccReg).

[1] Succession Without Disposition of Property

[a] Applicable Law

If the deceased person dies intestate, all of his or her property is governed by the law of the state where the deceased had his or her habitual residence at the time of death (Article 21 I SuccReg). Under the conditions set out in the exception clause (Article 21 II SuccReg), a different law may be applied.

[b] Choice of Law

The deceased may choose the law governing all succession property from amongst the laws of any state whose nationality he possesses at the time of making the choice or at the time of death (Article 22 I SuccReg). Choice of law must fulfill the formal requirements of a valid disposition of property (Articles 22 II and 24 I SuccReg). In Germany, a valid disposition may be made by a will certified (*beurkundet*) by a notary public or by a holographic will handwritten, located and dated, and signed by the deceased (§§ 2231, 2232 and 2247 BGB).

[2] Testaments (Wills)

The admissibility and substantive validity (*see* Article 26 SuccReg) of a will is governed by the law of the State which, under the SuccReg would have been applicable to the succession of the person who made the will if he had died on the day on which the disposition was made (Article 24 I SuccReg). In this disposition, the testator may also choose the law applicable to succession, admissibility and substantive validity, which can be chosen according to Article 22 (Article 24 II SuccReg).

[3] Agreement as to Succession (Erbvertrag)

[a] Succession to One Person

If the estate of only one person is concerned, the admissibility and substantive validity (*see* Article 26 SuccReg) and its binding effects between the parties, including the conditions for its dissolution, are governed by the law of the state which would apply if the deceased had died on the very day the agreement was concluded (Article 25 I SuccReg).

[b] Succession of Several Persons

The validity of an agreement regarding the estates of several persons is governed by the laws which, under the SuccReg, would have governed the succession of all the persons involved if they had died on the day the agreement was concluded (Article 25 II § 1 SuccReg).

The substantive validity of a will (*see* Article 26 SuccReg) and its binding effects between the parties, including the conditions for its dissolution, are governed by the law referred to in the first subparagraph, i.e., the law of the state the agreement has the closest connection to (Article 25 II § 2 SuccReg).

[c]   Choice of Law

The parties may choose the law governing their agreement regarding its admissibility, its substantive validity and its binding effects between them, including the conditions for its dissolution, from the laws available to each of the parties by virtue of Article 22, hence the laws of their respective nationalities (Article 25 III SuccReg).

Example: A Greek-German couple had their habitual residence in Athens and conclude an agreement as to succession. This agreement would be inadmissible according to Greek law, which governs their succession according to Articles 20, 25 II SuccReg. The couple, however, can choose German law according to Article 22 I § 2 SuccReg and German law allows for such an agreement.

[4]   Formal Validity of Dispositions of Property

Formal validity is extensively regulated in Article 27 SuccReg. With respect to form, a *favor negotii* applies under Article 27 I SuccReg.

[5]   Special Rues for Certain Assets

In Germany, agricultural property, because of economic, familiar, and social reasons, is always governed by German law, irrespective of the law applicable to the succession in other respects. This policy is preserved by virtue of Article 30 SuccReg.

[6]   Adaptation of Rights In Rem

According to Article 31 SuccReg, Germany is precluded from not recognizing a legacy "by vindication" on the only ground that, in German law, legacy only has the effect of a claim to transfer the object of the legacy to the person in favor of whom the legacy was made (ECJ ECLI:EU:C:2017:755, *Kubicka* C-218/16).

[7]   Commorientes

When two or more persons whose successions are governed by different laws die in a common disaster, there is uncertainty as to in what order their deaths occurred, and the laws applicable provide differently for that situation or make no provision for it at all, none of the deceased persons shall have any rights to the succession of the other or others.

[8]   Estate without a Claimant

If there is neither a claimant nor a legatee, the law applicable to succession does not preclude the respective state of the *rei sitae* to appropriate those assets of the estate that are located within their territory (Article 33 SuccReg).

[9]   Renvoi

Renvoi is only accepted in two incidents of referral to the law of a third state according to Article 34 SuccReg:

- if that law refers back into the law of a Member State, then the law of the Member State will apply;

  Example: A American citizen passed away in New York and left real estate in Germany. German courts, having limited jurisdiction according to Article 10 II SuccReg, are referred to the law of New York. Under New York conflicts law, the *lex rei sitae* applies, i.e., real estate in Germany is governed by German law. This *renvoi* of the law of New York will be accepted by German law according to Article 34 I lit. a SuccReg.

- if that law applies, the law of another third state which would accept the *renvoi* and apply its own law applies.

  Example: A Swiss citizen passed away in Turkey shortly after having abandoned his former habitual residence in Germany. German courts have jurisdiction according to Article 10 I lit. b SuccReg. As a result, Turkish law, the law of a third state, applies. Turkish law refers to the law of the deceased's nationality (Article 20 I § 1 Turkish PIL Act of 2007) for movables and for foreign immovable. Swiss law accepts the *renvoi* by virtue of Article 91 I IPRG and applies Swiss substantive succession law codified in the Swiss ZGB.

[10]   Public Policy

If foreign law manifestly violates public policy of the *forum* state, the *forum* state may apply its own law according to Article 35 SuccReg. If the law applicable to succession does not provide for a legitimate part of the estate to be accorded to close relatives, this fact alone will not render the rule manifestly incompatible with the public policy of the *forum*. If, however, the close relative who, under German law, would have been given his legitimate portion, is left without any share of the estate or legacy, and if there is no reason for excluding this person from succession, the will may violate the public policy of the *forum*.

[C]   Recognition of Foreign Decisions and Authentic Instruments

Foreign decisions and authentic instruments on succession are recognized, enforced and accepted by virtue of Articles 39–61 SuccReg.

[D]   European Certificate of Succession (ECS)

Courts or authorities having primary jurisdiction under Articles 4, 7, 10, or 11 SuccReg may issue a European Certificate of Succession (Articles 62–73 SuccReg). The ECS has considerable effects and protects parties acting in good faith. If the heirs dispose of the estate or receive payments due to the estate, parties receiving assets or making such payments are protected and need not return the assets or pay a second time if the ECS turns out to be incorrect (Article 69 SuccReg).

§12.07   COMPANY LAW

The EU has not yet passed a regulation with specific conflicts rules for companies. Apart from the *Societas Europea* (SA), a specific transnational corporate structure offered by EU legislation, the Commission has so far been too occupied to regulate the *lex societatis* of legal entities.

[A]   Jurisdiction

If Regulation Brussels Ibis and the Lugano Convention apply *(supra* §12.02[A]), companies or trusts must be sued at their statutory seat, the place of their central administration or at their principal place of business (Articles 63 I and 7 V Brussels Ibis and Articles 60 I and 5 V of the Lugano Convention). The now-outdated German conflicts law provided jurisdiction at the seat of a company or business trust as the factual center of administration of a company or trust. Apart from this general *forum,* a company may be sued in a state where the company has established branches, agencies or other establishments if the lawsuit is based on activities of these entities (Article 5 V of Brussels Ibis and the Lugano Convention).

[B]   Applicable Law

German conflicts law for companies consists of case law to a large extent. Jurisprudence has ruled so far that the establishment, the structure, organization and dissolution of companies are governed by the law of the state where the company's factual administrative headquarters are located: This is the principle of the factual seat *(faktischer Verwaltungssitz).*

These principles are now outdated under the influence of ECJ case law. Following the *Daily Mail* (ECR 1988, 5483), *Centros* (ECR 1999 I 1459), *Überseering* (ECR 2002 I 9943), *Inspire Art* (ECR 2003 I 10155), *Cartesio* (ECR 2008 I 9641), *National Grid*

Industries (ECR 2011 I-12273) and *Polbud* (ECJ ECLI:EU:C:2017:804, C-106/16) decisions of the European Court of Justice, every company duly registered in a Member State must be recognized in the other Member States. Therefore, within the European Union, the principle of the statutory seat applies as it already applies in relation to the United States under the 1954 Treaty of Friendship and Commerce between the United States and Germany. German courts are likely to follow up on these rulings even in cases where European law and international treaties do not apply.

[C]   Recognition of Foreign Judgments

The same principles apply as in the field of contract law (*supra* §12.02[C]).

§12.08   BANKRUPTCY AND INSOLVENCY

[A]   Jurisdiction

The recast of Council Regulation 2015/848 of May 20, 2015 on insolvency proceedings (InsReg) applies to an insolvent debtor with the center of his main interests in a Member State (except Denmark). According to Recital (28) of the Regulation, the "center of main interests" should correspond to the place where the debtor conducts the administration of his business on a regular basis and therefore is present for third parties, most importantly his creditors. In case of a company or legal person, the place of registered office is presumed to be the center of its main interest absent proof to the contrary (Article 3 I 2 InsReg). According to Article 3 I InsReg, German courts have jurisdiction to open the main insolvency proceedings if the debtor's center of main interests is situated in Germany. Such primary insolvency proceedings have universal scope and aim at dissolving the debtor's assets as a whole [Recital (23) 2 of the InsReg].

Secondary insolvency proceedings may be opened in another Member State if the debtor operates an establishment there, i.e., any place of operation where the debtor carries out a non-transitory economic activity with human means and goods (Articles 34, 3 II InsReg). Such secondary proceedings are restricted to the assets of the debtor situated within the territory of the Member State in which the establishment is located.

If primary insolvency proceedings have been opened in a non-Member State, German courts have jurisdiction to open secondary insolvency proceedings in Germany with respect to the debtor's assets located in Germany (Article 102 § 1 III Introductory Act to the German Insolvency Statute of 1994).

[B]   Law Applicable

Insolvency proceedings are governed by the *lex fori concursus* (Articles 7 and 35 InsReg). Article 7 II InsReg enumerates types of dispute covered by the *lex fori concursus*. Articles 8 et seq. of the InsReg regulate specific problems such as rights in rem, set-off, and the effect of insolvency proceedings on lawsuits pending at the time of opening of insolvency proceedings.

If a creditor takes advantage of assets located abroad and is paid out of the proceeds of the assets seized abroad, he is unjustly enriched and can be sued in German courts for unjust enrichment, provided that the liquidator can get hold of the creditor and seize a court having jurisdiction for this matter according to the German *lex fori concursus*.

[C] Recognition of Foreign Judgments

Any judgment opening insolvency proceedings handed down by a court of a Member State having jurisdiction pursuant to Article 3 InsReg must be recognized in all other Member States. Also, foreign decisions opening bankruptcy or insolvency proceedings in non-Member States will be recognized in Germany if the foreign authority had jurisdiction under the relevant German standards (domicile or seat of the debtor in bankruptcy). Therefore, a foreign trustee in bankruptcy may collect assets of the estate located in Germany and German creditors cannot enforce their claims in domestic courts. Instead, they are left with no choice but to take part in the bankruptcy proceedings administered abroad (Article 21 InsReg).

§12.09 INTERNATIONAL ARBITRATION

Germany is a contracting party to several international conventions on arbitration, especially to the New York Convention of 1958 on the Recognition and Enforcement of Foreign Arbitral Awards. Arbitration clauses are valid if they satisfy the conditions laid down in Article II of this Convention. Likewise, foreign arbitral awards are recognized and enforced according to the rules set out in the Convention.

If arbitration proceedings are governed by German law, the revised provisions of §§ 1025 et seq. ZPO [English translation in 37 I.L.M. 794 (1998)] apply. These are a faithful translation of the UNCITRAL Model Law on International Commercial Arbitration, with very few additions.

§12.10 INTERNATIONAL JUDICIAL ASSISTANCE

International judicial assistance is based on comity and granted by international conventions. Germany has ratified several Hague Conventions, e.g., the 1965 Hague Convention on the Service of Judicial Documents, the 1970 Hague Convention on the Taking of Evidence Abroad and the 1980 Hague Convention on the Civil Aspects of International Child Abduction.

Within the European Union, Council Regulation 1393/2007 of November 13, 2007 on the Service in the Member States of Judicial and Extrajudicial Documents in Civil and Commercial Matters and the Council Regulation 1206/2001 of May 28, 2001 on Cooperation between the Courts of the Member States in the Taking of Evidence in Civil and Commercial matters apply.

The European Judicial Network (EJN) in civil and commercial matters, established in 2001 (Council Decision 2001/470/EC), has been amended in 2009 (Decision

No. 568/2009/EC of the European Parliament and of the Council). The principles of the EJN must be implemented by the Member States.

Apart from these instruments and several bilateral treaties, German courts and authorities grant legal assistance to foreign courts under the applicable domestic rules, and with a commitment to comity. These domestic rules and the German implementation of the EJN are laid down in the Guidelines for Granting Legal Assistance in Civil and Commercial Matters *(Rechtshilfeordnung für Zivilsachen)*.

SELECTED BIBLIOGRAPHY

Hans Georg Bamberger & Herbert Roth (– Stefan Lorenz et al.), *Kommentar zum Bürgerlichen Gesetzbuch*, vol. 3 (3rd ed. 2012).

Christian von Bar & Peter Mankowski, *Internationales Privatrecht*, vol. 1 (2nd ed. 2003).

Adolf Baumbach/Wolfgang Lauterbach/Jan Albers/Peter Hartmann, *Zivilprozessordnung* (77th ed. 2019).

Alfonso-Luis Calvo Caravaca & Angelo Davì & Heinz-Peter Mansel (eds.), *The EU Succession Regulation. A Commentary* (2016).

Anatol Dutta (ed.), *Internationales Erbrecht. Kurz-Kommentar* (2016).

Walter Erman (– Gerhard Hohloch), *BGB Kommentar* (15th ed. 2017).

Reinhold Geimer & Ewald Geimer & Gregor Geimer, *Internationales Zivilprozessrecht* (7th ed. 2015).

Reinhold Geimer & Rolf A. Schütze, *Europäisches Zivilverfahrensrecht* (4th ed. 2017).

Rainer Hausmann, *Internationales und europäisches Familienrecht* (2d ed. 2018).

Maximilian Herberger/Michael Martinek/Helmut Rüßmann/Stephan Werth (– Markus Würdinger et al.), *Juris Praxis Kommentar BGB*, 6th vol. (7th ed. 2015).

Bernd von Hoffmann & Karsten Thorn, *Internationales Privatrecht* (10th ed. 2018).

Rainer Hüßtege/Heinz.Peter Mansel (– Peter-Andreas Brand et al.), *Nomos Kommentar, Rom-Verordnungen*, vol. 6 (2nd ed. 2015).

Gerhard Kegel & Klaus Schurig, *Internationales Privatrecht* (9th ed. 2004).

Jan Kropholler, *Internationales Privatrecht* (6th ed. 2006).

Jan Kropholler & Jan von Hein, *Europäisches Zivilprozessrecht* (10th ed. 2018).

Dirk Looschelders, *Internationales Privatrecht. Art.3–46 EGBGB* (2004).

Ulrich Magnus & Peter Mankowski (eds.), *European Commentaries on Private International Law, vol. 1: Brussels Ibis Regulation* (2016).

Ulrich Magnus & Peter Mankowski (eds.), *European Commentaries on Private International Law, vol. 2: Rome I Regulation* (2017).

Ulrich Magnus & Peter Mankowski (eds.), *European Commentaries on Private International Law, vol. 3: Rome II Regulation* (2017).

Ulrich Magnus & Peter Mankowski (eds.), *European Commentaries on Private International Law, vol. 4: Brussels IIbis Regulation* (2017).

Peter Mankowski & Michael Müller & Jessica Schmidt, *Europäische Insolvenzverordnung 2015* (2016).

Münchener Kommentar zum Bürgerlichen Gesetzbuch, vol. 11 and 12: *Einführungsgesetz zum Bürgerlichen Gesetzbuch. Internationales Privatrecht* (Jan v. Hein ed., 7th ed. 2018).

Heinrich Nagel & Peter Gottwald, *Internationales Zivilprozessrecht* (7th ed. 2013).

Otto Palandt (– Karsten Thorn), *Bürgerliches Gesetzbuch* (78th ed. 2019).

Hans Prütting/Gerhard Wegen/Gerd Weinreich (– Juliana Mörsdorf et al.), *Bürgerliches Gesetzbuch, Kommentar* (12th ed. 2017).

Thomas Rauscher, *Internationales Privatrecht* (5th ed. 2017).

Thomas Rauscher (ed.), *Europäisches Zivilprozess- und Kollisionsrecht, vol. 1: Brüssel Ia – VO* (4th ed. 2016).

Thomas Rauscher (ed.), *Europäisches Zivilprozess- und Kollisionsrecht, vol. 2: EG-VollstrTitelVO und Anderes* (4th ed. 2015).

Thomas Rauscher (ed.), *Europäisches Zivilprozess- und Kollisionsrecht,. vol. 3: Rom I – VO, Rom II – VO* (4th ed. 2016).

Thomas Rauscher (ed.), *Europäisches Zivilprozess- und Kollisionsrecht, vol. 4: Brüssel IIa – VO und Anderes* (4th ed. 2015).

Thomas Raucher (ed.), *Europäisches Zivilprozess- und Kollisionsrecht, vol. 5: KSÜ, EuErbVO und Anderes* (4th ed. 2016).

Peter H. Schlechtriem & Ingeborg Schwenzer (ed.), *Commentary on the UN Convention on the International Sale of Goods* (4th ed. 2016).

Peter Schlosser & Burkhard Hess, *EU-Zivilprozessrecht* (4th ed. 2015).

Kurt Siehr, *Internationales Privatrecht* (2001).

Johannes von Staudinger (ed.), *Kommentar zum Bürgerlichen Gesetzbuch mit Einführungsgesetz und Nebengesetzen* ("Neubearbeitungen" since 2005 et seq.).

All German cases on matters of private international law are collected in the annual publication "IPRspr." (= *Die deutsche Rechtsprechung auf dem Gebiete des Internationalen Privatrechts* = German Court Decisions in Maters of Private International Law). Many of these cases are discussed in comments published in the bi-monthly law journal "IPRax" (= *Praxis des Internationalen Privat- und Verfahrensrechts* = Practice of International Private and Procedural Law).

The most important memoranda, given to German courts by German university institutes and Max Planck Institutes are published in "IPG" (= *Gutachten zum internationalen und ausländischen Privatrecht* = Memoranda on International and Foreign Private Law).

CHAPTER 13

The Law of Civil Procedure

Wolfgang Hau

TABLE OF CONTENTS

§13.01   INTRODUCTION

Despite the general trend towards Europeanization of law within the European Union, the regulation of procedural law, at least for the most part, is still left to the Member States.[1] The law of civil procedure regulates the methods and procedures employed by courts to resolve private law conflicts that have given rise to civil litigation. The most important German body of law addressing this topic is the Code of Civil Procedure of 1877 (*Zivilprozessordnung* – ZPO). The ZPO covers the two main aspects of the law of civil procedure. First, it supplies the rules for the *Erkenntnisverfahren*, which denotes the procedural phase leading to a judgment or a settlement. Second, the ZPO provides the legal regime for the *Vollstreckungsverfahren*, i.e., the procedure aligned with the enforcement of judgments and settlements, as well as temporary attachment procedures and injunctive relief. Family proceedings as well as proceedings in matters of so-called non-contentious jurisdiction are dealt with in a Special Act of 2009 (*Gesetz über das Verfahren in Familiensachen und in den Angelegenheiten der freiwilligen Gerichtsbarkeit* – FamFG).

In recent years, special legislation has been enacted to cover various aspects of alternative dispute resolution, mostly based on EU law provisions. This holds true for the Mediation Act of 2012 (*Mediationsgesetz*) and the Act on Resolution of Consumer Law Disputes of 2016 (*Verbraucherstreitbeilegungsgesetz*). The law of arbitration, the third pillar of dispute resolution besides litigation and mediation, is again set out in the Code of Civil Procedure (§§ 1025 et seq.).

---

1. On this "principle of procedural autonomy" and its limits, cf. Nylund & Krans, *The European Union and National Civil Procedure.*

§13.02 PRINCIPLES

Although the Code of Civil Procedure has undergone remarkable changes since 1877 and especially during the last decades,[2] a number of principles can still be regarded as characteristic.[3] The *Dispositionsgrundsatz* (principle of free party disposition, or principle of party control), which is the procedural equivalent to the general principle of party autonomy, means that the parties rather than the court determine the beginning, subject-matter, and termination of the proceedings. Therefore, courts can neither initiate civil proceedings ex officio nor prevent parties from abandoning proceedings at any stage. The second principle, the so-called *Verhandlungsgrundsatz* (principle of party presentation) leaves it to the parties to present the facts and evidence to the court. There is no ex officio inquiry by the court in civil actions. Thus, the German law of civil procedure is "adversarial", and it would seem at least misleading to claim a fundamental difference between American and German law by asserting that the latter one is "inquisitorial". Another fundamental principle provided for in Article 103 (1) of the German Constitution (*Grundgesetz* – GG) is the parties' right to due process, in particular the right to be heard. This means that the parties in a civil action have the right to make motions, present facts, and submit evidence. Each party must have the opportunity to be appraised of the opponent's allegations and must be allowed to comment and to react accordingly. The right to be heard includes the right of the parties to present legal arguments, with the corresponding duty of the court to consider such arguments and allegations.

There are remarkable differences between the law of civil procedure in Germany (or, in a broader sense, Continental Europe) and in the United States, having caused reservations, if not frictions.[4] Many of these, however, may stem from the fact that German and American rules of civil procedure focus on different categories of cases: "The typical case at which the German system is aimed involves a comparatively small amount of money, raises no major issue of public policy, and is merely a dispute between private parties about private rights. In such cases it obviously makes sense to give the judge a leading role in the examination of witnesses and wider powers over the evidentiary process, thereby reducing considerably the amount of lawyer effort and cost in exchange for a modest increase in effort and activity on the part of the judge."[5]

---

2. For an analysis of recent reforms, cf. Lipp & Fredriksen, *Reforms of Civil Procedure in Germany and Norway*.
3. For a detailed account of these principles, see Koch & Diedrich, *Civil Procedure in Germany*, pp. 25 et seq.; Murray & Stürner, *German Civil Justice*, pp. 156 et seq.
4. See, e.g., Stürner, *Why Are Europeans Afraid to Litigate in the United States?* (2001), p. 15: "It is the combination of broad discovery, jury trial, American rule of costs, contempt sanctions, big and busy American law firms, extraterritorial application of law and broad personal and subject matter jurisdiction which characterises the American civil procedure in the eyes of European lawyers as a procedural monster which is feared because of its appetite, sharp teeth and capriciousness."
5. Cf. Kötz, 13 Duke J. Comp. & Int'l L. 61, 77 (2003).

§13.03   COURT PROCEDURE LEADING TO A JUDGMENT

[A]   Parties

Civil actions may be brought only by and against entities capable of being a party to a lawsuit (*Parteifähigkeit*) and having the legal capacity to conduct a lawsuit in their own name (*Prozessfähigkeit*). Every person having legal capacity (*Rechtsfähigkeit*) or possessing legal personality as a legal entity may become a party (§ 50 ZPO). In order to conduct legal proceedings in one's own name, a party must have legal capacity to contract (*Geschäftsfähigkeit*), otherwise a legal representative must act in the name of the party. Actions in one's own name but on another's behalf (*Prozessstandschaft*) are admissible either if permitted by law or if the agent himself has a proper legal interest in the action.

German civil procedure allows for a joinder of parties (*Streitgenossenschaft*) as plaintiffs or defendants. A joinder can merely be the result of considerations of expediency (simple joinder – *einfache Streitgenossenschaft*) or it can be compulsory if the decision has to be uniform for all plaintiffs or defendants involved (*notwendige Streitgenossenschaft*). A compulsory joinder brings about effects beyond the joint trial and the taking of evidence: When only one of the joint parties appears in court and pleads, no default judgment is admissible as to the other. Similarly, a time limit is met if only one of the joint parties adheres to it. Furthermore, §§ 72 et seq. ZPO allow for third-party notice (*Streitverkündung*) if a litigant is entitled to claim damages or indemnity from a third party should he lose the action. The third party is free to decide whether to join the action or not, but the outcome of the original litigation will be binding in an action subsequently brought by the defeated party against the third party.

According to § 78 ZPO, representation by an attorney (*Rechtsanwalt*) is mandatory in proceedings before regional courts (*Landgerichte*) and higher courts (higher regional courts and Federal Court of Justice – *Oberlandesgericht* and *Bundesgerichtshof*); the same holds true for certain family law matters which are dealt with by the local courts (*Amtsgerichte*, cf. § 114 FamFG). For lawyers admitted in other Member States of the European Union, EU law guarantees the freedom of establishment as well as the freedom to provide cross-border services (details are set forth in the German Act Implementing the Directives of the European Community Pertaining to the Professional Law Regulating the Legal Profession of 2000 – *Gesetz zur Umsetzung von Richtlinien der EG auf dem Gebiet des Berufsrechts der Rechtsanwälte*). Furthermore, special provisions regulate the freedom of establishment of lawyers from other Member States of the World Trade Organization (§§ 206 and 207 of the Federal Law on Attorneys: *Bundesrechtsanwaltsordnung – BRAO*).

An indigent plaintiff or defendant has a statutory right to legal aid (*Prozesskostenhilfe*, cf. §§ 114 et seq. ZPO).[6] If the prospects of a party's claim or defense are reasonably promising and the party cannot afford the costs of the lawsuit, the court

---

6. For details of the German legal aid system see, Blankenburg, 46 Am. J. Comp. L. 1 (1998); Hess & Huebner, in: Reimann, *Cost and Fee Allocation in Civil Procedure*, p. 159.

may grant legal aid upon application. Such a grant entails temporary or permanent exemption from court costs and fees for a court-appointed lawyer.

[B]   Courts

Civil courts are competent to decide disputes relating to civil law matters. Such courts adjudicate matters of public law only if explicitly assigned to do so by law (e.g., claims for damages for the violation of a public official's duties). For labor law, as well as administrative, social and fiscal matters, there are separate courts applying their own special codes of procedure.

In general, civil cases are decided by professional judges, without input of laymen or juries. Regional courts, however, comprise special litigation panels for matters of commercial law which are composed of a presiding professional judge and two lay judges (*Kammern für Handelssachen*).

At first instance, *Amtsgerichte* (local courts roughly equivalent to American-style county courts or municipal courts) have subject matter jurisdiction (*sachliche Zuständigkeit*) over disputes with an amount in controversy (*Streitwert*) of up to € 5,000 (§ 23 no. 1 of the Courts Jurisdiction and Organization Code, *Gerichtsverfassungsgesetz* – GVG) and matters specifically assigned to them (e.g., landlord and tenant disputes and domestic proceedings, § 23 no. 2 GVG). At the *Amtsgericht* level, cases are decided by a single judge.

Landgerichte (regional courts) have subject matter jurisdiction over all actions with an amount in controversy exceeding € 5,000, unless the case is assigned by statute to the local courts. At the *Landgericht* level, the case is decided either by a single judge (*Einzelrichter*) or, if the merits of the case affect special areas of law (such as banking, financing, or insurance issues), by a panel of three judges (*Kammer*). However, depending on the difficulties of the case in question, it can be transferred from the single judge to the panel or *vice versa* (§§ 348, 348a ZPO).

The rules concerning venue (*örtliche Zuständigkeit* – §§ 12 et seq. ZPO) distinguish between general and special venue. In principle, the court at the defendant's place of residence (respectively its seat if the defendant is a corporate entity) is competent to decide all claims brought against him. The Code also contains special venue rules for certain categories of disputes (cf. §§ 21–23, 27, 29, 29c–32, 33, 34 ZPO). Of practical importance are the *forum contractus* (the place of performance of a contractual obligation, § 29 ZPO), and the *forum delicti commissi* (the place where a tort was committed or the damage occurred, § 32 ZPO). Exclusive venue is provided for cases involving immovable property (§ 24 ZPO) and in landlord and tenant disputes (§ 29a ZPO). In principle, private parties may not enter into forum selection agreements (*prorogation* or *derogation*, § 40 ZPO). There are, however, important exceptions for merchants (§ 38 (1) ZPO) and stipulations made after the dispute has already arisen (§ 38 (3) ZPO); as regards international jurisdiction, in almost all relevant cases Article 25 of the Brussels Ibis Regulation (*see* below) takes priority over § 38 ZPO. Furthermore, venue can be established by submission if the defendant pleads in the hearing without reservation on the merits of the case (§ 39 ZPO). If the court chosen by the plaintiff finds that it lacks venue or subject matter jurisdiction, the court will, upon application, transfer the case to the proper court (§ 281 ZPO).

International jurisdiction of German courts is primarily governed by European law embodied in the EU-Regulation No. 1215/2012 on Jurisdiction and the Recognition and Enforcement of Judgments in Civil and Commercial Matters (so-called Brussels Ibis Regulation), or by international conventions (e.g., the Lugano Convention on Jurisdiction and Enforcement of Judgments in Civil and Commercial Matters). If neither international rules nor special German rules apply (such as §§ 98 et seq. FamFG for family law matters), international jurisdiction of German courts is determined by the same venue rules discussed in the preceding paragraph (§§ 12 et seq. ZPO). Once jurisdiction has been established, German courts have no discretionary power to decline it; in principle, there is no equivalent to the doctrine of *forum non conveniens*.

[C] Action

[1] Types of Action

German procedural law knows three classes of actions. First, if the plaintiff wants the court to order the defendant to do something or to refrain from doing something, he will file a so-called *Leistungsklage*. This action is available, e.g., if the plaintiff asks for performance of a contractual obligation (e.g., payment of a certain amount of money, delivery of personal or real property), claims damages, or demands that the defendant refrain from committing a wrongful act. If the plaintiff prevails, the corresponding judgment (*Leistungsurteil*) may be enforced against the defendant.

Second, an action for a declaratory judgment (*Feststellungsklage*) aims at obtaining a judicial declaration that an alleged legal relationship between the plaintiff and the defendant or an alleged right of one of the parties with regard to personal or real property does or does not exist. Since a declaratory judgment cannot be enforced against the defendant, actions for such judgments are only subsidiary, i.e., they are permissible only where a claim for money or other relief is not available. The plaintiff must prove the existence of a special legitimate interest in this kind of decision (*besonderes Rechtsschutzinteresse*), which is lacking if the plaintiff could file, as mentioned above, for a *Leistungsurteil* aiming at the performance of a duty arising out of the alleged legal relationship. Thus, e.g., the plaintiff may not bring an action for a declaratory judgment that a contract exists between him and the defendant if he could sue the defendant for performance of his contractual obligation.

The third class of actions includes petitions for a judicial modification of rights or legal relationships (*Gestaltungsklagen*). This is only available if statutory provisions require a court order to terminate, resolve or modify a legal relationship. Important examples are the expulsion of a partner from a general partnership or the petition for a divorce.

[2]   *Filing and Pendency of the Action*

Whether the action is properly filed depends on the mandatory requirements set forth in § 253 ZPO. The complaint (*Klageschrift*) has to specify the parties and the court applied to. Furthermore, it must indicate the subject in dispute and the cause of action. Indication of the cause of action requires specification of the facts which, in the plaintiff's opinion, provide the basis of his legal claim. The complaint has to contain a sufficiently definite motion (*Antrag*), which determines the form of action and the scope of judicial review.

Service of process to the defendant is regarded as an official act which is to be effected ex officio by the court (§§ 166 et seq., 271 ZPO). To the extent that legal representation is mandatory, the defendant will be requested to appoint a legal counsel admitted to the bar (§ 271 (2) ZPO). After service of process, the action is pending in a legal sense (*rechtshängig* – § 261 (1) ZPO).[7] Pendency may influence the legal position of a creditor or debtor, e.g., by interrupting limitation periods or triggering stricter liability in some cases. Furthermore, pendency pre-empts any other action involving the same matter in dispute (*lis alibi pendens* – § 261 (3) No. 1 ZPO) and locks in the jurisdiction of the court, even if the facts giving rise to jurisdiction or venue subsequently change (*perpetuatio fori* – § 261 (3) No. 2 ZPO). Service of process also determines the matter in dispute (*Streitgegenstand*), which later on may only be amended or modified with the consent of the defendant or upon court approval (§ 263 ZPO).

[D]   Trial

[1]   *Preparation of the Trial and Court Activity*

Under German law, the distinction between the trial and the pre-trial stage is less sharp than in common law countries. It has even been said that conducting a lawsuit in a civil law system such as Germany consists rather of piecemeal litigation characterized by the predominance of written elements and that there is nothing that could properly be called a trial.[8] Because there is no jury, there is indeed no need to conclude the matter within a single day in court or, for that matter, a continuous string of hearing days. Since, however, a hearing is normally required and it is considered desirable to conclude a suit in only one hearing (§ 272 (1) ZPO), the Code emphasizes the need for

---

7. For an analysis of the different styles of American and European procedural law regarding the commencement of litigation and the role of the parties and the courts, see Gerber, in: Nafziger & Symeonides, *Law and Justice in a Multistate World*, pp. 667 et seq.
8. Schlosser, 45 Kan. L. Rev. 9, 11 (1996); cf. Kötz, 13 Duke J. Comp. & Int'l L. 61, 72 (2003): "European civil procedure [...] is wholly unfamiliar with, and knows nothing of, the idea of a 'trial' as a single, temporally continuous presentation in which all materials are made available to the adjudicator. Instead proceedings in a civil action on the Continent may be described as a series of isolated conferences before the judge, some of which may last only a few minutes, in which written communications between the parties are exchanged and discussed, procedural rulings are made, evidence is introduced and testimony taken until the cause is finally ripe for adjudication".

a comprehensive and timely preparation of the trial. According to § 272 (2) ZPO, the Court of First Instance may choose between a preliminary hearing of the case (*früher erster Termin*, § 275 ZPO) or an exchange of written pleadings (*schriftliches Vorverfahren*, § 276 ZPO) which allows for a more detailed preparation of the hearing. Submission by supplemental pleadings further substantiates the presentation of facts and circumstances. Normally, the parties will also present their arguments on the legal issues involved even though they are not required to do so. In order to expedite the proceedings, the court will set a time limit for the defendant's response (*Klageerwiderung*) and the plaintiff's reaction to that response. Generally speaking, a failure to observe that time limit will preclude a party from presenting its allegations or arguments (§ 296 (1) ZPO). Therefore, it is not only useless but outright detrimental to withhold information in the hope of gaining tactical edge by only producing it at the oral hearing. The court may also disregard statements or evidence submitted in violation of the party's general duty to facilitate the proceedings in a timely manner. Before disregarding party submissions, however, courts must always ensure that such exclusions comport with due process, particularly with the right to be heard protected under the Constitution (Article 103 (1) GG).

The court has an obligation to prepare the trial. It has the power to demand that the parties fully elaborate on all relevant alleged facts. Within the limits inherent in the principle of party presentation (*supra* §13.02), the court will provide some guidance for the pleadings (§ 139 (1) ZPO) and, to some extent, will even assist a party that failed to present all relevant facts through oversight, inadvertence, or mistake (§ 139 (2) ZPO). Given the duty to remain impartial, however, a court treads a fine line when it intervenes. On the one hand, it has a duty to give directions; on the other hand, the court must avoid any appearance of partiality and therefore avoid helping a party to win. Of major importance is the court's power to demand that the parties supplement their pleadings (§ 139 (1) ZPO) and that they produce documents and things to which one of the parties has referred (§§ 142, 144 ZPO). It seems remarkable that the latter duties even apply to non-parties.[9] The court may also request public authorities and administrative agencies to produce documents or give information. Furthermore, it may issue summons to witnesses referred to by a litigant, effect court inspections, and obtain expert opinions or written statements by a witness (§§ 144, 273, 358a ZPO). Throughout the pendency of the action, the court is required to expedite the proceedings with a view towards a speedy disposition of the case.

[2]   Pleading and Defense

Due to a general duty of the parties to facilitate the proceedings (*Prozessförderungspflicht*), plaintiff and defendant must present everything in support of their claims or defenses as early as possible. Each litigant must give a complete and true statement on the facts of the case (§ 138 (1) ZPO) and must respond to all relevant allegations of the

---

9. For an analysis in English language, cf. Junker, *Access to Documentary Evidence in German Civil Procedure*, in: Peter Gottwald, *Litigation in England and Germany*, p. 51.

other party (§ 138 (2) ZPO). A party may plead lack of factual knowledge only if the facts are beyond his own personal knowledge and observation (§ 138 (4) ZPO).

There is, however, no obligation to defend in a strict sense: The defendant can neither be forced to appear in court (§ 141 ZPO) nor to react to the service of summons and complaint. Of course, such failure to act may result in a default judgment (§§ 331 et seq. ZPO), which may then be enforced against the defendant. A default judgment requires what is called "conclusiveness of the action" (*Schlüssigkeit der Klage*): The complaint must state all facts necessary to establish a cause of action.

If the defendant decides to defend the action, he may plead on procedural grounds and/or on the merits of the case. A motion for dismissal without prejudice will be successful if procedural requirements are not fulfilled. In most cases, the defendant will move to dismiss the case on the merits. He may present his own version of facts as a defense, contest plaintiff's allegations, raise legal objections to the claim, bring further evidence, or attack the plaintiff's evidence. The defendant is not restricted to a purely defensive role but may also bring a counterclaim (*Widerklage*). Under German law, such a counterclaim is always permissive, but never compulsory. If there is a factual connection between claim and counterclaim, the court applied to by the plaintiff has jurisdiction over the counterclaim as well (§ 33 ZPO).

The defendant may choose not to contest one or all of the plaintiff's factual allegations or may explicitly acknowledge their truth (§§ 288–290 ZPO). Facts admitted by the defendant are not subject to further evidentiary hearings and have to be treated as true by the court. According to §§ 288–290 ZPO, an admission (*Geständnis*) refers only to facts, not to the claim or legal arguments of the opponent. Even if all facts forming the basis of the claim are admitted, the defendant may plead for dismissal of the action on legal grounds. As a general rule, admissions are binding on the party who made them and may be withdrawn only if they were false and caused by mistake. The failure to contest factual allegations of the opposing party has the same effect as an explicit admission (§ 138 (3) ZPO). The party may, however, subsequently contest facts not explicitly admitted, but only within the limits set by § 296 ZPO (*see supra* [D][1]).

Litigation under German law is mainly left to the initiative of the parties. According to the principle of party presentation (*Verhandlungsgrundsatz, see supra* § 13.02), litigants have to present and prove all facts necessary to sustain their claim or defense. On its own initiative, the court will investigate facts and circumstances only in cases of public interest (e.g., in parent and child custody cases). Beyond the obligation to give a full and true statement on the facts (§ 138 ZPO), there is no general obligation of the parties to give information or disclose evidence in favor of the opponent's case. This is an important difference between German law and American civil procedure with far-reaching pre-trial discovery rules. The Code allows discovery of evidence held by the opposing party only to a very limited extent. In order to prevent civil actions from becoming a means of exerting pressure on the opponent, courts and the prevailing procedural doctrine reject any interpretation of the procedural rules that would create similarities to the practices occurring under American pre-trial discovery. On the other hand, a party may be entitled to information or to the production of documents and things on the basis of substantive law. These rights are sometimes granted generously by the courts and have become an important supplement to procedural rules. In line with the principle of party presentation, the court cannot take facts into consideration that the parties did not present. Personal knowledge on the part of the judge must not influence the court's decision. However, the judge's right and duty to direct pleadings in the form of "hints and feedback" (*richterliche Hinweispflicht* – § 139 ZPO) may significantly influence the presentation of the facts. Nevertheless, this influence does not restrict the freedom of the parties: When a party does not act upon a court's request or suggestion and does not supplement or improve its pleadings, the court remains bound by the facts as originally presented. In any case, the judge must remain impartial notwithstanding the duty arising out of § 139 ZPO and must not give cause to suspicions that he might be acting in favor of one of the litigants.

[3]   Hearing

§ 128 (1) ZPO requires an oral hearing of the case before a court may render its decision. Written proceedings are only allowed if stipulated by the parties (§ 128 (2) ZPO), or for very small claims (up to € 600) dealt with by the local courts (§ 495a ZPO). Apart from such exceptions, the parties make their motions and present the supporting facts orally in court, and the court may base its decision only on those presentations. Nevertheless, the parties are allowed to refer to their written pleadings (§ 137 (3) ZPO). In this way, the Code seeks to combine the advantages of both (traditional) oral and (modern) written elements. Hearings of the case are open to the public (§ 169 GVG), but *in camera* hearings may be ordered to protect individual rights or trade secrets.

After calling the case, the court introduces the matter at issue and communicates to the parties how it currently assesses the case both in fact and in law. At this point, the judge is required to discuss the possibility of settling the case (§ 278 (2) ZPO). If the parties are not willing to settle, and if the court has no reason to dismiss the case on procedural grounds (which it must consider ex officio), the parties will submit their motions. Motions may be read from the written pleadings or brought forward by referral to the respective pleading (§ 297 ZPO). The presentation of the facts, however, is done *ex tempore*.

[4]   Evidence

After discussing the subject matter with the parties, the court will hear the evidence to the extent it deems necessary.[10] As a fundamental principle of German civil procedure, evidence to be heard is restricted to the relevant facts contested by the opposing party, whereas facts not contested or admitted explicitly by the opponent must be accepted without further examination. This also applies to facts manifest and notorious (§ 291

---

10. In addition to taking evidence at the trial, the Code provides for an independent procedure to obtain evidence outside of or concurrent to the trial if there is concern that the evidence might be lost or its use impaired (*Selbständiges Beweisverfahren* – §§ 485 et seq. ZPO).

ZPO), i.e., facts obvious to the general public or facts notorious to the court from its official activity.

A party's motion to offer evidence requires a rather specific designation of the means of proof and the facts to be proven. Motions aimed at getting access to new evidence (e.g., a witness or documents) are regularly rejected as so-called fishing expeditions (*Ausforschungsbeweis*). On the other hand, it is not entirely clear which degree of specificity of factual allegations must be met by the party bearing the burden of proof. Even rather general or global allegations may be sufficient if they refer to facts within the opponent's private or commercial sphere to which the public or the adverse party have no access.

As a general rule, the taking of evidence must occur before the court rendering the decision (*Unmittelbarkeitsgrundsatz* – § 355 ZPO). The means of proof are inspection of land, chattel or persons, examination of witnesses or expert witnesses, production of documents, and party interrogation. Proof based on the presentation of documents is considered the most important and reliable evidentiary source. A document within the meaning of §§ 415 et seq. ZPO is every written statement in any language whatsoever. Official and private documents differ in their probative value with the former carrying more weight than the latter. The opponent of the party bearing the burden of proof is not generally obliged to produce documents within his possession or control. Documents must only be presented if referred to by the opponent himself (§ 423 ZPO) or if substantive law includes such an obligation (§ 422 ZPO). This principle applies to third parties as well (§ 429 ZPO). If disclosure is refused, the party bearing the burden of proof and being entitled to production by substantive law can bring a separate action for the production of documents.

The most common means of evidence is the examination of witnesses (§§ 373 et seq. ZPO). Every person capable of giving testimony on facts or conditions within his or her knowledge may be called as a witness. As a rule, parties to the action may not testify. For other persons, there is a general duty to testify, which includes the obligation to appear in court, to give testimony, and, when required, to take the oath. Privileged persons (e.g., spouses, fiancés and close relatives) need not testify, nor do persons entrusted with personal secrets by virtue of their profession or position (such as clergymen, physicians, lawyers, judges, tax consultants or certified public accountants). A privilege also exists for the protection of trade secrets. Furthermore, the law provides for a privilege against self-incrimination.

All witnesses are examined by the court, not by parties or their counsel. The parties may, and their counsel must, be given the opportunity upon request to ask additional questions (§ 397 ZPO), but such questions never amount to an American-style cross-examination.[11] An oath administered to the witness may follow the testimony, but it is within the discretion of the court and rather the exception than the rule. Testimony by witnesses is considered the most unreliable evidence due to imperfect observation, bad memory and the possibility that the testimony has been influenced. Naturally, then, it is an important task for the judge to conduct a thorough

---

11. Cf. Kötz, 13 Duke J. Comp. & Int'l L. 61, 63 (2003).

examination in order to elicit the truth and to evaluate the value and strength of testimony. From the continental European perspective, this is done better by a legally trained and experienced judge who renders the final decision without the input of a jury. Instead of questioning the witness orally, the judge may choose to ask him or her for a written statement (§ 377 (3) ZPO).

Expert witnesses are appointed by the court and must give a neutral opinion (§§ 402 et seq. ZPO).[12] It is their task to help the judge ascertain facts (or rules of foreign law, cf. § 293 ZPO) based on their expert knowledge. In any case, the judge remains the decision maker and is not supposed to delegate his power to the expert. Although, normally, expert opinions are rendered in writing, the court will summon the expert if either party so requests, and will require further explanation and responses to additional questions. Each party is free to hire its own expert and to submit his report to the court, but the opinion of a partisan expert is considered a mere party assertion and the party expert is not examined at trial.

Taking evidence from a party rarely occurs because such testimony runs counter to the rule that no one can be a witness in his own case. Therefore, interrogation of a party is only allowed to supplement evidence or upon request by the opposing party if no other evidence is available (§§ 445 et seq. ZPO).

German litigation is governed by the principle of free evaluation of evidence (*freie Beweiswürdigung*, § 286 ZPO): The court will decide according to its independent conviction whether an allegation has been proven to be true, taking into consideration the entire course of proceedings. In German law, there is no distinct law of evidence that, amongst other things, supplies detailed rules on the weighing of evidence. In principle, a fact is only proven if the court is convinced of its truth; due to this high standard of proof, mere preponderance of probability is normally not sufficient. Of course, there is no obligation for the judge to side with particular testimony, even if it is in conformity with that of other witnesses. Nor will the judge give credit to an inconclusive expert opinion. However, in rendering its judgment, the court has to set forth in detail the reasons for its evaluation of the evidence. The failure to prove an allegation to the conviction of the court will work to the detriment of the party bearing the burden of proof on that point. The allocation of that burden is a matter of substantive law. As a basic rule, each party has to prove the facts supporting its claim or defense.

[E]   Termination of the Action

[1]   Judgments on the Merits

The Court of First Instance may render a judgment on procedural grounds, i.e., dismiss the action as inadmissible (*Prozessurteil*). Ordinarily, however, litigation will be concluded by a judgment on the merits (*Sachurteil*). Once the legal dispute is ripe for

---

12. The difference between the role of experts in German and U.S. civil litigation is analysed by Timmerbeil, 9 Ann. Surv. Int'l & Comp. L. 163 (2003); Murray & Stürner, *German Civil Justice*, pp. 280 et seq.; Verkerk, 13 Int'l Journal of Evidence & Proof 167 (2009).

the final decision to be taken, the court is to deliver this decision by a final judgment (§ 300 ZPO). In its decision, the court may neither go beyond the motions of the parties nor award anything that has not been petitioned (§ 308 ZPO). The type of the judgment on the merits corresponds to the type of the action, i.e., judgments granting affirmative relief (*Leistungsurteile*) order the defendant to perform specific acts defined in the operative part of the judgment (e.g., to pay a sum of money to the plaintiff, to grant possession of personal property or to refrain from doing something). Such judgments are subject to enforcement, whereas mere declaratory judgments (*Feststellungsurteile*) and judgments establishing or modifying a legal relationship (*Gestaltungsurteile*) are only enforceable as regards the decision on costs.

The judgment must be rendered by the judge present at the final hearing of the case. If there is a panel of judges, they give only one judgment based on their deliberation of the case and, if necessary, a voting on the outcome. In principle, the decision must be delivered in a public hearing (§ 310 ZPO; § 173 (1) GVG), which may occur immediately after the closing of the trial or on a specially assigned date. After having rendered the judgment, the court becomes bound by its decree (§ 318 ZPO) and cannot retract or modify it – not even with the consent of the parties. § 313 ZPO specifies the form and contents of a court judgment. The caption (*Rubrum*) recites the parties, their counsel, the court and the judges participating, as well as the date of the final court hearing. The operative part of the judgment (*Tenor*) must be clearly displayed as being the authoritative ruling on the case. It includes a decision as to costs and as to the preliminary enforceability of the decree. The main part of the judgment contains the findings of facts and the legal reasons for the decision, summarizing the factual and legal considerations of the court. The judgment must be signed by the participating judges. In contrast to many other procedural regulations, civil judgments do not include instructions about a party's right to appeal.

[2]   Other Ways of Case Disposition

The litigants may agree to settle or otherwise terminate the dispute at any time so that the court does not have to decide the case on the merits. Again, this is a consequence of the principle of free party disposition (*Dispositionsgrundsatz, supra §13.02*). The court is bound by such acts of the parties even if it considers them inappropriate or wrong. If, e.g., the defendant acknowledges the validity of the plaintiff's claim in part or as a whole, the court must render a consent judgment without examining the merits of the case (*Anerkenntnisurteil* – § 307 ZPO). The plaintiff, on the other hand, is free to withdraw a pending claim (*Klagerücknahme*), unless the defendant has already pleaded on the merits in court (§ 269 ZPO). In that instance, the withdrawal requires the defendant's consent. As a consequence of withdrawal, there will be no judgment on the merits. The plaintiff bears the costs of the lawsuit, including those incurred by the defendant. However, terminating the action in this way does not prevent the plaintiff from initiating this same lawsuit later again. Such withdrawal must be distinguished from a waiver of action (*Klageverzicht*). In the latter case, the plaintiff no longer demands the relief originally sought and admits to not being legally entitled to the claim. On motion by the defendant, the court will render a judgment for the defendant without examining the merits of the case (*Verzichtsurteil* – § 306 ZPO). Because of the res judicata effect of this judgment, the plaintiff may not bring the same action again.

During litigation, issues underlying the controversy may have become moot. This happens, e.g., when the defendant pays the amount the plaintiff demanded or when the object claimed in an action to recover possession is destroyed. Both parties may then declare the dispute to be terminated, leaving the issue of costs to be decided by court order (*Erledigung der Hauptsache* – § 91a ZPO). The judge is bound by the conforming statements of both parties and will not examine their truthfulness. Litigation does not end if only one party declares the dispute to be terminated over the opponent's objection. If made to do so by the plaintiff, the court will treat this statement as a motion for a judgment declaring the action to be terminated. Such a decree will be rendered only if the action was initially admissible and well founded and has become moot after service of process has taken place.

At any time of the proceedings, the parties may reach a settlement in court (*Prozessvergleich*) and thereby terminate the lawsuit. A court settlement obviates the need for a judgment on the merits and, under German law, the court must encourage such a settlement throughout the course of the litigation (§ 278 (1) ZPO). An important psychological advantage of a court settlement is that neither party wins or loses face. Another benefit is that the parties may rearrange their entire legal relationship, even beyond the scope of the lawsuit, and even third parties not subject to the action may participate. Court settlements are regarded as contracts of a dual nature combining procedural acts and a contractual agreement. Therefore, in order to become effective, procedural as well as substantive law requirements must be met.

[3]   Res Judicata

The procedural instrument of res judicata (*Rechtskraft*) aims at public peace and legal certainty. If there is no more appeal from a court's decision (*formelle Rechtskraft*), it becomes final and absolute (§ 705 ZPO). Since the decision is of final force and effect, it binds the courts and the parties in any later action concerning the same matter (*materielle Rechtskraft*). Nevertheless, the binding effect of res judicata is limited: According to § 322 ZPO, the judgment becomes final and absolute only with respect to the claim (or the counterclaim), and it is only the operative part of the judgment (*Tenor*), not the findings of law that becomes res judicata. As a matter of principle, only the parties to the action are subject to the binding force of a decree. Furthermore, the judgment takes effect for and against the persons who have become successors in title of the parties after the matter has become pending, or who have obtained possession of the disputed object such that one of the parties or its successor in title has become constructive possessor (§ 325 ZPO). Judgments establishing or modifying a legal relationship (*Gestaltungsurteile*) have *erga omnes* effect.

A final and conclusive judgment cannot be reversed or changed in any way. It may be invalidated under the strict conditions of a motion for a new trial (§§ 578 et seq. ZPO), which will only be successful in cases of the most severe violation of procedural rights (petition for nullification of the judgment – *Nichtigkeitsklage*) or a serious tampering with the factual basis of the judgment (action for restitution – *Restitutionsklage*).

[4] Costs

Every final judgment must contain a decision on the costs of the proceedings which is rendered ex officio without motion by the litigants (§§ 91 et seq., § 308 (2) ZPO).[13] In principle, the losing party must pay for all costs, including court fees, costs for witnesses and expert witnesses, and the opponent's necessary expenses, including his attorney's fees. In exceptional cases, the prevailing party has to bear all or part of the costs, e.g., when the plaintiff has filed the action without due warning and the defendant has immediately acknowledged the claim. The amount of costs primarily depends on the amount in controversy (*Streitwert*) and is statutorily fixed in the Court Fees Act (*Gerichtskostengesetz* – GKG) and the Attorneys Remuneration Act (*Rechtsanwaltsvergütungsgesetz* – RVG). Attorneys can agree on higher fees with their clients, but such additional costs will not be borne by the losing party. Agreements under which remuneration shall depend on the outcome of the case or on the success of the attorney's work or under which the attorney shall keep a part of the award made by the court as a fee (contingency fees) are not permitted, unless the RVG provides otherwise (§ 49b (2) BRAO). Legal cost insurance is quite common in Germany.

[F] Appellate Remedies

Under certain circumstances, a party is allowed to appeal from a court decision to the court of next instance. The characteristic feature of such an appeal is that the judgment does not become final and absolute as long as the appeal is pending (suspensory effect). The Code of Civil Procedure establishes three types of appeal: first appeal (*Berufung*), appeal on points of law (*Revision*), and complaint seeking relief from a court order (*Beschwerde*). The success of an appellate remedy depends on its admissibility (*Zulässigkeit*) and its merits (*Begründetheit*). The admissibility requires statutory authorization and a filing in due form within the prescribed time limit. The appellant must have a legitimate interest in the appeal, which means that he needs to be aggrieved by the judgment from which he appeals. A party may waive its remedy, thereby losing the right to appeal, and a later effort to revive that right will be dismissed on procedural grounds. As long as only one party appeals, the appellate court is restricted by the principle that its decision may not put the appellant in a worse position than the judgment from which he appealed. Furthermore, the appellate court may not grant more or a different kind of relief than the appellant prayed for (§ 528 ZPO).

---

13. For details see Hess & Huebner, in: Reimann, *Cost and Fee Allocation in Civil Procedure*, pp. 151 et seq.; Murray & Stürner, *German Civil Justice*, pp. 341 et seq.; Wagner, in: Gottwald, *Litigation in England and Germany*, pp. 149 et seq.

An appeal aims at the reversal of a judgment. The dispute must be heard and decided by the appellate instance (§§ 511–541 ZPO). A first appeal (*Berufung*) can only be filed against a judgment of a Court of First Instance (*Amtsgericht* or *Landgericht*). The first appeal is admissible if the sum involved exceeds € 600. Alternatively, the Court of First Instance may explicitly permit the first appeal because the point of law in question is of fundamental importance or a decision by the appellate court could contribute to greater "unity of the case-law". The petition for first appeal must be filed by a lawyer within one month after the judgment was served or, in case it was not served upon the party, not later than five months after the judgment was delivered (§ 517 ZPO). There is an additional one-month time limit for filing a brief in support of the first appeal (§ 520 (2) ZPO). First appeals from the local courts (*Amtsgerichte*) are heard by the regional court (*Landgericht*), whereas first instance judgments rendered by the regional court will be examined by the higher regional court (*Oberlandesgericht*). Proceedings at the appellate level work as a continuation of the litigation of the first instance, which means that the case will be reheard on points of both fact and law. New facts, however, can only be presented if the party is able to sufficiently excuse itself for not having submitted them in due time at first instance or if the first instance court ignored those facts. The first appeal will be dismissed on the merits if the appellate court considers the judgment appealed from to be correct. If the first appeal is legally founded, the judgment will be vacated and the appellate court will render its own decision. It is only in very restrictive circumstances that the appellate court may not itself decide on the merits but remand the case to the Court of First Instance (§ 538 (2) ZPO).

The judgment of the appellate court (i.e., of the *Landgericht* or the *Oberlandesgericht*) may be subject to an appeal on a point of law (*Revision* – §§ 542–565 ZPO), which will be heard by the Federal Supreme Court (*Bundesgerichtshof*). Such further appeal is admissible only if the case is of fundamental legal importance or if a decision by the Federal Supreme Court is apt to create greater "unity of the law". The appeal on a point of law requires leave granted by the appellate court or, if denied, granted by the Federal Supreme Court. The appeal can only be based on a violation of procedural or substantive law. In principle, the parties are not allowed to present new facts. If the appeal is filed in due time and form and is well founded, the Federal Supreme Court will reverse the judgment. Under normal circumstances, the Federal Supreme Court will remand the case to the appellate court, which must base its decision on the legal conclusions formulated by the Federal Supreme Court (§ 563 (2) ZPO). The Federal Supreme Court itself will only exceptionally render a final judgment on the merits (§ 563 (3) ZPO).

Court orders, i.e., decisions other than judgments, may be reviewed on the basis of a complaint seeking relief from such orders. A so-called immediate complaint (*sofortige Beschwerde* – §§ 567–573 ZPO) is available against court orders defeating a motion on procedural issues without hearing the applicant or in cases explicitly specified in the Code. If the immediate complaint is admissible, the court order in question will be reviewed by the court of next instance on both fact and law. A further complaint on a point of law (*Rechtsbeschwerde* – §§ 574–577 ZPO) may be filed with the

Federal Supreme Court if the case is of fundamental legal importance or if a decision by the Federal Supreme Court could further the "unity of the case-law".

[G] Special Proceedings

[1] Proceedings Restricted to Documentary Evidence and Proceedings Based on a Promissory Note or Bill of Exchange

A claim for payment of a certain amount of money or delivery of a certain quantity of fungible things or securities may be asserted in an expedited trial by record if all facts necessary to establish the claim can be proven by documents (*Urkundenprozess* – §§ 592 et seq. ZPO). These fast and simplified proceedings are also available for claims based on a bill of exchange (*Wechselprozess*). All facts in favor of the plaintiff must be proven by documents, and all facts in favor of the defense must be proven either by documents or party interrogation. This restriction of available evidence intends to expedite the proceeding. In compensation, a judgment against the defendant will only be provisional and is subject to modification in subsequent proceedings before the same court: On the defendant's petition, the court will rehear the case without restrictions of evidence in order to decide whether the provisional judgment should be upheld unconditionally or rather be reversed.

[2] Summary Proceedings for Recovering a Debt or Liquidated Demand

A creditor may obtain an enforceable instrument without a court hearing by way of summary proceedings (*Mahnverfahren* – §§ 688 et seq. ZPO). These proceedings serve as an attractive alternative to the ordinary action. They are of great practical importance, particularly to enforce claims undisputed by the debtor. These summary proceedings are available for the recovery of a monetary debt or a liquidated claim. The creditor must file a motion with the local court (*Amtsgericht*), which is competent regardless of the sum involved. The court will examine whether the claim will be eligible for the summary proceedings but will study its merits only to a very limited extent. In essence, the claim must only be sufficiently identifiable, so that it can be distinguished from other claims, and valid on its face. If the motion meets these requirements, the court will issue a summary notice to pay (*Mahnbescheid*). Then the debtor may file an objection (*Widerspruch*) within two weeks. In case of such objection, the matter in dispute becomes *lis pendens*, and normal litigation proceedings will follow in the respective trial court having jurisdiction over the case. If the debtor does not file an objection in due time, the court will issue an enforcement order (*Vollstreckungsbescheid*). Again, the debtor may appeal within two weeks (*Einspruch*). If he does so, the matter is relegated to ordinary litigation. When the enforcement order becomes final and binding, the creditor may enforce it against the debtor.

[3]   ***Proceedings in Matrimonial Matters and Other Cases Involving***
        Family Law

The general rules of the Code of Civil Procedure also apply to proceedings in matrimonial matters and other family disputes (*Ehe- und Familienstreitsachen* – § 113 (1) FamFG). Nevertheless, there are some remarkable peculiarities. Exclusive subject matter jurisdiction lies with the family court (*Familiengericht*), a division of the *Amtsgericht*. Appeals are heard by the Court of Appeal (*Oberlandesgericht*). The proceedings are not open to the public. The principle of free party disposition (*Dispositionsgrundsatz, supra B*) is restricted. Therefore, the court is not bound by the statements or pleadings of the parties, and there is no obligation to treat undisputed facts as being true if the court is not convinced of their truth. There is no default judgment against the defendant (§ 130 (2) FamFG). The principle of party presentation of facts and evidence (*Verhandlungsgrundsatz, supra* §13.02) is also restricted (cf. § 127 FamFG).

§13.04   ENFORCEMENT PROCEEDINGS

If a defendant does not voluntarily comply with a judgment or court order, public institutions must help to enforce the creditor's claim. The rules relevant to the enforcement of judgments and court orders are set forth in Chapter 8 of the Code of Civil Procedure.[14]

[A]   Prerequisites for Execution of Judgments

The parties involved in enforcement proceedings are called "creditor" (the party holding a legally enforceable claim) and "debtor" (the party against whom enforcement is sought). Both must be capable of being a party in a lawsuit (*Parteifähigkeit*) and legally capable of conducting a proceeding in their own name (*Prozessfähigkeit*). Given the principle of party disposition, there is no ex officio enforcement of judgments. Therefore, the creditor must file an application for enforcement. The court competent for enforcement matters (*Vollstreckungsgericht*) or the enforcement officer (*Gerichtsvollzieher*) will examine whether the statutory requirements for enforcement are met. First, there must be a judicially enforceable instrument (*Titel* – §§ 704, 794 ZPO), i.e., a "title" specifying the creditor, the debtor and the kind and extent of the claim to be enforced. Second, that title must bear a court certificate of enforceability issued by the court (*Vollstreckungsklausel* – §§ 724, 725 ZPO), and third, the certified title must have been served upon the debtor (*Zustellung* – § 750 ZPO).

   In practice, important titles are final or at least provisionally enforceable judgments (§§ 705 et seq. ZPO). Provisional enforceability (*vorläufige Vollstreckbarkeit*)

---

14. This chapter does not deal with insolvency proceedings; these are not regulated in the Code of Civil Procedure but in the Insolvency Code, which entered into force January 1, 1999. The German rules on insolvency proceedings have been reformed to strengthen reorganization, enable discharge of the bankrupt and introduce special proceedings for consumers' bankruptcy.

means that the judgment is subject to enforcement even before it becomes res judicata. If the judgment is reversed on appeal, the plaintiff must compensate the defendant for the damage caused by the enforcement (§ 717 (2) ZPO). Therefore, the plaintiff effecting such preliminary enforcement does so at his own risk. In order to protect the defendant's claim for damages, most judgments may be provisionally enforced only upon payment of security (§ 709 ZPO).

According to §§ 794 et seq. ZPO, judicially enforceable instruments other than judgments include enforcement orders (*Vollstreckungsbescheide, supra* §13.03[G][2]), court settlements (*Prozessvergleiche*), special settlements between the parties represented by their lawyers (*Anwaltsvergleiche*), cost orders issued by the court (*Kostenfestsetzungsbeschlüsse*), and directly enforceable instruments drawn up by a notary (*vollstreckbare Urkunden*). A creditor intending to enforce a judgment rendered by a foreign court must file an action in order to obtain a writ of execution (§§ 722, 723 ZPO). If applicable, the summary enforcement proceedings under European Law (Brussels Ibis Regulation) or under specific treaties (e.g., the Lugano Convention) facilitate and expedite the enforcement process.

[B] Enforcement of Monetary Claims

Liquidated claims (*Geldforderungen*) will be enforced by attachment of property of the debtor and judicial sale in order to discharge the claim. The procedure varies according to the object seized (§§ 803–882a ZPO).

[1] Attachment of the Debtor's Movable Property

The attachment of movable property (§§ 808 et seq. ZPO) is within the responsibility of the enforcement officer (*Gerichtsvollzieher*). Enforcement begins with the attachment of the chattel in question, meaning that the debtor can no longer dispose of the chattel. In order to do so, the enforcement officer will take possession of the chattel that must be under the debtor's custody or under custody of a third party willing to give up possession. Since the enforcement officer normally does not examine the status of ownership, attachment of a third party's property which is found in the debtor's custody is effective. In this case, it is left to the third party to prevent alienation of the object seized by way of a third party claim (*Drittwiderspruchsklage* – § 771 ZPO).

Money, negotiable instruments and other valuables will be taken by the execution officer and held in custody. Other things are left in the debtor's custody, with an official stamp marking the attachment. In principle, the enforcement officer is allowed to search the debtor's apartment or premises. If the debtor objects, the enforcement officer must not enter the premises without leave of the court. In order to protect the debtor's basis of subsistence, the Code specifies chattels that are exempt from execution (§ 811 ZPO). The judicial sale of attached goods occurs by way of public auction. After deduction of costs, the creditor receives the proceeds of the sale while the debtor is entitled to any surplus.

[2]   Garnishment of Claims and Other Proprietary Interests

For the creditor it is usually more convenient and cheaper to initiate garnishment proceedings (§§ 828 et seq. ZPO) in which the debtor's claims, such as wages and salaries, are subject to execution. The court competent for this kind of enforcement is the *Amtsgericht* at the debtor's domicile or his general residence (*Vollstreckungsgericht*). The creditor must file a petition for enforcement identifying the claim to be garnished. The court will examine the general prerequisites for enforcement but will not inquire whether the claim actually exists or not. If the debtor does not hold a valid claim, the garnishment will be without legal effect. Another prerequisite is that the claim must be susceptible to enforcement. Only claims that are assignable are also subject to seizure by garnishment. The attachment of claims is restricted for socio-political reasons. Wages, e.g., are exempt from garnishment up to a certain limit in order to leave the debtor with the financial means needed to cover necessary expenditures.

If all prerequisites are fulfilled, the court will issue a garnishment order identifying the claim and forbidding the garnishee to pay the debtor. The latter will be ordered not to dispose of the claim in any way. The garnishment order becomes effective when served upon the garnishee. In a second step, often taken together with the garnishment order, the court will transfer the garnished claim to the creditor, who then has the right to submit the claim to the garnishee and to file an action if the garnishee does not pay voluntarily. Upon request by the creditor, the garnishee must declare whether and to which extent he accepts the validity of the garnished claim, but he may raise any pre-existing objection or defense. Particular rules apply to the garnishment of claims secured by mortgage and claims arising out of a bill of exchange or bank deposits.

A debtor's right to recover corporeal property from a third party is also subject to garnishment (§§ 846 et seq. ZPO). Rules of garnishment also apply if the creditor wants to attach property assets such as interests in an inheritance, portions of an estate or partnership interests.

[3]   Enforcement Proceedings Involving the Debtor's Immovable Property

The rules regulating the enforcement of a judgment against the debtor's real estate are set forth in the Act on Forced Sale and Forced Administration (*Gesetz über die Zwangsversteigerung und Zwangsverwaltung* – ZVG). The enforcement may be effected by a court officer by way of public auction in order to liquidate the substance value of the real estate and discharge the creditor's claim with the proceeds (§ 869 ZPO, §§ 15 et seq. ZVG). This must not affect security interests with priority over the creditor's claim. Consequently, all security interests in the property that are higher in rank, because they were recorded in the land register earlier than the judgment creditor's interest, continue to be valid and, despite the public sale, must be accepted by the highest bidder at auction. The highest bidder in the auction wins the bid, and legal title in the estate will be transferred to him by judicial act. Then the court officer distributes the proceeds among the judgment's creditor and the debtor's other creditors whose security interests did not survive the public sale because they were lower in rank. Another enforcement option is sequestration (§ 869 ZPO, §§ 146 et seq. ZVG): Upon motion of the creditor, the court will issue an order depriving the debtor of his right and authority to administrate his property. The court will appoint an administrator and the creditor will receive all income from the real estate. A third way of enforcing the creditor's claim is an execution lien on the debtor's land (§ 867 ZPO). Upon the creditor's motion, the land register (*Grundbuchamt*) will register a mortgage to enforce the judgment debt.

[C] Enforcement of Non-monetary Claims

Under German law, claims for the delivery or recovery of goods are enforceable (§§ 883–886 ZPO). On a judgment ordering delivery, the enforcement officer takes away the chattels in custody of the debtor and hands them over to the creditor. If the debtor has been ordered to vacate real estate, the enforcement officer restores it to the creditor's possession.

Judgments are also enforceable if they order the debtor to perform a certain act, refrain from a certain act or acquiesce in acts of the plaintiff (§§ 887–890 ZPO). Acts that do not require personal performance by the debtor (*vertretbare Handlungen* – § 887 ZPO) will be enforced by a court order authorizing the creditor to have the act performed by someone else. If the act must be performed personally by the debtor, such as the rendering of an account or providing a particular piece of information (*unvertretbare Handlung* – § 888 ZPO), the court will take measures to enforce compliance (i.e., penalties or coercive detention). Non-compliance with an enforceable claim to refrain from a certain act (*Unterlassungsanspruch*) or to acquiesce (*Duldungsanspruch*) will also be punished by fines or arrest for contempt of the court order (§§ 890 et seq. ZPO). If the plaintiff has obtained a decree ordering the defendant to make a certain declaration of will (*Willenserklärung*), this declaration will be deemed to have been made as soon as the judgment becomes final and absolute (§ 894 ZPO).

[D] Remedies in Enforcement Proceedings

If the enforcement is unlawful, the party affected has specific remedies that apply only as long as the enforcement proceedings continue, i.e., the enforcement process has been initiated but has not yet been completed. Objections may be raised if the enforcement agency (court, enforcement officer, or land register office) does not comply with the formal requirements of the enforcement proceedings (*Vollstreckungserinnerung* – § 766 ZPO). In this case, the court competent for enforcement matters (*Vollstreckungsgericht*) will examine whether procedural rules were violated.

The debtor may apply for a stay or provisional suspension of enforcement if its continuation would cause undue hardship due to exceptional circumstances (§ 765a ZPO). The debtor can also file an action with the trial court to challenge the enforcement of the judgment arguing that there are objections to the creditor's claim based on substantive law (*Vollstreckungsgegenklage* – § 767 ZPO). This action will be successful, and execution will be suspended, if the claim, in whole or in part, may not be enforced (e.g., if the debtor has satisfied the claim or obligation, or if the creditor has waived the claim after the final court hearing). Since the res judicata effect of the judgment must not be affected as such, the action needs to be based on circumstances that arose after the close of the trial.

A third party action against enforcement (§ 771 ZPO) offers a third party the opportunity to prove his rights in the property attached by the court or the enforcement officer. In this action against the creditor, the third party requests that the court declare the enforcement unlawful and suspend execution. As a prerequisite, the third party must have a right that operates as a bar against enforcement (e.g., a property right, security interest or lien). It is not sufficient that the debtor is merely obligated, e.g., under a sales contract, to transfer the property in question to the third party. Under German law, such a contractual obligation does not effect a change of ownership, but leaves the goods in the vendor's property until title is transferred through additional steps.

§13.05   ATTACHMENTS AND INJUNCTIVE RELIEF

Because lengthy civil proceedings may endanger the creditor's ability to enforce his rights, the German law of civil procedure offers relief through attachment remedies and temporary injunctions.

The attachment of property or arrest of the debtor (*Arrest* – §§ 916 et seq. ZPO) secures the future enforcement of a money judgment. This relief is available by way of summary proceedings. The creditor must set forth that he has a claim against the debtor (*Arrestanspruch*) and that there are urgent reasons for issuing the order (*Arrestgrund*). It is necessary to distinguish between the personal arrest of the debtor and attachment of the debtor's property. In order to state reasonable grounds for attachment of property, the creditor must set forth in detail that the debtor is removing or dissipating property dishonestly or secretly and is thereby frustrating future enforcement attempts. Only if attachment of property will not be sufficient to protect the creditor's rights, detention of the debtor will be allowed. The general rules for enforcing a judgment likewise apply to attachment orders and other orders for preliminary relief, but the resulting attachments operate as safeguards only: Thus, the judicial sale of the attached property cannot take place until the creditor has obtained a judicially enforceable instrument, e.g., a judgment against the debtor. If the arrest proves to be unjustified, the creditor is liable in damages (§ 945 ZPO).

Temporary injunctions (*einstweilige Verfügungen* – §§ 935 et seq. ZPO) are of even greater practical importance. They allow for a provisional regulation of legal relations or a safeguarding of non-monetary claims. German law offers three kinds of injunctions. So-called preventive injunctions (*Sicherungsverfügungen*) safeguard non-monetary claims (e.g., claims for the recovery of possession of personal property), whereas regulatory injunctions (*Regelungsverfügungen*) provisionally settle disputes regarding legal relationships (e.g., temporary regulations for the use of property by co-owners or regulations in landlord-tenant disputes). The third kind of injunction has developed through case law and, as an exception to the general rule, does not only safeguard the enforcement of a claim but results in an affirmative obligation forcing the debtor to render performance (*Leistungsverfügung*).

On a motion for a temporary injunction, the court has discretion to decide what kind of relief it will grant, but it must not go beyond the creditor's petition. A characteristic feature of summary proceedings is that the petitioner does not have to prove the prerequisites (claim and urgency of relief) to the full satisfaction of the court. It is sufficient to substantiate the claim by prima facie evidence (*Glaubhaftmachung* – § 294 ZPO). The scope of evidence is restricted to immediately available means of proof, including affidavits (*eidesstattliche Versicherungen*).

§13.06   ALTERNATIVE DISPUTE RESOLUTION

In recent years, special legislation has been enacted to cover various aspects of alternative dispute resolution, mostly based on EU law provisions. This holds true for the Mediation Act of 2012 (*Mediationsgesetz*) and the Act on Resolution of Consumer Law Disputes of 2016 (*Verbraucherstreitbeilegungsgesetz*).

Book 10 of the Code of Civil Procedure deals with the law of arbitration, the third pillar of dispute resolution besides litigation and mediation.[15] In this area, EU law is still of minor importance. For the most part, the German law of arbitration is modelled after the UNCITRAL Model Law on International Commercial Arbitration. The German rules apply when the venue of the arbitration proceedings is located in Germany (§§ 1025, 1043 ZPO). The requirements for a valid arbitration agreement are set out in §§ 1029 et seq. ZPO. The recognition and enforcement of foreign arbitration awards is governed by the New York Convention of 1958.

SELECTED BIBLIOGRAPHY

Official English translations of the most relevant German Acts are available online, *see* www.gesetze-im-internet.de/Teilliste_translations.html.

The leading textbooks on the German law of civil procedure are *Zivilprozessrecht* by Leo Rosenberg, Karl-Heinz Schwab & Peter Gottwald (18th ed. 2018), and *Zwangs-vollstreckungsrecht* by Leo Rosenberg, Hans Friedhelm Gaul, Eberhard Schilken & Ekkehard Becker-Eberhard (12th ed. 2010). Practitioners normally rather work with "commentaries" (*Kommentare*), i.e., editions of the Code of Civil Procedure with comprehensive annotations. Among the most widely used ones are Richard Zöller, *Zivilprozessordnung* (32th ed. 2018 – online accessible via juris.de), and Hans-Joachim Musielak & Wolfgang Voit, *Zivilprozessordnung* (14th ed. 2017 – online accessible via beck-online.de). The following list provides a short overview of literature on German law and/or on comparative aspects of civil procedure in English language:

---

15. For a detailed recent account of the German law of arbitration, cf. Rützel, Wegen & Wilske, *Commercial Dispute Resolution in Germany*, Ch. 2.

Michael Bohlander, *The German Advantage Revisited – An Inside View of German Civil Procedure in the Nineties*, 13 Tul. Eur. & Civ. L. F. 25 (1998).

Thomas Försterling, *Germany*, in: Alexander Layton & Hugh Mercer, *European Civil Practice* vol. 2 (2nd ed. 2004), p. 178.

Peter Gottwald, *Civil Procedure in Germany after the Reform Act of 2001*, 23 C.J.Q. 338 (2004).

Peter Gottwald, *Litigation in England and Germany – Legal Professional Services, Key Features and Funding* (2010).

Peter Gottwald, *The New German Procedure in Family Matters*, 198 Revista de processo 165 (2011).

Urs Gruber & Ivo Bach, *Germany*, in: Carlos Esplugues, José Luis Iglesias & Guillermo Palao, *Civil and Commercial Mediation in Europe, vol. I: National Mediation Rules and Procedures* (2012), p. 159.

Urs Gruber & Ivo Bach, *Germany*, in: Carlos Esplugues, José Luis Iglesias & Guillermo Palao, *Civil and Commercial Mediation in Europe, vol. II: Cross-Border Mediation* (2014), p. 155.

Burkhard Hess & Rudolf Huebner, *Cost and Fee Allocation in German Civil Procedure*, in: Mathias Reimann, *Cost and Fee Allocation in Civil Procedure* (2012), p. 151.

Burkhard Hess & Marcus Mack, *Germany*, in: Mads Adenas, Burkhard Hess & Paul Oberhammer, *Enforcement Agency Practice in Europe* (2005), p. 169.

Harald Koch & Frank Diedrich, *Civil Procedure in Germany* (1998).

Christian Koller, *Civil Justice in Austrian-German Tradition*, in: Alan Uzelac, *Goals of Civil Justice and Civil Procedure in Contemporary Judicial Systems* (2014), p. 35.

Hein Kötz, *Civil Justice Systems in Europe and the U.S.*, 13 Duke J. Comp. & Int'l L. 61 (2003).

Volker Lipp & Halvard Haukeland Fredriksen (ed.), *Reforms of Civil Procedure in Germany and Norway* (2011).

James R. Maxeiner, *Failures of American Civil Justice in International Perspective* (2011).

Peter L. Murray, *A Morning at the Amtsgericht*, in: James A. R. Nafziger & Symeon C. Symeonides, *Law and Justice in a Multistate World – Essays in Honor of Arthur T. von Mehren* (2002), p. 779.

Peter L. Murray & Rolf Stürner, *German Civil Justice* (2004).

Anna Nylund & Bart Krans, *The European Union and National Civil Procedure – A Smooth Process or a Rocky Road for Member States?* (2016).

Stefan Rützel, Gerhard Wegen & Stephan Wilske, *Commercial Dispute Resolution in Germany* (2nd ed. 2016).

Peter F. Schlosser, *Lectures on Civil-Law Litigation Systems and American Cooperation with Those Systems*, 45 Kan. L. Rev. 9 (1996).

Felix Schmidt, *A Critical Analysis of Recent Developments in German Law on Civil Procedure*, 28 C.J.Q. 273 (2009).

Astrid Stadler, *The Multiple Roles of Judges and Attorneys in Modern Civil Litigation*, 27 Hastings Int'l & Comp. L. Rev. 55 (2003).

Michael Stürner, *Litigation in the 21st Century: How Attractive Is the German Civil Justice System?* Tijdschrift voor Civiele Rechtspleging 145 (2016).

CHAPTER 14

Criminal Law

Tatjana Hörnle & Rita Vavra

TABLE OF CONTENTS

§14.01   CRIMINAL LAW IN GERMANY: FOUNDATIONS

Germany is a federal republic consisting of sixteen independent states or *Bundesländer*. German criminal law, however, is federal law only. Contrary to the United States, the German *Bundesländer* are preempted from enacting their own criminal statutes: the right to legislate on criminal matters is vested in the German Federal Parliament (*Bundestag*). Therefore, the same criminal statutes apply all over Germany.

German criminal law is codified. The most important source of substantive criminal law, the Criminal Code (*Strafgesetzbuch*, abbreviated as StGB), dates back to 1871. At the time of its enactment in 1871, the StGB was called "Criminal Code of the German Reich" (*Strafgesetzbuch für das Deutsche Reich*, abbreviated as RStGB). After the Second World War, the name was changed to the simple "*Strafgesetzbuch*" (StGB). Over the course of time, the Criminal Code underwent numerous significant changes, including important reforms in 1975 (reforming the General Part), 1998 (readjusting the punishments for crimes against property and crimes against persons) and, most recently, in 2016 (reforming the law of sexual assault[1]). New offense descriptions have been added in order to deal with new areas of criminality (e.g., cybercrimes) or to

---

1. For a discussion of the new law of sexual assault, *see* Tatjana Hörnle, *The New German Law on Sexual Assault and Sexual Harassment*, 18 German Law Journal 1309 (2017).

respond to societal problems such as stalking, environmental hazards or the support of terrorist organizations.[2] Despite the large amount of amendments and changes, the basic structure of the Criminal Code has remained largely unchanged. The German Federal Ministry of Justice and Consumer Protection publishes an English translation of the Criminal Code,[3] but the English version is not updated regularly.

The Criminal Code is the most important source of criminal law in Germany. For this reason, our introduction to German criminal law focuses on its provisions. It should nevertheless be mentioned that various supplementary statutes exist, some of which are of great practical importance – e.g., the Narcotics Act (*Betäubungsmittelgesetz*, abbreviated as BtMG). § 29 of the Narcotics Act, which, *inter alia*, sanctions the possession and sale of drugs, is a prominent charge in German criminal courts. Other criminal statutes cover traffic offenses (e.g., § 21 of the *Straßenverkehrsgesetz*, StVG, which criminalizes driving a vehicle without a driver's license) or tax crimes (e.g., § 370 of the *Abgabenordnung*, AO, which penalizes tax evasion). The Juvenile Court Act (*Jugendgerichtsgesetz*, JGG) deals with juvenile offenders and sets out specific criminal procedures and punishments for young offenders.

In the Criminal Code, offenses are classified into one of two categories: felonies (*Verbrechen*) and misdemeanors (*Vergehen*). Felonies carry a minimum penalty of one year imprisonment. The distinction between felonies and misdemeanors has consequences for the law of criminal procedure. For instance, with regard to felonies, prosecutors have no discretion to dismiss the case and the appointment of a public defender is mandatory.[4] A third category of sanctioned behavior exists outside of the StGB: regulatory offenses (*Ordnungswidrigkeiten*) that deal with misconduct of a less serious kind (e.g., speeding or parking violations). Sanctions are limited to fines: *Ordnungswidrigkeiten* cannot be sanctioned with imprisonment, not even in the case of persistent behavior. Regulatory offenses do not carry the same social stigma as crimes and the fines are not classified as criminal punishment. To distinguish these monetary sanctions from criminal fines, the former are called *Geldbuße* and the latter *Geldstrafe*. Many statutes (under both federal and state law) include the threat of *Geldbußen* as a regulatory instrument to prevent certain conduct. The general rules applying to regulatory offenses can be found in the *Gesetz über Ordnungswidrigkeiten* (Administrative Offenses Act, OWiG). Sanctions are not imposed by criminal courts but by administrative bodies, and they do not become part of a person's criminal record. Criminal courts only have to deal with *Ordnungswidrigkeiten* if the person concerned challenges the imposition of a *Geldbuße*.

---

2. For the impact of terrorism on German criminal law *see* Bernhard Kretschmer, *Criminal Involvement in Terrorist Associations – Classification and Fundamental Principles of the German Criminal Code § 129a StGB*, 13 German Law Journal 1016 (2012); Liane Wörner, *Expanding Criminal Laws by Predating Criminal Responsibility – Punishing Planning and Organizing Terrorist Attacks as a Means to Optimize Effectiveness of Fighting Against Terrorism*, 13 German Law Journal 1038 (2012).

3. *See* https://www.gesetze-im-internet.de/englisch_stgb/englisch_stgb.html.

4. *See* § 140 I No. 2 of the Code of Criminal Procedure (*Strafprozessordnung*, StPO).

The Criminal Code is divided into two parts: The General Part (*Allgemeiner Teil*) sets out general principles of criminal liability and sentencing, and the longer Special Part (*Besonderer Teil*) contains offense descriptions. The exact wording of the offense descriptions is of great importance in German criminal law because the principle of legality, as set out in Article 103 II of the German Constitution (*Grundgesetz*, GG), requires all criminal prohibitions and sanctions to be based on statutory, written law. The principle of legality prohibits judge-made criminal prohibitions or sanctions and unwritten customary law. Despite the constitutional principle of legality, many provisions in the Criminal Code need to be interpreted in order to be applied by the criminal courts. The General Part contains hardly any definitions: The meaning of important legal terms, such as, e.g., causation or intent, is not defined in statutory law. The sections on criminal liability in the General Part are rather short. Also, in the Special Part, offense descriptions contain vague terms and leave the criminal courts with a wide margin of interpretation. This is even true for murder (§ 211 StGB), a felony with a mandatory life sentence. The criminal courts have also reinterpreted existing criminal laws to a degree that changed the application of these criminal statutes.[5] Criminal courts therefore wield considerable power by defining legal terms. For this reason, it would be misleading to characterize German criminal law as exclusively determined by the contents of the Criminal Code (or other criminal statutes): Case law does play an important role. Also, criminal law doctrine as developed by legal scholars continues to be an important factor for court rulings. German criminal procedure (regulated in the Code of Criminal Procedure, *Strafprozessordnung*, StPO) does not include jury participation in criminal trials. Therefore, there is no pressing need to adapt legal reasoning to laypersons' understanding. Debates concerning details of criminal law doctrine figure not only in appellate court decisions, but also in the reasoning of trial courts. An important source for statutory interpretation are commentaries to the Criminal Code authored by scholars and/or judges from the highest courts.[6]

§14.02   GENERAL PART

The General Part of the StGB contains provisions applicable to all offense descriptions in the Special Part. The first provisions (§§ 1–10 StGB) refer to matters of international jurisdiction. The chapters that describe general features of criminal liability (§§ 11–35 StGB) are rather short. These parts of the StGB in combination with rules of legal doctrine are nevertheless of great importance for understanding German criminal law.

---

5. An example is the judicial reinterpretation of § 316 StGB (driving under the influence of alcohol or other intoxicants). In the past, drivers were conclusively presumed unfit to drive if their blood alcohol concentration was above 0.13%. In 1990, the German Federal Court of Justice lowered the threshold to a blood alcohol concentration of 0.11%. *See* BGHSt 37, 89.
6. *See*, e.g., Thomas Fischer, *Strafgesetzbuch* (65. Ed., C.H. Beck 2018); Schönke/Schröder, *Strafgesetzbuch* (29. Ed., C.H. Beck 2014); Münchener Kommentar, *Strafgesetzbuch*, Volume 1-8 (3. Ed., C.H. Beck 2017–2018); Leipziger Kommentar, *Strafgesetzbuch*, Volume 1-14 (12. Ed., C.H. Beck 2006 et seq.).

[A]   The Basic Structure of Criminal Offenses

Criminal liability is determined by a three-step test not explicitly mentioned in the Criminal Code but taught in law schools and applied by the courts. An offender first has to fulfill all the elements of the criminal offense as set out in the Special Part (*Tatbestandsmäßigkeit*). More specifically, this requires that the offender has fulfilled all objective elements of the crime as stipulated in the Special Part (this would be called *actus reus* in Anglo-American law) with the requisite subjective attitude such as intent or negligence (*mens rea* in Anglo-American law). In a second step, it must be determined whether the offender acted unlawfully or whether he was justified (*Rechtswidrigkeit*). If the actions of the offender were justified due to, e.g., self-defense or the valid consent of the victim, his actions are lawful and he cannot be punished under the statute. The third step (*Schuld*) is concerned with the offender's individual guilt, i.e., the question whether the offender is personally accountable. Personal guilt can be denied in exceptional circumstances such as when the offender is legally insane or acted under a high level of duress.

German criminal law strictly distinguishes between questions of lawfulness or justification (*Rechtswidrigkeit*) and questions of guilt or personal blameworthiness (*Schuld*). Conduct that is justified is not unlawful and is thus not considered legal wrongdoing. On the other hand, if a person is not justified, but only excused due to the fact that she cannot be personally blamed, the conduct remains a legal wrong. The law merely recognizes that the offender does not merit punishment because he could not have been expected to comply with the law under the special circumstances he found himself in. The distinction between justified and excused actions is not merely of theoretical importance: For example in the case of liability for participation in a crime, the prerequisite is that the principal actor acted wrongfully, i.e., without a justification, but it is not necessary that he is personally blameworthy. Moreover, whereas persons acting justified cannot be subjected to any kind of sanction under German criminal law, persons acting unlawfully but without guilt can be subjected to measures of rehabilitation and incapacitation (*Maßregeln der Besserung und Sicherung*) under § 63 StGB, *see* below §14.04[D].

[B]   Causation

The *actus reus* of most criminal offenses requires the offender to bring about a specific unlawful result (*Erfolgsdelikte*). In order to impute the result to the offender, the act needs to have caused the result in question. Whether a causal link between the act and the result exists is determined by the *conditio sine qua non*–test, asking if the act is a necessary cause for the result. In other words, would the same result have occurred if the offender had not acted the way that he did? If so, there is no causal link between the action and the result. However, if the action of the offender is a condition that cannot be disregarded, causation has been established.

Under German criminal law, the question of criminal causation is considered as an empirical connection between cause and result. If an act is a necessary prerequisite of the result, for judgments about causality, it does not matter how proximate to or far removed from the result the act was. The parents of a murderer thus set a cause for the death of the victim, as did the murderer himself when he fired the shot that killed the victim. Because this wide understanding of causation could lead to bizarre results in criminal law (e.g., holding the parents of a murderer responsible for the acts of their child), an additional normative test is common within criminal law literature. The "objective attribution" requirement (*objektive Zurechnung*)[7] asks whether the result can be attributed to the offender from a normative standpoint. This is the case if he created a legally intolerable risk which then materialized itself in the result. In some cases, the actor did not create a legally intolerable risk because the behavior was socially acceptable (thus, of course, the parents of offenders are not criminally liable). In other cases, a legally intolerable risk did not materialize itself in the result, e.g., when a third party or the victim acted in a way that broke the connection between the risk and the result. The criminal courts have not officially accepted the theory of "objective attribution." They prefer to deny criminal liability for remote causes by pointing to a lack of criminal intent.

[C]   The Necessary *Mens Rea*: Intent or Negligence

The default rule in German criminal law is that only intentional conduct establishes liability, unless the written statute explicitly extends criminal liability to negligent conduct (*see* § 15 StGB). For some crimes, particularly crimes against persons, merely negligent conduct suffices for criminal liability (*see* § 222 StGB, negligent killing; § 229, negligent infliction of bodily harm; or § 306d, arson by negligence). For most other kinds of acts, negligent conduct cannot be punished. Thus, for instance, negligent theft or negligent sexual assault are not criminal offenses. Strict liability offenses do not exist in German law, neither in criminal law nor in the Administrative Offenses Act (§ 10 OWiG).

German statutory law does not define which cognitive and volitional elements are necessary for intentional behavior. Within legal scholarship, there is an ongoing debate about these elements. Mainstream legal doctrine and case law distinguish three forms of intent: intention (*Absicht, dolus directus 1. Grades*), knowledge (*Wissentlichkeit, dolus directus 2. Grades*), and conditional intent (*Eventualvorsatz, dolus eventualis*).[8] For most offense descriptions, any one of these three forms of intent is sufficient to establish criminal liability, and the range of punishments prescribed in the statute is the same. However, some norms explicitly call for a specific version of intent, usually either intention and/or knowledge (*see*, e.g., § 226 II StGB, aggravated assault).

Intention (*Absicht*) requires the actor to purposefully fulfill the objective elements of the crime. In cases of intention, it is the objective of the offender to bring about the prohibited result, even if he is not sure if his actions are actually sufficient to

---

7. *See* for the theory of "objective attribution," Claus Roxin, *Strafrecht Allgemeiner Teil. Band I* (4. Ed., C.H. Beck 2006), pp. 371 ff.
8. *See*, e.g., Claus Roxin, *Strafrecht Allgemeiner Teil. Band I* (4. Ed., C.H. Beck 2006), pp. 436 ff.; Michael Bohlander, *Principles of German Criminal Law* (Hart Publishing 2009), pp. 60 ff.

achieve the result, such as the death of his victim. Intention can also be assumed if an offender has to achieve certain necessary interim results in order to achieve his main purpose. Thus, intention exists where an offender kills the only witness to one of his crimes, even though his main goal is more broadly defined as destroying all evidence connecting him to the original crime.

Knowledge (*Wissentlichkeit*) is characterized by the actor's certain knowledge that he will fulfill all elements of the crime. The cognitive element is prevailing here. As long as offenders have the certain knowledge that they are going to achieve the prohibited result, it does not matter if they are distressed by the outcome from a psychological point of view.

Finally, conditional intent (*Eventualvorsatz*) requires that the actor foresees the possibility of fulfilling all the elements of the *actus reus* and either accepts this possibility in an approving way (*billigend in Kauf nehmen*) or at least puts up with the result (*sich damit abfinden*) for the sake of pursuing his goals.[9] With this definition, German criminal courts require both a cognitive *and* a volitional element. The volitional element is important to distinguish conditional intent from negligence. If conduct was risky but the offender can convince the court that he trusted in a good outcome, he will not be convicted of a crime that requires intent. The establishment of conditional intent is thus of great practical importance in criminal proceedings. In most cases, it will be necessary to conclude from objective circumstances that the offender not only foresaw the outcome but also accepted it or put up with it. For example if a person undertook a very dangerous action, such as aggressively beating the victim's head with an iron pole, it can be assumed that she both foresaw and accepted the possibility of the victim's death. Nevertheless, all circumstances of the situation have to be assessed by the courts before conditional intent can be deduced from objectively life-threatening actions.[10]

Conditional intent is not the same as recklessness in Anglo-American law. In German criminal law, awareness of a substantial risk needs to be classified as either conditional intent – requiring the additional volitional condition that the offender approves of the result or puts up with it – or as advertent negligence. Advertent negligence is present if the actor, while foreseeing the possibility of achieving the prohibited result, honestly hopes for a harmless outcome. The distinction between conditional intent and advertent negligence is of great importance because the penalties diverge considerably. For example intentional killing triggers a minimum penalty of five years imprisonment (§ 212 StGB), whereas negligent killings are punished with a fine or a maximum penalty of five years imprisonment (§ 222 StGB).

In cases of negligence, the actor must have disregarded a duty of care and the harmful outcome, such as the death of the victim, must have been objectively foreseeable. The standards of care are established by reference to the conduct required from a reasonable person acting under the same circumstances as the individual offender. In addition to establishing objective features of negligence, "guilt" must be

---

9. *See* BGHSt 7, 363; BGHSt 36, 1.
10. *See*, e.g., BGH, NStZ 2009, 629, 630 (stabbing the victim's neck); NStZ 2012, 443, 444 (kicking the victim's head); NStZ 2015, 516, 517 (beating the victim's head against a cement floor).

established, requiring that the defendant was personally capable of fulfilling the objective requirements of the duty of care (*see* more below §14.03[A][3], negligent manslaughter). Under German law, the category of negligence encompasses both advertent negligence and inadvertent negligence. In the case of inadvertent negligence, the offender is not aware of the risks involved. Offense descriptions do not discriminate between advertent and inadvertent negligence, and the statutory punishment ranges thus apply to both. Some offense descriptions in the Special Part require an enhanced form of negligence, that is, gross negligence (*Leichtfertigkeit*), see for felony murder and some economic crimes below §14.03 [A][2], §14.03 [B][2].

[D]   Justifications (Justificatory Defenses)

Strictly speaking, there are no "defenses" under German criminal law. In criminal cases, it is not the duty of the defendant to submit defenses to escape criminal liability. It is always the task of the courts to establish all elements of the crime: the objective and subjective elements of the offense (*Tatbestandsmäßigkeit*), the unlawfulness of the act (*Rechtswidrigkeit*) and the defendant's guilt (*Schuld*). Once it has been established that the defendant has fulfilled the elements of the crime with the requisite *mens rea*, the question turns to whether he was justified in acting in the way he did. Some justifications (e.g., self-defense and necessity, §§ 32 and 34 StGB) are codified in the General Part. Other justifications can be found in other statutes (e.g., the permission to arrest a person in § 127 Code of Criminal Procedure) or in customary law. The constitutional principle requiring all criminal offenses to be established by statutory law (*see* above §14.01) is not applicable to legal rules that work to the defendants' advantage.

[1]   *Consent and Presumed Consent*

The Criminal Code does not explicitly name consent as a general justification. In fact, consent is only mentioned in § 228 StGB which deals with consent to bodily injury. It is nevertheless universally accepted that the valid consent of the victim renders the actor's conduct lawful if the crime in question attacks individual interests over which the victim was free to dispose.

Not all instances of victims' approval are legally relevant: valid consent needs to be distinguished from the victims' mere factual acquiescence. Declarations of approval do not always count as justificatory consent. Most importantly, a person cannot consent to her own intentional killing: According to § 216 StGB, it is a criminal offense to kill another person upon that person's express and sincere request (*see* below §14.03[A][4]). Furthermore, according to § 228 StGB, victims cannot consent to bodily injury in a way inconsistent with public morals (*die guten Sitten*). The German Federal Court of Justice (*Bundesgerichtshof, BGH*) interprets § 228 StGB narrowly, excluding consent only for particularly serious bodily attacks that involve the risk of maiming or death.[11] If there is no risk of this kind, consent can be valid, even if the injuring act or the injury itself clashes with widespread moral judgments, such as moral prejudices against sadomasochistic sexual acts.

The victim has to be competent to give valid consent. Factual approval is legally irrelevant if given by very young victims, victims with mental impairments or heavily intoxicated victims. The victim also has to act voluntary, i.e., not under duress or threats. Consent must be informed in order to be valid. No valid consent is given when the victim acted under the influence of a serious mistake. Lastly, consent has to be communicated verbally or nonverbally to the offender before or during the commission of the act. Subsequent consent does not render the prior actions of the offender lawful.

With regard to interferences with the body in form of medical treatment (which requires consent to be lawful), consent may also be presumed under certain circumstances, for instance if the victim is unable to declare consent explicitly (due to, e.g., a need for immediate medical treatment of an unconscious person). Presumed consent has to comply with the victim's known or presumed will. If it is known that the individual person would not consent to a specific medical procedure due to, e.g., religious reasons, her wishes have to be respected. The question of what a reasonable person would consent to only arises if the will of the victim is completely unknown and it is impossible to identify individual preferences.

[2] Self-Defense

If an offender acts in self-defense, as defined in § 32 StGB, his actions are justified and thus lawful. According to § 32 StGB, self-defense is defined as the "defense necessary to avert an imminent, unlawful attack from oneself or another person." The definition of self-defense thus includes acts meant to defend oneself as well as acts meant to defend another person. However, if the other person does not want to be defended and the actor knows this, his conduct is not justified under § 32 StGB. In all cases of self-defense, the attack has to be imminent or already ongoing. Preemptive strikes against dangerous individuals are not covered. Cases of defense against nonimminent dangers are dealt with under § 34 and § 35 StGB (necessity and duress).

In case of an imminent attack, the right of self-defense is far-reaching under German law. Not only personal interests such as one's bodily integrity, but also property interests can be defended. Moreover, there is no duty to retreat and the defender is not required to act in a manner proportionate to the attack. Because there is no general proportionality requirement, even property interests can be defended by – sometimes lethal – physical force. It is not prohibited to shoot (and even kill) a thief if this is necessary to protect one's property.

The question whether the defensive action was necessary thus carries considerable importance. An actor is only justified if the means of defense chosen by him were necessary to avert the attack. This means that there must be no alternative, milder modes of defense that would have ended the attack just as promptly, safely and

---

11. BGHSt 49, 166 (dealing with sadomasochistic actions such as bondage and suffocation).

definitively as the means actually chosen by the actor. Once again, there is no duty to retreat – even if retreating would have ended the attack with the least amount of injury, the defender is allowed to stand his ground. This wide applicability of self-defense as a justification in German criminal law stems from its double rationale: The actor not only defends his own rightful interests against the attack, but he is also seen as defending the legal order as a whole.[12]

Nevertheless, German criminal courts apply some restrictions to the right of self-defense. "Socio-ethical restrictions" (*sozialethische Einschränkungen der Notwehr*) are barely reflected in the statutory language and they could be criticized as conflicting with the principle of legality. Nonetheless, these boundaries are well established in case law. If an actor has intentionally or negligently provoked the attack against which he is now defending himself, he is not allowed to act with the full severity that the right of self-defense usually allows.[13] In the same manner, if the aggressor is a child, a legally insane, confused or highly intoxicated person, less aggressive means of defense must be employed, whenever possible. Only if there is no less harmful option, it is allowed to do what is necessary to stop the attack. Similarly, the right to self-defense can be restricted between persons in a close relationship who own each other a duty of care. This restriction is disputed, particularly in its application to spouses. The Federal Court of Justice has argued that the same forceful defense against violent attacks that would be permissible against strangers might not be permissible against one's spouse, provided that the couple still lives together with ongoing duties of mutual support.[14] Legal scholars argue, however, that in relationships characterized by (domestic) violence, the violent partner has suspended mutual duties and that the other partner must have unrestricted access to self-defense.[15] Lastly, there is no right to act in self-defense if the means chosen to protect one's interests are grossly disproportionate in relation to the value of the protected interests. There is thus no justification to shoot and kill, for instance, the thief of a single apple. However, as already mentioned, mere disproportionality between the harm caused and the harm to be expected from the attack does not stand in the way of self-defense. Self-defense is thus only prohibited in the case of an *extreme* imbalance between the interest protected and the means chosen.

If an actor exceeds the limits of necessary self-defense and thus does not act in a justified way, he still can be excused – if excessive self-defense was due to confusion, fear, or fright (see § 33 StGB).

[3] Necessity (Rechtfertigender Notstand)

§ 34 StGB stipulates that a person who, faced with an imminent danger to life, health, freedom, honor, property, or any other legal interest, which cannot otherwise be averted, commits an act to avert the danger from herself or another person, does not act

---

12. *See* Michael Bohlander, *Principles of German Criminal Law* (Hart Publishing 2009), p. 99.
13. BGHSt 42, 97.
14. BGH, NJW 1969, 802; BGH, NStZ 2016, 526, 527 (this restriction does not apply to cases of mere cohabitants in a shared flat without mutual duties of care).
15. *See*, e.g., Claus Roxin, *Strafrecht Allgemeiner Teil. Band I* (4. Ed., C.H. Beck 2006), p. 702.

unlawfully, if, upon a weighing of the conflicting interests, in particular the affected legal interests and the degree of the danger facing them, the protected interest substantially outweighs the impaired interest. The justification of necessity applies only if and to the extent that the act committed is an appropriate means to avert the danger.

The rationale for the justification of necessity is mostly seen in an obligation of all citizens to show – limited – solidarity with their fellow citizens. The owner of the impaired interest will be asked to relinquish his interest if a comparatively moderate sacrifice averts substantially greater harm. If both interests are of the same value, the actions of the offender cannot be justified by necessity under § 34 StGB. As an exception to this rule, § 228 Civil Code (*Bürgerliches Gesetzbuch*, BGB) stipulates that, in cases where the risk of harm was caused by the impaired interest itself (e.g., by an aggressive dog killed in order to prevent an attack), it is sufficient that the impaired interest does not disproportionally outweigh the protected interest. § 228 Civil Code only applies if the impaired interest is a property interest. However, actions that have harmed other interests can also be justified more easily under § 34 StGB if the person harmed by the criminal offense had caused the situation of necessity (these cases are called *Defensivnotstand* and are distinguished from the standard cases where solidarity is demanded from uninvolved individuals or the citizenry as a whole).

According to an almost universally shared opinion in German legal scholarship, the death of another person can never be justified by necessity. This is evident if one life would need to be sacrificed in order to save another life – the life of one person can never substantially outweigh the life of another person. However, a "sanctity of life"–rule is held to apply even where several or many lives could be saved by sacrificing one person. This restriction is not explicitly spelt out in § 34 StGB. Its widespread acceptance can be explained by the commitment to distance contemporary German legal doctrine from National Socialism, as it is prominently articulated by Article 1 I of the German Constitution ("Human dignity is inviolable").[16]

Lastly, the means used to protect the interest have to be "appropriate" (*angemessen*). This requirement is also interpreted in light of the constitutional human dignity-clause, bearing, *inter alia*, the consequence that the dignity of another person must not be compromised by measures such as torture, not even to save human lives.[17]

[E]   Guilt (*Schuld*)

After it has been determined that a person fulfilled the objective elements of a crime with the necessary *mens rea* and it has also been established that the person acted without justification, issues of guilt (*Schuld*) can also play a role.

---

16. *See* BVerfGE 115, 118.
17. *See* LG Frankfurt, NJW 2005, 692 (threat of torture).

[1]   Principle and Concept of Guilt

A person can only be convicted of a crime if she deserves personal blame. The German Federal Constitutional Court (*Bundesverfassungsgericht,* BVerfG) has reiterated the "principle of guilt" (*Schuldprinzip*) underlying this rule in several decisions.[18] The principle of guilt is not explicitly mentioned in the text of the German Constitution. The Federal Constitutional Court deduces it from other constitutional provisions: the rule of law (*see* Article 20 III GG), the human dignity clause (Article 1 I GG) and the provision that grants autonomy rights (Article 2 I GG). The principle of guilt is regarded as one of the most important cornerstones of German criminal law. A criminal conviction requires not only proof of *mens rea*, that is, intent or negligence (*see* above §14.02 [C]), but also proof of the fact that the offender had the possibility to act in a different way and that he can be blamed for not acting differently.[19] Usually, people can be expected to comply with criminal laws and in most criminal proceedings, questions of guilt will not be discussed as guilt is simply assumed. However, in cases of young age, incapacity/insanity, duress, or unavoidable legal mistakes, an offender might not be convicted to criminal punishment.

[2]   Children

In German criminal law, the age of criminal responsibility is fourteen. Children below the age of fourteen do not act with the guilt necessary for a criminal conviction (*see* § 19 StGB). If children under fourteen commit crimes, youth welfare services may intervene, but there will be no criminal charges. Juveniles (ages fourteen to seventeen) can be held responsible for their actions. However, their capacity to understand the wrongfulness of their actions and their capacity to act in accordance with such an understanding will be determined in each individual case (*see* § 3 Juvenile Criminal Court Act). By contrast, the guilt and criminal responsibility of adults (ages 18 and above) is only discussed if exceptional circumstances, such as insanity, are present.

[3]   Mental Incapacity/Insanity (**Schuldunfähigkeit**)

According to § 20 StGB, any person who, at the time of the commission of the crime, is incapable of understanding the unlawfulness of her actions or is incapable of acting in accordance with such an understanding due to a pathological mental disorder, a substantial impairment of consciousness, debility or any other serious mental abnormality, acts without guilt and can thus not be convicted of the crime. If the suspicion of insanity arises, criminal courts first have to establish that the offender suffered from one of the mental impairments just mentioned. Since judges do not possess the necessary medical expertise, experts will be asked to diagnose defendants. If it has been determined that the offender suffered from one of the mental defects stipulated by

---

18. *See,* e.g., BVerfGE 20, 323; 123, 267; 133, 168; 140, 317.
19. BGHSt 2, 194.

§ 20 StGB, the crucial question is whether the defect rendered him incapable of understanding the unlawfulness of his actions or of acting accordingly. If it has been established that an offender was unable to appreciate the unlawfulness of his actions or was unable to control himself, he cannot be convicted of a crime and punished, but he may be committed to a hospital of forensic psychiatry under § 63 StGB.

Debilitating intoxication can lead to a "pathological mental disorder" according to § 20 StGB. If, while committing a crime, an offender was so intoxicated that he could no longer appreciate the unlawfulness of his actions or act in accordance with such a belief, he did not act with guilt. Incapacity will be presumed if an offender acted with a blood alcohol concentration that exceeded 0.3 % at the time of the commission of the crime.[20] The presumption of incapacity is not conclusive: For example if the offender is an alcoholic and is thus used to high levels of blood alcohol concentration, it might still be possible for him to understand the unlawfulness of his actions and to act in accordance with this understanding. Attention thus has to be paid to all the circumstances of each individual case.[21]

For the defense of insanity, it does not matter whether the offender voluntarily caused the state of intoxication that rendered him incapable of acting in the state of guilt. Within criminal law doctrine, there is discussion about a narrow exception in constellations of a so-called *actio libera in causa*. The label *actio libera in causa* is reserved for cases in which the offender intentionally intoxicated himself with the preestablished intention to commit a specific criminal act. More important in practice is § 323a StGB which allows to convict an offender of having committed a crime in a state of drunken stupor (*Vollrausch*). Under § 323a StGB, the offender is not punished for the crime that he committed during his drunken stupor. He is only punished for the fact that he intentionally or negligently got so seriously intoxicated.

If a person's ability to understand the unlawfulness of her actions or her ability to act in accordance with such an understanding is merely substantially diminished, but not entirely absent, the person can be convicted of a crime. However, according to § 21 StGB, the sentence can be mitigated. In cases of intoxication, the courts presume that a defendant might have acted with diminished responsibility if his blood alcohol concentration exceeded 0.2 % at the time of the commission of the crime.[22] Once again, this presumption is not conclusive and the courts will consider all the circumstances in order to assess the diminished responsibility of the offender.[23] Mitigation of punishment is not mandatory according to § 21 StGB, even if it can be established that the offender acted in a state of diminished responsibility. In exercising their sentencing discretion with regard to intoxicated offenders, courts consider whether the defendant voluntarily caused his intoxication. If the offender voluntarily decided to intoxicate himself and if this intoxication foreseeably increased his risk of offending, § 21 StGB

---

20. *See* BGH, NStZ-RR 2013, 27; Claus Roxin, *Strafrecht Allgemeiner Teil, Band I* (4. Ed., C.H. Beck 2006), p. 890; Michael Bohlander, *Principles of German Criminal Law* (Hart Publishing 2009), p. 134. In cases involving intentional killings, the blood alcohol concentration has to exceed 0.33 % before the presumption is raised.
21. *See* BGH, NStZ-RR 2013, 27; BGHSt 43, 66.
22. *See* BGHSt 37, 231 (0.22 % in the case of crimes involving intentional killings).
23. *See* BGHSt 43, 66.

will usually not apply.[24] And even if the offender has not been warned by previous experiences that showed his tendency to become more violent or prone to committing crimes after consuming alcohol or other substances, courts may choose not to mitigate the punishment.[25]

[4]   *Duress* (Entschuldigender Notstand)

According to § 35 StGB, persons do not act with guilt if they commit an unlawful act in order to avert an imminent danger to life, bodily integrity or freedom from themselves, a relative or another person in a close relationship. The unlawful act has to be strictly necessary to avert the danger: If the danger could have been averted in another way, the excuse of duress does not apply. § 35 StGB does not render the act lawful. It merely negates the offender's personal blameworthiness under the special circumstances stipulated by the statute, acknowledging that the offender could not have been expected to act differently under these exceptional circumstances. Thus, for instance, a parent killing another person in order to save his child from imminent danger to life, bodily integrity or freedom does not act with guilt because, under such severe circumstances, it would not be just to attach personal blame to his actions.

§ 35 I StGB also stipulates exceptions for situations in which a person will *not* be excused despite imminent danger. For instance, if a person is responsible for creating the dangerous situation, she can be expected to withstand mental pressures of higher intensity. The same rationale applies to persons who are under a legal obligation to deal with dangerous situations such as policemen and policewomen. Accordingly, if such a person fails to comply with her professional duty, personal blame can be attached to her. Lastly, the harm done must not be grossly disproportionate to the protected interest. Thus, a person who kills another person in order to thwart the danger of a small injury to her bodily integrity will not be excused.

[F]   Mistakes

Offenders may have acted under a mistake of fact or a mistake that concerns the lawfulness of conduct (mistake of law). The legal consequences attached to these two types of mistakes differ considerably.

If an offender erred about facts concerning the *actus reus* of a crime, this mistake excludes a finding of intent (*see* § 16 I StGB). German law acknowledges mistakes of fact without applying a reasonable person-test. Even if the mistake was unreasonable, it negates intent as long as the mistake was honestly held. However, the offender may be punished for negligently causing harm if the criminal law includes an offense description for negligence. Accordingly, if the offender honestly, but mistakenly believes that he shot his neighbor's dog, when he in fact shot his neighbor's 5-year-old son, he will not be liable for murder, but can be convicted of negligently killing the boy.

---

24. *See* BGH, NStZ 2006, 274.
25. BGHSt 62, 247.

But in other constellations, if statutory law does not contain a fitting crime of negligence, unreasonable errors do not lead to any conviction. For instance, if an offender erroneously believed that the victim consented to what was in fact rape, he will be acquitted, even if this mistake was unreasonable – the German law on sexual offenses does not punish negligent conduct.

Factual mistakes as to the grounds of justification (*Erlaubnistatbestandsirrtümer*) occur, for instance, if the offender mistakenly believes that another person is about to attack him and he lashes out in purported self-defense. Details of the legal doctrine are contested but the courts and the majority of legal scholars in Germany agree that an offender acting under such a mistake cannot be convicted of an intentional crime. They apply § 16 StGB to these cases.[26] Liability for negligence remains. For instance, if the offender's belief in an imminent attack was unreasonable, he can be convicted of negligent bodily injury.

Mistakes of law are dealt with in § 17 StGB (*Verbotsirrtum*). Rules for mistakes of law are stricter than rules for factual mistakes. § 17 StGB exempts offenders from punishment only if they have behaved in a reasonable way. Thus, only those offenders act without guilt whose mistake of law could not have been avoided. The threshold for unavoidability is very high: A mistake of law is only considered unavoidable if the offender could not have arrived at the right conclusion through more careful delibera-tion. If the offender is uncertain about the legality of his acts or the content of criminal statutes, the courts require him to seek legal advice. And even if an offender had asked a lawyer and acted on the basis of this advice, an error about the lawfulness of his conduct still will be considered irrelevant if the suspicion of complaisance and unreliability arises. For avoidable errors, mitigation of punishment is an option but not mandatory (§ 17 Sent. 2 StGB).

If a person mistakenly believes that her lawful conduct was illegal despite the fact that it was entirely legal (imagined crime, *Wahndelikt*), she is not to be punished. For instance, a person who mistakenly believes that homosexual sexual relations are illegal under German law will not be criminally liable because sexual relations among same-sex partners are in fact legal.

[G]   Inchoate Offenses

Provisions on inchoate offenses attach criminal liability to an act even though no harm has occurred or before harm has occurred. The two principal categories of inchoate offenses under German criminal law are attempt and conspiracy.

[1]   *Attempt*

Under German criminal law, the attempt of a felony (*Verbrechen*; minimum sentence of one year imprisonment) is always punishable. In the case of misdemeanors

---

26. For a discussion of the legal principles surrounding the *Erlaubnistatbestandsirrtum*, *see* Claus Roxin, *Strafrecht Allgemeiner Teil. Band I* (4. Ed., C.H. Beck 2006), pp. 622 ff.

(*Vergehen*), attempt is only punishable if the criminal statute explicitly states so (which is the case for most misdemeanors). The sentence for an attempted crime can be mitigated according to § 23 II StGB. Mitigation is not mandatory. Offenders are also liable for attempt if their act was unsuitable to bring about the prohibited harm (*see* § 23 III StGB; *untauglicher Versuch*). Accordingly, an offender can be convicted of attempted murder for administering a substance that was harmless if he thought it to be poisonous. If the offender's plan was obviously unreasonable, the courts may mitigate the sentence or discharge the defendant without a sentence. Within criminal law doctrine, some argue that superstitious attempts do not compromise the law so that a person who attempts to kill another with "voodoo magic" should not be convicted for attempted murder.[27]

To be liable for attempt, an offender needs to have the necessary intent to commit the crime and he must have taken steps which will immediately lead to the completion of the offense as envisaged by him (§ 22 StGB). The "immediateness" requirement must be emphasized. Suspects who have successfully completed preparatory acts cannot be sanctioned for attempt if they did not come close enough according to the demanding standard of immediacy. German courts are rather restrictive with assuming that offenders' conduct would have immediately led to the completion of an offense. For example attempting to get access to a house in order to rape a person inside has not been punished as attempted rape.[28] German criminal law does, however, address at least some particularly dangerous preparatory acts in separate offense descriptions, *see*, for instance, § 310 StGB: acts preparatory to causing an explosion or radiation. Such preparatory acts can be punished, even if it would not be possible to hold the offender liable for attempted murder.

Once an offense has been attempted, an offender can still escape criminal liability if he abandons the attempt. According to § 24 StGB, a person who, of her own volition, gives up on the further execution of the offense or prevents its completion is no longer criminally liable for the attempted crime. If the offense is not completed regardless of the actions of the offender (because another person intervened, e.g., called an ambulance), the offender escapes liability if he has undertaken a voluntary and earnest effort to prevent the harm in question from occurring. Voluntariness will be assumed if the offender acted due to motives such as regret, shame or another self-chosen decision to revise plans. By contrast, voluntariness will not be found where the offender acted under strong external pressures, such as the arrival of law enforcement agents or other external or internal restraints that prevented autonomous choice.

The privilege of abandonment in § 24 StGB can be quite far-reaching. For instance, an offender can escape liability for attempted murder even after having tortured his victim for hours with an intent to kill if he finally just makes one phone call to emergency services and his victim can thus be saved (but he will be punished for the completed bodily injuries). If the offender does not believe that he has brought the victim into the risk of death with his actions (unfinished attempt, *unbeendeter Versuch*), he can even escape criminal liability for attempted murder by simply

---

27. *See* Claus Roxin, *Strafrecht Allgemeiner Teil. Band I* (C.H. Beck 2003), pp. 455 f.
28. BGH, NStZ 2000, 418.

refraining from further attacks. German courts interpret the requirements of § 24 StGB liberally in favor of offenders, assuming that this might give incentives to spare the victim additional harm by stopping further actions or contributing to the victim's rescue.

[2]   Conspiracy to Commit a Crime and Other Inchoate Offenses

According to § 30 I StGB, a person who attempts to incite another to commit a felony or to incite another person to commit a felony will also be punished according to the rules governing attempted crimes. § 30 II StGB covers conspiracies to commit a felony. Similar to conspiracies are the offenses of founding or joining criminal or terrorist organizations, §§ 129, 129a, 129b StGB.

[H]   Perpetration and Participation

Under German criminal law, not everyone who is causally responsible for bringing about a wrongful result is considered a perpetrator. The StGB distinguishes between perpetrators (§ 25 StGB) and participants (§§ 26 and 27 StGB).

[1]   The Distinction Between Perpetration and Participation

To draw a distinction between perpetrators (*Tätern*) and participants (*Teilnehmern*), the criminal courts have traditionally employed a subjective test: Offenders are classified as a perpetrator and not as a participant if they had the resolve to be a perpetrator (*animus auctoris*). Participants are characterized as merely possessing the mind-set of supporters of another person's crime (*animus socii*). Most criminal scholars in Germany are critical of this subjective approach, preferring objective criteria. According to the objective test, perpetrators are persons who take on a prominent or dominant role during the commission of the crime (*Tatherrschaft*), whereas participants play a merely supporting or subordinate role.[29] While the two ways of distinguishing between perpetrators and participants seem to differ widely in theory, they often arrive at similar results due to the fact that the subjective theory has to rely on objective indicators to establish the will of persons.

[2]   Types of Perpetrators

Perpetrators are divided into three categories: perpetrators acting on their own (*Alleintäter*; § 25 I Alternative 1 StGB), perpetrators acting through another person (*mittelbare Täter*; § 25 I Alternative 2 StGB) and co-perpetrators (*Mittäter*; § 25 II StGB).

    Perpetrators acting on their own are the main category of perpetrators. By contrast, in the rare case of perpetrators acting through another person, they commit

---

29. *See* Claus Roxin, *Strafrecht Allgemeiner Teil. Band II* (C.H. Beck 2003), pp. 9 ff.

the offense in question by making use of another person who is under the control of the perpetrator (indirect perpetration). In these cases of domination or control by an actor working in the background, the dominating actor can be punished as a perpetrator because he is the person that is truly responsible for the crime. Perpetrating a crime through another person usually requires that the agent carrying out the actual criminal act is not criminally liable due to some sort of personal defect (e.g., lack of intent because the agent was misled by the perpetrator or being a child). The perpetrator needs to mentally control or dominate the acting person. Mental domination can be established by controlling information (e.g., by deceit or exploiting errors) or by bending the actor's will (e.g., through threats). Under exceptional conditions, criminal liability for indirect perpetration can also be assumed even though the person carrying out the actual crime is fully liable as a perpetrator. Examples can be found within hierarchical organizations such as the military if the acting agent is under the full control of his higher-ups even though he does not operate under circumstances that compromise his own criminal liability.[30]

The third category is co-perpetration. Co-perpetrators jointly commit the *actus reus* of a criminal offense by acting together based on a shared plan. According to the subjective standard applied by the courts, it is also necessary that they act with the will of a perpetrator (*animus auctoris*). Whether all actors possessed the necessary resolve to be a perpetrator can be judged from circumstances such as their involvement in the planning or commission of the crime and their personal interests in it. If one person unexpectedly exceeds the parameters of the shared plan by, e.g., killing the victim instead of only beating him, the other co-perpetrators will not be held liable for the intentional killing of the victim. They can, however, be held liable for negligence if the excessive actions of the offender were fueled by the shared plan and not entirely unforeseeable.

[3]   Types of Participants (Instigators and Accomplices)

Participants can either be instigators (*Anstifter*; § 26 StGB) or accomplices (*Gehilfen*; § 27 StGB). Instigators are punished as severely as perpetrators (cf. § 26 StGB). They determine another person to commit a criminal act through their actions or words. If the offender was already determined to commit the crime, instigation is not possible. The perpetrator must commit the crime with intent and unlawfully, but not necessarily with guilt. Thus, it is possible to be criminally liable for instigating a child to commit a crime. The instigator himself needs to have intent to designate the other person to commit the crime and he must have a general understanding of the crime to be committed without necessarily being aware of all the details (e.g., the time and place of the crime or the means used).

Accomplices provide assistance to criminal perpetrators (cf. § 27 StGB). As in cases of instigation, the perpetrator of the actual crime act must act with intent and unlawfully, and accomplices need to have the necessary intent as to their own acts of

---

30. *See* BGHSt 40, 218 (concerning the shootings at the borders of the former GDR).

assistance as well as to the crime to be committed (again, a general understanding of the criminal act is sufficient). Assistance can consist of physical acts (e.g., providing the perpetrator with a weapon or a getaway car) or mental support (e.g., cheering on the perpetrator or strengthening his resolve). The assistance of the accomplice must have facilitated the commission of the crime. However, it is not necessary that the assisting actions were an indispensable component of the crime. A person can thus be convicted of assisting in the commission of a crime if the weapon provided was never used but offered the perpetrator a greater sense of security.

Difficulties arise in the case of so-called neutral actions (*neutrale Handlungen*). Neutral actions are everyday actions or actions that are part of one's legal professional activities that can nevertheless help the offender to commit his crime, such as providing him with a taxi ride to the location of a crime, helping him to transfer money abroad as a bank clerk or writing letters as a lawyer. In case of neutral actions, courts look at all the circumstances of the case and pay special attention to the subjective mental state of the person assisting the offender:[31] If the person knew that the offender planned to carry out a crime and intended to help him, seemingly neutral actions count as criminal aiding under § 27 StGB.[32]

[I] Crimes of Omission

A few offense descriptions make it a criminal offense to remain inactive in a certain situation ("real crimes of omission"; *echte Unterlassungsdelikte*). For instance, § 323c StGB stipulates that a person can be held liable for failing to render assistance to another person during an emergency if it was necessary to render such assistance and if helping the endangered person could be expected under the circumstances. These crimes of omission do not require a preexisting special duty of care toward the victim. Anyone can be criminally liable under the circumstances specified in the statute. However, crimes of this type are rare and usually carry rather low penalties.

Besides these "real crimes of omission," German criminal law also provides for a more general liability for omissions that cause harm (*unechte Unterlassungsdelikte*). According to § 13 StGB, a person who fails to avert a result prohibited by a criminal statute can be punished like the person who actively caused such a result. The requirement is that the offender by omission is legally responsible to ensure that the result does not occur, and that the omission is equivalent to the realization of the statutory elements through active behavior. A person can thus, e.g., be convicted of manslaughter or murder if she fails to prevent the death of the victim. The crucial question is who is legally responsible for averting the result.

Again, one can observe that the constitutional requirement of prior definition of crimes by statute (Article 103 II GG) is not taken very seriously. The Criminal Code gives no guidance regarding the question of legal responsibility for omissions. Courts and legal scholars assume a legal duty to avert the harmful result for two groups of

---

31. *See* BGH, NStZ 2004, 41, 42; NStZ 2000, 34; NStZ 2017, 461.
32. *See* Michael Bohlander, *Principles of German Criminal Law* (Hart Publishing 2009), pp. 172 f.

situations.[33] First, persons who carry a duty to protect the well-being of another person due to a special and close relationship between the parties (*Beschützergaranten*) can be guilty of a crime of omission. Duties of protection can stem from close family relationships (e.g., parents and children), from the shared participation in dangerous undertakings (e.g., members of a Himalaya expedition) or from the assumption of protective duties by contract (e.g., a bodyguard). Second, those who are responsible for a source of danger or a safety hazard are legally responsible for harmful outcomes (*Überwachungsgaranten*). Such hazards can be created through prior illegal actions or the responsibility to supervise dangerous machinery, premises or persons. In all of the aforementioned cases, great importance will be attached to the circumstances of the individual case. For instance, even though married partners usually have a duty to protect each other against harm, such a duty can be suspended, e.g., if spouses are estranged.

Criminal liability further requires that the offender could have prevented the result. If a person is under two equivalent duties to act (e.g., because a mother observes that both of her daughters are drowning at the same time) but can only fulfill one duty under the given circumstances, breach of the other duty, e.g., the failure to save the other child, is not unlawful (*rechtfertigende Pflichtenkollision*). Finally, according to § 13 II StGB, it is possible – though not mandatory – to reduce the sentence in the case of omissions, based on the assumption that a mere failure to act can be less severe than performing prohibited actions.

§14.03 SPECIAL PART

For a short introduction to German criminal law, it is impossible to cover all types of offenses. We can thus only briefly mention features of some crimes, that is, offenses against life, offenses against property and speech offenses.

[A] Offenses Against Life

[1] Murder and Homicide

Homicide (§ 212 StGB) is defined as killing a human being without being a murderer. *Mens rea* can be intention, knowledge or conditional intent (*see* above §14.02[C]). The sentence range for homicide is five years to fifteen years imprisonment. § 213 StGB deals with mitigating circumstances. If the victim provoked the offender (or a relative of the offender) by maltreatment or serious insult, and the offender lost his temper and responded immediately, or if the case is less serious for other reasons, the sentence range is reduced to a minimum of one year up to ten years imprisonment.

Killing another person (again with intention, knowledge or conditional intent) is sanctioned as murder if circumstances are present that aggravate wrongfulness or guilt (§ 211 StGB). The mandatory punishment for murder is life imprisonment (*see* below

---

33. *See* generally Claus Roxin, *Strafrecht Allgemeiner Teil. Band II* (C.H. Beck 2003), pp. 722 ff.

§14.04[B]). The circumstances that turn homicide into murder are listed in § 211 StGB. In contrast to homicide, the StGB does not include a clause that allows mitigation in unusual murder cases. Once one of the conditions listed in § 211 StGB is fulfilled, life imprisonment is mandatory. The elements of murder are either motives or objective factors. Motives that upgrade homicide to murder are: finding pleasure in the act of killing, sexual gratification, greed, committing homicide in order to facilitate or to cover up another offense, or other base motives. The description "base motives" (*niedrige Beweggründe*) is hard to reconcile with the principle of legality in Article 103 II German Constitution. The German Federal Court of Justice has developed case law that categorizes, for instance, anti-Semitic and racist motives,[34] blood feuds[35] and the defense of archaic concepts of male honor[36] as base motives. Objective circumstances that constitute murder are cruelty toward the victim (infliction of severe physical or psychological suffering), using means that create danger beyond the targeted victim for the public (for instance, a bomb) and stealth (*Heimtücke*). For several decades now, there has been an ongoing discussion regarding a reform of the definition of murder. The vagueness of the element "base motives" is criticized and the element "stealth" can lead to problematic results in the context of abusive relationships. If the weaker person (usually a wife, female partner or child) kills her former tormentor, this typically happens while he is asleep or inattentive. Thus, these killings which occur as a reaction to ongoing domestic violence typically are not only intentional homicides but, because of the "stealth"-element, also qualify as murder,[37] to be punished with life imprisonment. Self-defense is not allowed unless there was an imminent or ongoing attack by the future victim at that very point in time (*see* above §14.02[D][2]), and German criminal law does not encompass a justification or an excuse similar to what is discussed as the battered women syndrome in Anglo-American law. In a decision from 1981, the German Federal Court of Justice once deviated from the Criminal Code and decided against a life sentence in the case of a stealth killing (in this case, a man had killed his uncle who had previously raped the man's wife).[38] However, this obvious circumvention of statutory law has been met with criticism and did not lead to a chain of case law for domestic violence cases or other cases of stealth crimes.

[2]   Felony Murder

The Criminal Code contains some offense descriptions outside the Chapter on Offenses Against Life that resemble the so-called felony murder-rule in other countries in some ways. If the offender causes the death of another person during sexual child abuse, rape, abduction, hostage-taking, robbery, or arson, and if death occurred due to particular risks created through the commission of the felony in question, the minimum punishment is ten years imprisonment and the maximum is a life sentence (§§

---

34. BGHSt 18, 37; 22, 375; BGH, NStZ 1994, 124.
35. BGH, NStZ 2006, 284.
36. BGH, NStZ 2004, 332.
37. BGHSt 48, 255.
38. BGHSt 30, 105.

176b, 178, 239a, 239b, 251, 306c StGB, more offenses of this type can be found in the Chapter on Offenses Causing a Common Danger). With regard to the subjective element, the legislature has made an unusual choice: In these offense descriptions, *mens rea* can be *either* intent *or* a gross form of negligence (*Leichtfertigkeit*). *Leichtfertigkeit* has some features in common with recklessness in Anglo-American law. The risk of death must have been substantial and evident. Often, this will be advertent gross negligence, that is, the offender will be aware of the risk. However, this is not a necessary requirement under German law. It is sufficient that the conduct was grossly careless, even if the actor was subjectively unaware of this.

[3]   Negligent Manslaughter

Negligent manslaughter falls under § 222 StGB. The statutory penalty range is much lower than for homicide or murder: the minimum is a fine, the maximum five years imprisonment. Negligence requires disregard for a duty of care and, in addition, that the deadly outcome was objectively foreseeable. It is not necessary that the actor actually gave thought to the possible outcome of his careless act. § 222 StGB, like other descriptions of negligent crimes in German law, encompasses both advertent and inadvertent failures to behave with the necessary degree of care. Other than in the case of gross negligence (*Leichtfertigkeit*) mentioned above [2], it is not necessary that the deviation from the duty of care was particularly serious and evident. The offense description covers every departure from what the reasonable person-standard requires. The actor is, however, not liable if death could not have been avoided even by compliance with the duty of care (*rechtmäßiges Alternativverhalten*) or if the victim or a third party intervened in a way that broke the connection between the breach of duty and the outcome through, e.g., voluntary risk-taking. For instance, a person selling illegal drugs will not be punished for negligent manslaughter if the consumer had full knowledge regarding the risks involved and did not act in a state of mental disturbance.[39]

   Due to the strong position of guilt (*Schuld*) in German criminal law, with the culpa principle held to be a constitutional requirement (*see* §14.02[E][1] above), the objective person–standard must be complemented with an assessment of individual fault in a second round of assessments. In addition to the description of behavior as a deviation from the care that a reasonable person would have taken, it needs to be examined if the individual actor could have foreseen the risk and if he personally could have complied with the duty of care. This might not be the case with mentally impaired or young or inexperienced actors, or if someone is temporarily unable to comply with objective requirements due to, e.g., sudden illness. The assessment of individual fault, however, does not mean that many offenders who violate objective standards of care escape criminal liability. If someone is inexperienced or loses his capabilities, the content of blame can shift: For example if a young surgeon lacks the necessary experience for a complicated new procedure, or if an elderly colleague loses his

---

39. BGHSt 32, 262.

capabilities due to illness or old age, these persons will not be blamed for performing surgery but for accepting a task they are not or no longer capable of performing. The gap between a purely objective reasonable person-standard and the German approach that combines objective and subjective assessments is thus smaller than it might appear at first glance. Subjective incompetence will exempt actors from criminal liability only if they could not avoid becoming involved in the activity that over-stretched their skills.

[4] Suicide

Although the wording of the homicide provision (§ 212 StGB) does not explicitly demand that the offender must kill *another* person, suicide is unanimously excluded from criminal liability.[40] Therefore, a person who survives the attempt to take her own life will not be punished for attempted suicide. A person who incites another person to commit suicide is not criminally liable for incitement to homicide because participation presupposes an unlawful act of the main actor (§ 26 StGB). If, however, the person who kills herself suffered from a mental disease or was unaware that her actions would have deadly consequences, a person in the background who knew or who manipulated the actor can be criminally liable as a perpetrator acting through another person (*see* for this category of perpetrators above §14.02 [H][2]).

Supporting another person to commit suicide, e.g., by providing the means for suicide, is usually not a criminal offense. The reason is, again, that the general rules for participation require that the perpetrator acted unlawfully (*see* § 27 StGB). However, there are two situations in which the involvement in another person's wish to die can lead to criminal liability. First, the StGB contains an offense called "Killing at the Request of the Victim" (§ 216 StGB, *Tötung auf Verlangen*). If the offender was induced to kill by the express and earnest request of the victim, this is treated more leniently than ordinary homicide (the sentence range is six months to five years imprisonment) but, unlike merely aiding another to commit suicide, killing at the request of the victim is a criminal offense. The crucial difference is who performs the act that ends life. If the lethal act is committed by the suicidal person herself, the other person, who, for instance, provided drugs or a weapon, is a participant whose participation is not punishable. If, however, the dominant role (*Tatherrschaft, see* §14.02[H][1]) regarding the deadly act is taken by the second person, she will be punished according to § 216 StGB, and the express and earnest request of the person killed is only taken into account by way of more lenient punishment.

Secondly, as of 2015, even in the case of genuine complicity, e.g., by providing drugs, a person who gives another one the opportunity to commit suicide can be punished if she acted commercially (*see* § 217 StGB: Commercial Assistance to Suicide, punishment: fine or imprisonment for up to three years). The background for this new law was moral indignation about commercial associations with the sole purpose to offer assistance to persons wanting to die. While such organizations are legal in

---

40. *See* Michael Bohlander, *Principles of German Criminal Law* (Hart Publishing 2009), pp. 184 f.

Switzerland, they became a source of concern in Germany (again, a development that can be explained with a desire to distance German society from the German National Socialist past and a taboo against anything that might be labeled as euthanasia). Commercial in the context of § 217 StGB does not require the intention to make financial profit, but only the intention to offer assistance in a businesslike, repeated mode.

[5]   Abortion

Abortion, i.e., killing an unborn child, is a criminal offense in Germany (*see* § 218 StGB), for instance, if the offender intentionally hurts a pregnant woman in order to get rid of an unwanted child. The protected subjects of the law are embryos after their implantation into the uterus (§ 218 Sent. 2 StGB). There are, however, provisions that stand in the way of criminal liability if women voluntarily choose to have a doctor terminate their pregnancy. First, abortion is justified if it is very likely that the pregnancy was caused by a sexual offense (§ 218a III StGB) or if the life or health of the pregnant woman are at risk and this danger cannot be averted otherwise (§ 218a II StGB). Secondly, the law stipulates an exemption from criminal liability – without calling this exemption a justification – for abortions within the first twelve weeks of pregnancy (§ 218a I StGB). The requirement of this exemption is that the pregnant woman has visited a counseling center that encourages women to continue the pregnancy and helps her to clarify her prospects for a life with the child (§§ 218a, 219 StGB).[41]

[B]   Crimes Against Property and Economic Crimes

[1]   Theft, Embezzlement, Robbery

German criminal law distinguishes between simple theft of chattels with a punishment range from fines to five years imprisonment (§ 242 StGB) and aggravated forms of theft. Aggravated theft is assumed, for instance, in standard cases of burglarizing business and office buildings or the theft of items from sealed containers or of items with other protective equipment. Aggravated theft is punished with imprisonment between three months and ten years (§ 243 StGB). If a burglar carries a weapon or is a member of a gang, these aggravating circumstances lead to a punishment range between six months and ten years imprisonment (§ 244 I StGB). Since 2017, due to rising numbers of burglaries in Germany, breaking into a private home to commit a burglary is no longer a misdemeanor but a felony (*see* for this distinction §14.01). The mandatory minimum punishment is now one year of imprisonment, the maximum ten years imprisonment, § 244 IV StGB.

　　If the offender did not need to take away the item from another person because he had acquired possession otherwise – for instance, if the owner had lost it in a public

---

41. Concerning the constitutionality of these legal rules, *see* BVerfGE 39, 1; 88, 203.

space – he commits embezzlement (unlawfully appropriating chattels that belong to another person, § 246 StGB). The punishment is milder than the punishment for theft: a fine or up to three years imprisonment or five years imprisonment if the owner had entrusted his property to the offender.

The offense of robbery entails either the application of force against a person or the threat of death or bodily injury in order to take away chattels (§ 249 StGB). Robbery is, even in its simple version, a felony with a minimum of one year and a maximum of ten years imprisonment. Aggravations (leading to a minimum of three or five years imprisonment) are listed in § 250 StGB, such as carrying or using a weapon. For robbery with deadly consequences *see* above §14.03[A][2]. German criminal law distinguishes between robbery (coercion is applied before taking away chattels, §§ 249, 250 StGB) and theft with elements of robbery (applying coercion to secure possession of an item that the thief has already taken away, § 252). Punishment ranges, including punishment for aggravated cases, are identical. If the offender does not take away the items, but forces the victim to transfer them, this is a case of extortion with elements of robbery (§ 255 StGB).

[2]   *Fraud and Other Economic Crimes*

Fraud is defined in § 263 StGB. The offense description requires that the offender deceives another person about facts and thus creates an error with the intent of obtaining for himself or a third person an unlawful material benefit, and thereby harms the economic interests of another person. The penalty scale runs from a fine to a maximum of five years imprisonment; for more serious cases: six months to ten years imprisonment (for instance, if the offender acted as member of a gang or caused substantial financial harm, *see* § 263 II StGB). Computer fraud (§ 263a StGB) has become important because, in the age of automation, it is often no longer necessary to communicate with a human being and to deceive a real person in order to obtain unlawful benefits.

In addition to the general description of fraud, there are a number of more specific descriptions of fraudulent economic behavior in the German Criminal Code, such as subsidy fraud (§ 264 StGB), obtaining a loan by deception (§ 265b StGB) and capital investment fraud (§ 264a StGB). An offender commits subsidy fraud if he makes incorrect or incomplete statements to a public authority competent to approve state aid, in relation to facts relevant for the grant of it. Deception to obtain loans (§ 265b StGB) requires that the goal is to obtain a loan for a business or enterprise or for a fictitious business or enterprise (not included are consumer loans) from another business or enterprise, typically a bank. The criminal acts are submitting incorrect or incomplete documents, making incorrect or incomplete written statements or failing to inform about a deterioration of the financial circumstances represented in the information or statements already submitted. Capital investment fraud (§ 264a StGB) entails making incorrect favorable statements or keeping unfavorable facts secret in prospectuses, in representations or in surveys in connection with the sale of securities, subscription rights or shares intended to grant participation in the yield of an enterprise or an offer to increase capital investment in such shares. Subsidy fraud, capital investment fraud and obtaining a loan by deception are preparatory or abstract endangerment offenses. Other than in the case of general fraud, it is not a necessary feature that the victim is financially harmed.

Offense descriptions of fraudulent acts in relation to accounting and auditing can be found in the Commercial Code (*Handelsgesetzbuch*, HGB). According to § 331 HGB, it is a criminal offense for members of the managing board or the board of supervisors to misrepresent or conceal the state of affairs of a company (or company group) in the opening balance sheet, annual report, status report, etc. § 332 HGB addresses fraudulent statements by auditors.

Besides fraud, breach of trust (*Untreue*, § 266 StGB) is another typical economic offense. In contrast to fraud, this offense does not require intent to obtain unlawful benefits for oneself or a third party. Rather, the core of wrongdoing is the infliction of financial harm on a natural person or corporate entity with whom the offender is connected in a relationship of trust. Financial harm can be inflicted if the offender has the power to dispose of assets of another person or entity or to make binding agreements for the other person or entity. Alternatively, the offender violates his duty to safeguard the property interests of another person or entity. For example the German Federal Court of Justice approves of convictions under § 266 StGB if money from business enterprises or political parties is diverted into slush funds (for instance, for the purpose of paying bribes), even if the agent has no intention to enrich himself and the money is used to promote the economic or political interests of the firm or political party.[42]

Other economic crimes within the Criminal Code are money laundering (§ 261 StGB), bankruptcy offenses (§§ 283–283d StGB), bribery in the commercial sector (§§ 299–300 StGB) and bribery in the public sector (§§ 331–335a StGB), unfair competition through agreements in the context of public bids (§ 298 StGB). Outside of the Criminal Code, statutes that regulate economic activities in specific areas typically also include regulatory or criminal offenses, *see*, e.g., the regulatory offense in § 81 Antitrust Act (*Gesetz gegen Wettbewerbsbeschränkungen*, GWB).

Offense descriptions for economic crimes mostly require intent, which is the default rule for all criminal offenses unless statutory law explicitly states that negligence suffices (§ 15 StGB). Strict liability does not exist in German criminal law. Negligence rarely is sufficient for economic offenses, and if so, is limited to gross negligence (*Leichtfertigkeit*), *see* money laundering (§ 261 V StGB), subsidy fraud (§ 264 IV StGB), and bankruptcy (§ 283 IV No. 2, V No. 2 StGB).

[3]   No Corporate Liability

In contrast to other countries in Europe and the United States, German criminal law does not hold corporations criminally liable. Only human beings can be subjected to criminal punishment. The reasoning supporting the present state of the law refers to

---

42. BGHSt 51, 100; 52, 323; 55, 266.

the principle of guilt and its foundation in human dignity. In recent years, however, the idea that Germany should give up its traditional approach and introduce corporate criminal liability as a means to reduce corporate wrongdoing is gaining traction. In 2013, the Minister of Justice of North Rhine–Westphalia, presented a draft.[43] But despite ongoing discussions, no statute has been enacted so far.

Beyond criminal punishment, German law allows, however, to sanction companies for the misconduct of a chairman, authorized officer, leading employee, or other person representing the corporation. Benefits can be confiscated if the corporation has gained them through criminal acts of such an individual (§ 75 StGB). Confiscation is possible, even if the individual is not convicted for a crime (§ 76a StGB).

It is also possible to sanction the corporation not with criminal punishment but with hefty fines (*Geldbußen*), on the basis of the Administrative Offenses Act. For the liability of the corporate entity it is sufficient that the CEO of the company or another representative has committed a criminal offense or a regulatory offense in violation of duties imposed on the corporation or with the intention to enrich the corporation (§ 30 I OWiG). These fines can be substantial. According to § 30 II OWiG, fines up to €10 million for intentional criminal offenses and up to €5 million for negligent criminal offenses can be imposed. German courts have even imposed much higher fines against corporations (reaching hundreds of millions of Euros) as § 30 III and § 17 IV OWiG prescribe that the fine ought to be higher than the economic benefits. Fines can also be imposed on the owner of a company for her own fault in omitting supervisory measures required to prevent contravention of duties, including the appointment, careful selection and surveillance of leading employees (§ 130 OWiG).

With an eye to the substantial *Geldbußen* in the Administrative Offenses Act, it is not far-fetched to assume that sufficient deterrence might be possible without the label "criminal punishment." The more important factor for success in deterring corporate crime probably is the question of strict liability versus the fault principle. The German opposition against strict liability and the resulting need to establish a person's individual fault makes effective sanctions against corporations difficult. According to § 30 Administrative Offenses Act, sanctions against corporations require proof that a CEO or other representative intentionally or negligently committed a crime or regulatory offense, and proof of individual guilt is often difficult.

[C]   Speech Offenses

German criminal law includes a number of prohibitions that target speech (with the term "speech," we refer to all modes of communication, including communication via Internet and social media).

---

43. For a discussion *see* Karl-Heinz Krems, 10 *Der NRW-Entwurf für ein Verbandsstrafgesetzbuch*, Zeitschrift für Internationale Strafrechtsdogmatik 5 (2015).

[1]   Endangerment Offenses

Some speech offenses can be categorized in a straightforward way as endangerment offenses (*Gefährdungsdelikte*). Their rationale is to prevent remote harm to life, bodily integrity and other goods and interests of persons. Even if there was no concrete risk for a specific individual victim, the general risk is seen as sufficiently large to support abstract endangerment offenses (*abstrakte Gefährdungsdelikte*; this term does not appear in the StGB but is commonly used in German legal doctrine). Examples are prohibitions against offers to commit felonies (§ 30 II StGB), public incitement to crime (§ 111 StGB), public threats to commit serious crimes (§ 126 StGB), dissemination of instructions on how to commit crimes (§ 130a StGB) and calls for violence against a national, racial or religious group or a group defined by their ethnic origin (§ 130 I No. 1 StGB).

[2]   Protection of Honor and Human Dignity

For another group of speech offenses, it is less plausible that the conduct in question involves serious dangers of violent attacks on persons or other criminal harm. Speech in these cases is not considered a wrong because of future harm but because the content *as such* is considered offensive. German criminal law is based on the assumption that offensive speech can violate constitutional rights of targeted persons, that is, the right to personal honor (*Ehre*) and the right to human dignity. Both rights are mentioned in the German Constitution, honor in Article 5 II and human dignity in Article 1 GG. The Criminal Code contains a chapter on "Insults." §§ 186 and 187 address defamation and intentional defamation. Defamation means spreading factual information about a person that may defame her or negatively affect public opinion. This is a criminal offense if either the defendant cannot prove that the facts are true (§ 186 StGB) or he knows that the facts are wrong (§ 187 StGB). In addition to misrepresentation of facts, it is also a criminal offense to insult another person (§ 185 StGB). Insult, which can be punished with a fine or imprisonment up to two years, consists of abusive words and other negative opinions and assessments of a person that others would consider insulting in either content or formulation. The honor of dead persons is protected as well (§ 189 StGB). Insulting speech can be justified under certain circumstances, e.g., if negative opinions refer to scientific, artistic or commercial activities of the insulted person or if other legitimate interests justify this kind of assessment. However, even if the contents of the communication as such can be justified, formulations or other attending circumstances can still support a criminal conviction for insult (§ 193 StGB).

Human dignity is protected against verbal attacks that insult, maliciously malign or defame a national, racial or religious group or a group defined by their ethnic origin, or an individual because of his belonging to this group (*Volksverhetzung*, § 130 I No. 2 StGB). The punishment for such offenses that target groups is higher than for ordinary cases of insult or defamation, bearing a minimum of three months and a maximum of five years imprisonment. A second difference is that insult and defamation can be justified according to § 193 StGB with "legitimate interest"-clauses while *Volksverhetzung* under § 130 I StGB cannot. This criminal prohibition reflects widespread moral judgments, in Germany and elsewhere, that assess racist and xenophobic remarks as heinous and unacceptable. In Germany's contemporary situation with large-scale immigration and deeply split opinions about it, political demands to make liberal use of § 130 I StGB to suppress xenophobic opinions reflect the moral intuitions of many citizens. However, these demands also deserve critical assessment with regard to the values of free speech.

[3]   Offensive Speech: Holocaust-Denials and Insults Against Religions

German criminal law also penalizes speech that does not insult or defame human beings, as individuals or as a group, but consists of incorrect historical narratives or derogatory remarks about religious beliefs or customs. Denying the Holocaust is thus a crime (§ 130 III StGB). If someone publicly or in a meeting approves of, denies or downplays an act of genocide committed under the rule of National Socialism, this can be punished with a fine or imprisonment of up to five years. It is also a criminal offense with a punishment range from a fine to three years imprisonment to approve, glorify or justify violent and arbitrary National Socialist practices beyond genocide (§ 130 IV StGB).

The German StGB also still contains an offense that originates from the traditional crime of blasphemy: § 166 StGB, defamation of religions, punishable with a fine or imprisonment up to three years.[44] Today, the offense description does not refer to God, and besides religions, the norm also protects other comprehensive systems of beliefs (*Weltanschauungen*). Commentaries list, e.g., Marxism or anthroposophy as examples for *Weltanschauungen* – an entirely theoretical discussion as court decisions exclusively focus on religions. The existence of § 166 StGB does not mean that harsh criticism of religions, their institutions or customs will necessarily make the speaker criminally liable. Apart from § 130 StGB in all its versions, it is acknowledged that freedom of speech leaves some room for expressing skeptical views about religions, even if believers might feel offended. Convictions under § 166 StGB are very rare.[45]

In mainstream German legal doctrine and court decisions, the rationale of § 130 and § 166 StGB is explained as "protection of public peace." References to a (possible) disturbance of public peace also figure in the statutory text. It remains unclear, however, whether public peace can be disturbed below the threshold of actual violent protests – which are not to be expected in the event of Holocaust denials – and, more importantly, why violent protests against religious defamation should be attributed to the expression of the original opinion rather than to over-zealous demonstrators and protestors themselves. The more plausible explanation for these prohibitions points to

---

44. For a discussion *see* Christian Hillgruber, *Legal Limits of a Permissible Criticism of Religion*, 17 German Law Journal 265 (2016).
45. For instance, in 2015, only 6 persons were convicted under § 166 StGB, *see* Statistisches Bundesamt, *Rechtspflege – Strafverfolgung 2015*, Fachserie 10, Reihe 3 (2017), p. 31, under § 130 III and IV: 99 persons, *ibid.*, p. 29.

the hurt feelings of individuals who take offense at religious defamations and Holocaust denials.

The goal to regulate and suppress offensive remarks about religions and the German National Socialist past has encountered major difficulties since the Internet has made communication global. The German Federal Court of Justice argues that German courts have jurisdiction even where Holocaust deniers act from outside of Germany.[46] It is, however, obvious that German prosecution authorities are in no position to effectively control offensive speech on the internet. In 2017, the German parliament passed a law targeting social media platforms with at least two million registered users, demanding that they remove or block obviously illegal content (*Netzwerkdurchsetzungsgesetz*).[47]

§14.04 SANCTIONS

[A] Foundations

The Criminal Code and other criminal statutes stipulate upper and lower sentence limits, but these statutory sentencing ranges are typically wide. Thus, they leave considerable discretion for courts when deciding about the type of sanction and sentence length for individual cases. Sentencing guidelines do not exist in Germany. Courts decide about conviction and sentencing in one stage, not in two separate phases of the criminal trial. The German Federal Constitutional Court emphasizes that criminal punishment must be proportionate to the seriousness of the offense. The text of the German Constitution does not explicitly mention the principle of proportionality. The Federal Constitutional Court stipulates, however, that the right to dignity and the right to autonomy (Article 1, Article 2 I GG) demand that punishment must be proportionate to the seriousness of the offense and the offender's guilt.[48]

[B] Statutory Framework

For many misdemeanors, the statutory minimum is a fine. Some offense descriptions of misdemeanors prescribe a minimum penalty of three or six months of imprisonment, but there is a rule in the General Part that allows for conversion of sentences of less than six months of imprisonment into a fine (§ 47 II StGB). German law uses a day-fine system: The number of days must correspond to the relative seriousness of the offense while the amount of money for one day-fine depends on the offender's income (§ 40 StGB). If the convicted person does not pay the fine, one day in prison is substituted for every one day-fine (§ 43 StGB). In contrast to other legal systems, community service is not an independent sanction under German law. Persons who were sentenced to pay

---

46. BGHSt 46, 212.
47. *Gesetz zur Verbesserung der Rechtsdurchsetzung in sozialen Netzwerken* from 1 September 2017, BGBl. I, pp. 3352 ff.
48. *See* for instance BVerfGE 110, 1, 13; 120, 224, 254; 133, 168, 198.

a fine may, however, apply to do community service as a substitute for imprisonment if they experience financial difficulties.

For more serious misdemeanors and felonies, imprisonment is ordered in the form of a suspended sentence. Suspension of imprisonment is possible for sentences that impose imprisonment of not more than two years (§ 56 StGB), and suspension is the rule, not the exception for prison sentences of less than two years (*see* below §14.04[C]). For felonies, the minimum punishment proscribed by law often is one year of imprisonment, or in the case of aggravating circumstances two, three or five years imprisonment. Typical upper limits for misdemeanors are three or five years imprisonment.[49] The general upper limit for all felonies is fifteen years imprisonment (§ 38 II StGB); some offense descriptions set the upper limit at ten years. Even if offenders are convicted and sentenced for multiple offenses in one trial, the maximum sentence allowed by law is fifteen years (§ 54 II Sent. 2 StGB). German criminal courts thus cannot sentence offenders to more than fifteen years of imprisonment.

Only for murder, the penalty is higher: mandatory lifelong imprisonment (§ 211 StGB) or, in the event of felony murder (*see* above §14.03[A][2]), the option of life imprisonment. The Constitution prohibits capital punishment (Article 102 GG). Life imprisonment, however, does not mean that the offender will have to remain in prison for the rest of his or her life. The Federal Constitutional Court decided in 1977 that prisoners must have a chance to be released, arguing that the principle of human dignity prohibits life imprisonment without the possibility of parole.[50] Accordingly, the Criminal Code now allows early release if at least fifteen years of the sentence have been served, unless the particular seriousness of the convicted person's guilt or the risk of future serious offenses require continued imprisonment (§ 57a StGB).

The Criminal Code does not give judges much guidance on how to structure the decision when forming the sentence from the wide range of legal options. § 46 I StGB points out that the offender's guilt is the basis for sentencing, which means that wrongdoing and individual guilt are crucial. The second sentence in this provision stipulates that the effects of the sentence on the offender's future life in society shall be taken into account too. § 46 II StGB – in a rather unsystematic way – lists sentencing factors that courts may consider. In 2015, the legislature supplemented the component "motives" on this list of sentencing factors with "particularly racist, xenophobic or otherwise inhuman motives."

The Federal Court of Justice describes the relationship between retributive considerations and preventive reasoning by relying on a theory of margins (*Spielraum-theorie*). According to this margin theory, considerations regarding the offender's future life and general preventive reasons may be applied if the final sentence stays within the range of punishments that is fitting on desert-based grounds.[51]

---

49. In some offense descriptions one year or ten years imprisonment.
50. BVerfGE 45, 187.
51. *See* BGHSt 7, 28; 20, 264; 24, 133.

[C]   Sentencing Practice

The range of punishment in German criminal law and the sentencing customs of German criminal courts can be characterized as mild, at least in comparison with sentences in many other countries. The vast majority of criminal judgments (more than 80%, even if traffic offenses are excluded) impose fines.[52] Also, the overall severity of prison sentences is moderate. More than 90% of all prison sentences do not exceed two years, and only a tiny fraction of all prison sentences (less than 2%) goes beyond five years.[53] For the majority of all prison sentences (about 70%), courts suspend the actual enforcement.[54] Early release is possible after half (for first time offenders) or two-thirds of the sentence have been served (§ 57 StGB). Life imprisonment is very rare (for instance, in 2017, out of 437,159 criminal judgments, only 90 imposed life imprisonment).[55]

[D]   Measures of Rehabilitation and Incapacitation

Besides criminal punishment, the German Criminal Code provides a second track of state reactions to a crime: measures of rehabilitation and incapacitation (*Maßregeln der Besserung und Sicherung*). The most frequently used measure is the revocation of drivers' licenses as part of the sentence for a traffic offense if the convicted person is deemed unfit to drive a vehicle (§ 69 StGB). A similar incapacitating measure restricts professional activities if the offender has committed an unlawful act in abuse of his profession or trade or in gross violation of the attendant duties (§ 70 StGB). A mental hospital order is an option in response to an unlawful act committed in a state of insanity or diminished responsibility if future serious unlawful acts can be expected from the offender who therefore presents a danger to the general public (§ 63 StGB). In the case of addiction, a custodial addiction treatment order can be imposed (§ 64 StGB).

The most controversial measure is detention for the purpose of incapacitation (*Sicherungsverwahrung*). The rather complicated legal framework (*see* §§ 66–67h StGB) has recently been revised several times because both the European Court of Human Rights and the German Federal Constitutional Court had raised objections.

---

52. Statistisches Bundesamt, *supra* note 45, p. 92.
53. Statistisches Bundesamt, *supra* note 45, pp. 160–161 (even if traffic offenses are excluded, the percentage of long prison sentences does not exceed 2%).
54. Statistisches Bundesamt, *supra* note 45, p. 93. *See also* for German sentencing Stefan Harrendorf, *Sentencing Thresholds in German Criminal Law and Practice: Legal and Empirical Aspects*, 28 Criminal Law Forum 501, 519–530 (2017).
55. Statistisches Bundesamt, *supra* note 45, pp. 162–163.

Their rulings found fault with retroactive detention orders[56] and the way the detention was organized.[57] The last legislative reform, in effect since June 2013, took up the constitutional concerns and introduced a more therapeutic approach to enforcement (§ 66c StGB). Detention for the purpose of incapacitation is a measure applied not instead of, but in addition to criminal punishment, and is enforced after the prison sentence has been served. The requirements are, among others, that the offender has been sentenced to at least two years imprisonment for a serious offense and that it can be predicted that he will continue to commit serious crimes in the future, namely crimes that seriously harm victims physically or psychologically (§ 66 StGB). The duration of the detention is indeterminate. However, it must be assessed by annual review whether the risk of serious reoffending persists (§ 67e StGB). This measure is not chosen frequently: In 2015, it was applied in forty-seven cases only.[58]

SELECTED BIBLIOGRAPHY

Michael Bohlander *Principles of German Criminal Law* (2009).

Markus Dubber/Tatjana Hörnle *Criminal Law. A Comparative Approach* (2014).

Thomas Fischer *Strafgesetzbuch* (65th ed. 2018).

Bernd Heinrich *Strafrecht Allgemeiner Teil* (5th ed. 2016).

John Heller/Markus Dubber *The Handbook of Comparative Criminal Law* (2011).

Wolfgang Joecks/Klaus Miebach (eds.) *Münchener Kommentar zum Strafgesetzbuch*, vol. I–VIII (3rd ed. 2016 et seq.)

Urs Kindhäuser *Strafrecht Allgemeiner Teil* (8th ed. 2017).

Urs Kindhauser *Strafrecht Besonderer Teil*, vol. I (8th ed. 2017) and vol. II (9th ed. 2016).

Volker Krey *German Criminal Law. General Part*, vol. I (2002) and vol. II (2003).

Kristian Kühl *Strafrecht Allgemeiner Teil* (8th ed. 2017).

Heinrich Wilhelm Laufhütte/Ruth Rissing-van Saan/Klaus Tiedemann (eds.) *Leipziger Kommentar zum Strafgesetzbuch*, vol. I–XIV (12th ed. 2006 et seq.)

Reinhart Maurach/Heinz Zipf/Christian Jäger *Strafrecht Allgemeiner Teil* (9th ed. 2018).

Reinhart Maurach/Friedrich-Christian Schroeder/Manfred Maiwald *Strafrecht Besonderer Teil*, vol. I (10th ed. 2009) and vol. II (10th ed. 2012).

Rudolf Rengier *Strafrecht Allgemeiner Teil* (10th ed. 2018).

Rudolf Rengier *Strafrecht Besonderer Teil*, vol. I (20th ed. 2018) and vol. II (19th ed. 2018).

Claus Roxin *Strafrecht Allgemeiner Teil*, vol. I (4th ed. 2006) and vol. II (2003).

Adolf Schönke/Horst Schröder *Strafgesetzbuch* (29th ed. 2014).

Johannes Wessels/Werner Beulke/Helmut Satzger *Strafrecht Allgemeiner Teil* (47th ed. 2017).

---

56. ECHR, *M v. Germany*, 17.12.2009 – 19359/04; but *see also* ECHR, *Bergmann v. Germany*, 7.1.2016 – 23279/14.
57. BVerfGE 128, 326.
58. Statistisches Bundesamt, *supra* note 45, p. 341.

Johannes Wessels/Michael Hettinger/Armin Engländer *Strafrecht Besonderer Teil*, vol. I (41st ed. 2017).

Johannes Wessels/Thomas Hillenkamp *Strafrecht Besonderer Teil*, vol. II (40th ed. 2017).

CHAPTER 15

The Law of Criminal Procedure

Gerhard Dannecker & Julian Roberts

TABLE OF CONTENTS

§15.01   THE NATURE AND SIGNIFICANCE OF THE LAW OF CRIMINAL PROCEDURE

The provisions of criminal procedure govern the determination of whether and what crime a suspect has committed and how he is to be punished for it. The purpose of criminal procedure is to reach a verdict which is correct and just. The rules must ensure a factually and legally correct verdict. The guilty should be punished and the innocent should be protected against unwarranted punishment. For the accused, the process concludes with either a withdrawal of prosecution, an acquittal, or with a guilty verdict. In this manner, the rules of criminal procedure give effect to substantive criminal law.

Criminal justice is a matter for the state alone. It is the duty of the state to ensure justice (*Justizgewährungspflicht*). To prevent arbitrary action by the prosecuting authorities, all involved, especially the prosecuting authorities, must be bound by mandatory rules. The precise compliance with these rules is supervised by the appellate courts. In essence, criminal procedure consists of all those tried and tested rules to which all participants must adhere if arbitrary decisions are to be avoided and if the trial is to conclude with a correct and just judgment. These rules derive from centuries of experience. Thus, procedural rules are not a random technique but rather the essential components of any rule of law. According to contemporary notions of justice, the constitutionally guaranteed *presumption of innocence* can only be refuted by a regular criminal trial according to the rule of law.

In order to provide an effective criminal procedure under the rule of law, the prosecution must take account of a range of competing interests: the liberty of the citizen, the interests of persons not immediately involved in the process, the need for an efficient criminal procedure, and the state's interest in prosecuting crimes. Finding the appropriate balance is primarily the responsibility of the legislature. In the rules of criminal procedure, the legislature determines the appropriate manner and the extent of permissible interference with liberty. In addition, the courts must respect the freedom of citizens and ensure that the constitutional rule of proportionality is observed. The quest for the truth must not be pursued at *any* cost.

German criminal procedure combines principles of the inquisitional process with those of an accusatorial approach. The prosecuting authorities (state attorneys and the police) and the courts are independent of each another. By and large, the courts are not involved in the investigating procedure (*Ermittlungsverfahren*). The state attorney's office has to bring charges before a court may consider the case. Once charges have been brought, however, certain inquisitorial elements enter the picture. The judge now takes control of the proceedings. The court first decides whether the case will actually go to trial (intermediate procedure – *Zwischenverfahren*). At the trial itself, the judge is in charge of the proceedings as well.

§15.02   THE HISTORY OF GERMAN CRIMINAL PROCEDURE

Some familiarity with the historical development of German criminal procedure is helpful in understanding and evaluating the current situation. In the Germanic period, when there was no distinction between criminal and civil procedure, judgments were found by an assembly called a *Thing* at which the residents of a narrowly circumscribed region, or the members of a tribe, met and were guided by the advice of men knowledgeable in the law. The proceedings were oral and public. Criminal procedure was purely accusatorial. It was initiated by the injured person or his tribe, primarily in order to obtain monetary relief. In the most serious cases, the offender could also be excluded from the tribal community and declared an outlaw. The principal means of proof was the accused's oath of innocence (purificatory oath) which could be supported by compurgators. Ordeals were also common. For example in the trial by water, the accused was bound and thrown into a river or lake; if he sank, he was deemed innocent (the pure water accepted him) and fished out. If he floated on the surface (rejected by the water), he was considered guilty.

It was not until the second half of the Middle Ages, in the period after ca. 1100 AD, that the previous accusatorial proceeding was gradually replaced by a quasi-inquisitorial procedure ex officio, which occurred first in the cities. In such inquisitorial proceedings, the judge directed the investigation and played the role of both accuser and adjudicator. The injured party was now regarded merely as a witness while the suspect became the object of the investigation (inquisit). The rules of proof were designed to establish the factual truth. The compurgators disappeared and were replaced by people who testified according to what they had witnessed. Yet, the "queen" of proof was the accused's confession, and torture was often permitted to obtain it. Trials were increasingly conducted in writing and behind closed doors. Compensatory sanctions were replaced more and more by punitive measures which ranged from maiming to execution.

Toward the end of the 15th century, Italian law, whose superiority derived from its clear analytical and systematic structure, became increasingly influential on German criminal procedure and was eventually adopted in large part. This reception reached its high water mark in 1532 when Emperor Charles V introduced a penal court procedure for the entire German empire – the *Constitutio Criminalis Carolina* (CCC). Its procedure was written, by and large hidden from public view, and was largely inquisitorial. Preliminary investigations were initiated ex officio and the proceedings themselves were entirely under the control of the judge. He was bound by sophisticated legal rules of proof. A confession or proof by two unimpeachable witnesses was required for a guilty verdict. Torture was permitted only in order to obtain a confession and only within certain limits. It could only be used once there were already significant indications of guilt. The process ended with public and oral proceedings which, however, served only to pronounce the judgment and to set the stage for its public execution.

Criminal procedure did not change fundamentally until the age of enlightenment in the 18th century. In 1740, Frederick the Great of Prussia was one of the first princes to abolish torture. Subsequently, under the influence of Napoleonic legislation, criminal procedure in the various German principalities was increasingly shaped by the principles of publicity, orality, and immediacy of proof, by the participation of lay judges, by the creation of a separate state prosecution office, and by the abandonment of strict rules of evidence that determine the weighing of evidence. Especially after 1848, German criminal procedure was therefore substantially reformed.

After the unification of the German empire in 1871, a uniform criminal procedure eventually replaced the various procedural rules of the several states. It was codified in the Judicature Act (*Gerichtsverfassungsgesetz* – GVG) and in the Imperial Code of Criminal Procedure (*Reichsstrafprozeßordnung* – RstPO) of 1877, both of which came into force in 1879. Though modified and amended many times, they are still in force today.

Under the National Socialists (1933–1945), the law of criminal procedure was deprived of many of the safeguards of the rule of law. For example the finality (*Rechtskraft*) of certain decisions was restricted by statute on September 16, 1939 and by an administrative order of February 21, 1940 so that cases could be reopened, even after an acquittal. In a similar vein, the prohibition of the *reformatio in peius* was repealed by statute on June 28, 1935 so that on appeal, the trial court's judgment could always be changed to the disadvantage of the defendant.

After 1945, the occupying powers' control over criminal legislation initially led to substantial differences between the various zones of occupation and consequently to a considerable fragmentation of the law. It was only in 1950 that a uniform criminal procedure was restored in the Federal Republic of Germany – in essence by abolition of the changes made by the National Socialists. Thus, German criminal procedure was by and large returned to its pre–Third Reich state.

Since 1950, individual areas of criminal procedure have again changed, often several times. Most of these changes purported to accelerate the criminal process and to improve the position of the victims. In addition, in response to the terrorist activities of the "Red Army Faction" in Germany in the 1970s, wide-ranging changes affecting large-scale trials were implemented as well, and the conduct of the defense was more tightly regulated in some regards. Current reform initiatives concern measures against organized crime, reducing the work-load of the courts, and speeding up trials.

§15.03   SOURCES OF GERMAN CRIMINAL PROCEDURE

Although Germany is a federal state and there are concurring legislative powers in the field of criminal law, the States (*Länder*) themselves are not competent to legislate in the area of criminal law and procedure. Thus, the law of criminal procedure is entirely federal and hence uniform. The most important sources are the Code of Criminal Procedure (*Strafprozessordnung* – StPO) and the Judicature Act (*Gerichtsverfassungsgesetz* – GVG). As mentioned, they have been amended numerous times since they first came into force in 1879. Nonetheless, they still constitute the basis of modern German criminal procedure whose basic character has not been radically changed.

In addition, a few procedural provisions are contained in the Penal Code (*Strafgesetzbuch* – StGB), concerning, e.g., the right of the victim to seek prosecution (*Strafantrag* – §§ 77–77d) and statutes of limitation (§§ 78–79b). Regarding matters such as service of process and allocation of costs, the Code of Criminal Procedure also refers to the Code of Civil Procedure. More particularly, the costs of the criminal process are governed by the Act on Court Costs (*Gerichtskostengesetz* – GKG) and by the Federal Table of Lawyers' Fees (*Rechtsanwaltsvergütungsgesetz* – RVG). Special rules deal with the compensation of witnesses and experts. The Federal Central Register Act (*Bundeszentralregistergesetz*) contains provisions governing criminal records and access to the respective data. Finally, there are many other laws regulating questions relevant to criminal trials, e.g., in the Act on Judges of 1961 (*Richtergesetz*) or the Law on Attorneys of 1959 (*Bundesrechtsanwaltsordnung* – BRAO). The Juvenile Court Act (*Jugendgerichtsgesetz* – JGG) contains special rules for criminal proceedings against persons under the age of 21.

In view of the threats which criminal prosecution may create for fundamental human rights, the German constitution, known as the Basic Law (*Grundgesetz* – GG) with its catalogue of constitutional rights is also an important source of law. Both the general individual rights enshrined in Articles 1–19, and the special so-called judicial basic rights contained in Articles 101, 103 and 104, determine the boundaries which must be observed by a humane and just criminal process. Article 1 III GG binds all state authority to these basic rights as directly applicable law. Their infringement can be challenged through the regular appellate process as well as, ultimately, through a constitutional complaint to the Federal Constitutional Court (*Bundesverfassungsgericht*). This Court has shaped criminal procedure through many decisions. As a result, criminal procedure is, to a certain extent, "applied constitutional law." Yet, the regular criminal courts have to respect basic rights as well, and they must always construe and apply the individual provisions of the Code of Criminal Procedure in light of the Basic Law (interpretation in conformity with the constitution – *verfassungskonforme Auslegung*).

In addition, fundamental procedural guarantees are contained in the European Convention on Human Rights of 1950 as well as in the International Covenant of Civil and Political Rights. Both treaties have been ratified by Germany and thus have the rank of federal law. The guarantees they contain are essentially equivalent to those provided by the Basic Law. To the extent that the European Convention confers rights in greater detail, the Basic Law must be construed in the light of the value system of the

European Convention (interpretation in conformity with human rights – *menschenrechtskonforme Auslegung*).

§15.04 AN OVERVIEW OF CRIMINAL PROCEDURE

Criminal proceedings are divided into three phases: the investigative phase, the intermediate stage, and the trial itself.

[A] *The Investigation*

[1] Introduction

The investigative procedure has the function of preparing the state attorney's decision whether or not to bring charges (§ 160 StPO). The state attorney controls the proceedings (*cf.* §§ 163, 167 StPO) and may call on the police in order to carry out investigations. The prosecutor's role is to investigate matters of fact relevant under existing legal rules. In this context, he must collect and examine all evidence whether favorable or unfavorable to the suspect.

The investigative procedure can be initiated by the prosecuting authorities if they themselves learn of the commission of a crime, either through a formal notice about a potentially criminal act (*Strafanzeige*), or by the injured party's formal request for criminal prosecution (§ 158 I StPO).

If the state attorney concludes that formal taking of evidence before a judge is necessary, he will file an application with the local court (*Amtsgericht*) in whose area the evidence is located. The evidence will then be presented to a special pretrial judge (*Ermittlungsrichter* – § 162 StPO).

Once the state attorney's office has concluded its investigations, it indicates the close of investigations in the file (§ 169 a StPO) and then determines whether to bring charges.

[2] Indictment

Upon conclusion of the investigative process, the state attorney's office can either bring charges or drop the case. If the case is dropped before trial, the accused has no right to insist that the proceedings be continued so that he or she can be acquitted. Criminal proceedings are not intended to rehabilitate the innocent but only to produce a judgment on charges brought.

If the state attorney's office concludes on the basis of the investigation that the accused is likely to be found guilty at trial (sufficient suspicion – *hinreichender Tatverdacht*), it will file charges by submitting an indictment to the appropriate court (§ 170 I StPO). The indictment must meet certain requirements regarding its content (*see* § 200 StPO).

Upon filing the indictment, control of the proceedings shifts from the state attorney's office to the court. The subject matter of the proceedings is now fixed in the sense that further proceedings may only address the act charged in the indictment and the person accused. The person committed for trial is now referred to as the accused (*Angeschuldigter*) rather than as a charged person (*Beschuldigter*).

[3]   Judicial Review of the Decision to Prosecute

If the state attorney's office drops the case because the investigation fails to produce sufficient grounds for an indictment (§ 170 II StPO), the victim of the crime may, if he or she has sought an indictment, seek a review of the prosecutor's decision (§ 171 StPO, by initiating proceedings to force an indictment (*Klageerzwingungsverfahren*, §§ 172 et seq. StPO). These proceedings allow for judicial supervision of the principle of legality (forcing the prosecutor to bring charges if there is sufficient evidence to make a conviction likely) and also help to protect the injured party. The prosecutor's decision is initially reviewed by the state prosecutor general's office (*Generalstaatsan-waltschaft*) whose decision is, in turn, subject to review by the Higher Regional Court (*Oberlandesgericht*).

[B]   Intermediate Procedure

In the intermediate procedure, the court decides whether the case (or which parts thereof) should actually proceed to trail. The court acts as a body independent of the authority responsible for the indictment. It sits *in camera* to decide whether there are indeed sufficient grounds to support a criminal charge or whether the accused may be spared the rigors of a trial.

The court shall send the matter to trial if there seem to be adequate grounds of suspicion against the accused person (order committing for trial – *Eröffnungsbes-chluss*). The court will refuse to send the matter to trial if it concludes that the matter charged does not constitute a crime, if procedural conditions are not satisfied, if a guilty verdict seems unlikely in light of the facts (§ 204 in conjunction with § 203 StPO), or if there is any other reason why the case should not be tried. The state attorney may appeal this decision (complaint – *Beschwerde* – § 210 StPO).

[C]   The Trial

Further proceedings consist of two stages: the preparation of the trial and the trial itself.

The preparation of the trial is provided for in §§ 213–225a StPO. In the preparatory phase, all those involved in the trial must be summoned to appear (the accused, defense counsel, the witnesses, and potential experts). There must be at least a week between the service of the summons and the trial date (§ 217 StPO).

The trial itself mainly consists of a hearing which is the heart of the criminal process. The course of the hearing is provided for in detail by § 243 StPO. It begins when the matter is called. The presiding judge ascertains whether the accused and defense counsel are present and whether the evidence is available, in particular whether the witnesses and experts who have been summoned are indeed present. The witnesses then leave the courtroom as they must then be questioned individually and sequestered from witnesses who will testify later (§ 58 I StPO). Next, the presiding judge questions the accused about his or her identity. The state attorney then reads out the charges in the indictment. It is explained to the accused that he may choose whether to respond to the charges or to remain silent. If he is willing to respond, he is examined as to the matters charged.

The examination of the accused is followed by the presentation of evidence, which is directed by the court (§ 244 StPO). At the conclusion of the evidence- taking phase, the state attorney, defense counsel, and the accused present their closing arguments. The accused has the last word (§ 258 II StPO). The court then retires to consider the case and to make a judgment. The trial concludes with the pronouncement of the verdict (§ 260 I StPO). It may consist of a conviction, an acquittal, or an abandonment of the proceedings. The presiding judge reads the judgment which, in case of a conviction, contains the legal description of the act of which the accused is found guilty as well as the sentence. The reasons for the verdict are usually given orally at first and only delivered in written form after the end of the trial.

§15.05   THE COURT

[A]   *Independence of the Judiciary*

The Basic Law provides that the judges are independent and subject only to the law (Article 97 I GG). This means both personal independence guaranteed by an appointment for life (after a probationary period) and professional independence in the sense that judges are not subject to any substantive directions or recommendations.

[B]   Composition of the Courts and Involvement of Lay Judges

The court reaches its judgment as an institution. Its composition is determined by the crimes considered and the form of the proceedings. The court may consist exclusively of professional judges or of professional judges sitting together with lay assessors (*Schöffen*).

In courts of first instance – Local and District Courts (*Amtsgerichte und Landgerichte*) – lay judges are involved in many types of proceedings. These honorary judges need neither legal qualification nor even any basic legal knowledge. A committee formed at the Local Court (*Amtsgericht*) selects the lay assessors (*Schöffen*) from a list. Any German citizen may become a lay judge for a period of four years (§§ 36 et seq. GVG). The involvement of lay judges in criminal proceedings is thought to ensure democratic participation and control by the populace. In addition, it serves to keep the process and language of the law more comprehensible to the common people. Where lay judges sit on the court, they exercise the function of a judge to its full extent and have the same voting rights as the professional judges (§ 30 I GVG). Normally, they do not see the dossier before the trial. Thus their only source of information is the oral hearing, i.e., the trial proper. At the end of the hearing, professional and lay judges decide the question of guilt together.

[C]   Jurisdiction

The Judicature Act (*Gerichtsverfassungsgesetz* – GVG) determines the subject matter jurisdiction of the criminal (as well as the civil) courts, especially which court hears which kind of case at first instance. By a second step, cases are distributed among the various chambers or judges according to a predetermined system designed to prevent manipulation. Venue is governed by §§ 7 et seq. of the StPO. In addition, functional jurisdiction, e.g., the jurisdiction of the appellate courts.

Which court has jurisdiction at the trial level depends on the gravity of the offense. The various courts, in turn, can sit in a variety of compositions (single judge, three judge panel, etc.).

The local court (*Amtsgericht*) has jurisdiction at first instance in all cases in which the penalty does not exceed four years imprisonment (§ 24 GVG). A single professional judge has jurisdiction over minor criminal offenses, i.e., those amenable to private prosecution and cases in which the penalty is not expected to exceed two years imprisonment. In all other cases the *Amtsgericht* will sit with one (in serious cases two) professional judge(s) and two lay assessors (*Schöffengericht*, §§ 28 and 29 GVG).

In other cases, the District Court (*Landgericht*) has jurisdiction at first instance. The proceedings take place before the grand penal chamber (*Große Strafkammer*), which consists of two or three professional judges and two lay assessors (§§ 74 I and II, 74 a, c, 76 I and II GVG). The District Court (*Landgericht*) also hears appeals from the Local Court (*Amtsgericht*). The appeal is decided by the minor penal chamber (*Kleine Strafkammer*), which consists of one or two professional judges and two or three lay assessors (§§ 74 III, 74 c I, 76 I and III GVG).

The Higher Regional Court (*Oberlandesgericht* – OLG), whose chambers consist of five professional judges, has primary jurisdiction over certain crimes against the state (§§ 120 and 122 GVG). Most of the time, however, it hears appeals on fact and law from the District Court (*Landgericht* – § 121 GVG) as well as appeals of law from the Local Court (*Amtsgericht* – §§ 121, 122 GVG; in this case the OLG is composed of three professional judges only).

The Federal Supreme Court (*Bundesgerichtshof* – BGH), whose chambers are also composed of five professional judges, decides appeals on points of law from decisions of the District Courts (*Landgericht*) or State Supreme Courts (§135 GVG).

[D]   Exclusion of Judges

German criminal procedure provides for the possibility of excluding or rejecting particular judges. Thus, a judge who was himself injured by the criminal act, who has a close family relation to the accused or to the injured party or who had previously been involved in the case (e.g., in a court below or as a witness), can be excluded from the proceedings (§§ 22 or 23 StPO). Moreover, a judge can be challenged if there are reasons to suspect partiality. Whether that is the case is determined from the point of view of the observer: the question is whether an average person in the position of the accused would suspect the judge to be biased after reasonable assessment of the circumstances. The challenge has to be raised before the court to which the judge belongs (§ 26 I StPO). The challenger has to make a prima facie case (§ 26 II StPO); the detailed grounds for challenges are listed in § 27 StPO.

§15.06   THE LEGAL STATUS OF THE PARTICIPANTS IN THE PROCESS

[A]   The Accused

In a sense, the accused is an object of state compulsion, at least to the extent that he has to endure the criminal process as well as, under certain circumstances, serious restrictions of his rights (e.g., through pretrial detention). As a participant in the process, however, he also has numerous procedural rights and privileges, one of which is the presumption of innocence (Article 6 II European Convention on Human Rights) according to which all persons are deemed innocent until proven guilty.

The principle of legality (§ 152 II StPO) obliges the investigating authorities to declare a suspect an "accused" if the evidence against him provides sufficient grounds for suspicion (§ 152 II StPO). From this moment on, he can invoke all the rights of an accused person. Initial suspicion (*Anfangsverdacht*) exists as soon as available evidence suggests, in the professional view of the criminal investigators, that the suspect's behavior possibly warrants an indictment.

One of the most important rights of the accused is the right to be heard, as guaranteed by Article 103 I Basic Law. As a result, judicial decisions may only be based on evidence as to which the accused has been heard. The right to a hearing is governed by numerous provisions of the StPO. The accused also has the right to defense counsel at every stage of the proceedings (§ 137 StPO). Furthermore, he has a right to be present at the trial (§ 230 I StPO) the right to apply for the introduction of evidence (§§ 219 and 244–246 StPO), and to present questions (§ 240 II StPO). A further important right is provided by the rule against self-incrimination (*nemo tenetur se ipsum accusare*) which, however, is not enshrined in a statute. This rule is derived from the general right to personal integrity contained in Article 2 I in combination with Article 1 I 1 GG as well as from the rule of law principle contained in Article 20 III GG. As a result, the accused is not required to contribute to his own conviction. This engenders a right to remain silent as well as immunity from prosecution for perjury. If the accused invokes his right to remain silent, no adverse inferences may be drawn from this choice.

At the same time, the accused has a variety of duties. Under certain conditions, he is subject to various forms of compulsion and must participate in identity parades (line-ups) (§ 58 II StPO). Moreover, the accused is required to be present at trial (§ 230 StPO) and to appear before the investigating judge (§ 133 I StPO) as well as before the state attorney (§ 163a III StPO).

[B]   The State Attorney's Office and the Police

[1]   The State Attorney's Office

The state attorney's offices are part of the civil service of the respective State (Land). They are hierarchically structured and subordinate to the (State) Ministry of Justice. Only the federal state attorney's office, which is responsible for crimes against the state, is part of the federal civil service. In the context of criminal procedure, the state attorney's office has three primary functions: it is responsible for the investigative procedure, for representing the prosecution in intermediate proceedings and at trial and, finally, for executing the sentence. The state attorney is bound by the (lawful) directions given by his superiors (§ 146 GVG).

Only the state prosecutor's office can initiate a public prosecution (*see* § 152 I StPO, principle of officiality). At the same time, if there are sufficient grounds for suspicion, the prosecutor's office is obliged by §§ 152 II and 170 I to begin investigations on its own initiative and, should the suspicion be found to be substantial, to file charges (principle of legality). The state attorney's office must remain objective in its investigations. Thus, it must collect evidence both for and against the suspect.

The state attorney is continuously present during the trial hearing (§ 226 StPO). He acts as the representative of the state and must prove that the accused has committed an act triggering criminal liability. During the evidence-taking phase of the trial, the prosecutor has the right to ask questions (§ 240II StPO) as well the right to request that evidence be admitted (§ 244 StPO).

[2]   The Police

Police officers and agencies assist the state attorney's office in the investigation of the crime (§ 152 II GVG). Generally, officers will be members of the institutions of the general police service which belong to the States (*Länder*). Federal authorities get involved only in cases which transcend state boundaries – treason, terrorism, and organized crime – as well as in cases of unconstitutional activities.

The state attorney's office cooperates with the police during the course of an investigation. The police has to comply with requests from the state attorney's office (§§ 152, 161 GVG). Yet, the state attorney's power to instruct the police is limited to "repressive" functions, i.e., to the investigation of offenses that have already been committed. He has no power to get involved in crime prevention and in the general maintenance of public safety and order. The relationship between the prosecutor's office and the police is governed by the provisions of the StPO and the GVG, while the preventative functions of the police are regulated under separate state laws.

Police officers must initiate investigations of their own if there are indications that a crime has been committed (§ 163 I StPO). In cases of imminent danger, they are also entitled to use force, e.g., for purposes of arrest, searches and seizures. Yet, police officers may only take initial measures (§ 163 StPO). Thereafter, control over the investigative process has to be handed over to the state attorney's office without delay.

In practice though, the police usually carry out investigations independently up to the point where charges can be brought, simply because the police often has more experience in the investigation of crimes. As a result, the state attorney's office functions essentially as a legal supervisor of the police. The state attorney's office only becomes actively involved in the investigation in cases of particular public or political interest.

[C] Supporting Institutions

Section 160 III StPO permits the state attorney's office to call on special institutions to assist prosecutors and courts in investigating particular circumstances. These institutions (*Gerichtshilfe*) are staffed by social workers with the requisite psychological training and experience. They provide information about the personal circumstances of the accused which may be significant in assessing the degree of fault, the prospects for rehabilitation, and the danger represented by a convicted person. These investigations do not relate to the wrongful act itself.

The States (*Länder*) are responsible for creating such institutions although so far not all States have done so. In practice, their main activity has been in the context of proceedings against persons under the age of 21 (*see also* §§ 43 and 38 et seq. JGG). In proceedings under the Juvenile Court Act (*Jugendgerichtsgesetz* – JGG), these institutions always have the status of a participant and must therefore be informed as well as heard (§ 38 III JGG).

[D] Defense Counsel

Under the German law of criminal procedure, defense counsel is a participant with a particularly important role. The accused can demand legal representation at any stage of the proceedings (§ 137 I StPO). In cases in which the defendant must be represented by counsel, defense counsel will be appointed by the court of its own motion if the accused does not do so. Representation by counsel is mandatory, *inter alia*, in all cases in which the first-instance trial is before the District Court (*Landgericht*) or the Higher Regional Court (*Oberlandesgericht*); if the accused is charged with a felony; if the evidentiary or legal circumstances are difficult; or when the accused cannot defend himself (§ 140 StPO).

Even though the court and the state attorney must inquire into both incriminating and exonerating circumstances, defense counsel is essential for the protection of the accused and for establishing the truth. In particular, defense counsel can articulate the interests of the accused as they arise in the course of a trial. It is indispensable for the rule of law that the accused is able to respond effectively to the charges against him and to ensure that his version of the case is taken into account when judging the case. As a rule, lay persons are not able to present their views in the requisite manner, let alone guard against errors by the court. They normally have neither the necessary knowledge of procedural and substantive law nor the opportunity to take appropriate action especially if they are in custody. It is the role of defense counsel to remedy these problems.

Thus, the primary role of defense counsel is to represent the accused. As a matter of principle, counsel may only act on the accused's behalf. In exceptional circumstances, however, counsel may act contrary to the accused's wishes if this serves the interests of truth and of an effective defense.

The defense counsel's task is to advise the accused on questions of procedural and substantive law, to make declarations for the accused, to implement his own procedural rights and those of the accused, and to strive for a speedy resolution of the proceedings, where appropriate by getting the case dropped through other arrangements with the state attorney's office and the court. Unlimited and confidential contact between defense counsel and the accused must be ensured in order to guarantee the trust relationship that is indispensable for an effective defense (§ 148 StPO).

Defense counsel is independent. This means that he acts on his own responsibility and is not subject to supervision by the court. Neither is he or she bound by the instructions of the accused. Defense counsel must maintain the confidentiality of the information he acquires vis-à -vis the investigating authorities.

In addition defense counsel has a public function as an independent organ of the judicial process. This is connected with his duty to serve the establishment of the truth. Defense counsel is therefore regarded as someone who serves the interests of all citizens precisely by being partisan, by ensuring that all procedural rules are observed and that the discovery of material truth is pursued in a fair trial.

One of defense counsel's most important rights is to inspect the files (*Akteneinsichtsrecht* – § 147 StPO). This right is unrestricted once investigations are closed. In principle, the accused himself has no right to see the files. Yet, defense counsel may inform his client comprehensively of the content of the files as long as he does not reveal imminent investigative moves which are intended to work by surprise. In addition, defense counsel has a right to be present at the examination of the accused by a judge or state attorney (§§ 168 c, 163 a III StPO). At trial, he or she may examine and cross-examine individuals (§ 239 StPO), although cross-examination as such is not common practice in German courtrooms. Furthermore, defense counsel may make declarations on behalf of the accused at any stage of the proceedings. Finally, counsel has a right to request the admission of evidence. He or she must be accorded the right to make a statement after the hearing of each piece of evidence (§ 257 II StPO). Defense counsel may also appeal on behalf of the accused (§ 297 StPO) though not contrary to his client's express wishes.

Defense counsel has a right to take any action serving the protection and defense of the accused. This right, however, is limited by the provisions of the penal code. Furthermore, he is not allowed to obstruct the judicial process by inhibiting the discovery of the truth or by interfering with evidence. Still, he is not obliged to correct statements made by others if it becomes apparent to him that a witness or the accused are not telling the truth at trial. Even if defense counsel knows from personal conversation with the accused that his client is guilty, he may still request an acquittal in his closing speech if the guilt of the accused remains open to doubt.

[E]   The Victim

The victim has few rights in modern German criminal procedure. He or she is primarily a witness. In recent times, there has been a growing consensus in favor of extending more rights to the injured party. In April 1987, an amendment to the Code of Criminal Procedure entered into force which provides that the victim must be kept informed of the proceedings and must have access to the files. This right, however, can only be exercised through a lawyer (§§ 406f and 406g StPO).

Certain offenses such as libel (*Beleidigung*, § 185 StGB) and battery (*Körperverletzung*, § 223 StGB) may only be prosecuted upon application of the victim (*Antragsdelikte* – §§ 77 ff. StGB).

In the case of certain serious offenses, the injured party may also initiate proceedings by means of a private indictment (*Privatklage*) without seeking the assistance of the state attorney's office (§ 374 StPO). A private indictment by the injured party is most likely to occur in cases where the state attorney's office has dropped the case for lack of public interest in prosecution (§§ 374 and 376 StPO). Certain offenses enumerated in § 380 StPO (trespass, insult, infringement of the right to confidential mail, battery, threat of felony, intentional property damage) may only be prosecuted by private indictment if conciliation with the help of a special mediation service has failed. In proceedings according to a private indictment, the private prosecutor takes on the role of the state attorney though without being able to call on the assistance of the police. The state attorney's office can take over proceedings at any time (§ 377 II StPO).

§ 395 StPO permits victims or their personal representatives to join the public prosecutor in the role of an additional private prosecutor (*Nebenkläger*). This institution of "accessory prosecution" (*Nebenklage*) lets the victim play an active role in the proceedings for purposes of personal satisfaction. In the capacity as additional private prosecutor, the victim has access to the files (through his lawyer), is entitled to request the taking of evidence, and may appeal the judgment.

In addition, an "ancillary action" (*Adhäsionsverfahren*) enables the victim or his personal representative to pursue damage claims against the accused in criminal court as long as no civil suit has been initiated (§ 403 StPO). The conditions for such an action are laid down in § 404 StPO. If the outcome of the trial affirmes the damage claim, the court will enter a compensatory judgment in favor of the victim (§ 406 StPO). In practice, the "ancillary action" has little relevance in German criminal proceedings.

§15.07   PRINCIPLES OF CRIMINAL PROCEDURE

[A]   Principle of Fair Trial

The principle of fair trial (Article 20 III Basic Law, 6 I ECHR) states that the criminal proceedings must be fair at every stage. In particular, there must be equality of arms between the prosecution and the defendant or defense. This should prevent the exploitation of formal power positions.

[B]   The Principle of Officiality

The principle of officiality provides that only the state attorney's office may bring public charges (§ 152 I StPO). In other words, initiating a criminal procedure is a matter for the state and not for the individual citizen. Thus, it is irrelevant in principle whether the victim wants a case to be prosecuted or not. The state has a monopoly of prosecution in order to ensure public peace and order.

There are two exceptions to this principle. One is the institution of private indictment (*supra*). The other exception is that certain offenses will be prosecuted only upon application of the victim (*Antragsdelikte*, §§ 77 et seq. StGB).

[C]   The Principle of Legality

The principle of legality is the necessary complement to the state monopoly of prosecution. It requires the state attorney's office or the police to initiate an investigation once a sufficient suspicion exists. In short, the prosecuting authorities must investigate and prosecute all potential crimes. In principle, they have no discretion to drop a case as a simple matter of expediency.

In certain exceptional cases, however, the prosecuting authorities do have the option of desisting from prosecution for pragmatic reasons (principle of opportunity – *Opportunitätsprinzip*).

Section 153 I StPO allows the state attorney's office not to prosecute misdemeanors (i.e., offenses with a minimum penalty of less than one year imprisonment) if the defendant's guilt is slight and if there is no public interest in prosecuting the act. To determine the question of public interest it is necessary to take into account the goals of punishment, i.e., whether prosecution is required in order to deter the offender and others from committing similar offenses in the future. In cases of misdemeanors that do not carry an aggravated minimum sentence and where the consequences of the offense are only minor the court's consent is not required. After the offender has been charged, the court can still drop the case at any stage if the conditions just mentioned are met and if both the state attorney and the accused agree (§ 153 II StPO).

According to § 153 StPO, the state attorney or the court may also terminate proceedings where light misdemeanors are involved if conditions and instructions are imposed that eliminate the public interest in further prosecution. These conditions and instructions may include reparation to the victim, payment of a sum of money to a community organization or to the public purse, some other kind of community service, or meeting a maintenance obligation. In such cases, the initial public interest in prosecution is outweighed by other goals, such as compensation to the victim.

A provision on plea bargains, i.e., agreements between the accused, the state attorney, and the court about penalties, has recently been introduced by§ 257c StPO. According to this, the court may, in appropriate cases, agree with the parties on the progress and outcome of the proceedings. The subject matter of this understanding may only be (a) the legal effect of the judgment and of any related orders, (b) any procedural measures governing the underlying investigation of the facts, and (c) the procedural steps to be taken by the parties. A confession by the accused must be part of any plea bargain. The conviction as such and any measures of reparation and security may not be part of the plea bargain. The court announces the content of the agreement. It can also specify an upper and lower limit of the penalty. The parties must be given the opportunity to comment. The case is settled if defendant and public prosecutor agree with the proposal of the court. The official legal resolution is final, secret agreements (so-called deals) are inadmissible.

Under § 153a I 2 StPO the court has the power to make the following orders upon termination of the proceedings: reparation of the damage or other compensation of the victim, the payment of a sum of money to a charitable institution or the public purse, provision of other charitable services and the payment of maintenance to the mother of a child, If the defendant complies with the requirements and instructions, the proceedings are finally terminated. This means that the accused can no longer be prosecuted for the same facts. If the defendant fails to comply with the conditions and instructions within the set time limit, the proceedings will resume and charges will be brought and / or the oral hearing will be held.

Plea bargains most commonly reflect the punishment the accused would have had to expect if he or she had confessed. The public prosecutor's office and the court often have an interest in such an agreement because it can greatly reduce the complexity of the proceedings, in particular the duration of the main proceedings. The advantage for defendants is that on the one hand they obtain certainty about the outcome of the proceedings, and, on the other hand, they create a ground for leniency which carries considerable weight. In addition, the accused may spare himself a long and difficult trial.

Further options to drop charges on grounds of expediency are listed in §§ 153b et seq. StPO.

[D]   The Principle of the "Lawful Judge"

This principle is derived from a basic constitutional right contained in Article 101 GG which provides that nobody may be deprived of his or her "lawful judge." It means that the jurisdiction of a court and the designated judge(s) sitting have to be determined in advance by law. Ad hoc courts or the manipulated selection of specific judges are therefore forbidden.

[E]   The Principle of Accusation

The principle of accusation means that charges must be brought before any criminal court proceedings can be initiated (§ 151 StPO). Bringing charges is the privilege of the state attorney's office as an institution independent of the court (§ 152 I StPO).

This principle also entails that the court may proceed only with regard to particular the charges brought by the state attorney. If further offenses committed by the same perpetrator come to light in the course of the trial, it will be necessary to decide whether a potential verdict would cover these offenses as well (after the accused has been informed of this possibility according to § 265 StPO) or whether the state attorney will have to amend the charges by a so-called supplementary indictment (*Nachtragsanklage*, § 266 I StPO). To continue the proceedings without amending charges is only permitted if the additional offenses are part of the same set of facts (*see* §§ 155 and 264 I StPO) in the sense that the same historical event underlies the initial charges. Yet, even if the same facts are at issue and the additional offenses arise simply as a matter of legal interpretation, the court has a duty to bring this to the attention of the accused so that he or she can be heard accordingly.

[F]   Principles of Evidence

[1]   *The Principle of Investigation*

In contrast to civil procedure where it is for the parties to decide what facts they wish to put before the court (the principle of formal truth), criminal procedure is intended to establish what really happened (the principle of material truth). Thus, criminal proceedings are governed by the principle of investigation (*Untersuchungsgrundsatz*) that means that the court itself determines the inquiry into the case. It is not bound by the applications or submissions of the participants in the trial. This principle is applicable to all the prosecuting agencies (§§ 155 II, 160 II, 244 II StPO) and engenders a comprehensive inquiry to investigate the facts ex officio. For example the prosecutor must introduce exonerating evidence whether the accused has moved to do so or not. In practice, however, the prosecuting authorities are overburdened, and as a result, it is increasingly common (*praeter legem*) to handle more and more criminal cases by agreement with the accused. In such cases, there may be no full investigation of the facts. Thus the principle of investigation is threatened in practice.

[2]   *The Principle of Immediacy*

The principle of immediacy (*Unmittelbarkeitsgrundsatz*) requires the court to obtain the most direct and immediate impression of the events at issue (§ 261 StPO). This means, first, that the members of the court must be present during the entire course of the trial (§ 226 StPO). If any judge cannot continue to sit at trial, he may not be replaced by another who has not been present so far. Instead, the whole trial must be repeated. Thus, in larger trials so-called substitute judges (*Ergänzungsrichter*) are appointed (§ 192 II GVG) who may substitute for an unavailable colleague. The principle of immediacy also means that the court must rely on evidence closest to the facts. In the case of witness testimony, e.g., witnesses must be examined directly at the trial. As a rule, their examination may not be replaced by introducing the written record of some earlier examination or by a written statement (§ 250 StPO).

In light of this principle, it is somewhat problematic that the professional judges will usually have studied the file in some detail before trial, because there is a danger that they will already have reached their conclusions before the trial even begins.

Nevertheless, judges are expected not to allow themselves to be biased by knowledge acquired outside of the trial.

An exception to the principle of direct personal interrogation is supplied by § 247a StPO, which allows for audiovisual hearings both of factual witnesses and of experts. Here, the witness or expert stays in another place and is connected by simultaneous transfer with the main proceedings. The prerequisite for this is either (a) being questioned in the presence of the participants in the main trial would seriously endanger the wellbeing of the witness, or (b) if a hearing is necessary but either the witness cannot appear for reasons of illness, frailty or other insuperable obstacles, or his attendance appears unreasonable having regard to the distance he would otherwise have to travel. It is also permissible to rely on video transmission if the prosecutor, the accused and his attorney all agree. Outside the main hearing, an audiovisual witness hearing may be made at any time.

The use of so-called undercover agents (§ 110a StPO) poses further problems in connection with the principle of immediacy. Since there is an interest in keeping their identity secret, they may not be able to testify in person at trial. Decisions of the Federal Constitutional Court and of the Federal Supreme Court have permitted the introduction of indirect witnesses in such cases (e.g., a police officer who interrogated the undercover agent). The court, however, must take into account that indirect testimony carries less weight than direct testimony.

[3]   The Principle of the Free Assessment of Evidence

According to § 261 StPO, the court evaluates the evidence on the basis of convictions formed in the course of the proceedings. This is the principle of the judge's "free assessment of evidence" (*freie Beweiswürdigung*). In contrast to criminal procedure before the mid-19th century, the judge is thus not bound by any formal rules in deciding whether a fact has been proven or not. Yet, even today there are a limited number of rules of evidence. Thus, e.g., the Code of Criminal Procedure provides that the violation of essential procedural rules at trial can only be proven by means of the trial record (§ 274 StPO). In addition, certain important limitations on the principle of the free assessment of evidence are derived from various other procedural norms. They include the rules developed by the courts to exclude certain kinds of evidence (*see* below).

Finally, the accused's right to exercise certain rights requires that no negative inferences be drawn from his or her choice to do so, e.g., the choice to remain silent.

[4]   The Principle In Dubio Pro Reo

The principle *in dubio pro reo* means that, in criminal proceedings, the accused enjoys the benefit of the doubt. This can be deduced directly from the presumption of innocence in conjunction with § 261 StPO: If a guilty verdict requires the court to be convinced of the guilt of the accused, doubts as to this precondition must prevent such a verdict. Article 6 II ECHR also contains this principle. It is violated if the accused is found guilty despite doubt on behalf of the judge. As a result, the accused does not have to prove his innocence; on the contrary, the state has to prove his or her guilt. This applies to all issues pertaining to the question of guilt or innocence, such as alibis, justifications, excuses, or immunities.

[G] Formal Principles

[1] Orality

The principle of orality (*Mündlichkeitsgrundsatz*) requires that the judgment be based only on evidence introduced and discussed at trial. It may be inferred from §§ 261 and 264 StPO.

[2] Publicity

The principle of publicity (*Öffentlichkeitsgrundsatz*) is codified in §§ 169 et seq. GVG. It requires proceedings before the court, including the pronouncement of the verdict and any interlocutory decisions, to be open to the public. Its purpose is to prevent the secrecy of the process, common in earlier times. Television or radio broad-casts, as well as sound or film recordings of the trial, however, are prohibited (§§ 169 II GVG). In particular cases, the public may be excluded to protect a participant (*see* §§ 171a et seq. GVG), e.g., in proceedings under the Juvenile Court Act (JGG) or during the examination of victims of sexual offenses.

[H] The Principle of an Expeditious Proceeding

The rule of law enshrined in Article 20 III GG engenders the requirement that criminal proceedings should be conducted expeditiously (*Beschleunigungsgrundsatz*) (cf. Article 6 I ECHR). Also, the accused must be informed of the charges against him within an appropriate time.

Under current German law, however, excessive length does not require a mandatory termination of the proceedings under § 260 III StPO. Instead, the effects of an excessively long trial will be taken into account in determining the sentence. Yet, in particularly extreme cases, the court may conclude that the continuation of criminal proceedings is no longer tolerable under the rule of law. A further aspect of the principle of expeditious proceedings is the "maxim of concentration." It provides that the trial may only be subject to short interruptions (three weeks – § 229 StPO) and that exceeding this limit may require a completely new trial (§§ 228 and 229 StPO).

§15.08 PRECONDITIONS OF CRIMINAL PROCEEDINGS

Procedural preconditions determine whether a matter may go to judgment. The court has to consider them ex officio at every stage.

Procedural preconditions include, first, the court's jurisdiction. This encompasses the questions of whether the accused is subject to German jurisdiction (§§ 18 et seq. GVG), whether criminal procedure is generally admissible (§ 13 GVG), and whether the court has subject matter jurisdiction. A further question is whether the case is already pending elsewhere or the subject of an existing judgment (requirement of the *ne bis in idem*, Article 103 III GG comparable to the prohibition of double jeopardy). Other matters to be considered include the statute of limitations, statutory amnesties, the formal correctness of the indictment, and – to the extent required by law – the victim's application for prosecution (*Strafantrag*). In addition, the accused must be capable of standing trial, i.e., he or she must have the capacity to take care of his own interests, to conduct his defense in a rational manner, and to make and receive declarations relative to trial. Proceedings against children under the age of 14 are not allowed. It is controversial whether the fact that the accused will not live long enough to see the end of trial constitutes a bar to criminal proceedings.

If a permanent obstacle emerges during the preliminary proceedings, the state attorney's office drops the case in accordance with § 170 II StPO. If the obstacle is only temporary, a stay can be considered (*see* § 205 StPO). During the intermediate procedure, a permanent obstacle will lead the court not to proceed to trial (§ 204 StPO). If the obstacle is temporary, the court may close the case according to § 205 StPO. During the trial itself, the discovery of a permanent obstacle may lead to a judgment closing the case (§ 260 StPO).

§15.09 RULES OF EVIDENCE

[A] Purpose and Object of the Taking of Evidence

The introduction of evidence at trial serves the investigation of the facts and other matters relevant to the court's decision (§ 244 II StPO). Thus, presentation and evaluation of the evidence is the core of the trial and the primary task of the court.

Evidence can pertain to both internal and external facts. In addition, the principles of common experience are subject to proof as well because it is through these principles that individual facts are connected.

The rules governing the introduction of evidence are intended primarily to ensure that a complete picture of the underlying events is established. Even so, there are limitations on the permissibility of evidence due to rights which are considered more important than the discovery of the truth. If there is more than one source of evidence for a specific fact, the source with the greatest probative value must be preferred. As mentioned before, the evidence is to be freely assessed by the judge(s) (§ 261 StPO).

[B] Motions for the Introduction of Evidence

In criminal proceedings, the various participants must be allowed to introduce their individual perspectives on the relevant questions; only in this way it is possible to approximate the truth. In particular, the right of the accused to move for the introduction of certain evidence results from his or her position as an active participant. Moreover, despite the court's own ex officio duty to investigate the case, defense counsel also has the right to move for the introduction of evidence, as does the state attorney. The same right is accorded to private prosecutors (*Nebenkläger and Privatkläger, supra.*) where they participate in the trial.

A motion for the introduction of evidence must include a specific assertion of fact and a specifically identified form of evidence recognized by the Code of Criminal Procedure. Motions to introduce evidence in this manner may be made at trial until the time that judgment is pronounced. This enables the accused and defense counsel to obstruct the proceedings and, under certain circumstances, to delay them considerably.

Motions to introduce evidence may be denied by an interlocutory order and only on grounds provided by statute (§ 244 VI StPO). These grounds include the inadmissibility of the evidence, the fact that the matter is common knowledge (§ 244 III StPO) or the fact that the matter to be proven has already been established (§ 244 IV). The court may also deny such a motion if the facts to be proven are unrelated to the underlying events or if the means of evidence proffered is entirely unsuited for the purpose. Further grounds for denial provided by § 244 III StPO are the inaccessibility of the evidence, the intention to delay the proceedings, and presumptions of truth in favor of the accused.

[C]   Inadmissible Evidence

While the principle of official investigation (*see* § 244 II StPO) requires comprehensive investigation, it does not require the pursuit of truth at any cost. Instead, the principle of investigation is limited by rules of inadmissibility of evidence. These rules are designed to ensure respect for more important values and for rights guaranteed by the Constitution.

There is a distinction between provisions prohibiting the introduction of evidence and others that prohibit to take certain evidence into account. The former include rules against introducing evidence pertaining to specific topics, against certain means of evidence (e.g., the rule against hearing persons who cannot be summoned to appear), and against certain methods of obtaining evidence (e.g., the rule prohibiting certain techniques of examining witnesses). Where a rule against the taking of certain evidence was violated, the use of such evidence by the court may or may not be prohibited. It is not the purpose of these rules to discipline the prosecution. Nonetheless, investigative actions violating such rules may be grounds for disciplinary or criminal proceedings against the officials involved.

Only a few of the rules forbidding the use of certain evidence come in statutory form (*see*, e.g., § 136a StPO). In addition, there are a large number of exclusionary rules resulting from case law. The precise parameters of such rules and the exact criteria justifying the exclusion of evidence are often controversial. Results in particular cases often depend on the protective purpose of the infringed norm as well as on a balancing of the affected interests.

Case law has excluded evidence on the following grounds: Witnesses were not informed about their rights and duties (*see* § 52 III StPO); a relative of the accused refuses to testify at trial to a statement previously made; the accused was not informed about his rights (*see* § 136 I StPO); tape recordings were obtained without authorization (*see* § 100c StPO); the evidence consists of private diary entries; the evidence was obtained through illegal wiretapping (*see* § 100a StPO).

The reach of exclusionary rules is controversial. Courts have mostly held that evidence obtained on the basis of (other) excludable evidence may be used. In other words, the "fruit of the poisonous tree doctrine" has, by and large, been rejected by German courts. The main reason is that, as mentioned before, exclusionary rules are not meant to discipline the police or the prosecutor.

Since the exclusionary rules in the Code of Criminal Procedure are directed only at the prosecution, evidence illegally obtained by private persons may in principle be used, at least as long as it has not been obtained by serious infringements of human dignity and the use of such evidence would not itself engender yet another infringement of human rights.

[D]   The Accused and the Law of Evidence

The accused must be examined during the investigative procedure. Investigative examinations are carried out by the state attorney's office and the police (§ 136 in conjunction with §§ 133 et seq. StPO). Yet, it is also possible for the accused to be examined by a judge (*see* § 136 StPO).

Section 136a StPO prohibits certain methods of examinations. The freedom of choice and the capacity of the accused to exercise his or her will may must not be infringed upon by the examination. According to § 136a I 1 StPO, forbidden methods of examination include mistreatment, exhaustion, physical force, drugging, torture, deception (which includes the deliberate representation of untrue facts and the deliberately false depiction of the legal situation) and hypnosis. The second clause of this provision states that force may be used only to the extent allowed by law. The third clause forbids threats of measures not allowed by law as well as the offer of benefits not provided by law. Finally, § 136a II StPO prohibits measures affecting the memory or the intelligence of the accused. Despite this, tactics such as trick questions may be used. The use of lie detectors is not permitted because the results they produce do not derive from an exercise of the examined person's free will. According to § 136a III StPO, statements obtained as a result of violations of § 136a I and II StPO are inadmissible, even with the consent of the accused.

Section 136 StPO provides that the examination begins by informing the accused of the charges, i.e., of what he is suspected to have done and what penal consequences are at issue. The accused must then be informed of his or her right to remain silent and of the right to engage defense counsel. Next are questions pertaining to his or her identity. Thereafter, he or she is questioned regarding the subject matter of the proceedings. While the accused must identify him- or herself, there is no obligation to make any statements regarding the charges themselves.

Failure to inform the accused of the right to remain silent constitutes a form of deception under § 136a StPO. The general view today is that this failure entails exclusion of any statements made by the accused, at least where the accused's familiarity with his right to remain silent cannot be presumed.

[E]   Witnesses

Witnesses provide testimony about facts they have experienced. Matters that the witness has heard from another person as well as observations about the manner in which a person leads his or her life also count as facts in that sense. Thus, German law does not exclude hearsay evidence.

A properly summoned witness must appear before the judge (§§ 48–51 StPO) or state attorney (§ 161a StPO) and testify truthfully as to the object of the examination. False statements are punishable under §§ 153 et seq. of the Criminal Code (StGB). As a rule, witnesses do not testify under oath (§ 59 StPO) unless the court considers it necessary. In particular cases, witnesses may not be compelled to testify (i.e., if they have a privilege, *see infra*). If they testify regardless, they must do so truthfully. Section 52 StPO provides that certain relatives do not have to testify against the accused. A fiancé spouse, or near relative of the accused have an unrestricted privilege. The purpose is to spare the witness the conflict between the duty to tell the truth and the affection they have for his or her kin. The respective witnesses must be informed of their privilege before every examination (§ 52 III StPO).If this information is omitted and if this omission led the witness to testify, the testimony may not be used.

§ 53 StPO provides that certain other persons who are subject to professional rules of confidentiality enjoy more limited privileges. These protect members of clergy, the defense counsel, lawyers, accountants, physicians, members of counseling agencies, members of the press and media, and, by virtue of § 53a StPO, assistants to these professionals. These persons may refuse to testify regarding matters entrusted to them under confidentiality in the course of their professional activity, at least as long as they have not been relieved of the duty of confidentiality.

According to § 54 StPO, judges and civil servants are subject to a conditional prohibition to testify regarding matters within the scope of their official duties or classified material. They may testify only with permission from their superiors. Such permission may not be refused except where the welfare of the federation or of one of the States (*Länder*) or the performance of public duties is in jeopardy (§ 39 BRRG, § 62 BBG). Testimony given by public servants without such permission may, however, be used. Nevertheless, the official may be subject to criminal penalties (§ 353b StGB).

According to § 55 StPO, any witness may refuse to respond to questions if an answer could expose him or his near relatives to prosecution for an offense (privilege against self-incrimination). Witness have to be informed of this right as well.

Before being examined, witnesses have to be informed about their duty to tell the truth, about the significance of the oath, and about the criminal consequences of making false statements (§ 57 StPO). They must be examined individually and in the absence of those witnesses who are to be heard later (§ 58 I StPO). A witness is examined first as to his identity (i.e., his name, age, status or profession, and place of abode, § 68 I StPO). The duty to respond in this regard may be limited if it could expose the witness to danger (§ 68 II StPO). This is followed by the examination as to the events under investigation (§ 69 StPO). The judge is initially required to ask the witness for a coherent report about his knowledge. If necessary, further questions may be asked to clarify and complete the statement. The witness has a right to be treated fairly which, among other things, entitles him or her to be accompanied by legal counsel. Witnesses receive standardized compensation for lost time or income (*see* § 71 StPO).

[F]   Expert Witnesses

Expert witnesses are primarily assistants to the court. They provide expertise which the court lacks. The expert witness has three potential functions. He may acquaint the court with general matters of knowledge and experience established within his area of expertise. He may determine facts that may only be perceived, understood or assessed on the basis of particular knowledge. And he may use scientific principles and methods to draw inferences from facts.

The expert witness is to be distinguished from the regular witness who is also an expert, i.e., from someone whose testimony relates to past facts or circumstances the perception of which required a particular expertise. For such witnesses the normal rules on witness testimony apply (§ 85 StPO).

The expert witness becomes involved at the initiative of the court. He or she has a limited right of access to the file, and is allowed to be present at the examination of persons and to question them (§ 80 StPO). As §§ 72 et seq. StPO show, he or she has the duty to appear at trial, to testify truthfully and, upon motion by one of the participants, to testify under oath.

Except for specific cases listed in §§ 81, 87 et seq., 91 et seq. StPO, the court is under no duty to appoint expert witnesses. Yet, if the court overrates its own expertise, it may violate its judicial duties (*see* § 244 II StPO) which may be cause for appeal.

[G]   Corporal Evidence

Corporal evidence includes objects of observation and documents.

Observational evidence (*Augenscheinbeweis*) is derived from the sensory perception of persons or things. This includes corpses, tape recordings or situations, such as a busy intersection. The introduction of evidence by observation is admissible at every stage of the proceedings at the discretion of the court.

The term "documents" encompasses writings of any kind and any other materials which could be introduced as evidence by reading them in court (§ 249 StPO).

§15.10   COMPULSORY MEASURES AND RESTRICTIONS ON BASIC RIGHTS

The use of compulsion in criminal proceedings serves two primary purposes: the securing of evidence and the presence of the suspect whenever it is required. Compulsory measures are not penal in character.

Procedural compulsion entails a restriction of the involved citizen's fundamental rights, which may be necessary in the interest of effective prosecution. Yet, under the rule of law, this interest can never justify reducing a citizen to a mere object of state activity. Thus, a balance has to be found between civic freedom and the power of the state to prosecute criminals. The provisions of the StPO are designed to strike this balance. The legitimacy of any compulsory measures depends not only on the application of specific provisions of the StPO, but also on the constitutional principle of proportionality. The seriousness of the offense and the degree of suspicion, the likely utility of the measure for securing evidence or information and the damage or danger for the basic rights of the persons concerned have to be balanced whenever a compulsory measure is being considered. In any event, an interference with the basic rights of the person concerned is acceptable only if the same result cannot be achieved without such a restriction or with less intrusive means.

[A]   Custody

In criminal proceedings, keeping the accused in custody ensures that the process can be carried to its conclusion and that the sentence may be carried out. It represents a serious restriction of the right to personal freedom.

According to § 112 StPO, remand in custody requires that the accused is subject to a high degree of suspicion and that there is a special reason why custody is appropriate. There are four particular reasons why custody can be appropriate (§§ 112 and 112a StPO): the likelihood that the accused may flee the jurisdiction; the probability that he may tamper with the evidence; the suspicion of a capital offense, and the danger of committing further serious criminal offenses. In addition, remand in custody must comply with the constitutional principle of proportionality.

Remand in custody is ordered by a written warrant of a judge (§ 114 StPO) and is executed by arrest of the accused. Arrest is the task of the state attorney's office or of the police and is carried out by seizing the accused. Under § 115 StPO, the arrested person is to be brought before the judge who issued the warrant without delay.

The arrested person can challenge the arrest through a motion to examine (*Haftprüfung* – § 117 StPO) and by filing a complaint (*Haftbeschwerde*). The latter is subsidiary to the former and subject to the general rules on procedural complaints (§§ 304 et seq. StPO). An accused person in custody can file a motion for examination of custody (*Haftprüfung*) at any time. If custody has lasted for longer than three months, an examination has to take place ex officio if the accused has no defense counsel (§ 117 V StPO). After six months, a further examination is performed by the *Oberlandesgericht* (§ 121 StPO).

According to § 120 I StPO, the arrest warrant must be discharged, *inter alia*, when the conditions for remand in custody are no longer satisfied. As a rule, the warrant must also be discharged if the period of custody has exceeded six months unless one of several specific exceptions applies (*see* § 121 StPO). Exceptions apply if a judgment has been rendered and a term of imprisonment pronounced, if the investigations are still under way, or some other important reason justifies a further extension of custody. In light of constitutional rights, the concept of "an important reason" must be strictly construed.

[B] Temporary Arrest (*Vorläufige Festnahme*) and Compulsion of Attendance (*Vorführung*)

Section 127 StPO permits temporary arrest (*vorläufige Festnahme*) of suspects if there is no time to obtain a warrant. Under § 127 I StPO, anybody may arrest a person caught red-handed or in hot pursuit if it is likely that the suspect will otherwise flee or that his or her identity cannot be established. This right to arrest implies the use of force as long as it observes the principle of proportionality and is required for the arrest. In case of imminent danger, the state attorney's office and police officers also have a right to arrest based on § 127 II StPO. As mentioned, the arrested person must be brought before a judge without delay (§ 128 I StPO). If appropriate, the judge will then issue the necessary warrant (§ 128 II StPO).

Temporary arrest must be distinguished from compelling the attendance of the accused or summoning a witness. The judge (§ 134 StPO) and the state attorney's office (§ 163a StPO) may compel such persons to appear (*Vorführung*) but only if an arrest warrant could have been issued as well.

If the accused fails to appear at trial without an adequate excuse, the judge may compel his or her attendance or issue an arrest warrant (§ 230 II StPO).

[C] Institutionalization, Frisking, Fingerprinting, and Photographing

[1] Institutionalization

After hearing expert testimony as well as defense counsel, the court may order that the accused be confined in a public psychiatric hospital for observation. The purpose of this measure is the preparation of a report on the psychological condition of the accused (§ 81 I StPO). The maximum confinement period is six weeks (§ 81 V StPO).

[2] Frisking and Other Searches

A physical search of the accused may be ordered by the judge and, in case of imminent danger, by the state attorney's office (§ 81a StPO). Blood samples may be taken to test the blood alcohol level. It must be carried out by a physician according to accepted medical procedures. It may be performed even without the accused's consent but only as long as there are no foreseeable adverse consequences for his health. The accused is not obligated to participate actively; he must merely tolerate the procedure.

Since recent developments enable the authorities to perform so-called genetic fingerprinting, the question arises whether genome analysis is covered by § 81a StPO. Since the taking of DNA samples allows the discovery of a person's entire genetic make-up, it is doubtful whether the taking of such evidence is compatible with the principle of human dignity contained in Article 1 I Basic Law.

[3]   Fingerprints and Photographs

Section 81b StPO permits the taking of fingerprints and photographs of the accused even against his or her will if it is necessary for the criminal proceedings or for the purposes of identification. This may justify compulsory measures. It is even permissible in principle to alter an accused person's hair or beard for purposes of an identity parade (line-up).

[4]   Searching Third Parties

Under certain conditions, § 81c StPO permits the search of parties who are not under suspicion to have committed a crime and even without their agreement. They must be potential witnesses (*Zeugengrundsatz*) and the search must be directed when at the discovery of evidence of the crime on their person (*Spurengrundsatz*). If a witness has a right to refuse to testify according to § 52 StPO (*see supra*), he or she can also refuse to be physically examined (§ 81c III StPO).

[5]   Securing Objects

Objects may be seized in order to secure evidence (§§ 94 et seq. StPO) and for utilization during the procedure. In addition, the Code of Criminal Procedure permits the seizure of objects for purposes of forfeiture and confiscation (§§ 111b et seq. StPO, *see also* §§ 73 et seq. StGB).

Seizure of objects may be ordered by the judge or, in case of imminent danger, by the state attorney. It requires no more than an initial suspicion of a crime (*Anfangsverdacht*, § 152 II StPO). If the person in possession of the object delivers it voluntarily, the object is simply taken into possession by a police officer of prosecutor (§ 94 I StPO). Otherwise, a formal order will be necessary (§ 94 II StPO).

Section 97 prohibits the confiscation of certain objects. This prohibition results from the right of certain persons to refuse to testify. Thus, written communications between the accused and a person privileged under §§ 52, 53 I nos. 1–3b StPO may not be confiscated (§ 97 I no. 1 StPO). In a similar vein, notes and objects of persons enjoying certain confidentiality privileges may not be confiscated either (*see* §§ 53 I nos. 1–3, § 97 I nos. 2–3 StPO). These exclusions do not apply if the privileged persons are suspected of secondary participation in the crime, of obstructing the course of justice, of handling stolen goods, or if the objects to be confiscated are the subject of the offense (§ 97 II StPO). In addition, prohibitions of confiscation may derive directly from the constitution under the principle of proportionality or to avoid intolerable interference with core basic rights.

In principle, violations of these prohibitions lead to the exclusion of the evidence obtained.

[D] Intrusion into IT Systems

In particular cases, § 100a StPO empowers the prosecuting authorities to monitor and record telecommunications. This allows access to IT systems to investigate the source of existing information. The point is to circumvent protection by source-encrypted messaging services by accessing the unencrypted content in the IT system: The monitoring and recording of telecommunications may also be carried out by intervening with technical means in information technology systems used by the data subject, if necessary, in order to enable monitoring and recording, in particular in unencrypted form. Content and circumstances of the communication stored on the information technology system of the person concerned may be monitored and recorded if they could have been monitored and recorded in encrypted form during the current transmission process in the public telecommunications network.

[E] Online Searches

Legislators finally introduced the new §100b StPO for cases of serious crime: Even without the data subject's knowledge, technical means may intervene in an information technology system used by the suspect and data may be collected, if (1) there is suspicion that a person has committed a particularly serious offense or has attempted to commit it, (2) the act in the individual case weighs particularly heavy and (3) the investigation of the facts or the determination of the whereabouts of the accused would be considerably more difficult or hopeless.

[F] Searches, Checkpoints, Dragnet, and Profiling Techniques

[1] Searches

Searches (§§ 102 et seq. StPO) are intended to reveal evidence, or objects of confiscation. Private and other premises, suspicious and unsuspicious persons, as well as moveable property may be subject to searches.

In principle, searches may only be ordered by a judge, though in case of imminent danger they may also be ordered by the state attorney's office or the police (§ 105 I StPO). Persons entitled to refuse testimony may still be subject to search.

The requirements for a lawful search vary depending on whether the search concerns the suspect or some other person. A search directed against a suspect may aim at his or her arrest (*Ergreifungsdurchsuchung*) or at the discovery of evidence (*Ermittlungsdurchsuchung* – § 102 StPO). A search is admissible if there are reasonable grounds to believe that the search will succeed in producing the desired evidence. This belief does not have to be supported by concrete facts but it must be based on established criminal investigatory experience. The concept of a "suspect" must be strictly construed, i.e., a generalized and abstract suspicion is not sufficient to make somebody a "suspect." Searches directed against persons who are not suspects are permissible only if they are intended to effect the arrest of the accused or the discovery of specified objects and leads (§ 103 StPO).

If, by accidental discovery, the search reveals objects that indicate that yet another offense has been committed those may be confiscated provisionally (§ 108 StPO).

[2]   Checkpoints

Section 111 StPO permits the installation of checkpoints on public roads if there is a suspicion related to serious criminal offenses such as terrorism or aggravated robbery. At such checkpoints, all persons are required to establish their identity and to allow themselves and their property to be searched.

[3]   Dragnet and Profiling Techniques

According to § 163d StPO, personal data collected in the course of border and other controls may be stored and, to the extent that they match the criteria of the search for a suspect (e.g., height, hair color), may be matched by computer to existing data held by the prosecuting authorities (dragnet technique – *Schleppnetzfahndung*).

Section 98a and 98b StPO allow personal data stored in other databases, even though not acquired for the purposes of prosecution, to be accessed and automatically compared with the profile of suspects (*Rasterfahndung*). This requires an initial suspicion (*Anfangsverdacht*) under § 152 II StPO involving one of the serious crimes listed in § 98a StPO. The computer records must be erased once the investigative action has been completed (§ 98b StPO).

Section 161 I 1 StPO allows the state attorney's office to demand information about data of any kind held by all administrative bodies and collected for purposes other than criminal prosecution. Even unlawfully acquired data may be requisitioned on this basis.

[G]   Challenging Investigatory Measures

There are various options to challenge compulsory measures and interferences with basic rights in the course of criminal proceedings. These options are best divided into various categories, depending on whether the measures concerned are imminent, continuing or completed, and depending on who ordered them.

Challenges against imminent or continuing measures ordered by a judge are brought in the form of a complaint (*Beschwerde* – § 304 StPO). If such measures were ordered by the state attorney's office or the police, the Code of Criminal Procedure provides for an appeal to a judge in certain cases (e.g., §§ 98 II, 161a II StPO). In any event, the guarantee of judicial protection contained in the constitution (Article 19 IV GG) requires that all compulsory measures be subject to judicial review. Where the Code of Criminal Procedure contains no explicit provision, judicial review is available by way of analogy to § 98 II StPO.

There is no right to seek review of measures which were ordered by a judge and have already been completed. The prevailing view does not regard this as a violation of Article 19 IV GG because this provision guarantees review by the judiciary but not necessarily of judicial acts themselves. Nonetheless, there is a right to seek review *ex post facto* of completed measures, ordered by the state attorney or the police. Since completed measures can no longer be averted, the remedy is a declaration of its illegality. This remedy is available only if the applicant can demonstrate a special interest in such a declaration. Such an interest may exist with a view toward a damages claim against the state, or for the purpose of averting similar measures in the future, or due to a legitimate interest in personal rehabilitation.

§15.11 JUDGMENT AND RES JUDICATA

The judgment of the court must be delivered on the basis of the trial (§ 268 StPO). The judgment may declare the proceedings inadmissible (procedural judgment) or it may decide the merits of the case. In the latter case, it will acquit the accused or find him or her guilty and pronounce the sentence.

According to § 268 I StPO, the judgment is passed "in the name of the people." It is delivered by the presiding judge. The court's decision is read in open court and the essential aspects of the reasoning are delivered orally (§ 268 II StPO). After judgment has been pronounced, the accused must be informed of his right to appeal (§ 35a StPO).

The judgment becomes final if no timely notice of appeal is filed, if the right to appeal is waived, if an appeal is withdrawn, or if no (further) appeal is possible.

German law distinguishes between the formal and the substantive finality of a judgment. Formal finality means that the judgment can no longer be appealed. Substantive finality means primarily that no further punishment for the act(s) adjudicated is allowed (*ne bis in idem, see* Article 103 III Basic Law).

§15.12 APPEAL

The Code of Criminal Procedure provides for three types of appeal: Appeal on questions of fact and law (*Berufung*), revision, i.e., appeal on questions of law only (*Revision*) and complaint (*Beschwerde*). In all instances the case will be reviewed by a higher court ("devolutive effect"). Appeals on questions of fact and law, except interlocutory ones and complaints, suspend the judgment under appeal ("suspensive effect").

The right to appeal depends on several conditions. To begin with, an appeal must be admissible. In particular, the appellant must have a legitimate interest in an appellate review (*Rechtsschutzinteresse*). Such an interest exists if the appellant has been adversely affected by the judgment. The appellant must also have standing (*Anfechtungsberechtigung*). Parties with standing (*Anfechtungsberechtigte*) are the accused, defense counsel, the state attorney and, where appropriate, the victim. Finally, time limits and formal requirements must be observed.

A *reformatio in peius* by the appellate court is forbidden. Thus, where only the accused appeals the judgment, it may not be changed to his disadvantage (*see* §§ 331 I, 358 II StPO). This principle does not apply to interlocutory appeals.

[A]   Appeal on Questions of Fact and Law (*Berufung*)

According to § 312 StPO, an appeal on questions of both, fact and law, is permissible against judgments of the local court (*Amtsgericht*), i.e., of the single criminal judge (*Strafrichter*) and of the panel consisting of one professional and two lay judges (*Schöffengericht*). The appeal is admissible as long as it is not obviously unfounded (§ 313 II StPO). The appeal must be filed within a week of delivery of the judgment. It is to be filed either in writing or by notice to the court clerk with the Court of First Instance. The appeal does not necessarily have to state reasons. If the appeal is admissible, the case is essentially tried *de novo* before the higher court (*see* §§ 323 et seq. StPO). If the appeal is successful, the appellate court reverses the lower court's judgment and decides the case on the merits (§ 328 I StPO).

There is no appeal on questions of fact and law from the first-instance judgments of the district court (*Landgericht*). Instead, only appeals on points of law are permissible. As a result, the appellate process is simpler in more serious criminal cases. It has for some time been debated whether this is appropriate, especially whether it would not make more sense to provide for fewer appeals in the less serious cases handled by the local courts (*Amtsgerichte*).

[B]   Appeals on Questions of Law (Revision)

§ 333 StPO provides for appeals on questions of law only for judgments rendered by District Courts at first instance (*Landgerichte*, sitting as *Große Strafkammern*, standard format *Schwurgerichte*), i.e., in cases involving a high or even the maximum sanction, as well as from first instance judgments of Higher Regional Courts (*Oberlandesgerichte*). In addition, appellate decisions of the District Court (reviewing judgments of the local courts) are subject to appeal on questions of law. In fact, local court judgments can be appealed directly on questions of law only ("leapfrog appeal" *Sprungrevision*, *see* § 335 StPO). Appellate review on questions of law is limited to an examination of whether the lower court arrived at its decision on the basis of a correct procedure and of whether it applied the substantive criminal law properly. Appeals on questions of law are heard by the Higher Regional Courts (*Oberlandesgerichte*) or the Federal Supreme Court (*Bundesgerichtshof*) respectively. Appeals on questions of law have to be filed with the court whose judgment is being attacked, within a month of the written judgment. They have to state the reasons for appeal, i.e., the legal issues raised (*see* § 335 StPO).

If an appeal on a point of law is based on a procedural error, the appellant must show which rules of procedure have been violated; the record of the trial provides the evidence. For the appeal to succeed, the procedural error must have affected the outcome, at least potentially (§ 337 I StPO). According to § 337 II StPO, the law is violated whenever a legal provision is applied improperly or not at all. In addition, § 338 StPO contains a list of the most serious procedural errors. They are called "absolute grounds for appeal" because where they are committed, an impact on the outcome of the case is irrefutably presumed.

If, on the other hand, the appeal is based on errors of substantive criminal law, the appellant merely has to identify the law infringed (§ 344 II StPO). The court will then undertake a comprehensive review of the legal decision on point. This review will cover both the correct application of substantive law to the facts as well as the question whether the facts as found by the lower court support the legal result.

Once a preliminary review has established that the appeal is admissible and not obviously unfounded, its grounds will be argued at a hearing (for details *see* §§ 350 and 351 StPO). If the appeal is granted, the court will quash the judgment (§ 353 StPO). As a rule, the case will be remanded for a new verdict in compliance with the appellate court's decision (§§ 354, 358 StPO).

[C]   Complaint (*Beschwerde*)

Complaints can be filed against court decisions that precede the final judgment and do not involve compulsory measures (§ 305 StPO). They are available against decisions made by the courts of first instance or during appellate review of both fact and law (*Berufung*) as well as against decisions by the presiding judge, the investigating judge, and any requested judge as long as they are not expressly excluded (§ 304 I StPO). Complaints engender a review of questions of both fact and law. They are decided by the court immediately above the court whose decision is being challenged (§§ 73, 120 and 135 GVG).

§15.13   REOPENING A CASE

In contrast to the forms of appeal described above, the reopening of a case is an extraordinary remedy against final judgments (§§ 359 et seq. StPO). This may be required by the needs of justice inherent in the principle of the rule of law (Article 20 III GG). The Code of Criminal Procedure lists the reasons for which a case may be reopened and distinguishes between reopening a case in favor of the convicted person (§ 359 StPO) and to his or her disadvantage (§ 362 StPO). In practice, the most important ground is the discovery of new evidence (§ 359 no. 5 StPO) which, however, may not be invoked against an acquittal. Proceedings for reopening a case are divided into two stages: a stage determining the admissibility (*Aditionsverfahren*) and a stage dealing with the merits of the case (*Probationsverfahren*). If the application for resumption is admissible and substantiated the application is accepted. If the motion to reopen a case is successful, the case will be tried *de novo* (370 II StPO, for details *see* §§

371 et seq. StPO). The prohibition of a *reformatio in peius* applies here as well (§ 373 II StPO).

§15.14   SPECIAL FORMS OF PROCEDURE

[A]   Simplified Procedure

[1]   Accelerated Procedure

If the facts are straightforward so that it is possible to proceed to judgment immediately, the state attorney may apply to the local court (*Amtsgericht*, i.e., the *Strafrichter* or the *Schöffengericht*) for judgment according to accelerated proceedings (§ 417 StPO). The intermediate procedure (*supra*) will then be omitted (for details, *see* § 418 I StPO), and there is no need for a written indictment (§ 418 III StPO). However, the court can only impose either a fine or a prison sentence not exceeding one year (§ 419 I 2 StPO).

[2]   Penal Order

Another simplified way of handling less serious criminal cases is the penal order procedure (*Strafbefehlsverfahren*, §§ 407 et seq. StPO). Its purpose is to deal with simple cases in an expedient and uncomplicated manner, and it has considerable importance in practice. If the case falls within the jurisdiction of the local court (*Amtsgericht*), § 407 I StPO allows the state attorney to file an application for a penal order (*Strafbefehl*) recounting the facts alleged and specifying the legal consequences. The state attorney's office will use that option if it considers a trial unnecessary in light of the investigation. The state prosecutor's office may seek only a limited number of sanctions (§ 407 II StPO), including a fine, an order forbidding the accused to drive for a certain period of time, a revocation of his or her driver's license, or a suspended prison sentence of up to one year, provided that the accused is represented by counsel.

The ultimate decision still lies with the court. According to § 408 II StPO, the court may reject the application for a penal order if it considers the evidence insufficient. Yet, if there are no countervailing considerations, the court must grant the application and issue the penal order (§ 408 III 1 StPO). From the perspective of the accused, the major advantage of a penal order is that it spares him the cost of a trial, and the public exposure that comes with it.

The accused may file an objection to the penal order with the issuing court within two weeks after the order has been served (§ 410 I StPO) either through a written statement or by recording the objection at the court clerk's office. A timely objection essentially turns the penal order into an indictment and thus leads to the initiation of the intermediary procedure (*supra*) followed by a regular trial under the usual rules (§ 411 StPO). If the accused fails to object within the given time limit, the penal order becomes a final judgment (§ 410 III StPO).

[3]   *Proceedings* In Absentia

Proceedings *in absentia* are possible only for the purpose of preserving evidence, as there can be no trial against an absent defendant (§ 285 StPO). Such proceedings are governed by §§ 276 and 285 et seq. StPO. According to § 276 StPO, an accused is regarded as absent if his whereabouts are unknown or if he is abroad and it is impractical or inappropriate to bring him before the court. It is still possible, however, to confiscate the absent defendant's property (cf. § 290 StPO).

[B]   Proceedings for Forfeiture and Confiscation and Attachment of Property

Proceedings for confiscation (*Einziehung*) and attachment of property (*Vermögensbeschlagnahme*) are governed by §§ 111c et seq. StPO. According to §§ 73 et seq. of the Penal Code (StGB), objects that have been used or obtained in connection with crimes may be confiscated by the courts.

§15.15   COSTS

The costs of the proceedings consists of the fees and expenses of the public purse (§ 464a I StPO). In addition, there may be necessary expenses incurred by other participants (§ 464a II StPO). According to § 465 I StPO, the accused is liable for the costs of the proceedings to the extent that they were occasioned by an act of which he was convicted. Under certain circumstances, an apportionment between the public purse and the convicted person may be considered (§ 465 II StPO). If there is no conviction – i.e., if the accused is acquitted or the case is dismissed on other grounds – the costs of the proceedings and the necessary expenses of the accused are born by the state (§ 467). Under certain circumstances, a court may apportion the costs and expenses between the accused and the state here as well.

The costs of an unsuccessful (or withdrawn) appeal must be born by the appellant.

SELECTED BIBLIOGRAPHY

Anwaltskommentar Strafprozessordnung (Wilhelm Krekeler/Markus Löffelmann/ Ulrich Sommer eds., 2010).
Werner Beulke *Strafprozessrecht* (13th ed. 2016).
Hans Dahs *Handbuch des Strafverteidigers* (8th ed. 2015).
Ulrich Eisenberg *Beweisrecht der StPO* (10th ed. 2016).
Gerhard Fezer *Strafprozeßrecht*, vol. I and II (2nd ed. 1995).
Jürgen Peter Graf *Strafprozessordnung: StPO* (3. Aufl. 2018).
Klaus Haller/Klaus Conzen, *Das Strafverfahren* (7th ed. 2014)
Martin Heger *Strafprozessrecht* (2013).
Uwe Hellmann *Strafprozeßrecht* (2nd ed. 2006).

Heidelberger Kommentar zur Strafprozessordnung (Michael Lemke/Karl-Peter Julius/Christoph Krehl/ Hans-Joachim Kurth/Erardo Cristoforo Rautenberg/ Dieter Temming eds., 3rd ed. 2001).

Wolfgang Joecks *Studienkommentar Strafprozessordnung* (4th ed. 2015).

Jupp Joachimski/Christine Haumer, *Strafverfahrensrecht* (7th ed. 2015).

Karlsruher Kommentar zur Strafprozessordnung (Rolf Hannich ed., 7th. ed. 2013).

Urs Kindhäuser *Strafprozessrecht* (4th ed., 2015).

Bernhard Kramer, *Grundbegriffe des Strafverfahrensrechts* (8th ed. 2014).

Hans-Heiner Kühne, *Strafprozessrecht* (9th ed. 2015).

Heiko Hartmut Lesch, *Strafprozessrecht* (2nd ed. 2001).

KMR – Kommentar zur Strafprozessordnung (Gerhard Fezer/Rainer Paulus/von Bernd von Heintschel-Heinegg/Heinz Stöckel eds., 8th ed. 1990 et seq.)

Ewald Löwe/Werner Rosenberg, *Die Strafprozeßordnung und das Gerichtsverfassungsgesetz mit Nebengesetzen, Großkommentar*, vols. 1–6 (Peter Rieß ed., 27th ed. 2016 et seq.)

Lutz Meyer-Goßner/Gerhard Schmitt, *Strafprozessordnung* (61th ed. 2018).

Münchener Kommentar zur Strafprozessordnung (Hans Kudlich ed., 2th ed. 2018).

Heribert Ostendorf *Strafprozessrecht* (3rd ed. 2018).

Gerd Pfeiffer, *Strafprozeßordnung, Kommentar* (5th ed. 2005).

Holm Putzge/Jörg Scheinfeld, *Strafprozessrecht* (5th ed. 2013).

Henning Radke/Olaf Hohmann, *Strafprozessordnung* (2nd ed. 2019).

Otfried Ranft, *Strafprozeßrecht* (3rd ed. 2005).

Bernd Schünemann, *Strafverfahrensrecht. Ein Studienbuch* (29th ed. 2017).

Claus Roxin/Gunther Arzt/Klaus Tiedemann, *Einführung in das Strafrecht und Strafprozeßrecht* (6. ed. 2013).

Helmut Satzger/Wilhelm Schluckebier/Gunter Widmaier (eds.), *Strafprozessordnung: StPO* (3rd. 1918).

Gerhard Schäfer, *Die Praxis des Strafverfahrens* (7th ed. 2017).

Ellen Schlüchter, *Strafprozeßrecht* (3rd ed. 1999).

Friedrich-Christian Schroeder/Torsten Verrel, *Strafprozessrecht* (6th ed. 2014).

Systematischer Kommentar zur Strafprozeßordnung und zum Gerichtsverfassungsgesetz (Hans-Joachim Rudolphi/Wilhelm Degener/Wolfgang Frisch/Helmut Frister/ Hans-Ullrich Paeffgen/Klaus Rogall/Ellen Schlüchter/Petra Velten/Edda Weßlau/Wolfgang Wohlers/Jürgen Wolter, 5th ed. 2016).

Klaus Volk/Armin Engländer, *Strafprozessrecht* (9th ed. 2018).

Index